WITHDRAWN
No longer the property of the
Boston Public Library.
Sale of this material benefits the Library.

IMAGES OF JAPANESE SOCIETY

Japanese Studies
General Editor: Yoshio Sugimoto

Images of Japanese Society. *Ross E. Mouer and Yoshio Sugimoto*
An Intellectual History of Wartime Japan. *Shunsuke Tsurumi*

IMAGES OF JAPANESE SOCIETY

A Study in the Social Construction of Reality

Ross Mouer and
Yoshio Sugimoto

KPI

London and New York

HN723
.5
.M68
1986X

First published in 1986 by KPI Limited
11 New Fetter Lane, London EC4P 4EE
England

Reprinted 1986

Distributed by
Routledge & Kegan Paul
Associated Book Publishers (UK) Ltd.
11 New Fetter Lane, London EC4P 4EE
England

Methuen Inc., Routledge & Kegan Paul
29 West 35th Street, New York, NY 10001, USA

Produced by Worts-Power Associates
Set in Times
by The Design Team
and printed in Great Britain
by Dotesios Printers Ltd, Bradford-on-Avon

The publishers gratefully acknowledge the support of The Japan Foundation and La Trobe University in the publication of this volume

© *Ross E. Mouer and Yoshio Sugimoto, 1986*

No part of this book may be reproduced in any form without permission from the publisher, except for the quotation of brief passages in criticism.

ISBN 07103 0078-6

Contents

LIST OF ABBREVIATIONS xiii
LIST OF TABLES xvii
LIST OF FIGURES xxi
PREFACE xxv

1 JAPANESE SOCIETY: STEREOTYPES AND REALITIES 1
I The Recent Interest in Understanding Japanese Society 1
II Competing Images of Japanese Society 7
III Some Doubts Concerning the Consensus or Group Model of Japanese Society 10
IV Improving Our Perceptions of Japanese Society 12
V The Importance of Having More Accurate Images of Japanese Society 17

PART ONE: TWO VIEWS: COMPETING IMAGES OF JAPANESE SOCIETY 19

2 THE GREAT TRADITION: THEORIES OF UNIFORMITY AND CONSENSUS IN JAPANESE SOCIETY 21
I The Holistic Approach to Japanese Studies in English 22
A Anthropological Studies and the Search for a Rational Whole 23
B The Modernization Approach and the Conferences on Japan 27

C The Return to Neo-holistic Conceptions of Japanese Society 32
D The Learn-from-Japan Boom 36
II The Holistic View of Japanese Society in Japanese Literature 39
A 'National Culture' 41
B Democratization Theory 44
C Modernization Theory 47
D Neo-holistic Theories of National Character 49
E Theories of the Internationalization of Japanese Society 52
III Some Common Themes in the Holistic Approach 54
A An Overview 54
B The Promotion of Cultural Relativism 56

3 THE LITTLE TRADITIONS: THEORIES OF CONFLICT AND VARIATION IN JAPANESE SOCIETY 64
I Conflict as a Continuing Theme in Japanese Scholarship 64
A An Overview of Conflict in Japanese Society 64
B Citizens' Movements 69
II The Concern with Structured Social Inequality 71
A Social Policy 71
B Poverty and Economic Exploitation 74
C The Labor Movement 80
III Some Common Themes in the Little Traditions 82

4 THE DISTRIBUTION OF THE CONSERVATIVE AND RADICAL TRADITIONS IN JAPANESE STUDIES 84
I The Question of Larger Traditions and Paradigms 84
II The Distribution of the Two Paradigms in Japanese Studies 86
III Conflict, Class and Integration: the Limitation of Holistic and Conflict Models 91

PART TWO: SKEPTICISM: THREE REASONS FOR DOUBTING THE VALIDITY OF *NIHONJINRON* 97

5 SOME EMPIRICAL FINDINGS AT ODDS WITH THE GROUP MODEL 99

I Some General Findings 99
II The Presence of Conflict 106
A Popular Disturbances in Postwar Japan 106
B A Comparison of Industrial Conflict in Japan and Australia 111
C Rethinking Group Theories of Japanese Society 114
III Income Distribution 115
A Variation over Time 116
B Cross-sectional Variation 119
IV The Need for Empirical Research 128

6 SOME METHODOLOGICAL MISGIVINGS ABOUT THE GROUP MODEL 129
I Sources of Skepticism: Basic Methodological Lacunae 130
A Sampling 130
B Conceptual Ambiguity 133
C The Unconcern with Methodology 139
II Further Information on Methodology in Japanology 143
A *Nihonjinron* as a Methodology: a Content Analysis 143
B *Kotowaza* as a Data Base: an Evaluation 151
III Conclusions 155

7 TOWARD A SOCIOLOGY OF JAPANOLOGY 156
I Perspectives from the Sociology of Knowledge 156
II A Functional Framework for Evaluating the Comparative Study of Japanese Society 158
A Japanese Academic Life and the Generation of *Nihonjinron* 158
B The Foreign Researcher 163
III The Ideological Framework for Japanology 168
A In the Service of Specific Interests 169
B The Role of the Japanese Government 177
C The US-Japan Relationship 181
D Orientalism 185
IV Japan as a Self-fulfilling Prophecy 186

PART THREE: THE OBVERSE: TALES OF ANOTHER JAPAN 189

8 THE AUTONOMOUS INDIVIDUAL 191
I Introduction 191
II Leaders and Heroes 195
III Gravitation toward Individual Activity 200
IV Privacy and Private Property as Key Values 205
V Personhood and the Japanese Language 208
VI Conclusions 210

9 THE CONTRACTUAL RELATIONSHIP 211
I Introduction 211
II The Written Word 216
III The Contractual Relationship 219
IV Social Distance and the Struggle to Associate 227
V Some Cultural Origins of the 'Dry' Relationship 231
VI Conclusions 233

10 SOCIAL CONTROL: CORMORANTS OR FALCONS? 234
I Introduction 234
II Controls with Various Degrees of Coercion 239
A Watchdogs and Monitors 239
B Indicative Planning and Informal Direction 243
C Regulation 245
D Physical Violence 247
III The Fine Blend of Controls 252
A Controls within the Business Corporation 252
B Socialization and Social Control in the Educational System 256
C Minimal Deviancy and Social Structure 263
IV Cormorant Fishing and Falconry as Contrastive Analogies 264
V Conclusions 267

PART FOUR: MULTIPLE DIMENSIONS: TOWARD A COMPARATIVE FRAMEWORK FOR THE STUDY OF JAPANESE SOCIETY 273

11 SOCIAL STRATIFICATION AS A POINT OF DEPARTURE 275
I Introduction 275
II Social Classes in Japanese Society 277
III Social Mobility 279

IV Suggestions from Nakane and the Role of the Firm 281
V Toward a Synthetic Model of Social Stratification 288

12 A MULTIDIMENSIONAL STRATIFICATION FRAMEWORK FOR THE COMPARATIVE STUDY OF JAPANESE SOCIETY 292
I Societal Rewards and the Social Ranking of Individuals 292
A Societal Rewards: Toward a Definition 292
B Types of Reward 293
C Models Which Emphasize the Typology of Rewards 300
II Differentiation and the Stratification Variables 304
A Roles and Individuals 304
B The Agents of Stratification 306
C Models Which Emphasize Agents of Stratification 308
III Formalization of the Multidimensional Stratification Model 309
IV The Stratification Model and the Concept of Social Class 314
V Stratification and the Study of Japanese Society 322

13 THE STRATIFICATION FRAMEWORK IN A JAPANESE CONTEXT 328
I Societal Rewards in the Japanese Context 328
A Income as Specific to Time and Place 328
B The Importance of Particularistic Demands within the Japanese Setting 336
C Social Control and Reward Fungibility 338
II Inequality and the Differentiation of Behavior 342
A Political Attitudes 342
B The Male-Female Wage Differential 349
C Language 351
D The Crime Rate 352
E Other Applications 353
III Conclusions 356

14 TESTING THE STRATIFICATION MODEL: SOME EMPIRICAL EVIDENCE 360
I Introduction 360

II Some Initial Findings 364
A The Ranking of Job Situations 364
B Visual Associations 367
C Semantic Differentials 367
D Criteria for Choosing a Job 369
III Some General Conclusions 372

PART FIVE: RELEVANCE AND NEW DIRECTIONS: THE FUTURE OF JAPANESE STUDIES 375

15 INTERNATIONALIZATION AND JAPANESE SOCIETY 377
I Introduction 377
II Internationalism in Japan 379
III The International in Japanese Political Culture 383
IV Internationalization as a Problem of National Self-identity 388
V Internationalization and Japanese Society: an Australian Perspective Once Removed 393
VI False Images and International Isolation: Some Consequences 396
VII Internationalization and the Study of Japanese Society 400

16 THE FUTURE OF JAPANESE STUDIES 405
I *Nihonjinron* as a Social Construction: a Summary 405
II Methodological Considerations 408
III Toward a Methodology for the Study of Japanese Society 414
IV Toward the Internationalization of Japanese Studies 418
V The Study of Japan as a Personal Concern: Research as a Set of Choices 424
VI Toward a Moratorium on *Nihonjinron* 430

APPENDIX: METHODOLOGY FOR THE SURVEY OF JOB SITUATIONS 433
I Operationalization 433
II The Tabulations 442
III Sampling Procedures 444
IV Some First-order Statistics 447

NOTES 454
REFERENCES 473
INDEX 544

List of Abbreviations

AEN	*Asahi Evening News* (English-language newspaper in Japan)
AJ	*Asahi Jānaru* (Japanese-language weekly journal)
AMPO	*Anzen Hoshō Jōyaku* (Japan-US Mutual Security Treaty)
Anon	Anonymous (references without an author's name)
ASC	*Asahi Shinbun* (morning edition) (Japanese-language newspaper)
ASY	*Asahi Shinbun* (evening edition) (Japanese-language newspaper)
BSWS	Basic Survey of the Wage Structure (Chingin Kōzō Kihon Chōsa)
CPI	Consumer Price Index
CR	See GCR
Dōmei	Zen Nihon Rōdō Sōdōmei Kumiai Kaigi (All Japan Congress of Trade Unions)
Dōyūkai	Keizai Dōyūkai (Japan Committee for Economic Development)
DSP	Democratic Socialist Party
EEC	European Economic Community
EPA	Economic Planning Agency
FBI	Federal Bureau of Investigation
FEER	*Far Eastern Economic Review*
FIES	Family Income and Expenditure Survey (Kakei Chōsa)
GATT	The General Agreement on Tariffs and Trade

GCR	Gini Concentration Ratio
GNP	Gross National Product
ICFTU	International Confederation of Free Trade Unions
ILO	International Labor Organization
ITS	International Trade Secretariat
IMF-JC	International Metal Workers' Federation–Japan Council
JC	See IMF-JC
JCP	Japan Communist Party
JHC	Japan Housing Corporation
JIL	Japan Institute of Labor (Nihon Rōdō Kyōkai)
JPC	Japan Productivity Center (Nihon Seisansei Honbu)
JSP	Japan Socialist Party
JT	*The Japan Times* (English-language newspaper in Japan)
JTW	*The Japan Times Weekly* (English-language weekly in Japan)
Keidanren	Keizai Dantai Rengōkai (Japan Federation of Economic Organizations)
LAFTA	Latin American Free Trade Association
LDP	Liberal Democratic Party
MDN	*Mainichi Daily News* (English-language newspaper in Japan)
MITI	Ministry of International Trade and Industry
MS	Mouer and Sugimoto
MSA	Maritime Safety Agency
MSC	*Mainichi Shinbun* (morning edition) (Japanese-language newspaper)
MSY	*Mainichi Shinbun* (evening edition) (Japanese-language newspaper)
Nikkeiren	Nihon Keieisha Dantai Renmei (Japan Federation of Employers' Associations)
Nisshō	Nihon Shōkō Kaigisho (Japan Chamber of Commerce and Industry)
NKS	*Nihon Kōgyō Shinbun* (Japanese-language newspaper)
NKSC	*Nihon Keizai Shinbun* (morning edition) (Japanese-language newspaper)
NKSY	*Nihon Keizai Shinbun* (evening edition) (Japanese-language newspaper)
NORC	National Opinion Research Center

NRKZ	*Nihon Rōdō Kyōkai Zasshi* (Japanese monthly journal)
OECD	Organization for Economic Cooperation and Development
SES	Socio-economic status
SM	Sugimoto and Mouer
Sōhyō	Nippon Rōdō Kumiai Sōhyōgikai (The General Council of Trade Unions of Japan)
SRN	*Shūkan Rōdō Nyūsu* (Japanese-language weekly newspaper)
TDY	*The Daily Yomiuri* (English-language newspaper in Japan)
TMG	Tokyo Metropolitan Government
WPI	Wholesale Price Index
YSC	*Yomiuri Shinbun* (morning edition) (Japanese-language newspaper)
YSY	*Yomiuri Shinbun* (evening edition) (Japanese-language newspaper)

Tables

2.1 Some stages in the development of *nihonjinron:* periods, concepts and evaluations 57–8
2.2 Models of modernization emphasizing changes in social values and the nature of interpersonal relationships 60
2.3 Variables commonly used to indicate ideal types for industrial and pre-industrial societies 61
4.1 Two distinguishing features of the images of Japanese society presented by two traditions of scholarship 85
4.2 The distribution of the great and little traditions in English and Japanese literature on Japanese society 87
4.3 Bestsellers in the *nihonjinron* tradition 89
5.1 Technology and career patterns in Japan and the United States 105
5.2 Technology, career patterns and levels of alienation in Japan and the United States 105
5.3 The frequency of violent disturbances in four countries 107
5.4 The mean magnitude and intensity of different types of disturbance in Japan: 1952–60 110
5.5 Various Gini Concentration Ratios calculated from annual income groups in the FIES data, 1953–77 117
5.6 Firm-size differentials in working conditions: 1978 121
5.7 The correlation of household income and three life-cycle variables for households grouped according to a third variable: 1970 126
5.8 A comparison of the effect of eight variables on the distribution of income in Japan and the United States 127
6.1 Frequency of citation for major works and authors dealing with Japanese society, measured according to the *Social Sciences Citation Index* 144–5

6.2 The frequency distributions of four types of statement 146
6.3 The percentage of statements with and without evidence 148
6.4 The percentage of statements with evidence by type 149
6.5 Frequency of comparative statements by the comparative base 150
6.6 Distribution of samples used to make generalizations about Japan 150
6.7 The frequency distribution of 96 *kotowaza* from *iroha karuta* by value orientation 152
6.8 The range of scores and the frequency distribution of 50 *kotowaza* on scores for usage and support 154
7.1 Japanese language proficiency of Japan Foundation fellows (1972–7) surveyed in 1978 166
7.2 The titles of some publications distributed to non-Japanese 175
8.1 The uses of leisure time: 1976 202–3
8.2 A comparison of the number of compound words made with characters for the individual and for groups 209
11.1 Occupational distribution of the labor force: the percentage distribution of the gainfully employed by employment status, 1981 284
11.2 Occupational distribution of the labor force: the percentage distribution across occupational categories by sex, 1980 285
12.1 Types of reward 296–7
12.2 The relative solidarity of persons in a category defined by an agent of stratification 318–19
13.1 Economic demands during two periods in postwar Japan 329
13.2 The frequency of popular disturbances with particularistic and universalistic demands in Japan: 1952–60 338–9
13.3 Stratification variables and the perception of election issues related to the thirty-third general election for the House of Representatives (10 December 1972) 343–6
13.4 Stratification differentials and political preference and attitudes (in terms of percentage differentials) 347–8
13.5 The male-female wage differential in Japan: 1960–80 349
14.1 Ratio of standard deviation means for occupational criteria to those for firm-related criteria 366
14.2 Index of association involving pictures and job situations defined by occupation and firm-related factors 368
14.3 The mean of the standard deviations across occupations and firms for each of 25 semantic differentials 369
14.4 Relative weightings given ten criteria for choosing a job 370–1
15.1 Some definitions of the term *kokusaika* (internationalization) 381
16.1 Some fundamental concerns in evaluating theories of a society 410

16.2 Typology of methodologies for comparative research 420–23
A.1 Percentage distribution of the respondents according to sample and selected biographical characteristics 448
A.2 Index of rank order consensus for job situations 449
A.3 Mean rankings of occupations and firms on 25 semantic differentials 451–3
N.1 The number of citations of works by Dore 462

Figures

4.1 Some evaluative dimensions for assessing the great tradition and strategies for developing new models of Japanese society 94
5.1 Technology and levels of alienation in Japan and the United States 104
5.2 Prewar and postwar patterns of strikes in Australia and Japan 113
5.3 Age-earnings profiles in four countries 124–5
6.1 A causative statement 147
6.2 Survey form to indicate usage and general support for each of 50 *kotowaza* 153
7.1 The message in action-oriented *nihonjinron* 183
10.1 Societies with direct and indirect controls 266
10.2 The cultural control model of Japanese society 270
11.1 Configuration of social solidarity according to vertical and horizontal relationships which are delineated by attribute and frame 282
11.2 A two-dimensional distribution of the labor force 286
11.3 A stratification model in two dimensions 290
12.1 Reward-based models of social stratification 298–9
12.2 An interactive model for societal rewards 302–3
12.3 Distributive models of social stratification 310–11
12.4 The identification of social stratification subsystems 313
12.5 Three examples of stratification subsystems 315
12.6 Three-dimensional model of stratification and the comparison between Yamada Tarō and Watanabe Hanako 316
13.1 A comparison of old priorities and new demands 334
13.2 Scheme for six-way comparisons of the male-female differential among four subsamples varying by age and firm size 350

13.3 Third-level comparisons in cross-cultural research 358
A.1 Hypothetical contexts with sets of five job situations defined in one dimension 434
A.2 Hypothetical contexts with sets of five job situations defined in two dimensions 436
A.3 The definitions of one set of five job situations rotated to yield five sets 438
A.4 An example of a problem using picture identification 439
A.5 Semantic differentials and a job situation 440
A.6 Open-ended multiple response question 441
A.7 Some hypothetical rankings of job situations: three samples with indices of consensus 443
A.8 Examples of how to calculate the concentration index using percentage frequencies 445
A.9 Example of tabulations for semantic differentials for a sample of two 446

In this volume, Japanese names are given with the family name preceding the given name, in accordance with Japanese practice.

Preface

In Japanese there is a saying, '*kowai mono shirazu*'. The phrase is used to refer to those who dive into something without having a full appreciation of the consequences. While it connotes youthful courage and a refreshing openness to new perspectives, it also adumbrates the pitfalls which await the inexperienced. One could even say that it is an acknowledgement of nobility in failure, a recognition of both the promises and the frustrations associated with idealism.

This book began with a personal problem. Each author has lived approximately one-third of his adult life in Australia, Japan and the United States. A major aspect of grappling with the loss of national identity and of developing a new international or multicultural identity involves the need to translate across cultures when communicating with family and friends who continue to live in one culture. Why should it be so difficult to explain how or why one can move from one culture to another without any apparent sense of dislocation or discomfort? Why is it so difficult after living in a country for an extended period to answer the simplest, most honest questions? 'Do you like Japan? What are Australians like? How do Americans feel about Vietnam?' And then there are the most difficult questions of all. 'Don't you sometimes get homesick? How can you live in a society where you have no roots and everything is so alien?'

For two persons who consider three societies home, these questions produce a complex emotion, disdain mixed with anxiety: disdain toward others embued with a smug parochialism and anxiety about having lost the security of those shared meanings. The latter those ideas in English. Similar responses were received from outside Japan, many from young researchers invited to do research in Japan only to be told by their hosts that they could never understand Japanese society. In the words of C. W. Mills, our personal troubles seemed to intersect with a broader social problem, and our individual biographies came to have a historical context.

Confidence in that perception was reinforced by the fact that similar critiques were beginning to appear in various other forums. Further investigation also revealed that many of our doubts had been voiced as much as a decade earlier, although such statements seemed to have been left without further development. At the same time, the changes in Japan's international position had produced a new sense of urgency as Japan's trade surpluses, overseas investment and foreign aid introduced new dimensions.

That kind of information, along with a growing awareness of the ideological uses of the group model, and a concern for the artificial but none the less very real barriers it posed for Japanese wishing to communicate with people from other societies, encouraged us to systematize the critique. That was initially done in a series of publications over three years from June 1979. This book is an attempt to bring that work together and to reflect on what we have learned from the feedback received.

While debunking has been identified as a major motif of sociologists and perhaps social scientists in general (Berger: 1963), criticism alone is often a sterile activity. It sometimes results in a rickety crutch being thrown away, but not replaced when even a broken crutch would be better than none. It is at this stage that one begins to feel a sense of intellectual crisis. As Hidaka (1982a) has written, criticism is fine, but often the criteria used to criticize others come back to hound the critic.

In our work, three major sources of skepticism were identified: contrary empirical evidence, methodological sloppiness and the presence of social (especially ideological) factors shaping the formation of the group model of Japanese society. Although the first provides the primary grounds for accepting or rejecting a vision of society, the choice between conflicting evidence is often ultimately made according to consideration of the second and third. However, methodological purism and the rejection of socially produced knowledge soon become stumbling-blocks as one moves from the criticism of a theory to the construction of an alternative.

The demand for methodological rigor often gives way to a

narrowly defined empiricism and the postitivist's false sense of value-free objectivity. Social science is confused with natural science, behavior with ideas, and information with understanding. This is not to deny the importance of statistical logic and broader methodological concerns, but to keep them in perspective as a necessary but not sufficient condition for understanding. If there are to be cross-cultural comparisons, it may be that the body of definitions and the taxonomies which form the statistical logic of science will be the only *etic* or cross-cultural concepts which have universal application. At the same time, there is a need to realize that we live in a world of second bests; perfectly random samples often cannot be obtained, and the derivation of cross-cultural categories for classifying reality is not without serious difficulties. This is especially true when dealing with more abstract descriptions of evaluative thought processes.

The sociology of knowledge provides further reason for despair. Even minimal exposure to that perspective suggests that criticism too is ideology. It may well be impossible to be relevant without one's views being used ideologically by others. The failure to accept responsibility for the ideological uses of one's work is itself an ideological position, yet one is caught by the dilemma of not being able to predict how one's views will be used. That realization not only makes one humble about one's own creations, but also serves to weaken simple conspiracy theories about the creation of knowledge. As Glazer (1975) observed some time ago, although it is easy to see correlations between ideas and ideological positions, it is extremely difficult to demonstrate the causative relationship between the two.

With regard to the third criterion, research needs to be seen as a set of choices, some of which are enumerated in the final chapter of this volume. The problem is not solved but can perhaps be mitigated by making one's own choices as explicit as possible. This we have tried to do in numerous places, both in this volume and elsewhere. The application of the second criterion, methodological rigor, cannot, however, be resolved in such a straightforward manner. The authors have tended to fall back on the infant industry argument. According to that line of thinking, hypotheses are examined at two levels. The first level involves a decision as to whether a hypothesis deserves testing. Once accepted for testing, there is a second level at which hypotheses are scrutinized before they are labelled theories and accepted as a plausible explanation of the facts.

It is our contention that the tests are difficult at these two levels. In this volume the authors have hidden behind the infant industry argument in presenting two alternative models for examination at level one. The book argues that the group model of the Japanese has provided an interesting perspective, but that it does not qualify at level two. It argues that the model has been treated as though it has passed higher testing, and that frequent restatements of the interesting hypotheses have not moved the group model any closer to being tested at the second level. The models presented in this volume cannot be accepted as theory or as statements of fact. However, the authors hope that a basis has been established and that both the critique and the alternative propositions set forth are clear enough to allow for others to develop hypotheses in a fashion which will allow them to be tested at the second level in the future. It is only after such testing that an informed appraisal can be made of the two views of Japanese society presented in the third and fourth parts of this book. It should thus be clear that the ideas advanced in the pages that follow are seen by the authors as hypotheses for further testing, not as statements of some absolute truth.

Not unrelated to these goals, another object of this book is also to stimulate debate on the methodology and goals of area studies. Do area studies stand simply on the idea that there is a unity among the social sciences? Or does the very interest in society as the major unit of analysis mean that national character is seen as a major independent variable? What methodological considerations flow from an interest in cross-cultural comparisons? Do such comparisons mean that the methods of social science can be applied with the nation being seen simply as one additional source of variation? Or are there qualitative differences? If this volume serves only to stimulate debate on the methodology of area studies and the special problems involved in comparative research, the authors will be more than satisfied. In the process of writing, a concern with how to develop multicultural perspectives has emerged as important.

In large measure, this book is a record of ideas received from others. The intellectual debts begin with the growing body of literature about *nihonjinron* – the popular, stereotyped images of Japanese society. As a glance at the list of references will confirm, that literature is now quite extensive. We have also learned much and have received encouragement from those who have written to us during the three years between the publishing of our first joint effort in 1979 and the writing of this book in 1982. Our creditors in this category number hundreds and cannot easily be listed one by one.

We are especially grateful to the editors of journals and newsletters who have given us access to a mixed audience and who have kindly encouraged us to reformulate and to develop further initial ideas. Our ideas have changed greatly as a result of such valuable feedback; the fruitful process of writing, receiving feedback and rewriting has led us to value highly opportunities to publish in both English and Japanese. Over time we have come to see those opportunities as offering yet another research methodology; the 'final research report' has lost its finality and must now be regarded as a springboard for further discussion from which one can profit immensely.

Feedback has been received in other ways as well. Soon after the publication of the *Gendai no Me* series in 1979, the Australia-Japan Project at the Australian National University arranged a seminar which provided an open forum for the exchange of ideas. Generous financial support from the Australia-Japan Foundation, the Japan Foundation, the Utah Foundation and several other sources have made it possible to organize two international symposia in Australia: one in May 1980 in Canberra in conjunction with the first national conference of the Japanese Studies Association of Australia and the other early in 1982 at Noosa Heads (cf. SM: 1982c). These two gatherings brought together a number of scholars with similar concerns about the over-simplified view of Japanese society and with an interest in exploring the possibility of developing alternative models of Japanese society. Papers from the first symposium were published in a special issue of *Social Analysis* (nos. 5/6: December 1980) and invited other feedback. Finally, generous grants from Griffith and La Trobe Universities allowed our collaboration over four years which included frequent flights between Brisbane and Melbourne. The large number of opportunities for getting together at two- or three-month intervals, as well as overlapping sabbaticals in Tokyo in 1982, have resulted in truly collaborative interaction in which it has become difficult to distinguish clearly the ideas of one from the other, although Sugimoto's doctoral work on conflict (1981d) and Mouer's on income distribution (1980a) initially provided two different empirical bases for our original skepticism. In the final stages of writing the manuscript, the Faculty of Economics at Yokohama National University and the Department of Sociology and Anthropology at Tokyo Metropolitan University made office space available to us during our sabbaticals in Japan.

Debts to a few individuals require special mention. These begin and end with our wives, Elizabeth and Machiko. Earlier in our careers, as graduate students in the United States, considerable advice was received from our respective Ph.D. thesis advisers, Professors Alan B. Cole and Gilbert Shapiro. Thanks are also due to Sue Esdale and Pam Nichols at Griffith University and Norma Cann, Jill Gooch, Jan Lees, Bronwyn Bardsley and Barbara Matthews at La Trobe, who have typed manuscripts and correspondence over the past three years. In the final stages of editing this manuscript, suggestions from Frank Mouer, Frank Foley, Susan Wagner and Bruce Jacobs have been invaluable.

The support and assistance received from varied sources in several societies serves constantly to remind us that research is a cooperative enterprise. The attempt to take a multicultural perspective has simply made us more aware of that fact. This volume rests firmly on the belief that we can know ourselves and our own society better by studying other societies. It also emerges from a recognition that our perceptions of the world around us are shaped by our own self-image. Knowledge of our own society serves as the lens through which we see others.

In the world today, few men and few societies can cut themselves off from the rest of the world and be islands unto themselves. Rather, the global trend is toward increased contact. As many were reminded by the dispute over Japanese textbooks in the summer of 1982, no longer can educational policies be dismissed as merely a domestic matter. Education designed to produce responsible citizens aware of the forces shaping their society must include information on other societies.

At a time when Japanese society is characterized by reference to 'the move to the right' and when conservatism throughout the world is accompanied by a rise in parochial concerns, multicultural perspectives and a cosmopolitan tolerance for the views of others have an added significance for those interested in world peace and international understanding. Such a frame of mind, we believe, will help us to see beyond the narrowly defined goals of nationalism and the nation state. It is our hope that this book will encourage readers to develop further their own multicultural perspectives.

Ross E. Mouer
Yoshio Sugimoto
New Delhi and Tokyo

Chapter 1

Japanese Society: Stereotypes and Realities

I The Recent Interest in Understanding Japanese Society

Over the last two decades interest in Japanese society has grown remarkably, both within Japan and overseas. This development has resulted in part from Japan's emergence as an economic power. The apparent suddenness with which Japan appeared on the world stage stimulated many to ask how Japan's 'economic miracle' was achieved. During the seventies a large number of books on Japan were published. Many of these sought to make Japan's success story seem plausible by emphasizing the ways in which Japanese national character or Japanese culture had contributed to the process of modernization. The boom in literature emphasizing one unique facet of the Japanese character or another is evident not only in Japan itself but in other countries as well. Today there are not many disciplines in the social sciences in which the uniqueness of the Japanese is not stressed by at least some.

Significance has been attached to the study of Japanese society for a number of reasons. There are the mundane concerns of business firms competing against or negotiating with Japanese economic organizations. On the national level, there are the larger problems of dealing with certain domestic dislocations often blamed on Japan's aggressive marketing and social dumping, and with obtaining specific technologies being developed in Japan. In addition to these immediate concerns, the Japanese experience is also seen as significant in the study of some larger problems associated with industrialization.

1. *Interest in the Sources of Industrialization.* For many in the developing economies, Japan is seen as a model to emulate. The Karachi plan which emerged in the early sixties, for example, was based on the notion that the high levels of education attained in Japan were crucial to the nation's successful economic development (Duke: 1966; Nakayama: 1975, pp. 93–7; Toyota: 1970). China also has shown an interest in Japan's system of management (*NKSC*, 5 March 1980, p. 3) and in learning from Japan *à la* Vogel (*ASC*, 20 November 1980, p. 1). This interest is apparent in the images of Japan presented in the *People's Daily* (Zhang: 1982) and in the problem consciousness which Chinese scholars have in regard to Japan (Liu and Jiang: 1982).

Traditional societies facing the onslaught of the industrialized world have experienced the various tremendous psychological traumas described by Fanon (1965 and 1967a). Elsewhere Goulet (1971) has written about the 'cruel choice'. On the one hand, many in the 'less developed countries' feel that they must industrialize in order to prevent or at least limit the inroads made on their cultures by multinational enterprises and others from the 'developed countries'. At the same time, to absorb the required industrial technology and to achieve economic independence, many of these societies will have to sacrifice the very cultural heritage they seek to maintain. The belief that Japan developed successfully while maintaining its cultural integrity has shifted attention from narrow considerations of economic efficiency, competitiveness in international markets and protectionism at home to a whole range of sociological issues concerning the role of political organization and cultural continuity in industrialization.

In an effort to ferret out the main ingredients accounting for Japan's successes, scholars have compared Japan with various other countries (Beckman: 1962a; Ward and Rustow: 1964; and Black *et al.*: 1975). The literature on Japanese society now emphasizes the role of the governmental complex built around a highly developed bureaucracy, a strong sense of national identity, respect for education, paternalistic orientations behind the notion of labor-management cooperation and consensus in decision-making, enthusiastic acceptance of benevolent guidance, the work ethic and an inclination to save. Regardless of which aspect is emphasized, it is common for considerable attention to be given to the Japanese value system, and the Japanese are commonly seen as having economic values similar to those associated with Weber's Protestant ethic in the West (such as hard work and thrift). Yet the apparent absence of other values commonly associated with the West (such as individualism, rationalism and universalism) has also been frequently noted. Accordingly, many began to ponder whether there is in Japanese society a certain cultural predisposition which has promoted economic growth. This is true not only of the rather superficial discussion in Kahn (1970), but also of more sophisticated depictions of Japanese society. Although Vogel (1979a), for example, explains that his interest is in structures and not in values (p. ix), there is a tendency in the body of his argument to accept 'structured consensus' as a 'pre-programmed' or given cultural value.

2. *The Interest in Competing with the Japanese.* In recent years, many in the developed world also became interested in Japan. Confronted by the 'Japanese challenge', many realized in the late sixties and the early seventies that Japan was a force to be reckoned with not only in world markets overseas but increasingly at home in their own domestic economy (Kahn: 1970; Guillain: 1970; Hedberg: 1970: and von Krookow: 1970). The initial concern of policy-makers was the development of defensive strategies to deal with Japanese competition in the international economy, with domestic unemployment caused by Japanese imports, and with the prospects of Japanese involvement in economic decision-making resulting from growing levels of Japanese investment. The policies adopted to deal with these types of problem obviously emerged from some perception of how such a competitive advantage had been generated. In this regard, as a kind of solace for those suffering from economic woes in their own country, it was easy for authors to conclude that Japan's advantage resulted from social dumping, social orchestration and various other unacceptable practices.

3. *Japanese Lessons for the Industrialized World.* A more creative response to the Japanese challenge can be found in the suggestion that Japan's competitive advantage resulted from a better system of education, a well-designed program of tax incentives or from some other structural innovation. The solution lay not so much in defensive withdrawal but in learning from the Japanese. Some – including Dore (1973), the OECD (1973a and 1977), Clifford (1976), Vogel (1979a), Cummings (1980), Gibney (1982), Ōuchi (1981a) and Pascale and Athos (1981a) – have gone so far as to suggest that Japan has not only industrialized successfully, but also solved many of the

social problems associated with becoming a post-industrial society: alienation, crime, social disintegration and a certain loss of self-discipline. Dore even argues that as a 'late developer' Japan was able to adopt industrial technology and then create a post-industrial situation at the same time that an industrial society emerged. In other words, it developed initially with a 'culture lag' and was then already 'post-industrial' by the time that social changes began to occur. The Japanese economy progressed from being agrarian/feudalistic to being industrial/capitalistic to being post-industrial/welfare-coporate. However, the economy passed through the second stage so quickly that Japanese society did not really have time to develop social institutions commensurate with the intermediate type of economy. Moreover, some authors began to believe that many of the Japanese social structures found in the feudalistic stage are quite suited to the needs of post-industrial society, meaning that minimal amounts of social change and concomitant social dislocation have occurred in Japan.

4. *Assessing the Pluses and Minuses of Japanese-style Development.* In this fashion, then, the focus of attention has been shifted from considering the requisites for industrialization to considering how certain desirable features of Japanese society might be emulated in moving beyond industrialization. Despite these changes in focus, however, the major ingredients associated with Japan's success have remained unchanged: national independence, high levels of literacy and the ability to process information, a uniquely Japanese form of industrial relations, the central role of the bureaucracy and, behind all this, Japanese values, which emphasize group loyalties, consensus and service to society. From this perspective, the Japanese experience is seen as a forceful lesson in how to do it.

At the same time, attention has also been given to some of the demerits of the Japanese experience (Ui: 1968 and 1971–4; Woronoff: 1979 and 1980; Halliday: 1975; Bennett and Levine: 1976; and Halliday and McCormack: 1973). The demerits include

(i) pollution and the stand-offish attitude taken by bureaucratic and corporate organizations toward the victims of pollution;

(ii) the artificially high population densities and the loss of privacy resulting from excessive concentration of the population in a few urban areas;

(iii) the psychological pressures and pathological effects arising from the excessive weight attached to the merit-oriented, rationalistic, universalistic norms commonly associated with examinations in Japan's production-oriented system of education;

(iv) various forms of alienation common not only among factory and office workers alike, but also among senior citizens forced to retire prematurely without an adequate livelihood or sufficient opportunity to contribute to the larger community, and among students concerned about the scope and quality of their education;

(v) the utter imperviousness of bureaucrats to the aspirations and creative potential of local citizens who were seen as standing in the way of important national or regional development projects;

(vi) various types of invidious inequalities, not least of which is one concerning the status of women in Japanese society;

(vii) the extraordinary amount of social control which seems to characterize Japanese society–control that often dulls the rough diamonds which might otherwise inject into the postwar society that precious glitter associated with the idealism of youth culture in other societies around the world.

Putting aside for the moment questions concerning the accuracy of these images, it is clear that there are also those who view the Japanese experience critically, claiming that it also provides lessons in how not to do it.

5. *The Debates on Convergence and Divergence.* On a more theoretical level, the concerns discussed here have been central to the ongoing debate on convergence and divergence.[1] Condensed to its most common denominators, the debate originally revolved around the proposition of the convergence theorists, who suggested that there are two ways in which societies become increasingly alike as industrialization occurs. First, social structures become increasingly congruent. Second, the values of individuals in different industrializing societies become increasingly similar. Those emphasizing convergence argue that, despite dissimilar cultural origins and social traditions, societies with similar industrial technology will tend to produce common patterns in terms of the distribution of income and

status within society. Those emphasizing divergence stress the importance of cultural continuity and argue that individuals in different societies will be likely to perceive and evaluate the same physical environment (including the same machines, etc.) in very different ways.

Although both views can be found in the literature on Japanese society, it is our impression that the divergence theorists have prevailed in the English-language literature on Japanese society. Moreover, it is largely from this perspective that the mysteriously strange and quaint aspects of Japanese society seem to have received an inordinate amount of attention in the overseas media whenever Japan is featured. In recent years a small minority has voiced dissatisfaction with the predominant view of Japanese society, but thus far it has had little success in dislodging the divergence theorists from their accepted position as the true interpreters of Japanese social realities for those in the mass media and for those in policy-making positions.

6. *Internationalization and Japanese Society*. Finally, in recent years attention has been given to the cultural and social aspects of Japan's expanding presence around the world. The riots accompanying Prime Minister Tanaka on his visit to Southeast Asia in January 1974 seemed to jolt the nation's consciousness. Since then, Japanese intellectuals have increasingly sought to address the social problems caused by the economic inroads Japan was making overseas. In this context, increased foreign aid, cultural and academic exchange and a better grasp of the host nation's language were seen as solutions by some. In the meantime, others such as Nakane (1972a) and Kunihiro (1980) began to question whether some of these difficulties were the result of the Japanese having a unique set of social values and social structures. These scholars maintained that this uniqueness served to isolate Japanese abroad from the host society and to produce rather self-contained Japanese enclaves unable to interact with the local community. Others have begun to pay attention to the way in which the people of one nation come to form national stereotypes of the people in other countries (Iwao, Hagiwara and Mouer: 1980; Manabe: 1981; Broinowski: 1980; Chalmers and Mitchie: 1982; *AJ*, 26 March 1982).

Although observers have come up with different answers, there seems to have been considerable agreement as to what the central questions are. Obviously, the most pressing issues have changed over the years as the objective circumstances defining Japan's relations with the outside world have changed. During the occupation there was great interest in how to learn or absorb Western or democratic habits of thinking from abroad. Later, the focus shifted to ways of importing technologies and management techniques which had their origins largely in the West. The two Nixon shocks, the oil crisis and the normalization of relations with China, produced yet other concerns. At about the same time, the sudden increase in direct Japanese foreign investment and the continued drive to export Japanese goods drew attention to the problems of Japanese people having to live and work in other societies. This is turn created an interest in the cultural shock and dislocations experienced when Japanese re-enter their own society after a prolonged absence abroad (Hoshino: 1981; Nagata and Nagata: 1980; Kobayashi: 1981).

While Japan's overseas presence has been seen by many in the host countries as an economic challenge, some have been concerned with the social dimensions of the Japanese interface. In some countries, the Japanese are now taking their turn at carrying the 'ugly man's burden'. While the frequent and perhaps irksome clicking of cameras at tourist spots around the world may in fact be quite innocuous, the blatant commandeering of those visiting Korea, Taiwan and various Southeast Asian countries on 'sex tours' has aroused considerable anger. So too has the tendency of Japanese to establish enclave communities - behavior which is often interpreted as symbolizing total disregard of the local population, its traditions, its needs and its interests. One might also mention the changes which Japanese products and the accompanying commercialism have brought to lifestyles and ways of thinking in other societies. The Japanese presence is not yet as large or as conspicuous as that of American troops in various countries immediately after the Second World War. Nevertheless, the Japanese impact on specific societies has been considerable. Aware of these aspects of Australia's new economic relationship with Japan, both public and private parties in Australia have begun to give this dimension and the area of mutual perceptions more attention (Stirling: 1981; Broinowski: 1980; and Chalmers: 1981).

II Competing Images of Japanese Society

The reasons for studying Japanese society are numerous. Many are interrelated. Some involve complex psychological and ideological needs. The way in which such factors have shaped the perceptions of the Japanese provide interesting subject-matter for those interested in the sociology of knowledge. Although the significance of the Japanese experience for those in both the developing and the developed countries is clear, commonly held images of Japanese society continue to be dominated by a maze of apparent paradoxes which defy understanding. Some of these are captured by the imagery in the title of Benedict's classic, *The Chrysanthemum and the Sword* (1946). The development of this imagery in the English-language literature on Japanese society has been documented by Glazer (1975), Minear (1980b) and others. On the one hand, the Japanese are seen as being militaristic and ruthless. On the other, they are characterized as being mild-mannered, polite and peace-loving. Economic organizations are described as being both the most competitive and the best orchestrated in the world. Closeness to nature is contrasted with the world's worst examples of pollution. Some of the world's greatest eccentrics are produced by the world's most group-oriented society, where a supreme value is placed on conformity. One of the world's most conservative societies somehow also produces some of its most radical student groups. The contemplative self associated with the Zen heritage and many Japanese traditions somehow coexists with the materialistic and hedonistic self in one of the world's most consumption-oriented societies. While the list can be expanded *ad infinitum*, it is sufficient here simply to note that all these apparent contradictions are associated with one of the most stable societies in the world.

In the case of Japan, the paradoxical seems to be more pronounced by the ambivalence with which Japan's economic successes are evaluated by many in the West. As the title of one book on Japan, *The Fragile Blossom*, suggests, there is something ethereal about Japanese realities (Brzezinski: 1972). Although Japan's accomplishments are clearly perceived, many seem unwilling to acknowledge them publicly; accordingly, it is not uncommon for authors to suggest that the accomplishments may be fleeting. This equivocal view of Japan no doubt reflects the difficulty many Westerners have had in coming to grips with the Orient. Minear (1980a), for example, argues in his discussion of Said (1979) that scholarship on Japan has been colored by a notion of Western superiority which is commonly present in scholarly writing on other Asian societies. Those who admire Japan's success emphasize the accomplishments–the remarkable improvement in the standard of living, high standards of education, social equality, cleanliness, freedom of speech, high social mobility, low levels of deviant behavior and organizational loyalty. Those skeptical of Japanese success emphasize the failures – crowded housing, inflation, 'examination hell', the poor and forgotten minority groups, industrial pollution, various situational constraints limiting behavioral choices, the rigidities of a society structured around hierarchical bureaucracies, high levels of alienation, political corruption and closed labor markets. Although observers are not agreed as to whether the lessons from Japan concern that which is to be learned or that which is to be avoided, there is little doubt that something can be learned from the Japanese experience. As Johnson (1982: p. 24) writes, 'the impact of things Japanese on American society has never been more powerful, and the impact is spreading rapidly across American campuses'.

Though the significance of the Japanese experience seems to be widely recognized, Japanese society is perhaps the only major industrialized one for which there is no comprehensive textbook or set of readings in English. There are Befu's *Japan: an Anthropological Introduction* (1971a), Ishida's *Japanese Society* (1971), Fukutake's *Japanese Society* (1974); but these are all stop-gap measures to fill a need which was suddenly recognized at the end of the sixties. None is really comprehensive. The most all-embracing introduction to Japanese society is still Hall and Beardsley's *Twelve Doors to Japan* (1965), an excellent set of readings but one in which many of the pieces have been written more from the perspective of descriptive history than of social science.

Taking an overview of the popular literature, two contrasting views stand out as coherent schools of thought on Japanese society. One portrays Japanese society as an integrated whole; it seeks to extract unique aspects through social averages. It then uses such averaged behavior as the basis for international comparisons and for more limited statements and explanations about Japanese social phenomena. A second approach seeks to understand social realities in Japan by taking specific groups – particularly classes in the Marxist sense – as the major behavioral units by considering how inequalities in the distribution of wealth and power are related to conflicts of interest. This conflict-oriented approach, which in the broadest sense subsumes the Marxist viewpoint, focuses its attention on the causes, structure and dynamics of social class. The former approach is by far the most dominant in the Japanese-language literature, but in the Western-language literature on Japan it seems to hold a monopolistic position. Chapters 2–4 introduce these two approaches.

III Some Doubts Concerning the Consensus or Group Model of Japanese Society

In recent years many scholars have raised serious questions about the validity of the group model. This book is largely about these doubts. In particular, there are misgivings about the usefulness of referring to the Japanese as though all Japanese are uniform in size, shape, behavior and thought. Much of the literature tends to deal with the Japanese personality as though it emerges from a single cultural mold; the popular image suggests that Japanese behavior arises out of a common mental frame without individual idiosyncrasies. With English translations of several Japanese works in the same vein (including Nakane: 1970; Doi: 1973; and Bendasan: 1970) becoming available in the early seventies, this theory of Japanese uniformity has come to be accepted abroad even by many academics. Gradually, it seems to have become the dominant or mainstream view in English-language literature on the nature of Japanese society. It has been further reinforced by popular books written by well-known professors such as Reischauer (1978) and Vogel (1979a).

Explanations of Japanese society which emphasize the role of national character tend to play down the importance of social conflict and variation. They seldom mention the role of authority and power (particularly that of the nation state) in regulating social life. They fail to consider the ramifications of structured social inequality. They do not really come to grips with the presence of psychological manipulation or physical coercion, or the fact that power is concentrated in the hands of an established group in society. Conflict is seen as the exception in Japanese society, and open antagonism is interpreted as being the product of only a few social deviants.

The inability to explain conflict tends to characterize recent literature which stresses the uniqueness of Japanese society. One example is the way in which Doi (1973) has tended to dismiss student rebellion in Japan as being little more than mass or group hysteria.

Nakane (1970) has posited that the fundamental conflicts in Japanese society occur not among the capitalists and workers, who are respectively bound together 'horizontally' in their own classes, defined by their having a common 'attribute', but rather among 'vertically' structured groups, such as company A and company B, in each of which members relate on the basis of belonging to the same 'frame'. Basing its information on Nakane's book, the influential *Economist* even went so far as to describe Japan as being 'the most unMarxist society' (3 March 1973).

In the revised edition of *Japan's New Middle Class* (1970), Vogel has labelled one chapter 'Order amidst Rapid Change' and therein argues that Japan's extremely rapid industrialization was not accompanied by the great dislocations experienced by the West. His interpretation emphasizes how Japan's special group-orientation served to encourage a form of group-sponsored social mobility, which strengthened kinship ties, and to create an atmosphere in which human alienation was minimal. As a result, he argues, the sense of dislocation and disappointment arising from rapid industrialization was mitigated. This view appears again in his recent bestseller, *Japan as Number One* (1979a: cf. the review of that volume in Yoneyama and SM: 1980).

The theories and other explanations emphasizing the uniqueness of specific traits among the Japanese as the major determinants of Japanese behavior have held popularity for most of the postwar period. In recent years, however, the validity of such images has come to be increasingly questioned from a number of different directions. This questioning is now extensive enough to allow for some systematization. In this book several different kinds of reappraisal are discussed. Although each for a different reason finds the holistically inclined theories of Japanese society wanting, collectively they provide rather solid grounds for being skeptical about the flood of statements that either the social structure or the value orientations found in Japanese society are so unique. In particular, they raise doubts whether, in comparison with people in other societies, the Japanese are *more* group-oriented, place *more* emphasis on consensus and social harmony, value *more* deeply group membership or social solidarity, or are *more* accustomed to 'vertical' forms of organization. Certainly, every society is unique; but is Japanese society as 'uniquely unique' in terms of its levels of consensus and social integration as so many seem to suggest? This is the major question which emerges from this rethinking.

The major sources of doubt behind the reappraisal of the theory of Japanese uniformity are discussed in the chapters forming the second and third parts of this volume. They may be summarized as follows. First, empirical observation, it can be argued, does not support the holistic view of Japanese society (Chapter 5). Second, the methodology of those emphasizing the uniqueness of Japanese society is seen as having major weaknesses (Chapter 6). Third, from the perspective of a sociology of knowledge, the ideological uses of the consensus-oriented view of Japanese society also raise serious questions (Chapter 7). Fourth, the methodology used by many in arguing the case for the group model can also be used to produce very different results (Chapters 8–10). Finally, in recent years some work has been done to suggest that alternative models of Japanese society can be produced (Befu: 1974, 1977, 1980 and 1982a; Sone: 1982a; Marshall: 1981; Koike: 1982; Iida: 1979). Chapters 11–14 present a multidimensional model of social stratification as an alternative way of looking at Japanese society.

IV Improving Our Perceptions of Japanese Society

Concerted efforts have been made in recent years to rethink seriously popular images of Japanese society. Criticism of the consensus-oriented view of Japanese society began to appear in the late sixties and came largely from Marxists and other anti-establishment scholars. In the United States the anti-war movement against American involvement in Vietnam tended to promote such views. In Japan a long tradition of Marxist and anti-establishment literature seems to have resurfaced as a result of student demonstrations, the anti-pollution movement and other developments in the late sixties and the early seventies. In the mid-seventies others joined this questioning, and by the end of the decade a number of conferences were being organized to reconsider the holistic image of Japanese society. These gatherings have been basically revisionist, in the sense of trying to incorporate conflict in Japanese society as an aberration or as an exception to the basic model, rather than treating it as a fundamental and endemic manifestation of the society. None the less, they bear witness to the fact that the old images of Japanese society are sometimes or in some ways misleading and that more realistic images are needed if we are really to understand Japanese society better.

All of this seems to be moving us toward a major reappraisal which may result in the development of new models. Though it is too early to foretell the new image, it seems likely that the group model of Japanese society will be replaced not simply by another similarly restricting image, but perhaps by several competing images, and that the study of Japanese society will become manifestly multi-paradigmatic. For this reason, the next decade will be exciting for this field of study. Such a scenario will also be accompanied by the demand for up-to-date information, not the hackneyed clichés of the old Japan hands who peddle Japanalia.

In view of the various issues discussed above, which way should Japanese studies move? Although the authors consider some answers to this question in the latter part of this book, it is their feeling that at least three preconditions need to be met before there can be a clear breakaway from the current images of Japanese society.

The first is to recognize variation within the society. Regardless of how homogeneous Japanese society may have been before the war or before the Meiji Restoration (assumptions themselves open to debate), today it is not a simple society readily amenable to sweeping generalizations. It is a complex industrial society with differentiation occurring in many dimensions. Consequently, it behoves those speaking about Japanese society to eschew the use of randomly or arbitrarily chosen examples without paying careful attention to the problems of sampling. Much of the literature on Japanese society treats society as the major unit of analysis, abstracting 'cultural averages' or 'dominant value orientations' in an effort to define national character as the major independent variable. There is too much internal variation which national character cannot explain.

The second step is to be aware of conflict, which has been a dominant feature of Japanese society in every historical period. In this regard, it is especially important to study the role of ideologies in Japan and the various mechanisms by which some Japanese control others. While recognizing that the distribution of ideological socialization and authority relations will be closely related to various kinds of structured social inequalities, we must also consider how conflict on one level (e.g., among certain groups) exists at least in part as a result of strong solidarities and consensus on other levels (e.g., among members within each of those groups).

The third need is to accept the possibility that several models or theories may be equally valid, each allowing us to generalize about different types of behavior. The multidimensional stratification model presented in this volume seeks to highlight the ways in which variation in behavior and thought occurs according to gender, age, occupation, education, geographical location and other factors generally associated with stratification. As an elaboration of one component of that model, work by Befu (1974, 1977 and 1980) on exchange theory is of considerable interest. Another related framework is emerging out of work on the structure of interest groups (Sone: 1982a; George: 1982). Emphasizing the way in which interest groups were shaped by various institutional pressures, this approach focuses on the dynamics of inter-group relationships.

Common to these perspectives is the introduction of self-interest as a key concept. Attention is directed to the study of how individual self-interests aggregated result in collective self-interests being articulated, if not on a societal level then at least in terms of interest groups and/or social strata. Even without cross-cultural comparisons, the investigation of these kinds of phenomena within any single society is a formidable task. By focusing attention on power relationships and on the nature of authority in Japanese society, these approaches make one more sensitive to the ways in which concepts such as 'the *amae* psychology', 'vertical society', and 'the culture of consensus' are used ideologically. From this perspective, the truly unique feature of Japanese society becomes the way in which ideologically colored lenses have been used to give many Japanese a narrow view both of their own society and of the world.

In May 1980 a symposium was organized in Australia around the theme of 'Alternative Models for Understanding Japanese Society'.[2] The presentations focused on paradigms in the study of Japanese society, common images of that society, some political aspects of Japanese behavior and reappraisals of economic organization in Japan. At a time when infatuation with the unique features of Japanese society was at its height, and bestsellers describing Japanese society in terms of one national characteristic or another seemed to be appearing one after the other, the papers at the symposium examined Japanese society from a variety of perspectives. In doing so, many of the participants expressed their doubts about the validity of the group model and the associated set of images which portray the Japanese as having underdeveloped egos, as lacking an autonomous sense of self-interest, as behaving only in groups and as placing an exceptionally great emphasis on consensus. At the same time, participants also underlined the need for more rigorous international comparisons, for some recognition of how such images serve as ideology, and for the development of new or alternative models which might equally well explain Japanese society.

In considering possible new directions for the study of this society, it might be useful to review briefly some of the major themes which emerged during the three-day symposium. First, considerable attention was given to questioning the extent to which Japanese behavior is voluntaristic or spontaneous. Among the points discussed were the coercive and ideological dimensions of singing company songs at morning ceremonies, of taking overnight trips with members of the same firm, of socializing with other workmates or of working long hours of overtime. The difficulties of simply reporting such behavior at face value were made apparent. In this regard, a number of persons stressed the importance of institutional developments and argued that behavior could not be understood apart from the complex array of situational constraints which fostered and shaped the emergence and evolution of major social institutions. It was also suggested that more attention should be given to interpreting the symbolic interaction of individuals in order to delineate clearly between *tatemae* (the spoken principles) observed on the surface and *honne* (the inner feelings) found, for example, in the cynical humour of Fuji Santarō, Asatte-kun and other characters which appear regularly in the comic strips of the major Japanese newspapers. From this perspective, the Japanese are not seen as working actively or positively to promote consensus, but as passively responding to the ideological insistence of those in positions of authority. There was a call, then, to consider the possibility that 'groupism' or the group model is in fact an ideology, albeit a very successfully propagated one, and that as such it represents an example of how the Japanese elite controls or manipulates the rest of society.

Another theme at the symposium concerned the methodology behind comparative statements about Japanese society. Not unrelated to the idea that much of the popular literature on Japanese society is based upon or parallels the views of the elite in society, this perspective questioned the fruitfulness of describing societies in terms of national averages and national character stereotypes which do not include women and therefore do not relate to half the population. Even among males, the sizable number of individuals not affiliated with enterprise unions is commonly neglected. In other words, many commonly accepted images do not form an appropriate depiction of all Japanese. In this regard, it was argued that more attention must be given to delineating the subcategories or strata being compared cross-culturally. Until more rigorous comparisons are made 'Japanese groupism' will remain not as verified fact, but as a competing, though perhaps interesting, hypothesis.

Finally, attention was centered on comparative statements about Japanese society which are made without adequate reference to the comparative base. From the point of view of one Indian participant, for example, Japanese society is extremely materialistic and individualistic. Because the comparative base is often some idealized notion of the West, comparative statements about actual behavior in Japan are often worded to imply that Japan is unique, whereas in fact many similar cases often exist outside the West. Moreover, in treating the West as a monolith, individual cases paralleling Japan even in the West are overlooked. From this point of view, the need for a more diversified international comparative perspective was underlined.

The conception, construction and testing of even a single model is a huge undertaking which cannot be carried out by one individual. It will require the cross-cultural cooperation of many engaged in Japanese studies, and it is important that bridges be built. Such bridges must consist of common vocabularies and the development of commonly accepted criteria for verifying different types of statement about Japanese society. The process will certainly be facilitated by efforts to delineate clearly the behavioral units of analysis (individuals, groups, institutions, nations, etc.), the populations (universes) about which generalizations are made and the sample actually studied, the types of behavior about which generalizations are made (phenomenological/observable or ideational/non-observable), the assumptions which link concepts about ideas with observed behavior used as evidence, and different types of assertions (descriptive statements–which may make claims about 'absolute facts' on comparative relativities–and causative statements). In conclusion, social phenomena are complex, and their understanding requires careful research; there is good reason to be wary of those who claim to have gained access to the secrets which unlock all doors to understanding Japanese society. Gimmicks, we suspect, will remain as the major trademark of those interested in 'Japanology', but they will be viewed with caution by those interested in promoting Japanese studies that are firmly rooted in the social sciences and in carefully documented historical research.

V The Importance of Having More Accurate Images of Japanese Society

Japan's experience has a great, though often differing, significance for many around the world. As the only non-Western society to industrialize fully, Japanese society has often been considered as a critical case in the study of industrialization. Many in the Third World scrutinize the Japanese experience for a possible model. Those in the already industrialized world re-examine their own ethnocentrism and the essence of their own experience with industrialization, contemplating, like Vogel, whether the process is inevitably tied to some Western quality or whether lessons might be learned from Japanese society for structuring post-industrial institutions in their respective societies.

For those who deal with Japan on a commercial basis, different questions are asked. However, the sense of urgency seems to be more pronounced, since the accuracy of their answers will be assessed more ruthlessly in terms of profits and losses at the end of the financial year. For those involved in the formulation and execution of public policy, there may be less interest in understanding Japan and more interest in the extent to which the stereotypical images might be used in their own society as an ideology to prod along the masses. Nevertheless, in the long run politicians too may be brought to account by their public for their policies.

Japan has changed tremendously over the past two or three decades and, whatever the causes, it is clear that Japanese businessmen are better informed about their industries and products than ever before. For foreign businessmen to compete in Japan, the old stereotypes will no longer do. They must have a certain proficiency in the Japanese language in order to tap the wealth of information being created within Japanese society. Of even greater importance, they must realize, as Neustupný (1979 and 1982b) has advised, that even the language is quite situational. Surely it is time to see beyond the Japanese and to examine the sources of variation within Japan, now a society of well over one hundred million individuals who belong to many different types of often competing groups.

Finally, there are ordinary citizens for whom no tangible or readily felt sanctions are attached to the factual validity of their images of Japanese society. Simple concern for international understanding and the values of cosmopolitanism and cultural relativism requires that we all accept responsibility for our views. The alternative is to fall victim to the human factor, which Higgins (1980) has described as political inertia and individual blindness, and to the reactionary nihilism described by Naipaul (1980). From this perspective as well, then, our images of Japanese society matter.

Part One

Two Views: Competing Images of Japanese Society

Chapter 2

The Great Tradition: Theories of Uniformity and Consensus in Japanese Society

Interest in Japanese society has expanded considerably over the past twenty years. This trend is apparent both in Japan and abroad, and is no doubt closely connected with Japan's emergence as an economic superpower, reflecting the desire of many to explain its rapid economic growth. At the end of the sixties, numerous observers began to refer to Japan's economic growth as a miracle. The speed at which Japan industrialized was seen as being unprecedented.

Much of the effort to explain such special phenomena focused on unique Japanese cultural elements. In the late sixties and early seventies the literature emphasizing the unique features of Japanese culture and the Japanese personality came to enjoy a remarkable popularity, not only in the mass media but also among informed scholars as well. This was particularly true in the English-speaking world.

While these images of Japanese society highlight its paradoxical aspects, there seems to have emerged out of the emphasis on the cultural inevitability of Japan's modernization a coherent picture of the society and culture as a holistic entity. By focusing on those characteristics believed to be unique to Japanese society, considerable importance was attached to Japanese values or thought patterns as the major independent variables explaining Japanese economic development. This development is assumed to have occurred in a more or less spontaneous or voluntaristic fashion. Kahn (1970), Nakane (1970), Doi (1973), Vogel (1979a), Reischauer (1979) and many othrs have helped to paint a picture of Japanese society which leads us to believe that it is exceptionally well integrated. The message is that, compared with people in other similarly industrialized societies, the Japanese are more group-oriented and are more influenced by cultural norms placing a value on consensus and loyalty to the group.

In Japanese this literature has been referred to as *nihonjinron, shinfūdoron, nihonbunkaron, nihonshakairon* or simply *nihonron.* Although there is no one model of Japanese society in the *nihonjinron* literature, its various descriptions of the Japanese and the explanations it advances for their behavior seem to share a set of common properties. The composite picture of Japanese society which can be constructed from this set of common elements has variously been labeled 'the folk model' (Befu: 1982b), 'the group model' (Befu: 1982a), 'Japan Theory' (Davis: 1982), 'the model in the *nihonjinron* literature', 'the uniformity theory of the Japanese' (SM: 1979c) and 'the holistic model of Japanese society' (Mouer: 1980a). Although these terms are used more or less interchangeably in this volume, 'holistic approach' is frequently utilized as a convenient label. Although the term 'holistic approach' has been used variously to indicate quite different meanings, here it is used to refer to an approach which assumes that societies represent the major cognitive unit for analysis, that they have goals, ends and purposes which form the dominant components of the mechanism accounting for individual motivation, and that they are characterized by a high degree of consensus which means that variants in behavior may best be understood as 'deviant behavior'. This largely follows the usage of Cotgrove (1967, p. 35) who writes: 'The "holistic" approach which emphasizes the influence of the whole (society as an organic, though abstract, entity) over the parts (individuals) who make up society ... has come to be known as *functionalism.*'

I The Holistic Approach to Japanese Studies in English

Since the end of World War II, a considerable literature on Japanese society has appeared in English. Produced largely by American scholars, it reflects to a great extent the social milieu in America, shifts in America's international relations (particularly with Japan) and the dominant trends in American social science. While some emphases have changed, there is also a good deal of continuity. By looking at four stages in the development of this literature, the following sections identify several major themes which have, over the years, given Japanese studies outside Japan a certain degree of continuity. In delineating four phases in the development of Japanese studies, it should be noted that there are no neatly separated intervals. The periods overlap and the changes are more gradual. Yet the idea of stages may serve as a heuristic device which can capture some of the shifts which certainly have also occurred.

A Anthropological Studies and the Search for a Rational Whole

The emergence of a fairly intelligible and coherent image of Japanese society in the English-language literature is largely a postwar phenomenon. Certainly, a more general image of the Orient had taken shape some time before (Said: 1979) and some concept of Japan as a distinct social unit can be discerned in the early accounts of Western visitors to Japan (Wilkinson: 1981). By the thirties the work of Embree (1972) and Norman (1975) had become available. However, the war and its aftermath produced new concerns and new realities.

In surveying the postwar English-language literature on modern Japanese society, three major currents have been identified by Hall (1971): the anthropological approach, the developmental approach and the Weberian-Parsonian approach. In his view, postwar scholarship reflected a rather consistent effort to grasp the totality of the Japanese experience with a focus on the more positive aspects of Japan's 'drive to modern nationhood'. He also argued that this was owing to the continuing influence of the anthropological approach which is the heritage of Japanese studies in the United States.

On this point, Hall (1971, pp. 24–5) commented as follows:

> Benedict was not, of course, the first to apply the techniques of anthropological study to Japan. John Embree was surely the real pioneer in that respect. But Benedict, because of her wide reputation and because of the ambitiousness of her effort to understand the Japanese people as a totality, came to symbolize an approach which was, and still is, of prime importance to American scholarship. From this approach there flowed a large stream of village and community studies such as the University of Michigan group's *Village Japan* (1959), my own *Government and Local Power in Japan, 500*

> *to 1700, A Study Based on Bizen Province* (1966), and Ronald Dore's *City Life in Japan* (1958). More importantly, it was largely through a theoretical core provided by the cultural anthropologist that the whole area-study approach to the study of Japan was conceived and applied to the American academic scene. It is probably safe to say that during the 1950's in America, academic training about Japan was by and large dominated by the area-study approach – by which I mean Japan was to be studied as a cultural entity on a *separate* but *equal* basis with our own culture (cf. Kluckhohn's 'common humanity and diverse cultures'), and that through a pooling of separate disciplinary insights it would be possible to arrive at a coherent appreciation of the totality of Japanese culture. The emphasis was on knowing enough of the total context – historical and cultural – to explain Japanese behavior. The Japanese had to be made to appear reasonable both in the past and at present, whether living in village or city, whether dressed in *sebiro* or *kimono.* What the cultural anthropologist and the area approach did was to wipe out the basis for explaining the Japanese as exotic or inscrutable or as having in modern times a 'split level' existence.

While one may argue whether the area approach served to wipe out or to reinforce the notion of Japan as an exotic or inscrutable entity, there would seem to be little doubt that the tendency was to look for an all-embracing picture of Japanese society. This facet of studies on Japan was noted even earlier by Abegglen (1958, p. 5)[1] who wrote that

> in speaking of modern Japan there is a distressing frequency of sentences beginning, 'The Japanese are . . . ,' which treat the nation and its people as a compact and homogeneous unit with little or no note of the diversity and complexity of this modern nation.

The early attempts to grasp Japanese society as a totality had at least one major consequence. That was the predilection of many to avoid or to minimize the issue of conflict in Japanese society and the concomitant need to differentiate between different types of Japanese. This was often done by referring to the 'two-sidedness' of the Japanese character, or falling back on explanations which emphasize the importance of paradoxes as an inherent ingredient of Japanese society. In other words, the problem of differentiation – the fact that the observation of Japanese society at different levels results in conflicting views – has often been dismissed by the tautological assertion that Japanese society is paradoxical. While all societies are paradoxical, those promoting the group model as a basis for understanding Japanese society seem to begin with the assumption that Japanese society is more paradoxical than others. In this regard, Glazer (1974, pp. 22–5) argues that Japanese society has often been projected as being paradoxical or unpredictable, and that this view is reinforced by the tendency to stereotype the Japanese:

> The following points to my mind characterize the present attitude of the best-educated Americans toward Japan, on the whole: that they (the Japanese) are *characterized by radical paradoxes*; connected with this sense of radical paradox is a sense of *alienness* – and whether we see Japanese as alien because they are paradoxical, or paradoxical because they are alien, I am not sure; that one aspect of their alienness is their *insensitivity* to others, their peculiar relations to other people; that because of this paradoxicality they are basically *unpredictable* – they may change from one thing to another overnight; that because they are unpredictable one must approach their present prosperity, growth, and stability with a sense of extreme caution – in effect they are fundamentally *unstable*; since they are unstable, we must in particular be distrustful of the *Japanese commitment to democracy*. Admittedly, there are attitudes and images that run strongly counter to all these. These images are held not only by Americans who are fundamentally hostile to Japan and the Japanese – that would be natural – but by most American Japanese experts too, and therefore, those who help shape educated Americans' attitudes of Japan.

Finally, one should note the tenacity with which the imagery produced by the anthropological approach has survived through the postwar period, and the extent to which the production of such images has been characterized by conformity in opinion and approach. This point was also well articulated by Glazer (1974, pp. 17–19):

> What is striking when one reviews the central opinion-and image-makers about Japan in this country (America)–though admittedly all such conclusions must be, if easy to document, impossible to prove–is how much has remained constant between 1946 and 1972, even while such a fantastic change has taken place in the nature of Japan itself, in Japanese society, in the Japanese individual, in Japan's role in the world, and in its relations with the United States. Of course, this enormous change has had some effect. As we have seen from the *Asahi* poll, the feeling about Pearl Harbor has faded, and almost fully positive images about the Japanese now occupy first place in the American mind. This change has of course affected what the central shapers of opinion on Japan have had to say ...
>
> One would expect the general softening of language. Isolation now has positive as well as negative effects. But what is worth noting is how much remains the same: for example, the Japanese difficulty in relating to the rest of the world.

In evaluating the image of Japanese society produced by the anthropological approach, it is interesting to observe that the paradoxes described by Glazer are part of an image which Hall claims the anthropological approach was designed to correct. While the holistic approach tended to assume social integration, there were simply too many facets of an increasingly complex society which could not be fitted neatly into a single package. How much easier it would have been had the fact simply been recognized that within the same society different groups of people have different interests and goals. When these come into conflict, there is a process which sometimes shifts authority, power and other instruments of repression into the hands of one group or another. Such shifts have much to do not only with the well-being of each group involved, but also with its ability to express its own values. These simple points have consistently been played down in favor of the maze of paradoxes. Further, the image of Japanese society described by Glazer, which comes out repeatedly in the phrase 'they (the Japanese)', makes it difficult to explain changes in the power structure as an outcome of rational processes which lead to rational conflict.

B The Modernization Approach and the Conferences on Japan

The inter-disciplinarity and the all-encompassing overview associated with the anthropological approach were complemented in the sixties by a degree of disciplinary specificity. Theoretical concepts and the tools of each autonomous discipline came to be applied to the study of Japan with some rigor in the United States. Area studies were seen as a soft option which could coexist with the hard option offered by the various graduate departments in America's leading universities. Area studies by themselves never gained the respectability of the hard social sciences, but nevertheless produced people quite capable of pricking the most sophisticated generalizations and theories, which invariably deviated from some of the more minute particularistic facts. One accommodation was the disciplinary program with an area studies component. The concept which linked the two together was modernization. Accordingly, scholars could be encouraged to treat Japanese society as a discrete entity to be studied within each discipline. The focus was placed on Japan's century of modernization and on explaining Japan's emergence as a modern state. The emphasis shifted to the flow of historical events and the integrative forces which seemed to have bound the nation together in a more or less collective effort to achieve modern industrialization. Attention was given primarily to those elements which seemed to survive the Tokugawa period and to continue displaying a presence through the Meiji, Taishō and Shōwa years.

This predilection to look for a unilinear shift in 'dominant value orientations' was a major feature of the 'Parsonian school' which emerged in the United States in the late fifties. Though it is difficult to distinguish clearly between the ideas of Talcott Parsons and those of his more zealous students, it is not surprising to find that one of the earliest proponents of this view, Robert Bellah, concludes his work on Japan's version of the Protestant ethic with the statement that 'actually all the evidence available about popular sects and ethnic movements indicates that they taught a virtually identical ethic' (Bellah: 1957, p. 98).[2] The same conclusion was drawn ten years later by Marshall (1967, p. 114) who writes about the inability of the Japanese business community to establish an independent, self-legitimating ideology in prewar Japan.

Work on Japan's modernization culminated in the six volumes produced by a series of seminars known collectively as the Conference on Modern Japan. Although individual exceptions exist, the series as a whole relied heavily on the holistic approach. One volume on society, for example, focuses on ascertaining how industrialization occurred with the gradual evolution of societal values, which were defined in terms of the Parsonian pattern variables. This problem consciousness is clearly stated in the introduction (Dore: 1967, pp. 3–24). A similar concern with the integrated whole of society, sometimes referred to as the systems approach, can also be found in the introduction to the volumes on political development (Ward: 1968, pp. 6–9), social attitudes (Jansen: 1965, pp. 44–7) and Japanese culture (Shively: 1971, pp. xiii–xvii). In the volume on economic development, the interactions between various economic subsectors, particularly the rural and urban sectors, and the notion of duality are discussed. But the assumption of system integration is not seriously questioned as a core issue; nor is it seriously discussed in terms of a concept like exploitation. The paradigmatic parameters are fairly well spelled out in the preface (Lockwood: 1965, pp. 3–4) where the problem consciousness is discussed:

> From this book spanning a century of modern Japanese history one gains a sense of the essential continuity in the process by which Japan has transformed herself from a remote agrarian kingdom into the world's third or fourth largest industrial power. Persisting goals of national development and personal advance evoke recurrent patterns of thought and action amid changing circumstances. The sustained momentum of growth is striking, even more than the bursts of speed. A pragmatic instrumentalism in leadership and a resilient, cohesive response from the people are evident in the initial decades after 1868, and no less in today's resurgence from war and defeat.

During the latter part of the sixties, a reassessment of the 'modernization approach' can be detected, as suggested by the title, *Dilemmas of Growth*, which was given to the sixth and final volume of the modernization series. The earlier volumes were based upon assumptions of continuing prosperity and social stability, which seemed to characterize studies on Japanese society during the sixties. They began with Japan's achievements in the mid-sixties and tended to project those images back through time by tracing the positive undercurrents which had brought Japan to its present prosperity and seeming sense of societal consensus, or, at least, societal acceptance of the situation. Morley (1971, p. 9) describes this bias in the introduction to the final volume in that series:

> The earlier seminars, having been organized largely along disciplinary lines, had tended to emphasize the long flow of the modernization process, the deep continuities in separate spheres of life – intellectual, economic, political, social and cultural. At the same time, partly as a result of having tried too hard to look at the secular trends from the late Tokugawa to the present, the Conference has inevitably become impressed with the extraordinary overall success of various phases of the modernization effort in Japan and therefore has devoted considerable effort to trying to explain why things had gone so well.

In general, the modernization approach failed to deal adequately with questions of self-interest. The assumptions about social consensus and dominant value orientations were seriously undermined by events occurring in Japan in the late sixties and early seventies: the student demonstrations, the emergence of popular citizens' movements (*shimin undō* and *jūmin undō*), heightened emotions during the spring wage offenses (*shuntō*) and a prevailing sense of social uneasiness.

Somewhat outside the mainstream of the modernization school, Lockheimer (1969), for example, was one student of Japanese society who picked up the importance of these developments. As one of the Japanese participants in the Conference, Maruyama (1963 and 1965) quite early emphasized the importance of considering some of the dysfunctional aspects in the process of Japan's modernization. Another participant, Ishida, wrote somewhat later about the overemphasis on harmony and continuity in the following manner (1970, p. 10):

> Among some American scholars and some Japanese who have rather highly evaluated the century of Japanese modernization following the Meiji Restoration, there has been a marked tendency to ignore or play down the period of Japanese militarism as an exception to the general flow of Japanese history. Among these scholars the major emphasis has been focused on Japan's take-off to high economic

> growth rates and modernization following the Meiji Restoration and Japan's phenomenal economic growth in the postwar period. What lies in between, including the catastrophe of the Second World War, has more often than not been overlooked and neglected by these individuals. [Translated by the authors]

Many Japanese had been aware of these disruptive tendencies and the existence of considerable levels of conflict and coercion. It is, therefore, not surprising that the above caveats were lodged by Japanese and a foreign observer long resident in Japan. Although both Hall (1971, p. 32–3) and Reischauer (Anon: 1971) seemed to have been aware of the sudden increase in the number of young American scholars interested in conflict, both tended to dismiss that concern as a passing fad in work on Japanese society. Nevertheless, there seems to have been a greater willingness among scholars to question whether these kinds of happening were new to Japan and to consider whether they could be an integral part of Japanese society. It would also be incorrect to imply that reservations were expressed only after the fact as a reaction to these 'unexpected' events.

At the same time, the effect of this rethinking on the mainstream of American scholarship should not be overemphasized. The re-examination found in *Dilemmas of Growth* consisted mostly of balancing some of the pluses with a few minuses, and of describing dysfunctions without explaining the dynamics or processes which caused them. The failures found in Japan's modernization were conceptualized primarily as failures for the nation rather than as failures for some and benefits for others. Even Maruyama (1965, p. 493) refers to 'a traditional ethic which has been valid for promoting modernization at a certain stage' but then transforms 'itself into fetters when further modernization becomes necessary at a later stage'. He also argues for the need to understand 'the success and failure *of modern Japan* in terms of 'ambivalent possibilities' for democracy and authoritarianism.

The major correction was in the sum rather than the function itself; the change was in the overall evaluation of Japan, not in the approach. References to social tension were thus subsumed within a larger concern with the potential of the system to handle and resolve conflict rather than with the sources or meaning of the conflict itself. One wonders seriously whether instead it might have been more fruitful to examine Japan's 'modern' century of development not only in terms of commonly shared successes and failures, but also in terms of the relative successes it produced for some and the relative failures it held for others. Certainly it did not hold the same meaning for everyone.

In this regard, it seems particularly odd that in the introduction to *Dilemmas of Growth* Morley does not follow up the development of his major theme. Initially, he confronts the problem squarely in his rather general but none the less perceptive treatment of the Marxist position as a thorn in the side of the modernization approach (especially pp. 10–26). He identifies the central issue as the existence, dimensions and meaning of tension and conflict within the system. He also mentions several other approaches. But the matter is then suddenly dropped just when one might reasonably expect the discussion to move toward a resolution. The Marxist view seems to be dismissed simply because of some need for a more benign understanding of the Japanese themselves. With regard to the Marxist position, he writes (p. 12) as follows:

> It is not surprising that these works have been criticized as 'history without people' and have not yet found a grateful acceptance by most Japanese. The war was a personal thing, a time of grief through which all Japanese have passed, either in their own experience or vicariously in the experience of their fathers and brothers. Surely there is fault somewhere, but, in a land where group responsibility, the virtue of loyalty, and a consciousness of fate have been so interwoven in the sensibilities of the people, there has been a deeply felt demand for an attitude more humane than that of the victors or the Marxist-Leninists, and for a more humane history, one to be sure that will not deny the wrong paths taken, but one which will also build a bridge over the great gulf of defeat, so that surviving Japanese can live with themselves and so that future generations can look back on their ancestors with love and pride, or at the very least, understanding.

While the textbook issue in the summer of 1982 makes part of this statement appear naïve, there are also questions about the experiences of women during the war and about the distinction between those who sympathize with the peace movement and socialist causes and those who do not. Moreover, the analysis is clearly inconsistent with the first volume of the series in which Hall (1965a, p. 13) states that 'few other concepts of modernization have appeared to the Japanese so comprehensive and so capable of application to the Japanese experience as ... the Marxist approach.' However, the most basic shortcoming is the failure to question the assumption of consensus and homogeneity. Morley's Japanese included not only the victims of national policy but also those who consciously designed and perpetrated such a policy. The same tendency can be seen in the way Morley paraphrases one of Kawashima Takeyoshi's major premises as the assumption 'that democracy is an integral part of the good society that the Japanese have been and are striving for' (p. 4). The substitution of 'some Japanese' for 'the Japanese' would make all the difference in how one interprets Kawashima's point of view. Finally, one is unsure of how being able to look back on one's ancestors with love and pride is related to the accurate description of Japanese society. One is also unsure of why there is a need for scholarship which allows us to build bridges but not for scholarship which might promote democracy. Although these concerns are important, and are directly linked to the formation of problem consciousness, they do not form very firm grounds for accepting or rejecting the accuracy of statements about social reality.

C The Return to Neo-holistic Conceptions of Japanese Society

In the late sixties and early seventies interest in Japanese society as a totality seems to have reached a new level. In the English literature Nakane's typology for interpersonal relationships attracted much interest and was widely acclaimed for its insight into certain unique aspects of Japanese society. Her approach contrasted the importance of 'vertical' or hierarchical ties and group solidarity in the Japanese context with 'horizontal' or egalitarian ties and individualism in the Western setting (Nakane: 1965, 1970, 1971, 1972b). Although Ishida (1971: especially pp. 37–48) seems to have been much more aware of the need to deal with conflict in Japanese society, he nevertheless argued that such conflict must be viewed in terms of the uniquely Japanese concept of competitiveness resulting from strong ties of loyalty to concentric groups (the family, the village, the firm, the military, the *batsu* and the nation). In other words, competition is seen as being a by-product of group conformity and the lack of horizontal mobility within given occupational groupings, which makes competition among individuals within their organization all the more intense.

DeVos (1972), a social psychologist, argued that paternalism is still a most valid concept for understanding interpersonal relationships in contemporary Japan, following very closely the reasoning of Nakane. DeVos (1973: Chapters 7 and 14) also argued that the socialization experience of the Japanese leads them to sacrifice themselves and their own self-interest to maintain harmony within the group or organization to which they belong. Group loyalty is manifested in the strong achievement orientation of individuals who seek to perform for the group and for themselves through work. Japanese who are unable to experience a sense of self-realization at work often feel guilty of having failed to achieve their group's goals. They then work harder to achieve group goals and in the process become emotionally committed to a unique work ethic. Given the structure of Japanese self-identity, DeVos maintains that class conflict has never appealed to the Japanese and has not been significant in their society. Rather, the group-based achievement orientation is seen as the source of the high worker morale which has produced Japan's spectacular economic growth. It is also seen as the explanation for the relative absence of alienation among the Japanese.

In psychiatry, Doi (1962, 1967, 1973) has stressed the importance of the primary group in Japanese society, claiming that the constant dependence on these kinds of tie prevents the Japanese from becoming emotionally independent individuals, a trait commonly associated with Western people. He attempts to link the uniqueness of the Japanese psychology closely with the uniqueness of the Japanese language, focusing his analysis largely on the presence of one word in the Japanese vocabulary, *amae*. This kind of psychological dependency was also identified by Austin (1967) and referred to as the 'Izumi Syndrome' in a slightly different analysis. Nakamura (1974) writes that Japanese political behavior is dominated by the sense of fulfillment which the Japanese receive from selfless service to the group. This interest in the Japanese national character as the major explanatory device in studies on Japanese society will no doubt be further reinforced in the English-language literature by the recent translations of two older works on Japanese character, one written in the prewar period by Watsuji (1962 and 1971) and the other in the mid-fifties by Minami (1971). Another addition to this literature is the comparative study by 'Bendasan'

(1972) of Japanese and Jewish cultures and the impact of each culture on its respective society. Finally, Lebra (1976) has tried to capture the essence of Japanese society by focusing on the etymological origins of words such as *okagesamade, omoiyari* and *sumimasen.* The assumption is that the original meanings are still associated with the words, and that the words accurately reflect social norms about proper social relationships.

To a considerable extent, the plausibility of these explanations has been reinforced by the fact that most of the Japanese authors have been recognized scholars at reputable universities. It has often been said that Japanese academics often simplify and generalize too much when writing for foreign audiences. In the case of the items cited above, however, parallel versions can be found in Japanese (Nakane: 1967a; Ishida: 1970; Doi: 1971; Nakamura: 1973; Watsuji: 1935; Minami: 1953; 'Bendasan': 1970). This genre of writing is well entrenched, and to the extent that many of these scholars interact frequently with their counterparts overseas, their view of Japan is further reinforced through a vast network of informal interpersonal relationships. For example, one can cite the series of special contributions made by Tokuyama Jirō head of the prestigious Nomura Research Institute, to *Newsweek* during a good part of the seventies.

As the last statement suggests, the predominance of the consensus or group model of Japanese society is not found only in the vast array of academic literature, for it also predominates in the coverage given Japan by English-language newspapers and weekly magazines.[3] However, as Glazer (1974, pp. 12–13) notes, the opinions of those in the mass media and popular press are formed primarily from their understanding of what is written and said by the 'academic experts'. Book reviews in the mass media praise items like Nakane's *Japanese Society*, claiming that it is the key which 'unlocks Japanese society'.[4] Others continue to emphasize the resistance of Japan's unique values to the more superficial outward appearances of Western influence which have been introduced with rapid economic growth (Halloran: 1970, especially Part II). The conclusion is that the Japanese differ from other peoples, particularly in terms of their homogeneity and propensity for belonging to groups (Adachi: 1973).

Finally, the vogue which this approach has enjoyed is clearly reflected in two concepts which appeared at the end of the sixties: 'the Japanese superstate' and 'Japan, Inc.'. Kahn's argument that the twenty-first century would belong to Japan rested, in good measure, on the notion that Japanese economic activity was significantly supported by a unique set of social values. In Kahn's view, they accounted for Japan's social solidarity, stable labor-management relations and extremely high propensity for saving (Kahn: 1970).[5] Although Kahn has perhaps had the greatest impact on the American public, he certainly did not stand alone. A large number of similar books (Guillain: 1970; Hedberg: 1970; von Krookow: 1970; Brochier: 1965; Price: 1971; Eunson: 1965) appeared elsewhere in the West at about the same time, serving further to strengthen the images projected by Kahn. A survey of the Japanese economy by the *Economist* also emphasized the underlying sense of consensus which binds together the Japanese nation in its commitment to industrial activity.[6] Although a few have suggested that Japan's growth rate may slow down in the seventies (Brzezinski: 1972; Brooks: 1972), an image of unprecedented growth and national harmony continues to be projected in most forecasts even after the oil shock.[7]

At the same time, there has appeared in the United States the term 'Japan, Inc.'. This kind of label has often been utilized by those arguing that the Japanese have had an unfair advantage by developing and/or maintaining social organizations out of line with those generally found in Western society. These special forms of social organization, it is reasoned, are a major force generating Japan's excessively successful economic performance at home. The end result is seen as unemployment and other problems in the domestic economies of other nations. The idea of Japan as a corporate nation suggests that Japan is organized like one large corporation, with the government and big business serving as the board of directors and the mass of the people loyally filling the various roles of the accommodating employee. Although this term appeared in Kahn's *The Emerging Japanese Superstate*, it seems to have been made popular through the writings of Abegglen (1970a and 1970b).[8]

Two subtle changes in the literature can be discerned. One is the introduction of scare tactics to awaken the American public to the reality and, therefore, danger of Japan's sudden presence as a formidable competitor in the world economy. This is reflected in the subtitle given to one article published in the *Washington Post* (Abegglen: 1970b):

> The Japanese economy is now the third largest, its growth rate approaches 15% per year. If present trends continue,

> Japan will be the world's most affluent nation by the end of the century.

This theme can also be seen in the title given to the cover story in a special issue of *Time* (10 May 1972): 'Japan, Inc.: Winning the Most Important Battle'. The second development is the direct involvement of the US Department of Commerce in its own independent study of Japanese society in the name of the Director of the Far East Division of the Bureau of International Commerce (Kaplan: 1972). It should be pointed out that the Boston Consulting Group, with which Abegglen is associated as its most important specialist on Japan, did the three case studies which appear in the Department's report. Along the same lines are the publications by Van Zandt (1970 and 1972). These kinds of writing contained a number of unspoken assumptions about Japanese society which came to be embodied in criticism of Japan. When friction resulting from Japan's exports seemed to reach a new high in the early eighties, these assumptions appear to have been consolidated further. All of this coverage in the mass media might be passed off simply as propaganda or ideology were it not for the very active involvement of academics in promoting such views of Japanese society.

D The Learn-from-Japan Boom

Following the theories of modernization and the reappraisals of Japanese society it is not surprising that the idea of reverse convergence should emerge. Best articulated by Dore (1973), the argument is that Japan may have industrialized so fast that it achieved a post-industrial state without having lost its sense of cultural continuity or its basic respect for human relationships. Thus, while other industrial societies seem to be plagued by high unemployment, welfare programs they cannot afford, drug addiction and alienation, some have argued that Japan passed through the stage of industrialization and achieved a post-industrial situation so rapidly that it never had a chance to experience all the dislocations commonly associated with industrialization. It arrived on the doorstep of tomorrow with its social structure intact and its culture integrated. In looking at one aspect of Japanese society, industrial relations, Dore (1971) coined the term 'corporate welfarism' to refer to the sense of family and of looking after one's own which he felt characterized at least the large-scale sector in Japan.

Vogel's *Japan as Number One* (1979) puts the case more bluntly. Japan has been successful in a number of ways. While some have been critical of Vogel for overlooking some of the failures of Japanese society, the deterioration of America's competitive edge vis-à-vis the Japanese has lent credence to arguments that Americans need to learn from abroad and particularly from Japan. Few would dissent from the view that ethnocentric preconceptions have blinded many people in America to the possibility that other societies may have some useful clues for Americans on how to restructure their own. Following Vogel's bestseller, it has become fashionable to conclude academic treatises on Japan with a chapter on lessons from Japan. This can be seen, for example, in recent books by Cole (1979), Schonberger (1982), Cummings (1980) and Stucki (1978a and 1978b). Levine and Kawada (1980) also display a similar problem consciousness, although they tend to discuss the issue in the broader context of the debate on convergence and divergence and with less attention on lessons for America. In recent years, learn-from-Japan campaigns can be seen in Singapore (Kunugi: 1982; Awanohara: 1982), Malaysia (Takagi: 1982) and the Philippines (Salvador and Eduarte: 1982). This broader interest in lessons for development can also be seen in the symposium recently organized in Singapore around Vogel's book (Lim: 1982). Chinese translations of the most popular English volumes on Japanese society (e.g., Reischauer: 1980; Vogel: 1980b; and Nakane: 1982) and their own studies of Japanese management practices (Liu *et al.*: 1982) can be found on many shelves in China.

This trend seems to be particularly pronounced in the area where America and Europe seem to be having the most difficulties these days: firm management in the private sector. In 1982 Sharon Johnson made the following observation:

> The impact of things Japanese on American society has never been more powerful, and that impact is spreading rapidly across American campuses. Because many college and university officials believe their students' success as businessmen, lawyers and engineers depends on their understanding and in some cases borrowing of Japanese methods and philosophies, Japanese studies are becoming an important part of the curriculum of American schools.

Other journalists have also noted that a good part of America's trade imbalance with Japan is owing to inferior and short-sighted policies in America (Wade: 1982; Berger: 1982). The volumes of Ouchi (1981a), Pascale and Athos (1981a), Low (1982), Ohmae (1982), and Richardson and Ueda (1981) were designed to fill this need for quick information on Japan. Unlike the last item, which provides a more careful overview, the others (which are the bestsellers) package all the generalizations found in the neo-holistic view of Japanese society and argue for a spiritual revitalization of American management.

Pascale and Athos (p. 26) argue that 'managerial reality ... is socially and culturally determined' and seek to expose blind spots in American culture and society. While accepting that there are many similarities (p. 131), they argue that the crucial difference boils down to the American cultural emphasis on independence and the Japanese on interdependence. Ouchi also allows for American organizational features that strongly resemble Japanese firms (p. 60), but none the less underlines as the crucial differences the cultural characteristics of the Japanese corporation: consensus, collective values and management's 'holistic concern for the people' (pp. 33–47). In a cynical vein, Davis (1982, p. 254) notes the popularity of another volume:

> Misunderstandings of Japan are, and always have been, legion in the West. A good current example is the craze among Wall Street types for *The Book of Five Rings*, a classical manual on swordsmanship by the 17th century samurai, Miyamoto Musashi. Because the book was rumored to be a revelation of the spirit behind Japan's economic muscle ('Japan's Answer to the Harvard MBA'), American industrialists have been poring over the obscurity of its 96 pages in search of the samurai's power of positive thinking. Little do they know that in 1645, when the book was written, samurai were not allowed to engage in business, and that those who did give up their swords for the abacus usually went broke.

In the area of social order, the Japanese are seen as models by Clifford (1976) and Bayley (1976). Bayley discusses structural features related to the way police are organized, but in the end stresses the cultural dimensions: ethnic homogeneity, the absence of large or noticeable differences between social classes, family paternalism at work, the prevalence of group solutions as opposed to individual solutions. Clifford argues that Japanese cultural characteristics account for Japan's low crime rate. Relying almost entirely on sources in English, Clifford emphasizes the importance of conventional concepts such as face-saving, groupism, consensus orientation, and *amae*. His discussion seldom touches upon the political aspects of control or upon white-collar crime and hard-core political corruption.

Throughout this literature there is a mixture of new and old themes. Increasingly, there is a concern with national interest and stemming the Japanese tide. In the mass media there is still the hackneyed play on Japanese words: references to the Japanese *yen* for work, to the dark side of the *rising sun*, or to there being no *shame* in living well, or to the *suicidal* drive to world supremacy.[9] The picture of a kimono-clad young woman on a motorcycle still has the ring of reality for many foreigners. These constant retreats into the cultural grab-bag of the past underline the sense of paradox mentioned by Glazer. The emphasis on the human element in the personal relationships of Japanese businessmen is offset by innuendoes suggesting that Japan's *sararīman* works in a pre-programmed fashion to serve 'Japan, Inc.', the giant bulldozer mercilessly unearthing the world's last resources. Paradoxes in another domain, baseball, are emphasized by Whiting (1977).

The literature is also ambivalent on whether the differences between Japan and America (or the West) are structural or cultural. On one hand, the structural dimensions are underlined – either explicitly, as Vogel (1979, p. ix) does, or implicitly – by suggestions that there are organizational gimmicks which can readily be employed. At the same time, however, voluntaristic assumptions about Japanese behavior also abound and the power relations and coercive mechanisms which are also part of Japanese society are never discussed. The distinction between culture and ideology is seldom, if ever, made and the presence of the values attributed to the Japanese is never systematically studied.

II The Holistic View of Japanese Society in Japanese Literature

Japanese intellectuals have been addressing the question of Japan's uniqueness for several centuries. During the Tokugawa period, Kokugaku scholars such as Motoori Norinaga studied this problem

(Matsumoto: 1981). The word *wakon kansai* (Chinese learning with the Japanese spirit) came to symbolize both academic and ideological interest in the essence to Japanese society and culture.

In the Meiji period, enlightenment, which meant Western learning, was advocated by scholars like Fukuzawa Yukichi whose *Seiyō Jijō* (The Western Situation) came to dominate the intellectual climate of the times. The deeply felt need among intellectuals and leaders for Japan to compete with the industrializing nations of the West provided a backdrop for the popular discussion of theories concerning Japanese society. The need to Westernize and mobilize the nation created a difficult situation in which values and ideology were extremely difficult to disentangle. The new slogan was *wakon yōsai* (Western learning with the Japanese spirit). It is therefore not surprising that two distinct traditions emerged, one emphasizing the importance of cultural values shared by the common people in accounting for Japanese patterns of behavior and thought, and the other emphasizing the need to educate the people by disseminating ideas of enlightenment from above. In this context, the mood of the Japanese has swung back and forth between periods of inferiority complex and superiority complex. To some extent this has been a function of Japan's place in the international arena at any given time.

During the Meiji and Taishō years, one can discern phases in which attention was focused on the examination and preservation of Japan's 'unique national culture': *jōiron* (an argument for expelling foreigners) at the time of the Meiji Restoration, the rise of ultra-nationalism toward the end of the nineteenth century, and the propagation of the theory comparing the Japanese nation to the Japanese family system after the Russo-Japanese War provide ready examples (Hijikata: 1982, pp. 26–7). Interspersed between these nationalistic years, there were periods during which opinion leaders stressed the importance of transplanting universalistic values allegedly present in Western societies. The post-Restoration enlightenment movement (as symbolized by Rokumeikan and Meirokusha), and Taishō democracy (with its openness to ideas about universal suffrage and unionization) represent this line of thinking.

These fluctuations in the images of Japanese society were carried over into the Showa period, when the lines of difference between the two competing views – the theory of cultural uniqueness and shared essences and the theory of conflict – became clearly drawn. It was at that time that the historical development of these two views was being traced by Hasegawa (1966). Although a number of studies emphasizing ideological control were written even during the war (e.g., Tosaka: 1937; Ienaga: 1977; Sakaguchi: 1968), the position stressing the uniqueness and prime significance of Japanese cultural values held sway in both academic and journalistic communities. In focusing on the latter tradition, the account given here begins with a brief look at some of the views which prevailed immediately before the outbreak of World War II, and then considers how *nihonjinron* has developed in the postwar period. The discussion is organized according to the period divisions developed by Kawamura (1982a).

Reserving discussion of the literature produced by those emphasizing conflict until the next chapter, here we will focus on the view of Japanese society which has stressed the importance of a uniquely Japanese set of cultural values. In doing so, we begin by looking briefly at views which prevailed in the prewar period.

A 'National Culture'

Many of the basic ingredients of Japanology today can be discerned in the thirties. At that time theories of Japanese national culture seemed to attract the interest of both academics and the public at large. The period was also characterized by militant chauvinism and the denigration of Western culture. Within Japan white racism was seen as the dominant ideology of the international scene. The failure of the League of Nations to pass a resolution on racial equality tended to undermine its moral authority on other matters, such as Japan's activities in Manchuria. Under these circumstances, Japan withdrew from the League; many Japanese felt it imperative that other ways be found to provide Japanese citizens with a growing sense of pride (Takata: 1934). The sense of injustice and of being so clearly right on the issue of race also carried over to other areas and invited from the more romantic nationalists theories of Japanese superiority.

It was difficult, however, for the romanticists to argue on objective criteria that Japanese material culture (such as technology or military might) was superior, although some did make reference to advanced technologies in dyeing, spinning, pottery, lacquer ware and other traditional industries. With regard to military goods and household commodities, the items which seemed to count most abroad, Japan had not yet matched the West. However, by focusing attention on a number of intangible areas such as the spirit, the mind and emotional feelings, Japan's leaders implanted a belief that the inalienable superiority of these more fundamental traits would later manifest itself in material terms. Japan would win wars and industrialize! The relationship between *wakon* (the Japanese spirit) and *yōsai* (Western technology) was subtle but firm. Out of this milieu, three major themes emerged.

The first is the climatological analysis of Watsuji (1935). He linked Japanese culture and national character with the Japanese climate, maintaining that the East Asian monsoon climate was the major determinant shaping Japanese society and culture. According to Watsuji, the monsoon produced patience and a certain duality in the Japanese setting, where the tropical and the arctic were mixed together to produce clearly delineated seasons but also sudden unexpected changes. Watsuji sought parallels to the climate in the national character of the Japanese. On one hand, he argued that the Japanese possessed 'gentle passion' and 'militant open-heartedness'. On the other, he maintained that the Japanese climate had produced among the populace a unique way of living which consisted of delicacy, restraint and compassion. However, he did not carry out any systematic research to compare the characteristics of the Japanese with those of other nationalities. Nor did he seek to compare rigorously the different geographic areas in Japan. Nevertheless, to the end Watsuji maintained that Japan's climate was unique, and that the Japanese would be happiest adapting themselves to this reality and learning to love their climatological uniqueness. These ideas were later disseminated by Shiga (1937) and Haga (1938).

A second approach can be found in the ethnography of Yanagida. His aim was to establish an indigenous scholarship rooted in the world view and life experiences of the common people. He challenged Japan's academic scholarship, which relied heavily on abstract theories and concepts imported from the West. Yanagida collected and compiled a vast array of data from every part of Japan, including information on the customs, festivals and legends of the lower-class and non-urban population. Yanagida has had a lasting influence upon those with a serious interest in the social history of Japan. The publication of his complete works in 31 volumes in the sixties is one indication of the continuing regard for his scholarship. The work of Yanagida and others who followed his line of thinking, such as Origuchi (1972–4) seems to focus attention on Japan's uniqueness, and thus the need for indigenous concepts. However, given their commitment to establishing a genuinely Japanese scholarship which is constructed with Japanese cultural concepts and which is free from Western frameworks of analysis, these scholars rarely considered their findings in comparative terms. Apart from a few, such as Minakata (1971–5) who sought to place ethnographic observations within a more universal framework, the tendency was to refrain from making explicit inter-societal comparisons while arguing that the patterns they observed were uniquely Japanese. Perhaps as a result of this ambiguity, many in this school found it difficult to stand apart from the militaristic nationalism which swept the nation in the thirties.

A third prewar stream can be found in the rural sociology of Aruga Kizaemon. Inspired by Yanagida's ethnographic work, Aruga forged a rural sociology which was empirically grounded and theoretically informed. Family sociologists in postwar Japan have been strongly influenced by Aruga's conceptualization of the family and the idea of concentric loyalties. The notion of Japan being a vertically structured society had its origin in Aruga (1943: p. 33):

> I do not claim that there are no classes in Japanese society. However, I am of the view that one cannot analyse the nature of class consciousness in Japan in terms of the Western concept of it. Western social organization is based upon individuality. In the West, *horizontal* organization has been predominant, as observed in a parliamentary system consisting of representatives from various classes. On the other hand, Japanese social organization is based on the link between a superior and an inferior. In Japan, *vertical* organization has been pervasive, as is the case with the organization of the *dōzoku* manifested in the *oya-ko* relationship [between a leader and his follower]. This contrast highlights the difference in the national character of the Japanese and of Westerners. It is no surprise, then, that the theory of class struggle developed in the West. Taken up by the leftist movement as a kind of fashion, the theory of class struggle never became popular in Japan. This is because the Japanese national character and the characteristics of Japanese social organization hardly required these kinds of theories. [Translated by the authors with the italics added]

In this quotation two themes common to all three prewar traditions can be seen. One is the view that particular concepts and theories are applicable only to Japanese society. This view regards Japanese society as an integrated and harmonious whole and assumes that all or most Japanese possess the same national character. Based on this assumption, common denominators believed to operate throughout Japanese society were extracted. The second trend is to describe Japanese society in detail but without making systematic comparisons with other societies. In the prewar period, comparative findings without comparative research were supported by the ideological stereotypes which emphasized the superior qualities of the Japanese. These included *yamato damashii* (the Japanese spirit) and the *kokutai* (the Japanese body politic). Like Watsuji and Yanagida, Aruga also had a following. The work of Suzuki (1971) and Oikawa (1967) certainly contributed to establishing Aruga's ideas as a kind of paradigm.

B Democratization Theory

The policies for the democratization of Japan following the war created a new mood which could readily be seen in Japanese scholarship. The positive evaluation of the Japanese spirit and the confidence in there being a national body politic gave way to a concern for promoting democracy. Although there was a shift in the vision of reality, a larger change occurred in the value judgement being passed on Japanese society. Lamenting the wartime experience and all the suffering that it brought, many attributed the war to the feudal elements in Japanese society–elements which had been positively evaluated as Japan's unique heritage before the war. The major task of concerned scholarship became the exposure, analysis and dislodgement of such elements.

Maruyama (1956) was one of the leading intellectuals during this period. He saw democracy as a phenomenon which fought for survival against the encroachments of the state. For democracy to be realized, he argued, it was not sufficient merely to alter a few political institutions. Rather, the establishment of a new cultural value system was seen as necessary, with a new system to integrate the private and public lives of people. He saw democracy as a social system which allows private individuals to have a public realm without losing their individuality or their right to live independent of state controls. For Maruyama the difference in how the person was conceptualized in fascist and democratic systems was symbolized by the terms *shutai* (free subjects) and *kokutai* (the state) (1956, p. 29).

For such a democratic political culture to take root in Japan, Kawashima (1950) argued that the Japanese family system would need to change. Since culture is primarily a way of thinking about things, Kawashima argued that a kind of spiritual revolution was essential. His political message was quite clear: abolish the patriarchy which had been the corner-stone of the Japanese family system (1950, pp. 22–5).

Finally, the work of Ōtsuka (1948) should be mentioned. As a student of Max Weber, he argued that interpersonal relations in Japan had been dominated by emotional elements and underlined the need for Japan to develop a legal rationalistic framework which would define authority relations in a democratic or modern way.

Although all three scholars were professors at the University of Tokyo, their views can be found in the writings of many others such as Shimizu (1948) and Minami (1953). Along with the push for democratization there was a tendency to underline the feudalistic, the socially backward or semi-barbaric aspects of Japanese society. It is not surprising, then, that Benedict's *The Chrysanthemum and the Sword* was widely read in Japan. This kind of negative portrayal has remained as one major undercurrent in Japanese intellectual life. Even today it is not uncommon for the 'underdeveloped features of Japanese society – the low status of women, the presence of academic cliquishness, the blind eye turned to the grey officials involved in the Lockheed scandal and the exclusive nature of press clubs – to be contrasted with Japan's economic and technological achievements.

Along with the negative assessment of certain Japanese practices or thought processes, there was also a certain idealization of the West. As in the prewar period, the West is conceived as the mirror which would best reflect Japan's unique feudal backwardness. So after the war as well Japan continued to be described in comparative terms without explicit comparisons, although the textual studies of Nakamura (1960 and 1964) might be cited as semi-empirical. In the process of making these comparisons, there was a tendency to accept foreign statements about foreign ideals or values as statements of foreign realities. Few scholars in the postwar period were able to spend extensive periods overseas actually living as citizens in the foreign countries they wrote about, although most had made several trips abroad and could read one or more foreign languages. As a result, many descriptions of Japanese society were true to Japanese realities, but lost their validity because they were phrased as comparative statements suggesting that Japanese realities were more or less than something in an idealized West, which had never actually been carefully studied.

Although the research on democratization was in sharp contrast with prewar scholarship and was in many cases meant as a rebuttal of that scholarship, two points of continuity can be discerned. One is the assumption that all Japanese possess a common set of attitudes and share similar behavioral patterns. In this regard, Japanese scholars did not differ substantially from their overseas counterparts who were trying to understand Japan within an anthropological framework. The second carry-over from the prewar period was the tendency to conceptualize the West as a monolith. At the same time, the ideal was no longer the Japanese spirit; in the postwar years that ideal was replaced by the notion of Western democracy. The critical assessments of the West in the prewar period were replaced by critical assessments of Japan in the immediate postwar years. Constant throughout was the juxtaposition of the whole of Japanese society and the whole of Western society.

Particularly noteworthy in this context is the challenge to the assumption that Japanese modernization would consist largely of a process of imitating, emulating and catching up with the West. It was argued by some that Japan's development had been a rather autonomous process which paralleled, rather than followed, the Western European experience. According to Umesao (1957 and 1967) who presented an ecological theory of the history of civilizations, it is nonsensical to classify the world into the East and West. Even on the Eurasian continent, which he labelled the Old World (as distinguished from the New World which comprised North America, South America and Oceania), he argued that a fundamental difference existed between the 'offshore civilizations' such as Japan and Western Europe, on the one hand, and the 'inland civilizations' in continental Asia and the rest of Europe on the other. Umesao maintained that the former types of civilization attained high levels, and that Japan and Western Europe were fundamentally similar in having an internally stimulated process of 'autogenic succcession'. By contrast, in the latter area, the externally precipitated 'allogenic process of development' is predominant. Umesao's theory is that modern Japanese history is not a record of Westernization but of the more universal processes of modernization and capitalist development, which had occurred more or less simultaneously in Western Europe and Japan because of their similar ecological conditions. S. Katō's thesis (1956) that Japanese culture is fundamentally hybrid follows a similar line of reasoning. For him, even as a cross-breed, Japanese culture has a status equal to the pure cultures of the West, because the melting-pot phenomenon is in itself a cultural pattern which must be given a due place in comparative studies. With their emphasis on more universal trends, these arguments brought into clear relief the bias built into theories of democratization which tended to idealize the West. In so doing, the way was paved for broader theories of modernization and social change.

C Modernization Theory

The transformation of Japanese society which accompanied rapid economic growth invited new emphases in the analysis of Japanese society. On the political left, theories of mass society (e.g., Matsushita: 1959) came to the fore, and attention was directed to the analysis of numerous phenomena such as the rise of the new white-collar class, extensive unionization, mechanization, mass production and consumption, metropolitanization, bureaucratization and mass communications. Theorists of mass society attempted to throw light on a variety of manipulative techniques with which the authority of technocratic power elites increasingly came to regulate the life of the common citizen. There was a concern that what Maruyama called the 'sphere of the private citizen' had been invaded before it was even established.

In analyzing the changes in postwar Japanese culture, H. Katō (1957) argued that *chūkan bunka* (middle-brow culture) had become dominant since the mid-fifties. According to him, this cultural pattern could be observed most easily in the increasing popularity of weekly magazines, paperbacks and musicals which were neither high-brow nor low-brow. In Japan the fifties had witnessed the red purges, the reverse course, the split of the Socialist Party, the introduction of legislation to strengthen the discretionary powers of the police and the Government's steps to centralize the system of education. In the wake of leftist-inspired mass demonstrations against the US-Japan Security Treaty, however, other changes were also occurring.

The Hakone Conference was held in 1960 to prepare for a series of conferences on the modernization of Japan, which resulted in the Princeton Series. The gatherings facilitated contacts between Japanese and American scholars with an interest in applying modernization theory to Japan. Modernization theory was also being promoted at a time when State Department funds were being used to bring hundreds of Japanese trade-union leaders to the United States for some exposure to modernization- or convergence-oriented theories of industrial relations, which tended to shift attention even further away from notions of class interest to the benefits of productivity agreements in capitalist or mixed economies (Mouer: 1976).

With these broader developments in the background, Tominaga (1965) sought to apply Parsonian systems theory to the analysis of Japanese society. He attacked Marxist theories of social change, and set a guide-post for Japanese modernization theorists by explaining social change in Japan without reference to Marxist notions of class struggle. In the meantime, the convergence theory of industrialization (Kerr *et al.*: 1960) was translated into Japanese by Nakayama (Kerr *et al.*: 1963). The development of conciliatory relationships between labor and management was presented as a major index of modernization by Nakayama (1960 and 1974). In the sixties attention was increasingly given to the new middle class and mass consumption. Embourgeoisement of the proletariat was seen as one product of Japan's rapid economic growth. Japan was seen as having achieved both development and democracy. The analysis of Japanese society in terms of the dichotomy between capital and labor was held to be irrelevant for its study (Murakami *et al.*: 1979).

In the late sixties and seventies, Japan's system of industrial relations in particular began to receive academic attention. For example, Hazama (1964 and 1971), Tsuda (1968, 1976 and 1977), Iwata (1977, 1978, 1980 and 1982), Morikawa (1973 and 1980), Funabashi (1971b) and Hanami (1973) all wrote about the uniqueness of Japan's industrial relations. OECD reports (1973 and 1977) on Japan's manpower policies were translated into Japanese and given wide acclaim. Two major themes stood out. One was the emphasis on the uniqueness of three Japanese practices: seniority wages (*nenkōchingin*), lifetime employment (*shūshin koyō*) and enterprise unionism (*kigyōbetsu kumiai*). The second was the significance attached to informal relationships in the settlement of disputes. The Spring Offensive was treated as ritual behavior for public consumption (*tatemae*) while the real negotiations (*jissai*) and real emotions (*honne*) were said to be found only in semi-closed discussions which have been institutionalized in a complex system of joint consultations (*rōshi kyōgisei*).

As Japanese GNP continued to grow at a rapid rate and books abroad began to laud Japan's emergence as an economic superstate, some of the assumptions in modernization theory began to be questioned. One new argument was that the cultural characteristics commonly associated with non-modernized societies were the source of Japan's spectacular successes and present social stability. While some dismissed these as remnants of the past, which still remained behind as a kind of cultural lag, others came increasingly to evaluate them positively as the driving force behind Japan's economic miracle. Various kinds of social dislocation were dismissd as the temporary side effects of rapid economic and social change (Tominaga: 1965). The earlier emphasis on feudal elements was criticized; the rising standard of living was underlined. Japan's rising stature in the international community was also noted. Finally, there was a return to an earlier theme, that technology and machines alone will not produce growth; hard work and a certain social ethos are also seen as being important.

Still, despite criticisms of earlier scholarship, the break with the past was not complete. Many of the holistic assumptions were never questioned and comparisons between Japan as a whole and a monolithic West persisted. While theories of Japan's potential for democratization tended to be accompanied by a strong sense of inferiority towards an idealized West, the modernization theorists seemed more inclined to take a balanced view and at least to distinguish between ideals as values and as ideology, on one hand, and behavior as measured in national indexes, on the other. The distinction between values and ideology was not made, and this in part allowed many of the simpler holistic assumptions to remain unchallenged.

D Neo-holistic Theories of National Character

As continued economic growth thrust Japan even more squarely onto the center of the world stage in the late sixties and the early seventies, Japanese elites began to exhibit a renewed sense of self-confidence and optimism. Scholars increasingly tried to liberate themselves from the disturbing contrast between feudal Japan and the democratic West. There was a growing belief that Japanese economic growth was indeed unique. Where else had people been able to raise their GNP seven times in only two decades? For many observers, the achievement seemed so unique that only a particular explanation could adequately convey what had actually happened. For scholars who sought such explanations, earlier theories about Japanese national character provided an independent variable with only two cases, Japan and the West. Though insignificant, the correlation was bound to be clear: high growth and Japanese national character as opposed to lower growth and some other kind of character (e.g., Western individualism). Much that had flourished in the thirties was revived in a modified and slightly more sophisticated form. A string of popular publications appeared during this period, as academics and other intellectuals openly made a renewed claim that the uniqueness of Japanese society required unique concepts for its analysis. On this point, the new emphasis on national character made a sharp contrast with the democratization and modernization theories, which sought to utilize more universal concepts like civil consciousness and industrialization as principal tools for analysis. Nakane (1967a, pp. 12–13) for example, used a metaphor to make this point, arguing that metric measurement might be appropriate for making Western suits, but that measurement based on the *shaku* (a traditional unit of linear measurement in Japan) was the most appropriate for making a *kimono*. Finally, the tendency to describe Japan in comparative terms without making any explicit comparisons became more pronounced.

The neo-holistic view of Japanese society can be seen in the work of Nakane (1967a), Doi (1971), Ishida (1970), Nakamura (1973) and others whose translations were introduced into English. The view was reinforced by translations into Japanese of similar statements by Westerners (Milward: 1978 and 1980; Stucki: 1978; Clark: 1977; Vogel: 1979b; Abegglen: 1974; Reischauer: 1979). In addition to broader theories of Japanese society (Okonogi: 1978; Aida: 1970; Aizawa: 1976; Watanabe: 1980) we can also see attempts to relate these kinds of sweeping theoretical generalization to every conceivable aspect of Japanese behavior, including political behavior (Wakata: 1981; Nakamura: 1974 and 1976), political and legal institutions (Ōtsuka *et al.*: 1976), the Emperor system (Wakamori: 1973), industrial relations (Takahashi: 1970) and leadership (Aida: 1977; Nakamura: 1976), welfare (Baba: 1981) and the consciousness of young people (Matsubara: 1974).

An example of how far those associated with this genre have gone can be seen in a number of interesting statements by its proponents. Kunihiro Tetsuya, professor of psychology at the University of Tokyo, for example, reports that Americans must always call each other by their names so as not to offend each other's sense of individualism, whereas in Japan persons are called by the title of their position because individuals are submerged within the organizational structure of the group.[10] This is a theme described earlier by Mori

(1972) and can be referred to as the fragile eggshell theory. Higuchi (1972) begins his argument that the Japanese have a special way of thinking by underlining the importance of Japan's unique climatic factors and the racial characteristics of the Japanese. Namiki (1981) argues that social scientific economic theory does not apply to Japan and looks for explanations of Japan's economic structure which emphasize traditional consumption patterns for food, clothing and housing. Iwata (1980) also pushes a similar line. Hamaguchi (1982) argues that the Japanese have a special regard for interpersonal relationships and that the Japanese are basically inter-active persons (*kanjin shugisha*) rather than individuals (*kojin shugisha*). This is also the major theme of a special collection of essays (Hamaguchi, ed.: 1982). One can also mention the much cruder attempts of Watanabe (1980), Shinoda (1977 and 1979) and Masuzoe (1982), who tend to begin and end only with stereotypes.

It is noteworthy that some advocates of *nihonjinron* have used their cultural arguments to support the current political situation in Japan. In particular, Yamamoto (1979a and 1979b), Yamamoto and Komuro (1981), Watanabe (1976 and 1980), Komuro (1982), Takemura (1977) and Takemura and Clark (1979) have tended to support the policies and programs of the conservative government and the business establishment on key issues such as national defense, nuclear energy, environmental pollution and the control of education. It would seem that their emphasis on the uniqueness of Japanese society and culture is also tied to a political stance for the establishment. Another feature of this literature is the blurring of the distinction between journalism and fiction, on one hand, and serious scholarship on the other.

From a different angle, there has been interest in socio-biological theories which explain why the Japanese are different. Tsunoda (1978) presents the most scientific version of this claim in his work on the Japanese brain. On the basis of a series of experiments, Tsunoda has maintained that native Japanese speakers differ from persons with other mother tongues in the way in which their auditory functions are 'lateralized' in the brain. Linking this observation with the way in which vowels are used in Japanese, Tsunoda posits that the cultural uniqueness of the Japanese can be traced to the unique structure of their brain. Higuchi (1972, pp. 25–6) contends that the Japanese are a superior hybrid race, the result of the cross-breeding of contiguous but different races. Sameda (1966) attributes the thought patterns of the Japanese to the fact that they are traditionally herbivorous, a trait which distinguishes them from Westerners, who have developed a 'carnivorous culture'. Again one can see links with prewar theories, in that racial differences are easily translated into theories of racial superiority. The appeal of these theories can be seen in the public clamor made in Japan in mid-1982 about the report of a British research team, which found Japanese respondents outscoring respondents from other countries. Without any discussion of what an IQ score means, the findings were circulated in Japan as further evidence that the Japanese had superior intelligence, although some also commented cynically that the examination system had simply produced a large number of people trained to perform well on the types of test used for measuring IQ (*ASC*, 5 September 1982, p. 4).

E Theories of the Internationalization of Japanese Society

In recent years a large number of books have been written by Japanese with some overseas experience. This stream of publications reflects the fact that an unprecedented number of Japanese are now living and working outside Japan. The authors include professionals in business and journalism such as Fukada (1975 and 1976) and Shiroyama (1981), diplomats such as Ogata (1980) and Kawasaki (1969 and 1973) and translators such as Kunihiro (1980) and Nishiyama (1972) who have had intensive contact with people abroad. Common to their writings is the suggestion that Japanese must internationalize culturally and socially, in accordance with Japan's growing presence throughout the world. Nakane (1972a), the Nagatas (1980), Toba (1978) and others (e.g., Mainichi, ed.,: 1977) have focused on ways in which uniquely Japanese cultural patterns have made it difficult for Japanese to interact abroad. Others, such as A. Hoshino (1981) and Ono (1979), for example, have dealt more specifically with problems related to Japanese investment overseas, such as reverse culture shock when returning to Japanese society or conflict between Japanese management practices and local customs in host countries where Japanese have joint ventures or other investments. Finally, one can cite the way in which the teaching of English in many schools and on NHK educational television has become in part a lecture on speculative cultural anthropology.

Although the question of internationalization is dealt with in more detail in Chapter 15, several common themes may be emphasized. One is concern with changing Japanese behavior to facilitate the overseas expansion of Japanese economic interests. This is not necessarily a new theme. Similar arguments were used in the early sixties in prodding Japanese to accept the inevitability of a certain amount of liberation of Japan's economic protection and to tell Japanese that they would now have to work harder than ever to win in international competition (Yoshimura: 1961; Tanaka: 1963; Miyaji: 1963). In recent years, however, the problem areas seem to be more diffused. In addition to the personal problems of the predominantly upwardly mobile *sarari man* stationed overseas with Japan's larger firms and the exclusiveness of the Japanese business and diplomatic community abroad, concern has also been expressed about unthinking tourists on sex tours and the textbook issue. Novels and other written material, including the conversations of Japanese overseas, have increasingly portrayed the existence of the overseas Japanese businessman as one of rational behavior amid irrational surroundings, having to deal with local people in America and Australia, not to mention Europe and the Third World, who are seen as being less agile in processing the massive reams of information believed to be crucial to life in Japan and who are usually less refined in terms of the human courtesies expected in Japan. Conspicuous is the cultural apology for insensitive individuals. Rather than reprimanding such individuals for behavior that is not universally accepted even in Japan, the uniqueness of the Japanese is lamented and a plea is made for a change in the way of thinking of all Japanese (e.g., Japanese culture). At the same time, there are also allusions to the failure of others to accept Japanese cultural norms and the Japanese *modus operandi.* The unfairness, the unnaturalness and even the impossibility of conforming to other cultural norms is underlined. These observations have not yet been fully documented, but nevertheless form part of the *Gestalt* collected by the authors from their reading.

The other major theme is the greater willingness of academics to rise to the defense of Japanese interests in the international arena. In the first half of 1982, for example, when trade friction (*bōeki masatsu*) received so much attention, there was a great clamor about cultural misunderstanding. While some (such as Katō and Miyazaki: 1982) have advocated the need for a more positive approach to public relations, which would help foreigners to understand fully the cultural essence of Japanese society, others have engaged in overseas surveying and interviewing to show how uninformed foreigners were about Japan or how uninformed foreign leaders were about public opinion in their own countries (*AJ*, 26 March 1982). In June, when two Japanese were arrested by the FBI in America for illegally buying industrial secrets stolen from IBM, an editorial in the Yomiuri newspaper complained that the arrests were unfair because the FBI used tactics which Japanese police used only in narcotics investigations. Cultural differences were underlined but no concern was really shown for whether the Japanese were guilty of such behavior or not, or whether the alleged behavior itself was something to be proud of even in Japan (*YSC*, 26 June 1982, p. 4; also cf. *TDY*, 26 June 1982, p. 2). In these briefs for the defense of Japan's national interests, the common cultural stereotypes of Japanese and Western societies are expediently produced and used as convenient ammunition to defend the home team. At the same time, however, deeper sources of tensions arising from conflicts of interest owing to shared values tend to be ignored.

III Some Common Themes in the Holistic Approach

A An Overview

Although the literature emphasizing uniformity among the Japanese is quite varied and appears to have been written with several different aims in mind, a number of common themes can be identified. One is the assumption that the Japanese find their *raison d'être* in group activity. They feel no need for any explicit demonstration of individuality. Prime value is attached to loyalty to the group. It is argued that subjection of oneself to the promotion and realization of a group's goals gives Japanese special psychological satisfaction. In this regard, the Japanese are seen as attaching greater importance than other peoples to the maintenance of harmony within the group. Relationships between superiors and inferiors are carefully cultivated and maintained, and one's status within the group is seen as being a function of the length of one's membership. Self-effacing, polite expressions serve to reinforce these values in everyday life; such language is seen as a direct expression of the Japanese psychology.

From this perception, then, the Japanese are seen as maintaining particularly strong interpersonal ties with those in the same hierarchical chain of command within their own organization. In other words, Nakane's vertical loyalties are dominant, and in this regard the vertical organization of the Japanese is contrasted with the horizontal consciousness found among Westerners. Unlike the Japanese, it is assumed that Westerners define their membership in terms of skill-related or other functional criteria which supersede affiliation with other types of group.

Widespread acceptance of these and other cultural values is seen as having facilitated the efforts of Japanese leaders to organize or mobilize other Japanese. Moreover, it is posited that the ease with which the energy of the Japanese can be focused on one task contributed in no small measure to Japan's remarkably rapid economic growth during the first quarter-century after the war. Because their cultural, linguistic and social homogeneity is particularly pronounced, the Japanese are acutely conscious of being Japanese; they are easily spurred to support nationalistic causes. When comparing themselves with other nationalities, the Japanese are prone to see their differences and act according to that awareness. Given this strong sense of national identity, Japanese society is closed to outsiders.

On the surface, it is argued, Japanese society has been Westernized by its rapid economic growth and high level of urbanization. Beneath the surface, however, there appears to be a more intimate level at which Japanese society operates. Knowledge of this level is seen as being central to an understanding of how Japanese society really operates. The secrets of Japan's rapid economic growth can be discovered only if one becomes familiar with how Japanese society works at this more intimate level. This proposition is often extended to include the notion that Western society can somehow more easily be taken at face value.

The world of work and industrial relations is one place where these images have been most readily associated with concrete examples. The interpretation of Japanese society described above is seen as being consistent with fewer strikes, lower labor turnover and lifetime employment, group decision-making from the bottom up and the Japanese system of *ringisho* (formal memoranda), company unions, greater social equality in terms of the distribution of income and wage differentials, a greater sense of national identity and lower levels of alienation. The world of work is also an area where the debate on convergence and divergence has been most vigorous. In this area, there seem to be some differences based on academic discipline, with anthropologists tending to argue for the consensus model and Japanese uniqueness (Abegglen: 1958; Nakane: 1970; Rohlen: 1974 and 1975; Clark: 1979) and sociologists attempting to fit Japan into a more universal framework (Inkeles and Rossi: 1956; Ramsey and Smith: 1960; Cole: 1971a and 1979; Marsh and Mannari: 1976 and 1977).

In the holistic approach two major assumptions stand out. One is that Japanese society can best be understood in terms of a monolithic concept of the individual. In a manner not too dissimilar to the way in which economic man and political man are conceptualized, we are given a rather uniform Japanese man. The probability that any two Japanese may have been produced from different molds is never seriously examined. The tendency to focus attention on the Japanese is as much a characteristic of this body of literature today as it was thirty years ago when Abegglen first drew attention to this predisposition. The second is that whole societies are the most important unit for analysis. Little attention is given by those recommending the group model to other variables which cut across cultures and produce variation within societies. Few of the sweeping statements about national character are readily amendable to the careful analysis of cross-sectional or time series data gathered within Japan.

Finally, the interaction of the English-language and Japanese-language literature should be noted. Although there are leads and lags, the periods tend to be congruent. The parallels also extend to the concepts used and the evaluative judgements of Japanese society as described by the *nihonjinron* theorists. Based on earlier work by Kawamura (1982a, pp. 58–9), Table 2.1 helps to clarify these relationships.

B The Promotion of Cultural Relativism

Since this volume focuses on some of the shortcomings of the group model and of the *nihonjinron* literature in general, this chapter concludes with some mention of the contribution made by this tradition to the promotion of cultural relativism and to the campaign against parochial myopia. The contributions are of at least two types.

One is in the form of support for the idea of learning from other nations. Several books which have pushed this theme have been mentioned. This emphasis is particularly noticeable in publications written for businessmen and public policy-makers. In other words, the audience consists largely of individuals who are able to make decisions about the flow of information at various levels. To borrow the vocabulary of Magofuku (1981), there seems to be a discernible shift, at least in the English-speaking world, away from teaching others to learning from them. Regardless of whether one agrees with the view of Japan presented in this literature (and the authors

Table 2.1 *Some stages in the development of* Nihonjinron: *periods, concepts and evaluations*

	Images of Japanese society in Japanese literature			Images of Japanese society in English literature		
Stage and rough dates	Major themes	Evaluation of the ideal type presented as Japanese society P = positive evaluation N = negative evaluation	The nature of the major concept(s) used: P = particularistic concepts U = universal concepts	Major themes	Evaluation of the ideal type presented as Japanese society: P = positive evaluation N = negative evaluation	The nature of the major concept(s) used P = particularistic concepts U = universalistic concepts
I 1930–45	Japanese national character (family and climatology)	P	P	'Orientalism' as presented in travelogues and the popular media	N	P
II 1945–60	Japan's prospects for democracy and the problems of feudal remnants	N	U	Japanese society as an integrated cultural whole	P/n	U
III 1960–75	Japan's modernization	P	U	Japan's modernization	P	U

Table 2.1 *(contd.)*

	Images of Japanese society in Japanese literature			Images of Japanese society in English literature		
Stage and rough dates	Major themes	Evaluation of the ideal type presented as Japanese society P = positive evaluation N = negative evaluation	The nature of the major concept(s) used: P = particularistic concepts U = universal concepts	Major themes	Evaluation of the ideal type presented as Japanese society: P = positive evaluation N = negative evaluation	The nature of the major concept(s) used P = particularistic concepts U = universalistic concepts
IV 1967–80	Japanese national character (groupism and consensus)	P	P	Japanese national character (groupism and consensus)	P	P
V 1975–	The internationalization of Japanese society	P/n	P/u	Lessons from Japan	P	P/u

Notes: (1) The first four periods for Japanese literature were taken from Kawamura (1982a, p. 58). The fifth stage and the American data were added by the authors. For a slightly different approach to periods see Neustrupný (1982a).

(2) Where P, N and U appear with a slash (/), upper case is used to indicate the dominant trend and lower case to indicate that a particular theme could be discerned in some of the literature, but with less conspicuousness.

certainly do not), few would argue with the idea that there is a need to be better informed about other societies. Some of the learn-from-Japan literature makes a forceful case for opening our eyes to the world around us.

Chapter 2 of Vogel's *Japan as Number One* must surely bring home to most readers (American or otherwise) a powerful message: there are many criteria for judging success and the Japanese will be successful according to some.[11] The reader is also encouraged to learn how apparently unrelated behavior can play an instrumental role in the achievement of longer-term goals. This realization is certainly vital if more cosmopolitan attitudes are to spread. One could argue that it is a pre-condition for lateral thinking.

There is certainly room for more discussion of the various issues involved in the debate on reverse convergence. There is also the fundamental question of whether Japanese practices can be transferred elsewhere, and there would certainly be contention as to exactly what features ought to be borrowed, even if it were possible. Although major structural changes seldom occur in societies without some process of diffusion, the conditions under which societies open themselves up to foreign ideas need to be studied more carefully. Also, to the extent that true consensus depends upon informed and voluntary choices and is desirable, the move to experiment with alien forms of social organization is best accompanied by a reasoned and unimpassioned attempt to collect all the facts. Both halves of reality must be carefully recorded and interrelated. In the words of V. S. Naipaul (1980), to deny the value of such learning is to deny oneself the fruits of civilization and instead to cultivate a step backwards to philistine, fundamentalist parochialism and a 'pride in being stupid'.

Another contribution to cultural relativism is the insistence that we rethink the framework, problem consciousness or predisposed views we bring with us to the study of other societies. Specifically, the emphasis on Japan's uniqueness in much of the *nihonjinron* literature is a challenge to half the notion of Orientalism which has been described by Said (1979) as an entrenched Western view of Asia. This message seems clear to the authors in their reading of Nakane's *Japanese Society*. Out of Max Weber's concern with the Protestant ethic and the comparative sociology of religion was born a large number of studies of the way in which interpersonal relations and the notion of social roles in society change as industrialization occurs. A number of these schemes are given in Table 2.2. This approach to understanding social change and venturing comparative statements

Table 2.2 *Models of modernization, emphasizing changes in social values and the nature of interpersonal relationships*

Originator	Pre-industrial communal societies with informal organization	Post-industrial associational societies with formal organization
Herbert Spencer	militant	industrial
Henry Maine	societies based on status	societies based on contractual relationships
Ferdinand Tönnies	*Gemeinschaft*	*Gesellschaft*
Emile Durkeim	mechanical solidarity	organic solidarity
Howard Becker	societies based on sacred ties	societies based on secular ties
Robert Redfield	folk (rural) society	urban society

about societies at different stages in the process of industrialization culminated, perhaps, in the perceptive taxonomy developed by Talcott Parsons. For reasons not discussed here, the dichotomous types (which came to be known as 'Parsonian pattern variables') were treated by many of his students and others interested in social change as ideal types on monolineal continua, which were useful for making generalizations about pre- and post-industrial societies. These are shown in Table 2.3.

Although Nakane (1970, pp. 141–51) does not explicitly mention Parsons' pattern variables, her concern with Western evolutionary models emphasizing the inevitability of 'Parsonian democracy' is quite explicitly stated. Nakane seems to be saying that Japan does not fit the model developed to explain change in Western society. Modernization theory suggests that industrialization in Japan will be accompanied by growing individualism, greater functional specificity, and contract-based and universalistic interpersonal relations (as opposed to emotionally intimate and particularistic ties). These are also not infrequently projected by the modernization theorists as being the essence of democracy, but they are precisely the traits Nakane finds missing in Japanese society, a fact which causes her to stand up and say: 'No! Japan is different! The Japanese are not individualistic! They do not employ such universalistic standards! They are bound by emotional ties! Although the Japanese are very conscious of hierarchy, they are conscious in a way which promotes

Table 2.3 *Variables commonly used to indicate ideal types for industrial and pre-industrial societies*

A Parsonian pattern variables

	Pre-industrialization (pre-modernization)	Post-industrialization (post-modernization)
1	traditional	rational
2	particularistic	universalistic
3	functionallly diffuse	functionally specific
4	intimate	avoidant
5	collectivistic	individualistic
6	non-hierarchical	hierarchical
7	egalitarian	non-egalitarian

Notes: The first six are from Levy (1969, p. 137). They are derived from Parsons (1951). The seventh item was suggested by Lipset (1963). On the final item, see Parsons (1970, pp. 13–14).

B Some common attributes associated with *Gemeinschaft*- and *Gesellschaft*-types of interpersonal relationships

	Gemeinschaft-type groups (community)	*Gessellschaft*-type groups (society or association)
1	personal	impersonal
2	informal	formal, contractual
3	traditional	utilitarian
4	sentimental	realistic, rationalist
5	general in purpose	specific in purpose
6	private	public
7	exclusive or closed	open
8	conscriptive	voluntary
9	ascriptive-oriented	achievement-oriented
10	ties based upon emotional feeling or gratification	ties based on rational agreements, self-interest and comparative advantage
11	members look for satisfaction of all goals	members look for the realization of partial and specific ends
12	found in communal societies	found in associational societies

an egalitarian groupism which knits together closely all the members as a family!'

Chapter 5 argues that many of the comparisons with the West are not supported by valid empirical evidence. However, it is quite possible that many of the comparisons in the *nihonjinron* literature are misleading not because the facts about Japan are particularly wrong, but rather because they are based upon assumptions that Western theories do indeed fit Western experience. Not only may the Japanese be more individualistic than is made out in most of the *nihonjinron* literature, but so may the Westerners be more group-oriented than imagined.

For some reason the *nihonjinron* theorists tend to accept that Western sociologists or social anthropologists are experts on their own respective countries. However, this overlooks much that is written about cultural imperialism in the sociology of knowledge, a perspective developed in Chapter 7. It also seems to ignore the fact that there are various conflicting interpretations of social reality in the West. It is difficult to account for the reason why only a particular type of interpretation has been imported to Japan. In his perceptive study of Benedict and her writing of *The Chrysanthemum and the Sword*, Lummis (1982) addresses himself to the sudden shift which resulted in her strong emphasis on the contrast between 'modern and democratic American values' and 'feudalistic and fascist Japanese values'. He makes it clear that there is in these contrasts a retreat from her earlier commitment to cultural relativism. There is also the suggestion that the individual motivations of authors need to be set against larger historical trends, in this case the milieu created by the Second World War and America's adversary relationship with Japan.

Finally, while *nihonjinron* often confuses anecdotes passed on by respectable individuals, national character stereotypes and social reality, an issue dealt with in Chapter 6, there is an important message. Had Japan won the war and had the *nihonjinron* theorists actually had the necessary financial resources and ideological support, one wonders what splendid findings might have been produced by the consistent application of the methodological strategies and concepts used for analyzing Japanese society to the Western societies referred to as the comparative base in most of the *nihonjinron* literature. Here the limits of naïvely subscribing to the doctrine of cultural relativism can be seen. There are some complacent aspects of a gentlemen's agreement when the chantings of foreign high priests must in their own culture be taken at face value by would-be observers from the outside. The victor's justice extends to the writing of history and to decisions about the *lingua franca*. Nevertheless, the major challenge made by the *nihonjinron* literature and the emphasis on learning from Japan is clear: don't assume that all societies will follow the same path in experiencing social change.

Chapter 3

The Little Traditions: Theories of Conflict and Variation in Japanese Society

I Conflict as a Continuing Theme in Japanese Scholarship

Consensus and homogeneity are not the only features of Japanese society to receive attention. Numerous accounts of conflict and brutality also exist. Indeed, as the authors have been reminded by historians, the social history of Japan is largely a history of conflict.[1] From the peasant uprisings during the Tokugawa period to the anti-pollution movements of the seventies, popular demonstrations against the authorities or the establishment are well documented. This chapter introduces some literature emphasizing conflict in Japanese society. The discussion begins with some information on the tradition of conflict-oriented scholarship in Japan, and concludes with a summary of some major themes common to the literature emphasizing conflict.

A An Overview of Conflict in Japanese Society

As some of those participating in the Conference on Modern Japan noted (Hall: 1965, p. 13; Morley: 1971, p. 66), it is difficult to comprehend contemporary Japanese scholarship without knowing about the Marxist perspective. Thus, although American participants at the Hakone Conference on the Modernization of Japan in the summer of 1960 'hesitated to introduce any ideologically charged concepts into the definition of modernization, the Japanese side in the main insisted that it would be meaningless to discuss modernization, especially that of Japan, without paying due consideration to these concepts' (Maruyama: 1965, p. 65). The concern with social tension and conflict is part of an established tradition in Japanese scholarship. This concern can be seen in Marxist economics. Economists of this line have in many ways adopted an approach more commonly associated with sociology than with economics, sensitive to the existence of opposing classes and class interests. Although there is considerable disagreement as to the exact nature of class interests in the Japanese setting, even in the prewar period both parties to the '*rōnōha-kōzaha* debate' agreed that there was a ruling elite. This was seen as being composed of big business, lesser capitalists, the *samurai*-dominated bureaucracy, the military, the wealthier landlords and the nobility. The elite was seen as making a more or less coordinated effort to repress the political and economic aspirations of the then still embryonic working class, the semi-proletarian peasants in agriculture and the petty bourgeoisie.[2]

Defeat in the Pacific War, however, brought rapid changes to Japanese society. The postwar reforms removed from public affairs the major feudalistic elements which provided the nucleus for the traditional set of elites. The reforms also replaced the family-oriented and particularistic *zaibatsu* (the prewar conglomerates) with a more universalistic *zaikai* (the community of big business interests in postwar Japan). The significance of the debate thus receded. However, the scholarship it stimulated left an important heritage for postwar scholars interested in studying social conflict within the Japanese context. This tradition can be found in the work of postwar Marxists like Inoue (1963–6 and 1969) and Suzuki (1956) who provided an important foundation for scholars preferring to emphasize these aspects. In addition to several monumental works on the history of Japanese capitalism (including Yanaga *et al.*: 1965; and Kajinishi *et al.*: 1970), a variety of authors continued to view power relationships between ruling or capitalist groups and the great mass of the working people as a dominant force within the Japanese economy (e.g., the edited compilations by Ikumi *et al.*: 1966; Okakura *et al.*: 1973; Kōza Konnichi no Nihon Shihonshugi Henshū Iinkai: 1982).

The rapid economic growth of the sixties produced a considerable shift in Marxist scholarship. Scholars such as Masamura (1968, especially pp. 141–3) came to contend that there was a need to take off the blinkers of a narrowly defined and rigidly applied orthodox Marxism. They argued that the prewar oligopolists have been replaced by a new ruling class (*shihai kaikyū*) headed by a new group of managers (*keieisha*) and administrators (*kanrisha*) who represent capitalist interests without necessarily owning large amounts of capital themselves. In criticizing standard Marxism and developing his own methodology, Masamura (1972: especially pp. 154–223) gave full support to Uno Kōzō's insistence that scholarship must be separated from party politics and that social realities in Europe need to be differentiated from those in Japan. According to this position, many situations in Japanese society cannot be explained by the simple, mechanical application of European Marxist political doctrine. Although recognizing the role of rapid economic growth in lifting the absolute living standard of the average worker and equalizing the distribution of earnings among members of the working class, Masamura (1972, pp. 150–3) argued that the income differential between those receiving wages and salaries and those living on property income has become larger. Finally, he attributed the rise in the absolute standard of living not to the merits of any economic policy, but rather to the pressure put on management by the growing awareness and assertiveness of the working class as evidenced in the labor movement, particularly the spring wage offensive, and the conscientious use of the right to vote (pp. 153–4). Nagasu (with Masamura: 1966, especially pp. 37–41), Horie (1962 and 1969), Yamazaki (1966), Nozawa (1965), Ōuchi Tsutomu (1970 and 1971) and others have also emphasized these points.

In the postwar period the conflict approach to understanding Japanese society has no doubt found a receptive audience among those sympathetic to the opposition parties. The Japan Socialist Party and the Japan Communist Party in particular provide a political tradition not institutionalized in the United States. Efforts of the Occupation authorities to democratize Japan gave many scholars an opportunity to expose anew the history of censorship and repression to which they had been subjected in the prewar years. However, rapid growth and the tremendous across-the-board improvements in the standard of living shifted attention away from theories stressing the exploitation and impoverishment of the proletariat. The simplistic assumptions and seemingly repetitious arguments associated with the conflict approach were further undermined in the sixties as 'Parsonian theory' and the value-orientation approach, which looked for dominant value clusters or patterns in the national character, were introduced (e.g., Tominaga: 1965).[3]

The conflict tradition seemed to find renewed vigor and a new rationale in the student movements at the end of the sixties. In the early seventies additional momentum for the conflict approach was generated by several new phenomena – the anti-pollution, consumer and citizens' rights movements, the stepped-up efforts of employees in the public sector to regain the right to strike and the emergence of reformist coalition governments at the local level. It thus behoves us to be more aware of this other tradition. Finally, one should not be blind to the forces which have tended to dampen the popularity of this approach in the late seventies – the second oil crisis, Russian involvement in Southeast Asia and Afghanistan, the Four Modernizations in China and its *rapprochement* with the United States, and perhaps the world-wide move to the right. While the careful observer will be alert to those forces which may again promote the popularity of the conflict approach in the future (such as the anti-nuclear movement, the attention given to violence in schools and the trade war with the United States and Europe, and concern about the textbook issue) it would seem that the move to the right (*ukeika*) will persist for the foreseeable future in Japan.

Among the better known cases of recorded conflict and the social tensions which have accompanied it are the *hyakushō ikki* (peasant rebellions) of the Tokugawa period (Kokushō: 1928; Aoki: 1971). In the early Meiji period, disturbances against land tax reform and compulsory conscription swept the nation (Aoki: 1967). As landlords began to enlarge their holdings, tenant farmers and poor peasants increasingly fell into debt, and protests erupted mainly in the Kantō region, culminating in the Chichibu Rebellion in 1884, the most revolutionary revolt in modern Japan (Irokawa: 1979). The repression of socialists during the Taishō period is also well documented (Large: 1972). Rice riots followed the end of World War I (Inoue and Watanabe: 1959–61), and the Communists were shackled during the thirties (Okudaira: 1973; Kakegawa: 1976). The prewar history of the labor movement is also well documented (Aoki: 1978; Ōkōchi: 1952b, 1958 and 1970; Ōkōchi and Matsuo: 1965–73).

The postwar period has also had its share of conflict: a militant labor movement, the red purges (Johnson: 1972), the *ampo* demonstrations (Hidaka: 1960; Packard: 1966), the student movement (Tsurumi: 1968; Kitamura: 1972; Krauss: 1974; Dowsey: 1970), the anti-pollution movements (Ui: 1968 and 1971), the anti-Vietnam War movement (Oda: 1969 and 1974), consumer movements (Takeuchi: 1972; Nihon Hōsō Shuppan Kyōkai: 1980; Kokumin Seikatsu Sentā: 1981) and the struggles between the Japan Teachers'

Union and the Ministry of Education (Thurston: 1973).

An examination of this literature reveals at least three common themes. First, although much of the research is focused on a particular incident, careful historical analyses show that many incidents represent the long culmination of tensions and that open conflict seldom resolved the issues involved. Second, many of the conflicts revealed a very clear sense of self-interest on the part of those initiating the protest. Sometimes the focus of the dispute involved a tangible economic good (like water rights, higher wages or an improved standard of living); but in many cases protest was spurred by a deeply felt resentment about being disenfranchised. In the latter case the demands were invariably for structural changes in the system. Third, most conflicts were brought to a head by the use of power. Solutions through consultative mechanisms are few, although third parties often became involved in mediation. Power took several forms. One, of course, was the brutal repression of dissidents with physical force. Another was the ability of the authorities to control the flow of information to dissidents and potential dissidents. Finally, the authorities or other representatives of the establishment were able to achieve a temporary cessation of hostilities by buying off the dissidents one by one or by convincing them that their true interests lie elsewhere.

Three elements seemed to be present in varying degrees and to contribute to the development of a strong sense of solidarity among the dissidents. One was the sense of deprivation, the feeling among a group of people that they have received an unreasonably small share of social rewards. This perception is often linked to the demand for tangible compensation. The second was the people's sense of political inefficacy and often surfaced as a deep resentment against regulations and other controls that were decided by some distant authority, often without accurate knowledge of the local circumstances. Third was the existence of some form of organization. Few outbreaks of violence occurred on the spur of the moment. Many movements were characterized by organizations which have produced a leadership, spokespersons and considerable functional specialization. Although this has been particularly true of postwar movements, it can also be seen in prewar movements. The constitutions for local government uncovered by Irokawa (1970) and dating back to the middle of the Meiji period demonstrate this potential for organization.

While noting the presence of varying degrees of organization and solidarity, we can also observe a tendency for some types of movements to split and be undermined by factional in-fighting. This can be seen in the student movements (Nakajima: 1968), in the movements of the atomic bomb victims (Imahori: 1974, pp.192–231), the efforts of the *burakumin* to organize (Buraku Kaihō Kenkyū-sho: 1981; Buraku Kaihō Dōmei: 1974; Kitahara: 1975; Shimahara: 1971, pp. 47–8) and in some of the pollution movements (Okamoto: 1972; Hayashi and Sano: 1974). Although there are few careful studies of this factionalism, a casual reading of the literature on these movements leads one to consider the extent to which a well-developed sense of self-interest makes it difficult for the interests of a large number of people to be aggregated. It should be pointed out that although there often is some level of organization on the part of the dissidents, their organization is seldom as tightly knit as that of those who form the establishment. This, in part, reflects a great difference in access to the resources necessary for an organization to develop and to be maintained. It may also be a phenomenon produced by the constant pressure kept on these movements by members of the establishment.

B Citizens' Movements

As the preceding discussion suggests, popular opposition to authority has taken many forms in Japan. Citizens' movements (*shimin undō*) can be said to represent the prototype for conflict-oriented behavior in Japanese society. The writings of both researchers and participants repeatedly highlight several features common to many of these movements – features which distinguish them from the more institutionalized or organized protest groups such as the labor movement, the communist movement and many of the new religions.

First, many of these movements have had an extensive history. Though the term *shimin undō* has been popularly used only since the late fifties, the movements themselves have existed in a variety of forms since the Meiji Restoration. The concept of civil rights (*minken*) was given popular political support as early as the 1880s. The classical debate on civil rights occurred between Ueki (1879) and Katō (1882). Ueki argued that such rights are inalienable and natural, whereas Katō stressed the importance of the rights of the nation state (*kokken*) and promoted the acceptance of social evolution, in which the strong are supposed to win and the weak are expected to lose. Behind this exchange was the political clash between the emerging nation state of the Meiji Oligarchs and the grass-roots interest groups which were losing ground. This basic division persisted throughout the subsequent years and was itself the focus of many civil protests in prewar Japan (Aoki: 1967, 1968 and 1977).

A second property of these popular movements has been their spontaneity. Affiliation was voluntary and mass participation tended to limit the extent to which they could be pre-programmed. Often independent of established political parties and institutionalized labor movements, the citizens' movements depended largely on the individual initiative of the participants. The food riots which swept the nation in 1918 originated with a handful of fishermen's wives congregating on the seashore in Toyama Prefecture (Inoue and Watanabe, 1959–61). The Japanese postwar peace movement was started in the fifties by a small number of housewives in Tokyo's Suginami Ward. Contact with peace movements around the world was made on their own initiative (Imahori: 1974). The Koe naki Koe no Kai (Group Representing the Voiceless Voices) was initiated in 1960 by a housewife who started a march by herself, with only a protest flag and an invitation for anyone to participate. Hundreds spontaneously joined her march (Koe naki Koe no Kai: 1962).

A third common feature is the amorphous way in which these movements are organized. Because they express views about a specific issue, their life-span tends to be limited, ranging from several months to a decade or so at the most. Leadership positions are often rotated among the members. By definition these movements are those in which the energy is generated from democratic organizational arrangements which give each member an equal say; such movements lose one essential characteristic when Michels' 'iron law of oligarchy' starts to operate. The Yamagishikai movement best embodies this principle. A communal movement based on participants having no property, its members move freely from one position to another, from one commune to another, and from one job to another (Yamagishikai: 1973; Niijima: 1978). Most of these movements have emerged outside the work setting. Accordingly, non-occupational variables tend to explain the way in which solidarity emerges among the participants: sex in the case of women's movements, age in the case of senior citizens' movements and geographic area in the case of anti-pollution movements and other residents' movements.

In some movements, participants represent a wide spectrum. This is particularly true of voluntary associations addressed to universal issues. Beheiren (Citizens' Group for Peace in Vietnam) drew its membership from professionals, students, unionists, housewives, Koreans and the unemployed (Tsurumi *et al.*: 1972). In recent years this feature has also been visible in the conservation movement (Ui *et al.*: 1971), the movement against noise pollution (Hayashi and Sano: 1974), and the movement against nuclear weapons (*AJ*: 4 June 1982, pp. 6–15; Kodomotachi: 1978).

The spontaneous quality of these movements is in contrast to the more established, often more radical, movements headed by liberal intellectuals and other elites, whose vocabulary is often imported from abroad. As populist expressions of the people at the grass-roots level, these movements are more solidly linked to the masses of people who make up the bulk of Japanese society. In addition to the widespread appeal to ordinary citizens, the fierce independence of those involved and their refusal to be drawn into larger organizations on the right or on the left also underlines a strong individualistic or even anarchistic tendency. It is at this level that the demand for an occasional voice in the running of things and the suspicion of established authority has a more universal message. It is thus not uncommon for persons involved in a regionally based small-scale protest against a specific source of pollution, for example, to be able to see in their activities certain global concerns. It is in this context that citizens' movements have attracted the interest of those studying mass culture.

II The Concern with Structured Social Inequality

A Social Policy

Another group of scholars concerned with conflict are known as the social policy theorists (*shakai seisaku ronsha*). Inspired by the German school of social policy around the turn of the century, these scholars had a deep interest in the role of public policy as a device for mitigating social tension. Although this concern seemed to wane as the union movement and the ideas of socialism were revived after the First World War, it did not die. Rather, it lay dormant until the early thirties, when the labor and socialist movements came under increasing pressure from more conservative and rightist elements (Sumita: 1965, pp. 84–8).

Some, like Mori (1951) argued that the government ought to act as a neutral party which could mediate class interests. In favor of a policy for redistribution (*bunpai seisaku*), Mori argued that the process of capital formation in capitalist society tended to concentrate economic wealth in the hands of the capitalist class (*shihonka kaikyū*), thereby creating considerable social unrest among the underprivileged members of the working class (*rōdōsha kaikyū*). He maintained that social policy would allow society to continue with capitalist processes of production by redistributing or channelling back to the working classes some of the wealth generated by their economic activity.

A second group of social policy theorists formed around the work of Ōkōchi (1940, 1949 and 1952a). He explained why capitalists would find it in their own interest to improve the quality of their most important input (i.e., labor). Ōkōchi argued that capitalists would increasingly give way to the demands of labor for better working conditions and a higher standard of living simply to improve economic efficiency and thereby long-term profits. In some ways this position agreed with the work of Dunlop and others who spoke of the theory of countervailing power and the balance of power between big business, big government and big labor. This school tended to see the historical processes of capitalism as producing progressive development. It recognized the strong, nationalistic role of the government in initiating industrialization, including its support for capital; the emergence of a labor force, its organization and the subsequent changes in the consciousness of some workers; and, finally, the role of government in taking positive steps to set up a legal framework in which labor-management disputes could be settled in the interests of both parties and of the broader public. Although Ōkōchi gave attention to the historical context in which these kinds of relationship emerged, this approach none the less has much in common with the views on convergence set forth somewhat later by Kerr and his associates (1960), Levine (1967), Karsh and Cole (1968) and others. In the last analysis, Ōkōchi presented a model of how conflict is institutionalized.

A third body of opinion is represented by Kazehaya (1973)[4] and Kishimoto (1955 and 1967). This viewpoint argues that governments are never neutral, but rather exist to serve the ruling class. In a capitalist society this means that the government will always act in collusion with the business community to help create and maintain an adequate supply of efficient and obedient manpower. Scholars of this persuasion, therefore, have argued that the task of researchers interested in social policy is primarily to provide an accurate social history and to prick the social conscience. Their task has been to expose to the public the unseemly relationships which actually exist between the ruling class (primarily representing business interests) and the government.

Despite variations in the explanations as to why and for whom social policy is formulated, there was consensus among prewar scholars that the need for social policy inevitably arises in capitalist society as the interests of business and labor come into conflict (Sumita: 1965, pp. 26–32). Postwar scholars have tended to become bogged down in theoretical discussions concerning the nature of the parties (*shutai*) to the conflict. In other words, the focus has been on who belongs on which side of particular divisions. This has entailed distinguishing the capitalists from the laborers and delineating more sharply the role of the government. In reaction to this trend, scholars like Sumiya (1954, 1965 and 1974) have argued for a shift in emphasis, asking how the interests of workers as members of the labor force related to their interests as social entities outside the labor force. Sumiya has argued that the conventional Marxist theory says little about the actual composition of the working class and the way in which it is shaped by the labor market. In other words, even if the writings of Marx tell us something about the worker's interests in his contractual or productive relationship with the capitalists at work, Sumiya argues that Marxism does not adequately analyze the worker's interests as a member of the larger society outside, and separate from, his place of work. Sumiya (1954) earlier argued in the mid-fifties that there was a need for a behavioral approach perhaps similar to that found in the American sub-discipline known as labor economics. At that time, he wrote, 'the debate among the social policy theorists . . . has not made any useful contribution to the study of labor in terms of objective social science research.' Twenty years later he was able to conclude that since 1955 much research had been done along the lines he originally proposed. He cited how detailed research on the labor market, the wage system, the labor union movement and labor-management relations had shifted attention from social policy (*shakai seisaku*) in the narrower sense to labor problems (*rōdō mondai*) in the broader sense. He asserted that the basis for profitable discussion within the framework of the social policy theorists had been established, and called for a return from these microscopic studies to macroscopic theory building.

Although there is not space here to examine each of these developments between 1954 and 1975, the interesting work of Matsubara (1973) might be mentioned. In the field of lifestyles and living patterns (*seikatsu kōzōron*), he used the A-G-I-L subsystems approach of Parsons to illustrate how the average person seeks to fulfill these functions through production, political activities, family life, education and leisure (the subsystem R is added for relaxation). Matsubara goes beyond a mere application of Parsonian doctrine, and presents a wide variety of interesting modes. From this perspective, two related areas, namely poverty and the labor movement, are particularly relevant to the arguments of the conflict theorists.

B Poverty and Economic Exploitation

A contention of many conflict theorists is that Japan's economic growth has consistently benefited certain sectors of Japanese society at the expense of other sectors, thereby resulting in greater income inequality. One segment of society which has had to pay a disproportionately large share of the price for rapid economic growth has been the poor. One group of scholars specializing in research on the poor has concluded that poverty is chronic, and that it is the result of a structured system of inequality which discriminates against specific elements of the working class.[5] The working class is seen as being divided not only psychologically but also in terms of the labor market. This duality, it is argued, has produced a group in society with a level of wages considerably below the level which would otherwise prevail. The division in the labor market also accounts for the apparently low level of class consciousness. In other words, although the high rate of savings and investment in Japan may have facilitated rapid economic growth and thereby a higher standard of living for all Japanese workers, the savings mechanism is seen as being essentially coercive, not voluntary. It was also seen as serving over time to shift ownership of the country's wealth to a small, but powerful, elite.

Yokoyama (1949 reprint of 1899 original) and Kawakami (1949 reprint of 1916 original) mingled among the working classes in Meiji and Taishō Japan, using household budgets and other materials to describe the dire poverty of the times. Ishihara (1913) and Hosoi (1947 reprint of 1926 original) recorded the lives of young girls who worked under conditions similar to those usually associated with forced labor. These conditions are vividly described in the proletarian literature of Kobayashi Takiji and others. Then there was also rural poverty among tenant farmers.

In the postwar period, Mori (1953) argued that Japan responded to the international capitalist order by pursuing capitalist development at home, and that this was done by taxing the lower strata of Japanese rural society unduly. The result was that many continued to live in poverty despite the overall record of economic growth. He described this process as follows (p. 17):

> Because capitalism in Japan emerged rather late (compared with its development in the other advanced [imperialistic] countries of the world), it developed upon the feudalistic institutions of the past without clearly differentiating classes in a modern way. Nevertheless, Japanese capitalism soon came into direct conflict with the other capitalist countries. . . . In order to meet this challenge and survive, it had to compensate for the fact that its capital stock was very poor. In essence it had to catch up. The means of speeding up the process of capital formation in Japan was, of course, embodied in policies to expand the population and to maintain Japan's low level of wages. The result was a system which paid wage rates similar to those given to slaves, feudal serfs, or people in the colonies. Because of these low wages, social dumping could occur, involving the export of goods which were undervalued (in terms of the labor input). These goods were known as 'starvation exports' [*kigateki yushutsu*]. For example, it is common knowledge that the spearhead of Japanese industrial capital was the textile industry, which was built upon the low wages born out of the excessive supply of labor in the extremely poor peasant strata in the rural agricultural villages and the seasonal workers who sought to earn additional income to help make ends meet in those poor households. The conditions of those times are clearly recorded in the frequently cited *Menshi Bōseki Shokkō Jijō* [Working Conditions in the Cotton-spinning Mills], *Ki-ito Orimono Shokkō Jijō* [Working Conditions in the Silk-spinning Mills] and Yokoyama Gennosuke's *Nihon no Kasō Shakai* [The Lower Class in Japanese Society]. . . . This, then, was the beginning of what would lead to a great tragedy for the girls who were brought to labor in the textile factories. [Translated by the authors]

In this regard, one might also consult the work of Ōkōchi (1964, pp. 73–91).

In the early postwar years, several million Japanese were repatriated. Many returned after the war without any economic base in Japan, and soon found themselves living in relative and absolute poverty (Ōkōchi: 1964). Accordingly, literature in this period focused primarily on the identification of a minimum standard of living (*saitei seikatsuhi*). As the economy began to recover with the change in occupation policy and the Korean War, attention shifted to the sociological dimensions of the chronically poor. This required a closer look at the lifestyles and social position of the unemployed (*shitsugyōsha*), the fatherless household (*boshi katei*), the social migrant or vagabond (*furōsha*), the temporary worker (*rinjikō*), social outcast groups (such as the *mikaihō buraku*) and the prostitute (*baishunfu*).

Much of this work was connected in one way or another with the formulation of government policy and counter-proposals by those outside the government. Late in 1950 the Government set up a council to study the feasibility of establishing a minimum wage and a social security and social insurance system. In 1952 and 1953 these studies were given further impetus by the charge of the leftists that Japanese rearmament would serve again to impoverish the masses. One expression of this latter concern is Kishimoto's work (1955) on impoverishment and social policy. Although his theoretical treatment of how the working class is impoverished in the capitalist system is borrowed largely from studies of social policy and poverty in Britain, it is clear from his preface (pp. 1–15) that Kishimoto believes this analysis also applies to Japan.

Rapid economic growth, which began in the mid-fifties and continued until the early seventies, led many to believe that poverty was a thing of the past. Certainly this was the impression given by the flood of books on Japan's 'new middle class' and frequent reference to surveys conducted by the Prime Minister's Office in the seventies, which consistently found that about 90 per cent of the population placed themselves in the middle class (Osada: 1981). Despite the general shift in academic interest away from poverty, books on the subject continued to appear (Akiyama *et al.*: 1960; Isomura: 1962; Ōhashi: 1962; Teihen no Kai: 1961). In 1964 Ōkōchi wrote as follows:

> In the postwar years as well, the kind of lower class (poverty) which we saw in prewar Japan has not disappeared one bit. Rather, it survives in a new form. Thus, the kind of poverty

reported on in the *Welfare White Paper* is at best only part of the story. The real source of poverty lies elsewhere. (p. 74)

An important shift in emphasis can be detected in the early sixties as scholars began to delve into the culture of poverty. The nature of this shift can be detected in the introduction to a four-volume series on poverty which appeared in the early sixties:

> We already have many studies of poverty. Some employed laborious and painstaking surveys and used reliable materials. Both the methodology and the writing show conscientious concern. With these studies an unsparing examination of the contradictions in capitalist society was launched. The researchers have sought to cut out and place before society the diseased portion which is poverty, and have argued passionately that there cannot be a solution of this problem until the social structure itself is reformed.
>
> Nevertheless, to be frank, we still somehow feel ill at ease with these studies. *The problem is that all this research has been done by outsiders*–people who are called scholars and professional researchers. *Research done by outsiders invariably has inherent biases and errors.* This shortcoming is probably not the fault of those on the outside alone. None the less, the fact is that *the unfortunate of mankind close up tight when confronted by surveys from the outside.* Even before the questions start to flow from the outside investigator, the respondent has already prepared an innocuous answer. Knowing the kind of answer the investigator and his assistants expect, the respondent cannot help but be cynical. He can pretty much tell beforehand the kind of answer which will result in any particular report. This response is born out of the very fact that he is poor. To close up and give prepared answers repetitiously like a parrot is one sure way that the poor can protect themselves. It is a kind of wisdom born out of poverty and a long history of oppression and humiliation. It is also a subtle expression of reproach against those who come to ask questions in their new suits and student uniforms, and who somehow stand out apart from the poor. Then again, it's also a passive expression of anger against this kind of concern which mixes pity and curiosity.

> People from the outside are usually inclined to deal with poverty as a corpse (e.g., by looking at the results of poverty). *Opposed to this approach, we wish to deal with poverty as a way of life. By doing so we can go behind the ordinary investigation* which seeks merely to assess the state of things. Rather, *we look for the social consciousness of the lower class*, making clear the kind of tension and conflict which exist at this level. [Translated by the authors from Akiyama *et al.*: 1960, vol. 1, pp. 1–3]

The message was clear: there needed to be an examination of the methodology from a phenomenological or sociology of knowledge perspective. It was also clear that such questioning could not help but throw doubt on the superficial surveys of the Prime Minister's Office, which showed more and more people identifying with the middle class.[6]

The new approach tended to remove the study of poverty from the realm of statistical surveys and to place it clearly in an ethnographic framework focusing on a particular subculture and way of life. This is an extremely important development in the methodology related to the study of inequality. It demonstrates how anthropological methods of study can be used without the encumbering assumptions usually associated with the holistic approach. The movement was away from the immediate postwar concern with delineating the poverty line, and interests shifted from the hard to the soft economics of poverty (Ogawa: 1969; Kagayama: 1970). While many have pointed out that poverty in the traditional sense remains even after nearly two decades of rapid growth (Horie: 1969; Takano: 1970, pp. 2–26 and 91–184), more important perhaps is the marked change in the concept of poverty.

In writing about the impoverishment of the working class and the antagonism it breeds between workers and capitalists, Ogawa (1969) has suggested that

> the return to labor must not be evaluated only in the narrow sense as wage income, but must be understood in terms of wages and various other conditions of employment such as working hours, the intensity of the work load, and so forth. (p. 33)

In 1970 Takano wrote in his preface that

> the working masses in contemporary Japan are now threatened by a new type of poverty: the deterioration in the goods and services for common social consumption which go to meet fundamental human needs such as housing, education and transportation. . . .

Although this emphasis can be found in Kishimoto's earlier work (1955, p. 4), it is interesting to note here that Takano seems to have backed down from his insistence on the inevitability of the working class becoming impoverished in absolute terms (e.g., a drop in the real standard of living) and has come instead to view impoverishment in relative terms (cf. Sumiya, 1974, pp. 742 and 744 and especially footnote 8). Funabashi too has explained the difficulty of estimating necessary living expenses. Discussing how such difficulties complicated his study of working-class households in the Yokohama area (1971a, pp. 6–7), he commented that

> a simple calculation of the cost of maintaining physical existence is not enough. Rather, the cost of participating culturally in society at its given level of historical development must be included. . . . When increases in the wage level have not been able to keep up with the sharp increases in living expenses (for these kinds of socio-cultural needs), workers acutely feel a new kind of 'modern poverty', and this anxiety soon breeds alienation and a sense of deprivation (*yokkyū fuman*).
>
> Moreover, . . . there is a deterioration in the ability of the labor force to reproduce itself. In 'reproducing itself' we mean not only its physical (quantitative) dimensions but also its cultural and educational (qualitative) dimensions.

This new concept of poverty has been skillfully employed and further developed in a number of recent studies of the working class in the early seventies. In discussing the impoverishment of the working class, many writers began to focus attention on excessive rationalization through larger-scale production, intensified work loads, longer hours of work and inconsiderate personnel transfers. They mentioned industrial accidents, pollution, the problems of the small subcontractor and his labor force, discrimination against women in the work force, the under-populated areas, alienation and the sense of impotence among workers unable to determine the ends of their economic activity (Kozeki: 1960; Kojima, 1973; Kamata: 1973 and 1974; Asahi Shinbunsha: 1975; Naruse: 1982). There seems to be in this literature, then, a new realization that the power inequalities paralleling income inequalities have unmistakable consequences which affect the ability of particular social classes to express their respective sets of values. Consequently, much of the literature on poverty stresses the need for completely new kinds of social legislation. In this sense, the literature shares concerns expressed earlier by the social policy theorists.

C The Labor Movement

The history of the Japanese labor movement has also provided conflict theorists with good material for the argument that conflict is an inherent part of Japanese society. In addition to the general histories of the prewar years (e.g., Ōkōchi: 1952b and 1970), there are many case histories of particular unions such as the Japan Machinists' Union (Ikeda: 1970) or the 1921 strikes at the shipbuilding yards in Kōbe (Ikeda and Ōmae: 1966). Whereas very little, if any, of the literature on social policy and poverty is available in English, a fair amount has been written in English about the labor movement, to which readers can refer (Harada: 1968 reprint of the 1928 original; Ōkōchi: 1958; Levine: 1958a, 1958b and 1967; Ayusawa: 1966; Cook: 1966; Large: 1972; Kublin: 1964) and a summary of some of this literature can be found in Evans (1971). In addition, leftist political parties have also received considerable attention (Beckmann: 1969; Scalapino: 1967; Cole *et al.*: 1966). Much of this literature, however, has tended to describe institutions or personalities, and has not really developed broader theories to explain conflict, violence and the sense of confrontation which is thoroughly documented in the more critical Japanese literature. To present a history of exploitation, police harassment and repression, and the Government's failure to take a progressive stance on many issues involving the human rights of workers, Japanese scholars have also drawn heavily upon the writings of labor leaders, journalists and socialists in the prewar period.[7] In comparison with those written in English, however, Japanese scholars have tended to limit themselves primarily to substantiating the claim that considerable tension and social cleavage exist in this arena as well. There has been a tendency to fall back on imported Marxist explanations whenever more generalized theoretical statements are needed.

Legislation in the immediate postwar years extended to labor the right to organize, to strike and to bargain collectively. It limited considerably the discretion of those representing the state to call in the police or to use other coercive forms of repression or physical brutality to suppress the outspokenness of labor unionists. However, the more militant and insistent union leaders were put on the defensive by MacArthur's decision to ban the general strike planned for 1 February 1947. The campaign against labor was stepped up with four laws taking away the right to strike from employees in the public sector. This campaign was given momentum by occupation-inspired efforts to enforce the Ordinance for Organizations, to disband Zenrōren and to disrupt Sanbetsu Kaigi. Occupation authorities also promoted the red purge which resulted in many communist sympathizers being removed from their work-place, and in the publication of *Akahata* (the official newspaper of the Japan Communist Party) being suspended (Rōdō Undōshi Kenkyūkai: 1972 and 1973; Takemae: 1970; Shiota: 1969, especially pp. 74–109). Mass dismissals and the establishment of company-sponsored unions were policies designed to weaken the more assertive, leftist-oriented unions in the fifties. The history of labor and management in those years provides necessary background for understanding the union movement today. A classic study of how leftist unions (*daiichi kumiai*) have been isolated and replaced by unions favorable to the company (*goyō kumiai* or *daini kumiai*) was written by Fujita (1955).

There is a sizable literature on labor-management relations which tends to stress the commitment of the Japanese worker to his company and the existence of some kind of symbolic relationship between the union and management. Conflict-oriented scholars, however, have consistently argued for a careful analysis which considers the real intentions of labor leaders in establishing enterprise unions in the chaos following defeat in 1945. They have also drawn attention to the reasoning behind initial demands for a system of seniority wage payments and for the use of average wage rates in bargaining at a time of extreme economic privation. Further, many have noted the development of *shuntō*, the emergence of the 'second union', and the various political forces which were very much present in Japan in the seventies (Nishimura: 1970, pp. 1–130; Fujita: 1972; Kishimoto: 1969, pp. 251–301).

III Some Common Themes in the Little Traditions

There are, of course, a number of other areas in which the presence of considerable tension and conflict can be easily documented. Starting with the work by Ui (1968 and 1971–4), the literature on anti-pollution movements provides one ready example. One could proceed to list the literature on the anti-war movement, dissatisfaction with American military bases in Japan, the student movement, the consumer movement, the activities of various citizens' groups, and the confrontation between new reformist governments and the old political establishment controlled by the conservatives. In the early eighties, the anti-nuclear movement and the activities of Nihon wa Kore de Ii noka Shimin Rengō (the Citizens' Group to Rethink Japanese Priorities) emerged. However, the foregoing discussion provides sufficient evidence that there exists another tradition of scholarship not so well known outside Japan.

The view of Japanese society which emphasizes variation and conflict is quite diverse and has grown out of a number of rather distinct traditions. Nevertheless, in this complex intellectual tradition some common themes can be discerned. Most conspicuous is the willingness to accept conflict as a consistent feature of Japanese society. It is asserted that conflict in Japan delineates the basic tensions which exist among various organizations, groups or social classes. Violence and physical repression are seen as being isolated phenomena underlying more extensive conflicts and tensions in Japanese society. Much of this conflict is seen as arising from a concern with inequalities in the distribution of economic rewards. In referring to economic rewards, reference is made not only to cash income but to economic utility in general, including the right to capital ownership, differences in working conditions and the provision of social welfare. The conflict theorists see a close correlation between the amount of income a person receives, his or her ability to influence political processes and the making of socially significant decisions, and his or her access to socially relevant information.

Taken as a whole, the literature on conflict in Japan suggests that each individual can differentiate between his or her own interests and those of others. While the way in which individuals define their self-interest varies, this variation has not been fully systematized. There does, however, appear to be common agreement that structural inequalities and the way in which people view their own interests change as industrialization proceeds. In this regard, then, attention is focused on the processes shaping the capitalist approach to production and on the way economic ownership is defined in Japan. From this perspective, the fundamental conflicts are seen as occurring not so much in terms of competition between economic enterprises, as suggested by those emphasizing consensus in Japanese society, but rather between capitalists, management, landowners and conservative bureaucrats, on one hand, and organized and unorganized labor, tenant farmers and the poor, on the other. It is in terms of these two groupings that conflict must ultimately be understood.

Finally, it is held that when conflicts of interest arise between labor and management or between consumers and producers, members of the political establishment will invariably work to bolster the position of large capital and land-owning interests. Conservative bureaucrats, politicians and management are seen as working to prevent, or at least to retard, the development of groups which would unify labor or other anti-establishment elements. Were this constant pressure or control to be removed, competing political and economic ideologies would receive a much broader following among the public. According to the conflict theorists, the ruling elements in Japan are in a decidedly advantageous position in terms of manipulating the present system to their advantage, and they will quite naturally continue to maintain their position in every way possible.

Chapter 4

The Distribution of the Conservative and Radical Traditions in Japanese Studies

I The Question of Larger Traditions and Paradigms

In the preceding two chapters, two differing views of Japanese society have been outlined. One stressed the high level of social consensus in Japan and the other stressed the presence of conflict. Based on their reading of Neustupný (1982a), Said (1979), Davis (1982) and Bix (1979), the authors are inclined to conclude that the two views are not simply different interpretations of the same data or even of the same phenomena. It would appear that the differences in viewpoint are part of a more fundamental or more general difference in the paradigm: a system of thought characterized by similar descriptions of social phenomena, a common problem consciousness and shared methodological assumptions and strategies.

In the preceding chapters two general views of Japanese society were presented. In one tradition Japanese society and culture are treated as a coherent, integrated whole; it stresses the 'Japaneseness' of Japanese society and seeks to contrast societal values in Japan with those found in other societies. The second tradition underlines the importance of social tensions, especially those which seem to exist between dichotomous classes in the Marxist sense. It tends to take a phenomenological view of knowledge and to be skeptical of survey research. Despite the inclination of some to depend upon a generalized statement of Marxism for theoretical or explanatory insight, the research of many promoting this view has relied heavily on the historical, case-study approach which emphasizes particular settings.

The two general approaches have been labelled 'the great tradition' and 'the little traditions' respectively. The reasons for using these terms will become more apparent as the reader progresses through the book. Each has a sizable literature and a fairly distinct ideological position. As Table 4.1 indicates, the two perspectives provide very different views of Japanese society.

Table 4.1 *Two distinguishing features of the images of Japanese society presented by two traditions of scholarship*

Variable applied to Japanese society	The stream of scholarship	
	The great tradition	The little traditions
amount of internal variation	little (homogeneity)	much (variation)
amount of agreement on social values	high (consensus)	low (conflict)

The existence of these two antipodal models no doubt reflects, at least in part, a perdurable antithesis in the social sciences as a whole: the dichotomy between the conservative and radical traditions as defined by Lenski (1966, pp. 1–23). This bifurcation of social science into two traditions of scholarship has been widely noted, and the relative merits of each approach have been vigorously debated in the postwar years. They have been referred to variously as integration and conflict theory (Allardt: 1968), the utopian and the rationalist (Dahrendorf: 1969a and 1969b), the nominalist and the realist (Wrong: 1969), the operational model and the deterministic model (Wessolowski: 1969), functional schemes and dychotomic schemes (Ossowski: 1956 and 1963), equilibrium theory and the conflict theory (Tumin: 1967), the holistic approach and the action approach (Dawe: 1970), and the American approach and the European approach (Béteille: 1969).

One approach places a major emphasis on the way in which the individual is integrated into the nation, the state or just society in general. The individual's sense of affiliation to the social system is seen as a logical outcome of reasoned thinking which recognizes the necessity of social differentiation and the basic efficiencies produced by social specialization. The second approach attaches considerable weight to the individual's awareness of self-interest and the ways in which this awareness tends to divide or segment society into conflicting social classes as defined below in Chapter 12 (Table 12.2). The emphasis is often on the dysfunctional aspects of differentiation which are exploitative or alienating, and which are, therefore, the source of considerable tension and disintegration. The ideal types suggested by these two viewpoints would perhaps be purblind, romantic obsessions with nationalistic or societal ends at one extreme, and narrow, militant class consciousness and coldly calculated self-interest with no room for altruistic aims at the other (Tumin: 1953).

II The Distribution of the Two Paradigms in Japanese Studies

In the Japanese-language literature, two very different images of Japanese society seem to coexist. Although those emphasizing variation and endemic conflict in Japanese society represent a minority, their views frequently appear in the Japanese literature (perhaps owing to the more established position of Marxist or socialist viewpoints in Japan) even though they tend to be ignored by the 'academic establishment'. Nevertheless, while recognizing the presence of a literature in Japanese which focuses largely on tension and conflict, one should not lose sight of the fact that the holistic view is clearly dominant. In the English-language literature, the holistic approach described above seems to have an even more pronounced dominance. Though there are a few noticeable exceptions, the group model has almost attained a monopolistic position in the coverage of Japan found in Western languages. If this assessment is correct, it might be argued that it is those who have to read about Japanese society in English who have a limited number of viewpoints, and that it is in English that more debate is needed (Table 4.2). To avoid misunderstanding in this regard, further explanation may be necessary.

The first reason for believing that the holistic view is dominant in Japan is the publishing figures. Nakane (1967a), Doi (1966), Vogel (1979b) and Reischauer (1979) have all sold more than 400,000 or

Table 4.2 *The distribution of the great and little traditions in English and Japanese literature on Japanese society*

		Language in which the literature on Japanese society appears	
		Japanese	English
View of Japanese society	The great tradition: the holistic model of Japanese society	A long and established tradition occupying a very dominant position in the media Receiving support from business and government circles	Monopolistic position since the end of the war
	The little traditions: the conflict model of Japanese society	A number of long and established traditions among a minority of scholars Receiving some support from anti-establishment groups	Almost non-existent although a small trickle begins in the seventies

500,000 copies. The figure for Nakane is reported at over 760,000 and that for Doi is over 1,250,000 (Dōmeki: 1982). None of the best-known works by the conflict theorists come close to those sales. The popularity of the holistic view is also illustrated by the dozens of books in the same vein in Western languages which are immediately translated into Japanese (and with such speed that quite often the Japanese version appears even before or at least simultaneously with the overseas edition). As early as 1963, the Science Council of Japan published a bibliography of several hundred items in this vein which had been published in Japanese, including a number of prewar items (Nihon Gakujutsu Kaigi: 1963). In 1978 the Nomura Research Institute published a report listing merely a sample which included nearly 700 items in this genre (Nomura Sōgō Kenkyūsho: 1978). Yasuda (1980) later compiled a substantial list of the more academic work in that vein, and Tsukushi (1982) published a list of over 60 volumes which had been translated into Japanese. A look into any bookstore would confirm the above information; in the locations where the bestsellers appear, a large number of books espouse the group model's description of Japanese society. A look at how major issues are interpreted in the mass media will also reveal the pervasiveness of the great tradition. For example, the discussions of *bōeki masatsu* (trade friction) with the United States in 1982 tended to dismiss completely foreign criticism of Japan's trade policies; instead the problem was consistently presented as one of cultural misunderstanding. A major emphasis in NHK's programs teaching English continues to be that of cultural differences: one learns to speak English by thinking like a Westerner.

Has the importance attached to the group at least by informed Japanese been exaggerated? At academic gatherings, for example, the old clichés are heard much less frequently. Papers explaining everything Japanese by reference to unique Japanese cultural characteristics have largely disappeared, although one can still occasionally find such phenomena mentioned as background in the footnotes.[1] At the same time, several facts suggest that *nihonjinron* literature is still viewed seriously by many established and influential academics. In Japan it is well known that Reischauer and Vogel are professors at America's most prestigious university, and that Doi and Nakane are professors at Japan's corresponding institution, the University of Tokyo. Among the lesser foreign stars are academics such as Ballon (1969) and Clark (1977) who teach at Sophia University. Table 4.3 lists a dozen other authors of bestsellers; all are university professors. The group model is also well enough established for serious intellectuals to have begun to write overviews of that literature as a distinct intellectual and academic tradition (Minami: 1980; Tsukushi: 1982; Nomura Sōgō Kenkyūsho: 1978; Aizawa: 1976). Some have even begun to formulate meta-theories about *nihonjinron* (Kawamura: 1982b; Fujiwara *et al.*: 1982; Yamamoto and Komuro: 1981; Matsumoto: 1981). A special issue of a leading sociological journal also contains similar discussions (Gendai Shakaigaku Kaigi: 1980). Finally, as we mention elsewhere in this book and as Minami (1980), Yamamoto and Komuro (1981), Kawamura (1982a and 1982b) and Koike (1982) have observed, this stream of scholarship has a long history in Japan, going back at least to the prewar period if not to the entire *kokugaku* movement in the Tokugawa period.

Cannot many examples also be found in the mass media which openly expose conflict and corruption in Japanese society? This kind of question is more difficult to handle. On one hand, there is such coverage and it provides an important source of data, some of which

Table 4.3 *Bestsellers in the* Nihonjinron *tradition*

Author	University(a)	Publisher	Date of original publication	Number of editions
Nakane	Tokyo	Kōdansha	1967	63 by 1982
Doi	Tokyo	Kōbundō	1971	128 by 1981
Aida	Kyoto	Kōdansha	1970	23 by 1982
Araki	Ehime	Kōdansha	1973	16 by 1982
Hanami	Sophia	Nihon Keizai Shinbunsha	1973	5 by 1976
		Kōdansha	1982	First edition in October 1982
Itasaka	Harvard	Kōdansha	1971	23 by 1982
Kamishima	Rikkyō	Kōdansha	1975	11 by 1981
Katō	Sophia	Kōdansha	1976	11 by 1982
Masuzoe	Tokyo	Kōbunsha	1982	
Ozaki	California	Kōdansha	1980	5 by 1982
Shinoda	Sophia	Kōbunsha	1977	29 by 1982
Takatori	Kyoto Joshi	Kōdansha	1975	7 by 1982
Watanabe	Sophia	Shōdensha	1980	4 in the first four months
Yoneyama	Kōnan	Kōdansha	1976	6 by 1981

Note: The universities listed are those given in the author's introduction in each book examined. In some cases, the affiliation has changed since publication.

is cited in the chapters which follow. Also, as suggested above in Chapter 3, there is, to be sure, a full-fledged alternative approach in Japan which stresses conflict. Finally, some of the muck-raking in the popular press must have been written by persons associated with, or sympathetic to, one or more of the little traditions. On the other hand, however, the mainstream magazines and journals which have dealt with the more unattractive aspects of life in Japan have not presented those views as a coherent picture or macro-societal theory of Japanese society. Incidents or scandals are, for the most part, described in isolation. They are, at best, given a micro-sociological explanation quite specific to the events, individuals or groups discussed. Seldom are generalizations about Japanese society drawn from press coverage regarding Ikeda Daisaku, the Red Army siege at Mt Asama, the frequent sex tours to other parts of Asia, or the Kanehira incident. Discussions of events like Tanaka's resignation and the baseball-bat patricide in December 1980 resulted in temporary discussions of certain problem areas and even an institution or two, but did not produce sustained interest and new or seriously competing views of society, aside from those already developed by the conflict theorists.

The abridged discussion in Chapter 3 of the literature dealing with conflict in Japan should verify that there is a sizable literature in Japanese which underlines the presence of conflict in Japanese society. Its authors tend to be associated with various opposition parties and publish in well-established journals which, on the whole, have much smaller circulations than do those carrying the great tradition. They can be said to represent a minority voting bloc in the departmental faculties of many large universities. Within departments, they tend to have their own research seminars; outside the university they tend, in many disciplines, to have their own research organizations and academic associations. At the same time, their visibility tends to fluctuate over time. At the time of the anti-pollution movements, the anti-war movement and the *ampo* demonstrations in the early seventies, it was more pronouced. In the late seventies and early eighties the conflict theorists have been less vociferous. Given their political associations, they perhaps had good reason to reflect on the activities of the Soviet Union in Vietnam, Kampuchea and Afghanistan. Given the long tradition of this stream of scholarship, however, it would be premature to say that it has expired.

The situation is somewhat different in English-speaking countries where a mixture of the group model and the paradoxical contrasts tends to dominate views of Japan. Several considerations lead to this conclusion. One is the association of university academics with this view, as indicated above. While not all academics readily accept that view of Japanese society, comprehensive alternatives have not been presented. Moreover, the support for the holistic image of Japanese society has also received support from persons outside academic life – those working for governments, business and consulting agencies. Finally, the group model was also presented in heavy doses by correspondents like Bernard Krishner, who wrote for *Newsweek* over a long period in the seventies.

In Australia, the group models of Japanese society seem to be eschewed. None the less, they can be seen in a recent issue of *Australian Business* (Stirling: 1981) and in the work published by two leading research centers (cf. March: 1982; Davis: 1978; McDonnell: 1980). They can also be seen in the seminars organized by the Japanese Economic and Management Studies Centre at the University of New South Wales. A recent project by students in Queensland confirms that the views presented in Chapter 2 are also held by many in the general public. Finally, a perusal of the *Far East Economic Review* (or items mentioned in the discussion in Chapter 1 on learning from Japan) will suggest that those views have been distributed far and wide.

As previous publications have pointed out (Sugimoto: 1975b, 1978a and 1981d; Mouer: 1973a and 1978; MS: 1979a, p. 137; and SM: 1979c; 1980a, p. 33), consensus and integration are not the only aspects of Japanese society described in the English-language literature. For example, the peasant riots in the Tokugawa period, the brutal repression of dissidents in the thirties, and the *ampo* demonstrations and anti-pollution movements have been well documented in English. Nevertheless, because the literature on conflict has tended to concentrate on particular events without developing comprehensive or systematic overviews of Japanese society, non-Japanese wishing to have a general theory of Japanese society have turned for inspiration to the work of those emphasizing consensus.

Finally, compared with the Japanese-language literature, the conflict tradition in the English-language literature is rather meager. Ōhashi's *Nihon no Kaikyū Kōsei* (1971) and Horie's *Nihon no Rōdōsha Kaikyū* (1962) have no counterpart in English, although work by Norman (1975), Halliday (1975), Koschmann (1978), Hane (1982), Steven (1979 and 1980) and others immediately comes to mind. The solid Marxist/socialist tradition in Japanese scholarship on Japanese society is not matched either in volume or in creative diversity by the small amount which comes through from *AMPO, Ronin* or the *Bulletin of Concerned Asian Scholars.*

III Conflict, Class and Integration: The Limitation of Holistic and Conflict Models

In focusing on the formation and breakdown of consensus, conflict models immediately address themselves to universal social phenomena: conflicts of interests and power relationships. However, there is a tendency for those taking this approach to overestimate the ability of the individual to know his true interests, to stress the importance of occupational position and the relationship of the individual to the means of production in determining economic interests and power relationships, and to overlook the forces which work to resolve conflict and maintain high levels of social integration. These problems stem in part from an abstracted concept of class which tends to be reduced to its simplest form. Often a clear distinction is not made between classes as statistical categories (*Klasse an sich*) and classes as antagonistic groups within society (*Klasse für sich*). Indeed, in much of the conflict-oriented literature on class in Japanese society, there is a tautological quality; statements often posit that conflict is generated by income inequalities between people with resources and those without them. The link between inequality and conflict is, more often than not, assumed; seldom is it spelled out in empirical terms.

Given these shortcomings, there is first a need to define interests not only in terms of the individual's proximity to or control over income-producing resources and consumer goods, but also in terms of his or her life cycle, reproductive needs and other non-material concerns. In a sense, the literature on the 'new poverty' is one step forward in trying to fill this gap. Within this broader framework, there is a need to define more adequately the concept of social rewards and to study their interconnection. Finally, there is a need to study the sources of conflict, the variables which transform *Klasse an sich* into *Klasse für sich*.

It is at this point that the holistic approach relates to the problem of stratification and social tension. Without going into the complexities of system integration, the presence of which is assumed in the group model of Japanese society, it is important to be aware of how class cleavage is bridged by a common ethos, though not necessarily a common ethic, which binds together a society. First, there is the presence of nationalism and recognition of the nation state as a viable geographical unit for social organization. Second, there is a similar expressive vocabulary which emerges from a similar culture regardless of whether common values exist throughout society. Accordingly, even if economic growth did promote certain changes which might contribute to a rise in social tension and disagreement concerning the goals of economic activity, it is quite possible that the same changes have been accompanied by a rising sense of nationalistic pride and the rapid diffusion of a common culture. Thus, these two factors no doubt serve to minimize the spread of social tensions which were created by other more powerful variables.

In suggesting that conflicts of interest are an important force in society, we are, none the less, left with the question of whether *Klasse für sich* emerge in Japanese society. It is difficult to judge the amount of antagonism, cohesiveness or awareness which is necessary to claim that classes exist. Given the state of research on Japanese society at this stage, one must fall back on one's own findings (which in part are based upon one's own subjective judgements).[2] In the case of Japan, it is clear that considerable conflict and tension exist. The pollution movement and the student movement provide just two examples of the emotional tension which can suddenly be released. Although various control mechanisms keep these kinds of outburst at a minimum, Japanese society is very open and free, and one would expect that open class antagonism would be more evident were conflicting values really held by people in distinguishable social classes. Thus, while tensions exist, revolution does not occur. It is at this point, perhaps, that the group model may throw some light on the problem: its major concern is social values and the Japanese cultural vocabulary. At the same time, social structure is complex; it is more than a reflection of dominant cultural values. As Chapter 13 illustrates, the multiple dimensions of stratification produce a number of cross-cutting subcultures which tend to pluralize the political consciousness of persons who belong to a given sex, who share the experiences of a particular generation, who identify with a specific work organization and a certain occupational activity, and who find themselves putting down roots in a clearly demarcated geographic area.

Political constraints, social structures and culture: these elements are present in every society. Accordingly, in considering the lessons to be learned from Japan, rather than concerning ourselves with whether the motivation of Japanese to industrialize emerged spontaneously from an existing set of values or even from a sudden nationalistic but consensual response to a foreign threat, or whether it was forged out of the coercive relationships defined by a given political milieu, the real questions concern the ways in which these elements were combined in the Japanese case.

This book does not seek to resolve the conservative-radical dichotomy in the social sciences. It does not seek to pit one paradigm against the other or to argue for one as opposed to the other. Nor does

Figure 4.1 *Some evaluative dimensions for assessing the great tradition and strategies for developing new models of Japanese society*

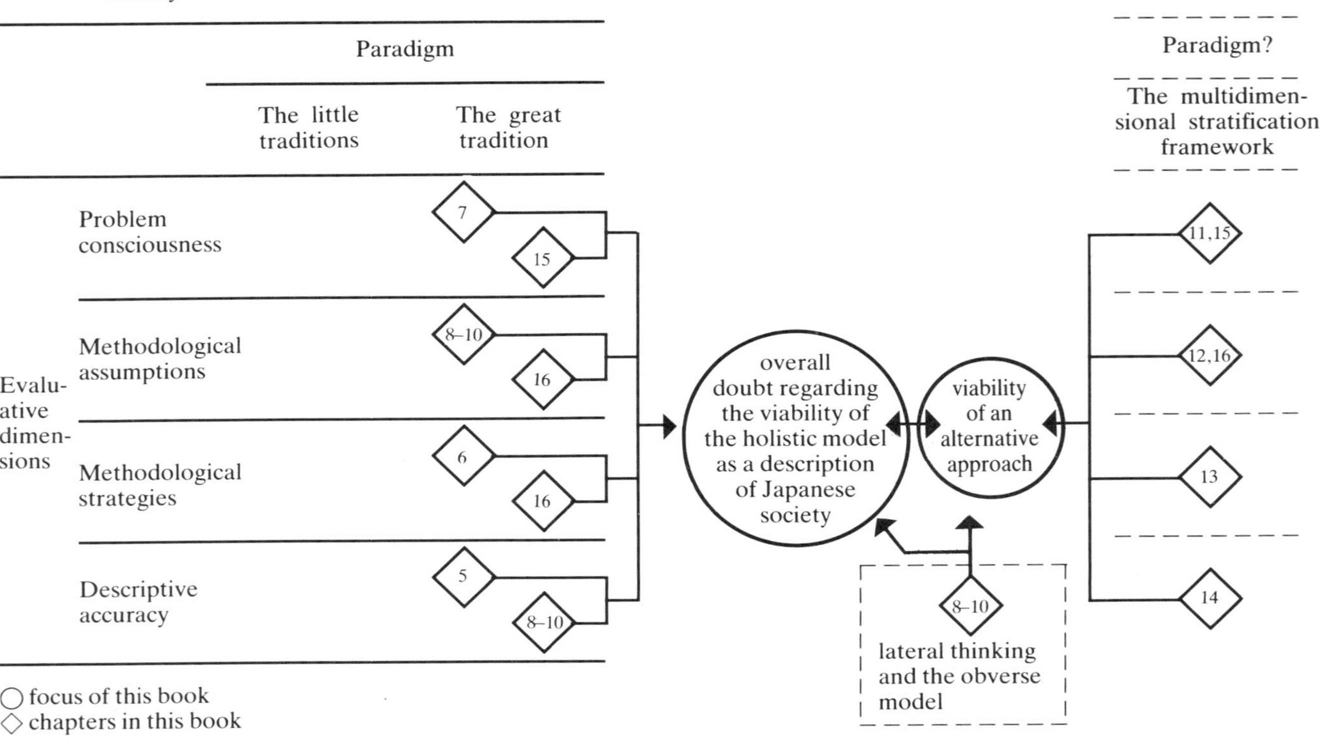

it pretend to compare the validity of one view of Japanese society as opposed to the other. Its goal is more limited. It is an attempt to understand some major descriptions of Japanese society as social phenomena. Introducing two traditions of scholarship on Japanese society, as an initial exploration it deals primarily with one one, the great tradition. Raising doubts about the methodology of those in that tradition, it offers no alternative, aside from a bland proposal for eclecticism. Exposing a certain amount of moralizing and ideological advocacy in that tradition, it contains its own partisan viewpoint and does not provide a way around the Mannheimian dilemma.

The overall structure of the book is shown in Figure 4.1. The specific aims are two; they are represented by the circles. One is to explain reasons for being skeptical of the holistic or group model of Japanese society. The chapters in Part Two argue that there are three reasons for doubting the descriptions of Japanese society presented by those working in the great tradition: conflicting empirical findings, a lack of concern for methodological rigor and certain reservations from the perspective of a sociology of knowledge. The chapters comprising the third part of this volume introduce a variety of examples to suggest that data can be selected in an arbitrary manner to obtain an image of Japanese society which is considerably at odds with the group model. That such an obverse model can be constructed not only raises doubt about many of the methodological or paradigmatic assumptions on which the group model rests, but also offers another promising direction for future research. Finally, as an effort to accommodate both traditions, a multidimensional model of stratification is presented in Part Four. Although the model is not fully developed and many of its potential uses are not discussed, it is conceived out of the little traditions and is sensitive to variation, inequality and authority relations. However, it also poses some interesting explanations about how consensus is formed. The final two chapters seek to return to some of the questions of significance raised in the first chapter and to air some ideas on the comparative study of Japanese society as a set of options.

Part Two

Skepticism: Three Reasons for Doubting the Validity of *Nihonjinron*

Chapter 5

Some Empirical Findings at Odds with the Group Model

In recent years a growing number of scholars have begun to question the holistic image of Japanese society. In particular, they have come to doubt whether, in comparison with people in other societies, the Japanese are more group-oriented, place more emphasis on consensus and social harmony, value more deeply group membership or social solidarity, or are more accustomed to 'vertical' forms of organization. These scholars have come to be skeptical about the flood of statements alleging that Japanese social structure and value orientations are unique. Certainly, every society is unique; but is Japanese society, as so many seem to suggest, 'uniquely unique' in terms of its levels of consensus and social integration? This is the major question which emerges from this rethinking. Given the cultural uniqueness of any society, the other major question emerging is whether those adopting the holistic view of Japanese society have correctly grasped its unique features.

The first part of this chapter presents some empirical findings of other scholars which do not coincide with the group model of Japanese society. The latter part of the chapter introduces work by the authors themselves, looking first at social conflict and then examining some data on social inequality.

I Some General Findings

Chapter 3 discussed the scholarship of Japanese working in sub-disciplines such as Marxist economics, the history of the labor movement, the history of popular movements, social policy and poverty. The accumulated research in all these fields provides a detailed record of the exploitative relations and inter-class tensions which have accompanied the process of industrialization. In addition to these accounts of conflict, there are also studies which examine analytically many of the explanations which tie together the holistic view of Japan.

Some have criticized directly the factual descriptions of the holistic theorists. Recent essays by Shimada (1980), Umetani (1980), Sumiya (1981) and Pucik (1980 and 1981) on labor-management relations undermine many of the stereotypes about this subject. Work on income distribution, including that of Koike (1976 and 1981) and Shimada (1974) suggests that wage differentials in Japan are similar to those found in other societies. Moreover, a careful survey of documentary evidence of economic priorities also underlines certain fundamental disagreements and very real conflicts of interest. Umemura (1967) argues that the commonly accepted explanation of the seniority wages system as a uniquely Japanese practice is difficult to substantiate logically, and with others he has presented data which show that pay according to age and seniority can be found in other societies as well (1971). His findings corroborate the general theories of those studying the economics of education (Blaug: 1976). Levine and Taira (1978) observe that there has been considerable industrial unrest, and Chalmers (1981) argues that cross-cultural differences in the level of disputation at a given time can be partially accounted for by differences in industrial structure, thereby throwing doubt on the idea of national character being the major variable. Taira's careful study (1970) of the labor market in Japan suggests that many Japanese respond to economic incentives in a manner similar to that found in other societies of Asia and the West. Sano (1970), Ono (1973) and Ishida (1976) have all conducted very detailed studies of wage determination in Japan without relying on national character. Arisawa (1955), Obi (1968), Nishikawa (1974) and others have shown that, as in other industrial societies, the willingness of women to work is shaped not so much by cultural values concerning the proper place of women, but by more general economic considerations associated with the so-called Douglas effect (i.e., the observation that the willingness of wives to work is inversely related to their husband's income) and by the age of the women themselves (which produces the so-called M-shaped age-participation curve for women as opposed to the inverted U-shaped curve for men).

Although much new questioning has occurred with regard to Japanese economic behavior, particularly in the labor market, perhaps owing to the good comparative data which has become relatively plentiful in recent years, a growing number of scholars have become skeptical of the alleged Japanese uniqueness in other areas as well. Befu (1974 and 1977), for example, has presented evidence that self-interest is a most important factor accounting for social exchange in Japan. This general theme can also be seen in the work of Marshall (1981) and Sone (1982b). In a historical study of decision-making in Japan and the West, Rikō and his associates at Keiō (1980) show that unanimous consensus has been the exception rather than the rule in Japan. The findings of Inoguchi (1981) and Watanuki (1967) suggest that occupation and Marxist concepts of class are useful in explaining voting behavior in Japan.

While underlining the reluctance of Japanese to deal with outsiders (*tanin*), Yoneyama (1976) emphasizes the particularly fluid nature of group consciousness (*nakama ishiki*), and criticizes Nakane's vertical structure for ignoring the fact that individuals often belong to several different types of group simultaneously. Atsumi (1975 and 1982) argues that many of the ties described as friendship and as being voluntaristic actually involve elements of social control and are often an instrumental means to achieve more personal goals linked to some concept of self-interest. Befu (1982a, pp. 31–2) cites a number of examples of 'paternalistic neglect'. Although the image of the loyal worker is usually one of a contented worker, there is good evidence to suggest that there is a good deal of alienation in many of Japan's firms (Kamata: 1973 and 1974; Sengoku: 1982). Pucik (1980 and 1981) reports on his research showing that there is not one Japanese style of management but several, which range from the dictatorial control of a single individual to various forms of collective decision-making.

Another area of debate concerns the importance of university cliques (*gakubatsu*) in determining career patterns. The commonly projected image centers on the fiercely competitive examination system to get into a famous university, a success which sets one up for life. Coupled with this are the notion of difficult entry into and easy exit from the Japanese university and the assumption that career patterns are fixed by educational background upon entry. Takeuchi and Aso (1982) and Koike and Watanabe (1979a and 1979b) have argued that the importance of the university has been exaggerated and that it has in any case diminished over time. Ono *et al.* (1976)

have documented the extent to which income differentials between company executives (a very high percentage of whom are university graduates in Japan) and ordinary employees have narrowed considerably over time and especially so in the postwar period (also cf. *NKSC*, 5 July 1981, p. 11). At the same time, the rebuttals by Takeuchi (1980), Iwata (1981) and Iwauchi (1980) suggest the phenomena are complex enough to require more careful consideration. In the debate it is crucial whether one samples large firms or small firms; company presidents, senior executives, top management, middle-level management and supervisory personnel may all be company officers in large firms, but each concept yields a different sample and different findings. It would seem that graduates from some of the prestigious universities surprisingly have a much lower rate of success in being promoted to a certain level of management, but that among those who attain that level they are much more successful in making it to the next level. The end result, then, is a phenomenon at the second level which is more in line with popular expectations. However, the overall debate has certainly underlined the danger of generalizations which are too sweeping.

From a more macroscopic viewpoint, Iida (1979) argues that more or less universal economic values characterize economic behavior in Japan and that the basic concept of rationality central to modern economic theory underlines the economic choices made by most Japanese. Surveying European literature on economics, Nishibe (1975) reaches similar conclusions. The critique presented by Kōsai and Ogino (1980) also raises serious questions concerning the cultural uniqueness of Japanese economic behavior. In this regard, the careful study of debt-equity ratios in Japan and the United States by Inoguchi (1980) tends to draw into question major assumptions found in common theories regarding the behavior of Japanese firms.

Perhaps the emphasis on the uniqueness and the incomparability of the Japanese experience is a natural reaction to, and a logical escape from, a hundred years of being compared against foreign, and especially Western, standards which cannot be met because they are so ethnocentrically defined.

The dislocations experienced by those wrapped up in endless imitation of foreign culture and by those searching blindly for a unique national identity are poignantly captured in the movie *Nantonaku Kurisutaru* (Nevertheless Glistening). Produced from a novel by Tanaka Yasuo, the scenes at the piano bar show how the importation of an entirely new world of cultural symbols (e.g.,

American songs and jazz) has resulted in an artificial situation in which those 'high on English' have difficulty communicating both among themselves and with those left behind in the 'ordinary world of Japanese'. In trying what one cannot do with one's own limited Japanese (perhaps because language alone is a limited medium) or with one's own basket of other things Japanese (e.g., music, dance, painting, etc.), it is easy to believe the adoption of foreign symbols will provide a solution. While the movie takes a critical view of those who think 'internationalization' is simply the adoption of material cultural paraphernalia from abroad and who believe that Western culture is imbued with some kind of universal value, one is sharply reminded that the Japanese experience also includes some broader, universal meanings by a later scene built around the lecture of a drunken *sararīman* on the unique spirit of Japanese folk songs (*enka no kokoro*), a scene which parodies the absurdity of parochial theories of 'the Japanese essence'.

Finally, there are a number of studies which recognize peculiarly Japanese behavioral phenomena but argue that such behavior can be explained by more universal processes. Examining the lower rates of job turnover or labor mobility in Japan, Marsh and Mannari (1977) dispel the notion that the answer will be found in social values emphasizing the culturally unique aspects of Japanese society. Kōshiro (1982a) argues that population densities and the relative scarcity of good jobs are important variables accounting for behavior in the Japanese labor market. A study by Phelps and Azumi (1976) suggests that many aspects of organizational behavior in Japan can be explained better by theories which do not emphasize the culturally unique aspects of Japanese society.

An example of the way in which differing social contexts can produce phenomena subject to more general explanations can be found in a recent paper by Azumi and Hull (1982). Focused on industrial organization and alienation, their research suggests that technology in Japanese and in American factories relates in opposite ways to levels of alienation: low- and high-grade technologies are associated with relatively low levels of alienation in the United States and relatively high levels in Japan whereas medium-level, process-oriented technologies seem to produce higher levels in the United States and lower levels in Japan (Figure 5.1). However, Koike (1976 and 1981) has observed still other differences related to the level of technology, differences in career patterns in the United States and Japan (Table 5.1.).

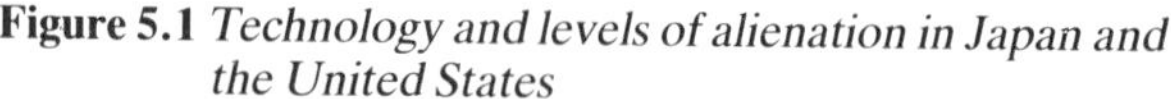

Figure 5.1 *Technology and levels of alienation in Japan and the United States*

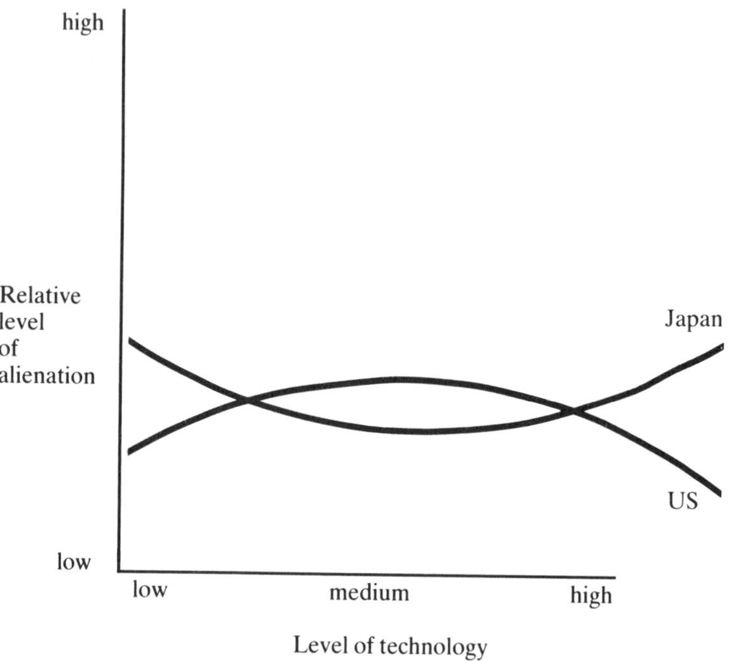

Considered alone, theories of alienation or career patterns do not provide a generalized explanation. However, when considered together they provide a very powerful general explanation in which technology and career patterns together explain changes in the level of alienation. Koike's explanation is that higher technologies produce higher levels of alienation and deeper career structures lower the levels of alienation. In Japan a major difference between firms with low and medium technology is the introduction of in-depth careers which more than overset the increase in levels of alienation due to the change of technology. However, when we move to firms with high technology, technology is the only variable and alienation rises. In the United States, however, in-depth careers appear only in firms with higher technology. Accordingly, in moving from industries with low technology to those with medium-level technology, the

Table 5.1 *Technology and career patterns in Japan and the United States*

Type of technology	Career pattern	
	Japan	US
low	type B	type B
medium	type A	type B
high	type A	type A

Type A: in-depth careers with considerable opportunity for upward promotion tied to a more diffuse range of jobs.

Type B: limited careers tied to the performance of specific jobs.

technology is the only variable which changes and alienation increases. In the United States, however, the next shift in technology is accompanied by a change in career patterns as the shift is made to firms with high-level technology. The combined effects of these two variables are shown in Table 5.2.

The shortcomings of the holistic model are most striking in two areas. One is its emphasis on consensus in Japan when conflict can readily be seen. The other is its assumption that the Japanese are more homogeneous than other peoples, when marked inequalities

Table 5.2 *Technology, career patterns and levels of alienation in Japan and the United States*

Change in the level of technology	Changes in career patterns and the effects on levels of alienation	
	Japan	US
low → medium	T↑ → A↑ ΔC → A↓	T↑ → A↑
medium → high	T↑ → A↑	T↑ → A↑ ΔC → A↓

Note: T = level of technology
C = depth in the career structure

characterize the distribution of income. In the following two sections of this chapter, the research of the two authors is introduced to throw light on the question of consensus and uniformity.

II The Presence of Conflict

A number of studies recording conflict were introduced in Chapter 3. The research of one author (Sugimoto: 1975a, 1976, 1977a, 1978a, 1978b and 1981d) is introduced here to underline two points. One is that a time perspective is needed. When a longer time perspective is taken, the present low levels of conflict in Japan are offset by the higher levels which were recorded immediately after the war. A second need is for more sophisticated definitions of conflict. Frequency, participation, duration and intensity are each different aspects of conflict; each needs to be considered when overall levels of conflict are discussed.

A Popular Disturbances in Postwar Japan

One project involved the study of popular disturbances between 1 January 1952 and 30 June 1962 in 44 prefectures (excluding Tokyo and Hokkaidō); 53 national and local newspapers were inspected for cases of popular disturbance which was defined as 'collective coercion that threatens the existing control of legitimate means of coercion in the political system'. 'Collective coercion' was judged as having existed either when the dissidents committed physical violence, injuring other people or damaging their property, or when the conflict developed to a stage where police intervention occurred. A total of 945 such cases were identified over eight and a half years; 385 involved violence.

These findings can be compared with those for other societies collected on the basis of similar criteria. For example, Charles Tilly (1975, p. 56) defined collective violence as 'any event in which at least one group of fifty persons or more directly took part in an action resulting in some persons or objects being damaged or seized'. He gathered cases for France over six decades in the nineteenth and twentieth centuries. Based on a similar definition (with the number of participants being set at 20) Richard Tilly (1975, p. 208) produced data for nineteenth-century Germany. Using much the same criteria, Douglas (1979) collected data on demonstrations in Australia between 1968 and 1972. Table 5.3 compares these findings with the Japanese data. The highest number of recorded incidents occurred in the data for Japan.

Here several points need to be kept in mind. First, the editorial policy of papers varies from paper to paper, from country to country and over time, even within the same country. Further, the data of both Charles and Richard Tilly were based on a reading of only national newspapers. However, the evidence still shows beyond doubt that the first decade following the restoration of Japan's sovereignty was characterized by very high levels of conflict.

In some ways the period under consideration is comparable to the decade after the Meiji Restoration, another period of rapid and pervasive change for which reliable information about social

Table 5.3 *The frequency of violent disturbances in four countries*

Society and investigator	Operational criteria	Period	Number of incidents
Japan (Aoki)	Unspecified	1868–77	523
Japan (Inoue and Watanabe)	Human injury or property damage	1918	248
Japan (Sugimoto)	Human injury or property damage or police intervention (50 participants or more)	1952–60	945
	Human injury or property damage (50 participants or more)	1952–60	385
France (Charles Tilly)	Human injury, or seizure or damage of property (50 participants or more)	1830–9	258
		1840–9	293
		1850–9	116
		1930–9	336
		1940–9	93
		1950–60	163
Germany (Richard Tilly)	Human injury, or seizure or damage of property (20 participants or more)	1816–47	323
		1848–9	197
		1850–81	236
		1882–1913	214
Australia (Douglas)	Human injury or damage of property	1968–72	75

Source: Sugimoto (1981d, p. 67).

disorders is available. Reading from the exhaustive chronological tables of Aoki (1971) the decade 1868–77 recorded 499 peasant uprisings (*hyakushō ikki*) and 24 urban mass disturbances (*toshi sōjō*). Aoki defines these incidents as protests against the power establishment at the time, without specifying any substantive criteria for the number of participants or visible indicators, such as physical violence and police intervention. His definition is more liberal and less restrictive than that used in the research reported here. At the same time, it should be pointed out that the postwar Japanese data do not include incidents in Tokyo or Hokkaidō. Accordingly, in terms of the frequency of incidents, the fifties appear to be even more turbulent than the years following the Meiji Restoration.

On the other hand it seems to be widely acknowledged that the rice riots (*kome sōdō*) which swept Japan in 1918 did result in the greatest amount of social upheaval in Japan's modern history. These were sparked off by a sharp upswing in the price of food, especially rice. The incidents began in a town in Toyama Prefecture, with the wives of fishermen forming a small picket line to obstruct the shipment of rice to other areas. They attributed the sky-rocketing rice prices to the scarcity of rice in their own prefecture. Soon rioters throughout Japan demanded cheaper rice. Inoue and Watanabe (1959–61) recorded 570 cases of disorder between 23 July and 15 October 1918. The riots occurred in 42 prefectures. Clear evidence of human injury or property damage was recorded in 248 cases. During the turmoil the police forces were temporarily paralyzed and the army was mobilized in 70 locations, including 33 cities, 23 towns and 14 villages. In terms of the number of violent incidents, the data indicate that 1918 was probably the peak year of political violence in the entire history of modern Japan.

There is strong evidence, then, to suggest that the notion of Japan as a cohesive and tightly knit society based on a single value system requires reassessment. Some conceptual confusion has perhaps contributed to the unbalanced picture. Researchers have often confused governmental stability with mass contentment. However, absence of change in the political establishment does not necessarily mean that there is little popular dissatisfaction. The decade of unrest which culminated in the *ampo* demonstrations in 1960 failed to produce a change in the government.

Contrary to the assertions made by the majority of specialists on Japanese society, data produced by this research suggest that the political cleavage between superordinate and subordinate groups is sharp and ubiquitous; that these rival groups have competing interests which involve exclusive values; that competition between these groups often manifests itself in open and direct confrontation involving consciously formulated but contradictory goals; and that the contending groups feel strongly enough about their interests to substain and/or inflict serious bodily injury or property damage. Observing that Japan recorded more incidents of unrest than some major societies in Europe, one finds it difficult to sustain the view that competition between vertically structured groups of equal status takes precedence over conflict between superordinate and subordinate groups.

The overwhelming majority of the disturbances were the result of pressures being brought to bear on the system by special-purpose associations organized at the national level. Labor union members, especially unionists in the public sector, were the principal dissidents during the fifties. The demands were largely for improvements in the dissidents' standard of living. They were highly political in that they often laid responsibility for their plight with the government. While disturbances against the Security Treaty with the United States involved mass demonstrations and therefore registered high average magnitudes, they were largely based in the urban centers and never really spread into rural areas. On the other hand, disturbances related to education resulted in relatively mild action, but they were waged in both urban and rural communities.

The most violent confrontations were triggered by police involvement, a fact which is consistent with the idea that at the grass-roots level there is sharp resentment against control from above. Among the different protest groups, students were most militant. Whenever police and students were both involved in a disturbance, considerable violence was likely to occur. Finally, disturbances involving Koreans were numerous, indicating that political cleavage along ethnic lines is not absent from Japanese society.

Disturbances involving labor unions most frequently involved particular demands, although those where universal goals were sought tended to register greater magnitudes in terms of the numbers involved (see Table 5.4). The involvement of workers in universalistic causes is particularly significant, given the alleged pervasiveness of Japanese values supporting the system of permanent employment and enterprise unionism, both of which are designed to promote particularistic orientations among employees. Despite these structural factors, however, unionists seemed to entertain strong political

Table 5.4 *The mean magnitude and intensity of different types of disturbance in Japan: 1952–60*

Disturbance type	Number of cases	Magnitude	Intensity measures			
			Number of serious injuries	Number of slight injuries	Extent of property damage	Number of arrests
All disturbances	945	225	0.53	6.69	2.12	3.60
Classified by issues:						
pacifist disturbances	76	870	1.08	11.33	1.47	6.29
anti-Security Treaty	39	1,288	1.51	17.72	0.72	3.44
Disturbances:						
anti-police disturbances	141	721	1.69	24.06	4.63	8.71
education-oriented disturbances	152	156	0.50	5.76	1.02	1.00
Classified by participants:						
unionists	628	270	0.58	8.12	1.09	2.96
students	119	779	1.53	17.72	3.18	8.28
Koreans	98	283	1.15	12.17	6.11	14.84
farmers	91	125	0.24	2.39	1.59	2.01
Disturbances with police intervention	664	289	0.71	8.90	2.76	4.84
Disturbances involving both students and police	103	869	1.75	20.31	3.68	9.56

Source: Sugimoto (1981d, p. 85)

aspirations which cut across particular company lines and were able to identify with universally conceived grounds for worker solidarity. The data corroborate other studies which flatly contradict the proposition that Japan is a status-based society rather than a class-based one. Many of the popular disturbances in Japan involve conflict between superordinate and subordinate groups with competing interests and contradictory goals concerning the distribution of society's scarce resources. The data show that rival groups often resort to violence or other forms of physical confrontation to achieve their interests.

Significantly, protesters in postwar Japan frequently formed alliances cutting across company, occupational and community lines. With varying degrees of solidarity, unionists, students, Koreans, unemployed workers, victims of pollution and other community groups have united nationally on numerous occasions to attain a common goal. This can be seen in the demonstrations against the Subversive Activities Prevention Act in 1952, the increase in the Government's control of education, the Police Duties Act in 1958 and 1959 and the revision of the Security Treaty in 1960. Movements against military bases, movements to protect the environment and movements against the testing of atomic and hydrogen bombs have also produced similar coalitions. In industrial conflict, industrial federations and national centers have played crucial roles. The spring wage offensive and May Day demonstrations are instances where 'horizontal' affiliations are highlighted. These movements and demonstrations were most certainly organized by protesters with shared ideological convictions, not by people floating about in an anomic state. However, the underlying network of 'horizontal' alliances is not explained by the holistic model of Japanese society. It is also quite clear that groups with power formed alliances to contain the anti-establishment forces. Despite factional strife and sectarian conflict, conservative parties, central government and bureaucracies and the large corporations have consistently assisted each other, and have seen the enforcement of their claims and legal rights against the various opposing and subordinate groups as falling within the duties of the police.

B A Comparison of Industrial Conflict in Japan and Australia

A second research project on conflict, relevant to the debate on the nature of Japanese society, concerns industrial disputes in Australia and Japan (Sugimoto: 1977b). Because the underlying populations and the number of unionists differ substantially between the two countries, all figures were converted to a per capita basis. The study was designed to gauge the relative militancy of Japanese and Australian unionists.

The overall level of disputation was defined as the product which results by multiplying the frequency rate, the participation rate, the average duration, and the volume. Each component is defined as follows:

$$\text{Frequency Rate} = \frac{\text{number of strikes}}{\text{number of unionists}}$$

$$\text{Participation Rate} = \frac{\text{number of persons participating in strikes}}{\text{number of strikes}}$$

$$\text{Duration} = \frac{\text{total number of working days lost}}{\text{number of strikes}}$$

$$\text{Volume} = \frac{\text{total number of working days lost}}{\text{number of unionists}}$$

The separation of strike activity into these dimensions is useful in studying the morphology of industrial disputes, and allows a visual picture to be presented as a three-dimensional solid with frequency, participation and duration as the three coordinates. The size of the solid may be thought of as one measure of the overall level of disputation.

To examine changes over time, the data for the prewar period (1921–45) and the postwar period (1946–72) were examined separately. The results are shown in Figure 5.2.

The Australian and Japanese data share three similarities. First, strike intensity is lower in the postwar period. The average number of days lost dropped by nearly two-thirds from 10.1 to 3.4 in Japan and from 9.2 to 2.4 in Australia. Second, the strikes were larger in the postwar period. The number of participants per strike increased from 298 to 351 in Australia and from 122 to 1400 in Japan. Finally, the volume of strike activity (working days lost per unionist) declined

Figure 5.2 *Prewar and postwar patterns of strikes in Australia and Japan*

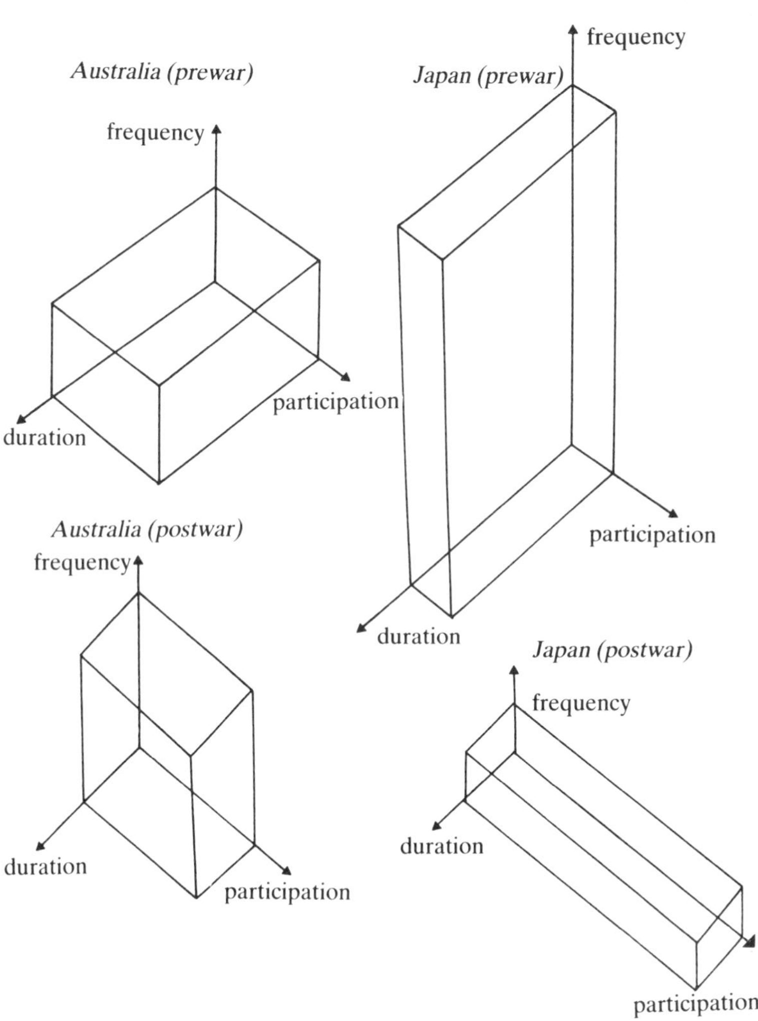

from an annual average of 1185 to 642 days in Australia and from 2285 to 714 days in Japan. These indices suggest that industrial disputation has levelled off over time in both countries, but that the factors accounting for this decline are more complex than has been maintained by proponents of the theories emphasizing the institutionalization of conflict.

It is interesting to note that, with the exception of participation in the prewar years, all the scores both before and after the war are higher in Japan than in Australia. This point is clearly at variance with commonly held beliefs about the respective social characteristics of the two societies under examination. As we have pointed out, Japan has been portrayed as a highly integrated society where the powerful mechanism of value consensus and social solidarity predominates in social relations. On the other hand, Australia has been considered as a society in which 'strikes are a major feature of life' (Iremonger, Merritt and Osborne: 1973).

Although the figures show significantly higher levels for Australia during the seventies, empirical data for the longer-term period following the war do not support the suppositions of the holistic theorists which underline the idea that the Japanese possess a culture of consensus. The Japanese past is too strewn with examples of conflict to attribute the present situation to traditional cultural traits. Because the low level of industrial conflict in Japan is a relatively new phenomenon, its explanation is likely to lie in more recent developments.

C Rethinking Group Theories of Japanese Society

In the group model of Japanese society, the distinction between intra-group and inter-group levels of analysis is never clear. The existence of intra-group consensus does not mean there is inter-group consensus. The study of intra-group dynamics has tended to result in conflict between groups being overlooked or dismissed euphemistically simply as competition. Intra-group integration increases the likelihood of inter-group conflict.

When each of several competing interest groups is particularly well integrated internally, the likelihood of there being confrontation between them is, *ceteris paribus*, increased. Conversely, when groups with contradictory goals are pitted against each other, intra-group solidarity is often heightened by the inter-group conflict. In future, conflict between groups needs to be carefully studied. Specific interest groups relevant to the study of conflict include: unions, management organizations, high-level officials in the public bureaucracy, agricultural co-operatives, political parties, community groups, voluntary associations, student groups and minority organizations.

Those stressing groupism often refer to the group as an abstract. As Yoneyama (1976) has observed, there tends to be an assumption that each individual belongs to one group. The proliferation of interest groups in Japan suggests that many Japanese may belong to several groups simultaneously. It is also consistent with the idea of syncretism associated with Japanese religious practices (Befu: 1971a, pp. 96, 100–01; Earhart: 1974, pp. 82–4). To what extent does multiple membership result in role conflict? Consider the businessman who is a member of the Japanese Communist Party, or the university professor who is a consultant both for a large petrochemical firm and for an anti-pollution group, or the tea girl in a large firm who is also a member of a feminist organization. How are these cross-cutting memberships resolved? At the present we know very little about the extent to which individuals in Japan experience role conflict. It would not be surprising that the more devoted an individual is to multiple groups, the more he or she would suffer from role conflict if the goals of the different groups diverge. Again, there is the need to distinguish between different levels. Does conflict within or even among individuals serve to constitute conflict at the societal level?

Finally, there are even more basic problems of conceptualization. For example, what distinguishes conflict from competition? Are these concepts merely two points on the same continuum, or are they qualitatively different? Can competition in one society be regarded as conflict in another? These lines of inquiry indicate directions in which research might profitably be pursued by those interested in formulating theories based on the empirical study of social and organizational dynamics. They are directions away from simplistic theories relying only on the culture of consensus to explain what has not been adequately researched.

III Income Distribution

Although the question of income distribution was set aside by many mainstream economists during the period of high economic growth, since the early seventies studies of income distribution have proliferated. Much of that recent research has been summarized by Takayama (1980). Four general conclusions emerge. One is that the distribution of income has been more egalitarian in the postwar period than in the prewar years. Second is that overall levels of income inequality are extremely difficult to grasp. Third is that the period of rapid economic growth during the sixties seems to have produced a more equal distribution of wage income but a widening of the gap between wage and property income. Finally, there is not full agreement about the mechanism which accounts for the widening and narrowing of measurable income differentials. To throw further light on these issues, the findings of one author on the distribution of income in Japan (Mouer: 1973b, 1973c, 1974a, 1974b, 1975a, 1975b, 1980a, 1980b) are introduced below.

Several different surveys may be used for the study of income distribution in Japan, each having different features and yielding different results. Here results primarily from the Family Income and Expenditure Survey (FIES) are presented. Although the survey also has a number of shortcomings (Mouer: 1973c), it includes both annual income by recall and monthly income for the households of employees.

A Variation over Time

Regardless of the type of income chosen, the classification used, or the type of household considered, during the sixties there appears to have been a pronounced drop in the Gini Concentration Ratio calculated from the Lorenz curve (hereafter referred to as the GCR; see Table 5.5). Lower GCRs are associated with greater equality. Since 1970, however, there appears to be no significant change in the GCR. Because of the change in the survey format in 1963, earlier results are not shown, but it seems that there was a widening of income differentials during the fifties.

These general conclusions are also set forth by Takayama (1980, p. 23). In this regard, three additional points require mention. One is the fact that wealth-generated income is not included. It is believed by some that the inclusion of wealth or property income would have resulted in an overall increase in inequality over time (Sano: 1972, p. 51), although Takayama (1980, p. 37) suggests that, even with wealth income included, the sixties produced an overall narrowing while the seventies were characterized by an overall widening of differentials. Given the general widening of differentials in the wage income of

Table 5.5 *Various Gini Concentration Ratios calculated from annual income groups in the FIES data: 1953–77*

	Number of annual income classes	Quintiles			16 income-size groupings		
	Type of household	All households		Employee households	All households		Employee households
Year	Type of income used in calulat-ing the GCR	Annual income estimates A	Annual income estimates B	Monthly income estimates C	Annual income estimates D	Annual income estimates E	Monthly income estimates F
1963		.3118	.2603	.2153	.3345	.2753	.2258
1964		.2976	.2490	.2057	.3182	.2636	.2157
1965		.2827	.2412	.1980	.3023	.2559	.2081
1966		.2849	.2449	.2023	.3037	.2597	.2140
1967		.2801	.2380	.2061	.2980	.2519	.2175
1968		.2666	.2276	.1930	.2832	.2405	.2036
1969		.2568	.2195	.1792	.2729	.2319	.1889
1970		.2533	.2178	.1787	.2681	.2294	.1878
1971		.2587	.2203	.1788	.2740	.2322	.1874
1972		.2562	.2230	.1797	.2704	.2350	.1887
1973		.2606	.2234	.1792	.2776	.2366	.1889
1974		.2686	.2412	.1879	.2886	.2592	.1994
1975		.2765	.2492	.1883	.2971	.2682	.1974
1976		.2668	.2294	.1861	.2840	.2435	.1962
1977		.2578	.2227	.1844	.2726	.2335	.1928

employees in the old FIES series (1953–64) (Murakami: 1967), it is difficult to evaluate the observation originally made by Takahashi (1959) and confirmed by Taira (1970, p. 27) that wage differentials tended to narrow in periods of economic growth and increase during periods of recession.

The consensus among experts would be that the fifties saw some widening of differentials, the sixties considerable narrowing, and the seventies little change, or even some widening if property income were included. Although the distribution of income in the postwar period seems to be considerably more egalitarian than that existing before the war (Hitotsubashi Keizai Kenkyūsho; 1961; *NKSC*, 5 July 1981, p. 11), and although a number of postwar reforms introduced by the occupation, as well as the general fluidity resulting from several dislocations caused by the war itself, would seem intuitively to warrant such conclusions, there is a need for further research before definite statements can be made about the distribution in the immediate prewar, wartime and immediate postwar periods. The wartime period is in need of particular attention. Many changes and policies were introduced to put the Japanese economy on a wartime footing, and the Government became involved with the wage system (Magota: 1972). On this subject the work of Choo (1975) on Korea suggests that historical disruptions such as foreign occupation can cause considerable upheaval which results in new, often more egalitarian patterns of distribution, which are for some time quite fluid, and that it is some time before the new patterns are institutionalized and can be fully discerned.

Much of the difference between the prewar and postwar distributions lies in the dislocation caused by the war and in the occupation policies themselves. The authors know of no scholars who would seek to explain variation in the level of inequality (i.e, fluctuations in the value of the GCR) over the past three decades by reference to changes in the cultural values or attitudes of the Japanese. Finally, in this regard the great difficulty of making cross-cultural generalizations about the relative equality of Japan's distribution needs to be underlined. While many of the methodological problems are common knowledge, the reader is referred to Kuznets (1963), Wootton (1962), Allison (1978) or Alker and Russett (1968). Both the findings to date and the methodological problems with relatively tangible data underline the need for considerable care when making sweeping statements about the greater homogeneity of Japanese society with regard to income shares.

B Cross-sectional Variation

Given the difficulty of making cross-societal comparisons of overall levels of inequality, as well as some of the conceptual problems involved even if comparable data were available, a more sociological approach was advocated some time ago by Spengler (1953).[1] The FIES data are analyzed according to six variables; data on two other types of differentials can be found in the Basic Survey of the Wage Structure (BSWS).[2] Looking at the FIES data, three patterns can be discerned. One is the consistent long-term decline in the GCR for both city-size groupings and geographic regions. Both have dropped from intermediate levels (with the GCR above .0500) to low levels (with the GCR below .0200). The second is the relatively stable GCRs of an intermediate value recorded for industrial groupings until 1973, after which the GCR increases slightly. Finally, the third pattern is of fairly stable high GCRs for firm-size, age and occupational groupings. Each variable is discussed briefly below.

1 City-size Differentials. The conspicuous decline in the GCRs for city-size groupings and geographical regions is related to the fact that the households are classified by residential address, whereas many household members (and particularly household heads) are employed in urban areas or geographic regions which are in another classification. This is particularly true for the city-size groupings; for example, commuters working in Tokyo (which is classified as a large city) live in smaller communities in Saitama, Chiba and Kanagawa Prefectures. The fact that the volume of this commuting has increased significantly between 1960 and 1975 is important.

2 Distribution among Geographic Regions. In the case of geographical regions, the net flow in the population from rural to urban areas is important. With the exception of the Yokohama area, the increase in the labor force in urban areas between September 1965 and September 1970 is far above that for the country as a whole. Thus, to some extent we can say that the law of diminishing returns is at work. The flow of factors of production (in this case, labor) from areas or uses where marginal productivity is low to locations where it is high will serve to level differences in marginal productivity. The continued advance of regional development projects and the emergence of large industrial complexes (*konbināto*) during the sixties also contributed to the narrowing of regional differentials in productivity.

3 Industrial Affiliation of the Household Head. The inter-industry differentials arise from a number of sources. Sano (1967) recognizes the importance of the differing occupational composition of each industry, arguing that, as in other industrial societies, skill differences perhaps explain the constant presence of such differentials but do not explain their variation over time. Somewhat paralleling the work of Reder on such phenomena in the United States, Sano argues that both competitive forces, as measured in the ability to pay, and union influence are important factors shaping the size differentials.

4 Occupational Differentials. Occupation has consistently been a fairly important source of differentiation. In this regard, one might also consider the BSWS data on the income of *buchō* (division chiefs), *kachō* (section chiefs), *kakarichō* (subsection heads) and, where applicable, *shokuchō* (foremen). GCRs were also calculated for these three (or four) groupings for differently sized firms and different industries. Given the general belief that occupational differentiation is less important in Japan, it is interesting to note that inequality caused by such differentiation varies directly with firm size; differentials are largest in the large firm, where the rhetoric of groupism and team work as the major component of Japanese society is most vigorously disseminated. It is also the sector where these features are believed to be most entrenched. Finally, it should be noted that several surveys, including the BSWS, provide excellent data on occupational differentials for 50–100 categories, showing that such differentials are not insignificant.[3]

5 Firm-size Differentials. That firm-size differentials are also significantly large should be no surprise, as much has been written about dualism in Japanese industry. These differentials remained fairly constant during the decade of rapid growth, but have increased to some extent during the seventies. Although good comparative data are difficult to find, firm-size differentials in Japan are not insignificant, as shown in Table 5.6. The data for 1978 concur with those gathered in the late fifties by Broadbridge (1966, p. 51) and those published in the mid-sixties in the report on a jointly sponsored study of wage structures by the US Department of Labor and the Japanese Ministry of Labor (1966, p. 87). The findings suggest that the firm-size differentials have consistently been larger in Japan, that the firm-size differentials have been rather stable over time and that the rank order in terms of earnings from large to small firms is the same in both countries. The social significance of these differentials is perhaps made greater in Japan by the sizable portion of the labor force employed in small-sized establishments (cf. Tokyo Metropolitan Government: 1972, Yamanaka: 1971).

Table 5.6 *Firm-size differentials in working conditions: 1978*

Firm size (number of employees)	Percentage of employees in private enterprises	Monthly hours worked per person in all secondary and tertiary sectors excluding personal services	Monthly hours worked per person in all manufacturing industries	Index of average wage rates	Index of productivity	Index of fixed capital per employee
1000+	12.03	171.8	171.7	100.0	100.0	100.0
500–999				85.5	89.3	83.3
300–499				81.9	81.3	77.6
200–299	18.54	175.1	174.4	74.7	72.6	57.8
100–199				67.6	64.2	46.3
50–99	22.28	180.5	182.8	60.3	53.0	36.4
30–49				57.8	48.6	33.1
20–29	34.12	184.6	184.5	54.2	46.6	28.6
5–20				n.a.	n.a.	n.a.
1–4	13.02	n.a.	n.a.	n.a.	n.a.	n.a.
N	29,838,000					

Sources: Rōdōshō (1982), pp. 162 and 130; Yano (1981), p. 43.

6 Age and the Seniority Wage System. For a long time the seniority wage curve has been considered a peculiarly Japanese practice. More recent research, however, has tended to explode this myth.[4] Indeed, similarly arranged data on household income for the United States results in a GCR of .1485, a figure which is considerably above the levels shown for Japan.[5] A closer examination of age-earnings profiles in Japan with the BSWS data suggests that age differentials are more pronounced in the larger firms and for those with more education; the age-earnings curve is steeper and the peak occurs at a later age. It should also be noted that occupational differences produce similar patterns of variation in the seniority wage curve. This is not surprising since major occupational groupings tend to correspond to groupings based on the level of education. Finally, the age-earnings curves are flatter for women.

Two additional points should be made. First, while age-earnings curves are similar in the United States and Japan, some attention should be paid to differences in their historical evolution. Immediately after the war the Marxist labor unions fought hard to obtain a living wage by demanding age-based wage schemes which would tie the wages of the household head to the reproduction costs of his household. As a result, in many cases women did not qualify directly for the special payment based upon the age-tied component, because they were not household heads. Employers (who today seem to espouse the virtues of groupism and the system of seniority wage schemes) initially opposed these moves and a compromise was reached in many firms, with an age-based payment and a length-of-employment payment being combined. Where Marxist unions were stronger the first component was more important; where management was stronger the second was more important. The relative shift of power from labor to management and the emergence of the 'number two unions' resulted in length of employment with the same firm starting to receive greater weighting. However, the present system of seniority wage rates was not really institutionalized until the late fifties or early sixties. Again, this history raises serious questions about explanations which emphasize the cultural value orientations of the Japanese. In this process, women with careers interrupted for childbirth and family duties lose out considerably. [6]

The second point has to do with the abundance of evidence indicating that similar age-earning profiles exist in many other countries, as shown in Figure 5.3. This is not to say that this common phenomenon is not viewed differently in Japan. Indeed, the rich vocabulary in Japanese for talking about *nenkō joretsu chingin* (the seniority wage curve) points to a special concern with it. The point to be made, however, is that there is not a one-to-one correspondence between language and reality. Moreover, reality at one level (e.g., behavior) does not necessarily reflect reality at another (e.g., language and ideals).

7 Level of Education and Earnings. As Figure 5.3 would lead one to expect, the GCRs calculated with the BSWS data show that education also accounts for significant income differentials. The GCR for groupings by level of education is significantly higher for males than for females, except in small firms. Also, education becomes increasingly important for males as firm size increases. This is in line with the expectation that growing bureaucracy will result in greater weight being placed on the role of formal education in certifying the qualifications of persons joining the organization (Clark: 1968). However, the reverse seems to hold for women: the importance of education as a determinant of wage rates varies inversely with firm size. This is certainly a feature requiring future study by those interested in male–female wage differentials.

Education seems less important in accounting for inequality in Japan than in the United States. Data collected in 1974 and 1975 from American households, categorized according to the education of the household head (as opposed to the BSWS data for individuals in Japan) yield a GCR of about .1600, three or four times as high as the figures for Japan.[7] It should be noted, however, that the American data are for males and females, whereas the Japanese data are divided by sex. With women having lower overall levels of formal education, combined figures for both sexes would yield a higher GCR. Another factor accounting for the lower GCR in the Japanese data involves postwar changes in education. Until recently the average income earned by Japanese in the education group next to the highest (graduates of special technical institutes before the war and junior colleges after the war) has been above that of those in the highest group (university graduates) largely because of the seniority factor. Although many institutions previously classified as special technical institutes were officially recognized as universities in the postwar period, in the late sixties postwar graduates had not yet attained positions of authority in large enough numbers to reverse the pattern. Between 1970 and 1975, however, the younger generation of postwar university graduates began to emerge as the highest paid group. This process of closing and then widening differentials has no doubt kept

Figure 5.3 *Age-earnings profiles in four countries*

A United States of America (1949)

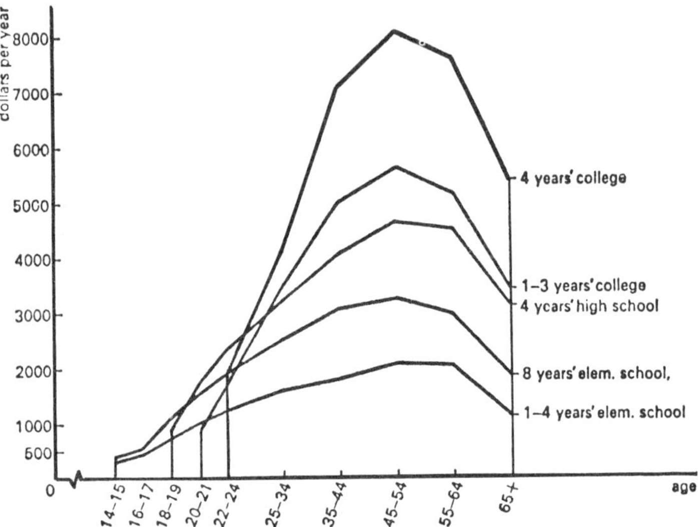

B United Kingdom (1964)

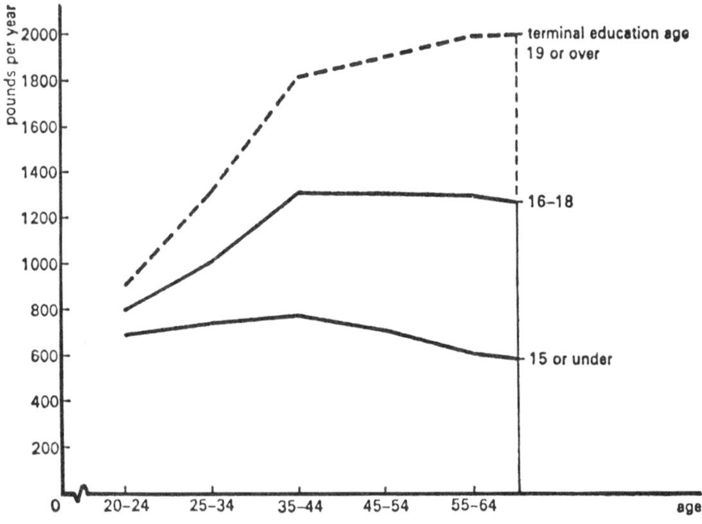

Source: Blaug (1976), pp. 24–5.

C Mexico (1963)

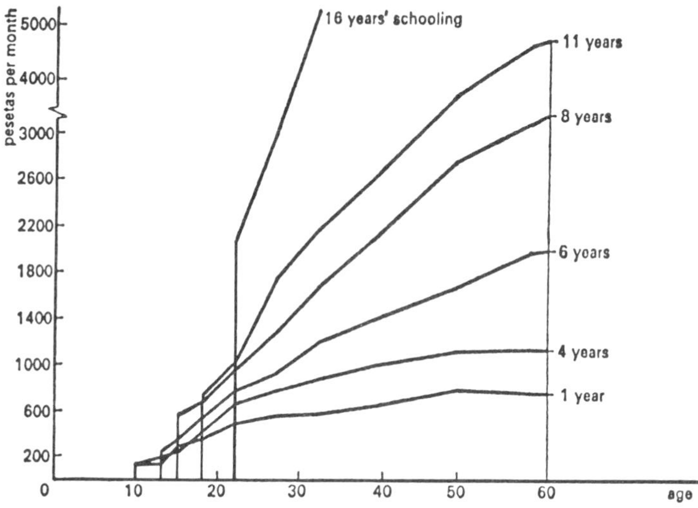

D India (1961)

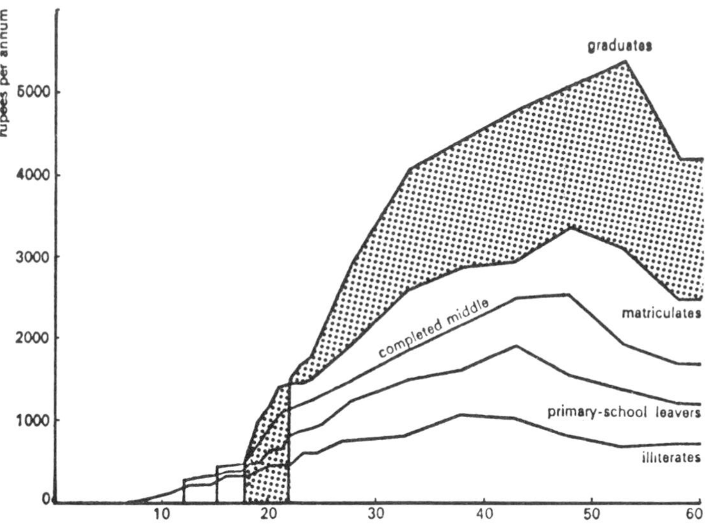

Table 5.7 *The correlation of household income and three life-cycle variables for households grouped according to a third variable: 1970*

Pairings of life-cycle variables	City-size groupings	Geographical regions groupings	Firm-size groupings	Industrial categories	Occupational groupings
Income and age	very negative	none	none	slightly negative	fairly negative
Income and household size	very negative	slightly positive	fairly positive	none	slightly positive
Income and labor force participation	very negative	slightly positive	fairly negative	none	fairly negative
Household size and labor force participation	very positive	fairly positive	slightly positive	fairly positive	very positive
Age and household size	fairly positive	none	slightly positive	slightly positive	fairly positive
Age and labor force participation	fairly positive	none	slightly positive	fairly positive	fairly positive

the GCR artificially low for the period under examination, and it would seem plausible that the GCR will rise in the future. Because the labor market has been institutionalized around the annual hiring of new graduates, for some time it will still be plausible to talk of separate labor markets for middle-school and high-school graduates. With the high percentage of middle-school graduates continuing on to high school, however, the relative shortage of middle-school graduates may push their wages up relative to the wages received by high school graduates.

8 Sex Differentials based on Gender. A number of factors complicate the study of sex as a determinant of wage differentials: differences in job responsibilities, hours of work, length of employment and educational background (Takahashi: 1975). Nevertheless, marked differences in the earnings of men and women do exist. Since these differentials are examined in Chapter 13, further discussion is omitted at this point.

The preceding discussion yields three conclusions. One is that the distribution of income results in numerous cross-cutting differentials. Explanations which stress only age or seniority as the major variable are misleading; it is not clear that age is even the most important among several variables. The summary in Table 5.7 makes that clear. The second conclusion is that the overall patterns of inequality in the distribution of income are remarkably similar to those found in the

Table 5.8 *A comparison of the effect of eight variables on the distribution of income in Japan and the United States*

Stratification subsystem	The nature of variation: rank order correlation of average income for subsystem categories in Japan and the United States	Comparison of the amount of inequality caused in Japan and the United States
1 City-size groupings	high	smaller in Japan
2 Geographical regions	not applicable	smaller in Japan
3 Industries	low	lower in Japan
4 Occupation	high	similar
5 Firm size	high	higher in Japan
6 Age	high	similar
7 Level of education	high	slightly lower in Japan (similarity likely in the future)
8 Sex	high	similar

United States (Table 5.8). Finally, the available research contains no evidence that there is through time or among different areas in Japan any correlation between the levels of inequality and the cultural characteristics associated with the group model. Nor is there any indication that Japanese society is structured to provide even marginally more rewards to those possessing such characteristics.

IV The Need for Empirical Research

The authors' research in the two areas examined in this chapter is rudimentary and incomplete. So too is much of the research introduced at the outset. Nevertheless, the empirical findings at hand suggest that the realities of social life have little to do with the images projected by the *nihonjinron* theorists.

Although the above findings require further verification, if they are generally correct two criticisms of *nihonjinron* can be made. First, its emphasis on consensus needs to be reconsidered; conflict is too often ignored or simply dismissed with euphemisms. Second, the emphasis on homogeneity needs to be reformulated. A rather high level of racial homogeneity and the use of the Japanese language by all citizens of Japan is often confused with ethnic or cultural homogeneity. The question of structured social inequality is not discussed by the advocates of *nihonjinron* except to allude to certain dimensions of inequality in isolation as uniquely Japanese features embedded in the Japanese cultural tradition. The research introduced above leads to the conclusion that any adequate theory of Japanese society must in part account for two kinds of variation over time and among the various sub-populations: differences in the level of conflict and in the access of individuals to social rewards.

Chapter 6

Some Methodological Misgivings about the Group Model

A second source of skepticism with regard to the group model of Japanese society is the methodology used by its proponents. The conflicting findings presented in the preceding chapter raise a number of issues about criteria for asserting that one image of a society is better than another in terms of factual accuracy. Although correctness in this regard is not the only standard for judging the full validity of an image or theory of society, it is an important consideration.

As an initial step to forming an opinion about the factual accuracy of *nihonjinron*, the authors began to look for the evidence being presented. This sometimes involved simply a closer reading of footnotes and appendices; at other times it required some background reading of earlier work. The overall impression was that there is little hard empirical evidence in the books themselves. In many cases, the reader is simply asked in good faith to accept statements at face value, a reasonable request perhaps when made by well-known scholars in this age of specialized knowledge. In some cases, authors referred readers to earlier publications. However, in many instances the cited items were merely an earlier statement of the same views without additional evidence or further information on the methodology employed to reach the conclusions. In some cases the empirical research cited was actually on another topic. A broader reading of several dozen items from the *nihonjinron* literature suggested that there was a certain amount of circular referencing. This broader reading suggested two hypotheses. One was that a more careful analysis would reveal that the methodology of the *nihonjinron* theorists is seldom explained. The second was that methodological shortcomings could be found in many of the works reviewed. These problems are enumerated and briefly explained in the following section. The initial findings presented in the overview served as hypotheses for a detailed content analysis of specific books, which is presented in the second section of this chapter. Finally, an analysis of Japanese proverbs, one data base commonly used by the *nihonjinron* theorists, is analyzed.

I Sources of Skepticism: Some Basic Methodological Lacunae

On a number of occasions the authors have discussed different methodological problems associated with *nihonjinron* (SM: 1979a, 1979b, 1979c, 1980a; Yoneyama and SM: 1980; MS: 1979a, 1979b). Here some general impressions about the methodological weaknesses of *nihonjinron* are summarized. These can be grouped into three categories: problems involving sampling, the lack of conceptual clarity and the absence of methodological concerns.

A Sampling

The problem of sampling occurs at several levels, and arises when generalizations are made about all Japanese society from a limited number of observations. While many of the *nihonjinron* theorists address themselves to questions about the whole of Japanese society, their concrete discussions often relate only to white-collar males in large firms or the upper levels of the bureaucracy. The experiences of women, blue-collar workers, deviants and certain minorities are ignored or discussed in euphemistic terms. One criticism of Doi's work is that the psychology of *amae* attributed to the Japanese people comes from the study of a limited number of psychiatric patients as though they were representative of the Japanese population.

Part of the problem lies in the failure to consider even the most basic aspects of sampling. Because the universes about which generalizations are to be made are seldom clearly specified, and because many implicit comparisons are not explicitly treated as comparisons, it may be that many of the *nihonjinron* theorists are not even conscious of the problem. Conceptual ambiguity is not unrelated; for example, the distinctions between behavior and ideals or between the words people tick when surveyed and their true value orientations are seldom discussed. Failure to come to grips with the problem of sampling at this more general level often leads to a series of related problems. Three will be discussed briefly here.

1 'Anecdotism' and 'Episodism'. Many of the *nihonjinron* theorists use a liberal dose of arbitrarily chosen anecdotes and metaphorical examples to prove their propositions. When arguing that the Japanese are group-oriented, reference is made to the fact that one has seen Japanese travelling abroad in groups, that one has seen Japanese bathing together in groups, or that many Japanese festivals involve a group of young men carrying a portable shrine. When arguing that the Japanese have a comparatively underdeveloped ego, it is pointed out that a word like *amae* exists only in Japanese, that some Japanese have been observed crying when they saw the image of a mother in a film, or that Japanese did not criticize the presentation of a senior professor at an academic gathering. Based on his viewing of the movie *Love Story*, the film made from Erich Segal's popular novel, Kunihiro Tetsuya concluded that Americans can never say they are sorry because to say so would be an admission of guilt or fault which would put the cold, calculating individual in American society on the defensive and hinder his ability to maximize his own self-interest (*NKSC*, 22 January 1972, p. 22). In arguing that the basic difference between Western and Japanese systems of industrial relations lies in their different social structures, another author cites an anecdote from Shiloh (1976, pp. 197–9) to support his conclusion that the result of a strongly implanted set of ownership categories is a respect for public property which cannot be seen in Japan. He argues further that this trait can be seen in Western children and cites the fact that they do not spit on the street or tease animals at the zoo because both the street and the animals are clearly conceived as public property. In adults, he goes on to point out, the end product is Western individualism, a characteristic which focuses discussions between labor and management on the rights of each party. The contractual notion of labor-management relations in the West is contrasted to the emotional or humanist relations which prevail in Japan, where the notion of rights is not very developed (Iwata: 1977, Chapter 2 and especially p. 39).

Sengoku (1974, pp. 43–5) argues that Western society is characterized by antagonistic relationships (*tairitsu kōzō*) whereas Japanese relationships are marked by the value placed on self-effacement. To demonstrate this he contrasts the need of American women to wear make-up in order to impress their husbands, with the acceptance of a uniform standard by Japanese women who do not feel the need to compete with other women to impress their husbands.

Such examples sometimes provide useful illustrations which facilitate explanation across cultures. However, when used as evidence, there is the shortcoming that an endless number of counter-examples can be presented. Anecdotes and examples to support a particular view can be cited endlessly. There are always enough exceptions to any rule about social behavior to allow for a large absolute number of carefully chosen examples to support a variety of conclusions. The problem involves more than numbers, which could partially be resolved simply by enlarging the sample of examples; it also involves qualitative judgements as to which examples are more representative of the truth. Accordingly, while examples and anecdotes are sometimes useful to illustrate a point, they do not convincingly demonstrate much unless a fair number of randomly selected cases are thoroughly analyzed, or some other ideas are presented to persuade one that careful thought has been given to the problem of adequate representation.

2 Views of a Monolithic West. A further shortcoming of the *nihonjinron* theorists is their tendency to conceive of all Western societies as a monolith. Japan is contrasted with an ambiguously defined West. According to the context and the convenience of the author, the West may refer to America, England, Italy, France, Germany or any other European society or grouping of those societies. Just as the Filipinos, Chinese, Koreans, Indians, Malaysians and Japanese resent being lumped together simply as Asians by many Westerners, it is natural that many Europeans are skeptical about the usefulness of theories which seek to throw all Europeans together into a single unit. A recent book edited by Sturmthal and Scoville (1973), for example, shows clearly how much variation exists among the labor movements in different Western European countries. We suspect that a comparison of each European society with Japanese society would yield unique sets of similarities and differences.

In addition to the treatment of the West as a monolith, there is a tendency to exclude altogether certain Western nations, such as Portugal or Yugoslavia (not to mention most of the nations in Africa, Latin America and Asia) from the comparisons. Lee (1978 and 1982, pp. 12–13) has suggested that the Korean language contains more ways of expressing *amae* than did Japanese. From this perspective, what seemed like a Japanese love for nature to an artistically sensitive person raised on the cold concrete sidewalks of New York appeared to many Koreans to be nothing more than a Japanese penchant for artificiality and for rearranging nature (Lee: 1982, pp. 127–8). If it is indeed true that beauty is in the eye of the beholder, then it behoves us to look for truth with more than one pair of eyes.

3 The Comparison of Non-parallel Universes. When making cross-societal comparisons, it is important that the actual groups studied be controlled in terms of several significant variables, the common ones associated with social stratification being perhaps the most important. Consider the systems of life-time employment and seniority wages which have often been introduced as uniquely Japanese features and as evidence of group-orientation in Japanese society. The comparisons more often than not contrast employment practices for regular employees in Japan's largest enterprises and public bureaucracies (which employ less than 30 percent of the Japanese labor force) with practices for the entire labor force only in the private sector of some other society.

One of the first tasks in comparative research is the delineation of the relevant sub-populations in each society. The goal is to align universes in terms of such demographic or stratified variables as age, occupation, level of education, sex and social class. To the extent that the sample from each society is chosen according to a different set of criteria, the value of the comparison is diminished. How useful is it to study differences in national character by comparing a group in the French film industry with a group of Japanese academics, as Nakane (1973, pp. 77–8) does? What do we learn from Bayley's comparison (1976, p. 117–18) of the Japanese public's approval of Premier Tanaka's sex life and the American reaction to Kennedy's accident at Chappaquiddick? In relation to the discussion of conflict in the preceding chapter, how meaningful is it to contrast low levels of industrial conflict within Japanese automobile industry groups to the high levels of conflict between two different groups in Poland? Nevertheless, *nihonjinron* is replete with examples of such comparisons.

B Conceptual Ambiguity

Another set of problems relates to the use of undefined concepts. Some *emic* concepts like *amae, tate* and *yoko, uchi* and *soto, tatemae* and *honne, tanin*, or *haji* are alternatively used as *etic* or abstract concepts for comparative statements and as *emic* or descriptive terms for labelling supposedly unique features of Japanese society.[1] Other concepts–such as class, modernization, feudalism, democracy – are also used to describe a mixture of phenomena. Sometimes they are labels for institutions or practices abroad; at other times they serve to indicate ideals associated with the West in general. The list of concepts frequently used but seldom defined also includes loyalty, consensus, cultural homogeneity, group orientation, lack of individualism, emotionalism and paternalism.

Even when presented as a description of the Japanese, *nihonjinron* is often implicitly comparative. When the descriptive concepts are not defined, and comparative adjectives (such as 'tall' or 'short') are used instead of absolute units of measurement (such as centimeters), the problems of definition become even more important. They are further aggravated by the tendency of *nihonjinron* theorists to argue with isolated examples or metaphors and by the tendency to illustrate rather than define concepts. This can be seen in Nakane's use of *ba* (frame) and *shikaku* (attribute). 'Frame' is tied to words like 'vertical' and closely associated with Japan; 'attribute' is linked to 'horizontal' and West (ambiguously seeming to mean 'not Japanese' in some places where Chinese and Indian examples are interlaced). The precise logic behind the association of frame with vertical ties and attribute with horizontal ties is not clear. Vertical tends to indicate ties between persons in a hierarchy, and is connected with belonging to firms in which some have more power, income and status and others have less. But hierarchies also exist within Nakane's horizontal categories. The problem of conceptual clarity has been discussed by a number of other observers, including McCormack (1982) on fascism and McGown (1982) on paternalism. Three types of conceptual ambiguity are discussed briefly in the following paragraphs.

1 Linguistic Reductionism. Related to the use of examples or anecdotes as evidence is the identification of words unique to Japanese in order to prove that the behavior described by the word is also uniquely Japanese. This method takes a number of forms, one being the citation of *kotowaza* (proverbs or wise sayings) as sources of authority. Citing well-known Japanese *kotowaza* such as *saru mono hibi ni utoshi* (which means 'out of sight out of mind') or *deru kui wa utareru* (which suggests that forwardness will cause trouble or that one will get along best by conforming or not making waves), some go on to argue that the Japanese place great emphasis on proximity in human relationships or that the Japanese tend to conform to the expectations of those in authority. It is often assumed that words or expressions possessing nuances particularly difficult to translate are especially representative of the Japanese national character. *Nagai mono ni wa makareyo* (which means 'take the easy way out and bow to authority') and *yoraba taiju no kage* (which means 'rely on someone big and powerful') are often cited as evidence of authoritarian strands in the Japanese personality.

The major problem with this reasoning, however, is that, like many languages, Japanese contains numerous pairs of opposites, equally difficult to translate. One can just as easily cite *haragei* (emphasizing the merits of emotional persuasion) and *ron yori shōko* (which calls for proof rather than mere abstract arguments), or *bushi wa kuwanedo takayōji* (which refers to the putting on of airs to protect one's name or nominal status at any cost, even if such pretensions mean starving) and *hana yori dango* (which refers to those who would openly seek materialistic enjoyment without any such pretensions). Which of two antonyms is more representative of the sentiments of the Japanese? The Japanese language also contains expressions of anti-establishment sentiments such as *hanganbiiki* (which calls upon one to side with the underdog) and *ippiki ōkami* (which romanticizes the lone wolf or maverick). Rather than arbitrarily selecting only phrases which support one's own views, it is important that random or controlled samples be used, and that the criteria by which samples are chosen from a language be made explicit.

The etymological approach is apparently somewhat more sophisticated. Discussion of the origins of a key word is not uncommon. For example, the literal translation of *sumimasen* is 'I am not finished', and to render the full meaning of such a term one might explain that it once meant 'I have become eternally grateful for your kindness, and nothing I can do will repay my debt to you.' Arguing that the frequent exclamation of *sumimasen* reflects this deeper meaning, some (e.g., Lebra: 1976, pp. 92–4 or Ozaki: 1978, pp. 187–8) assert that this kind of analysis uncovers subconscious traits of the Japanese national character, such as the importance Japanese are alleged to attach to returning social favors or the handling of guilt by working or studying hard for others. Another example can be found in Lebra's interpretation of *okagesamade* (which she translates as meaning 'thanks to your protection or benevolence') as demonstrating the extent to which Japanese tend to depend upon others (Lebra: 1976, p. 50).

The selection of isolated phrases, often out of context, has been a useful device for pulling the wool over the eyes of foreign scholars who are not fully versed in the intricacies of the Japanese language. Even when the correct etymological origins of a particular expression are introduced, the extent to which people today are cognizant of such origins is quite problematic. In English there is the expression 'good-bye', which is a colloquial contraction of 'God be with you' (Skeat: 1910, p. 245). However, to conclude from the frequency with which such a phrase is used that English speakers are the most religious people in the world would certainly invite skepticism. So too would the suggestion that the Japanese are more aware of the etymological origins of the words and phrases they use than are English speakers of the expressions they use.

The use of *kotowaza* and special words as evidence for generalizing about the national character of a people raises several difficulties. First, similar meanings are commonly expressed in different ways in other societies. Second, many languages contain a full range of expressive vocabulary, including a large number of antonyms. Without careful records of the frequency with which each item is used, it is difficult to gauge carefully their relative importance. Third, without in-depth studies involving interviews and various projective techniques, it is difficult to know how particular words or phrases are evaluated. Which ones represent normative statements of how things should be and which ones behavioral statements of how things actually are? Simply to accept the full range of *kotowaza* at face value may well force us to conclude that many societies, including the Japanese one, emphasize similar values. From this perspective, we would be likely to lose sight of that which is unique to Japanese society. While a careful analysis of *kotowaza* and other similar expressions may yield considerable insight, the necessary records have in any case not been kept. Given the arbitrary way in which linguistic expressions are chosen and the failure to adhere to any recognized procedure of selection, it seems to us that the use of rigorous linguistic analysis in the study of the Japanese is at best a speculative activity.

2 Tautologies and Paradoxes. Definitions are devices which improve the logic of a language when it is used as a medium for debate. It is not surprising, then, that conceptual ambiguity is also accompanied by several forms of logical inconsistency. Tautologies are sometimes offered as logical arguments or evidence, whereas they are in fact true by definition. Consider the following arguments in Nakane (1973):

(a) 'Inside it [the group within a given frame], a sense of unity is promoted by means of the members' total participation, which further strengthens group solidarity' (p. 24).

(b) If members are organized in an occupational group, they tend to be isolated from the firm (paraphrased by the authors from p. 26).
(c) 'The range over which the leader exercises authority is determined by the relative balance of abilities and personalities which the leader and his subordinate bring into a given group' (p. 73).
(d) 'Without either "frame" or "vertical links", it seems to be almost impossible for the Japanese to form a functional group' (p. 62).
(e) 'Employees in an enterprise must remain in the group, whether they like it or not: not only do they not want to change to another company; even if they desire a change, they lack the means to accomplish it' (p. 21).

While statements of this kind are simply tautological, there are also more blatant contradictions. Vogel (1979a, p. 158), for example, introduces Japan's tremendous achievements in education with a statement to the effect that ten Japanese journalists produce coverage comparable to that given by a single American journalist. This kind of efficiency contrasts with those cited in Chapter 2 (e.g., pp. 10–17). Vogel's discussion of education also contains a statement that American teachers are more prepared to accept that some students are unteachable (p. 175) whereas further along the teachers are commended for spending a lot of time helping students from diverse backgrounds catch up (p. 180). Entrance exams are seen as being necessary to maintain standards (pp. 165–6) whereas the threat of failure is not necessary to maintain standards (p. 175). Although the Ministry of Agriculture is subordinate to the LDP in one location (pp. 80–1) the ministries are seen as being independent of the LDP in other passages (pp. 60, 61 and 67). It is also not uncommon to see an emphasis on consensus (e.g., pp. 95–6) followed by an emphasis on coercion or the use of power (e.g., pp. 60–1).

In Nakane's *Japanese Society* (1973), the difficulty of lateral entry into the higher positions of organizations is stressed in two locations (pp. 109–11 and 118) while elsewhere the high rate of mobility into top firms through *amakudari* (the transfer of high government bureaucrats to the private sector) is mentioned (p. 121). In-fighting and opposition to authority are described at some length (pp. 49 and 107), whereas the golden rule is said to be obedience (pp. 36–7 and 54–5). Elements built into the body of the group are seen as being virtually unable to be changed (p. 102) whereas some groups, like subcontractors, are easily cut loose [and replaced] (p. 98). One statement suggests that members of a group argue in front of outsiders (p. 78) whereas another indicates that they do not (pp. 71–2). Although a very deeply felt consciousness of and concern for rank is seen in one passage as affecting relationships between all members of the group (pp. 26–42), on other pages these aspects are also passed off as only an image projected for outside consumption (pp. 71–2). Although the power of the Japanese leader is restricted by the communication of group consensus from below (p. 59), the system is characterized by the extreme efficiency of communicating from the top downwards (p. 54). Although it is impossible for two or more persons to stand in parallel or equal positions (p. 46), an *oyabun* is normally shared by equals (p. 46). Although there is only one ranking order for a given set of persons (p. 31), a platoon that lost its head could not figure out who was next in line to be leader (p. 46). Although the Japanese ethic puts a high value on the harmonious integration (*wa*) of group members (p. 50), somehow people are not sufficiently aware of these values for persons lower in an organization to obtain enough social recognition to assuage their resentment (pp. 51–2).

There are also internal contradictions in the literature as a whole. To justify the importance of *amae* as an analytical tool and as a valid or significant descriptive category, Doi (1971, pp. 69–78) cites work by Whorf and Sapir to argue that the meanings embedded in the peculiarities of a given language are crucial to in-depth psychoanalysis and the understanding of a cultural milieu. Elsewhere, however, Okonogi (1978) uses an Indian word (*ajase*) to express another key idea for which there is no Japanese. The difficulty in translating *nenkō* or *nemawashi* from Japanese is often cited to infer the uniqueness of certain behavior in Japanese firms. Conversely, the absence of a certain word, the fact that it was coined only recently (e.g., since the Meiji Restoration in 1868) or the practice of writing it in *katakana* to set it aside as a foreign derivative is commonly cited to indicate that the concept really does not exist in Japanese or to emphasize the distinction between surface Westernization and deeper Japanese psychic structures. The fact that *Puraibashii* is a borrowed word from English and therefore not truly Japanese is often cited to suggest there is not a native concept of private property. At the same time, English words of recent origin such as ‘individualism’ are used as though they reflect meanings deeply implanted in the minds and psychological make-up of Westerners.[2] The authors did not in their reading run across any examples discussing the alienation Japanese felt in owning a *terebi* (television), a *kā* (car), a *kūrā* (cooler or air conditioner) or their own private *hōmu* (home). Finally, the question of Greek and Latin derivatives in English, such as 'democracy' or 'modern', is not considered when using them to capture some deeper essence of the Western character.

Judging from these and other writings constituting the *nihonjinron* literature, it is difficult to conclude that the authors are illogical or disorganized persons. Rather, it is simply that these apparent contradictions are more likely to occur when concepts are not clearly defined.

C The Unconcern with Methodology

The list given above does not include all the methodological problems found in the *nihonjinron* literature. Nevertheless, each reflects a general nonchalance with regard to the methodological considerations and rigor commonly associated with social science. This does not mean that there are not other valid methodologies. However, it is difficult to find any systematic explanation of the methodologies or of how the *nihonjinron* theorists reached their conclusions.

1 The Absence of Statements on Methodology. The authors spent some time looking for independent methodological statements by the proponents of *nihonjinron*. For example, a book by Watanabe (1976) with the enticing title, *Chiteki Seikatsu no Hōhō* (Approaches to an Intellectual Life) was found. However, this volume gives only more general advice such as 'know thyself', 'buy lots of books', 'use your time wisely' and 'organize your information.'

In the preface to *Japanese Society* (1973) Nakane writes that she will use 'some of the methods which I am accustomed to applying in examining any other society' (p. i). There are also some references to 'suggestive evidence' (p. ii). Unfortunately, the process by which suggestive evidence is generated remains unexplained. Attention is often directed away from questions of methodology by the statement that one has simply laid aside any concern with rigor or scientific explanation in writing the particular book in question. In *Japanese Society* (1973), Nakane explains that her book is not 'a scientific thesis' (p. i), and that it uses 'evidence drawn almost at random from a number of different types of communities' (p. i). How random is random and what are the criteria for selecting 'suggestive evidence'?

The only essay on methodology the authors could find by Nakane (1975) is a personal account and throws little light on problems of this kind.

Vogel (1979a) claims that he is 'more interested in Japan than in social science generalizations' (p. vii). Ozaki (1978, pp. 13–14) is a bit more dramatic in his disclaimer:

> It pretends to be neither a scientific treatise introducing a seductive hypothesis on the social psychology of the Japanese nor a recondite inquiry into some sublime aspects of their history. It merely purports to draw in broad strokes a representative landscape of Japan, to compose an amplified free haiku that will reveal the distinguishing features of the Japanese character.

By omission, statements like this invite the reader to believe that scientific evidence and bases for conjecture lie elsewhere. The suggestion is that the scientific stuff would be too deep for the ordinary reader, who is interested primarily in general findings. An aura of scientism is lent to the work by phrases such as 'the vertical relation which we predicted in theory' or 'in the foregoing discussion it has been shown that . . . '. The scientific mood is reinforced by an occasional reference to some very precise figures – often the percentage who chose a particular answer in a public opinion poll.

Finally, given this atmosphere, the introduction of unique Japanese phrases helps to fix the spell. It is easy to be cynical about the intentions of those who use this 'sleight of hand'. However, it would be fair to say that the warnings are there in clear print: 'Beware: not scientific!' If there is a fault, it may lie rather with uncritical readers, who in their own spheres of influence repeat and disseminate interesting speculations as fact. Despite the honest attempts of an author to affix carefully worded caveats at regular intervals, it is not unusual for his or her message to be taken out of context and used by others to promote specific ideological goals. In the process the message changes. Even Marx is claimed to have said, 'I am not a Marxist.' At the same time, however, some authors have contributed to the aura of discovery without having done anything except contemplating. Ozaki claims he does not present hypotheses but 'landscapes'. Nakane begins a later book (1972a, p. 4) on the Japanese in Southwest Asia with the sentence, 'Japanese society and the Japanese that have produced the vertically structured human relationship demonstrated in my book *Japanese Society*', and a hypothesis is transformed into fact.[3]

2 Moralizing. Methodological sophistication does not mean the pretension that research is or should be value-free; it is, however, associated with researchers being aware of the differences between their values and those of their subjects, of the misunderstandings caused by reifying society, and of the moral implications of recommending one's own values to those with different ones. Ideals and reality are not congruous, but ideals can be used to shape reality, a phenomenon observed by many and labelled 'self-fulfilling prophecy' by Merton (1957, pp. 421–36). The *nihonjinron* literature is characterized by the tendency to moralize by mixing statements about Japan with statements about how things should be. This is a problem not unrelated to the frequent use of *nihonjinron* as ideology, a problem discussed in the following chapter.

Although the aims of Reischauer's many writings are less explicitly stated, they are none the less woven into his books. Quite apart from his unique mixture of academic life with political involvement, as the American Ambassador to Japan in the sixties, he is well known for his stance on the Vietnam War and for his impact on American foreign policy as the head of the 'Reischauer lobby', following his return to Harvard. With a commitment to the concept of cultural relativism, international understanding and the tenets of humanism, Reischauer has worked hard to present Japan as a understandable whole to the American people. In doing so, however, there has been a certain commitment to seeing Japan from an anthropological, holistic perspective tended to highlight the great tradition and overlook the minor ones or aberrations. They lack the documented continuity generally associated with the culture of the elite (Asahi Shinbunsha: 1975). At the same time, the political messages have been clearly identified in his other work (see, for example, Glazer: 1974).

While the notion of value-free research has lost its appeal for many, the importance of having values lies in their being clearly stated. Because modernization, capitalism, democracy, improved international communiction, nationalism, winning in international competition, cosmopolitanism, and having close ties with nation X are never explicitly mentioned as the goals of the *nihonjinron* theorists, it is difficult to judge the adequacy of such scholarship. As a result, the assumption that *nihonjinron* serves a useful purpose is never seriously challenged. One is given as fact certain descriptions of reality, but not the goal of knowing about Japanese society, against which the usefulness of the descriptions can be evaluated. Finally, to the extent that there are value orientations to promote and ideologies to push, one wonders about the development of Japanology as a religion, and recalls undergraduate lectures on the problems of distinguishing between religion, ideology and even knowledge itself. Each is a kind of belief system. When institutionalized, each tends to be disseminated by a chosen few who often come to constitute themselves as a self-appointed inner circle.

3 Cliquish Intuitiveness and the Chosen Few. If there is a major methodological assertion in the *nihonjinron* literature it is the emphasis placed on a kind of mystical empathy. Although cultural immersion and a sense of the social milieu or cultural ethos are crucial when it comes to translating between *etic* and *emic* domains (cf. Befu: 1982d), there seems to be an underlying methodological assumption that only Japanese and a few select foreigners (who share their views) are able to understand Japanese society. The intuitive insight necessary to make reliable pronouncements about the essence of Japanese society seems to be reserved for this small priestly class. The use of a word such as Japanology to describe the study of Japanese society tends to buttress the belief that intuition is the key to understanding it. Like Kremlinology or Sinology, it suggests the study of something wrapped in mystery.

There is in this way of thinking a logical contradiction. The assertion that only Japanese or Japanologists can understand Japan leads one to the proposition that only individuals native to a society can have more than a superficial understanding of that society. Although this may be true to some extent, this line of reasoning leads one to expect that there would be little value in the classics by Marx (a German) on the French Revolution, by de Tocqueville (a Frenchman) on American society or by Malinowski (a Polish migrant, first to England then to the United States) on primitive societies. To insist that the major sources of sociological understanding must come from a member of the society studied tends to deny the possibility that an individual can do comparative research. Nevertheless, this view is often advanced by those who constantly use comparatives and superlatives to describe Japanese society. It also raises the question of how Japanese scholars claiming that foreigners cannot understand Japanese society qualify to write volumes based on the assumption that they understand Western society.

II Further Information on Methodology in Japanology

The characteristics listed above were compiled and systematized from a general reading of the *nihonjinron* literature. There is then the question of whether these impressions stand up under closer scrutiny. A number of tests can be derived to test these impressions; two are presented here. One consists of a content analysis of four volumes representing the *nihonjinron* literature. The second is a study of *kotowaza* which seeks to examine their usefulness as a reliable source of data.

A *Nihonjinron* as a Methodology: a Content Analysis

The first experiment was designed to ascertain whether argument consisted of anecdotes and isolated examples and to examine whether methodological tendencies could be found. The sample, the unit of analysis and the findings are briefly introduced.

1 The Sample. Four books were chosen for the study: Doi (1971), Nakane (1973), Reischauer (1979) and Vogel (1979a). Several considerations motivated this choice. All four have appeared in both English and Japanese. All four are by established professors at renowned universities. Among the various contributions to the *nihonjinron* literature, these are the bestsellers. A scan of the *Social Sciences Citation Index* (as indicated in Table 6.1) suggests that these authors have also had considerable influence in academic circles.[4] Finally, all four have been widely reviewed in both academic and popular media. Both the Japanese and the English versions of each book were read, although the findings for only one version are presented. In addition, as background the authors examined several other items published by each author and these are included in the list of references. Several people were employed as referees, although the recording of data for any given volume was done by the same person.[5]

2 The Unit of Analysis. Four types of statement were recorded. Descriptive statements involved assertions that some property of one population was significantly different from that for another population. For example, 'the Japanese are shorter than Europeans.' Causative statements implied some explanation of a given social phenomenon. For example, 'the phenomena described immediately above occur *because* the Japanese eat seaweed.' In other words, 'the quality of height (dependent variable) is less likely to be present when

Table 6.1 *Frequency of citation for major works and authors dealing with Japanese society, measured according to the Social Sciences Citation Index*

Author	Book (date of the original publication in parentheses)	Number of citations											
		1970	1971	1972	1973	1974	1975	1976	1977	1978	1979	1980	1981
1 Harumi BEFU	*Japan: an Anthropological Introduction* (1971)				1	4	1	4	1	1	1	1	3
	Total for all publications	6	9	4	6	9	7	8	14	4	12	5	13
2 Ruth BENEDICT	*The Chrysanthemum and the Sword* (1946)	8	11	7	11	4	13	14	18	13	13	18	16
	Total for all publications	44	52	36	51	22	57	65	55	57	65	65	65
3 Robert COLE	*Japanese Blue Collar* (1970)		1	2	6	7	4	5	6	6	4	8	3
	Total for all publications	2	5	3	10	10	6	8	10	17	16	20	21
4 Takeo DOI	*Amae no Kōzō* (1971)			1	2	1	1	1	1			1	1
	Anatomy of Dependence (1973)					4	2	8	8	10	7	6	8
	Total for all publications	9	4	2	11	13	12	11	17	13	10	12	12
5 FUKUTAKE Tadashi	*Man and Society in Japan* (1962)	2						1			1		
	Japanese Society Today (1974)						2		1	2	1	3	
	Total for all publications	4	3	2	1	5	7	8	6	4	4	8	4
6 John HALL and Richard BEARDSLEY	*Twelve Doors to Japan* (1965)	3	1	1	1	1	1	3	1	1		2	1
	Total for all publications of J. W. Hall	16	19	20	17	18	14	16	16	19	24	29	31
	Total for all publications of R. K. Beardsley	5	7	5	7	5	6	6	4	7	4	8	4

Table 6.1 *Continued*

Author	Book (date of the original publication in parentheses)	Number of citations											
		1970	1971	1972	1973	1974	1975	1976	1977	1978	1979	1980	1981
7 ISHIDA Takeshi	*Japanese Society* (1972)				2	2	3	4	2			1	
	Total for all publications	1	6	1	4	4	4	7	5	6	1	4	7
8 NAKANE Chie	*Tate Shakai no Ningen Kankei* (1968)	2	1	2	1	1			1	1		1	2
	Japanese Society (1970)		10	4	6	13	18	16	19	19	14	15	19
	Human Relations in Japan (1971) and/or *La Société Japonaise*						2				1	1	
	Total for all publications	10	15	10	14	21	24	22	26	23	17	23	27
9 Edward NORBECK	*Changing Japan* (1976)									1	1	1	1
	Total for all publications	8	17	16	15	32	6	18	14	9	11	14	12
10 Edwin REISCHAUER	*Japan: Past and Present* (1946)	2	1	2	1		2	1			1		
	Japan: the Story of a Nation (1970)	1	1	3		1	1	3	1				
	The Japanese (1978)											7	6
	Total for all publications	20	9	10	11	15	24	22	14	10	19	14	11
11 Ezra VOGEL	*Japan's New Middle Class* (1963)	6	3	2	11	10	7	7	8	9	1	6	6
	Japan as Number One (1979)										4	22	19
	Total for all publications	13	18	15	29	28	24	35	35	34	20	54	59

Note: The totals given for all the publications for each author include the frequencies for the specific publications mentioned. For Hall and Beardsley, the citations for *Twelve Doors to Japan* are included only in the total for the author under which the specification appeared.

seaweed is eaten (independent variable).' Definitions refer to statements which elucidate or define (implicitly or explicitly) some concept employed in a descriptive or causative statement. Finally, statements concerning methodology were recorded in a slightly different manner. They included statements about the methodology actually used or about methodology in general; on the other hand, they may be statements by the referee about some methodological implication in the work examined. The frequency of each type of statement is given in Table 6.2.

Table 6.2 *The frequency distributions of four types of statement*

Type of Statement	Author			
	Doi	Nakane	Reischauer	Vogel
Descriptive statements of a comparative nature	29.1	56.8	70.1	59.4
Statements about causation	16.3	20.6	29.3	40.4
Definitions	15.3	6.7	0.6	0.2
Statements indicative of methodological concern, problems or issues	39.4	15.8	0.0	0.0
TOTAL	100.0	100.0	100.0	100.0
N	320	461	174	443

A few other comments should also be made about the scheme for classifying types of evidence. First, a clear distinction is made between evidence for descriptive statements and evidence for causative statements. For example, the descriptive statements related to the dependent variable in Figure 6.1 may be supported by statistical evidence showing that the economic growth rate in postwar Japan was above that in another country, and the descriptive statement related to the independent variable may be supported by solid statistical evidence showing that the amount of personal savings has also been greater. Even so, it is possible that there is no indication as to why or how these two facts are related, except for the author's statement that they are. Degrees of rigorousness aside, the referees were asked to determine whether causal statements were accompanied by some evidence that a correlation existed between the two variables. Evidence simply that two properties were present in one

Figure 6.1 *A causative statement*

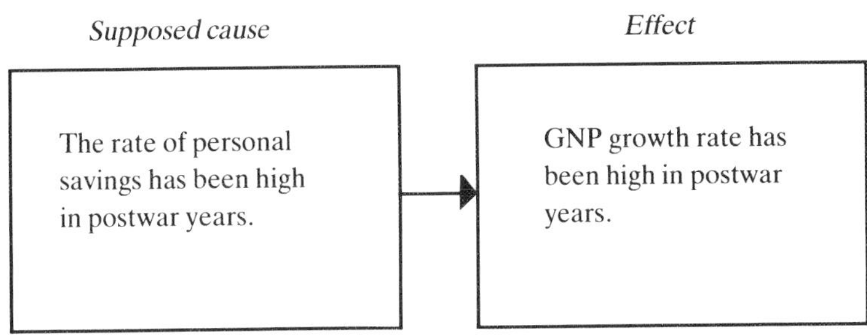

particular case was not considered evidence of causation. Evidence of variation involving at least two cases was necessary. Second, with regard to the classification of evidence, there were some ambiguities in the categories and in the counting of pieces of evidence. For example, the referees were able to define clearly the line between 'no evidence' and 'personal authority'; it sometimes seemed logical that statements without tangible evidence would have been based on personal authority. However, in most cases 'personal authority' was reserved for those statements which presented a view either with some elaboration or with some vague reference to the author's having talked with 'many people' or to having acquired the knowledge from 'long experience over the years'. Another ambiguity lies in how a single item of evidence was defined. For example, the Japanese might be said to like green tea more than the Americans because the per capita intake of tea in Japan is 7.6532 cups per day whereas the level in America is 2.3487 cups per day. Although each figure may have come from independent surveys on habitual tea-drinkers, the two figures were counted as one piece of evidence (that the Japanese drink more green tea). When the source of the evidence was not given, a third difficulty involved the distinction among 'personal authority' or 'own data', 'someone else's data' and government survey data.

3 Some Findings. The four books shared certain similarities (Tables 6.3–6.5). First was the fact that the vast majority of statements have no solid evidence and lack a firm empirical base (Table 6.3). Many statements which are classified as having some kind of evidence are, in fact, supported only by isolated examples and personal authority. Second was the heavy reliance on illustrative examples rather than carefully gathered data (Table 6.4). Third was the failure to cite the sources of evidence. Although Vogel appends a bibliography for each

Table 6.3 *The percentage of statements with and without evidence*

Author	Doi		Nakane		Reischauer		Vogel	
Type of statement	DS	CS	DS	CS	DS	CS	DS	CS
Number of cases	93	52	262	95	122	51	263	179
Statements with some type of evidence	51.6	32.7	31.3	14.7	45.1	39.2	53.2	32.4
Statements with no evidence at all	48.4	67.3	68.7	85.3	54.9	60.8	46.8	67.6

Note: DS = descriptive statements
CS = causative statements

chapter, seldom is explicit reference made to specific items in the bibliography. This may be related to the use of many illustrative examples, since such evidence inevitably involves informants and the problem of confidentiality. Finally, considerably more 'evidence' was found for descriptive statements than for causative statements (Table 6.3). The proponents of *nihonjinron* tended to speculate about causation without having a solid, social-scientific framework for analyzing it. Often a rich variety of extremely interesting hypotheses was provided; seldom, however, were hypotheses rigorously tested.

There were also some contrasts between the Japanese and American scholars. Most significant, perhaps, was the more frequent use of statistical data by Vogel and Reischauer (Table 6.4), although the absence of any rigorous examination of the statistical sources is a conspicuous deficiency in their work. The two American scholars also eschewed anecdotes and linguistic reductionism, although other types of more or less isolated examples were used.

Table 6.5 gives information about the other societies mentioned in comparative statements. The comparative base was given for only 15–30 percent of the statements. However, this figure is difficult to interpret because some statements are absolute and not comparative descriptions, even though all four books focused on identifying unique Japanese features. Nevertheless, the tendency to refer largely to the United States or to vague notions of the West was pronounced in all four volumes. Nakane, who was the most insistent about Japan's uniqueness, was the least likely to mention her comparative base. At the same time, however, the cases in which that base was stated suggest that her comparative base was the most diversified.

Table 6.4 *Percentage of statements with evidence by type*

Author	Doi		Nakane		Reischauer		Vogel	
Type of statement Evidence	DS	CS	DS	CS	DS	CS	DS	CS
A Examples								
1 Stories, episodes and personal anecdotes	8.9	10.0	6.2	11.7				
2 Special words and expressions in Japanese	29.7	16.7	9.7	5.9				
3 *Kotowaza* (proverbs)	2.0	6.7	4.4	5.9				
4 Other kinds of examples	25.7	20.0	40.7	29.5	87.8	84.9	78.9	82.4
B Historical materials					1.8	3.8	0.3	
C Statistical sources					9.0	11.3	14.7	11.4
D Own research data								
E Other researcher's data							1.9	
F Quotations from other authorities	19.8	20.0	3.5		0.6		4.3	6.5
G Author's own authority	13.9	26.7	31.5	35.3	0.6			
H Other			4.4	11.7				

Note: DS = descriptive statements
CS = causative statements

For the Reischauer and Vogel books data were also recorded on the Japanese samples from which generalizations were drawn. Table 6.6 shows that Vogel in particular drew heavily from the elite sector for his examples. Neither author included more than a handful of isolated examples from union members or leaders of protest movements. Whereas Reischauer made frequent reference to the Japanese as a homogeneous whole and did not distinguish between sub-groups within Japanese society, Vogel was more cautious in this regard, but clearly extracted his conclusions from information about big business and the government, suggesting that his contacts may

Table 6.5 *Frequency of comparative statements by the comparative base*

Society compared with Japan in the comparative statement	Author			
	Doi	Nakane	Reischauer	Vogel
America		22.7	35.2	87.5
The West	92.9	22.7	50.0	8.8
Britain		9.0		0.1
India or the Hindu civilization		20.5		
China	3.6	13.6		0.1
Other	3.6	11.4	15.0	2.9
TOTAL	100.0	100.0	100.0	100.0
N =	28	44	54	136
Percentage of total statements for which the comparative base is not clear	80.7	87.7	68.8	69.2
N =	145	357	173	442

Table 6.6 *Distribution of samples used to make generalizations about Japan*

Sub-universe	Authors			
	Reischauer		Vogel	
	DS	CS	DS	CS
Japan	73.3	50.7	40.1	37.6
Business organizations			8.6	17.3
Individuals in big business	0.1	9.0	6.1	6.4
Government organizations			12.7	8.7
Individuals in government			10.2	16.8
Others	21.7	40.2	22.3	13.3
TOTAL	100.0	100.0	100.0	100.0
N =	120	67	197	173

have been skewed in that direction. This problem is no doubt accentuated by the 'semi-case-study' or 'extended-example' approach used by Vogel without any real explanation as to why one case or example better substantiates the point than another, a shortcoming related to the absence of explanation regarding methodology. Minorities, the non-respectable, anti-establishment types, women and the average person in the street tend to be overlooked.

B *Kotowaza* as a Data Base: an Evaluation

The methodological overview identified *kotowaza* and special linguistic expressions as a type of evidence frequently utilized in *nihonjinron*. The discussion suggested that a number of terms or phrases with opposite meanings could easily be found, and that it was not obvious that a representative sample would yield results consistent with the holistic image of Japanese society. In order to test this hypothesis, Sugimoto (1980c) obtained a full list of Kantō and Kansai *iroha karuta* from the appendix in *Kotowaza-Meigen Jiten* (A Dictionary of Proverbs and Famous Sayings, Tokyo: Sōgensha, 1978) and examined their distribution across several categories of meaning.

The study was very simple. The 96 proverbs were sorted into a number of categories, as shown in Table 6.7. The initial results were interesting and showed in a very preliminary way that the arbitrary use of *kotowaza* involved certain dangers. At the same time, however, the paper raised two problems. First, the *kotowaza* in the *iroha karuta* set do not all have the same degree of currency. Second, many *kotowaza* could be interpreted in several ways, meaning that the sorting of a single researcher was likely to be biased and unreliable.

1 The methodology. To supplement the first study the authors conducted a further one. The experiment was structured around a survey and an interview schedule was built around yet another set of *iroha karuta*. The basic format is given in Figure 6.2. The survey was distributed to 854 students at four high schools in a large urban area. Each student filled in four answers for each of 47 *kotowaza* from the *iroha karuta* set and for each of three *kotowaza* taken from Nakane (1967a). The form in Figure 6.2 was used to test for the usage and general support each *kotowaza* received.

Another form was created to ascertain the meaning associated with each *kotowaza*; 15 adults were interviewed for roughly two hours, although some respondents were not free for the full time required

Table 6.7 *The frequency distribution of 96* kotowaza *from* iroha karuta *by value orientation*

Rank order	Idea expressed by *kotowaza*	Number of *kotowaza*
1	Ridicule of futile or meaningless action	14
2	Mockery of the powerful and the wealthy	12
3	Importance of economic rationality and efficiency	12
4	Utility of perseverance	11
5	Importance of achievement and accomplishment	7
6	Praise of good interpersonal relations and harmonious groups	6
7	Importance of precautions	4
8	High frequency of unexpected situations arising in life	4
9	Necessity of the aged following the instructions of the young	3
10	Burden of child-rearing	2
11	Virtue of being ignorant	2
12	Other	19
TOTAL		96

Source: Sugimoto (1980c), p. 3B

and agreed to complete the forms on their own and to return them to one of the authors at a later date. The survey questions and interpretative scales were created without reference to the *kotowaza.* Rather, they were created with the major assertions of the *nihonjinron* literature in mind. Again, each respondent gave his or her interpretation for each of the 50 items used in the survey. Finally, 15 university students and staff members administered the interview schedule as a survey.

2 Initial Findings. The scales were treated as intervals and the average was calculated for each question for each *kotowaza.* In Table 6.8 the range and the average scores are given for each question. The extent to which the *kotowaza* were not heard or used is conspicuous. The three used by Nakane had scores of 3.127, 3.640 and 3.505 for the first question and 3.518, 3.767 and 3.772 for the second, suggesting that

Figure 6.2 *Survey form to indicate usage and general support for each of 50* kotowaza

---

Please answer the questions below with regard to the following *kotowaza*:

さ

猿も木から落ちる

Homer also nods sometimes, *or*

The best horse stumbles, *or*

The best cart may overthrow.

A How often have you heard this *kotowaza*?

1. Very often
2. Sometimes
3. Seldom
4. Never

B How often do you use this *kotowaza*?

1. Very often
2. Sometimes
3. Seldom
4. Never

C To what extent do you think this *kotowaza* expresses a fact of life or some kind of social reality?

1. Very well
2. To some extent
3. Can't say
4. Not very well
5. Not at all

D To what extent do you feel that the *kotowaza* advises people to do the right or moral thing?

1. Very much so
2. To some extent
3. Can't say
4. Not very much
5. Not at all

Note: Each booklet consisted of 50 duplicate sheets, each with a different *kotowaza* entered in the space provided.

Table 6.8 *The range of scores and the frequency distribution of 50* kotowaza *on scores for usage and support*

Score	Questions on survey form			
	A Usage (as receiver)	B Usage (as sender)	C Reliability or truth value	D Extent of approval
Lowest score	1.407	1.957	1.835	1.725
1.0–2.0	15	2	4	4
2.0–2.5	8	7	7	4
2.5–3.0	7	9	20	24
3.0–4.0	20	32	19	18
Highest score	3.710	3.854	3.272	3.126

they are not representative. Also noticeable is the fact that only four *kotowaza* out of 50 received reasonably warm support (the fourth question) or were seen as being reliable reflections of social reality (the third question). Scored on a five-point scale, it is interesting to note that none had a mean over 4.0. The low standard deviations suggest that the differences are minimal and cast doubt on the singling out of one *kotowaza* to represent Japanese value orientations. In other words, the rather clear-cut differences in usage do not necessarily translate themselves into social values (i.e., approval and disapproval), although there seems to be a correlation between usage, the feeling that a *kotowaza* reflects reality and the normative evaluation given to the advice contained in the proverbs.

The two proverbs which register the highest usage support and truth value are *nen ni wa nen o ireyo* (look before you leap) and *yudan taiteki* (always be alert and careful). Both advise the individual to watch out for his or her own interests by protecting or defending himself or herself. They show a sharp contrast with Nakane's proverbs, which ranked low on all indices. Taking a closer look at the two popular proverbs, the only significant demographic variable seemed to be school. This variable is particularly interesting, as higher frequencies were recorded in schools where college preparatory courses were emphasized. Overall, this raises questions about the extent to which the frequency distribution might vary by age, since high-school students have an exceptionally strong concern with entrance exams and having to compete with their fellow students. In this regard, however, it is interesting to note that a survey of 300 salaried employees aged between 35 and 50 yielded similar results (Taishō Kaijō Kasai: 1981). The father's education, the size of the father's firm, the mother's education and the mother's employment status seem to have no influence on the scoring of these two proverbs.

Finally, the respondents to the interviews were unable to agree on the messages contained in the *kotowaza* and most felt that the vast majority of them said very little about the propositions advanced by the *nihonjinron* theorists. This finding is also supported by a survey among middle-school children by Inagaki *et al.* (1981). The suggestion is clearly that great care is required in interpreting such phrases and that there is a danger of reading too much meaning into even frequently used sayings.

III Conclusions

A perusal of the *nihonjinron* literature suggests that it has a very shaky methodological foundation, if any at all. Although various traits are claimed to be uniquely Japanese and to have been produced out of Japanese cultural traditions, the proponents of *nihonjinron* do not seem to be concerned with the logical format generally accepted in the social sciences for demonstrating either that differences exist between two or more societies or that correlation exists between two variables. Problems in sampling are particularly obvious, and the failure to deal with the issue of variance within Japanese society throws into stark relief the frequent references to the Japanese as though they are all interchangeable. There seems to be a simple assumption that the Japanese do not have individual personalities and can be treated as cogs or replaceable parts in a much larger social machine. The heavy reliance on a sample of examples drawn largely from establishment-oriented contexts is also related to the question of ideological bias, an issue dealt with in the following chapter.

Chapter 7

Toward a Sociology of Japanology

I Perspectives from the Sociology of Knowledge

People thinking about the social and physical world around them are influenced by the social milieu in which they are born and raised. At one time there was a general consensus that the world was flat and that it was circled by the sun. Today the earth is seen as being a sphere which orbits the sun. In most societies only a small number of persons have the time necessary to confirm their perceptions. While given knowledge may be broadly shared by nearly all members of a particular society, it is not uncommon for the generation of such knowledge to be entrusted to a few persons, with its truth being accepted by other members of society merely on the word of the elected few. At the same time, the insistence of a very small number of people, which is generally accepted as fact or even as common sense in one era, is rejected in the next.

Today Toyota and Sony are known as Japanese companies by millions of people; at the same time there are also millions of people who do not even know that a country called Japan exists. While many Japanese consider *sashimi* (raw fish) to be a delicacy, people in some societies cannot imagine anyone wanting to eat such a slimy, oily substance. Each culture tends to embody its own images of reality.

The sociology of knowledge is the study of why particular knowledge exists in a specific culture at any given time. The range of knowledge is seen as extending from nuclear theory to the maximum of common sense built into the everyday lives of ordinary citizens. It includes the natural sciences, philosophy, religious beliefs and popular myths.

There are two major views about how knowledge develops. One stresses the cumulative nature of knowledge, the idea that each new generation receives from the previous generation a store of knowledge to which additions are made before it is again passed on. Merton (1957, pp. 456–88) has been associated with this perspective. Another suggestion is that bodies of knowledge compete in the political arena, some receiving the favor of the powers that be and others being repressed by those with political influence. From this viewpoint the building of knowledge is not simply a matter of addition; it is also a complex process whereby various groups with competing economic and political interests advocate different interpretations of reality. Accordingly, the knowledge which is seen as prevailing at any given time can be said to reflect the social structure at that time. Scientific revolutions and changes in paradigms are associated with the second view (Kuhn: 1970).

Central to both perspectives is the idea that those subscribing to a body of knowledge will improve their understanding of the potential and limitations of that knowledge by taking a reflexive stance. As a product of society, knowledge should be amenable to the same analysis given to social phenomena in general. Just as there are several theories of society, there are also several theories of knowledge. The two mentioned above seem to parallel the larger dichotomy existing in the social sciences between the consensus oriented functionalists and the conflict theorists (cf. the first section of Chapter 4). Depending upon the emphasis, then, knowledge is seen not only as liberating enlightenment which can free one from the myths of the past and some of the weight of tradition, but also as a means of ideological control which is designed to keep people ignorant by replacing old myths with new myths in the name of science.

In Chapter 15 the link between the social milieu in Japan and the appearance of *nihonjinron* is approached from a slightly different perspective which emphasizes the impact of Japan's internationalization and questions of national self-identity. In this chapter, the *nihonjinron* literature is examined from the two viewpoints of gradual accumulation and paradigmatic change. It begins by considering some functional requisites for developing a comparative knowledge of Japanese society. It then deals with the question of ideological uses and looks at the way in which the larger social setting may have been conducive to the development and diffusion of *nihonjinron*.

II A Functional Framework for Evaluating the Comparative Study of Japanese Society

The ability of scholars to engage in comparative research will to a large extent be shaped by their training in certain skills. Cross-cultural research requires special skills. These include a second language, a sensitivity to culture and its relationship to language and some knowledge of field research techniques. When the study of a society is formulated within a comparative context, skills in measurement are also useful. In this section some aspects of the Japanese academic climate relevant to *nihonjinron* are discussed; attention is then directed to the training of foreign researchers for the study of Japanese society.

A Japanese Academic Life and the Generation of *Nihonjinron*

The wartime experience, particularly the inability of Japanese intellectuals to resist effectively the repressive measures of the Government, led many to query the elitist assumption that intellectuals are better critical thinkers than others. Evaluating some elements of the Chinese intellectual tradition, Takeuchi (1952) advocated solidarity with Asian peoples and attacked Japanese intellectuals for being oriented almost exclusively toward the West. Tsurumi and his associates in Shisō no Kagaku Kenkyūkai (Research Association for the Science of Thought) addressed themselves to the way in which thought patterns were shaped by the state and its coercive forces. They scrutinized a wide range of 'forced conversions' during World War II (Tsurumi: 1982; Shisō no Kagaku Kenkyūkai: 1959–62). Their massive collaborative work threw light on the weaknesses of elitist intellectuals detached from the everyday realities of the masses. It emphasized the vitality and creative vigor of thinkers and activists living as common people, and demonstrated that there was a good deal of variation in the thought patterns of the Japanese. From a slightly different angle, Yoshimoto (1959) provided a philosophical foundation for the non-affiliated left. He too argued that aloofness from the common people was the major reason why intellectuals were so likely to be co-opted under a minimal amount of pressure from the state. These studies challenged the elitist bias long embedded in both rightist and leftist writings, and presented populist alternatives for the analysis of Japanese society.

A major fact of Japanese intellectual life is its division into Marxist and non-Marxist camps. This is particularly evident in faculties of economics, where one is classified as *marukei* (a Marxian economist) or *kinkei* (a modern or non-Marxist economist). In many disciplines two academic associations exist, the Marxist and the non-Marxist. These tend respectively to be anti-establishment and pro-establishment in orientation. Those in the second group are invited to participate in various government advisory councils and in research groups organized by the councils. Those who are Marxists are generally not invited, although there are exceptions. There is also a large number of scholars who fit into neither camp. Despite their exclusion from officially sponsored research, anti-establishment scholars have a significant and institutionalized existence in Japan. Even rather conservative scholars can converse in 'Marxianese' and are quite sensitive to the hermeneutic tradition. For some conservatives, the end product is a cynical rejection of all logical arguments about the nature of phenomena and an escape to intuitive understanding. For others it may be a naïve belief that tangible evidence is the only thing one can rely on; the escape in this case is to simply worded questionnaires about the likes and dislikes of the man in the street. Input of the latter type can be seen in the massive surveys conducted by the Prime Minister's Office and often reported in *Gekkan Yoron Chōsa* (the Monthly Review of Survey Data). Such data are frequently used to argue that the Japanese have no sense of class consciousness or that they have some uniquely Japanese set of values.

The aloofness of Japanese academics from the people they study has several consequences. Although some may engage in extensive interviewing and may have frequent conversations with contacts in various organizations, participant observation is seldom used (cf. Cole: 1971a, pp. 42–4). The most probing ethnographies have been written by Japanese journalists such as Kamata (1973, 1974 and 1982) and Honda (1968, 1970 and 1979) or by novelists such as Ariyoshi (1972 and 1975), Sumii (1961) and Yamazaki (1965 and 1969). There are perhaps a number of reasons for this reluctance, including the difficulty of maintaining confidentiality in a densely populated context. Nevertheless, the relative aloofness in research is compensated in two ways. One is active participation in policy-related activities. With a large number of political parties and a wide range of interest groups, there are ample opportunities to be involved. Though political study groups may not always be conducive to objective research, they provide an important means by which scholars can keep in touch with their constituencies. Obviously these opportunities are more numerous for those oriented toward the establishment, as there are many semi-official research organizations (*gaikaku dantai*). Another means of obtaining feedback is the mass media. The publishing industry in Japan is extensive and competitive; nearly every aspect of popular culture is covered in one form or another. Academics are often able to float their ideas in the mass media. While not being a forum conducive to rigorous discussion along strictly academic or scientific lines, it is a good place for testing one's grasp of the *emic* vocabulary.

Japanese academics have traditionally placed great emphasis on the absorption of foreign theories and their introduction into Japan. It has been common practice for tenure-track appointees to translate at least one book into Japanese early in their careers. Many will do a good deal of reading in a foreign language, often focusing on the work of a specific individual and producing a small volume which introduces that person's thought in a systematic fashion. Well-known scholars abroad often have their shadows in Japan. The translation syndrome is further reinforced and institutionalized by those who mobilize their students to translate the works of their mentors abroad. The result is that foreign societies are often understood only through classics and other official documents.

This approach to scholarship has several consequences. One is exposure to a foreign language in its written or formal style, without much accomplishment in the spoken word. Since many Japanese can read English, and it is widely believed, perhaps owing to the emphasis on importing technologies, that knowledge can be acquired through books, the need for going overseas has never been fully recognized and an established system of sabbatical leave has never been institutionalized. Accordingly, opportunities to study overseas for long periods are minimal. This is further reinforced by the fact that universities tend to be tenure-track institutions with career employment patterns. It is difficult for Japanese to give up their employment and to find other means of support to extend their stays overseas as there is little hope that they can later go back to Japan and compete in an open labor market.[1] When sabbatical leave is given, it is not uncommon for the individual to confine his work to the library, to have a very narrow circle of friends located primarily in the host university, and to relax by socializing with other Japanese exiles. At the same time, most Japanese scholars have some information about at least one foreign society, either from their reading at home or from these limited experiences abroad. The superficiality of their exposure to everyday life experiences abroad means that they are seldom in touch with the living culture. While hundreds of books about Japanese society by foreign scholars have been thought to be valuable enough to be translated into Japanese, few if any by Japanese about American or European society have been considered to offer enough insight to warrant their translation into one of those languages.[2] The translation between *etic* and *emic* levels remains difficult. As a result, when inter-societal comparisons are made, there are basic asymmetries in both the volume and quality of the information held on Japan and on the other societies with which Japan is compared.

This means that the interpreter has a special role to play. The interpreter is, first of all, the person who can handle foreign visitors who do not speak Japanese. Such persons are also chosen to represent Japan overseas. It is not uncommon to meet foreign scholars studying in Tokyo and to know, only from their discipline and from the language they speak, the dozen or so Japanese they have met. To participate in world affairs in the international language of the day (e.g., English or other Western European languages) Japan has produced official guides who serve as the major point of contact for many foreign researchers. There are many stories of official interpreters who have added to and changed the content so that things will go smoothly (e.g., cf. Nishiyama: 1979, pp. 150–3 and 228–32). A study of the culture of interpreters, from Nitobe Inazō onwards, would be extremely interesting. There are other criteria in addition to foreign-language proficiency which determine their selection, and one suspects that their status is precarious. One would also not be surprised to find that they have a special interest in their country being as different from Japan as possible.

Two other characteristics of Japanese scholarship are salient. One is the extent to which the interests and problem consciousness of scholars is shaped by immediate events. In many cases it seems to be directed by a market orientation rather than a firm philosophical base. In this regard, Yamagishi and Brinton (1980), Aoi and Naoi (1974) and Takasuga and Teranishi (1974) point to the importance of larger structural changes occurring in Japanese society and changes in the international situation which have shaped the development of the social sciences in general in Japan. This tendency to move with the times builds into Japanese scholarship the same weaknesses which are associated in the media with the notion of *zeze hihishugi* (middle-of-the-roadism) as discussed by Hidaka (1982).

Another feature of Japanese scholarship is access to financial resources. Salary levels for university staff and research personnel in Japan are neither high nor low. However, it is generally expected that the competent ones will augment their income in several ways. One is to publish superior books over a long period, so that one receives a considerable income from accumulated royalties. Another is to use the mass media. Much of the *nihonjinron* literature has been geared for the bestseller market; a good deal also appears in weekly and monthly magazines. However, heavy writing schedules tend to cut into research time. Moreover, copy is usually accepted not on its truth value but on its appeal to the general public. Catch-phrases, nationalistic symbols and the novel twist tend to attract readers. It is not surprising, then, that Befu (1982b) has referred to *nihonjinron* as a 'folk model'. *Nihonjinron* theorists are not the only ones to publish for mass consumption. While there is a full range of magazines, they tend to thin out and have much smaller circulations as one moves to the left.

The major sources of research funds for academicians have been outside the university. The research context in Japan cannot be understood apart from the large number of research organizations established by the government. While many have been established as independent foundations, most are dependent on annual allocations from the Ministry responsible for their activities. They are also a haven for retired Ministry officials and for a few on secondment from the Ministries. Since most of the institutes work on annual budgets, so too are research grants tied to the fiscal year. This makes it difficult to obtain the longer-term commitments often necessary for comparative research and tends to limit the depth with which one can investigate a given area. In addition there are a number of private research organizations, such as the Japan Economic Research Center. Although these are tied to interests at both ends of the political spectrum, the resources of those representing conservative interests and large capital are many times those of organized labor or of other interests not affiliated with the establishment. By and large, it is the conservative organizations with which the *nihonjinron* scholars are most frequently associated.

Many of the private research bodies have referred to themselves as 'think tanks', a label which helps to legitimate their activities in the eyes of the ordinary citizen. However, as one study shows, the extent to which most of the think tanks are engaged in thinking may be questioned. Most are involved primarily in supplying more mechanical services like data processing, market surveying and publications (Takahashi: 1983). The result is a series of research organizations competing to sell information; facts are packaged in such a way as to attract buyers. In the rush to circulate information, both the producers and the consumers come to equate information with understanding and to believe that the facts speak for themselves. The argument here is that a conservative interpretation is invariably attached to the presentation of the data and that research is so organized that other views do not have an equal opportunity (of financial and other forms of support) to be represented or to have a full public hearing. The connection of many conservative research bodies to policy-making organs means further that the conservative interpretations have a much higher chance of being implemented, and that they often become a *fait accompli* and thereby self-fulfilling prophecies.

Yet another aspect of academic life has to do with personal networks. Some of these have been discussed in the study of the academic labor market in Japan by Cummings (1972). Kawamura (1982a) has noted certain continuities in the development of *nihonjinron*. The major figures have come from the University of Tokyo, although in recent years Sophia University seems to have had its own pool, including foreign stars such as Gregory Clark, Robert Ballon and Peter Milward. In terms of publishers there has been a shift from Iwanami to Kodansha and Saimaru. A large number of the *nihonjinron* scholars have been involved in government research projects or in projects organized by various semi-official research organizations. Conflict theorists are usually excluded from such involvement. The political connections of the two groups result in two very different networks being formed.

B The Foreign Researcher

The non-Japanese researcher has a different set of problems in studying Japan. Some may be understood as being the inverse of those faced by Japanese studying abroad. Some are peculiar to foreigners in Japan. Three are touched upon briefly here.

1 Getting to Japan. Time and money are both constraints. Given that funding from foundations is limited for both students and professionals, the criteria used in selecting recipients of grants is crucial. Networks are fairly important and these generally result in there being in-groups and out-groups. One study of Japan Foundation dissertation fellows from America indicated that graduate school affiliation was an important factor determining employment for eight out of ten recipients (Downard: 1978, p. 14). Again, the ideological climate in the United States and Japan, where most of these foundations are located, should be mentioned. Despite a rather active anti-war movement and the emergence of the new left in America during the sixties, scholars working in that vein have received a disproportionately small share of the grants. For the most part, graduate students need sponsors. The most effective mentors are those who have themselves become part of the networks and are acceptable. Departmental seminars and regional colloquia are often used as formats where graduate students and junior members of faculty are examined. As an established academic at one of the chosen ten universities in America having programmes in Japanese studies commented to one of the authors at the end of the seventies,

> it takes a lot of guts for a non-tenured person either to get up and criticize one of the old Japan hands or to report on some kind of airy-fairy speculative research. The pressures to get tenure are now so great that one cannot afford to offend anyone or to appear unsophisticated in front of tenured peers. It is too bad, but a good deal of creative thought is sacrificed to dogma.

The time required for careful comparative research is also difficult to acquire. Graduate students who are able to engage in fieldwork are usually encouraged to return after two years. The search for employment is fairly structured and job applicants who spend longer overseas seem to impart an image of doubt and indecisiveness rather than one of confidence and competence. The pressure to complete one's dissertation often means that foreign researchers coming to Japan must take a narrow view of things and bury themselves in their research. This in turn means that few are able to develop primary ties. Those who are full members of the trade also have their constraints. There seems to be great variation among universities in the provision of sabbatical leave and generalizations are difficult. Family commitments and summer sessions often limit visits during the inter-semester breaks, although it was found in the study mentioned above that the majority of professional fellows commented on the difficulty of getting away for longer periods and welcomed the idea of having more short-term fellowships (Downard: 1978, pp. 15–16). In this regard, it is interesting to note in Downard's findings the concern with teaching and the belief that a major value of a short-term trip to Japan was not research but inspiration, refreshing their Japanese and lifting their motivation.

2 Language. Although the teaching of Japanese has become widespread in universities around the world, and has even become a part of the secondary curriculum at many schools in Australia and North America (not to mention Korea and other countries in Asia), few scholars are fluent in the language. Surveys of language skills have been taken in the United States but they have relied on self-evaluations. In the survey mentioned above (Downard: 1978), for example, 12 of the 55 respondents claimed they could write Japanese with little difficulty and 16 answered that they could do so with ease. As one might expect, reported fluency is even higher for reading and speaking. However, when native speakers, language teachers and individuals who have lived in Japan for long periods are excluded, the performance is much more modest (Table 7.1). The same data suggest that there has been a great improvement in the language ability of those entering the profession (assuming that the self-ratings are reliable). However, those surveyed by Downard are primarily young scholars who have yet to make their contribution to the literature on Japanese society.

Difficulty with language is underlined in several ways. Very few non-Japanese write regularly and publish their research results in Japanese, although a good number have had their books translated into Japanese by someone else. Of the 130 items about Japan by foreigners which are available in Japanese and listed in Tsukushi's compilation (1982), only a handful were written by the authors, and those authors were Chinese or Korean. Three of the four books examined in the previous chapter were all available in the other language as a result of translation. What kinds of bias are introduced in the research of foreigners reluctant to utilize fully the abundance of materials available in Japanese? Of 91 items mentioned in the bibliography to Vogel's volume (1979a), for example, only seven were in Japanese. Of nearly 250 correspondents in Tokyo in the early seventies, perhaps only a dozen could converse in Japanese and only two or three could read Japanese.

The Hakone Conference held in 1960 to launch the modernization

Table 7.1 *Japanese language proficiency of Japan Foundation fellows (1972–7) surveyed in 1978*

Level of proficiency	Dissertation fellows				Professional fellows			
	Writing ability	Reading ability	Speaking ability	Speaking ability, excluding native speakers and language teachers	Writing ability	Reading ability	Speaking ability	Speaking ability, excluding native speakers and language teachers
with difficulty	8		2	2	27	8	9	7
with little difficulty	13	11	10	3	12	16	13	5
with ease	—	10	9	5	16	32	34	2
TOTALS	21	21	21	10	55	56	56	14

Source: Downard (1978), pp. 10–12

series stipulated that the official language be Japanese. Perhaps for the first time the principle of working in Japanese was acknowledged. Unfortunately, one participant confided, with the exception of only two or three, the foreign scholars conducted business as usual in the designated unofficial language, English. While there are problems related to who has the money and who wants to control discussion in these international forums, Miller (1982, pp. 271–2) argues that there are also problems of foreigners constantly being taught *nihongo* while Japanese learn *kokugo*, a point which has also been made by Neustupný (1979) who has argued that there is a need to go beyond the teaching of *hyōjungo* (standard Japanese) by making students aware of the variations which result in most Japanese speaking a non-standard version of their own language.

3 Isolation in the Japanese Context. A third problem affecting the foreign researcher is the very awkwardness of just being there and confronting constant reminders that one is not part of that society. The conspicuousness of one's presence, coupled with the general absence of participant observation in the Japanese intellectual tradition, means that intrusion into a situation invariably changes it. This is a problem even in researching one's own culture; it is even more of a problem in Japan, partially because of the special attention accorded the foreigner and partially owing to his or her frequent dependence on methods which minimize the full use of the language. In describing his experience as a participant observer, Cole (1971a, pp. 48–51) suggests that the foreigner also has some advantages. These include special cooperation and a view of the researcher as an outsider not interested in affecting the interests of the actors being observed. Although no evidence is given to support his views, there is clearly room for looking at both the merits and the demerits. Without a more careful assessment of how the situation is affected by the presence of the foreign observer, however, it is difficult to evaluate accurately data obtained by methods such as participant observation and interviewing.

At the same time, few foreigners have independent access to the media. Only recently is it possible for non-Japanese scholars long established in Japanese academic life to hold tenured positions at Japan's national universities; moreover, few, if any, have ever been invited to participate in the government's advisory boards. One must rely on personal friends for a sense of the cultural ethos or social milieu. However, in the limited time one has even as a graduate student, it is difficult to build up an extensive network of such friendships. Pressures of time result in friends being used as informants, a problem which raises still other issues. As guests with a language problem, most foreign researchers are left with the official interpreter and others who can speak English. Contacts in Japan tend to be not with a cross-section of Japanese but with counterparts at similar institutions: academics with faculty members at Japanese universities, businessmen with businessmen, and correspondents with Japanese newsmen. Although there is some cross-fertilization, the overall pattern is one largely of elites obtaining information from elites. In Vogel's volume (1979a), for example, the publications listed in the bibliography which were published in Japan were nearly all authored and/or published by the Japanese Government or some management-affiliated body. This may be an effective way to obtain data in a limited amount of time, but to the extent that power differentials and relations of authority are an integral part of the phenomena being studied, it is a bit like running door-to-door and surveying parents to find out if child abuse is a problem. The telltale signs are usually the bruises which are seen only by doctors, teachers or others who come into direct contact with the child. Although this may be less of a problem to the extent that power inequalities are not involved, the fact still remains that those riding the bullet train to Osaka and those living and working under the guard rails often see Japan in very different lights. This may in part account for the failure of many researchers to distinguish clearly between *tatemae* and *honne* (the official interpretation and the reality) or between the part and the whole. Conceptual ambiguity, mixed levels of analysis and non-parallel comparisons are no doubt related to this problem of getting under the surface. In addition to the problem of access, dependence on an established host also tends to inhibit the foreign researcher's ability to be critical. After having received many kindnesses, it is often difficult to write things which may embarrass one's host or suggest that he was less than competent in showing what needed to be seen in Japan. The same holds for Japanese going abroad.

III The Ideological Framework for Japanology

The sociology of knowledge can foster a very cynical view of human behavior when its attention is focused exclusively on the ideological uses of knowledge, or on instances where the selection of data or the choice of methodology has been determined not by criteria relevant to discovering the truth, but by the relative political influence of those who advocate the different approaches. It does not take much imagination to visualize the situation described by those in the hermeneutic (Connerton: 1977) and symbolic interactionist (Phillips: 1971) traditions, whereby at an even earlier stage the political presence of the researcher shapes the very data he or she collects. In this section, the discussion focuses on several ways in which ideology seems to impinge upon the study of Japanese society and works to shape its popular images.

A In the Service of Specific Interests

In some contexts *nihonjinron* has been used as an ideology to enhance the interests of those in control within Japan. These interests can be seen on two levels: the maintenance of social order at home and the promotion of Japan's economic interests abroad.

1 Domestic Stability. Marx once wrote that religion is the opiate of the masses. At times *nihonjinron* (for which there is the synonym *nihonkyō* meaning the teachings on Japan) has been used to alter the image which ordinary Japanese have of themselves and their society. The idea of one's nation being number one and having a mystique of uniqueness placing it beyond the understanding of outsiders has an attraction for many people, including Japanese. Spreading the belief that Japan's unique approach to personnel management has given the Japanese the world's most sophisticated system of industrial relations is bound to contribute to the *esprit de corps* of the labor force and to distract the attention of the workers from some of the less happy aspects of their everyday lives. At the same time, attributing Japan's remarkable economic growth largely to uniquely Japanese cultural traits encourages workers to accept other forms of discipline associated with tradition and this acceptance in itself can shape the work force into something more closely resembling the ideal worker advocated by management. That in turn can indeed serve as a fillip to behavior supportive of economic growth.

Yamamoto (1979) argues that Japanese traditional values have been important ingredients accounting for Japan's rapid growth. While noting that these may have been used by misguided militarists to lead Japan into the last war, his emphasis is on how these traits have also accounted for Japan's many successes. Another Yamamoto (1980, pp. 196–9) relates how in more recent years the stress on the uniquely Japanese elements (e.g., the vocabulary) of management's paternalistic philosophies and techniques has served as the major factor accounting for the high level of commitment among employees to winning the competitive edge in world markets. Crawcour (1977) and others have discussed in more concrete terms the way in which images of the unique Japanese are promoted as part of management ideology. Today, reference to the unique features of Japanese society *à la nihonjinron* is common at morning ceremonies (*chōreikai*) in many Japanese firms.

It is not surprising, then, that the Personnel Development Office of a corporation like Nippon Steel (1982) should publish and market its own *nihonjinron* guide to Japan, which presents the group model of Japanese society in capsule form. The important point, as stated in the foreword (p. 7), is that the material was prepared for the education of its own employees who were to work overseas and would otherwise find it difficult to answer properly the questions foreigners are always asking about Japan. Over time those employees shared the book with members of their families and other businessmen who saw the book as useful in that regard. Today the book is a bestseller; after all, if a reputable firm like Nippon Steel encourages its employees to read such material, many are inclined to accept its truth value.

Since the Tokugawa period it has been widely asserted that the essential elements in Japanese culture can be grasped only by Japanese with a deep understanding of the Japanese mood, *yamato damashii*, the Japanese spirit, the national essence, Japanese ways of doing things, and Japanese tradition in general. Before World War II, this position was openly promoted by the state and presented as part of the ideology associated with the imperial interpretation of Japanese history. Although Japanese bestsellers in the seventies use a different vocabulary, many seem to be quite similar in their emphasis on the presence of Japanese characteristics absent in other societies and in glorifying the apparently paradoxical elements of Japanese culture. In short, they often celebrate the *status quo* or supply historical precedents for changes advocated by the conservative elements in Japan.

Nihonjinron has thus become a major point of reference in justifying the conservative policies of the LDP. This fact becomes more obvious when we examine the publications in which *nihonjinron* appear. They are primarily the establishment-oriented media. When the unique aspects of Japanese political processes are isolated from the political practices found in other countries and the entire political system is then referred to as a uniquely Japanese approach to decision-making based on traditional notions of consensus, unsubstantiated assumptions about the nature of decision-making in Japan are glossed over and the entire system is legitimized in the minds of many citizens.

Nihonjinron can also be used in support of the 'banana theory', the idea that there are two categories of Japanese: the real Japanese who are above suspicion and those who only have Japanese skin. Social critics influenced by Marxism are often dismissed as not being truly Japanese. The exclusion of Ainu, *burakumin* and Koreans is not unrelated to this general attitude. Japanese women marrying white Westerners are treated as international persons, linked to the positive reference group but none the less denied Japanese citizenship for their children until recently.

In this regard, it is interesting to note the dual meaning attached to the word *kokusaijin* (international person). It can refer positively to those who bring in technologies and other ideas useful to achieving the goals of industrialization and national independence. It can also refer to naïve persons who have gone native in their enthusiasm for Western things, dangerous elements with romantic notions of changing the sacred elements in Japanese society. This duality is shrewdly but sensitively captured by Genji Keita in his humorous short story, 'The Translator' (1972). The professional translator's services are indispensable to his firm, but he is for all other purposes isolated from the company's activities and treated like a pariah with a mixture of embarrassment and lack of interest. From this perspective, then, *nihonjinron* can also be seen as a way to minimize foreign influences.

2 Ploys in International Negotiations. The interests of Japanese abroad are also served by *nihonjinron*. In the game of cultural understanding, disagreement is put forth as an instance of ethnocentrism on the part of the other party. The failure of the foreign negotiator to understand all the nuances of Japanese culture and the generally accepted principles of cultural relativism are thrown on the bargaining table like trump cards. The foreign negotiator is often put in an awkward position where he can remove the label 'ignorant and ethnocentric' only by agreeing with the Japanese negotiators. Another device is the diversionary tactic which allows the Japanese negotiator overseas to wriggle out of a tight spot by claiming that his decision must in fact be made by the group back in Tokyo. Expressed as an apology with lavish praise for the foreign concept of individualism, this maneuver is difficult to counter. The claim that group decision-making is a Japanese cultural trait is also used to create an awkward situation in which a single foreign negotiator is surrounded by a Japanese team of 10 to 15. To be sure, businessmen from large Japanese firms are the product of such situations in Japan and it is reasonable to expect that they would feel at home in the company of their colleagues and perhaps even feel that such a gathering was quite natural. The argument, however, is not simply that such patterns are followed in the specific firm in question, but that the patterns are culturally dictated and that they cannot be changed. The result is an excuse for any insensitivity to the discomfort caused for foreign negotiators.

Another tactic may be illustrated by an example from Australia. Several years ago the sugar dispute captured the headlines in Australia and Japan. Australia's first long-term contract had called for a stable supply of raw sugar to the Japanese refineries. However, when world prices dropped, stability was no longer valuable to the Japanese; cheaper imports were. The Japanese made a good deal of publicity about the need for cultural understanding. It was suggested that in Japan the notion of contracts was underdeveloped or was tied to some sense of *amae* which allowed one party to get out when the going got too tough. From that perspective it is incumbent on the other party to acquiesce magnanimously. Australians were accused of trying to impose their rigid Western-oriented concept of a contract or agreement on the Japanese, and therefore of being ethnocentrically insensitive to the idea of cultural relativism and the notion of give and take (March: 1979). More recently, however, when shipments of iron ore were delayed by industrial disputes late in 1980, Japanese executives representing steel interests came to Australia and released statements about the importance of stability and of honoring contracts (*The Australian*, 16 November 1980, p. 1). In this case it was Australians who could lament the aggressiveness of the economic animals from Japan who seemed to have no sense of mateship and no human warmth when it came to business dealings. The Japanese were obviously seen as being second to none when it came to materialistic instincts and rigid contracts. Taken together, these two examples illustrate how images are created and manipulated in order to obtain advantage in negotiating and in domestic politicking.

In 1982 a good deal of attention was given to *bōeki masatsu* in the Japanese media. While the difficulties experienced by the Japanese in communicating abroad and the consistency with which Japanese intentions are misunderstood by foreigners were often cited as a major source of the problem, the overwhelming message was that the problems arose from cultural differences rather than from conflicts of interest. The idea was that cultural relativism could be used to defeat the viciousness and ethnocentrism behind accusations that Japan's trading practices were unfair and based on a national policy of social dumping.

The learn-from-Japan boom may also be partially understood as a craze for new symbols abroad. In today's world the factors which affect the self-images of one people are likely to affect the self-images of other peoples as well. Reflecting on the Miyamoto Musashi boom as described by Davis (1982, p. 254), (cf. Miyamoto: 1982; Yoshikawa: 1981), several possible latent functions of the English-language translation come to mind. Although the reading of Miyamoto may contribute little to the understanding of contemporary management practices in Japan, it may serve, however, as a symbol to distinguish the in-group from the out-group in the foreign community residing in Tokyo. It may also provide American businessmen with an example of Japanese folklore around which they can build an inspiring message for the *chōreikai* which they are planning to institute in their own company upon returning home from their latest tour to Japan.

Other examples from the Australian experience reveal ways in which the promotion of *nihonjinron* can be used as a mirror to promote a specific ideology at home. Although disadvantaged in negotiations with their Japanese counterparts who come to Australia full of cultural theories as to why Australia (with a strike ethic) ought to sell at lower prices its resources to Japan (which is said to place a high cultural value on stability), some Australian businessmen found the stereotypes of Japanese society a convenient perspective for bashing Australian unions. The cultural understanding game is also sometimes played in reverse when negotiating with the Japanese. Cultural relativism may mean that leniency is expected when it comes to respecting strikes as a unique Australian tradition.

In recent negotiations the Japanese have all the statistics; figures from the Japanese Minister of Labor and the Australian Bureau of Statistics clearly show that Australian workers strike more frequently, a phenomenon which is interpreted as being consistent with an Australian culture emphasizing individualism and strong class consciousness. However, no mention is made of the fact that the two data-collecting bodies use different definitions of strikes and collect data in different ways. No mention is made of the fact that it was not long ago that Japan had many strikes and that Australia had relatively few. No mention is made of the fact that national averages are deceiving; Australia's strikes happen largely in the mining sector (Chalmers: 1981), a sector which Japan does not now have but one which is characterized by higher levels of disputes in all societies, including Japanese society in the past if the Miike strikes are only recalled.

Finally, the refusal to accept refugees from Indochina might be cited. Japan is presented as a racially and ethnically homogeneous society in which others could not possibly live. The same apologists, however, are quick to point out that the refugees would make a great contribution to the cosmopolitanization of a white Australia which, after all, has lots of unused land which is *mottainai* (going to waste). Again, parallel shifts in the way national interest is defined are interesting. This argument did not appear in the prewar period when Chinese and Koreans were brought to Japan to provide cheap labor.

The whole range of euphemisms and cultural exotica can be seen in the comments of the Japanese interviewed by Stirling (1981). Many of the pieces submitted by Tokuyama Jirō to *Newsweek* during the seventies contained the same hackneyed stories. Again, however, it is difficult to pin down responsibility. As one Japanese intellectual recently conceded to the authors,

> On reflection it may have been wrong, but it was lots of fun flying around the world and the preparation was so easy because everyone wanted to hear the same old stuff. I had only to come up with a new catch-phrase on each trip. I think the hosts were generally happy with my jokes and everyone had a good time.

Certainly one should not be faulted for being friendly or cooperative, but it is easy for otherwise sophisticated persons to be complacent with the material they felt obliged to 'mass produce'.

Intentions aside, the fact remains that the foreigner is constantly bombarded with the holistic view of Japanese society. Even before reaching Japan, the old clichés are presented in the many industrial journals distributed freely overseas. A cross-section of English-language material provided to foreign correspondents and researchers by the information centers in Tokyo is shown in Table 7.2. By and large, this literature portrays Japanese society in the same way (i.e., as a holistic entity), although the *Japan Quarterly* and the *Japan Interpreter* might be considered exceptions. The reference to Japanese society is often sandwiched among more technical, industry-related information, but for many readers functions subliminally as their only source on Japanese society. Although *AMPO, RONIN* and *SOHYO News* are published in Japan, seldom if ever are they available at the major information centers.

As brief examples randomly chosen to give some idea of the views presented in publications of this kind, two magazines might be mentioned. One is *Winds*, the inflight magazine of Japan Airlines, which greets many of those traveling to Japan. One article in recent years introduced the passenger to the delights of Narita, the land around Tokyo's new international airport. The area's history is

Table 7.2 *The titles of some publications distributed to non-Japanese*

General publications	Publications of corporations and other business organizations
PHP	The JAMA Forum
Look Japan	Tradepia International
Japan Pictorial	The Wheel Extended
Japan Echo	Sumitomo Scope
Entrepreneurship: the Japanese Experience	Steel Today and Tomorrow
Journal of Japanese Trade	Information from JGC
Energy in Japan	Hitachi Zosen News
The East	Nissan International Graph
Business Japan	Nippon Steel Forum
Business View	Dentsu Japan: Marketing/Advertising
The English Journal	Sumitomo Quarterly
Press Guide	
Japan Society Newsletter	
Japan Quarterly	
Japan Interpreter	

described in glowing terms, without any reference to the fierce struggles waged to prevent the airport's construction in the seventies. The recommended tour included lots of temples but was designed to avoid any of the monuments to that struggle. The pictures of the airport had been carefully cropped so that the miles of barbed wire are not seen. In past issues of *Winds* the same old stereotypes can also be seen repeatedly in the serialized interviews of Fukada Yūsuke which were carried for some time under the title *Sekaishi Taidan* (Dialogues with the World in View).

Those who fly by other means will still find the message tucked away in the pouch in front of them on their ride to the city on the limousine bus, which has its own magazine, *City Guide*. The names and places change, but the message is invariably the same:

> President Hashiguchi Shunya, a former Dentsū man, emphasizes that to do business in Japan there must be lasting personal ties – that partners cannot rely on the cold logic of short-term mutual advantage alone. 'Westerners are very clever, but in Japan, and particularly in the ad business, the problem is getting to be trusted and liked.'
>
> Hashiguchi boasts, 'Our new joint venture has the best of both worlds – Western marketing strategies backed by scientific methods, along with the great talents of Japanese creators, who are experts at dealing with raw imagery in very human terms.'
>
> This difference, in analytical and intuitive logic systems, is said to derive from a contrast in brain hemisphere differentiation. It is reflected in the way Japanese and Americans approach any joint project, in particular, the time frame involved. (Plimpton: 1982, p. 4)

Sumitomo's guide (1982) to Japan for its foreign customers sketches the same picture.

Given that the means have been institutionalized to bombard foreigners constantly with this kind of establishment-oriented information, it is not surprising to find, as an article in *Shūkan Bunshun* (6 January 1983, pp. 32–5) notes, that a considerable stir is made both in Japan and abroad when books like Kamata's *Zetsubō Jidōsha Kōjō* (Deadend at the Auto Plant) are finally translated into English and other European languages. The original publication in

Japan nearly a decade earlier, on the other hand, hardly raised an eyebrow there.

B The Role of the Japanese Government

The ideological uses of *nihonjinron* as 'scientific nationalism' before and during the Pacific War have been mentioned by Crawcour (1982) and require no elaboration. To the extent that Japan as a civilization has a history of several centuries, it is easy to choose selectively particular aspects of the Japanese tradition which link with present phenomena (such as Japan's economic successes). The image of Japan as a uniquely unique entity tends to give such a phenomenon a sacred quality. At the same time, the portrayal of Western decadence as an inevitable outcome of Western culture lends credence to the idea that culture is a racial or biological property. Miller (1982) discusses how the Japanese language has been treated by many Japanese as being a biologically determined ingredient in the make-up of every Japanese. This is an interesting reversal of Said's Orientalism, which tends to assert that Asians are a breed which has not been able to keep up with the evolutionary developments occurring in the Western races.

The Japanese Government has for a long time had a hand in promoting certain images of Japan. This can be seen in several ways. One is the active role of the national government in controlling textbooks and education. The problems of indoctrination and censorship in the prewar period are well known. The Japanese Government has also taken a keen interest in presenting the holistic image of Japanese society overseas. Although Nakane's *Japanese Society* (1970, 1971, 1973) had already appeared in several English editions, the Foreign Ministry decided to produce its own version, *Human Relations in Japan* (1972b), and to distribute thousands of copies to schools and other bodies in Europe and Southeast Asia. Nakane's book, however, is only one of a series. Yakabe's volume (1977), for example, explains the secrets of industrial harmony in Japan. For some time the Japanese Government has also channeled money through the Ministry of Education to make the *nihonjinron* classics available in English. These include works by Nakamura (1960), Nishida (1960), Watsuji (1962) and Hatano (1963)–all published by the Japanese Government. In general, it has also supported the efforts of other unofficial bodies (such as the Japan National Commission for UNESCO) to translate into English many of the *nihonjinron* classics, while deliberately not lending financial or other support to translations of the work of Marxists and others documenting conflict in Japanese society.

Some, such as Cole (1972a) have noted that part of the responsibility for distorting the image overseas of Japan's labor-management relations lies in Japan. A close look at cultural exchange reveals that many of the Japanese organizations working for international understanding are in fact public agencies affiliated with the Government: the International Society of Educational Information; the Japan Foundation and its predecessor, the Kokusai Bunka Shinkōkai; the Japan Culture Institute; the Institute for Developing Economies; the Japan Society for the Promotion of Science; the Science Council of Japan; the Japan International Cooperative Agency and the National Language Research Institute. The responsible ministries keep a watch on the activities of the agencies and are careful to provide guidance when it seems they might deviate from the accepted path. This pastoral care takes several forms, including the perusal of certain publications before they are sent to the printers.

The Japanese Government has in recent years also taken positive measures to create specific images abroad of Japanese society. In the name of cultural understanding, the Japanese Government and related bodies continue to send abroad *nō, kabuki* and *kyōgen* troupes, flower arrangers, tea masters and martial arts instructors who invariably imbue foreigners with the sense of Japan's cultural uniqueness. Amano (1982) reports that the Foreign Ministry spends $400,000 annually to bring foreign correspondents to Japan for short-term visits. Its activities are supported by the Shinbun Kyōkai (Association of Newspapers) which has set up programs to bring 70 persons a year from designated countries, including America, the Soviet Union, Australia, and several in Europe, Southeast Asia and South America. The Foreign Press Center has also been created by the Government (as a semi-official body under the auspices of the Foreign Ministry) to specialize in the dissemination of information on Japan in English and a few other foreign languages. A perusal of its basic information series reveals a heavy input of the *nihonjinron* viewpoint and the absence of opinions stressing conflict as a theme in Japanese society. For the Symposium for Editors in America, Europe and Japan, organized by the Shinbun Kyōkai in October 1982, the Foreign Press Club organized trips for foreign correspondents to see Japan at first hand. The itinerary included the normal show-places: the Nissan Motor plant in Kanagawa, the main office and factory of Matsushita Electric in Osaka, Nippon Steel in Kawasaki and the factory of Fanakku Fuji in Yamanashi. The Japan National Railways and other troublesome locations were predictably not visited.

One piece of evidence consistent with this interpretation is the lack of seriousness with which many of the Japanese foundations promote Japanese studies. More concretely, over the past decade how many of the students invited to Japan by such foundations have become fluent in Japanese? How many QC circles have been established to ensure that they receive high-quality education? How many fellowships are given to scholars with a superficial knowledge and a minimal command of Japanese as opposed to scholars who can do serious research? To what extent are Japanese nationals based abroad (sometimes for 20–30 years) excluded from receiving support from many of these organizations? How seriously are the research activities and other contributions of recipients later followed up? Miller (1982, Chapter 12), for example, argues that the Japanese are not really interested in having foreigners learn the Japanese language.

Although very sophisticated techniques have been devised to improve and to maintain a high standard of quality control in Japan's leading export industries, the organizations concerned with improving the knowledge which foreigners have of Japanese society have not shown much interest in such approaches. One is reminded of Miller's comments (1982, p. 262) on earlier attempts to internationalize, when the Dutch were allowed to trade at Nagasaki but were prohibited from learning the language. Roy Lockheimer recently noted that there are fewer foreign students in Japan today (7,000) than before World War II (12,000) and that the figure is minuscule compared to the numbers presently studying in the United States (350,000) (*MDN*, 20 October 1982, p. 10).

Foreign researchers are also subjected to a constant barrage of opinions which essentially serve to discourage them in their efforts to know Japan. Whymant's caricature (1982a) of the foreigner as the puzzling creature Extra-Nipponica strikes a familiar chord for many non-Japanese trying to do research in Tokyo. He argues that the Japanese build a psychological wall to keep the foreigner forever on the outside of Japanese society. Cole (1971a, pp. 12–13) reports that throughout his study people went to great lengths to impress upon him their uniqueness. The Japanese too have their stereotypes of how the West and the Orient ought to differ and these are constantly used as a mirror for visitors who forget their Western identity. Most foreigners are familiar with the treatment. It comes in many forms and in various degrees. Horvats (1978, pp. 73–4) gives one account of a foreigner's taxi ride upon arriving in Japan:

> Tourists passing through the grey concrete valleys from Tokyo's International Airport to their downtown hotels often complain they feel cheated out of an exotic Oriental experience. Looking out of their taxi windows, these one-time visitors are likely to say, 'Take away the strange neon signs and we could be in Pittsburgh.' But the foreign resident, who can exchange a few words in Japanese with the taxi driver, will discover that the cabbie too feels very much the same way.
>
> 'It was difficult for you to learn Japanese, wasn't it?' the eyes enquire from within the rear-view mirror. 'Japanese is the most difficult language in the world. Isn't it?' The next question is predictable. 'Can you also eat raw fish? And what about *nattō* (the cheese-like, slightly fermented soya bean that people used to have for breakfast before switching to bacon and eggs, toast, and coffee)?'
>
> The variety of the questions will differ depending on the imagination of the taxi driver, but the nature of the answers the man wants are all the same. The cabbie would like to be told that Japan is the most unique place in the world and despite the skyscrapers, the steel elevated highways, the profusion of cars and electronic appliances, there is not another country anywhere in the world that is remotely similar. The foreigner does not have to praise Japan. On the contrary, criticism will often please more because it will show that the foreigner cannot fit into Japan's unique world. For example, if the foreigner in the back seat replies, 'Raw fish? Disgusting! Impossible to eat!' the driver will sigh sympathetically and murmur to himself, '*Yappari*', or '*Naruhodo*' (But of course, after all, one cannot expect . . .). Conversely if the foreigner says that he likes tuna medium fatty but the marbled white *otoro* is too rich for everyday consumption, the driver is likely to be terribly disappointed. 'A know-it-all,' he will mutter to himself.

As Horvats goes on to explain, the above anecdotes are totally unfair to taxi-drivers; if anything, the more educated a Japanese is, the more he feels himself obliged to know the various special characteristics of foreigners, and the more sophisticated his arguments become concerning the uniqueness–real or imagined–of his own nation. One would think, though, that if the Japanese were so convinced of their uniqueness they would not be constantly wanting to hear of yet more ways in which they differ from everyone else.

At the same time, there are those sincerely concerned about these problems. In recent years there have been significant moves toward the opening of Japanese public universities to foreign staff. The Japan Foundation has in its publications encouraged debate on these and other issues. The study of the dissemination of Japanese culture in America by Murakami (1982) is useful, as many of the people working in these bodies are sensitive enough to foreign opinion to respond to suggestions. Finally, the Japan Foundation, for example, has pretty much given foreign institutions a free hand in selecting the books to be purchased with library grants and the Japanese professors who will lecture overseas. At the same time, one can still find foundations donating thousands of dollars of beautiful picture books on flower arranging, packaging and the Japan Alps to an American university, at the request of one of its professors who wanted to teach postgraduate courses on Japanese society and Japanese management techniques.

C The US-Japan Relationship

The symbiotic relationship between the United States and Japan has had a very decided effect on images of Japan. This is in no small measure the product of several related phenomena: the predominance of American scholarship in Japanese studies, the Pacific War and subsequent occupation by the American forces, the continued economic ties between the two countries, the importance of America as Japan's positive reference group, the cold war and the role of American English as the means for disseminating information about Japanese society to the rest of the world. The close connection between images of Japanese held by the Japanese and those held abroad was discussed in Chapter 2. It is noteworthy that the crucial turning points which make period divisions possible correspond loosely with changes in the US-Japan relationship. Not only the image itself but the ideological message associated with it has changed over time, as suggested in Figure 7.1. The message derived from *nihonjinron* depends upon the country in which it is expounded. The message has changed through time, reflecting shifts in the value attached to Japan (e.g., Japan's position in the world at a given time). This can be seen clearly in surveys taken at regular intervals by NHK since the early fifties (NHK: 1975, pp. 208–9). As the economy began to sustain high growth rates, the Olympics were successfully held, and the bullet train service opened between Tokyo and Osaka in the mid-sixties. The percentage of people feeling that the Japanese were superior rose sharply and confidence in America began to decline (NHK: 1975, pp. 208–11). Davis (1982, p. 254) had an even longer time perspective when he commented on this phenomenon:

> During the Meiji period, Japanese intellectuals began to convert to Christianity in their search for the secrets of economic and military strength. When success finally did come to Japan, Christianity, of course, played no role at all. But time, fortune and fancies change and now it is Americans who are seeking after 'strange gods'.

Schweisberg (1982) notes a number of other ways in which 'the "Japanning" of America' is taking place, and Matsuyama (1982) discusses the problem of Japan's being understood within the context of a changing international situation.

In this regard it is as well to note that the learn-from-Japan campaign and the idealization of certain Japanese behavior in America largely reflects a change in the way in which the American problem is defined. As George Kennan observed recently, with regard to the American image of the Soviet Union, it is the constant reiteration of American weaknesses which has made the Soviet Union appear so formidable, not Soviet military might *per se*. It is an image which has been created, he argues, to mobilize Americans and to justify large defense budgets (American Public Broadcasting Network, 7 January 1983).

Today attention is directed at areas where America is weak and Japan is strong. The successful quality control circles sold as uniquely Japanese phenomena are taken from the automobile and electrical goods industries. Why this particular approach and a flood of bestsellers on Japanese management when reference could have been made to America's best-run companies, as suggested by Peters and Waterman (1982)? Even if this were a phenomenon only to be found in Japan, why is it attributed to a uniquely Japanese personality and cultural orientation? Very little is said about the inefficiencies in other Japanese industries. Industrial relations in the Japanese public sector

Figure 7.1 *The message in action-oriented* nihonjinron

		Audience	
		Japanese (the Japanese-language literature)	Westerners (e.g., Americans and Australians) (the English-language literature)
Society and culture to which superiority is attached	One's own	STAY THE SAME Strengthen the uniquely Japanese features (teach the West) (late 1970s) ↑	STAY THE SAME Invite the Japanese over and help them to Westernize their society and to become a 'fortress of Western democracy' (1950s and 1960s) ↓
	The other	CHANGE Modernize Japan and work for economic growth (1950s–1970s)	CHANGE Learn respect for nature and spirituality (1950s and 1960s) Learn Japanese management style (late 1970s)

Note: The arrows indicate the direction of change during the seventies in the percepton as to which society was superior.

(see Kōshiro: 1980) which employs persons from the same Japanese society, are not mentioned.

The safety record of Japan Air Lines, until recently inferior to that of many other international air lines in the industrialized countries according to one careful study (Barnett *et al.*: 1979), tends to be overlooked. Few have looked at the perfect flying record of Australia's national carrier, QANTAS, and suggested a campaign of learning from Australia. When the need arises to mobilize other industries to compete with industrial giants in other countries and the interest in Japan wanes, it is likely that the image of Japanese society will change to coincide with the new ideological line.

Reminded of Glazer's comments about the paradoxical image of the Japanese (as discussed above in Chapter 2), one wonders whether people are somehow more easily mobilized to adopt a particular strategy when it is presented as part of a total package, which includes a global and definitive statement on the mentality of the competitors. To what extent is the paradox produced by the attempt to develop an image of the Japanese which can be used to justify enthusiasm for things Japanese at one point in time and then criticism at other junctures when it is convenient? In any case, the significance attached to Japanese paradoxes and the aspects which are emphasized seem to change rapidly over time, not only as Japanese society itself changes but also as its relations with other societies ebb and flow.

During the fifties and sixties Japanese social science was influenced in several ways by developments in America. One was the importation of American methods, especially empiricism and a faith in behavioral research. Second was the development of the Fulbright program and the allocation of other funds through the State Department to invite labor union leaders and others in industrial relations to the United States.[3] American support in setting up the Japan Productivity Center and the Japanese Government's role in establishing such agencies in Japan served to promote the idea that the institutionalization of industrial conflict was inevitable. These programs tended to isolate Marxists and other anti-establishmentarians from a major arena of academic debate. Finally, there was modernization theory. As Dower (1975a and 1975b) has argued, the ideological content is again difficult to ignore, although the extent to which there was a conspiracy may be debated. Although, there was little agreement on how to define modernization at the Hakone Conference, as the series of conferences progressed, a rather firm conception somehow emerged and the ideological message became more pronounced. By the late sixties even an uninformed observer of Japanese history could detect a certain ideological bias. Moods come and go, but during their life a momentum often develops which can leave lasting images on the minds of several subsequent generations.

However, a more lasting heritage may be the tremendous network of interpersonal relationships which has been fostered. In some ways this has been rather healthy and has allowed each nation to have its own set of trouble-shooters, persons with trusted friends on the other side who can assist in smoothing over small but potentially explosive problems. In academic circles it has meant that certain professors are able to give their graduate students immediate access over there. At the same time, the door is opened to a certain amount of inbreeding and the exclusiveness of a bilateral inner elite. It is not surprising, then, that Japanese OB's arrange the translation and publication of books written by the American professors they studied with or under. Although the flow of publications to America from Japan has not been as great, visiting fellowships and professorships have been arranged for Japanese counterparts to facilitate writing and outlets have been made available for the English versions of their work. It is also interesting to note, for example, that two of the four authors whose works were originally published by the Ministry of Education afterwards had their work published by the East-West Center and University of Hawaii Press (Nakamura; 1964; and Nishida: 1973).

D Orientalism

Quite apart from ideological tendencies, there seem to be deeper images on the back roads of our minds. Said (1979) argues that Westerners have had and continue to have an ethnocentric view of the Orient. The rose-colored lenses through which Japan in particular has been observed over at least the last several centuries are amply described in Wilkinson's study (1981). Pulvers (1979), Minear (1980b) and Lummis (1982) have suggested that the narrow ethnocentric visions of Western industrial society in general and romantic notions of what has been lost to materialism in the process of industrialization interact to create in our minds images of something traditional that we want Japanese society to have been in the past or to be now and in the future.

In another direction modernization theory fashioned its ideal types around self-images born in the West and largely consistent with the way in which the American experience was interpreted by Americans: individualism as represented by the American pioneer, rationalism and specificity as seen in American factories, non-affectivity as observed in the litigation associated with American courts and contracts. It is no wonder, then, that *nihonjinron's* great contribution was to draw attention to this ethnocentrism. However, the realization that Japan did not fit the model was not accompanied by the same scrutiny being applied to whether it fit the Western experience. As a result, Japan was suddenly seen as being out of line. Rather than re-examining the concepts assumed to be corner-stones of Western history, it was easier simply to dismiss Japan as being unique.

IV Japanology as a Self-fulfilling Prophecy

One source of skepticism concerning findings by scholars associated with the two approaches identified in Part One is their close connection with ideologically oriented groups within society. Such associations are frequently assumed to be obvious in the case of Marxist scholars, many of whom have openly affiliated themselves with Marxist or socialistically inspired political parties in Japan. Less attention, however, has been paid to the political and ideological ties of the more conservative mainstream sociologists or others whose work is within the holistic framework. Without discussing the intellectual history relevant to the study of scholarship on Japanese society, two conclusions may be stated. One is that there is a positive relationship between ideology and views of Japanese society. The other is that such a relationship is maintained by a complex network of interpersonal and inter-institutional relationships which in many cases means that research biases are built in, despite high levels of individual integrity.

One type of evidence in this regard is the distribution of views on Japanese society. As shown above in Table 4.2, there is clearly an imbalance between the Japanese-language and the English-language literatures on Japanese society. The holistic approach has tended to dominate the English-language literature. With a few notable exceptions, one could even go so far as to say it holds a monopolistic position. Approaches which emphasize variation or endemic conflict in Japanese society are largely absent from the English-language literature produced in America, where there is no established tradition of socialist political parties. Although the holistic view of Japanese society is not quite so pervasive in Japan, it is none the less clearly in a dominant position. Despite the fact that Marxist and other conflict approaches tend to be ignored by the social science establishment in Japan, they are quite institutionalized in the Japanese intellectual tradition. The strength of the conflict theorists fluctuates over time with the overall level of support obtained by opposition parties of a socialist bent.

From among several possible explanations as to why the consensus-oriented view of Japanese society has prevailed outside Japan, the cold war and its impact on America (where much of the English-language literature was generated) immediately come to mind. As America was the leader of the free world in the war of propaganda with the socialist bloc, it perhaps seemed wise to many Americans that problems arising from class conflict be played down or even overlooked. It is hard to imagine that this intellectual climate in the United States did not affect those who studied Japanese society. From a somewhat different angle, Stockwin has suggested that the holistic image of Japan has also been made to appear authentic by the fact that the LDP has been able to maintain political control in Japan over the past 30 years, a fact which has given the appearance of there being a stability based upon consensus.[4] Finally, changes in the economic relationship between the United States and Japan and shifts in the international political arena seem to have affected both American and Japanese scholarship. However, in both cases the major changes have occurred less in the image of Japanese society and more in the significance attached to the given image.

The preceding sections have raised a number of problems, some common to any comparative research and others more specific to the study of Japan within a comparative framework and to the production of *nihonjinron*. Self-criticism is never fun. When it involves a group of people it is even less fun. The tendency is to be quiet and to hope that the discussion does not come around to oneself. However, the sociology of knowledge can help by highlighting the way in which differences in goals and basic assumptions account for much of the disagreement with regard to the facts. As Chapter 16 concludes, there are many possible, sometimes conflicting, goals which might be served by comparative research and the study of Japanese society. At the same time, an improved understanding of Japan in comparative perspective is such a mammoth task that cooperative and cumulative efforts are required. One of the future tasks of those interested in the study of Japan will be to bring together not only those with different images of Japanese society but also those with different goals. With this problem of ideology in mind, several possible goals are explored in the last two chapters of this book.

While the development of a sociology of knowledge perspective is important, the fruits of such efforts will appear as meta-theories. Such a perspective will not in and of itself produce the theories which explain Japanese society, although the meta-theories will certainly help to improve the first-order theories. More positive steps are necessary to improve our understanding of Japanese society. It would be rash on the basis of the preceding discussion simply to ignore the work of earlier social scientists, however we may question their motives or their methodologies. The authors would argue that a two-pronged strategy is desirable, one involving a careful assessment of the claims made by earlier theorists, in order to retrieve as much useful insight as possible from the two views of Japanese society discussed in Chapters 2 and 3, and the other moving toward the development of alternative models for understanding Japanese society.

As part of the search for new models, the chapters in Part Three present some attempts at lateral thinking by considering what the obverse of the group model might be. In doing so, attention is given to the multi-faceted nature of the concepts we commonly refer to as values. The suggestion is that there may be many dimensions to individualism, and that different societies develop the concept of the individual in different ways, given the symbolism in their own culture and the environmental constraints limiting choices at various historial junctions. Part Four presents a framework for comparative research and tests that framework as an alternative model for understanding Japanese society.

Part Three

The Obverse: Tales of Another Japan

Chapter 8

The Autonomous Individual

I Introduction

Chapter 4 suggested that one strength of the holistic model was the internal consistency with which it linked individuals, interpersonal relations and social phenomena. One test of a model is to examine the viability of its inverse. If after exhaustive brainstorming no alternative interpretation emerges, the original interpretation can be said to stand as the only candidate and to have a certain attractiveness, if only by default.

In the preceding three chapters a number of questions were raised concerning the group model of Japanese society. While methodological concerns and the perspective of the sociology of knowledge provide some initial reasons for being skeptical, the most telling arguments will focus on whether or not observed realities are consistent with the model. The research findings of the authors and others which did not support the model were presented in Chapter 5, and it was also argued in Chapter 6 that the absence of a sampling procedure resulted in the use of examples for which there were counter-examples. The next three chapters present some of these counter-examples. The major task is to construct a comprehensive picture of Japanese society which is significantly different from the group model and which fits together in a logical fashion. The three chapters use the device of *arbitrarily choosing isolated examples and anecdotes* to show that an alternative picture of Japanese society and the Japanese can be drawn. Given the goal of producing alternative models and new frameworks for viewing Japanese society, these chapters may also function to free us from some of the more commonly accepted stereotypes, which often inhibit our ability or willingness to set out in new directions. The sketch of the Japanese which emerges is drawn *using the general methodological guide-lines which seem to be followed by the* nihonjinron *theorists.* The propositions are based on arbitrarily chosen facets of Japanese life to provide some idea of the range of Japanese behavior and values and to show that intuition alone can be used to produce a portrait of Japanese society quite at odds with the group model of the *nihonjinron* theorists.

To summarize Chapter 2, *nihonjinron* presents a vision of Japanese society with propositions about three levels of social existence. With regard to the individual, it is commonly posited that the Japanese ego is underdeveloped and that the Japanese tend to conform to group norms or otherwise lose themselves in group activities, to be emotional and to have a weak sense of self-interest or of privacy. Interpersonal relations are seen as requiring frequent face-to-face encounters, and as being characterized by non-verbal communication and a loose give and take arrangement with the emphasis on giving and repaying. Finally, groups are seen as being bound together by some voluntaristic commitment or loyalty which results in there being very high levels of consensus and intra-group harmony.

The obverse of the holistic model is pursued on these three levels. This chapter considers statements about the individual; the next, some general notions about interpersonal relationships; and the third, suppositions about the internal social dynamics of Japanese society.

Much has been written about the homogeneity of the Japanese. To the foreign executive who has just visited Japan, Japanese businessmen may all look alike: dark suits, black shoes, black hair, short stature, undistinguished ties of the same cut and company pins on the lapel. On a school visit, students are seen wearing the same uniform. Shopping at a large department store, the female assistants are dressed alike, bend up and down in unison and chime together, '*irasshaimase!*' The familiar signals identifying the individual are missing: hair, eye and skin color, accent in the language and clothes. However, were the Japanese to appear as uniform to themselves as they do to foreigners, one would expect to see frequent apologies for having approached the wrong person and for having called a person by the wrong name. The impression of the authors is that Japanese have no more difficulty identifying a date in front of Hachikō at Shibuya or the Wakō Building on the Ginza than would an American at Rockefeller Center in New York City or an Australian at the Opera House in Sydney.

This individualism comes through in a number of ways. A visit to a department store will reveal the extent to which product differentiation occurs in Japan. Tourists planning to do their shopping at the last minute are overwhelmed by the choice they have in cameras, watches or accessories. This is not simply the result of affluence, although that has been a factor. Over 4000 periodicals have been marketed over the past century, an average of 40 major new periodicals per year for a hundred years running (Ōyama: 1979; or the special series during 1982 in *Dakapo* entitled 'Omoide no Zasshi' (Magazines of the Past)). This vast array of magazines and journals reflects very different intellectual tastes, variation in the needs of different age groups and divisions between male and female subcultures. In *How to Wrap Five Eggs*, Oka (1967 and 1975) shows how the individualism of store owners and craftsmen is expressed in their wrapping of packages. At a tea ceremony where formalized etiquette seems to be the rule, the host takes great pains to choose teabowls and to offer sweets which will be different and distinguish his or her ceremony from others. The same will be true of not only the choice of *kimono* but also the way in which it is worn (Shiotsuki: 1972).

Although the Japanese have rather well-defined individual identities, the symbolic behavior which delineates one person from another is very Japanese. Individualism is expressed in other ways. It might be argued that physiological differentiation allows for individuals to be adequately distinguished one from another in a rather passive manner and without any real effort in American or Australian society; conversely, in a society like Japan a concerted effort must be made to distinguish other individuals and to set oneself apart from them.

There are many ways to ride the train. Although the options are crowded out during the rush hours, a ride on any train toward the end of the day on a warm summer evening will reveal two facets of that identity: one is the full expression of one's self and the other is obliviousness to others. Someone opens the window; someone else gets on at the next station and closes it. A slightly overweight young woman wears a red T-shirt embossed with green lettering reading 'slippery when wet'. The music from her radio is contained by headphones, but her body wiggles limply and she smiles blandly.

Next to her is a middle-aged businessman; dressed in a high-quality suit, he wipes sweat from his forehead, studies the daily financial newspaper and then takes out a textbook on Japanese chess. Across the aisle another middle-aged salary man chews gum noisily; picking his nose and flicking his diggings onto the floor, he reads a pornographic magazine. The cover-girl is tied in a contorted posture, but the contents seem to arouse the man's sexual fantasies. Another man stands, despite the fact that there are empty seats; actually he half sways from the hand-belts overhead. In a low but contented voice he sings the refrain to a *karaoke* (melody) he had only half-finished at the last bar. At the far end, four students are dressed for mountain climbing. They talk and laugh loudly, joking about events in class earlier in the week.

Part way down the aisle on the other side rides a young boy and his girl friend. Wearing his all-black leather pants and an embroidered shirt with a safari cut, his key holder hanging conspicuously at his side, he is too young to be called a *chinpira* (a young punk) and is probably a *banchō* (head of a gang) at a junior high school. He may feel out of place, but he doesn't flinch and pretends not to notice that his leather pants don't breathe and are the major reason his shirt is soaking with perspiration. If he were older and more confident, he might ignore the no-smoking sign. His arm is propped up on the aluminium reinforcement pipe and he curls his hair with the end of his index finger. His girl friend, in black slacks but a colorful shirt, rocks her ankles back and forth, her high cork sandals serving as a fulcrum. She sits quietly; her fingers dance up and down his smooth arm. They never talked once during the twenty minutes they rode the train.

At the other end of the carriage a girl is throwing up in a corner. One friend pats her soothingly on the back while another finds a discarded newspaper on the luggage rack and tries to cover up her mess with the Giants' star pitcher and a well-known pro wrestler who share the front page. Across from them a man lies on his back with his feet propped up through one of the cross-bars. His tie is half undone, as is his zipper, but he blissfully sits with closed eyes, cherishing the evening at his favorite bar where the younger fellows in his office had called him *shachō* (company president) and *meiyo kyōju* (distinguished professor emeritus, a title meaning 'great leader'). These expressions of fondness offset the relatively low status accorded his lackluster career and the sad fact that he had to return home by train rather than in an air-conditioned taxi. 'No,' he consoles himself, 'promotion is not the only source of happiness,' although unfortunately his family and many in society at large have still to be convinced of that general truth.

Each passenger possesses a unique personality; it is inconceivable that one would be mistaken for another. Although they are all coping with at least two shared problems, heat and fatigue, each shows a highly individualistic way of coping. It is a peaceful train and no one feels threatened by the others' very different expressions of individualism. The golden rule is *jūnin toiro* (different strokes for different folks). In recent years there has also been the phrase *karasu no katte desho* (literally, 'as the crow pleases') which indicates that one can have one's own reasons for doing things. Just as the crow does not need to explain why or when he caws, so too is it unnecessary for individuals to behave according to a logic that everyone around them can understand. This chapter considers some expressions of individualism in the Japanese context.

II Leaders and Heroes

The Japanese have long had a tradition of individual responsibility and a strong sense of the importance of individual effort and willpower. As the proverbs *seishin ittō nanigotoka narazaran* (where there's a will, there's a way) and *jigō jitoku* (one must pay the consequences of one's misdeeds) suggests, it is *jishukisei* (self-discipline) which steels the individual and makes him great. That certainly is the theme which comes out in the biographies of Japan's great leaders. No two are alike and all tried to be individuals in their own way. This individualism can clearly be seen in the accounts given by Craig and Shively (1970), Morris (1975), Murakami and Harper (1978) and Kinmonth (1981). Although the study by Litton *et al.* (1979) has a pronounced emphasis on cultural factors, reflecting largely the input of Katō Shūichi, each of the persons studied had unmistakable identities. Any number of well-known persons could be chosen and the same message would come across. The Asahi Shinbun's two volumes on intellectual history (1974) also show this facet of personhood in Japan, as does Cooper's sketch of 50 top businessmen in Japan (1976). A survey by Dai-hyaku Seimei (1981) among about 400 housewives in Tokyo's 23 wards revealed that the ideal woman by far was Ichikawa Fusae, a tough-minded woman who never married but fought single-handedly against the establishment. Others in the top ten include a free-lance cartoonist, a leader of citizens' movements, a movie actress, a novelist and a social critic. All are out-going, individualistic women.

In literature for management and career businessmen, considerable attention is given to the idea of *jiko-hatten* (self-development), *jiko-hakken* (self-discovery), *jiko-kaizō* (self-renewal), *jiko-handan* (self-evaluation), and *jiko-kaifuku* (self-recovery). A good number of books are written to give individuals a fuller sense of *jishin* (self-confidence) and an *ikigai* (a clear personal goal in life and a sense of meaning), and to improve their *jigazō* (self-image). Advice abounds on how to overcome *rettōkan* (feelings of inferiority) or to achieve *jiko-jitsugen* (self-realization). Mothers are advised in various ways to develop their children's *seishin kōzō* (psychological state) or *shinri kōzō* (psychological composition). The emphasis in child-rearing is on the production of creative and self-reliant individuals. From childhood Japanese are praised for being *shikkari shita* (courageously strong-willed and stout-hearted) or for having *jitsuryoku* (the individual ability to carry out projects on their own). Those who try to conform or fit in by pleasing everyone (*happō bijin*) are looked down on for being timid and lacking self-confidence. The emphasis on individual initiative can also perhaps be seen in the smaller budgets allocated for social welfare and the tendency to rely on private solutions for old age.

One might argue that this emphasis on the individual is a new phenomenon produced by rapid economic growth and the wholesale exposure to Western influences after the war. To some extent Japan's emergence as a world economic power has fostered a renewed sense of confidence. However, one must also note that the change has been more in the environment which has allowed Japanese to express their individuality more openly, not in the value placed on doing so. Nakamura (1973: pp. 17–18) wrote in the early seventies that students were much more outspoken and articulate in expressing their own views in the prewar period. If the groupism-individualism continuum is a valid concept, it would seem that individualism has been expressed most openly in the immediate prewar period and in the late seventies, not immediately after the war, when American influence and the euphoric interest in Western democracy were at their height.

The renewed emphasis on a vibrant macho brand of individualism can be seen in the leadership boom at the beginning of the eighties. The win-at-all-costs philosophy being adopted in many firms and also being promoted by the leadership campaign developed by the mass media calls for aggressive individuals and the transformation of 'shall-men' into 'will-men', as though the secret of success lay in subtle semantic manipulation. Of course the linguistic approach in some *nihonjinron* would suggest that by their very existence these concepts embody the individualism being sought by so many Japanese males.

This strong emphasis on the individual, albeit on an individual more refined than the rugged pioneer or rough diamond associated with American culture, can also be detected in Japan's popular heroes: Miyamoto Musashi, Ishikawa Goemon, Kogarashi Monjirō, Nemuri Kyōshirō or Zatō Ichi. None were hermits, but each moved about through society on his own. In the comics, consider Fuji Santarō, Asatte Kun, Mappira Kun, Pēsuke, Tetsuwan Atom, Doraemon, Dr Slump or Hoshi Hyūma. Their strong sense of self or of having an internal gyroscope cuts a sharp contrast with Western heroes, who seem to come in teams or in pairs such as the Lone Ranger and Tonto. Roy Rogers and Dale Evans, the Three Musketeers, Abbott and Costello, Sherlock Holmes and Dr Watson, Mickey Mouse and Minnie, Donald Duck and his three nephews, Hansel and Gretel, Popeye and Olive and Robinson Crusoe and Friday. Even when attention is given to an individual, in the Western context it is often in the context of a supporting group, as in the case of Robin Hood and his merry men, Snow White and the Seven Dwarfs, the Hobbit and the dwarfs, or even Santa Claus and all his helpers and the reindeer.

These same themes come across in television drama and the cinema. For the last decade or so historical plays have been very popular: *Kunitori Monogatori* (a story about the era before the Tokugawa period), *Ryōma ga Iku* (the tale of a highly individualistic revolutionary on the eve of the Meiji Restoration) or *Katsu Kaishū* (an account of how the Japanese navy was formed). In each case the hero is a strong individual who stands by himself. The same could be said of the heroes in the novels of Matsumoto Seichō, the leading author of detective stories in postwar Japan. Invariably the plot involves an individual who is dissatisfied with the organization or group with which he is affiliated and seeks to put down those who control the organization and hide behind their authority and status. These contrast greatly with the situation comedies popular in the US (*Taxi, WKRP in Cincinnati, Lou Grant, MASH,* or *Barney Miller*) and the everyday life dramas on Australian television (*Prisoner, Cop Shop, Number Ninety-six,* the *Sullivans,* or *Skyways*). In looking back on the seventies, Murray Slaughter (*Time*, 24 May 1982, p. 72) commented as follows on American television dramas:

> What these shows told you was that being on top of the career heap wasn't as important as being with people you liked, who kept you amused and alive through the long day–and, if you needed them, through a longer night.

The strong sense of an individual surviving on his or her own (sometimes referred to in Japanese as *seishin*) can also be seen in the behavior of adventurer Uemura Naomi who, by himself, has made a solo trip to the North Pole, lived by himself in the world's northernmost village in Greenland and, again alone, has ridden a raft 6,000 kilometers down the Amazon. He died alone on another trek in North Canada. Moreover, he is not simply an odd-ball. His exploits are read with enthusiasm in Japan and he is famous as one kind of hero (e.g., see his bestseller, Uemura: 1980). So too is Egawa Taku, the baseball star of the Yomiuri Giants who refused to go along with the system that drafted him to another team. Although he was initially criticized for being impertinent and foolish enough to challenge a national institution, his superior *jitsuryoku* (ability as recorded in wins and losses) in the face of criticism and the psychological pressures that entailed earned him the respect and love of many Japanese. The verb *egawaru* was coined to express this person's type of individuality. Finally, this same *seishin* can also be seen as a major driving force in the lives of Yokoi Shōchi and Onoda Hiroo, the Japanese soldiers who held out on their own on the long-forgotten battlefields of the Pacific for over twenty years (Onoda: 1974; Asahi Sinbunsha: 1972).

This emphasis on individualism can also be seen in the large number of biographies and autobiographies found in bookstores throughout Japan. Children are encouraged to keep diaries as a permanent record of their existence. Publishers make available to children, in easily read Japanese, the biographies of famous persons (including many foreign figures). Many of these are available in series which number from 50 to 100 volumes. The biographies exploit the theme of the rugged individual: success by perseverance in hardship, by tenacity and firm commitment to a personal goal and by determined hard work. In this regard it is interesting to note that the most common posters in the rooms of Japanese teenagers are portraits of individuals. Groups and scenery are much less frequently shown.

This concern with biography often becomes an obsession with autobiography as individuals age. In no other country is there such a penchant for the individual to publish his own book or periodical. The publish or perish syndrome in some university systems abroad is limited to that sector and as a social phenomenon often reflects conformity rather than individualism. In Japan it is seldom necessary for university staff to publish for tenure yet many do. There is also a sizable number engaged in unaffiliated intellectual activity: social critics (*hyōronka*), commentators (*kaisetsusha*), free-lance journalists (*furī ransu*) and persons who simply establish their own research institute and serve as its head (*shochō*). The vitality and sense of personal statement is also evident in Japanese cinema. It would be difficult to find a more individualistic lot of film directors than in Japan (cf. Satō: 1982). In many other societies it would be difficult to find a novelist as popular as Mishima who was so introverted yet so militantly insistent upon communicating his own personal message and exploring in public his own sensual and psychological world. In Japan, however, this tradition of the personal exposé has a long history in *shishōsetsu* (the private novel) which focuses on events and happenings in the everyday life of the novelist.

Every year thousands of *dōjinzasshi* (private magazines) are published for private circulation and self-edification. There is also the practice of publishing *chosakushū* or *zenshū* (the collected works of an author), *kanreki shuppan* (volumes for professors on their sixtieth birthdays) and *koki shuppan* (volumes for professors on their seventy-seventh birthdays). To be sure, in the West one can find series of collected works and *Festschriften.* The difference, however, is one of degree and intent. In the West, collected works are usually compiled in the literary field as a convenience for readers, normally after the author has died, and only a few professors are honored with a *Festschrift.* In Japan, *chosakushū* and *zenshū* are often published for someone still living to symbolize his current stature in the field. They serve as a tribute to the man as an individual *Festschriften* in the form of *kanreki ronbunshū* and *koki ronbunshū* are a much more common occurrence and usually end with a complete listing of everything the person has ever published, often including one-page greetings from in-house publications and similar newsletters. Similar arrangements are occasionally made yet again for those who are fortunate enough to be alive and still active at the age of 88 (*beiju*).

One source of Japanese individualism can be found in religious tradition. Given the syncretic nature of Japanese religious practices and a tradition of many gods, each individual is able to choose a unique combination of gods and practices to suit his or her own individualistic needs. In many homes there is an altar where one can pray and confront God or Buddha on a one-to-one basis. The Western custom of collective worship in church or even of saying grace together as a family while everyone folds hands is quite alien to the Japanese. In Western societies the individual is seen as being weak in the sight of God and this weakness is symbolized in the notion of sin and in submission to someone else's authority rather than reliance on one's own intellect. This view of personhood is succinctly stated in the refrain of one common hymn which children learn in Sunday school: 'We are weak but He is strong; this I know because the Bible tells me so.'

From childhood Westerners are taught to depend upon an intermediary to intercede on their behalf, and the mediating role of the clergy is more established in Western society. This can be seen in the Catholic tradition, with its emphasis on confessionals and the intercession of the priest. It can also be seen in the popularity of the more fundamentalist sects in America, which provide for large rallies so that the individual does not have to face God alone. Billy Graham's rallies and the group atmosphere created by the Humboldt Singers on television have no counterparts in Japan. In America, the sense of group hysteria generated by this activity can sometimes be so great that whole congregations will migrate *en masse* or even commit group suicide, as was seen in the Jonestown tragedy.

On a more philosophical level, the notions of *wabi* and *sabi* emphasize the importance of personal or even solitary contemplation. In Buddhist temples, individuals sit next to each other for hours without saying a word. In the *Zen* tradition, inspiration comes from a quiet stroll in the gardens of a monastery or in quietly contemplating the sound of a frog jumping into an old pond. In the West there is much more emphasis on the notion of fellowship and the Greek idea of *agape*.

III Gravitation toward Individual Activity

One result of rapid economic growth and the attainment of higher standards of living has been an increase in leisure time. In this regard, it is instructive to look at the activities Japanese choose when they do have free time. One characteristic stands out: the extent to which individuals engage in activities by themselves.

Some of these features are shown in Table 8.1. The figures are from a survey of 76,000 households covering 258,000 persons, which was conducted by the Prime Minister's Office in 1976. The amount of time spent watching television, listening to the radio, reading the newspaper or simply relaxing is noticeable. These are activities people do primarily by themselves. Although the uses of time do not vary greatly according to sex, the somewhat derogatory phrase *sanshoku-hirune-terebitsuki* (three meals, a noon-time nap and television) captures the housewife's day at home alone, not in association with other women. In the case of both males and females, free time is devoted primarily to the pursuit of personal interests (hobbies) rather than sports. Hobbies are done largely at home. A camera buff buys his own equipment and takes his own pictures; the idea of joining a photography club does not occur to most Japanese.

This preference for playing alone can also be seen in other Japanese pastimes: calligraphy, taking care of one's car, pottering around home, cooking, fishing, photography, watching television, listening to music, sewing and embroidery, gardening, hitting golf balls or tennis balls in a cage by oneself or practising Japanese chess or *go* by oneself. By contrast, in the West a good deal of one's free time is spent doing things with others in cub scouts, boy scouts, girl guides, De Moleys' fraternities, junior chambers of commerce, Lions, Kiwanis, Rotary, Masonic orders, bowling leagues, various church groups and church-organized sports teams, and all kinds of voluntary groups and charity work. It is not surprising, then, that *pachinko* and electronic games such as space invaders, which pit one individual against a machine or an array of aliens, are popular pastimes in Japan. One might mention *mahjong*, but here too the players are individuals and the idea of playing with partners as in bridge has never really caught on.

Given the considerable amount of time spent viewing, listening or reading, it is interesting to consider briefly the kinds of music and sport which are popular enough in Japan for professionals to be able to make a living at them. In music, aside from the Dark Ducks and perhaps Los Indos, there are no Japanese groups which have consistently recorded popular songs over a long period of time. Although the West has its single performers such as Frank Sinatra, Elvis Presley, Cliff Richard or Edith Piaf, the popular music scene has also had a large number of groups: the Platters, Bill Haley and the Comets, the Beatles, the Rolling Stones, Jefferson Airplane, the Bee Gees, Manhattan Transfer, the Kingston Trio, the Kinks, Fleetwood

Table 8.1: *The uses of leisure time: 1976*

A Time used in various activities (unit: hours)

Activity	Average time spent in activity	
	Males	Females
study	.11	.08
hobbies	.35	.25
sports	.12	.05
service	.05	.04
socializing	.29	.27
travel	.18	.14
radio/television newspapers/magazines	2.26	2.22
relaxing	.56	.58
visiting a doctor	.12	.13
other	.17	.19
unaccounted	1.20	1.19
TOTAL	5.41	5.14

B Some aspects of hobbies (unit: percentages)

		Males	Females
Type of activity	1 viewing, sightseeing	22.7	22.4
	2 creative activities:	33.7	65.2
	tea, flower arranging, Japanese dancing	.5	13.4
	3 non-creative activity (*pachinko*)	43.6	12.4
	4 competitive activities	39.0	5.8
	5 other	4.7	6.6
Type of persons involved	1 other family members	14.8	19.5
	2 persons from work	11.2	3.4
	3 school chums	2.3	3.4
	4 neighbors	1.6	3.9
	5 other friends/acquaintances	14.5	15.4
	6 others	1.2	3.7
	7 no others involved–activity done by oneself	53.6	50.1

Table 8.1 *Continued*

		Males	Females
Place of activity	1 home	42.3	59.4
	2 company facilities	6.5	2.6
	3 school facilities	2.0	4.0
	4 public facilities	4.5	5.3
	5 private facilities	12.5	11.5
	6 other	30.4	15.3
Affiliation	1 done as part of a group	6.1	12.1
	2 done without any group affiliation	92.8	81.3

C Some aspects of sport

		Males	Females
Type of sport	1 individual sports	6.6	8.0
	2 team ball sports	32.1	25.0
	3 one-to-one competitive ball sports	8.2	14.0
	4 other competitive sports	4.5	1.0
	5 outdoor sports	34.2	21.0
	6 other sports activity	14.4	31.0
Type of persons involved	1 other family members	10.8	23.3
	2 persons from work	29.4	11.4
	3 school chums	16.1	22.2
	4 neighbors	5.6	8.0
	5 other friends/acquaintances	22.6	15.8
	6 others	2.3	2.3
	7 no others involved–activity done by oneself	12.2	16.0
Place of activity	1 home	13.2	29.4
	2 company facilities	14.6	8.5
	3 school facilities	21.4	27.1
	4 public facilities	7.6	5.8
	5 private facilities	16.5	6.7
	6 other	24.4	20.4
Affiliation	1 done as part of a group	24.9	17.1
	2 done without any group affiliation	73.9	81.3

Source: Sōrifu (1981a), p. 308.

Mac, the Village People, the Osmonds, and Peter, Paul and Mary. In Japan there is nothing which comes close to the choruses, gospel groups or barber-shop quartets which so openly exude their own rapport and the fun they are having by simply being together. In the area of classical music, the Japanese have tended to prefer instruments played largely by themselves (such as the *shakuhachi*, the *shamisen* or the *koto*) or instruments which, at least to the Western ear, sound so discordant (as in *gagaku*). Traditional songs in the genre of *nagauta, enka*, and *minyō* are typically sung by a single individual. There is no tradition of large groups like the Western orchestra. In dancing, the traditional *buyō* has tended to focus attention on individual performances, whereas ballet has tended to blend individual performances with the dancing of a large number of others.

Social gatherings are also revealing. Japanese bookshops have a large number of books on how individuals can make formal individual speeches at parties; in the West the books are more about how to tell jokes or start games which will break the ice and get everyone laughing and interacting together. One of the most difficult situations for the average American or Australian to handle in Japan is a *bōnenkai* (year-end party), *sōbetsukai* (farewell party) or similar gathering where they may be called on to sing or perform by themselves in front of everyone else. While their uninhibited Japanese friends have no problem getting up in front of others and singing or dancing, many foreigners somehow feel very uncomfortable and look for some reason to beg off. For many Westerners there is an immediate sense of being exposed and of losing face in front of the group. For many it is their first exposure to uninhibited and explicit individualism, and they come away with a new respect for the Japanese as individuals and an envy for their openness. Perhaps for this reason, the tradition of having professional toast-masters is more established in the West.

Sport is another area in Japan where strong individualism is readily evident. Japan's traditional sports are those which pit one person against another in a manner which produces a clear winner: *sumō, jūdō, kendō, kyūdō, go* and *shōgi*. Even among the most recently imported sports, the most popular are golf, tennis, gymnastics, skiing and pro wrestling. These have not, on the whole, been the most popular spectator sports in the West, although there are exceptions among some countries. Rather, the most popular sports in the West have been team-oriented: soccer, rugby football, basketball, baseball, hockey and cricket. The only one among these which is popular as a professional sport in Japan is baseball, the team sport requiring least interpersonal interaction. On completion of a baseball game, Japanese broadcasters like to single out a hero for each game and to have a special interview with him on the field; the American approach is to move to the dressing-room where the team atmosphere is preserved and several persons can be interviewed.

IV Privacy and Private Property as Key Values

In discussing the concept of the individual in Japan, some have argued that the Japanese word for privacy, *puraibashī*, was borrowed from English to express the concept of there being a private self. However, two doubts immediately come to mind. First is the presence in Japanese of a good number of other words to express the feeling of privacy: *nawabari* (one's own territory), *mongai fushutsu* (not to be taken outside the house), *minomawarihin* (one's personal effects), *jinushi* (landowner), *chosakuken* (copyright), *shiyūken* (the right of private ownership), *shiseikatsu* (one's private life), *shidan* (a private conversation), or *shiji* (a personal affair). One can also go back a thousand years and find many terms to indicate boundaries and units of land associated with ownership (Senda: 1980). Moreover, careful records were kept of the ownership of land (Kanda: 1978). While land was often registered in the name of the family, the family system made succession very clear. Accordingly, the individual's rights (or absence of rights) to control or command property were explicitly defined and known to members of the family and to the broader community. The construction of walls and gates and the notion of trespassing (*shinnyū* or *shingai*) can also be traced back through time. For those with status, a private garden was often a place to contemplate without being disturbed. The phrase *urusai* is often commonly used to delineate the individual's sense of private space and to warn others when they are invading that territory. To respect this privacy, the practice of knocking or making a noise before entering or even approaching an individual's room, is well ingrained in Japanese culture.

A second reason for being skeptical of the etymological approach (which tends to associate a specific orientation with individuals using a particular word or phrase, identifying the value by examining the intent with which the expression was originally used) is the speed with which certain foreign words are adopted. [1] To be sure, in the process of borrowing a word, the meaning assigned to the word in Japanese is often different from that expressed in the original language. Nevertheless, while the nuance of the word changes and the forms which privacy takes are different, borrowed words are often used simply to introduce more variety to the vocabulary and to add delicate nuances quite apart from the concept of privacy or private ownership. A word like *mai* (my) is seen as a convenient prefix for other English derivatives: *maikā* (my car), *maihōmu* (my home), *maipēsu* (my pace), *maiuei* (my way), *maidārin* (my darling), *maibēbi* (my baby), *maibōto* (my boat) and *maipurēn* (my plane).

The concern with privacy begins at home. For example, it can be seen in the practice of having a *genkan* where people must wait while someone inside decides whether or not they can come in. This contrasts with the West where even strangers are often immediately invited into the home. When guests do visit, there is the practice of using *oshiire* (large closets with sliding doors). One's private things are usually put away in the *oshiire* before guests come. The home is a private world, and one's bedroom an inner sanctum. This contrasts with the West, where it is not uncommon to have friends come into one's room and even sit on one's bed. There is also a great emphasis on children having private rooms. Rather than studying at the kitchen table, the ideal is that each child should have his or her own desk. Although there are many children who do not have their own rooms, this is because their family cannot afford such luxuries, not because a lesser value is placed on attaining that goal.

The tendency to have private property in the home is also conspicuous. Whereas families in Western societies, such as those in the United States and Australia, tend to use cutlery and crockery interchangeably, it is the practice in most Japanese families for each person to have his or her own teacup, rice bowl and chopsticks.

Practices learnt at home often affect behavior later in life. In general, university students are reluctant to room with other students in flats or other accommodation which requires any degree of communal living. In the early seventies, the self-defense forces had great trouble retaining graduates from their high school. In surveying the graduates to see why they left after having received a free education, they found that the largest number had left because they didn't like the living arrangements. In short, they felt that life in barracks did not afford them the privacy they needed. Japanese exchange students staying in private houses often find it difficult to adjust to lots of traffic in the bathroom. Such group activity is alien to most Japanese.

Many Japanese also find it difficult to adjust to Western toilets which require them to place a private part of their body where someone else has. One Japanese exchange student confessed that she made a practice of waiting 15–20 minutes for the seat to cool off, as if whatever there was to catch would not be incubated at lower temperatures. In many high schools and universities in the United States athletic facilities are provided so that there is a common hamper full of jock straps, socks and towels, which the athletes use interchangeably. This is unthinkable to most Japanese; indeed, they would feel anxious about simply mixing the clothes together in the wash, let alone wearing undergarments previously worn by somebody else. The Japanese idea of privacy in some of these areas can be traced back to much older traditions, and the concern with oneself becoming contaminated can today be seen in a number of facets of Japanese life (Befu: 1971a, pp. 104–08).

Related to the discussion of privacy is the practice in public bathing areas of covering or protecting one's private parts from view. Even after a team victory, the Japanese bath is a private affair. Athletes often sit in a row facing the wall, each with his back to the group. In other countries where showers are used, one's back is to the wall and showering is often associated with singing, playing around and snapping towels at each other. The sense of camaraderie and open interaction is in marked contrast to the seriousness and privacy of Japanese dressing-rooms. In this regard, it is interesting to note that the number using *sentō* (public bath-houses) declines each year as more individuals can afford their own private baths. Not unrelated to these practices is the provision of leisure facilities. Here too, marked cultural differences exist. Tennis courts, golf courses, pools and other facilities are largely privately owned in Japan; one can gain access to them only by having a private account with the firm running them. This gives individuals considerable control over whom they will mix with and limits the number able to infringe their territory. By contrast, in America facilities like this are often publicly owned and open for everyone and anyone to share and to enjoy. Finally, the preference of the Japanese for private education should be noted. In 1980, for example, a large percentage of school students attended private as opposed to public institutions. Each private school will have its own motto and individual character. There is a feeling among parents that at a private school their child will receive more individual attention, will have more opportunity to develop his or her own personality (*kojinsei*), and will be more refined (e.g., not exposed to mass culture, a theme related to the idea of private cleanliness). Among 446 universities in Japan in 1980, 319 were private institutions, a situation which contrasts with that found in Australia and many other Western countries, where all the universities are public.

Another example of the concern for the individual's privacy is the general resistance to Government involvement in the lives of private citizens. In 1982 there was a great outcry against the proposed introduction of the 'green card system' which was to be somewhat similar to the United States system of giving everyone a social security number for identification purposes. It was seen by too many people as an invasion of the privacy of their financial affairs.

V Personhood and the Japanese Language

One approach to the study of how personhood is conceptualized in a given society is to consider how members of that society refer to themselves. There are many ways to look at the expression of individualism in the language.

One is to look at the number of pronouns used to describe the self. In English there is only one word ('I'), whereas in Japanese the ability of the individual to express his personality and to differentiate himself from others is enhanced considerably by the wide range of words available for reference to the self (*watashi, watakushi, boku, ore, washi, jibun, uchi, shōsei* and *atai*). If we consider the great amount of regional variation in Japan and the vocabulary found in the various dialects (*hōgen*), the contrast between Japanese and English is even greater.

This ability of the Japanese to give specific definition to themselves can also be seen in the vocabulary for defining others. Whereas English is limited to 'you' (and perhaps the outdated 'thou'), Japanese offers a wide range of second person pronouns (such as *anata, kimi, omae, temae, kisama* and *otaku*) with further choices again being added by the dialects. In referring to a third person, again the subtlety with which persons can be distinguished in Japanese is unmatched in English.

With regard to vocabulary, it is interesting to note the extent to which *kanji* (Chinese characters) for expressing the self are used. As shown in Table 8.2, a large number of *jukugo* (compound words with two or more *kanji*) are formed from characters indicating the individual or the private as opposed to the number of characters referring to groups of people or the public. A consideration of the frequency with which these are used and the positive and negative nuances attached to the various compounds in mass culture, for example, will underline the amount of attention given to the individual in Japanese society.

Table 8.2 *A comparison of the number of compound words made with characters for the individual and for groups*

Chinese characters representing the individual			Chinese characters representing the group		
Character	Reading	Number of derivatives (*jukugo*)	Character	Reading	Number of derivatives (*jukugo*)
私	Watakushi SHI	102	組	Kumi SO	9
自	Onozukara Mizukara JI	70	群	Mure GUN	23
独	Hitori DOKU	43	団	DAN	22
長	Nagai CHŌ	123	隊	TAI	20
民	Tami MIN	54	公	Ōyake KŌ	111

Source: Compiled from Nagasawa (1982).

Another example might be the richness of the Japanese vocabulary (euphemistic and otherwise) for describing an individual's sexual behavior (*Dakanno*, 20 January 1982, pp. 98–9). Many examples can be produced to show ways in which a rich vocabulary has developed in Japanese to allow a distinction among individuals by reference to the complex collage of characteristics which go together to form the overall *Gestalt* or image which is associated with a specific individual's behavior and overall performance in this area.

VI Conclusions

The preceding discussion has focused on ways in which individualism is expressed in Japanese. The image of personhood presented here contrasts sharply with common notions of the Japanese as a people without fully developed egos or a well defined sense of self-interest. The discussion suggests, however, that the Japanese have rather developed, though different, concepts of privacy and the self. It argues that a close look at Japanese society will reveal healthy expressions of self-interest, nonconformity and the differentiation of one individual from another. The argument is not that the Japanese are more individualistic than Westerners on a quantifiable scale, but that Japanese have developed in their own culture a number of ways, some qualitatively different, by which they can express their individualism. Ideas about nudity and sexuality are a good example of how difficult it is to draw simple conclusions about the Japanese possessing more or less of a particular quality when cross-cultural comparisons are actually made. In some contexts Japanese are very open and liberal while Americans and Australians seem prudish; in other areas the Japanese seem more reserved. While Japanese may have a fetish for one type of cleanliness, Americans see the problem of pollution as involving different matters. There is a need, as Lee (1966) argues, to see the multifarious orientations of people in their own culture. More attention must also be paid to the fact that even in a single society there may be many different kinds of hero and that the array of heroes may change over time (cf. Gerzon: 1982). Simply concluding that one people is more liberated, more hygienic or more individualistic than another, using only one standard, is misleading. In many cases, such judgements simply reflect the application of very ethnocentric or otherwise narrowly defined standards. Cross-cultural research is more complex and involves more subtle translation between the *emic* and *etic* levels of analysis. The task at hand, however, is to explore further the ramifications of Japanese individualism in interpersonal relationships and social organization.

Chapter 9

The Contractual Relationship

I Introduction

The formation of the individual's personality and system of values is in many ways shaped by the social environment, and the concept of the individual outlined above has rather profound consequences for the way in which interpersonal relationships develop in the Japanese context. The major unit of analysis in examining such relationships is the dyad. Groups and organizations represent complex networks of criss-crossing and complementary relationships. Before dealing with these more complex phenomena, however, it may be useful to sketch in the consequences of strong individualism and the cultivated sense of drive and purpose (*seishin*) for the individual's interpersonal relationships with other Japanese. In this regard, two major themes stand out. One is the emphasis on written forms of communication. The other is the pervasiveness of contractual ties. The net result is that the Japanese have difficulty in forming groups spontaneously.

A look at the collected wisdom found in the proverbs associated with mass culture helps us to see how the ideas outlined above have been institutionalized. While *kaji to kenka wa edo no hana* (fires and arguments: the joy of the true Tokyoite) emphasizes the preference of Japanese for open argument, a contrast is the wisdom found in the English phrases 'don't rock the boat' or 'don't make waves', which counsel getting on with others and warn that individuals who express contrary views endanger not only themselves but those around them as well. The Biblical story of the Good Samaritan stands in sharp contrast to the advice given in the Japanese proverb *sawaranu kami ni tatarinashi* (don't bother those who have no relationship to oneself). Overall, involvement with others is discouraged by any number of proverbs: *hito no inochi wa isha no terai* (beware of doctors; they'll use your life for their experiments), *hito no kawa o kaburu* (watch out for a wolf in lamb's skin), *kyōdai wa tanin no hajimari* (strangers start with one's siblings), *hito o tanomu wa mizukara tonomu ni shikazu* (don't ask others to do what you can do yourself), or *hito o mitara dorobō to omoe* (if you meet another person, treat him like a thief; he that trusts the world is sure to be deceived). This fundamental lack of trust is also seen in the frequent requirement in Japan that one have a *hoshōnin* (guarantor or patron) or *baishakunin* (a go-between) who is known to both parties meeting for the first time. One Japanese traveller to the United States was surprised to find a handout at Greyhound Bus depots which was entitled 'Don't Rely on Strangers: Tips for Teenage Travellers'. For a Japanese this seemed to be common sense, and the visitor could not understand why in a sophisticated society like America it was necessary to educate grown teenagers about something so basic. In Japan children are much more likely to be socialized to look after themselves.

There is also an emphasis on using others, as expressed in the following sayings: *hito no nasake wa yo ni deru toki* (don't bother with those who are over the hill), *hito no fundoshi de sumō o toru* (use other people's things for your own good), *hinsen tomo sukunashi* (the poor have few friends), *baka shōjiki* (it's shortsighted to tell others too much), or *na o sutete jitsu o toru* (don't be fooled by the applause of others; go for your own profits instead). Finally there is counsel to ignore those around oneself if they are of no consequence for one's self. In contrast to the English maxim, 'When in Rome do as the Romans do', which counsels the individual to fit into other groups, the Japanese say *tabi no haji wa kakisute* (people can do as they damn well please when away from home).

Japanese tourists travelling abroad are often singled out for moving about *en masse*, blindly following a leader with a flag on a pole and madly taking photographs of themselves as a group in front of every historical monument along the way. Although the presence of the Japanese group is made more conspicuous by the flag-waving, the commanding voice of the leader, the clicking of cameras and the sometimes aggressive shoving as members struggle to keep up, the behavior is often interpreted by the foreign observer as an example of the tightly knit Japanese group. On closer inspection, however, it is often all the tour guide can do to get his or her group through the course on schedule, and he or she is grateful for all the artificial gimmicks – including badges, hats and flags – which will somehow hold the group together until the tour is finished.

This aspect of Japanese group activity can be seen by observation of a tourist group which recently passed through the international airport at Hong Kong on their return from a seven-day trip to China. As they approached the seat allocation lounge, a young Japanese woman of about 30 was at the head of the group. She suddenly turned around and addressed twenty others through a mini-loudspeaker:

> The plane is scheduled to leave in one hour; the attendants will begin to issue seat placements in about half an hour. Please have your tickets in the green folders ready at that time. Don't forget to tell them whether you want smoking or non-smoking. Also don't be careless and lay your hand luggage somewhere you're likely to leave it. I'm sorry that the authorities here at Hong Kong were so very strict on the size of your carry-on baggage and that the extra charges were not covered in your contract. And please let me remind you further that ...

Her voice went on but it was obvious that few were listening.

The group was an odd assortment. Some of the men wore unusual hats, including a beret: some were without hats. Some had ties, others did not. One wore a dark suit in the sweltering weather, another was more coolly dressed in a colorful short-sleeved shirt. The purple shoes of one of the older gentleman looked as though they would shine in the dark. The women were in slacks, skirts and dresses. Each had his or her own tote: a shopping bag with various strange works in English, a leather shoulder-bag, a wicker basket, a duffle bag. Each had a green 'Tours to Heaven' badge stuck in or on a different place: one squarely in the middle of his baseball cap, another tucked in the band around her sun-visor, a third on the breast-pocket, a fourth just above the hem of her dress and several others on various parts of their luggage.

Efforts to get a group picture proceeded slowly. A German bystander was summoned to take the picture and was immediately flooded with cameras and a flurry of instructions. Just when he seemed ready to snap the first picture, yet another individual would break ranks and bring him another camera or simply utter an additional instruction about one of the settings he'd forgotten. Five times the leader used her speaker in the restricted area to urge her charges to get in the group picture. But just as one returned with some American cigarettes and French perfume, another decided to go off and take a picture of the plane standing on the other side of the window about 15 meters away. She then returned to the fold just as another wanted to go to the toilet. The first five automatic cameras were clicked in rapid succession with two or three missing; just when it seemed that they were all together and the lens focused, the camera's owner came out and muttered something the German could not comprehend. They discussed the matter. Those whose cameras had been clicked slowly came forward, picked up their cameras and drifted away as the group began to disseminate. Those whose film had not been exposed came up sheepishly to retrieve their cameras with a look of resignation.

It was just as well as another group was coming down the hall. The men all had short-sleeved shirts, open with no ties. Although each had his own tropical design, they were all wearing the same kind of brightly colored shirts which blurred together to form a collage and give the group an instant identity. None wore hats, but all had blue and white Pan Am shoulder-bags. They were a much more distinct group, clearly Americans. Whereas the Japanese tended to look at things or to talk quietly in twos, the Americans interacted all the way around, hugging each other and already making plans for a reunion at the end of the year. When the time came to board, the leader of the first group announced to the Japanese that it was time to go, reminded them to show their tickets clearly and then gently nudged her charges along with her open arms if they stalled. She watched until the last was out of sight. The Americans had no announcements; in fact, they had no leader. They just stood up together and moved slowly to the chute with their tickets clearly displayed.

Inside the plane, the American males helped not only the women but themselves as well. Each Japanese took care of his or her own hand luggage, except for the oldest woman who received some help from the young girl seated next to her. Somehow the Americans were all seated together in the middle of the non-smoking area, a bit rowdy, perhaps, as all seemed to be talking at once. Everyone's shopping and photographs were shared with the others. Members of the group were constantly moving about and changing seats so that the same story was sometimes retold two or three times to different audiences of four or five. Those who had heard the story before were kind enough not to interrupt. Although they had only met two weeks before at the San Francisco international airport, they had developed an *esprit de corps.* As the plane taxied to the runway, some took out cards for games which could be played in twos, threes or fours. The Japanese sat here and there, some in smoking and some in non-smoking, but each preoccupied with personal thoughts; as the plane began to move some were reading Japanese newspapers or weekly magazines while others sat with their eyes closed, waiting patiently for music to flow through the earphones they had already put on. One clipped his nails, something he had been unable to do while in China. As they landed on the runway at Narita, the Americans all of a sudden applauded in unison, as though they had received a secret signal. Although somewhat surprised by this spontaneous outburst, most of the Japanese continued checking through their personal luggage to make extra sure that they had not forgotten any valuables and to see that everything was in order for disembarking.

The contrast in the patterns of American interaction and Japanese lack of interaction is striking. Although the Japanese may have formed the more conspicuous group at the airport, it was largely because of the assertive role taken by the tourist guide and the slight disruption caused in trying to get everyone together for the photographs. The Americans had bidden their guide farewell when they got off the bus; yet, as though by tacit understanding or some form of telepathy, they all moved together. Although they moved at a slower pace, they were constantly interacting and openly enjoying the sense of belonging to their group. For the Japanese, the old saying seemed still to hold true: *hito aru naka ni hito nashi* (a group is not company).

This does not mean that the Japanese do not form groups. They obviously do, but in different situations and in a less spontaneous fashion. When they do form a group, however, the value placed on affiliation in Japan is much more likely to be instrumental and the roles tend to be more clearly defined. In the snapshot just presented, most of those pictured had travelled in the group simply to obtain a cheaper fare, not for the joy of being with other people and interacting in a group. This chapter discusses some of the ways in which a firmer contractual basis for interpersonal relationships can be seen in the Japanese context.

II The Written Word

In some descriptions of the Japanese, emphasis has been placed on the ambiguous nature of the Japanese language and the ability of Japanese to communicate through *haragei* (psychological empathy) or *ishin denshin* (a form of unspoken communication). However, such descriptions tend to overlook another Japanese form of communication: the explicit and unequivocal written word. When a new idea is put to one's boss in Japan, the most common response is *bunsho de teishutsu shite kudasai* (Put it down in writing!). In fact, a core element in Japan's decision-making apparatus has been the *ringisho* (a written memorandum, not simply to communicate information, but to make it clear that all involved in the decision have indicated with their personal seal their own approval). Given that self-interest is so clearly defined in the Japanese situation, this semi-legal arrangement seems to be necessary to make it clear beyond doubt who participated in the decision and with what information or ideas.

In many other societies the sorting out of interests (known as *nemawashi* in Japanese) is usually done orally and without careful written records. It is often done on the phone, in the corridors, in the shower room, over a beer at one's club or at a pub. If a signature is required, several illegible initials are scribbled on the paper with an air as if to say that all the formality is really not necessary at all and that it goes against the grain of the person involved. In Japan, an informal, illegible signature which can be forged is not good enough. Each employee is required to use an official seal to formalize the document.

The preference for a written record can also be seen in the most conspicuous behavior of Japanese travelling: taking pictures. Their photographs of an overseas trip surprise the foreigner in two ways. One is the large number of photographs taken; two or three of the same subject are often taken with different settings to make sure that there will be a record. The second is the emphasis on photographing oneself. A look at the albums of many Japanese reveals a low level of concern with the historical monuments themselves. The captions not infrequently read 'me at the Acropolis', 'me at the Eiffel Tower', 'me in Spain', 'me on the *Mayflower*'. There is a personal satisfaction in seeing oneself at all these places, and it is as though that feeling will be enshrined by making a proper documentary record. It would seem psychologically that the photographs provide a sense of security in a way that an oral account could not; they are undeniable proof that one has in fact visited all the places on one's itinerary. In Japanese there is the popular phrase, *ron yori shōko* (let's not talk about it, let's simply see the proof).

In addition to the practice of keeping diaries, there is also the practice of keeping engagement books (*techō*) and household accounting and budget books (*kakeibo*). In these rather carefully laid out books, a fairly clear plan of future behavior is recorded. The businessman knows exactly where, at what time and with whom he will meet, often for several months in advance. The housewife carefully plans her menu and shopping schedule as well. While these practices can be found in Western societies and there are certainly Japanese who do not follow them, the important difference is one of degree: the greater frequency with which Japanese keep these kinds of written record, and the attention given to making entries in a correct or standard manner.

Another typically Japanese practice is the exchanging of *meishi* (name cards). In the West, calling cards or business cards are used, but as the words themselves suggest, their use is limited to specific times and places. In Japan, however, these are used by nearly everyone with an affiliation outside the home (e.g., including students but not housewives) as a part of the formality of introducing oneself. Some other features also distinguish the Japanese practice. Whereas in the West it is common to have a calling card with only one's name, in Japan a good deal more detail is given: the address and phone number is often given both for one's home and for the place(s) where one is affiliated. One's official position in one's association is also given. It is not infrequent for a more established person with two affiliations to have two *meishi*. Further, in the West a person often disposes of a card when it has been received or shortly after the acquaintance is established. In Japan, however, these cards are treasured and kept for long periods. Special filing systems have been developed for keeping these cards as a permanent record, and there are people who have all the *meishi* they have received over the past 30 years. Related to this record-keeping is the custom of informing people whenever one changes companies or shifts house. Japanese businessmen are likely to run off several hundred of these *tsūchijō* (notification postcards) and mail them to everyone from whom they have received a *meishi*. When shifting house, it is not uncommon for a map of the way to the new residence to be included in the announcement. In other societies few people tell more than their closest friends and relatives. Printed announcements are rare except for those with a significant social position or salesmen (e.g. estate agents).

Another example of this *meishi* consciousness can be found in the practice of *kanban* (shingles) or *menkyo* (licenses). In the West, people often engage in their hobbies simply for the enjoyment. While the Japanese also experience the joy which comes from having made something with one's own hands, they still feel a need for some written evidence to prove to others that they have such and such a level of proficiency. This tendency is particularly pronounced in the more commercialized traditional hobbies where the *iemoto* system is strong and Japanese are most likely to pay large amounts of money for tuition: flower arranging (*ikebana*), tea ceremony (*sadō*), calligraphy (*shodō*), Japanese dancing (*buyō*), Japanese singing (*nagauta*), the playing of Japanese musical instruments (*koto, shakuhachi* or *shamisen*). In some of the martial arts, as well as *go* and *shōgi*, the awarding of *dan* (rankings) is also accompanied by tangible proof. The *kanban* are not slight pieces of paper; they are fairly expensive wooden plaques on which the school, the individual's name and level of proficiency are engraved. Perhaps in imitation of this tradition, the practice of giving certificates can also be found in hobbies of other kinds, like woodcarving and lacquering (*kamakurabori*), knitting and sewing (*doresumēkingu*), cooking (*ryōri*), pottery (*tōgei*) and weaving (*hataori*).

This preference for the written word is reflected in Japan's traditionally high literacy rates. It is estimated that the literacy rate for males at the end of the Tokugawa period was over 40 percent (Dore: 1965, pp. 20, 31 and 317–22). Today Japan enjoys one of the highest literacy rates in the world. Moreover, despite the popularity of television, a look at the number of papers read and the number of books and magazines published will certainly substantiate that the Japanese form a well-read public. According to one survey in 1980 by NHK's Institute for Public Opinion Research, the average adult in Japan spends about 40 minutes reading every day. Without a basic knowledge of how to read and to write it is nearly impossible for one to survive in Japanese society. Each day there are numerous forms to complete and announcements to be read. This contrasts sharply with the United States and Australia, where the need to read and to write is less pronounced and where large numbers of migrants are able to go about their daily lives without ever becoming proficient in written

English. The Japanese emphasis on writing can also be seen in the great attention given to calligraphy. Students are taught to write not just clearly but with an artistic touch which will emboss the document with their own individuality.

III The Contractual Relationship

Another characteristic often attributed to the Japanese is sentimentality, a concern for *ninjō* (human feelings) and an ability to identify emotionally with others. While these facets of interaction can certainly be observed in Japanese behavior, it is the extensiveness of the 'dry' or calculated relationship which seems to set them apart from other peoples. This aspect of Japanese life can most easily be seen in the pervasiveness of the contractual relationship. The whole idea behind basic concepts such as *giri* and *on* is that of reciprocity or social exchange.

This binding sense of reciprocity can also be seen in the internal dynamics of organizations like business firms, hospitals and universities. It has been described in a number of novels, including Yamazaki's *Shiroi Kyotō* (Power in the Great White Tower) (cf. Befu: 1977). This instrumentality in human relationships can also be seen in the need to give presents when asking an acquaintance for even the smallest favor and in the common exchange of money for acts which would simply symbolize friendship in other societies. The concept of a bribe and the idea that such an exchange is socially unacceptable are not firmly established in Japan. Indeed, such payments are often seen as the oil which allows smooth interaction. The factions in each of Japan's political parties are not bound together simply by loyalty to the faction or the leader; there are instrumental rewards as well and those without money often find it difficult to maintain a following (Naka: 1979, pp. 123–4).

As the selection of a successor to follow Suzuki Zenkō as Prime Minister reveals, it is not consensus but the balancing of interests among various factions that counts, and the balance is worked out among leading individuals with strong personalities. Power brokerage is not a game of entrusting balloons to the winds of public opinion. Politicians will want to know about public opinion and will want to give the impression of party consensus when in power, but those are not the phenomena which most frequently determine the selection of the leadership or the policies they will follow.

Proceedings in the Diet are often characterized by boycotts, with the opposition parties walking out because legislation is rammed through. The case of the hearings in 1982 on the LDP's proposed legislation to alter the election system for the Upper House is one example. The refusal of the LDP to budge on the request by the opposition parties to investigate further the implications of its members in the Lockheed scandal is another. This contrasts sharply with the elaborate devices developed in the United States Senate to facilitate consensus. One observer of American politics commented on the American system as follows (Will: 1982, p. 10).

> Senate rules that allow filibusters reflect accommodations that are more subtle than some senators. Senate procedures measure the intensity of feeling as well as numerical strength. The filibuster, an expression of intense opposition, is used frivolously when the intensity is disproportionate to the principle at issue.

Given the careful division of powers to ensure a balance of interests and a certain continuity over time, the successful American President is the one who knows how to forge consensus among those in the different public offices. Greenstein (1982) writes of the 'hidden-hand presidency' in arguing the greatness of Eisenhower. The most important technique, he argues, is the ability to be laid back and to let it appear that others are making the decisions that one wants made.

Finally, in business, the scandal involving the Mitsukoshi department store in 1982 provides some unique insight into how management is chosen in Japan. The vote of the board of directors to depose the former president, Okada Shigeru, was unanimous, 16–0. However, it is widely believed that the vote itself was only a formality after a considerable power struggle. Moreover, on the point of consensus, it is now clear that a number of the store's high officials were involved in extensive secret and/or underhand activities (cf. the various weekly magazines and monthly journals in Japan during September, October and November, 1982).

These were activities in which secrecy was paramount because there was not a consensus which allowed others to be trusted. The area of corporate secrecy and the prevalence of scandals and *kuroi kiri* (black mist) still awaits careful comparative research. There is a wealth of vocabulary in the Japanese language for describing such behavior. While careful comparative research is not likely to expose such scandals as a uniquely Japanese trait, they would contribute to an understanding of Japanese decision-making which would be more sophisticated than the common explanations, which underline the importance placed on consensual values.

In some ways this all boils down to the matter of trust. As observed above in many proverbs which caution Japanese to beware of others, the general level of trust in one's fellow human beings is low in Japan. Japanese companies hire security firms to investigate prospective employees, whereas their foreign counterparts are happy to accept at face value the material submitted by the applicant and the comments of references. Personal checks are not used in Japan even for local shopping where one is well known. Because of the care with which money is counted and handled in Japan, and the need to make thorough security checks, the cost of using bank checks is considerable. The *Economist* (4 December 1982, pp. 90–1) reported on a volume by Frazer and Vittas (1982) revealing that the Japanese, on the average, use only four checks a year as compared to the 154 used by Americans. Foreigners in Japan are surprised to find that the pay-on-demand check sent to them from a friend who spent two hours in a large American city in order to draw it on a major Japanese bank such as Mitsubishi or Sumitomo cannot cash it in Tokyo at a Fuji or Sanwa bank, except by paying a considerable fee and waiting three to five days before being able to use the money. Their travellers' checks are good only in large hotels and a few stores for tourists, whereas in other countries they never had a problem regardless of where they went. Although the money card system came into use in Japan some seven or eight years before it did in Australia, the money vending machines cannot be used on the weekends or after 6.00 p.m. on weekdays in Japan. Where they have been installed in Australia, they are now readily available at all hours (including the weekend).

The contractual relationship can be seen most clearly at work. Compared with the view of American business given by one executive, who observed that his business was carried on in a social environment and that it was rooted in conversation and verbal dialogue and in the way in which 'industry folks' mix a bit of socializing and the doing of business (Shaw: 1982), Japanese business is rooted in the *ringisho, shuisho* (a written prospectus for presenting a new idea), *shintai ukagai* (a written intention to resign which is clearly different from the resignation itself), *shimatsusho* (a written apology for being late for work or for a small slip on the job) and *kyūka negai* (a written application for permission to take a day off or to engage in some activity apart from one's normal job). This can also be seen in the procedures for taking leave or for borrowing company property. One tends to sign for things and to keep a record of things, whereas in the workshop in Australia or America a welder simply walks out with a tool, waving it in the air with one hand and pointing to it with the other, and receiving the nod from the tacitly acknowledging foreman who makes a mental note. Sometimes the relationship is so informal that even the body language is done away with and the tool is simply said to be missing. This kind of loose give and take arrangement is unthinkable in Japan.

Upon being appointed to a job, the employee is given a contract. The permanent or regular male employee knows full well that he must retire at 55 and that the company is obliged to retain him until that age. Reflecting the power relationship, contracts written in the last 20–30 years are worded ambiguously to give the employer a decided advantage. Although the actual contract is fairly short, as Rohlen (1974, pp. 18–19) observes, it obliges employees to follow the firm's by laws or regulations (shūgyō *kisoku*) which are often very detailed and form a substantial written document.

Numerous surveys have shown that many employees would like to change jobs and would if it were possible to do so. However, despite a certain naïvety on the part of the prospective employee (which contrasts with the scrutiny given the applicant by the company), once the contract is signed and its consequences fully appreciated, Japanese are less inclined to leave the firm. To leave a firm with which one has a contract is seen as bad etiquette (e.g. the breaking of one's contract). As indicated above in Chapter 5, a full career with the same firm is rare in Japan; what should be emphasized, however, is that the rate of labor turnover is considerably lower in Japan than in many other industrial societies and that the notion of contracted obligation is one factor accounting for this difference.

In the West it is common for one to accept a job and then to quit after a few years' free training in order to take up employment elsewhere. Because the expectations of both the employer and employee are never clearly written down, this is less likely to be perceived as a blatant breach of contract, although a too cavalier or frivolous manner in this regard may be frowned upon, and there are firms which work hard to develop an atmosphere which will communicate management's desire for a longer-term relationship.

The origins of these contractual relations, as Nakane (1967b and 1973) suggests, can perhaps be found in the notion of the *ie*, the family which is tied together as an organization by instrumental relationships and by a specific set of goals as an economic enterprise, not as an emotionally based kinship unit linked primarily by blood and sexual intercourse. The way in which the contractual principle of the Japanese family (*ie*) has been carried over into the firm is explained by Kaneko (1980, p. 108) in the following manner:

> The system of career employment is closely linked with paternalistic management and the family system. Once the firm is seen as a united, family-like group, the transition to being an organization with a built-in system of retirement is easy. When the head of a family has served his full time as head of the family, the eldest son will have been nurtured to maturity and the senior figure will be able to hand over his position as household head to his son and look forward to a comfortable life in retirement. In the same fashion, the older worker in the firm hands over his position to a younger employee. In return, the enterprise awards the older worker with a lump sum payment on retirement to show its gratitude for his many years of hard work. In other words, the retirement system has emerged as a way of handing down the top positions from one generation to the next. The original rationale for this system can be found in the proposals for a typically Japanese system of remuneration based upon scientific principles and the concept of a lifetime earnings profile (the so-called 'livelihood wage').

The rights and obligations are clearly defined. Reference to tradition also brings to mind the surveys by Wigmore (1967–70) on the early days of the Meiji period. Taken among all the commercial guilds in the Tokyo area, they reveal a well-developed set of commonly agreed principles for carrying out business. When a mishap occurred in shipping or an account was not paid, the procedures to be followed were clear to all parties involved and were often spelled out on paper. Bills of sale and lading were used, and a careful system of accounts was maintained at all times. One is also reminded of local government constitutions drawn up in the Meiji period and later given considerable publicity by Irokawa (1970).

This concern with the specifics of a written contract can also be seen in one issue of *Torabāyu* (23 April 1982), a magazine for working women. Rather than criticizing employers for being misleading or taking advantage of a housewife's unfamiliarity with the terminology in the job advertisements, the magazine took the line that each woman must be responsible for knowing her own legal status and for reading carefully her employment contract; 13 cases were introduced where a woman employee felt she had been treated unfairly. A random sample of the advice includes the following:

1 The term 'office consignment' (*gyōmu itaku*) refers to an employment status which is different from that of those who have a contract with the company. [In other words, it sounds like a job description but is an employment status description.] . . . Because you do not have a contract with the firm, it is obvious that you should not be treated like those who do have a contract [even though you are made to work like the others]. . . . If you start work without being fully aware of your contractual status, and continue working under the assumption that you are an employee, you have only yourself to blame in the end (case no. 12, p. 12).

2 Some firms have a trial period (*shiyō kikan*) of one to three months, although this is not always stated in the advertisement. Technically, although you may think you are an employee qualified for the pay advertised, you are not in the position described in the advertisement (*honsaiyō*) until you've successfully completed this period. You'd better find this out for yourself when you go for the job interview (case no. 2, p. 8).

3 Some firms pay long-term irregulars a bonus. However, you'll have to look at the contract signed when you took up the job. The payment of bonuses can take many forms and it will all be spelled out in your contract (case no. 13, p. 12).

While non-Japanese might think that this was simply a conservative magazine speaking out for the prerogatives of management, that is obviously not the case. Rather than trying to change the legal system, the magazine is doing the most rational thing, simply teaching women how to read the advertisements more accurately in terms of the clear legal meaning. Rather than trying to create a new situation with new ambiguities, it is trying to elucidate further and therefore build onto the legal understandings which already exist and are already clear for certain members of society.

The idea of a contract can be seen in other areas as well. In August 1982 the Indian Government sponsored a large gathering of 400 Japanese and Indian businessmen in Tokyo. The intention was to raise Japanese interest in making private investment in the Indian economy. The interviews on television (the Nine O'Clock News, NHK, 5 August 1982), however, revealed a considerable gap in the thinking of the two sets of businessmen. The Japanese wanted the Indian Government to lodge written guarantees with the Japanese Government, clearly protecting their investments and insuring them that there would not be unrest or other demonstrations in India at a later date, accusing the Japanese of exploiting India's cheap labor. The Indian businessmen and government officials, however, took the line that problems would not arise and that such guarantees were unnecessary if the parties themselves were fully committed to truly mutual purposes. Formal contracts were seen as a sign of mutual mistrust rather than the goodwill which should characterize the launching of such enterprises.

In recent years the idea of marriage as a contract has been given some attention in the West. Many Japanese are puzzled by this, as marriage has always been much more of a contractual arrangement in Japan. There are, of course, the commonly cited examples (which often exaggerate the extent) of arranged marriages through *miai* (an arranged meeting) and the fact that individuals actually bring two households together. There is, however, a much more pervasive way in which the idea of contract is shown in Japanese households: the division of labor. The roles of husband and wife, for example, are much more clearly defined than in the West. Someone once described this with the phrase *dansei wa katoku, josei wa setsuyaku* (the man's job is to bring home an income and the woman's job is to manage it wisely).

Traditionally men were able to dismiss a wife with a written summons (*mikudarihan*), the idea being that the contract was for certain services. In return for her services as a wife, accommodation was provided. If a wife performed well enough during the trial marriage period, her status as a full employee (i.e., the wife) was then confirmed in a number of ways. This transition has sometimes been symbolized in a formal way by the handing over of the *shakushi* (rice scoop). There is thus the expression *shakushi jōgi na hito* to refer to a person who follows the rules. While this type of contract may seem unfair to many of today's young women, it should be pointed out that in Japan much more attention has been given to the training of women to perform their duties properly. Also, the rights of women in the household have also been fairly clearly delineated. In addition to having a resolute hold over the purse-strings and a firm say on how money will be spent (with their husbands having to ask for weekly or monthly allowances for extra outings), women also have the decisive voice regarding their children's upbringing and what the family will do when it is together (e.g., whether to visit relatives, go to a park with the children or go for a picnic).

A few examples may further illustrate the differences. Borrowing money from friends in Japan is also a quite limited practice. When one Australian correspondent in Japan once asked a good friend of six or seven years to borrow $150.00, the friend very quietly assured him that there would be no problems, immediately took the money out of his pocket and then asked that the Australian sign a written IOU. This same person later had another occasion to ask for money at home in Australia, asking a migrant whom he had known for only two years, with much less frequent interaction, for $1,000.00. The money was advanced straightaway with only the simple verbal request, 'Please return it when you can.'

The same can also be seen in renting. Whereas it is common to post one month's bond when renting a flat or apartment in many other countries, a quick perusal of any of several weekly magazines with rentals being advertised will show that the most commonly demanded bond (*shikikin*) in Japan is three months, and that it is in addition to one or two months' non-returnable contribution known as *kenrikin* or *reikin*. Foreign students coming to Japan are often surprised by the long and very complex contracts they have to sign when renting a flat. Many comment that they simply had a verbal agreement to rent before coming to Japan.[1]

Another example will illustrate this very loose attitude toward money in the West. In Australia there is a program called *This is Your Life*. It is a program to honor persons who have made significant contributions to Australian life. On one program the man responsible for creating Sea World on the Gold Coast appeared. When asked for the secret of his success, he commented that it had been in having the type of relationship with people which never required a contract. He was proud to be able to say that he had made many verbal business deals, often for hundreds of thousands of dollars, with only a handshake and no written document. When this story is told in

Though conductors and ticket-takers are quick to match the skill of even the most adroit passenger, the cleverness and facility with which youth adopts new challenges mean that high school and university students tend to excel in these maneuvers.

Although the constant attention given by the Japanese to their high population density might lead one to expect crowding together to result in a certain acceptance of physical contact, in Japan physical distance seems to be the rule. Japanese businessmen bow rather than shake hands. Friends wave and give a nod-like bow, but they do not embrace and exchange a friendly kiss the way people do in many Western societies. Traditionally, the girl walked so many paces behind the male. Folkdancing in Japan is also for the most part done without touching. Unlike the cheek-to-cheek two-step, square dancing or even ballroom dancing, the traditional Japanese dance involves people in a line following one after the other, waving their hands in the air rather than linking them with someone else's.

This difference in how people behave in groups can also be seen in eating arrangements. The Japanese have traditionally had a culture where people ate from separate dishes – one dish for each item, which allowed each individual to be sure of getting his or her share. This contrasts with the traditional Chinese custom of eating out of the same dish, or the European smorgasbord which is said to have had its origins in the banquets of the Vikings. The Romans also had feasts where they drank out of the same cups. Although Americans tend to have their own plates at a given meal, it is common for them to serve themselves from a larger bowl from which everyone else also helps themselves. There is still nothing in Japan like the Australian barbecue or the American potluck where people all bring different foods and then enjoy eating out of each other's pots. Although a very small number gather at locations like Ueno Park to drink, sing and dance under the cherry blossoms each spring, they are often looked down on by many other Japanese who happen to be passing by, as being a bit rowdy and lacking self-discipline. It is also difficult to find Japanese children sipping a drink or biting an apple and then passing it to another child. The practice of cooking *sukiyaki, okonomiyaki* or *teppanyaki*, from which everyone helps himself is a more recent introduction which developed in the late Edo period or after the Meiji restoration and perhaps was inspired by Western ideas. *Naberyōri* or *mizutaki* developed in the Edo period among the common people as a cost-efficient way of eating, but for a long time was looked down on as unrefined (*gehin*) by those better off in society (Tada: 1975a and

1975b). A survey by Taishō Kaijō Kasai (1981) of 300 *sararīman* (who were aged 35–55, had children and lived in Tokyo) indicated that *sushi, sashimi*, noodles, *tempura* and steaks were the top five favorite foods. All are served as individual helpings. *Sukiyaki* (a fried mixed dish with meat and vegetables: ranked sixth) and *yakiniku* (barbecued pieces of meat: ranked ninth) were the only group or shared dishes which involved eating from a common bowl.

Much attention has been given to the commitment of the Japanese employee to his firm; it has also been rather well substantiated that the Japanese employee changes firms less frequently than his American counterparts and that he works longer hours and more days for his firm. However, there is little good comparative data on his motivation to behave in that way. With regard to his interaction with the group at work, several considerations suggest that there is less spontaneity in his association with the firm than is generally assumed. Employees seldom know the names of the children of their workmates or much about their family life. They are reluctant to talk about their personal problems at work and will speak in a very low voice or go outside to a private phone when calling home or conducting other private business. As Atsumi (1982, p. 65) notes, in writings on Japan the distinction between spontaneous friendship (*yūjin kankei*) and obligatory relationships at work (which she calls *tsukiai*) is seldom made. It should also be noted that relationships are often terminated when one leaves the company. This is a serious psychological adjustment that people retiring must make in Japan (Sparks: 1972). Befu has also noted this phenomenon and called it 'paternalistic neglect' (1982a, pp. 31–2). It is also a major theme in Shiroyama's novel, *Mainichi ga Nichiyobi* (Every Day a Sunday). Finally, a program on NHK in July 1982 on the future of medical services in Japan lamented the fact that specialist teams (such as the cardio-vascular units which have emerged in America) have been so slow to develop in Japan, although it introduced one attempt to adopt that approach at Toranomon Hospital in Tokyo, which brought in an American team to teach the Japanese the fundamentals of working together.

Change is occurring, but it is slow. Young males and females, for example, have become much more blatantly physical in their associations. Higher standards of living have also freed young people from many of the financial constraints and worries which made the previous generation more careful. Emotional relationships sometimes result in individuals being hurt psychologically and financially, but young people can now cover much of the latter type of cost. One can also see a great deal of spontaneity in the Sunday gatherings of the *takenoko* (young kids in colorful garb) near Harajuku station in Tokyo. Although most industries are still very competitive, firms now feel they can offset a certain looseness in strict cost accounting and written memoranda with other types of efficiencies. As the strong individuals born in Meiji Japan were replaced in managerial positions during the sixties and seventies by those who grew up during the occupation and the early fifties and have a rather positive image of American democracy and teamwork, Japanese organisations may come to allow for more group spontaneity.

V Some Cultural Origins of the 'Dry' Relationship

The Japanese emphasis on contractual or unemotional relationships can be traced to certain elements in the society's cultural traditions. The most important may be the emphasis placed on logic and on thinking of people as replaceable and therefore expendable modules over the centuries. The result is a lucid understanding of functional relationships, the ability to deal with abstractions and to see other persons not sentimentally as particular or otherwise irreplaceable units, but as units of labor or as numbers of votes which are interchangeable and can be utilized to accomplish one's own goals.

In dealing with the abstract rather than the concrete, there is an emphasis on the universal and on roles rather than on the particular person. This trait is shown in several ways. One is the importance attached to mathematics in Japanese education. As Vogel (1979, p. 18) points out, the Japanese consistently obtain outstanding results in international comparisons of students' mathematical abilities.

The Japanese preference for abstraction can also be seen in other areas as well. A comparison of Japanese and Western chess is interesting in this regard. In contrast to Western chess, where each side is distinguished by color and where the pieces are shaped so that their physical appearance serves as an aid to help their functions being memorized, in *shōgi* (Japanese chess) all pieces are the same color and the same pentagonal shape. They can be distinguished only by Chinese characters and the direction in which one of the five corners points. Moreover, whereas captured pieces are simply removed from the board and die in Western chess, allowing the situation to become increasingly clear and concrete, in the Japanese version one is able at any time to use as one's own pieces the pieces one has captured from the opponent. In other words, there is a tremendous amount of fluidity and functional interchangeability, and a considerable capacity for a logical memory is required.

The Japanese game of *go* does not even have a counterpart in the West. Here color is used to distinguish the two sides, but all 361 pieces are round and exactly the same size. It is a game of calculated probabilities which, unlike chess, has so many permutations that it cannot be programed in a computer. Both *shōgi* and *go* are given a special column in all leading newspapers and in terms of abstraction and difficulty really have no rival in the West.

This high level of abstraction can also be seen in the Japanese language. While all language represents some form of expressive logic, the Japanese language seems to excel in that particular dimension. The use of singular and plural forms for nouns, which often involves repetition (as in *two chairs*) does not occur in Japanese. As in mathematics the expression is simply 2x (or *two chair*). The unnecessary personification of objects through the use of masculine and feminine genders is also avoided. The redundant use of a period and a capital letter to indicate a break in sentences is also avoided; so too is the unnecessary use of both quotation marks or underlining and capital letters to indicate titles of publications. Verb tenses and conjugations are also kept to a minimum. A fixed set of prepositions is used rather than cumbersome declensions to indicate relationship. The phonetic sound is associated with a unique pair of *kana* (like upper- and lower-case letters in the alphabet) to express it. The possibility of one *kana* being read in several ways does not exist. Finally, there is the use of Chinese characters, which as *jukugo* can be combined in an endless variety of ways (like Greek and Latin derivatives) to express almost any idea. It is this high level of abstraction in the language which has lent Japanese its tremendous flexibility, making it possible to introduce not only foreign ideas and concepts, but, as *gairaigo*, the very foreign words themselves.

The ability to deal in abstracts has also made it possible for Japanese to excel in learning foreign languages. Nearly all students at university study a foreign language in Japan, whereas only 8 percent of American universities require a language for graduation. As Magofuku (1981) observes, it is estimated that there are 10,000 Japanese businessmen in the U.S. with a working knowledge of English, whereas only a handful of the fewer than 900 American representatives in Japan have a working knowledge of Japanese. Nor is this a postwar phenomenon. The ability of Natsume Sōseki, Mori Ōgai, Fukuzawa Yukichi and Suzuki Daisetsu to read and translate foreign languages is legendary. Moreover, their achievements occurred long before there were good dictionaries or grammar textbooks. Few other people can match the Japanese in their ability to translate foreign books into their own language. It is also instructive to note that a significant portion of the Japanese literature available in Western languages was translated by Japanese. To translate into one's second language is no mean accomplishment.

VI Conclusions

It is difficult to bring persons with a strong sense of self-interest and individuality together to form a group. In Japan the well-developed notion of the contract has facilitated this process. The Meiji Government inherited a long bureaucratic tradition based on meritocratic principles, which emphasized individual ability, and on minute record-keeping, which fostered an acceptance of written records and explicit, contractual relationships. Perhaps because of the Government's strong role in fostering enterprises and then turning them over to private ownership in the Meiji period, Japan's new enterprises emerged with the social infrastructure necessary for modernization and with the ability to maintain the large organizations necessary to exploit fully the economies of scale associated with industrialization and economic development in general. Other groups which sought voluntary membership therefore found it much more difficult to bind their members together to the same extent. Entrepreneurs compensated by utilizing *emic* terms describing contractual relationships in the *ie* or family. Efforts to promote the notion of the contract, first as a particular concept arising out of the family and then later as a universal concept legitimized by emperor worship (*tennōsei*), have continued to be a major feature of Japanese paternalism. As a bureaucratic system, however, the normal red tape and other devices to check the intrusion of private interests and to keep people in line are needed. These controls are the subject of the following chapter.

Chapter 10

Social Control: Cormorants or Falcons?

I Introduction

The preceding chapters have touched upon the strong commitment of many Japanese to the achievement of their own personal goals, the developed sense of privacy, the importance attached to contractual relationships and the preference for written records. It was suggested that social exchange based upon the calculated maximization of self-interest was an important element in the interpersonal relations of many Japanese. One key to understanding these views of interpersonal relationships is the idea of scarcity. Those in countries with low population densities and an abundance of resources, like America or Australia, have tended to view their lives as a series of opportunities and their societies as having frontiers. In more recent years, however, the attention given to endemic poverty in the land of hope and to diminishing resources on a global scale has tended to foster even in those societies the notion that life is part of a zero-sum game played with others living in the same world. However, the Japanese have long held this view which has, as part of a cultural tradition, been encapsulated in the notion of *higaisha ishiki* (a kind of persecution complex) which emphasizes that Japan is a small island country with no resources, surrounded by a number of fairly hostile, or at least aggrandizing, other nations to which Japan must react as an integrated whole if it is to survive. Given these perceptions, Japanese leaders have cultivated a neo-Confucian or functional view of the world which has emphasized a positivistic, logical-empiricist framework for manipulating not only the environment in which Japan finds itself, but Japanese society as well. This view, then, is linked with a highly developed ability to deal in abstracts.

When mixed together, these various ingredients produce a peculiarly Japanese blend of competition. As mentioned in the preceding chapter, from childhood males learn to compete in successive examinations to obtain one of the limited places in the prestigious middle schools, high schools and universities. Businessmen work long hours and compete for promotion within their firm. Poor retirement benefits and an underdeveloped pension system have meant that at retirement small margins in performance may be crucial in giving the individual another two or three years with the firm or in making possible a smooth transfer to a managerial post in a smaller subsidiary or subcontractor. Competition within the firm in part accounts for their competitiveness in both domestic and foreign markets. The extension of the idea of competition allows many to see the nation of Japan as their interest group in the league of nations, where resources are scarce and where one national team is able to move up only at the expense of others.

With stiff competition among the Japanese, how is the society held together? What keeps the centrifugal forces of self-interest from whirling apart? One key to this problem is control. In this chapter, four types of control are discussed. The four types illustrate that much of the behavior commonly cited as examples of spontaneous consensus in Japanese society is in fact produced by a fine blend of manipulative and coercive controls. A model of social control in Japanese society is then contrasted with the voluntary or consensus model applicable in many Western societies. Finally, some thought is given to the need for several models in explaining Japanese society.

Some of the control mechanisms discussed below can be seen in the life of Morioka Hiroshi, a young man of 22 who had been working for six months in the Maruse department store in one of the prefectural capitals. One summer day he was suddenly informed that his superior, the chief of the storage room, had lost his father and that Morioka would be expected to attend the funeral as it was to be held in a small village only two hours from the city. Morioka did not have a black suit, but dutifully borrowed a black arm-band from his brother. He arranged to meet at the station some of his workmates under similar orders, and together they caught the train. He and the others were wet with perspiration by the time they arrived at the local station. The twenty-minute bus ride was like a mobile sauna. They all agreed not to put on their jackets for the ceremony.

As Morioka stood in the hot sunshine, many thoughts raced through his mind while the priest droned on and on with the sutra. First was an unkind gesture to the dead, which soothed his own anger for wasting his only day off that week for some old man he had never met or a supervisor he did not feel too sorry for. 'Why couldn't the old geezer have dropped over in the spring or the fall when the weather would be half-way decent?' Only three or four others had come from the company. One of the others, Akiyama Minoru, worked in the men's clothing department. They had immediately become good friends, since they had both entered at the same time, were the same age, and had worked elsewhere before.

They had talked a bit the night before and had lamented the fact that as re-employed newcomers (*chūto saiyōsha*) they were particularly weak when pressured by superiors to go beyond the call of duty. Misery likes company, and they had had a good laugh at their work experience. Several weeks ago Akiyama's number had been called; this meant that he had to get up in front of everyone at the Monday-morning ceremony to open the week. He was to recite the store's motto for everyone. Unfortunately, under the pressure his mind suddenly went blank; after an embarrassed silence, accentuated by the exaggerated movement of lips from which no voice emerged, he had been replaced by one of those slick new grads straight out of the university and working in the sports department. His supervisor was furious, and he was immediately summoned to the supervisor's office once the ceremony was over. Akiyama had been relieved of work that day and required to write the motto a hundred times before being sent home. It reminded him of his punishment for breaking a window at school when he was a kid in Nakano.

Morioka had poured himself another beer and then laughed, 'Akiyama, old boy, you did look a bit stupid up there, though!' However, a few drinks later it was Morioka's turn to remind Akiyama how funny he had looked the week before with his new butch haircut, which had lowered his ears so that they glowed in the lights above the door where he had had to stand for two days with the girls bowing and yelling all day, 'Welcome! Welcome! Please come in! Thank you for being such a good customer! Welcome! Welcome! Please watch your step! Please watch your step! Welcome! Welcome! Welcome! Please watch your step! Welcome! Welcome! Welcome! This is the door in . . . . ' Akiyama said he looked like a dodo bird, and that the customers were equally dense to need such constant prodding. He must have repeated the same thing several times to each customer, probably over a thousand times in the course of a single day. No wonder he had been hoarse for three days afterwards and his lower back had ached for a week! All of that was for his having stood at a morning ceremony without his heels properly together and his toes at a thirty-five-degree angle, and for having forgotten to wear his company pin the week before. He wondered whether the trouble had been brought on by his earlier failure to have his hair trimmed a bit. A clip around the ears had been suggested to him one day in May, when the head of the customer services section had taken the seat next to him in the cafeteria. The same person had also been right in front of him at the morning session. If the business about his hair had been an official order, the guy should have said so. Morioka was about to get married and wanted this job to go smoothly; he needed the money.

Several weeks ago the two had been invited out drinking by one of the floor managers who had entered the firm the same way. In his forties, Tanaka Ichirō had not been particularly successful in the firm, but his dour face brought a seriousness onto the men's clothing floor which the management liked. After getting fairly drunk, the three had gone to the park, where they began to ride around on some bicycles which had been left there. Unfortunately, they were stopped and questioned by a policeman making his rounds. The officer was friendly enough, but hauled them down to the station to make out a report. The lecture was bad enough, but the requirement of having a guarantor come down to sign the *mimoto hikiukenin-sho* (the guarantor's form) was an even more bitter pill. They had missed the last train, and it cost Tanaka ¥23,500 to have his wife come all the way from their home by taxi; money aside, she had had to wake the neighbor to ask her to keep an eye on the house, as their two children were still only in primary school. Morioka had had to raise his father, the president of a local bank, and his driver to come and pick him up, all to sign that stupid *mimoto hikiukenin-sho.* The two had become somewhat upset and said a few rude things to the policeman they later regretted but for which they were excused, owing to their slight intoxication. Akiyama had tended to take it all in stride. He philosophized and for some reason seemed able to identify with the policeman. After all, he argued, they could have been planted by another department in the police force to make sure that the fellows at that particular precinct had been doing their job. Be that as it may, good honest Tanaka had to blab the story all over the store the next day. What mental notes would the people in the personnel department make for the future when his round for promotion came up?

The two often reminisced about their earlier jobs, Morioka at a small record shop and Akiyama at a small men's clothing store. Both had fond memories of their previous employment. They were sometimes late at work after a rough night with the boys, but neither could recall having been penalized. The hours were much longer, sometimes 60 a week, but there was no bloody time clock and they were free to come and go as they wished and could let their hair down a bit, privileges not to be abused but none the less ones showing respect for their integrity and discipline. Also, they were able to joke and even fool around. Now they were afraid a friend would come in and talk to them while they were working (which was behavior strictly against the regulations). Now they had to punch a time clock and obtain written permission just to leave the building during lunch. The store's cafeteria for employees was good and cheap, but sometimes a change would be nice. However, by the time one made up an excuse to go to the bank and filled out the proper form, and then waited 20 minutes for the form to be processed, the lunch period was almost gone. There was certainly no time to go out and eat. Morioka suddenly commented, 'If only they had paid more at the other job or offered more of a future. That's the problem with the small family-run stores.' Akiyama nodded; he could afford to be complacently sympathetic since he would one day return to run his father's business in Nakano. He was, in a sense, being made to travel before taking over the reins of his father's business.

'Once I get into the family business,' he sighed, 'maybe I'll write a book about Maruse department store, all the bullshit that goes on at the *chōreikai* and that stupid company song! Anything I can write to help you get promoted?'

'No, not really; fat chances for a high-school graduate.' As his groan gave way to a sheepish smile, he added, 'Don't forget to write about the motto if you can still remember the words! And don't forget to include our lovely company song. . . . Especially the refrain: "And the Sun rises again to shine on Maruse where the customers are King!" Didn't the composer know that the customers would be housewives and that a king is a man? Ha, Ha, Ha! But make sure you've finished at Maruse before you publish it. Also, mind you, also don't forget what happened to that Takashima fellow.'

Akiyama had not yet heard the story; someone named Takashima had worked for the firm for 20 years and had been active in the old union. Morioka did not know all the details and the union no longer existed. However, when the company had stored large amounts of sugar in the warehouse for men's clothing after the first oil shock, Takashima (who had worked his way up to be assistant warehouse manager) let it be known that the company had hoarded sugar in the warehouse. The manager had been demoted and officially reprimanded; he was shifted to another part of the company where he seemed to have exonerated himself and was now a *buchō* (division head) in charge of purchasing. Although Takashima got promoted to manager, he shortly afterwards resigned; it was rumored that he'd been intimidated and pushed around in the warehouse when he had worked late one night, and that the promotion itself had been set up. Morioka liked Akiyama's openness, but was bothered by the thought that his association with Akiyama might later become a liability. He felt some of that *giri-ninjō* tension he'd read about in his Japanese literature class in high school.

The lives of both Morioka and Akiyama are controlled in a number of ways, although neither has been directly forced to do anything against his will. Both feel a certain amount of subtle coercion, although neither would publicly say so. For that reason in particular, it is difficult to know how much coercion actually is involved or how typical the experiences are. Without further research it is difficult to argue convincingly on this point. However, even the new recruits entering after graduation soon have a clear idea of what they can and cannot do, and the experiences of the two people described can be understood from the broader perspective of social controls in Japan. The following paragraphs introduce a number of examples of social control which warrant further investigation. The examples are organized into four tentative categories based on the degree of coercion. Some other dimensions of social control in terms of the distribution of social rewards and the uses of social resources are discussed below in Chapter 12.

II Controls with Various Degrees of Coercion

A Watchdogs and Monitors

In her work with Japanese in detention camps in the United States during World War II, Benedict (1946) detected among the Japanese she observed a peculiar concern with being watched. It is likely that many of those who agreed to be interviewed by her and who were most open to her questions were those who had migrated from Japan precisely to escape the various controls which had been structured into Japanese society. Coupled with their present dependence on their American supervisors and the likelihood of reward for praising American ways, it is not surprising, therefore, that they emphasized aspects of control in the accounts of Japanese society they gave to Benedict. However, not being a serious student of Japanese language, it may be that she was unable to get a firm grasp of their moral sense of right and wrong. Her conclusion was that Japanese were motivated by constant reference to others and what they would think, rather than by some overriding or transcendental principle. She attached the label *haji* (shame) to the reported anxiety which Japanese felt at being observed or at having been said to have acted contrary to the rules of *on* and *giri*. However, her concern with patterns of culture, democracy and the word for democracy (cf. Lummis: 1982; Minear: 1980b) seems to have produced a firm conviction in Benedict that this anxiety was born out of an internalized set of norms. No mention was made of ideology or of the *tennōsei* (the political culture of the Emperor system). No mention was made of the sanctions awaiting those who failed to adhere to the guidelines for behavior which were set down by the Emperor's official overseers. Rather than as a functional equivalent for guilt, *haji* can be better understood as a response to the omnipresent watchful eye of the state.

The concern with being watched is not something which grew out of the militarism of the thirties and the *tennōsei*, although the surveillance of the private lives of many Japanese was surely extended at that time. In the Tokugawa period there was a system of gates (*seki*) through which all travelers had to pass. People had to have passports or papers from their *han*, and these were checked and rechecked at each gate along the way. The use of spies by the *bakufu* during the Tokugawa period is well known. This, it is commonly said, was one reason that *hōgen* developed as a means for local people to distinguish between outsiders and those from their own region.

Following the Meiji Restoration a number of new devices were adopted. A national police force was established, the system of education was centralized, a system of universal military conscription was introduced in 1873, and the Government became very involved in economic activity. The Public Security Police Act (*Chian Keisatsuhō*) of 1900 gave the Government the right to censor publications and have the police sit in on private gatherings.

During the thirties the Government's ability to supervise was further strengthened by the implementation of the *tonarigumi* (five-person brigades), the establishment of the special censorship boards to review all publications, the organization of Sanpō (National Association of Patriotic Workers) and the placement of military personnel (usually veterans) in all schools.

While many of the more conspicuous forms of surveillance seem to have disappeared in postwar Japan, more subtle forms remain. One tab on people is the family register (*koseki*) and residential registry (*jūmin tōroku*). These are part of an elaborate system of files which records information on each family. The file lists convictions, previous addresses, marriage particulars and other information; behavior is recorded on a family basis so that the peccadilloes of each individual are recorded with those of other family members. Despite a person's desire to assume individual responsibility, his indiscretions will always affect some other people. The consultation of these records in decisions relating to marriage and employment are well known, although public pressure has, in recent years, resulted in some restrictions being placed on their accessibility.

Japanese who go overseas are required to fill out an overseas residence card at the nearest Japanese embassy or consulate. Japanese do not have a right to passports and the application for a passport is a kind of passing through another check. Until the seventies severe foreign exchange restrictions also made it impossible to leave without approval from other quarters to take out the currency necessary to live abroad. Of course, this approval was always readily forthcoming for those employees going abroad for large business firms. Concern with Japan's image abroad and with controlling the emigration of those who would damage it is recorded even from the Meiji period (Wilson and Hosokawa: 1980, pp. 30–53).

A major organizational unit accounting for the effectiveness of the police in Japan is the *kōban* (the police box) in urban centers and the *chūzaisho* (the residential police post) in rural areas. Bayley (1976, pp. 13–14) states that there are 5,800 *kōban* and just over 10,000 *chūzaisho* in Japan. The simple gathering of information is the most important function of those attached to these units. In fact, the Japanese word for policeman is *omawarisan* which literally means 'person who makes his rounds'. Most *kōban* are strategically located at the entrance to a railway station or strategic intersections where their presence will be conspicuous. Those manning the police box do not ask for papers or travel documents (except from unfortunate foreigners who happen to get up late and leave without their passports or residence registration documents), but they do watch people come and go. They are trained to remember faces, where people live and what their routines are. One person told us of returning to an old residence he lived in for a year after ten years' absence and having a policeman come up and inquire after his well-being, calling him by his name. A very nice policeman, but a very watchful one as well. The police officer stationed at *kōban* or *chūzaisho* is free to do what he wants as long as he makes some kind of minimal contribution to the overall workings, including the paper work and other office work, of the police force. He is a generalist and does not have to have the knowledge of a specialist. His major job is simply to watch and to report those who are dressed suspiciously or who are carrying suspicious bags. The officers also have a list of persons who need special looking after and keep careful notes on others who accompany them. Nearly ten years after the riots of the late sixties and early seventies, it is not uncommon to find outside the gate of a large university one or two policemen standing, all day every day. They simply watch and wait. Although the Japan Communist Party is legal, it is treated as a dangerous element and is kept under constant police surveillance. Beiheiren, the anti-Vietnam War group, also came under police surveillance. Their coffee shop, 'The Hobbit', at Iwakuni was frequently visited by police with search warrants, on the suspicion that guns were illegally being concealed. No such weapons were ever found, but the same warrant was issued numerous times.

Finally, some mention should be made of the generally high level of security consciousness. Japanese are careful to lock doors before leaving. Many wealthier Japanese have dogs, not as pets to come into the house but as watch-dogs confined to a small kennel near one of the gates to the house. Whereas people in other societies often go out with the windows open in the summer, or leave them open at night for fresh air, Japanese invariably close the windows and the shutters in order to keep *dorobō* (burglars) out. Simply to lock up the doors and windows is often not enough if Japanese are going away overnight. The practice of house-sitting *(rusuban)* is an old tradition in Japan. Only in recent years have Americans become so security conscious, despite having higher crime rates for years. Most Japanese companies have watchmen situated at their entrances. Many have a system requiring one or more employees to stay at the firm overnight (*shukuchoku*). Most factories are fenced and have a gate at which one waits for the host to appear in person. Visitors are often required to sign in and then to wear an identity pin with a specific number on it.

With all of this watching, it is interesting to note that some are above the system. Although very clearly involved in the Lockheed scandal, many politicians or gray officials have been protected from investigation. The LDP is not subjected to the same kind of surveillance given the JCP. Only a few of many electoral violations alleged to have been committed by conservative politicians are carefully investigated. Right-wing activists who disrupt the national conventions of the Japan Teachers' Union are not given the same scrutiny as leftist student activists.

B Indicative Planning and Informal Direction

Specific direction is given to social activity in several ways. One practice frequently commented on by foreign observers is *gyōsei shidō* (administrative guidance). As a bureaucratic style, this phenomenon has been noted by numerous persons (Vogel: 1979a, pp. 65–6, 108–10 and 122; Johnson: 1982, pp. 242–274; Abegglen: 1970c, pp. 71–9; Hadley: 1970, pp. 380–6; Ojimi: 1975, pp. 106–09; and Miyazaki: 1980). This kind of guidance is facilitated by the existence of rather cohesive enterprise groups (*keiretsu kigyō*) and an elaborate system of consultative bodies (*shingikai*). In the context of Japan's financial markets, reference is often made to 'indirect financing' and 'window operations'. In the narrow sense, *gyōsei shidō* refers to the administrative guidance given by individual Ministries to the private sector or to lower administrative units. In the broader sense, however, it is a style of indicative planning which can be found in many of Japan's organizations.

Suzuki (1974, p. 29) describes the essence of *gyōsei shidō* as follows:

> Government bureaucracies and agencies have authority. If a private party does not cooperate with one of the governmental bodies, it is able to make its influence felt in other ways and in other places. This idea is captured by the kotowaza '*Edo no ada o Nagasaki de utsu*' (Enemies in Edo (Tokyo) are taken care of in Nagasaki). [In principle,] if a firm is large enough and fairly self-sufficient, it can resist the government's initiatives without worrying constantly about its future. However, if we look at the economic situation in

> which most firms have found themselves in the postwar period, it is clear that their existence would be in jeopardy were they not to comply with such directives.

The smack on the hands of a large firm like Sumitomo Metals in 1965 (Yamanouchi: 1977, pp. 29–30) served as a good reminder of the authority described by Suzuki in the preceding quotation. Because of the depressed steel market in the mid-sixties, MITI requested in the spring that steel firms cut production to a level 10 percent below that recorded in 1964. Sumitomo followed the recommendation for domestic production but insisted on maintaining export levels. Its quota for export was soon cut from its requested level of 47,000 tons to 9300 tons. In November Sumitomo was denied the foreign exchange necessary to maintain its production levels. By January 1966 it had come around to seeing things the way MITI did.

NHK, Japan's major radio and television broadcasting station, is a public corporation. While it has a healthy budget and can afford to produce rather lavish programs, it is very sensitive about its dependence on annual allocations from the Government to top up its revenues from the television tax and to change the amount of the tax which can be levied. It is thus notorious for its bland reporting of Government policy. Many research bodies which are *gaikaku dantai* (semi-official public bodies) are in a similar position. Their research activities and publications are carefully scrutinized, and directions which will win budgetary allocations are often openly suggested by officials in the ministry responsible for overseeing their activities.

Reporters writing material unfavorable to the Government have often found it difficult to obtain inside information on a par with other reporters. Some idea of how censorship worked before the war can be found in Mitchell (1976), Huffman (1980), Shillany (1982) and Bix (1978). Although the crime of *fukei* (*lèse-majesté*) does not exist now as in the prewar period, publishers printing books or articles unfavorable to the Emperor or related institutions are often singled out for special treatment and subjected to various types of intimidation. The *Chūō Kōron* incident is but one such case. Laws on pornography are also enforced in selected areas.

Jishukusei (the system of self-censorship) does not require the constant surveillance of every publication. People are led to know what will happen. Nor does the Ministry of Education have to be so crude as to make outright rejections. All it has to do is to ask publishers and authors to think about something. The delays themselves are so crucial in the publishing world that the effect of simply having to think about it (even if, in the end, no change is made) is that the whole project loses money while the Ministry appears only to have been making constructive suggestions. One author (Professor Kojima Yoshio at Nippon University) revealed another facet of this problem when asked about recent attempts to change his portion of a textbook written with several others. He said he felt compelled to go along with the changes advocated by the Ministry because of his fear that the publisher and the other writers would suffer losses if he rejected the proposal of the inspectors (*JT*, 9 August 1982, p. 2). At the same time, the official position of the Ministry of Education is that the publishers and authors made all the decisions and that it only gave advice which they were free to reject.

Gyōsei shidō also takes many other forms. As mentioned in the two preceding chapters, emphasis on individual self-interest and on the contractual tie (where money is the binding agent) means that Japanese society is characterized by a good deal of corruption. The dealings in Mitsukoshi department store (Nakano: 1982; Ōshita: 1983), the Lockheed Scandal involving the nation's Prime Minister (Fudesaka: 1983; Sekiguchi: 1983) and the complex rebate schemes worked out between local public officials and construction companies (Minami: 1980) might be mentioned. When people refuse to move, those around them are often bought off and various bureaucratic and private moves are made to obstruct the efforts of ordinary citizens to obtain justice by simply having a fair public hearing of their ideas. During the struggles over pollution (cf. Ui: 1968 and 1971–4), collusion between companies and Government officials was frequently uncovered, as were efforts by business firms to buy off victims of the anti-pollution movement and to have relevant documentary evidence destroyed. The essence of these moves is not physical violence against individuals. It is rather the psychological wearing down of their ability to resist. Things are made to appear so difficult that the ordinary person will simply give up. That defeat is then used as a symbol to signal to recalcitrant individuals that certain behavior is expected and that the cards will be stacked against them should they decide to behave otherwise.

C Regulation

Japan is a society of signs and announcements saying *suruna* (don't): Don't step off the path! Don't cross here! Don't step on this dirt!

Don't enter! Don't sneak under the crossbars! Don't stand inside the white line! Don't run out suddenly! Don't forget your umbrella when you get off the train! Don't linger here! Don't put your cigarette butts here! Don't stand on the toilet seat! Don't do this and don't do that! People are either not given much credit for thinking or taking initiative on their own, or it is simply assumed, perhaps correctly, that they have their own values and will go off and do something else. Japanese are pushed through life by a great number of regulations. Foreign students visiting Japanese universities on exchange programs have tremendous difficulties adjusting to the rules: don't go off campus without permission, lights out at 22:30 every evening, breakfast between 07:00 and 07:30 only, no eating in your room, no electrical appliances in your room, no Japanese students to use the Western toilets, no phone calls after 20:00.

Two things stand out. One is the amount of detail and the other is that the regulations are invariably worded to specify not what one may do but what one may not do. While the purpose is clearly to control certain types of behavior, a good deal of latitude is given to the entrepreneurial spirit. While there is the constant reminder about too much of a good thing, there is no fear that one commits a crime by simply being clever. Because additions can be made to the regulations, a certain amount of self-discipline is encouraged; so too is discretion and secrecy in the doing of good things. Of course, good things are good only for some people. By taking a low profile on pollution, for example, it was 10 or 15 years after serious pollution emerged before the Government was abruptly made aware of the problem by various citizens' movements. By being quiet about pollution, firms made it as difficult as possible for citizens' movements to obtain information about it. It also meant that managers of polluting firms were legally obliged only to avoid the types of pollution which were specifically mentioned in outdated regulations for older technologies or for industries not currently in production.

Regulations are not new in Japan. They emerged some time ago, no doubt with the phrase *kanson minpi* (the bureaucrats are respected but the ordinary people despised). The best-known of the control mechanisms of the *bakufu* (military government) during the Tokugawa period was the *sankin kōtai* system, which required that all *daimyō* live at least part of the year in Edo, and that they leave part of their family in Edo whenever they returned to their provinces. This in itself placed a great financial burden on the various *han* and ensured that they did not amass too much wealth or power. Other regulations spelled out the privileges and duties of those in each of the four recognized social classes. Only *samurai* and those with special permission could carry swords. Ōe (1978) describes in detail how *kaigenrei* (martial or emergency law) developed in Japan from the Meiji period through the assassinations of the thirties. In postwar Japan regulations have been extensive, although they have certainly been revised to suit the new circumstances.

The details of regulations often appear absurd to non-Japanese. Some hotels have their regulations laid down in the form of a constitution with 12–15 articles, each with subsections. Although it would take the normal visitor an hour or so to read the entire document, it spells out numerous grounds on which the hotel's management might legally refuse to serve guests or ask them to leave – nothing as ambiguous or as sweeping as the simple statement often found in other countries, about the management reserving the right to refuse service. Coin lockers, which at bus and train stations in the United States have a simple set of pictures explaining their operation, in Japan have posted on each door a list of a dozen or so stipulations for the user, including sub-paragraphs telling him or her that corpses should not be left in the locker and that the management will not be responsible for anything lost or damaged in the lockers. At coin laundries as well, there are lots of instructions on how not to use the machines and very clear statements that the management will not be responsible for any damaged clothing.

D Physical Violence

Japanese history contains many examples of how the state has used violence to control the behavior of citizens. It also contains examples of popular rebellion against such controls. Sometimes violence is used to combat violence, and sometimes it is used simply as a pre-emptive measure to quell the voice of the opposition. The brutal suppression of the peasant uprisings during the Tokugawa period need no special mention. Following the Meiji Restoration, the way in which factory girls (who were supposedly volunteers from *samurai* families (Kano: 1974)) were beaten and locked in insanitary dormitories is well known. The Taigyaku Jiken, which involved the framing and subsequent execution of Kōtoku Shūsui and other anarchists in the early Taishō period, and the killing of Ōsugi Sakae and Itō Noe by police immediately after the Kantō earthquake in

1923 are also examples of how state power was misused. During the thirties the assassination of democratic leaders was accompanied by imprisonment, torture and physical hardship inflicted on communists and others who spoke out against state fascism.

During the war, the great emphasis on the spiritual essence of the nation (*kokutai*) and on voluntary service to the Emperor was accompanied by the greatest amount of physical violence. Not only was violence seen as the way of leading or teaching the Chinese and others living in Asia, it was also a major device for fostering consensus (i.e., compliance) at home. Corporal punishment was common in schools and even more common in the military, which was supposed to epitomize this spirit of voluntary service. Accounts of the training and of the internal group dynamics among those in Japan's Imperial Army and Navy are fragmentary. Pieced together, however, they reveal that force was used extensively.

Novels like Ōoka Shōhei's *Nobi* (Fires on the Plain) reveal this dimension in stark terms:

> 'You shouldn't tag along with us the way you do, saying "Yes, sir," "No, sir," "Thank you, sir" every few minutes to the squad leader. I've been with the corporal ever since we landed on New Guinea and I wouldn't treat a dog the way he's treated us. He's never done one single thing for his men. He wasn't so bad when we were stationed at headquarters, but as soon as we got to the front, he became a real bastard. Just because he thinks he knows something about fighting, he feels he can treat us all like dirt. He'll do the same thing to you. If you keep tagging along like this, he'll clean you out of all your salt and in the bargain he'll probably . . . he'll probably get rid of you.' (Ōoka: 1978, p. 151).

> 'Hey, you!' barked the corporal's voice. I turned around and found the muzzle of his rifle pointing straight at me.
>
> 'If you think you can surrender, just try doing it!' he said. 'You really figure you can get away with it, do you, you shameless bastard? Well, you can't! You tried dropping out of ranks once before, but now I'm going to see that you get to Palompon if I have to drag you every inch of the way myself . . . ' (Ōoka: 1978, p. 154).

There is little evidence of decision-making from below or of the consultative sessions or the quality control mechanisms frequently singled out in recent years as being particularly Japanese contributions to the art of management. Rather, the record suggests that the more universal regimentation found in the military organizations of other societies also propelled the Japanese soldier.

The *kamikaze* suicide pilots are often taken as an example of Japanese spirit and the willingness of the Japanese soldier to die for his Emperor. However, although research in this area is not very advanced, we do know that there is a great discrepancy between the Japanese records of *kamikaze* hits and the American naval records. The Japanese records appear to show that pilots reported attacks which never appeared even as sightings in the logs of American vessels in the reported area (Inoguchi *et al.*: 1958). We also know from the letters of pilots and from the unwillingness of those connected with the operations to talk about them that decisions to sacrifice their lives were not as voluntary as one is commonly led to believe (Nihon Senbotsu Gakusei: 1949).

There are many who believe that the Japanese experience holds more general lessons for others as to what war and military organizations can do to the men involved. Accounts of the biological experiments using Chinese civilians in Manchuria are significant, not only as a history of Japanese atrocities during the war but as a story of how group cohesion was maintained among members of 731 Regiment. It would be naïve to believe that all members of the Ishii Unit volunteered to do human experiments because of a general value orientation common to Japanese. Many were repelled by their work, but were silenced or compelled to go along by the fear of violence and other sanctions against themselves (Morimura: 1981 and 1982). Even as Morimura wrote in 1980, operations carried out 40 years earlier are still shrouded in secrecy and many are still afraid to speak out.

Similar accounts of violence as an internal dynamic in the Japanese military can be found in the stories in *Peace is Our Duty: Atrocities caused by the War* (Sōka Gakkai: 1982), in Yūki's novel, *Gunki Hirameku moto ni* (Under the Unfurled Flag) or in Nitta's novel about the forced march in Aomori which left so many dead on the snowy slopes of Mt Hakkōda in the winter of 1901. Disregard for human life and the meting out of physical violence as a motivating device were taught from the start in the basic training of the military and were part of the curriculum in the military training which was introduced into Japanese schools during the thirties. These attitudes regarding human motivation and organizational effectiveness can also be seen in the way in which Koreans and Chinese were organized to do forced labor during the war (Tsurumi: 1982). Moreover, as numerous Japanese have argued in reacting to accusations of racism in the brutalized treatment of their prisoners of war, the same principles and logic were applied in running the Japanese Army.

In the civilian sector laws were passed in the early forties in order to limit opportunistic labor mobility. A complex pay system with many allowances arose, in part as an attempt by management to avoid taxation and other regulations designed to direct more of their resources to the war effort (Magota: 1972, pp. 169–73). The resistance of those in Tōdaisha (the Lighthouse Society) to conscription in the face of brutal torture (Inagaki: 1972) makes it almost impossible to comment on *tenkō* as any kind of serious conversion involving the selling out of one's beliefs (cf. Tsurumi: 1982, pp. 87–99; and Bix: 1978). As Hidaka (1980, pp. 3–10) has observed, the unnecessary death of Miki Kiyoshi, who was still in jail as late as October 1945, could be attributed in part to the hatred, brutality and determination with which the war had been prosecuted at home.

The end of the war is often painted as a watershed for Japanese fascism and the militarists. Following the war, attention was initially focused on the occupation reforms. Gradually public interest was shifted from the issue of democratization to modernization, industrialization and high growth. In the process, the virtues of supposedly traditional Japanese management practices suddenly surfaced. Mention of the violence associated with the *ampo* struggles, the student movement, the anti-pollution movements, or the struggles at Sanrizuka (where the new Tokyo international airport was built) is brief. Phenomena seen as being central to prewar fascism are dismissed as peripheral aberrations, no longer central to an understanding of Japanese society. While Japan has been one of the great postwar democracies, and police or militia have not been used freely as before the war, the frequent presence of the *kidōtai* (combat police units) on the streets of Tokyo, and the barbed wire and police patrols at the new Tokyo international airport serve as constant reminders that the limits of dissidence are finite.

Gangs (*bōryokudan*) have also been prominent in the postwar period. Their involvement in drugs, gambling and prostitution is known, and the violence they use is a major theme in comic books. Some, like *Hana no Ōendan* (which is about the male cheer-leader groups at universities) even make violence look like fun. The general acceptance of violence can also be seen in the status accorded *banchō* (the leaders of middle-school gangs) and Japan's version of Hell's

Angels (the *bōsōzoku*). The ethic of violence can also be seen in some of the training programs for sports teams.

While the organized and systematic use of violence has been restricted in postwar Japan, sporadic accounts remind one that violence is still seen by many as the ultimate means of effecting change. Yokota Testuji, who published an exposé of the Japanese meat industry in 1977, was intimidated with threatening letters and phone calls and in the end was beaten up by administrative staff members for being disloyal to his company, an organization designed to gather information and publish a journal for the meat industry (*TDY*, 27 December 1981, p. 2).

Another individual who brought a suit against the Governor of Hyōgo Prefecture in 1970, in an effort to receive welfare payments, began to receive intimidating phone calls and mail. Her case is recorded by Yoshisato (1982), and the *Asahi* editorialized, 'When weak persons insist on their rights in public, they are frequently harassed and intimidated by anonymous and cowardly parties' (*ASC*, 8 July 1982, p. 1).

Another example can be found in the way in which Chisso employees beat up the internationally renowned photographer, Eugene Smith, for taking photographs of pollution in Minamata (cf. Smith and Smith: 1975).

There are a large number of cases where the victims of pollution have been physically intimidated by employees and hired 'professionals' once they had made demands on the polluting firm. This action was also taken with the unofficial approval of management, which often feigned ignorance publicly but took no steps to reprimand employees for defending the interests of the firm in such a loyal manner.

These aspects are touched upon, but generally glossed over, in accounts of decision-making in local communities in Japan. Smith (1961), for example, writes about institutionalized penalties 'supported by an effective consensus of society' but does not define the key word 'effective' or explain why there is a need for sanctions if there is consensus. The creation of consensus and the stacking of public opinion against households are mentioned, but are not really explored as manifestations of shifting power alliances and as an ideological phenomenon. In this regard, it should be observed that the use of violence is a cultural pattern, not simply a device used only by the establishment to control the masses. Its use as a major motivator can also be seen in the brutality with which the Red Army was run, in the assassination of Shimoyama in the early fifties, in the in-fighting among factions in the student movement, and, as mentioned below, among workers in the labor movement. One major difference which distinguishes crime patterns in Japan from those in the United States is the relative absence of random violence. Even when the most sadistic mutilation is involved, seldom is violence perpetrated simply for the sake of violence. Rather, it is committed with a clear aim in mind: the attainment of self-interest or organizational goals. In other words, physical sanctions are seen as a viable way to obtain behavior consistent with one's needs.

III The Fine Blend of Controls

Seldom are Japanese exposed to just one of these controls in its pure form. Rather, they are constantly controlled by a fine blend of all four mechanisms (as are people in most societies). Little research, comparative or otherwise, has been done on the topic of social control in Japan. Yet without paying any attention to the matter of control and power relationships, many authors have made sweeping statements about Japan's exceptionally high levels of social consensus and the relatively central role played by a rather homogeneously distributed set of cultural values as the major determinant of social behavior in Japan. Several short examples, however, may illustrate how the presence of various controls underlines the need for more careful comparative research before firm conclusions can be drawn.

A Controls within the Business Corporation

Individuals begin to feel the control of their prospective employers even before they are employed. This comes in the form of background investigation of prospective employees. Some companies, especially during the period when the student movement was active, spent considerable sums to hire private detective agencies to investigate applicants on their short lists. In both written and oral examinations, employers inject subtly worded questions to draw out the political ideology and value inclinations of applicants.

Once employed, individuals are placed in a work situation conducive to group pressures and group policing. White-collar employees are not given private rooms or even partitioned work space. Rather, under the *ōbeya* (large stable) system, they are required to work under the watchful eyes of their workmates. Employees are often required to complete a good deal of paper work to account for money and stock or materials which they have handled. In some banks and retail stores all employees in a branch or a division will be required to stay until every yen is accounted for. In America and Australia supervisors are often given a margin of error: 'As long as it's under five dollars, forget it.' Missing stock is also much smaller in Japanese wholesale and retail operations, and surveillance for shoplifting is often much more sophisticated. In applying for vacation leave, employees are often asked to indicate their reasons and/or destinations if travelling. Many larger companies organize trips and other leisure-time activities for employees. While they may be cheap ways of doing things, unionists have been quick to raise doubts about the use of these activities to monitor what little free time employees have. Studies show that many employees do not particularly enjoy all the group activity and that in some cases those forced to play along end up with higher levels of alienation.

Rather than being given initiative, workers are often prodded to work harder, with supervisors constantly circulating and looking over their shoulders. It is thus not uncommon for employers to think they are free to squeeze as much energy as possible from employees during their time at work. Where physical labor is involved, it is common for the supervisor to single out those who are a bit slack and to chastize them in front of others, saying, '*nani o guzuguzu shite irunda*' (What are you fiddling around with over there?) or '*hayakushiro*' (Hurry up!). The practice around the turn of the century of beating factory girls for not working harder was poignantly shown in the film *Ah Nomugi Toge* (*The Nomugi Pass*) made from Yamamoto's account (1972). Although this brutality is often dismissed as something from the distant past, the same approach to personnel management could still be seen in the fifties, when the union movement for human rights at the Ōmi Spinning Mills was crushed. However, the movement uncovered a secret company operation in which girls were followed by detectives (Nihon Rōdō Kumiai Sōhyō Gikai: 1974, vol. I, pp. 586–7).

Employees are often informally advised to follow a particular course of action and their behavior is frequently channelled in a number of ways. The most blatant cases involve the creation of *goyō kumiai* (company unions) or *dainikumiai* ('second unions' favorable to company policy). In order to undermine the influence of the leftist-controlled unions which grew up in the years immediately after the war, management often took promising defectors aside and offered them promotion and other rewards for establishing an alternative union. Once created, it does not take much insight for new employees to figure out which union will give them a future in the company. The classic study of this phenomenon was made by Fujita (1955). Cole (1971a, especially Chapter 7, pp. 225–70) also discusses this phenomenon.

In the fifties and early sixties management felt that stiff measures were called for to rid companies of leftist dissidents; today management is again squarely in the driver's seat and it can afford more sophisticated devices. Nevertheless, nights out drinking with the boss, invitations for weekend golf or inclusion in special training sessions often serve as an important means of tapping the selected few. These and other cues signal go. Unpleasant assignments or, even worse, no work often signal the reverse. Such sanctions also serve as a constant reminder to other employees that they have been successful so far, but that they too are still vulnerable.

The way some of these symbols are used has been discussed by Gunji (1982, especially pp. 110–16) in his report on personnel practices at NHK. Pucik and Hatvany (1982) discuss the use of training sessions (*shain kenshū*) to implant the proper image of the company man. At the same time, it is common for employees to work ten years or so for a company without any clear sign as to their chances for promotion, although those on the elite track have already been chosen and subtly informed of their privileged status. Until the early seventies, companies often sent married men overseas by themselves for two or three years. While this in part reflected stringent foreign exchange policies, the system worked very much like the *sankin kōtai* scheme to ensure that the man returned to his company and that the nation experienced a minimal brain drain.

In recent years, Japan's quality control (QC) circles have received considerable attention from overseas, and are being introduced in one form or another into several societies, including the Philippines, Singapore and the United States. Little attention, however, has been given to QC circles as a form of management, an organizational device to ensure that workers will perform in a certain manner. While there is a good deal of rhetoric about shared profits, participation, teamwork and consensus, even the most superficial perusal of any of dozens of Japanese-language textbooks on QC circles (such as QC

Sākuru Honbu: 1971) clearly indicate that the goal is to create structures which will ensure that certain goals are met regardless of whether there is consensus, participation, etc.

The opportunities for channeling persons in one direction or another are greater in company towns. The documentary film *Polluted Japan*, and studies of company towns like Toyota and Hitachi reveal the way in which informal guidance can work. In most firms, even the decision to retire is not left to chance. Management talks about recruiting voluntary retirement, but what is meant is counseled retirement. This involves management approaching an employee and telling him that his retirement benefits will not be improved by staying with the firm. Given high rates of inflation, this means that the real value may even be lower if the employee does not leave on schedule. Management may also offer other small financial incentives to win the person being encouraged to retire over to its way of thinking.

Work is an area where regulations seem to proliferate. Upon entering a company, new entrants are required to sign a contract, and to submit a résumé, a certificate of health, a diploma, their official transcript, additional proof that they have graduated, a signed pledge, a personal guarantor's statement, written evidence of a clean criminal record and a photograph. They are usually given a book of over 100 pages which spells out the company's regulations (*shūgyō kisoku*). Again the extent and the detail would startle most foreign employees. Many Western firms have some regulations, but employees seldom read them, even when they are asked to sign a sheet saying that they have. In Japan employees are often required to memorize them and are sometimes even examined on them.

The regulations range from those on obtaining permission to leave the premises at lunch-time to requirements that employees obtain affidavits from train companies if they are late at work because of a breakdown or other failure of a train. Some clauses require that employees use only the employees' elevators and toilets, others forbid socializing with customers or bringing personal articles (such as bags with knitting, etc.) to work, except with special permission. The rules of one company carefully laid out 14 different situations in which the employee would lose his status with the company. In addition to *shūgyō kisoku*, employees are also given various texts on bylaws and procedures: how to wear the company pin, how to bow, what phrases to use with customers, how to position one's feet when standing, various particulars about singing the company song and attending morning ceremonies, the dos and don'ts of eating in the cafeteria, etc.

One area in which violence has abounded in the postwar period is industrial relations. Although this area has commonly been overlooked in recent years because of the general accolade given the Japanese system of personnel management as a major facet of the learn-from-Japan campaign, it is of considerable interest to note that the industrial peace of the seventies followed two decades of considerable unrest. The *seisankanri* movement immediately after the war was accompanied by the physical takeover of plants. Nakayama (1975, p. 178) relates how workers marched onto the president's nice *tatami* mats with muddy boots, something they had never even dreamed of doing before the war. The red purges and the Shimoyama and Matsukawa incidents also suggested how state power could be used to suppress certain elements in the labor movement. Soon came open struggles between first and second unions. Quite apart from those struggles which culminated in the Nissan and Miike strikes, one can cite the petty destruction of property and the constant annoyance of antagonists described by Hanami (1973, pp. 9–68). There has been a fair amount of violence among workers themselves. This has happened between members of number one and number two unions in some cases (as in the JNR) and among workers from different geographic areas in other cases (as at Toyota in the mid-sixties). Violence between railmen working to rule and the general public, or between pollution victims and company employees has also happened. Although foreign attention has been focused largely on the private sector and the industries which have made inroads into America and Europe, even today there is considerable tension between labor and management throughout much of the public sector, in which workers continue to strike without the right to do so. Postal workers, teachers and railway employees provide ready examples.

B Socialization and Social Control in the Educational System

An area in which Japanese society has received considerable praise is its system of education. Few would argue with the view that Japan has one of the most literate populations in the world and one of the most skilled and adaptable (e.g., retrainable) labor forces. However, little attention is given to the fact that these results have been produced on a battlefield scarred by one encounter after another between the Japan Teachers' Union (JTU) and the Ministry of Education. Many of the controversies have focused on the philosophy of how children should be educated, and the need for a proper balance between the guidance of teachers and the state and the freedom of children to develop in their own directions. The central issue is control, the Ministry of Education and conservative politicians arguing for more and the JTU for less.

It is difficult to make a simple summary of the ways in which the ideological outlook of children and young people is shaped by the system of education. There is a vast array of both private and public schools; organization and the general thrust also vary from one level to another. In public schools at the primary and secondary level, one major trend stands out over the past 30 years: increasing centralization. Early moves to centralize education in the fifties are summarized in Hall (1965b, pp. 415–26). Developments since then have been described in some detail by Miyanohara *et al.* (1979).

The arbitrariness with which American-inspired reforms were introduced into Japan (cf. Nishi: 1982) meant that certain revisions were in train when Japan regained its independence. However, the revisions were motivated less by an interest in creating institutions in line with the aspirations of the Japanese people and more by a desire simply to strengthen control of what was being taught. There were several moves to increase centralized control.

One was the introduction of *gakushū shidō yōryō* (guidelines for instruction). Although such material was initially distributed by the Ministry to supplement textbooks, adherence to the guidelines was made compulsory in 1958. Another is the *shuninsei* (system of responsible persons) which was implemented from 1975. Before, the *kōchō sensei* (principal) and the *kyōtō* (vice-principal) were the only administrative officers. Under the new system, however, the discretion of principals was increased by providing for them to select suitable persons as deans for various activities. Since 1977 these persons have been able to receive a special allowance, which has set them apart from other teachers.

The system of *kinmu hyōtei* (teacher evaluation) also served the same end. Rather than having outside assessors, principals were given a free hand in evaluating their own teachers. In 1958 the *zenkoku gakuryoku tesuto* (national equivalence examinations) were introduced to ensure that every student was judged by the same criteria. The resultant ranking of schools has further contributed to the idea of there being *de facto* a national curriculum. The idea of the modular individual for slots in the economy was further developed in the early sixties, with the notion of manpower planning. In January 1965 the *Chuō Kyōiku Shingikai* (Central Education Consultative Council) circulated its plan for producing the ideal person. It called for moral education to create citizens who would love and revere their homeland and the Emperor, a goal captured by the phrase *sokoku keiai tennō keiai.*

The resistance of the Ministry of Education to the decentralization or democratization of education could also be seen in 1978, when it fiercely opposed a decision by the Nakano Ward Council in Tokyo to select its school committee by elections. After a two-year struggle, a compromise was reached by which the chairman of the ward council would continue to nominate members of the school committee on his own authority, but that he would in the future also take note of the results of a public opinion poll on who should be on the committee.

The struggle at the Yōka Prefectural High School in Hyōgo Prefecture in 1974 also illustrates the tight reins on which students are kept. An application from students from the local *buraku* community for the school's recognition of a *buraku* study group brought out into the open not only antagonism between *buraku* factions, but also the fears of educationists representing the conservative establishment that things might get out of hand. Consciousness raising is not seen as a useful way to foster ideal types; lots of rote memory work and authority are.

One practice which is fairly standard in both private and public schools is the keeping of *naishinsho* (confidential appraisals of the students). In addition to performance in the entrance examination, high schools also consult the *naishinsho* from an applicant's middle school. Teachers are free to write their own feelings about a student. Inquisitive students in good standing with a teacher may receive some comment like 'healthy curiosity' or 'an exploring mind' whereas those seen as questioning the teacher or disrupting the class will be labeled impertinent. Students are thus in a position of having to calculate what a particular teacher may write on their *naishinsho* before acting. From an early age, attempts are made to remove spontaneity from their behavior. The control mechanism here is not shame, but rather the threat that the door to upward mobility will be closed to them. One recent case involving a middle-school activist refused entry to high school because of negative comments on his attitude toward authorities received considerable attention in the national media (e.g., *AJ*, 18 June 1982).

Another device is the *mondaiji tsūhō seido* (system of listing problem children) which is used in Nagoya (Kataoka: 1982). Principals submit lists of troublesome students (*mondaiji*) and those who are potential problems (*mondai yobiji*) to the educational committee of the city government. Students who are seen as likely trouble-makers are those who disrupt the rhythm of the class by forgetting things, by being restless, by using impolite expressions or by not doing their homework. Those coming from single-parent homes are also suspect from the beginning. Whereas in many other countries children of this type are tolerated and even given special attention to help them lead a normal student life and to locate not only their needs but also their special strengths, in Japan these children are labelled as deviants from the start and the idea of special education is given little consideration. They are constantly told that their name will be sent to the city office if they don't mind their P's and Q's. The education system may thus be seen as being a mechanism for breaking down the strong individuality of most children in order to produce more uniform human beings suitable for the technologies of mass production.

Another indicator of the trust and rapport between students and teachers is the way examinations are supervised in Japan. A good example of this can be seen in the way that university examinations are invigilated. To prevent students from cheating, a number of university officials wander about the room, pretending to be looking at the ceiling or out of the window but all the time keeping a sly but careful watch over the students out of the corner of their eye, while the students struggle to look innocent, to collect their thoughts and to put their answers on paper. This contrasts greatly with the American honor system where students are given their examination papers and then often left to complete the examinations on their own. The students are left to supervise themselves. The penalties for cheating may not be different if they are caught, but the overall view of the student as a human being is very different. It is also not infrequent in Japan for grades to be determined largely by attendance. Somewhat similar to the counting of heads at a nursery school to make sure all the children are accounted for, an attendance list is passed around and each student is required to sign his name. In a required subject like English, it is not uncommon for professors to check the roll by calling out the name of students and having them stand to read a passage from the textbook. At the same time, students too are clever at devising ways to cheat, to have their attendance recorded without attending class or to appear not to be reading a comic book during a boring lecture.

A more subtle form of control from the vantage point of the children is supervision of textbooks. Although the occupation reforms resulted in the direct censorship apparatus which existed in the prewar period being dismantled, and in local school boards deciding on textbooks, since the early fifties control over textbooks has been increasing. The Ministry of Education has resumed certain earlier censorship functions, now having the right to approve all textbooks. Its insistence on petty changes to hinder publication of a high-school history textbook by Ienaga Saburō (a renowned liberal historian) are well known (Kyōkasho Kentei: 1967–81). So too are its more blatant attempts in recent years to change the account of Japan's involvement in China during the thirties and forties (*AJ*: 13 August 1982, pp. 122–31).

Attempts to influence the curriculum and the climate in the classroom can be seen in other ways as well. One is the controversial system of teacher evaluation mentioned above. Less direct are political pressures brought to bear on teachers through the PTA. The promise of receiving (e.g., the suggestion that they may not receive) a swimming pool or various other facilities to improve the quality of their children's school (e.g., by attracting good teachers which might improve the chances that their children will succeed in entrance examinations for the next level) can be used by politicians to mobilize parents against teachers who in their teaching stray too far from accepted political ideologies (Miyanohara *et al.*: 1979, vol. II, pp. 208–22).

Control of foreign ideas entering Japan is also an area of growing concern. Attempts to internationalize public education in Japan have consistently been blocked. Although the Diet finally passed legislation in August 1982 to enable national and other public universities to appoint foreigners as tenured professors, the new law still provides that such appointments can be made only with the approval of the Ministry of Education and that foreign staff cannot head a department (*MDN*, 25 December 1982, p. 12; *ASY*, 2 November 1982, p. 5). Moreover, the Ministry of Education was quick to send a circular to administrators of secondary schools, asking that they should not hire foreign staff. Given the fact that the number of prefectures doing so has increased rapidly over the past few years and that approximately 30 foreigners were so employed by October 1982, the move is interpreted by some as an attempt to reverse the trend toward providing students with a more international education and to keep out a small Korean minority, for whom teaching is one avenue of upward social mobility and assimilation (*ASC*, 3 October 1982, p. 3).

Numerous other practices are used to regiment children. Prizes are given for perfect attendance, a status denied to children with weaker physical constitutions who are prone to illness. Until recently many high schools refused to accept physically handicapped children, on the grounds that they would be unable to pass the physical education courses necessary for graduation. Yakura *et al.* (1982, pp. 240–1) report that in Aichi Prefecture students are forced to take *okazu*, bread and milk in that precise order, continuing to rotate from one to the other until all is finished. It is reported that some teachers even use physical force to stuff the food into the mouths of children unwilling to eat, in order to inculcate the habit of *sankakutabe* (triangular eating). Children are also made to clean the classrooms in silence. They are told to wear reversible hats, red on one side and white on the other. All start with the white side out, but they are made to wear the red side out if they are caught talking. The principal and vice-principal then walk around, and teachers in classes which consistently produce red hats are called in for a warning that stricter supervision is necessary. In this regard, there is a good deal of emphasis on military order. Attention is given to *kiritsu* (standing), *rei* (bowing) and *chakuseki* (sitting). Outside the classroom, students are often told '*ki-o-tsuke*' (Stand at attention!) or '*mae ni narae*' (Get your lines straight!) (cf. Sugimoto: 1980a, p. 14).

Many schools have strict dress codes which specify hair length and how uniforms should be worn. Although universities tend to be somewhat more relaxed in this respect, junior colleges for women place special attention on the private lives of their young ladies. Even in 1982 some student dormitories continued to require that twenty-year-old coeds be back by 10.00 p.m. every evening (11.00 p.m. on Saturdays). The girls are forbidden to drink either in the dorm or outside.

As part of the regimentation of students, one could mention various types of physical violence which are used as sanctions. The most widespread are in many cases not punishments at all, but part of a toughening-up process. For 'cream puffs' and others with delicate constitutions, this emphasis on virile physical fitness and the macho cult is seen as a form of coercion which attempts to instil in students (especially male students) competitive values and a hard-nosed outlook on human nature, values which are, no doubt, of considerable importance in creating an ethos conducive to hard work and the later mobilization of the work force behind nationalistic economic policies and personnel practices. The national baseball tournaments for high-school students in the spring and summer breaks have further reinforced that ethic.

Although corporal punishment is not officially recognized now, teachers are able to enforce situations in which considerable physical discomfort is experienced by students. Sport is one area where such sanctions are visible, but the use of force extends to other areas too. The forced feeding mentioned above is only a simple example from some schools. Others can easily be cited. At one school in the Tokyo area, for talking and playing around in a class on modern dance, a woman teacher made her female students sit in formal Japanese style on the ground for an extended period of time, until the knees of some students were bruised or even punctured by small stones on the hard surface. Although in recent years a good deal of publicity has been given to student violence in schools (*gakunai bōryoku*), one survey by the Education Office of the Tokyo Metropolitan Government (Tokyo-to Kyōiku Kenkyūsho) revealed that teacher violence was much greater than that of the students. Moreover, it was reported that nearly all the students who had been classified as problem children had at one time or another experienced a beating at the hands of their teacher (*AJ*, 14 May 1982, p. 15). Kamata (1982) reports from Aichi Prefecture the practice of *jishu kanri* (personal management) in which middle-school students are compelled to shave their heads. Although the shaving of one's head is not compulsory in the strictest sense, teachers take an active role in organizing students so that considerable pressure (including their social exclusion) is brought to bear on children who do not go along with the habit.

As for the teachers themselves, the antagonism between the Japan Teachers' Union (JTU) and the Ministry of Education is well known. Aside from the indirect uses of administrative guidance to sort out those whose thinking is acceptable to the Ministry from those who are not, some mention should be made of right-wing violence against the JTU. Every year its annual convention is disrupted by right-wing groups. Owners and staff at hotels where the convention is to be held are intimidated in numerous ways. Local politicians in towns hosting the convention are also pressured. Loudspeakers are used to make it difficult for the JTU to carry on its deliberations. JTU members are jostled on their way into and out of the convention venue. On the pretext that rightists also have a right to organize and to express their political views, police have been reluctant to curb right-wing excesses or to do anything which would facilitate the activities of the JTU. Their behavior toward right-wing demonstrations to disrupt JTU activities contrasts greatly with their unwillingness to confront openly left-wing student groups in the late sixties and early seventies.

Finally, within the realm of education there is student violence. It sometimes involves attacks against the establishment (as on issues such as the war in Vietnam, the security treaty with the United States and various citizens' movements). Sometimes it is more localized and focused on a particular university for changes in the decision-making apparatus, tuition fees and regulations.

C Minimal Deviancy and Social Structure

The low crime rate in Japan has often been cited as evidence of relatively high levels of social integration. Most treatments of this issue in both English and Japanese have focused on the role of social values as the major independent variable. Given the recent attention to violence in schools (*gakunai bōryoku*), Japan's version of Hell's Angels (*bōsō zoku*) and the middle-school gang leader (*banchō*), it is meaningful to look at some of the controls in this area. According to the cultural explanation, low crime rates are primarily the result of conformity, consensus, professionalism in the police force, the absence of alienation and high overall levels of decency – all factors tied to the orientation of the population on the ideational level. However, these are not the variables which have changed in recent years and which could therefore account for the change in the level of violence in the schools.

Discussions of deviance in Japan have generally failed to consider many of the important structural features:

- (i) schooling on Saturdays (keeping students off the streets but also boxed in and frustrated),
- (ii) the large number of employees involved in security activities (e.g., *shuei, rusuban, keibiin* and the *shukuchokusei*),
- (iii) security systems for industrial installations and offices, for residences and for schools,
- (iv) the absence of a natural economy sufficient to support social drop-outs or to allow for sufficient public recreation facilities,

(v) the physical cost of living in prison,
(vi) the relatively large number of small shops,
(vii) the keeping of permanent family registers which are like centralized data banks, where dossiers on families record each individual member's indiscretions,
(viii) the extent to which elite firms hire detectives to investigate the background of all potential employees,
(ix) the effect of very strict gun control,
(x) the way in which police boxes are located in front of most urban stations and other key intersections in the transportation system, a fact which takes on added significance when we consider the society's dependence on rail transport,
(xi) the extent to which the vastly superior weaponry and authority of the police intimidates people in society.

A major shortcoming of the type of discussion of deviance which relies on *nihonjinron* for inspiration is the way it glosses over numerous control phenomena central to the issues being studied.

IV Cormorant Fishing and Falconry as Contrastive Analogies

There are a number of terms which might be used in referring to the way in which people form groups. One set of terms from Japanese might be *kumi shakai* (the organized society) and *mure shakai* (the associated society). Although both terms refer to societies composed of groups, the first uses a character with the rope radical, which symbolizes that members are bound or even tied together by some means physically restraining the individual. There are those who control and those who are controlled; those who do the binding and those who are bound. People who are controlled in this manner find it very difficult to separate themselves from the group. Military and police organizations provide good ideal types for conceiving such tightly disciplined groups, which are characterized by very clear-cut notions of hierarchy and of ranking based on differentiated authority.

The second type of group is expressed by the character which is written with the second person radical and the ideograph for sheep. It symbolizes groupings made by birds, deer and sheep. Although there are hierarchies in these groups, particularly among males, the animals are wild and may roam as they choose. Although there may be a psychological or instinctive drive which results in the animal staying with one group, times when one animal may keep another from joining his or her particular group, and pecking orders indicating clear lines of stratification, there are few group mechanisms to prevent one from straying. If young ones are nudged along it is usually by their mother, not by some group-operated mechanism, and occasionally deviant mothers simply let the young ones go unattended.

The first type of society is organized so that every aspect of an individual's life is circumscribed by a comprehensive set of supervisory monitors. The second type of society is much more fluid and the controls are fragmented and partial. The motivation of the group member and his or her sense of loyalty derive from different premisses. In the first type of society, loyalty is more likely to be assessed in terms of instrumental contributions to the group; in the latter type, more weight will be given to the spontaneity of a gesture rather than to its calculated timing.

To alter the metaphor slightly, the organizational principles found in the two kinds of society might be seen in the way in which birds are trained. The basic psychology of the first type of society may be found in the traditional Japanese art of cormorant fishing. The keeper of the birds has each cormorant on a leash, and trains them to respond to the most subtle tugs and pulls. It is impossible for the cormorants to escape and they learn to accept the teasing which almost gives them a meal before they are forced to hand it over to their master.

The rationale for the second type of society can be seen in the Western art of falconry. In this case the bird also responds to the directions of a master. However, the bird is much freer to come and go as it pleases; it is allowed much more discretion. This same principle can be seen in the use of homing pigeons. They are released and free to fly as they wish. Some never return, but most do so on their own volition.

The two types of society are shown in Figure 10.1. The *kumi shakai* corresponds to the way in which cormorants are herded about on a little boat and sent out on a leash to fish; even after they have caught the fish, the master pulls the string and constantly supervises them to make sure they do not eat their prey but obediently turn it over to the master. The *mure shakai* corresponds more to falconry; the bird is released on trust, and is free to fly away. Although both types of organization involve control, the manipulation of the subjects

Figure 10.1 *Societies with direct and indirect controls*

The *Kumi* society

The *Mure* society

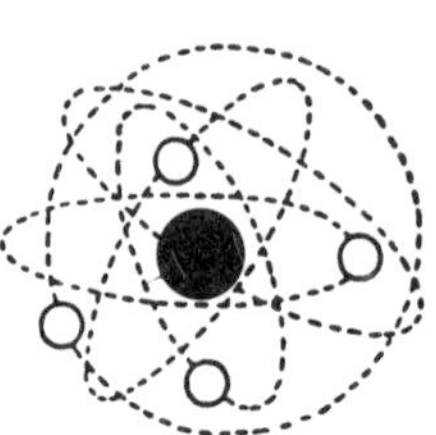

Controls in cormorant fishing

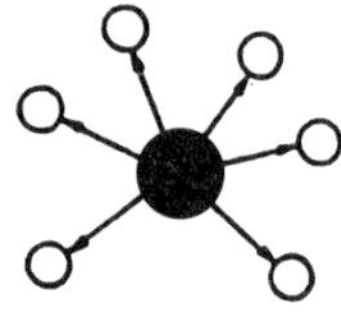

Controls in falconry

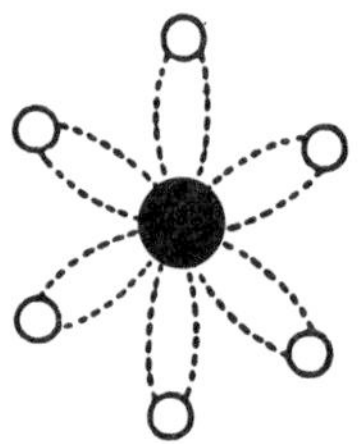

● those who control ⟶ direct controls and physical links

○ those who are controlled ...... gravitational forces and orbits

involves more physical constraints and direct intervention in the former situation and less so in the latter. The differences are both qualitative and quantitative.

Each represents an ideal type; no society will be purely of one type or the other. Nevertheless, the discussion in this chapter has suggested ways in which the Japanese approximates the first type. However, the strong sense of individualism discussed above in Chapter 8 suggests that many Japanese would prefer the latter type if given a choice. For the person in control the differences may not be so important, but for those who are controlled, the style of the master is of crucial importance. To the extent that the person in control has a contractual view of human relations and in general feels unable to trust his fellow men, the more direct mode of control is seen as producing a more satisfactory arrangement. Some people may still want to confront authority even after there is a noose around their necks, but one yank on the rope will usually straighten them out and put them in their place.

V Conclusions

Japanese history is full of examples of brutal oppression and fanatical resistance to authority. As Sugimoto (1981d) has observed, popular disturbances in Japan fit various general theories on such uprisings: explanations stressing discrepancy or relative deprivation, those emphasizing the role of repression, and theories focused on organizational features built into the social structures of those controlled. However, rather than a more exhaustive typology of specific types of conflict, a more general model is required which will link forms of social control, cultural norms and emphases on individual freedom. There is a need to explain how these different elements exist simultaneously, and how control, culture and the notion of the individual vary through time and from one social stratum to another. What is sought is not just a theory of manipulation, but one of social mobilization which can explain both nationalism and social class.

In particular, it is useful to get away from notions of dominant culture and to consider subcultures and counter-cultures as spontaneous or true reflections of the inclinations of one or more segments of the Japanese population. From this perspective attention should be shifted from the slogans of political parties to bathroom graffiti, from bronze statues of Ninomiya Sontoku to comics such as Fuji Santarō, from Miss Japan contests to the scandals reported in the weekly magazines, and from public lectures on traditional culture to *manzai* and *rakugo*. Such a shift will serve to highlight two points. One is that the link between values and behavior in much modernization literature is at best tenuous. Behavior which appears to be individualistic, contractual or coercive in the eyes of one person often turns out to symbolize conformity and strong group orientations, spontaneity and freedom of choice from the vantage point of someone else. This is particularly true if the observers are from different cultural traditions.

The second conclusion is that models or theories do not need to explain everything. There are aspects of Japanese society which might be explained by the obverse of the group model. In many cases, the choice of a single model is a choice of which phenomena will be overlooked or simply ignored. Although more research is needed, and will probably reveal other aspects of society amenable to the control model, it is unlikely that the control model will explain everything. One important task, then, is to sift through phenomena more carefully and delineate those which can be explained by the control model and those which cannot. In this task care and consideration must be given to the processes through which ideology becomes culture and the ways in which cultures and particularly dominant subcultures are used as ideology. Lilian Smith's *Killers of the Dream* (1961) about growing up in the American South before the war, is very sensitive to subtleties of this kind. Although much of one's socialization is never explicitly verbalized, she argues that it would also be naïve simply to accept as culture everything that somehow just oozes forth from the walls. Clever people have a canny ability to make arrangements promoting their own interests look quite like the natural order of things. Is the ethnocentric universalism of the walls a cultural perspective or an ideological insistence?

The second conclusion contains an invitation to move away from the notion of national character stereotypes. Rather than saying that all Japanese are this or that, it may be more revealing simply to admit that some Japanese are very group-oriented while others are very individualistic. In terms of Nakane's vertical and horizontal consciousness, Hasegawa (1966) pointed out a long time ago that both exist as distinct traditions in Japanese history, one associated with the ruling elite and the other with the common people.

It has often been mentioned that the Meiji Restoration led to a homogenization of Japanese society, with the elites imposing their vertically oriented subcultural values on other Japanese. The full-scale mobilization of Japanese society, which was the goal to be achieved by this adoption of the elite's subculture, invited a good deal of opposition from below. If the socialist movements which sprang up one after the other in prewar Japan also had an artificial element, it was largely in their foreign vocabulary, not in the horizontal values themselves. It was largely foreign to those imbued with the vertically oriented subculture of the elites. One reason for its quickly taking root in Japan was that it spoke to others in Japanese society, who found hope and optimism in the values of a horizontally based subculture. As a reading of Mannheim (1954) might suggest, this should not be a remarkably surprising discovery, although the specifics of the Japanese situation inevitably means that a uniquely Japanese set of cultural symbols is developed to express the ideas associated with ideology ('ideal situation I') and utopia ('ideal situation II'). At the same time, it would again be erroneous to rely on Mannheim's model alone; there are many elites not strongly aligned with the ruling ideology and many in the lower reaches of society who have fully internalized such ideas as their personal philosophy and values.

Figure 10.2 illustrates some of these ideas. While accounting for social conflict, Mannheim's dichotomy and Mills' tacit agreements, it also allows for cultural and ideological bonds which will cement society together. A major difficulty of this model is the extreme complexity of both the communication and the control networks involved. There are so many particular elements involved that attention is shifted from the goal of making generalizations to the goal of documenting history. One is also left with some very vague concepts, such as tacit agreement, which caused Mills trouble in *The Power Elite*. Something more convincing, more tangible, but less complex is needed than the model in Figure 10.2. As one framework for conceptualizing society, as opposed to being a theory for explaining it, the possibility of developing a multidimensional model of social stratification is explored in the next part of this book.

At this stage the important point is not that Japanese society is characterized by more control, stronger contractual ties and more frustrated individualism than is the case elsewhere. The careful comparative research necessary before any firm conclusions can be drawn has still not been conducted. The obverse model of Japanese

Figure 10.2 *The cultural control model of Japanese society*

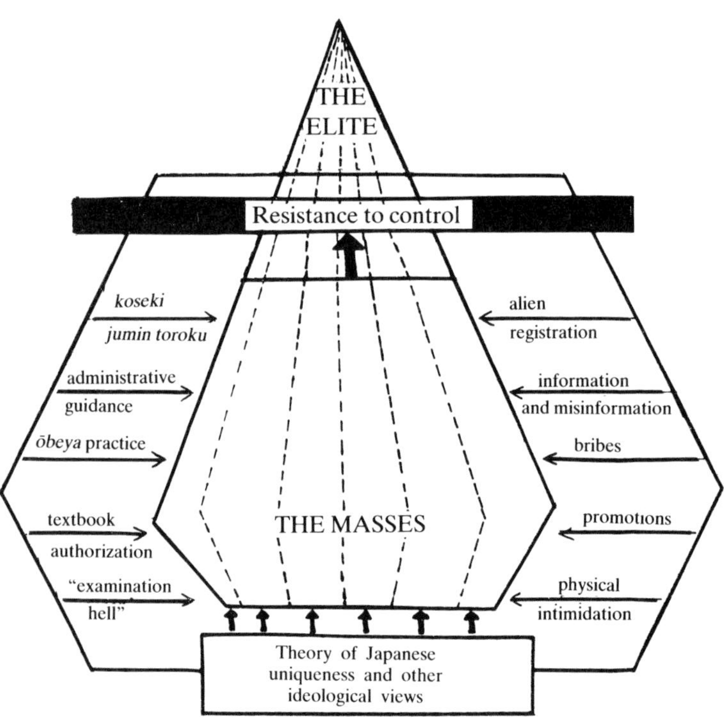

society is presented largely to illustrate the limits of theories based on narrowly defined concepts. In this regard, more attention needs to be paid to the way in which certain abstract concepts are represented by key words. The work of Needham (1979) suggests that the same key word can be used in the construction of an ideology to advocate one type of concrete behavior at one point in time or by one individual and then be used by someone else to advocate a very different type of behavior in another situation or at another time. As Wilson (1978) illustrates, even in a single society police control alone may take many forms, some involving physical violence and others administrative procedures and counseling.

In concluding the three chapters on the obverse model of Japanese society, *the fact that arbitrary examples have been chosen must be underlined.* The authors do not see the model as a fair representation of Japanese society nor yet as an empirically validated view of how Japanese society is structured. It is, however, viewed by the authors as being a model which is at least equally as valid as the group or consensus model so frequently presented in the *nihonjinron* literature. The three chapters are seen as offering a vision of phenomena commonly overlooked by those working in the *nihonjinron* tradition. Any adequate model of Japanese society must include these rather important aspects of social reality in Japan.

Part Four

Multiple Dimensions: Toward a Comparative Framework for the Study of Japanese Society

Chapter 11

Social Stratification as a Point of Departure

I Introduction

In Part One two rather different ways of looking at Japanese society were introduced. Each of the chapters in Part Two dealt with a particular skepticism regarding the group model. Although the conflict model was not similarly scrutinized, and attention was focused on the more dominant and influential set of images in the popular stereotype of Japanese society, the conflict model also deserves close examination. It too must certainly have an ideological element. Its proponents may have presented a better documented description of historical facts (as suggested in Chapters 3 and 5), and would be in agreement with many of the points made in Part Three (especially with regard to social control), and must therefore be seen as having tabled a formidable criticism of the consensus model. Yet the conflict theorists do not link their particular facts rigorously with the broader generalizations often associated with conflict theory. A major problem in collecting historical facts is that of selection. The anecdotes used by the consensus theorists were questioned not as to their accuracy but as to their representativeness and the failure to make explicit the criteria used in their selection.

In evaluating the merits of the conflict approach, many scholars would argue that the functional differentiation of roles results in a graduated continuum with individuals being spread out rather than bunched in terms of the amount of social prestige, power or income they receive. It has been suggested that the distribution is not such as to warrant the use of the catch-all categories usually associated with notions of class. The existence of several nodes or looser groupings, commonly referred to as strata, is emphasized by critics of the conflict or class approach; further, considerable mobility between the various strata is seen as a factor strengthening the sense of gradation. It is thus argued that class consciousness is weak in a complex industrial or post-industrial society like that found in contemporary Japan, and that the bases for such consciousness are at best problematic. To these doubts may be added the observation that inequality and social identification exist in dimensions other than those defined by occupational categories, and that these other loyalties and commitments cut across all occupational groupings.

The sense of dissatisfaction or at least mild skepticism with regard to both consensus and conflict-oriented models underlines the need for others. The preceding discussion, however, suggests that such models must pay careful attention to two phenomena. One is differentiation within Japanese society. It is apparent that differentiation occurs in several, cross-cutting dimensions, and that the number of significant categories defining such differentiation in most dimensions is, for the most part, arbitrary. The second is appreciable conflict. Every period in Japanese history contains its stories of struggle. In many cases the central issue involves the extent to which one party can control another; the efforts of individuals to articulate self-interest and aggregated interests are never-ending.

A brief comment is needed concerning the nature of the model developed in the next four chapters. The term 'model' is an ambiguous one in the social sciences. It is often used interchangeably with 'theory' to indicate a set of ideas which not only describe a social situation but also seek to explain it. It is also used in a less constrained fashion to indicate a visual depiction of how society is structured. In this sense a model may serve as a framework or heuristic device to facilitate research and understanding. It is primarily in the second sense that the word is used in referring to the model presented here. It provides a map of the structure of a society or, more precisely, some ideas on how to draw such a map. Accordingly, it provides not a theory but rather a framework for making cross-cultural comparisons. It is the belief of the authors that the debate on the uniqueness and universality of Japanese society or of certain features of that society would benefit by reference to such a framework when comparisons, implicit or explicit, are made.

This short chapter begins by introducing some literature generally associated with work on social stratification in Japan. Some of this work is in English, and where possible the English-language literature is cited. The chapter concludes by introducing some of Nakane's ideas as a spring-board for developing a more comprehensive model for dealing with Japanese society. The full development of that model is left for the following chapter.

II Social Classes in Japanese Society

Using a relatively loose definition of class,[1] Cole (1956) identified a number of strata or classes relevant to the comparative study of Japanese society in the prewar and postwar periods. His analysis dealt with nobility, the bureaucracy, the military, business elites, urban middle class, labor and those involved in agricultural activities in rural areas. These groupings had been noted much earlier by Norman (1975) among others, and were differentiated primarily in terms of functional or occupational criteria. It was more or less assumed that occupation is loosely, though reliably, associated with income, education and status within the total society.[2] In Cole's work two other important observations were made. First, the existence of further stratification within each of these groupings was noted. Second, some ways in which stratification can be both integrative and disintegrative were mentioned. Although it was researched nearly 30 years ago, Cole's study remains as the only account in English which attempts to sort out the whole of Japanese society in terms of stratification.

There are, however, a number of studies which examine particular social strata. In his study of the salary man, Vogel (1963) distinguishes between the old middle class (small independent businessmen and landowners) and the new middle class (white-collar employees of large business corporations and government bureaucracies), a distinction made earlier by Aonuma (1962), Hazama (1960) and others.[3] Looking even more closely at the composition of the new middle class, Ishikawa and Ujikawa (1961, pp. 4–5) identify three substrata: the lower supervisory staff, those doing technical or skilled work requiring a certain mental input, and the ordinary office worker whose primary input is physical. Others such as Miyagi (1970) suggest that those doing highly technical or semi-scientific work constitute an entirely new and self-contained class.

Although following Marxist practice in not using the term 'class' to refer to this stratum, Yamaguchi (1972) does identify and clearly differentiate between a new stratum of white-collar workers and the stratum of the older, traditional white-collar workers. Ōhashi (1971), Horie (1962) and Kawai (1973) also stress the multi-operational framework as the most important dimension in the way in which they conceptualize class or strata-based groupings. However, it should be pointed out that the emphasis of the former two and that of the latter are quite different. Ōhashi and Horie attempt to show how marginal class groupings (in agricultural or entrepreneurial activities, for example) are breaking down, while the number of white- and blue-collar workers is increasing. They also suggest that mechanization of office work and the resultant monotony have served to close the psychological gap between the blue- and white-collar strata. Kawai, on the other hand (especially pp. 39–44), suggests that the most important phenomenon is the increase in the number of white-collar employees.

This attempt to make refined distinctions can also be found in work on elites and studies of the working class. Among researchers on elites, for example, Curtis and Stockwin have suggested that it is important to distinguish between big business, the bureaucracy and the ruling party.[4] At the other end of the class continuum a series of case studies conducted in Toyama, Iidabashi and Shizuoka by the Social Research Center at the University of Tokyo in the mid-fifties focused on the importance of small amounts of mobility among occupations at the lower end of the occupational scale. Here the researchers argued for the importance of distinguishing between upper, middle and lower poverty groups. Kagayama (1970, pp. 206–87) reports on other work conducted in 1964 which took a similar tack. However, Shimodaira (1973) tends to deny the usefulness of these small differentiations, arguing that overemphasis on these refined distinctions in income and social status serves to draw attention away from more fundamental discontinuities.

Stratification occurs in other dimensions as well. Although ethnic groups in Japan are small, the plight of Koreans (Mitchell: 1969) and *burakumin* (DeVos and Wagatsuma: 1967) is well known. Another important variable is sex. Large male-female wage differentials, for example, can be easily documented (Shinotsuka: 1980; Fujii and Takahashi: 1972), and male and female subcultures can readily be identified. The dualities between large and small firms are also conspicuous. Finally, the importance of rural-urban and regional differentials has also been underlined by numerous scholars.

III Social Mobility

A second body of literature relevant to the study of social stratification deals with social mobility. Contrary to the opinion that modern Japanese society is characterized by relatively distinct classes, those dealing with social mobility argue that extensive mobility occurs on an inter-generational basis, with less but still significant mobility occurring within the lifetime of the individual on an intra-generational basis. Analysis of the data gathered by a research team of the Japanese Sociological Association from the mid-fifties indicates that Japanese society allows for mobility in a manner similar to that found in most Western societies (Nihon Shakai Gakkai: 1958; Odaka and Nishihara: 1965). Another study in 1965 suggested that Japanese society had become even more open (Tominaga: 1969, 1970a and 1970b). Tominaga (1973) later singled out four major factors accounting for extensive mobility in modern Japan: individual motivation or the desire to get ahead, differentials in the rates of fertility, structural change in the industrial and occupational composition of the labor force and changes in the institutional structure.

Finally, attention should be given to studies of business elites. The existence in Japan of a power elite as defined by Mills (1956b) is described in a comprehensive, though dated, survey by Yanaga (1968). As Mosca (1939) and Pareto (1935 and 1968) observed, societies may be characterized by the extent to which this very important group is open. The studies of Mannari and Abegglen (1971), Mannari (1974), Asō (1967) and Aonuma (1965) suggest that Japan's prewar and postwar business elites have come from a rather broad cross-section of Japanese society.

Two major questions remain unanswered in the literature on social mobility. Although changes in occupational and industrial structures have tended to open up society and to create opportunities for movement from one occupation or industry to another, comparisons over time are fairly difficult. As the whole society moves upward from an earlier set of occupations (such as farming and unskilled blue-collar work in the factory) to a new set characterized by relatively less physical labor and more intellectual input (such as white-collar or technical work), the new occupational categories (to which the prestige of being associated with the modern sector is attached) are diluted; over time they subdivide and new lines of stratification appear as those with less status in the new sectors are identified and finer distinctions are made to delineate truly prestigious jobs. Accordingly many have enjoyed mobility in absolute terms without being upwardly mobile in terms of their rank order or relative position compared with others in the same society.

A second problem concerns the role of education. In his interpretation of the data, Tominaga (1970b, pp. 134–5) places considerable importance on education as the most significant prerequisite for social (i.e., occupational) mobility. In another study on the recruitment of business elites, Azumi (1969, pp. 15–29) argues that education is the major channel for social mobility. However, one could argue that entrance into the University of Tokyo and employment as a top bureaucrat forms one set and that the real question concerns the factors determining entry into this stream. In this regard, educational attainment must be conceived not just in terms of years of schooling but also in terms of the particular school or university attended; many schools, and particularly the better universities, are relatively closed institutions. While the number of those going on to receive a university education has increased remarkably, the elite universities have become relatively more difficult for those from lower social strata to enter. For example, although the University of Tokyo is a public institution and sets low tuition fees, the necessity of attending expensive private preparatory schools before taking the entrance exam has resulted in a situation where the average income of the parents of entering freshmen at the University of Tokyo exceeds that of their counterparts at much more expensive private universities like Keiō and Waseda.[5]

The use of data grouped simply according to the level of education (middle school, senior high school and university) results in these phenomena being overlooked. Greater access to tertiary-level education and diminished income differentials between statistical groupings based on levels of education (or between their related occupational groupings) do not necessarily mean that the relative position of those graduating from the half-dozen or so elite schools at any given level has changed or that mobility into and out of this elite set has increased. By raising questions of this kind, the literature on social mobility shifts our attention from narrow concerns with occupational categories to the level and place of education.

Tominaga (1970b, p. 133) cites the work of Hayashi Megumi, Moriji Shigeo, Tachi Minoru and Kuroda Toshio in writing that 'social mobility in the broad sense has been defined to include population movements from rural villages to the cities.' He also mentions the work of Ujihara Shōjiro, Nishikawa Shunsaku, Yamamoto Kiyoshi, the Ministry of Labor and others in pointing out that 'social mobility in the broad sense also refers to the movement of labor from one locality, industry or firm to another' (pp. 133–4). Nevertheless, Tominaga tends to limit the concept of vertical mobility to changes in social status as defined by occupation, level of education and income; inequality and mobility in other dimensions generally remain ambiguous, as does the concept of social stratification. In explaining why class consciousness is so underdeveloped in Japan, Yasuda (1973) is more explicit. He mentions the importance of different dimensions as they set in motion a complex matrix of cross-cutting considerations in terms of the way individuals conceptualize self-interest (pp. 206–08). It is a view which recognizes that income, social status and power are societal rewards and that an individual's relative access to these rewards varies with his or her position in terms of numerous stratification variables including, but not limited to, occupation or level of education.

IV Suggestions from Nakane and the Role of the Firm

In the first chapter of *Japanese Society* Nakane develops a typology for classifying solidarities in any society. One category is for solidarities growing out of relationships between individuals who belong to the same frame (*ba*). The other is for solidarities which arise among individuals who share the same attribute (*shikaku*). She later goes on to characterize relationships associated with the former type as vertical and those with the latter type as horizontal. Although these concepts are not adequately defined, Nakane's examples suggest that she is referring primarily, though not exclusively, to organizational principles of affiliation characterized by the firm and to solidarities based on the notion of occupation. These two types of solidarity are shown diagrammatically in Figure 11.1. Two hypothetical societies, each with a population of 20 persons, are considered. The first is characterized as one in which individuals are tied together by vertical solidarities (↕) and competition occurs between firms (⬌). The other is characterized as one in which individuals are linked by horizontal identities (↔) and competition occurs between hierarchically ranked occupational groupings (⬍).

Figure 11.1 *Configuration of social solidarity according to vertical and horizontal relationships which are delineated by attribute and frame*

A Solidarities based on vertical ties arising from belonging to the same situation (e.g., being employed at Firm I, II, III or IV)

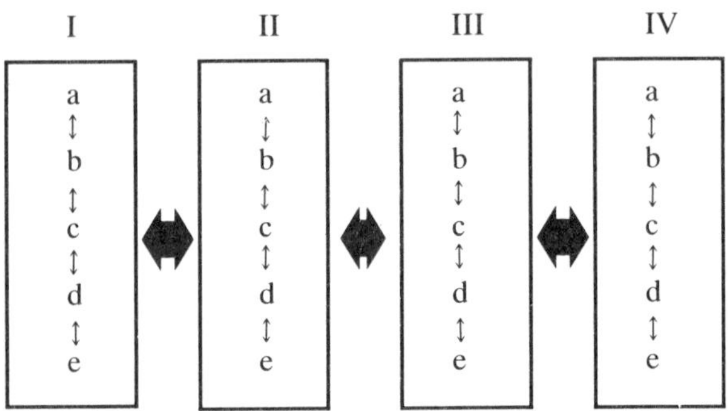

B Solidarities based upon horizontal ties arising from possession of similar attributes (e.g., belonging to occupation A, B, C, D or E)

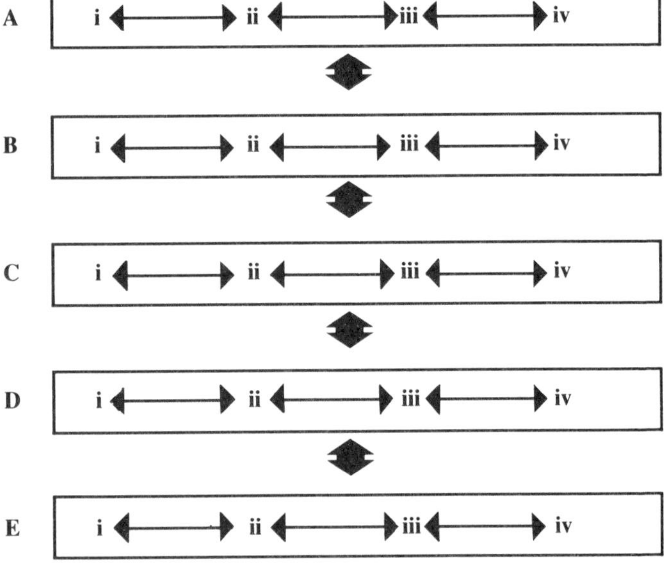

Attribute and frame are essentially meta-theoretical or umbrella concepts for categorizing the different criteria (i.e., stratification variables) by which populations are divided into social classes.[6]

Although the conceptual consequences of this formulation are not fully developed by Nakane, she seems to have presented clearly the rudiments of a two-dimensional stratification model which is, as a theoretical construct, superior to the single-dimension model based on occupational groupings or class alone. There is a certain rationale to emphasizing the importance of the firm. Before discussing the role of the firm, however, it might be useful to consider a problem concerning the association of the two types of solidarity with verticality and horizontality.

Nakane is not the first to make such an association. In the twenties Sorokin (1959) wrote about vertical and horizontal mobility. Aruga also spoke of the vertical (*tate*) and the horizontal (*yoko*) in his work on social structure in rural Japan (see Kawamura: 1975, vol. 2, pp. 196–7).[7] Although the rationale for their having been chosen is not explained, vertical seems to imply hierarchy and horizontal to imply equality. However, just as various occupational positions are hierarchically ranked within a given firm, so too can those within a given occupational group be ranked according to their places of employment. The hierarchical relationship between firms by size and subcontracting is well institutionalized in the *keiretsu* relationships which characterize not only Japan's major industries (Noguchi *et al.*: 1973) but also many of its *jiba sangyō* (local industries) (Ide and Takeuchi: 1980). If rankings are conceived more generally in terms of social rewards (to use a term from the literature on social stratification) and if we consider only one type of reward, income, it is readily apparent that just as there are occupational wage differentials, so too are there firm-size differentials. It thus occurs to us that a vector analysis might provide a more fruitful approach. Such an analytical framework allows for social mobility to occur as a result of a change in either the frame in which one is situated or the attribute one possesses.

In Figure 11.2 the two dimensions shown in Figure 11.1 are superimposed to create a matrix which is roughly scaled to approximate the distribution of the Japanese labor force. To the extent that Nakane writes about permanent employees in Japan's large firms, she is writing about a rather small group in Japan. Table 5.6 suggests, less than 20 percent of the labor force is employed in firms with over 300 employees. Although several ways of considering occupational groupings are common in Japan, the figures in Tables 11.1 and 11.2 suggest that the percentage of the labor force in the occupations described by Nakane is limited to 25 percent at the most.

Figure 11.2 is drawn on the dubious assumption that the same occupational composition exists in firms of all sizes. The shaded area in the upper right-hand corner of Figure 11.2 represents less than 5 percent of the entire labor force. One might also argue that some in categories C and G and most in categories F and I should be added (bringing the occupational total to a maximum of 50–60 percent); the total then rises to 15 percent at most. However, when one is reminded that Nakane was writing about men in certain age groups living in particular geographically defined areas in Japan, it can easily be seen that the sample from which she sought to generalize about Japanese society was even further restricted. This discussion relates to the problem of variation and sample representativeness discussed above in Chapter 6 (pp. 130–3). Although Figure 11.2 shows only two dimensions and underlines the importance of the firm as a significant variable, it does by omission direct attention to other dimensions. Before turning to consider some of the other dimensions, such as sex, age or geographical location, the firm might well be discussed in further detail.

Table 11.1 *Occupational distribution of the labor force: the percentage distribution of the gainfully employed by employment status, 1981*

I	Entrepreneur		13.79
II	Family workers		7.03
III	Regular employees		71.65
	A White-collar	31.07	
	B Blue-collar	40.58	
IV	Irregular employees		7.50
TOTAL			100.00 (N = 5071)

Note: The breakdown in category III is estimated by using the ratio given in the Kakei Chōsa (Family Income and Expenditure Survey) in 1980.

Sources: Sōrifu Tōkeikyoku (Bureau of Statistics, Office of the Prime Minister), *Rōdōryoku Chōsa* (Survey of the Labor Force), as reported in Rōdōshō (1982), pp. 22–3.
Sōrifu Tōkeikyoku (1981b), pp. 120–1.

Table 11.2 *Occupational distribution of the labor force: the percentage distribution across occupational categories by sex, 1980*

	Occupational categories	Males	Females	Both sexes
A	Professional and technical personnel	4.79	4.48	9.27
B	Administrative personnel	5.24	.28	5.52
C	Clerical personnel	10.79	11.28	22.07
D	Sales personnel	8.66	4.00	12.65
E	Miners and masons	.10	.00	.10
F	Transport workers	5.47	.36	5.83
G	Skilled and ordinary process workers	24.08	7.99	32.08
H	Laborers	2.39	1.37	3.77
I	Public order and other service workers	4.28	4.43	8.71
TOTAL (N = 39,280 million)		65.80	34.19	100.00

Source: Sōrifu Tōkeikyoku (Bureau of Statistics, Office of the Prime Minister), *Rōdōryoku Chōsa* (Survey of the Labor Force), as reported in Rōdōshō, Fujin Shōnenkyoku (1981), pp. 54–5.

There are several reasons why the firm is important to our understanding of social stratification in Japan. The first has to do with the large amount of attention given to the dual structure of Japan's economy (Broadbridge: 1966; Yamanaka: 1971; Tokyo Metropolitan Government: 1972). The term 'dual economy' or 'dual structure' is sometimes used in referring to differentials between the agricultural sector and the industrial sector or between the traditional sector and the modern sector (see, for example, Shinohara: 1972), phenomena not at all unrelated to our discussion here. Nevertheless, the most common reference in the Japanese literature is to the large differentials which exist between a privileged few who are employed in elite corporations with over 1000 employees and those employed in very small entrepreneurial firms and shops with less than, say, 50 employees.

Another interest in the firm lies in the fact that it is an important arena where the two groups seen by conflict theorists as being most fundamentally antagonistic to each other (workers and capitalists) are brought together. It is at work, many such theorists would argue, that workers come to feel alienated as a result of work-loads being intensified in the name of greater productivity or efficiency, while an increasing amount of their surplus is distributed to other members of society. In contrast, those inclined toward the group model of

Figure 11.2 *A two-dimensional distribution of the labour force*

Note: The occupational categories correspond to those in table 11.2.

Japanese society have argued that the firm is the key organizational unit in Japanese society. In particular, literature on labor-management relations tends to stress the commitment of the Japanese employee to his company and the existence of some kind of symbiotic relationship between the union and management. The company union, lifetime employment and the seniority wage system are seen as being the key concepts. This interpretation has been made popular in English by Abegglen (1958 and 1973). Similar generalizations may be made from another study of large firms in Japan and the United States by Whitehill and Takezawa (1968, particularly pp. 344–63). The strongest statement of this view is in books edited by Ballon (1969) and an OECD study team (1977). The most articulate Japanese emphasizing this dimension have been Hazama (1964 and 1971), Iwata (1977, 1978 and 1980) and Tsuda (1968 and 1976). It is a view also promoted by Nakayama (1972) and Yakabe (1977). Low strike rates and low rates of labor turnover, as well as some of the cultural value-orientations commonly associated with the group model, have often been cited in further support of this thesis. Meanwhile, a thorough debate has gone on for a number of years as to how this system in general, and the seniority wage schedule in particular, came into being.[8] However, the emphasis has continued to be on how Japan's labor-management relations and the employee's commitment to his firm are rooted in Japan's cultural values, with the firm replacing the family as the major social unit in Japanese society.

Dore (1973) referred to this arrangement as 'welfare corporatism', noting that it provides many Japanese male employees with a particularly strong sense of belonging. Earlier he wrote that 'the viability of Japanese patterns of welfare corporatism throws doubt on the assumption that individualistic market-oriented contractual relationships in employment are essential to efficient industrialization' (1971: p. 125). As the most important predisposing factor, he stressed Japan's 'traditional ethic which lays an overwhelming stress on group loyalty and the subordination of individual interests to the interests of the group to which the individual belongs' (p. 120).

The emphasis on the firm as the social institution which best serves the individual's need for group identification means that it must be seen as an important source of differentiation within society. It is not, however, the only source of differentiation; nor is it necessarily the group with which most Japanese will readily identify. For example, Tominaga (1968) reports that only 12.1 percent of all employees stay at the same firm throughout their careers. The point is also made by Cole (1972b, pp. 616–18) who cites a number of other sources in making his point. Three considerations suggest that the importance of the firm should not be exaggerated.

First, many institutions previously thought to be unique to the Japanese firm have been shown not to be so. Scholars like Shimada (1974) have shown that similar seniority wage schedules can be found in other industrial societies. Other data also suggest that lifetime commitment is not uniquely Japanese.[9] Finally, Umemura (1967) argues that the theory of a unique seniority wage system does not stand up on logical grounds.

Second, commitment to the firm is not complete. Although occurring at a slower pace than in some other industrial societies, mobility between firms does occur; very few people work 30 or 40 years with the same firm.[10] Authors like Odaka (1965) point to the existence of split loyalty; workers feel torn between their sense of commitment to both the company and the union. Okamoto (1971) takes an even stronger stance, arguing that employees, particularly the younger generation, have become indifferent toward both. Kojima (1973) uses some of the same data, but concludes that alienation among the young has led not to apathy but rather to greater militancy. Kamata (1973 and 1974) emphasizes indifference as a major theme among employees in many of the large firms where commitment to the firm is supposed to be most entrenched. Behind this indifference, he argues, there is widespread alienation and a deep sense of inefficacy.

Finally, there are the *objective* differentials between the firms themselves. These are not small and there is a general awareness of which firms or types of firm get what. Consequently, one's sense of *subjective* identification with one's firm is partially dependent on the *objective* or *subjective* ranking of that firm relative to all other firms. Accordingly, the sense of identification with the firm and the nature of that identification will vary according to the firm's size and performance.

V Toward a Synthetic Model of Social Stratification

The literature introduced in this chapter provides a useful point of departure in the search for more sophisticated models of Japanese society. In developing alternative views, however, several points should be remembered. First, there is a certain artificiality in the construction of occupational categories; they can be arbitrarily subdivided to give the appearance of forming a graduated continuum. Despite the attempts of Landecker (1960 and 1963) and others to develop a framework for identifying significant categories in terms of class or status crystallization, Wild (1974) still raises the question of whether the significant categories are in fact nothing more than statistical artefacts. He argues that they allow those studying social mobility to expend considerable energy on statistical exercises which do not yield an understanding of the real essence of social stratification.

Second, other variables also explain access to social rewards and societal cleavage. The level of educational attainment is one such variable, although it correlates rather well with occupational grouping. The firm is another such variable, significant because it cuts across occupational groupings. Managers, secretaries, manual operatives or janitors work at different firms; the access of those in the same occupational grouping to social rewards and their consciousness will in some measure be affected by the particulars of the firm in which they are employed. Although much of the literature on industrial relations and personnel practices emphasizes the impact of the firm on the *subjective* consciousness of the employee, it is also important to delineate precisely those aspects of the firm which shape the employee's *objective* well-being. One must also recognize, however, that within firms a number of practices, such as the seniority wage system, produce similar patterns of differentiation according to other variables which supersede differences among firms. In short, we are compelled to consider both inter- and intra-firm inequalities. An awareness of these additional kinds of differentiation makes one less inclined to accept the simple explanations which result in holistic generalizations about all of Japanese society and culture and exaggerate the importance of variation in only one dimension of social stratification.

A third issue is the considerable social mobility existing in most complex industrial societies. It is exceedingly difficult to judge the significance of a given set of categories in determining the choices of the individual. To what extent does each variable delineate behavioral choices? To what extent does each parameter limit choice and constrain behavior? Cleavages caused by occupational differentiation may be bridged by considerable mobility and the presence of

Figure 11.3 *A stratification model in two dimensions*

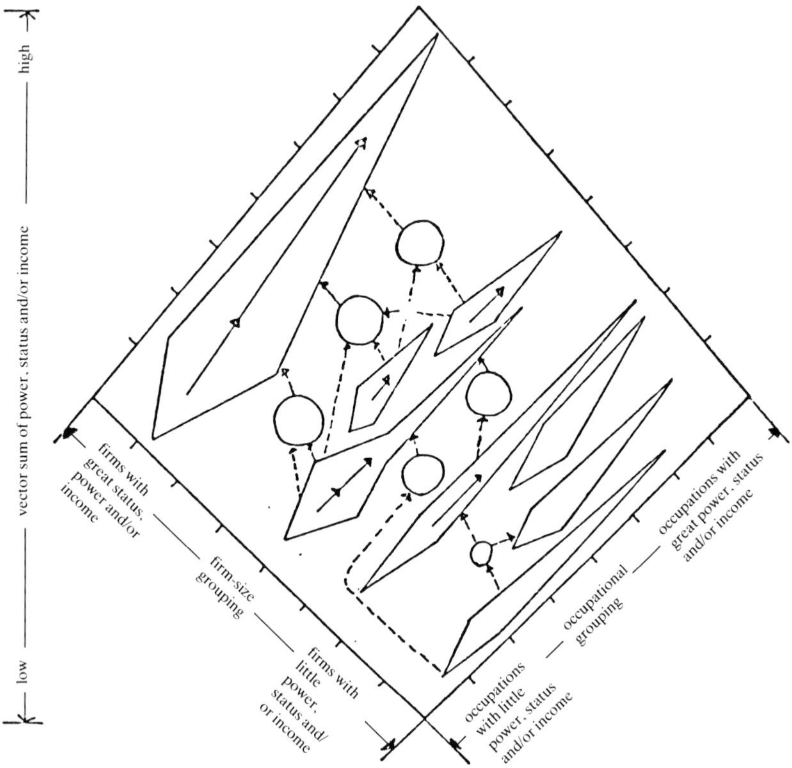

low
vector sum of power, status and/or income
high
firms with great status, power and/or income
firm-size grouping
firms with little power, status and/or income
occupations with little power, status and/or income
occupational grouping
occupations with great power, status and/or income

○ school

◊ firm

⟶ upward intra-generational mobility, primarily among occupations within the same firm

- - → upward inter-generational mobility between firms, with or without occupational mobility

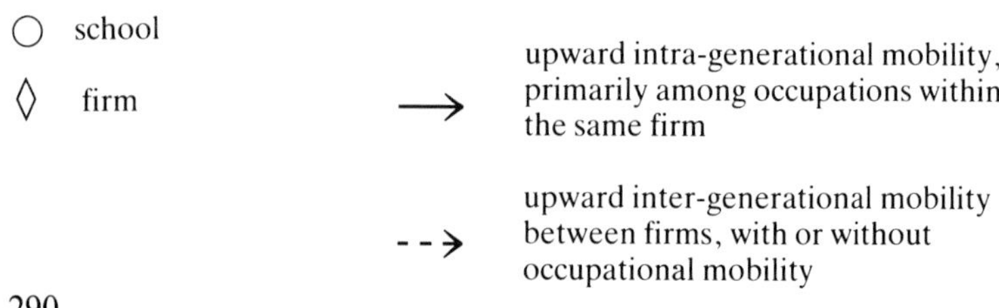

other cross-cutting differentiations based on the level of education and firm affiliation. Other sources of differentiation (including sex and spatial location) must also be considered. A closer look at organizational structures within the firm would reveal their importance.

Consideration of only two dimensions–occupation and the firm–yield the map of Japanese society presented above in Figure 11.2. This can be redrawn as Figure 11.3 to highlight further the sense of there being a matrix built on vectors. One task for the following chapter is to show how additional vectors or dimensions can be incorporated within the model and to explore further the notion of hierarchy in the ranking of the categories in any given dimension.

Chapter 12

A Multidimensional Stratification Framework for the Comparative Study of Japanese Society

The preceding chapter identified some major variables accounting for differentiation. It did not, however, discuss the criteria used in ranking individuals in any particular dimension. This chapter deals first with the ranking criteria and then develops a fuller set of demographic variables associated with social differentiation. The third section suggests how these two aspects are related. The chapter concludes with a brief discussion of the relationship of the stratification model to the understanding of social class.

I Societal Rewards and the Social Ranking of Individuals

In Section II of the preceding chapter the notion of hierarchy was mentioned, and the terms hierarchy and vertical principle were used somewhat interchangeably. It was suggested that the horizontal also had an element of hierarchy, and that in the broadest sense hierarchy could be understood as being a ranking in terms of access to social rewards.[1] While shifting to a term with a slightly different nuance, 'societal rewards',[2] this section will seek to define the concept more fully.

A Societal Rewards: Toward a Definition

Societal rewards are here defined to include both returns to the purposive activity of the individual and any other incidental gains relevant to the welfare or well-being of the individual. They are societal to the extent that they result from activities involving social arrangements or having social implications.[3] In complex societies, rewards are usually created by the interaction of two or more persons. Rewards include tangible or material goods and more intangible or psychological returns associated with social position. Finally, rewards may in many cases be used as resources; they may be reallocated to other persons in exchange for certain behavior or for other rewards, a phenomenon not unrelated to that of reward fungibility which is discussed below.

The value of any given reward will vary from person to person. Although in a given society there may be general agreement on the value associated with different rewards, there may still be considerable variation in the marginal utility which a given reward has for any given individual. Distribution may be evaluated on two levels; the uniform distribution of goods does not always guarantee that egalitarian goals have been achieved. Accounts of both foreign aid and social welfare abound with examples of how well-intentioned donors have given items of great value to themselves but of questionable value to the recipients.

Purposive activity involves a cost calculation. An individual's net intake of rewards is equal to the gross intake minus the costs. Costs include both real costs and opportunity costs. For example, to earn an income to purchase a home and to feed and clothe a family, one may also have to cover transport costs and expend many hours of physical and mental energy that might also be spent in political activity, reading technical journals or mere relaxation. To enjoy status and psychological satisfaction from one friendship or association, one sometimes has to sacrifice that derived from another relationship. One's well-being is also affected by a nearby factory which releases pollutants that disturb all living in the vicinity, but which also constructs a new road that all may use freely.

B Types of Reward

As a heuristic device, many writers have sought to develop a typology for societal rewards. It is argued that rewards are best studied together with other rewards which have similar properties.

One early effort along these lines is found in the work of Weber (1958). In rejecting Marx's emphasis on monocausal economic forces, Weber sought to distinguish between three areas of purposive human activity – the economic sphere, the political sphere and the sphere of social status.[4] This same approach has generally been followed by succeeding scholars, but for the most part has not undergone close scrutiny. Runciman (1967) considered the desirability of adding a fourth category for information, but in the end stayed with Weber's classification (see the selection from Runciman in Béteille: 1969, pp. 45–63). Tumin (1967) also retains the so-called Weberian triad, referring to the three as property, power and prestige, but adds a fourth category, psychic gratification, as a kind of catch-all for any other rewards. Although a detailed discussion of each kind of reward is beyond the scope of this chapter, the authors propose to continue the discussion using a four-category typology: income (W), power (X), information (Y) and prestige (Z).[5] Each has been studied in depth by different disciplines in the social sciences (Table 12.1) and is discussed briefly below.

1 Income. Income accrues to people in several forms: wages, interest and rent are the components commonly discussed in introductory economics. Some minimal amount of income is essential, not only to obtain many daily necessities but also to enjoy life and to have some freedom of choice. Among the four rewards, income seems to be the most tangible and the most readily quantified. Perhaps for that reason, its distribution is most frequently used as an index of social inequality in empirical studies. Moreover, it is commonly assumed that income is a fairly good indicator of the relative amount of one's other societal rewards. Finally, a special importance is attached to income inequality and the economic structure by many proponents of the conflict model.

2 Power. The essence of power lies in the ability to cause other people to do things, either against their will or in a manner contrary to their true self-interest. Here too various subcategories exist: physical power, authority, influence and persuasion. Politicians, elite businessmen and top bureaucrats all have fairly large reserves of power. So too, though perhaps to a lesser extent, do leaders in labor unions, the mass media and various social movements. Those who are not affiliated with any social organization, especially those who do not belong to politically oriented groups, are usually characterized as having small amounts of power.

3 Information. Knowledge, learning, common sense and perception are all forms of information. Some information will be of better quality and provide the individual with more satisfaction than other information. Concepts such as the 'age of information' or the 'information society' direct attention to the importance of information, not only as an end in it itself but also as an important resource which can be used to generate upward social mobility. People in the media, those able to speak a foreign language, academics, bureaucrats and others in positions of authority generally may be considered to have disproportionately high access to information. People who are at the forefront of their occupation or who are in control at their place of work generally have access to information and are even able to generate information. To some extent they can also control the quality and quantity of information others receive.

4 *Prestige.* It is common in literature on social stratification for there to be a rather open or catch-all category for the various kinds of satisfaction people receive from being favorably evaluated by those around them and especially by those commonly referred to as significant others. The idea of such positive evaluations is partially captured by terms such as: fame, honor, esteem, respect, laurels, regard, approbation, acclaim, kudos, glory, veneration, applause and popularity. School headmasters or principals, public figures, statesmen, stage performers and athletes often enjoy a good deal of prestige. Those who are ostracized from society are usually denied access to this resource.

Each category of rewards can be further broken down as suggested in Table 12.1. Before considering some societal macro-models utilizing the notion of rewards as the key variables, two additional comments should be made.

First, the term societal reward is not used to imply that the recipient is deserving in a moral sense or that there is social agreement on the criteria determining who should (in a normative sense) be rewarded more or who should be rewarded less. Rather, the word is used as a generic term to indicate anything that has a utility for someone, the creation of which involves interaction with one or more other persons.

Second, whenever there is disagreement with regard to the goals (production priorities) of social interaction, the distinction between distribution and goals becomes less clear; the achievement of person A's goals at the expense of achieving B's goals results in the distribution of societal rewards which have relatively more utility for person A. In other words, the composition of any individual's rewards markedly influences the total value or utility of his share. As Nakayama (1975) suggests, there is probably a trade-off between efficiency in terms of producing some type of material satisfaction, on one hand, and the level of non-material satisfaction and the sense of

Table 12.1 *Types of reward*

Reward cluster	Vocabulary associated with each reward dimension			Examples of each kind of reward	Academic disciplines in which the reward is most studied
	Runciman	Tumin	Mouer-Sugimoto		
Economic rewards	wealth	property	income	salary pension environment employment security job safety public recreation facilities leisure bribes	economics urban planning conservation ecology engineering
Political rewards	privilege	power	power	charisma influence authority contacts guns and tanks army or police force votes publicity posters slush funds information and intelligence	political science sociology of man's social movements law and jurisprudence military history

Table 12.1 *Continued*

Reward cluster	Vocabulary associated with each reward dimension: Runciman	Tumin	Mouer-Sugimoto	Examples of each kind of reward	Academic disciplines in which the reward is most studied
Psychological rewards	rank	prestige psychic gratification	prestige	status prestige honor esteem fame publicity recognition charisma friends conspicuous consumption	sociology in general psychology and psychoanalysis theology sociology of religion
Information-based rewards			knowledge	knowledge specific skills social awareness technical know-how patents and copyrights inventions instruction and education industrial property intelligence access to mass media books, papers, manuscripts	education educational sociology sociology of knowledge communications theory journalism

Figure 12.1 *Reward-based models of social stratification*

A Power model (Lenski)

power
privilege
prestige
altruism
x, y, z
relative degree of economic inequality determined by economic surplus

B Power model (Dahrendorf)

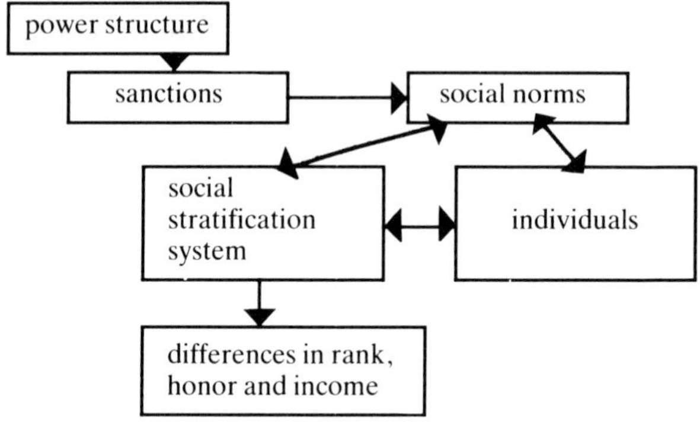

C Economic model (the Lynds)

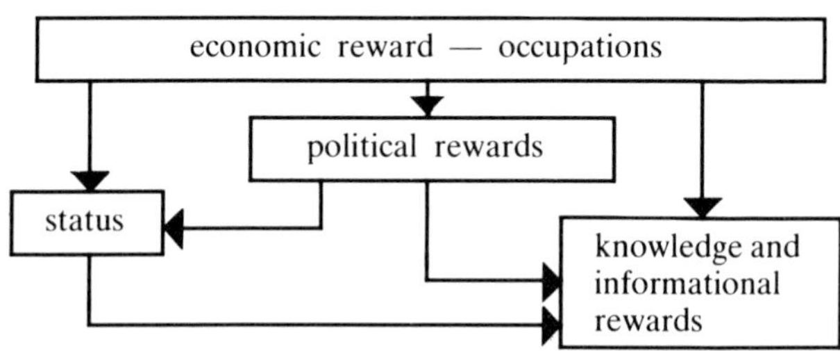

D Economic model (Wessolowski)

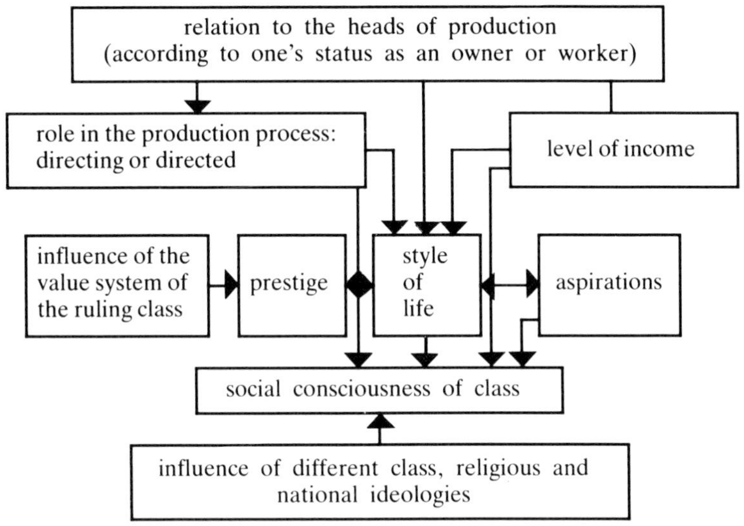

E Status model (Warner)

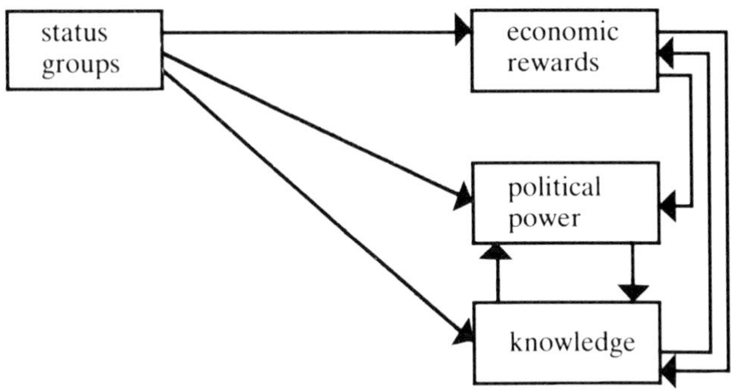

Sources: A Lenski (1966), pp 45–6;
B Dahrendorf (1969b);
C Lynd and Lynd (1929) as explained in Gordon (1958), pp. 122–48;
D Wessolowski (1969), pp. 122–48; and
E Warner's Yankee City series as presented by Gordon (1968), pp. 89–100.

psychological well-being which accompanies active participation in the decision-making processes, on the other.[6]

C Models Which Emphasize the Typology of Rewards

Many of the familiar models in the literature on social stratification pertain to the delineation of rewards and the ways in which different types of reward interact. Several of these reward models are presented in Figure 12.1. Two are power-based models (Lenski and Dahrendorf); two are economic models (the Lynds and Wessolowski); and one is a status-based model (Warner).

In the first two, power accounts for the distribution of economic and status rewards. The economic models view the distribution of economic rewards as the determinant or independent variable. The status-based model similarly attaches prime importance to status.

The most conspicuous aspect of these five models is their monocausal or uni-directional flow patterns. The emphasis is on one type of reward, suggesting that access to one type of reward leads to the acquisition of other rewards. However, when discussed on a general level with only the most crude distinctions being made, such as grouping all rewards into four categories, arguments as to whether power creates economic advantage or whether economic advantage gives way to power is in many ways like arguing whether the chicken or the egg came first. In general, three conceptual problems characterize these models.

1 Definitional Problems. One problem concerns definitions. Most of these models of stratification expand the definition of one type of reward and reduce the scope of definitions of the other types. Exponents of the power-based model, for example, define power in such a way as to subsume economic privilege or status symbolism. Distribution of many economic goods is seen as distribution of the right to command the services of those goods; status is interpreted as being the power to control ideological symbols. Proponents of the economically based model extend the realm of economic activity to include the production of the instruments of coercion, monopolistic behavior and secret price cartels, and the psychological manipulation of advertising to produce conspicuous consumption. The concept of status as a total judgement can also be cited.[7]

Although these models raise a number of questions with regard to the definition of societal rewards, they focus attention on the need to be concerned with the dynamics of cause and effect. In the end, rather than presenting precise and clear-cut definitions of four mutually exclusive reward categories like those in the models in Figure 12.1, it might be better to recognize the fact that such neat definitions are at this stage difficult to derive, and that many rewards will fit into more than one of these categories. Military equipment is both an economic good and an instrument of power. A book may be evaluated as income (for the publisher or the author), knowledge (for the student), political power (for the politician wanting to generate an ideology) or status (for the author of a bestseller). Conspicuous consumption provides yet another example. This type of overlapping among reward clusters is illustrated in Figure 12.2.

2 *Feedback and the Fungibility of Rewards.* A second problem is the failure to identify more carefully dynamic interaction among various reward clusters. The causal relationship between two clusters is usually interactive or two-way. An integrated approach might better suggest a complex network of interrelationships. Income can generate power and power can generate income. Income can be used to set up a political organization, to buy publicity, to make bribes and to purchase various instruments of coercion. Power allows one to pass legislation which alters the demand for certain goods, regulates or permits certain kinds of economic behavior which have external signs, levies taxes on certain kinds of income and/or provides for certain transfers of income, like those through a welfare system. In this way there seems to be a certain amount of fungibility which allows an individual to shift his or her holdings in one reward to another reward. By breaking down each cluster into its components, these relationships are perhaps easier to see. Perhaps certain types of income may be converted into status, while other types cannot be so easily transformed. While there would seem overall to be a high degree of fungibility or reward liquidity, different rewards are not equally convertible. While recognizing the existence of reward inconsistency (which is, in Lenski's terms, one type of status inconsistency) whereby a person might have a large income but little status or power, the authors are inclined to believe that there would be a high, though by no means perfect, correlation between individual holdings of different rewards, and that reward consistency would be the norm.

3 *Distribution.* Reward models do not answer one major question: which individuals receive how much of which societal rewards and why? At best these models seem to indicate only that those who somehow obtain access to one reward will also be able to obtain other

Figure 12.2 *An interactive model for societal rewards*

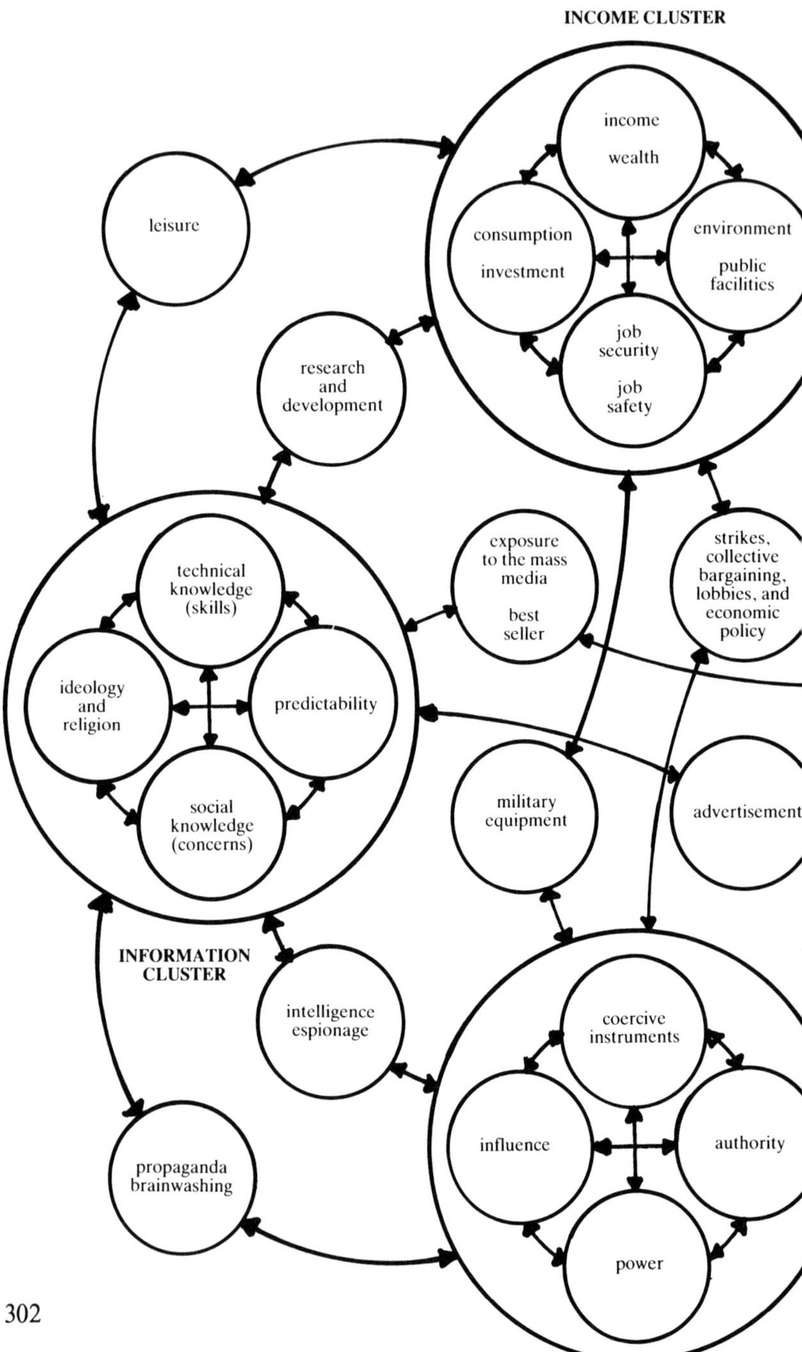

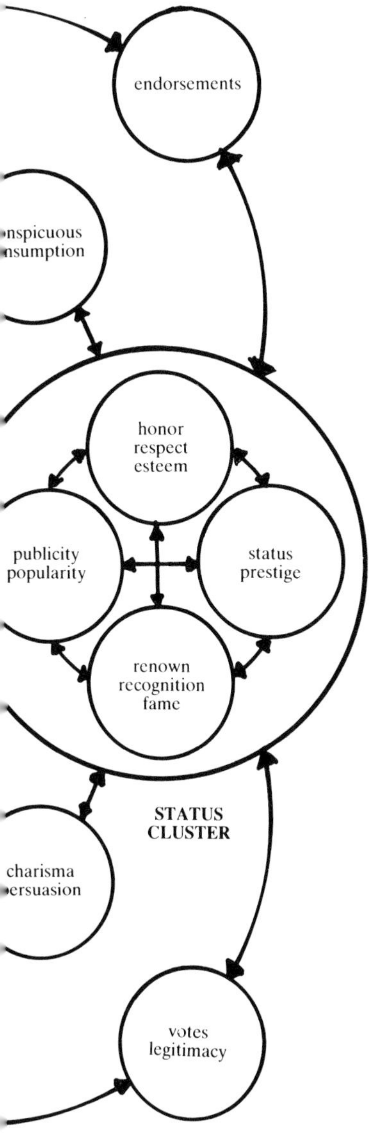

endorsements
nspicuous
nsumption
honor
respect
esteem
publicity
popularity
status
prestige
renown
recognition
fame
STATUS
CLUSTER
charisma
ersuasion
votes
legitimacy

kinds of reward: to him who hath shall even more be given. The recipients of various societal rewards are simply not identified. For this purpose, reward models must be combined with some consideration of stratification variables to obtain a fuller picture as to how societies are stratified. By themselves these models tell us a good deal about interrelationships among the various rewards. However, they tend to leave us with the tautological conclusion that the total social position (TSP) of the individual is defined as his or her total access to societal rewards. One is not told how to distinguish between one individual with a large share of rewards and another individual with a small share, apart from measuring their shares.

II Differentiation and the Stratification Variables

Differentiation involves decisions about who receives how much for doing what (achievement criteria) or for being what (ascriptive criteria). Both the group and conflict approaches described in the preceding chapters agree that differentiation occurs primarily in terms of occupational roles ranked in a functional hierarchy. They disagree as to the nature of the relationships between roles and between persons filling different roles. The integrationists argue that those lower in the hierarchy share goals with those higher up the ladder and thus value the overall efficiency gained from cooperating voluntarily with their superiors. The conflict theorists argue that coercive mechanisms and exploitative relationships characterize the system.

Also stressing the importance of occupational differentiation as the prime source of inequality, the literature on social mobility goes further and suggests other dimensions in which mobility occurs. These include education, the firm and geographical location. It is surprising that few have sought to incorporate the notion of multiple, cross-cutting hierarchies or inequalities in their models of social stratification.[8] Accordingly, it is necessary to develop a model which will identify the major types of differentiation.

A Roles and Individuals

Some stratification theories seek to explain how societal rewards are distributed among individuals and how individual behavior reflects or relates to certain specific patterns of distribution. Unfortunately, the distinction between individuals and roles is not always clear in the literature on stratification. Indeed, many of the functionalists tend to focus almost wholly on the process of rewarding differentiated roles or positions. Davis and Moore (1945, p. 242) state that stratification relates to a 'system of positions, not to the individuals occupying those positions'. Other writers continue using the same terminology, albeit in a more ambiguous fashion and with less explicit differentiation between the two concepts. Heller (1969, p. 3), for example, writes that social stratification involves the 'separation of positions and roles'.

Those critical of the functionalist position have attempted to relate these roles to individuals. Dahrendorf (1969b, p. 12) states that 'the hard core of social inequality can always be found in the fact that men as the incumbents of social roles are subject ... to sanctions.' Tumin (1967, p. 12) goes further, perhaps, when he defines social stratification as 'the arrangement of any social group or society into a hierarchy of positions'.

It is important to remember that any concept of role or other means of considering individuals collectively involves an abstraction. Such abstractions may be essential to the understanding of functional relationships which constitute social organizations, and may therefore be central to the analysis of bureaucracy as an end-product of organizational efficiency. However, their fruitfulness is often diminished to such an extent that one cannot work back to the human actors. Several considerations suggest that more care should be taken to link roles with individuals.

The tendency to define roles in terms of responsibilities and obligations frequently results in an inordinate emphasis on functional roles and occupational structures. While this has a certain value in identifying achievement criteria relevant to the attainment of commonly accepted goals, it sometimes means that politicking and relationships of hierarchy are often overlooked as key elements shaping the choice of goals. Also, the non-functional roles associated with informal networks and unofficial relationships tend to be disregarded.

It is also easy to demonstrate that individuals may be differentiated by ascriptive criteria not related to functions (e.g., responsibilities and obligations) or even by criteria not yet institutionalized so as to define a role *per se* (as might occur when there is not full agreement on the goals). In contrast to functional divisions of labor according to achievement criteria, there exist many kinds of trait or ascriptive criteria which differentiate individuals in terms of their access to societal rewards. Race, religious affiliation, membership in various ascriptive groups, or age do not *per se* define roles in a functional sense, but are often criteria for differentiating among persons in the same role. More important than the distinction between roles and the individuals who fill them is recognition of the fact that there are many ways of defining roles. This awareness, coupled with adherence to the accepted criteria for constructing typologies (mutual exclusion and collective inclusion) results not in one typology of roles but in many.

Another problem concerns the fact that individual behavior seldom aligns with the average or ideal commonly associated with a given role. The individual more often than not occupies many roles at the same time, some formal and others informal. Moreover, the complex of roles which one shares is constantly changing. It is not uncommon to find a disproportionately large number from one ethnic or educational group in certain occupations. Accordingly, we sometimes talk about syndromes or clusters of roles which go together. One's overall status within the social system must be understood in terms of the total combination of statuses associated with each role occupied by the individual at specific points in time. In this light the concept of roles may be valid, provided that a formula of addition or a weighting scheme is available so that a sum total can be calculated for the role cluster of each individual. However, although much time has been spent constructing indices of socio-economic status, it is, unfortunately, difficult to grasp the individual's overall access to societal rewards by simply analyzing his position in a limited number of roles. Indeed, the roles defined in one typology often account for variation among those sharing a common role as defined in another typology. As suggested in Figure 11.3 at the end of the preceding chapter, a vector approach is required to add up the individual's relative well-being in each of perhaps a dozen dimensions.

B The Agents of Stratification

Among the various roles, traits and physical features which define the individual as someone unique among thousands of human beings in society, certain ones have repeatedly been shown to have a high correlation with the individual's access to societal rewards.[9] The variables which are associated with differential access to societal rewards are referred to as the agents of stratification.[10] To the extent that a given distribution represents an evaluative judgement about the relative merit of individuals in social terms, persons sharing the same roles, traits and features tend to have a common basis for communicating, associating and forming groups. A sense of community is fostered by the awareness that a role, trait or feature systematically gives them a disproportionately large or small share of the societal rewards. The objective fact of differentiation is thus linked with the subjective dimension. Social stratification, then, is defined as the phenomenon which results from the *objective fact* of systematic or structured differentiation being coupled with the shared *subjective awareness* of the roles, traits or features accounting for such differentiation.

It is clear that inequality is patterned. Certain *types* of people consistently receive disproportionately large or small allotments. Other things being equal, employees in large firms receive more of all four rewards than do employees in small firms. Those living in Tokyo and Osaka tend to have more access to information and various kinds of authority than do persons living in the countryside. Company presidents are more generously compensated than ditch-diggers. Every individual can be characterized in an endless number of ways, and it is the overall combination of the characteristics that determines his or her access to rewards.

While differentiation occurs in many dimensions, agents of stratification common to most societies include sex, age, spatial location or residence, ethnicity and educational background. At work, occupation, industry, firm size and organizational style seem to affect one's access to rewards.

Each agent can be expressed as an ordinal variable. Further, the categories associated with any given scale can be ranked according to the average amount of rewards received by the incumbents in each of the respective categories. For the variable of sex, there will be the male and the female category. For business firms, it is often meaningful to talk about large, medium and small firms, although firm size is usually conceived on a graduated scale and exact cut-off points are usually arbitrary. Age, industry and occupation are often thought of in terms of scales with considerably more categories.

One's access to income, power, information and prestige is influenced by the category to which one is affiliated in each dimension. A middle-aged male bureaucrat is likely to have more rewards than a temporarily employed young female factory worker. The total of all rewards will be a function of an individual's vector location in this multidimensional space. Accordingly, a career manager with a university education in a large firm may well earn more than a company president with a high-school education heading a small firm. However, there are exceptions, and many of these can be accounted for by considering other dimensions such as sex, age and industry.[11]

The idea of a vector space can be easily understood if we consider briefly a diagram with only two dimensions, occupation and firm size. For occupation, five groups are given in rank order from that with the largest share of rewards to that with the smallest: executive managers and supervisors, white-collar clerical workers, blue-collar factory workers and janitorial staff. For firm type, four groupings are given, based on size: large, intermediate, small and very small. Figures 11.2 and 11.3 in the preceding chapter illustrated how these two dimensions might be represented together as a vector space. In combining occupation and firm size, the figures represent only one of many possible two-by-two pairings which include sex and age, level of education and location of residence, or industry and ethnic background. With just ten variables, 45 unique pairings are formed. If all ten are considered together, a complex vector space is created, one which can easily be represented mathematically but not visually.

C Models Which Emphasize Agents of Stratification

As with models using societal rewards, numerous observers have attempted to single out one agent of stratification and assign it primary importance. Several models based upon various kinds of differentiation are presented in Figure 12.3. These models by no means exhaust the number of possibilities. Similar diagrams could be drawn showing the relative access to rewards enjoyed by those affiliated with different industries or enterprises, different sex categories or different levels of education. The emphasis in each model is on delineating who gets societal rewards, with little attention being given to a precise definition of the rewards or a careful delineation of various kinds of rewards. In most cases, models of this kind do not include more than two agents of stratification. Perhaps the difficulties of visual presentation have been one consideration limiting the development of more complex multidimensional models. In the remainder of this chapter, Section III presents an integrated model of social stratification and Section IV addresses the question of class.

III Formalization of the Multidimensional Stratification Model

The next step is to consider how reward models and agent models can be combined to obtain a full-fledged model of stratification. One attempt to do so can be seen in efforts to construct socio-economic indices. However, in addition to the problems mentioned above, such indices have often led to confusion of the rewards with the agents of stratification; generally, these indices have not contributed to the analysis of class conflict. After formalizing the aggregate model in this section, the question of social class will be discussed.

The first step is to consider how multidimensional models account for the distribution of societal rewards. In Chapter 5 it was shown that the individual's access to income in both Japan and the USA is affected by the following seven attributes: occupation (O), industrial classification (I), the firm or enterprise (E), age (A), geographical location in terms of population density (D), geographical location in terms of regions (G) and sex (S). Although not explicitly dealt with in this study, race, ethnicity and language (R), religious affiliation (B), family (F), the level of educational attainment (L), the place of education (P) and physical features (C) might also be considered. The total social position (TSP) of any given individual (H) with regard to his total access to societal rewards may then be written as a function of the various groupings to which he belongs:

$$TSP_h = f(O, I, E, A, D, G, S, R, B, F, L, P, C)$$

In the same fashion, the social position (SP) of any individual (H) with regard to income (W) may be written as follows:

$$SP_h^w = f(O^w, I^w, E^w, A^w, \ldots, C^w)$$

In the same fashion, the social position of any individual (H) with regard to power (P) may be written in the following manner:

$$SP_h^p = f(O^p, I^p, E^p, A^p, \ldots, C^p)$$

For a given agent of stratification, there may be any number of groupings, ranging from two groupings in the case of sex to many in the case of, say, occupation. In the case of a trait like sex, the number

Figure 12.3 *Distributive models of social stratification*

A The ethno-religious model (Baltzell)

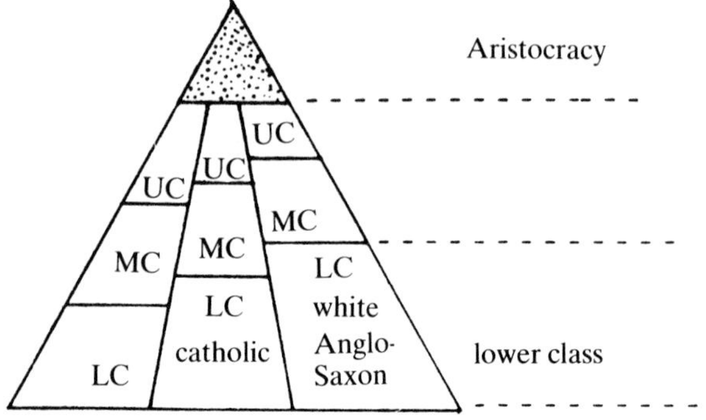

B The racial or ethno-linguistic model

white

non-white

White Anglo-Saxon

East Europeans

Southern Europeans

Orientals

Blacks

C The institutional sector model = Strategic Elites (Keller)

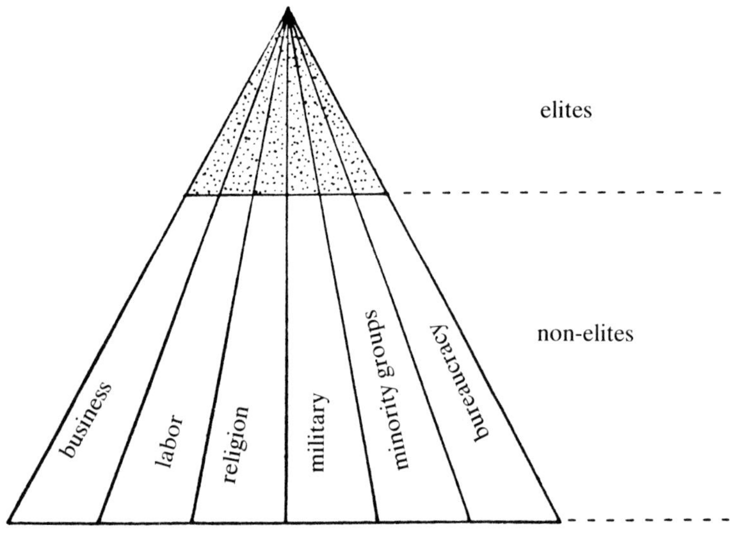

D A geographical model (ecological school)

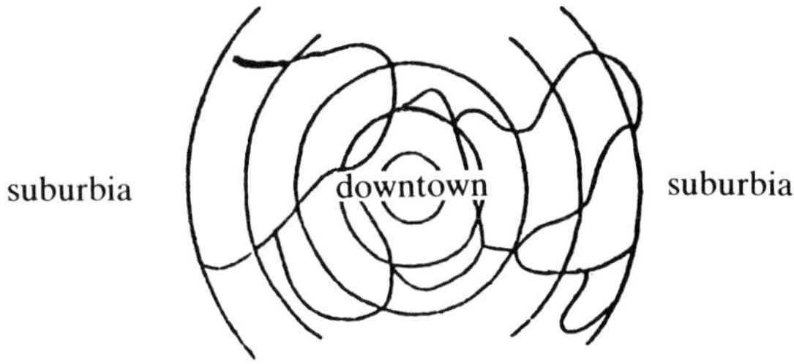

E Occupational models

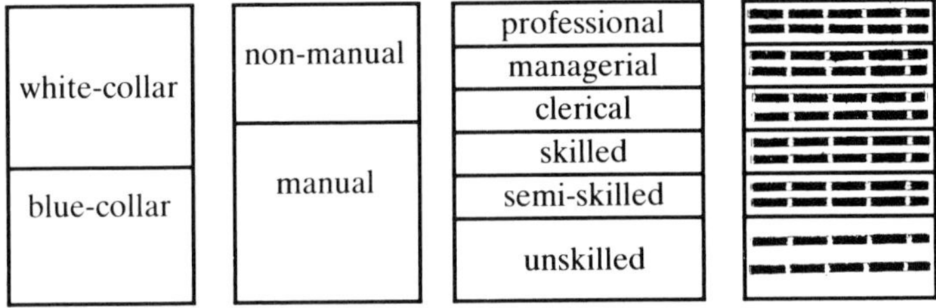

F Two factor race-occupational model

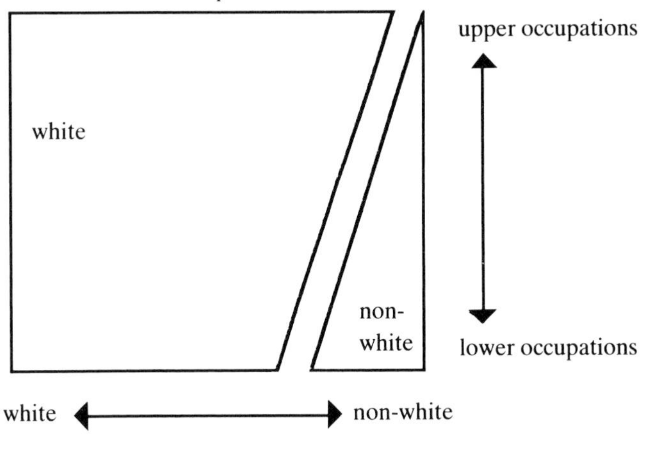

Sources: A Baltzell (1964)
C Keller (1963)

of possible groupings is more or less fixed. In the case of a set of roles such as occupations, the number of significant groupings may vary from society to society. In practice they will often be determined by the data available.

Each grouping delineated by a given agent of stratification may possess its own expressive vocabulary and subculture. For example, men and women, college graduates and primary school graduates, company presidents and janitors, persons at one end of the country and those at the other, believers of one religion and those of another all use slightly differing linguistic expressions and have different lifestyles. Moreover, certain norms develop to define relationships not only among those in the same subgroup, but also between the subgroups associated with a given agent. Because inter-group and intra-group relationships are often institutionalized, and because they often involve the division of labor, they form a kind of system. This kind of system may be called a stratification subsystem. For each agent of stratification there is a corresponding stratification subsystem. In any given subsystem the major subsystem categories or subsystem groups may be conceived in several ways. For example, one's income is in part a function of the firm or enterprise (E) in which one is employed. However, in identifying the individual with a firm, one is in fact identifying the individual with some aspect of the firm, such as its size in terms of the number of employees, its capitalization, the number of years it has been in business, or its organizational style. The individual may thus belong to the large-scale sector or the small-scale sector, an established firm or an unestablished firm, an organization directed by a committee or an organization led by one man.

If the patterns of stratification in a given society are related to the values in that society, as many seem to think they are, then it might be useful to delineate more carefully the manifold ways in which stratification occurs as one avenue to understanding social values. To do so requires an examination of both the reward dimensions and the various agents of stratification which characterize the subsystems. The overall model can be broken down for closer analysis in several ways.

One way is to consider each reward separately, examining how each agent of stratification relates to its distribution. Following this line of reasoning, a framework consisting of M rewards and N agents of stratification would have M × N components. Figure 12.4 shows how a typology of four rewards and seven agents would yield 28

Figure 12.4 *The identification of social stratification subsystems*

types of reward \ agents of stratification or types of stratification subsystem	sex (G)	age (A)	location of residence (G)	level of education (L)	industry (I)	occupation (O)	Firm size (E)
income (W)							Example A in Figure 12.5
power (X)		Example C in Figure 12.5					
information (Y)	Example of Yamada and Watanabe in Figure 12.6		Example of Yamada and Watanabe in Figure 12.6	Example of Yamada and Watanabe in Figure 12.6			
prestige (Z)				Example B in Figure 12.5			

distinct pairings if we study the distribution of each reward in one subsystem at a time. Possible findings for three pairings are shown in Figure 12.5. For each pairing data are gathered on how the subgroups delineated by the agent under consideration correlate with the amount of a particular reward each subgroup's incumbents receive. For the pairing of income and sex, for example, the distribution of males and the distribution of females according to income are compared. The shaded areas in Figure 12.5 show the mode for each distribution. In diagrams A and B a simple linear relationship exists. As we move from one category to another in the order given, we see a steady increase in the amount of rewards received. In both cases the largest number of employees in each subgroup is such that they fall into the shaded boxes on the diagonal; among persons in large firms the largest number have high incomes whereas among persons in smaller firms the largest number have low incomes. In diagram B, persons with more education enjoy more prestige. The relationship between power and age in diagram C is curvilinear; it is the familiar seniority responsibility curve. As age increases, so too does the responsibility of most persons up to a certain age, after which it tends to decline. Similar two-dimensional diagrams could be drawn for the remaining 42 pairings, with a variety of relationships being discovered.

Taking just one reward (information), we can see how three agents of stratification shape the access to rewards of two individuals: Yamada Tarō and Watanabe Hanako (Figure 12.6). Mr Yamada is aged 45, lives in Tokyo, and has graduated from a university. He works as a section chief (*kachō*) in a medium-sized bus company in the private sector. Ms Watanabe is aged 19 and lives in the town of Hino in Hino County of Tottori Prefecture. After graduating from middle school she found work with a fruit-vendor. Three years later she became the receptionist at a small timber-yard. Considering only three agents of stratification – level of education, sex and the size of the city in which they reside – the stratification model would yield the prediction that Watanabe has less access to information than does Yamada.

IV The Stratification Model and the Concept of Social Class

Differentiation does not always produce social stratification. Differentiation may be random; even when it occurs in a systematic

Figure 12.5 *Three examples of stratification subsystems*

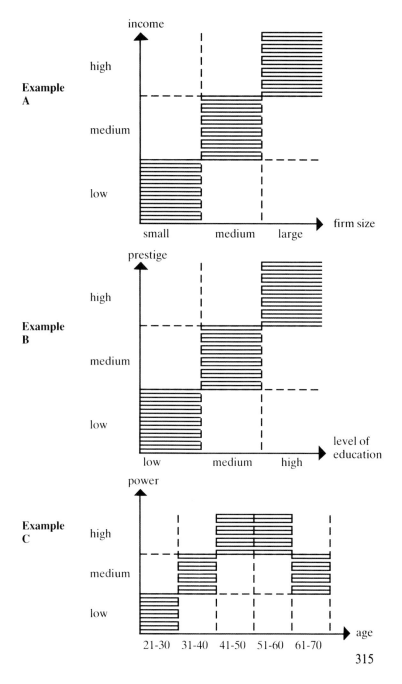

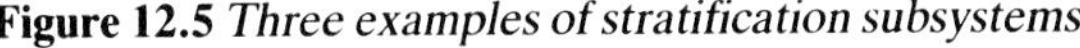

Figure 12.6 *Three-dimensional model of stratification and the comparison between Yamada Tarō and Watanabe Hanako*

Societal reward: income

Agents of stratification: place of residence, level of education, and sex

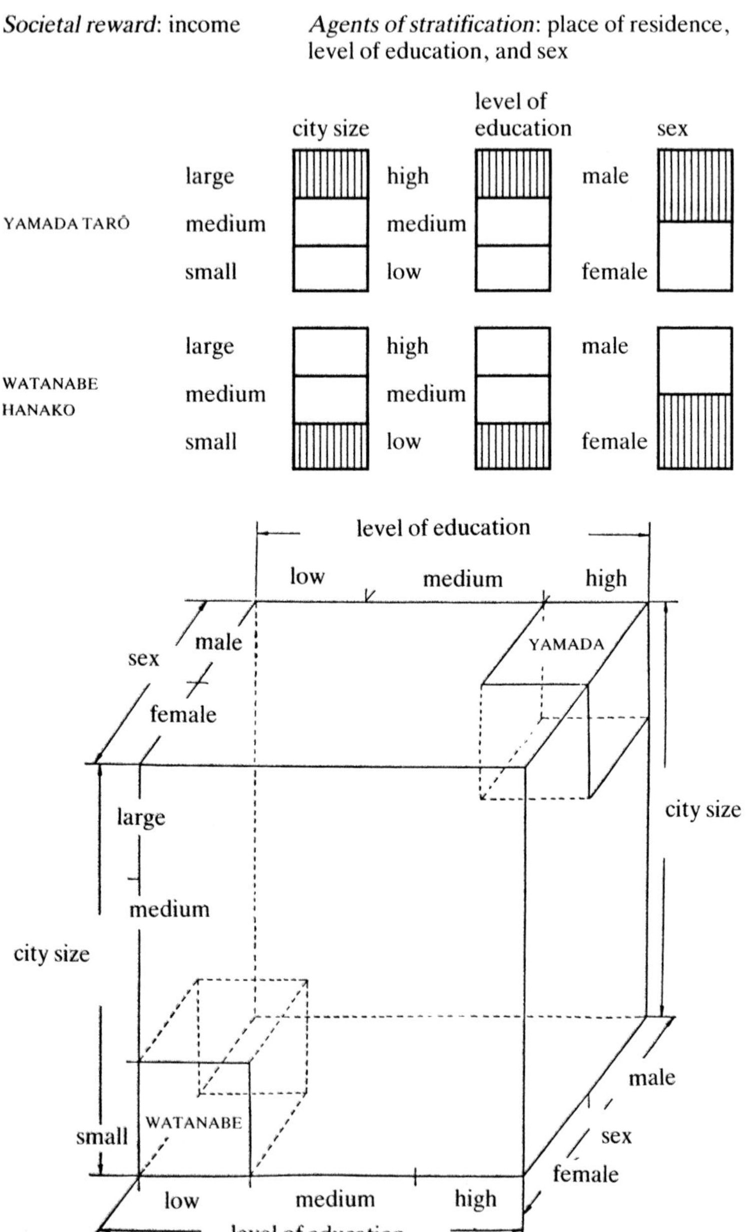

fashion, it may not be generally perceived. The formation of a distinct statistical group does not necessarily mean that group consciousness exists. Groups may be organized to meet short-term needs quite irrespective of distributive patterns. The phenomena of social stratification and the existence of social strata or classes as defined below are produced by the existence of aggregates of individuals who are tied together in a loose fashion by some common sense of identity. This common identity is born out of an awareness that one shares with others a common existence which is defined by one or more agents of stratification.

The dynamics of social stratification are found in the processes which determine the relative strength, vitality and cohesion of those who are in a similar category. The mere presence of systematic differentiation without awareness results in statistical groups which can be identified by the social scientist, but which have little subjective meaning for the persons belonging to them. However, when there is an awareness that being in a particular category produces a certain similarity with other persons in the same group in terms of the distribution of societal rewards, such groups take on added significance. People in a particular group develop common communicative symbols and subcultures which serve to make the quantitative lines of differentiation more qualitatively permanent. As the overlapping characteristics related to language patterns, lifestyles and ideology become more pronounced and the sense of group solidarity increases, these groups come to be recognized as social strata. The most cohesive of these groups are here referred to as social classes. The conceptual scheme developed here is shown in Table 12.2. Defined in this fashion, the meaning of social class is close to that given by Marx when he used the term *Klasse für sich*, but without Marx's causative explanation. The main elements are consciousness, cohesion and conflict.

The student of social inequality is interested in identifying the agents of stratification which delineate statistical groups, social strata and social classes. For Marx, the most important factor differentiating individuals in a way producing social classes was the individual's relation to the means of production and his functional role in economic activity (e.g., occupational role in the broadest sense). While one may question whether groups based upon occupational differentiation actually become social classes as Marx envisioned, the important fact is that occupational differentiation does often result in groups which are sufficiently cohesive to produce friction,

Table 12.2 *The relative solidarity of persons in a category defined by an agent of stratification*

Kind of social amalgamation	Degree of cohesion and solidarity	Defining characteristics
Social class	Much cohesion; strong solidarity	1 Systematic differentiation 2 Common awareness of differentiating trait(s) 3 Common culture with others sharing the same trait(s) 4 Low mobility–considerable difficulty in changing trait(s) (inter- and intra-generational) 5 Common sense of antagonism versus persons with dissimilar trait(s) 6 Quasi-organizational ties with those sharing the same trait(s)

Table 12.2 *The relative solidarity of persons in a category defined by an agent of stratification*

Kind of social amalgamation	Degree of cohesion and solidarity	Defining characteristics
No grouping	No cohesion; no solidarity	No systematic differentiation
Statistical grouping		Systematic differentiation
Social grouping		1 Systematic differentiation 2 Common awareness of differentiating trait(s)
Social stratum		1 Systematic differentiation 2 Common awareness of differentiating trait(s) 3 Common culture with others sharing the same trait(s) 4 Low mobility–some difficulty–in changing trait(s) (inter- and intra-generational)

tension and even open conflict within industrial society.

Nevertheless, social institutions and relationships between occupational groups have remained rather stable over the longer period. Here two developments come to mind. First, industrial societies, or at least the upper occupational groups in such societies, seem to have been able to institutionalize or regulate conflict. Second, as Galbraith (1956) suggests, the balance of power between, say, management and labor has been more equal than perhaps was anticipated by many earlier, more doctrinaire Marxists. Finally, and perhaps most important, one should recognize other grounds for social differentiation which may produce groups which are almost equally disruptive. Racial, ethno-linguistic and religious groups have demonstrated their potential for splitting societies wide open. Many other types of social groups do not often develop sufficient cohesion and solidarity on the subjective level to be classified as social classes. Still, they are important enough to contribute significantly to the pluralization of society by cutting across other types of social strata or social classes based, say, on occupational differentiation or firm criteria.

The multidimensional class concept of Lenski (1966) is of particular interest. Although the meaning of 'class' as used by Lenski is closer to the concept of social group or social stratum as defined in Table 12.2, he describes the importance of differentiation based upon age, for example, in the following way:

> Of all class struggles in modern societies, the most underrated may prove to be those between *age classes*, especially those between youth (in the sense of adolescents and young adults) and adults. The importance of this struggle is so underestimated, in fact, that its existence is typically overlooked altogether in discussions of class struggles, or confused with economic class struggles. Nevertheless, there is considerable evidence to indicate that the struggle between age classes is a distinctive class struggle in its own right and, furthermore, is one of the more serious and least tractable (p. 426).

Lenski writes similarly about classes based upon differentiation between the sexes:

> Another much neglected aspect of the distributive systems of modern societies is the large class system based upon sex.

> This neglect has been due in large measure to the tendency of sociologists to treat families, rather than individuals, as the basic unit in systems of stratification (p. 402).

Parsons (1954a, pp. 418–27) also identifies a number of dimensions in which differentiation occurs among different subgroups; he emphasizes agents of stratification which delineate groups functioning or otherwise interacting to form a subsystem in terms of his own framework. As relevant sources of differentiation, Parsons discusses enterprise affiliation, occupation, family kinship ties, sex, ethno-racial status, religion and education. Elsewhere (1954b) he defined one type of class system in terms of the family kinship unit:

> A class may then be defined as a plurality of kinship units which, in those respects where status in a hierarchical context is shared by their members, have approximately equal status. The class status of an individual, therefore, is that which he shares with the other members in an effective kinship unit. We have a class system, therefore, only insofar as the differentiations ... involve differentiations of family living (pp. 328–9).

The importance of a given agent of stratification depends upon a number of factors. One is the extent to which the categories associated with it account for overall dispersion in the distribution of societal rewards. This is the relatively objective aspect of stratification and determines the relative importance of the subsystem in terms of systematic differentiation, the minimal criteria for constituting even a statistical group as defined in Table 12.2. A second concern is the extent to which some or all of the members in a particular category are bound by a sense of solidarity. This is the subjective aspect of stratification and largely determines the amount of friction or tension which will occur among groups in a particular dimension. For example, four rather loosely defined occupational groups which in some societies might qualify as strata are capitalists and managers, white-collar and non-manual employees, manual and blue-collar workers and farmers and peasants. Depending upon the society and the historical setting, they might even be potential classes. When racial discrimination or religious fanaticism reaches exaggerated proportions, the agents referred to as race and religion can be said to define class-like cleavages. Other groups, like those based on sex, may best be categorized as social groups which might aspire to becoming social strata when the women's movement becomes active. Generation gaps also produce social groups. Groups based upon firm and industrial affiliation no doubt lie somewhere between statistical groups and social groups. Those based upon geographical regions may fluctuate all the way between being mere statistical groups and being social classes (as in the case of a civil war). Finally, the importance of a given agent of stratification will depend upon the extent to which there is mobility between the various categories which define it. Increased mobility may reduce the importance attached to systematic differentiation in terms of access to societal rewards on the objective level, and thereby also serve to weaken the individual's cohesive bonds with, and psychological commitment to, other individuals in a particular category of which he or she is only a temporary affiliate.

In summary, numerous traits, roles and features account for systematic differentiation among individuals in terms of their access to societal rewards. The more important of these define somewhat cohesive social groups. Each is seen as a distinct dimension in the overall stratification matrix. The categories (or subgroups) within each dimension (or stratification subsystem) can be identified and ranked in terms of some variable which has been called an agent of stratification. Subsystems change over time. Sometimes they are associated with considerable dispersion in the distribution of societal rewards and high levels of cohesiveness and solidarity within some or all of their groups. At other times this association will be weaker. To the extent that social groups delineated by a particular agent of stratification come to have their own subcultures and to the extent that a special subculture defining relationships between groups in the same dimensions emerges, a stratification subsystem can be said to exist. Individuals participate consciously or unconsciously in many stratification subsystems. This fact results in a number of social phenomena such as role conflict and status inconsistency, and in their total access to societal rewards being a function of the various subsystem groupings to which they belong.

V Stratification and the Study of Japanese Society

Mechanical applications of the model are misleading. Although the basic list of agents of stratification and the typology of rewards will make sense in most societies, each society or culture produces its own unique mosaic. One important variable is a population's demographic composition. Although industrialization seems to be accompanied by certain demographic transitions which form one difference between more developed and less developed economies, among more industrialized societies there are differences in industrial structure and the deployment of the labor force. France, the United States, Japan, Britain, Germany, the Soviet Union and Australia all have their demographic peculiarities.[12]

Many of the categories associated with a given agent of stratification are defined slightly differently from one society to another. Because we are interested in identifying groups with subjective dimensions (such as class consciousness), attention must be paid to the perceptions of people. What groups do they define as significant? It is often said that the Japanese identify with a firm and not with occupational categories, or that seniority criteria, such as age or years of continuous employment rather than occupation, determine one's income. While there may be some uniqueness in the case of Japan, it lies not in the actual distribution of societal rewards according to age, but in the development of an extensive and uniquely Japanese vocabulary for discussing more universal phenomena.

Culture also influences the use of occupational classifications. Many Japanese occupational categories do not have ready counterparts in America or Australia. In Japan the distinction in status between temporary and permanent employees is important. So too is the breakdown of temporary employees into *arubaito, shokutaku, komon, pātotaimā, rinjikō, dekasegi* and *haken*. Although these are not occupational groups in a functional sense, the occupational nuances are nevertheless clear. A *komon* does not operate a cash register; a *rinjikō* is not an accountant; a *shokutaku* is not a factory worker. Related to the problem of definitions is the rank order in a given dimension. The ranking of industries in terms of status or even income, for example, will differ from one country to another. A growth industry in one society may be in decline or even non-existent in another society. Even when an industry seems to have a similar position in two economies, in each it is characterized by a different history and a distinct technology. These differences give birth to a distinct ethos and set of traditions.

The influence of culture may be even more pronounced in the definition of societal rewards. Cultures are distinguished in part by different tastes, different notions of utility and different preferences.

Electric blankets and room heaters are not commonly seen as treasure by those living in hot climates. Status symbols and expressions of conspicuous consumption have considerable cultural content. The trade-off between longer hours and higher income, on one hand, and shorter hours and leisure, on the other, is well known. However, the combination of work and leisure judged satisfactory in one society may be rejected by another. The value attached to leisure may also depend upon the availability and cost of leisure facilities and upon other situational constraints.

In Japan a large body of literature called *seikatsu kōzōron* deals with lifestyles and daily customs. The study of mass culture (*taishū bunkaron*) and ethnology (*minzokugaku*) also throws light on these aspects. Wage negotiations in the seventies introduced the concept of life-cycle needs. The idea of changing needs as one ages is not particularly Japanese; however, the perception of what those needs might be and the idea of a standard family are. The life trajectories of Australians and Japanese are certainly different.

While the given social milieu or cultural context needs to be carefully considered, the model developed in this chapter is based upon a number of more universal assumptions. Here two are discussed in further detail.

1 Motivation and the Nature of Self-interest. In considering social values within a comparative framework, there is likewise a need for sharper conceptual clarity. The holistic or integrationist approach argues that there is consensus on societal goals but does not really define these social values. Those adopting the conflict approach also assume consensus, but are even more vague in their discussion of human values, often falling back on concepts of narrowly defined materialistic needs considered common to all humans. Some time ago Birnbaum (1953) discussed this basic problem with regard to motivation. The explanation of motivation in the literature of the Japanese Marxists was also something which concerned Sumiya (1954 and 1974) as discussed in Chapter 3. To achieve universal applicability, a broad framework is necessary for considering the notion of self-interest within a cultural context.

A general premiss of the stratification model is that individuals will seek to maximize their self-interest. Self-interest is defined as the acquisition of societal rewards which include not only economic profit or income but also power, status and information. In order to maximize self-interest, individuals normally engage in some rational calculation.[13] That individuals seek to maximize self-interest does not mean that they are always successful in doing so. Here we are talking about motivation. Another way of saying this is that the individual seeks to minimize his or her losses.

In looking for definitions of self-interest, one needs to be sensitive to cultural, subcultural and individual elements. Self-interest will probably be defined differently for each individual. For some it may mean the accumulation of money (even if it is only kept somewhere in a vault) while for others it will mean a rising social position and the prestige associated with honorary titles. From this perspective, overseas group tours of Japanese can be seen less as an expression of collectivist orientation or blind groupism but rather as the cheapest means of traveling. Members can be seen as having made a rational calculation as to how to obtain the best accommodation and see the most interesting sights for the least amount of money. In the labor market, people tend to move when their pay, responsibilities and status are improved by doing so.

From the perspective of building a stratification model, it is recognized that in many cases the experience of group behavior and coordinated interaction on the surface is maintained not so much by a common value placed on doing things together, but rather as the result of individual members seeking their own self-interest and coming together to maximize their comparative advantage. This sometimes occurs simply through individual exchange with other individuals; at other times it occurs through the aggregation of interests with others to effect collective exchange. A good example of this is the behavior of the so-called *sararīman*. Much of their willingness to work extra time each day, to spend hours in bars with associates, to give gifts for *seibo* and *chūgen* can be seen in terms of their keeping a very carefully balanced account with each of a large number of individuals in their world of work.

The assumption that individuals maximize self-interest is also basic to the exchange model of Befu (1974, 1977 and 1982c) and Marshall (1981). It is an assumption accepted by Marx and Weber, forming a central proposition upon which a good deal of modern economic theory rests. Given the idea that self-interest is conceptualized in many ways even with a single society, a major concern in applying the stratification model is the delineation of self-interest. In this regard a good deal of attention has been paid to the idea of subculture. To some extent, a good deal (though not all) of intra-societal variation in definitions is accounted for when we consider smaller aggregates of persons sharing a given subculture. There may also be some debate as to whether at the individual level the important information we need to know concerns the self-interest of the individual (either true self-interest or the individual's perception of self-interest) or the extent to which individuals seek to maximize their self-interests.

2 Volition, Culture and Ideology. Another assumption concerns the way in which volition is shaped. Although Camus observed some time ago that individuals can will what they do but cannot will what they will, and we have come to eschew placing too much emphasis on the individual, there is still little agreement as to the forces shaping the human will. Unlike the consensus-oriented view of Japanese society, which posits that culture determines behavior by shaping the consciousness of individuals socialized in a given culture, the stratification model rest on the idea that culture is distinct from ideology. It sees ideology as being a phenomenon produced largely by power inequalities. The model is built on the notion that the power inequalities inherent in societies with social stratification are in part maintained by ideological elements which shape the thinking and behavior of individuals. This distinction between culture and ideology is often absent from the consensus model.

One major difficulty associated with the consensus model has been its failure to clarify cause and effect relationships. Instead it has tended to replace causation with tautologies. In the case of Japanese society, 'Because the Japanese are group-oriented, they like behaving in groups,' or 'Because Japanese culture is based on the notion of consensus, agreement between people is given a high normative value in Japanese society.' While this type of descriptive statement may be logical, indeed axiomatic, it does not yield explanations of cause and effect as the wording would seem to suggest.

Behind tautologies of this kind is the belief that culture and a predisposed social psychology are the important independent variables which explain social structure and social institutions. That the culture and consciousness of a people are important variables cannot be denied; however, two points require careful thought. First is the fact that culture is not rigid. It changes over time; some elements are shaped by the specific policies of specific people or classes (i.e., ideology) while others seem simply to have been there always or to have emerged more spontaneously. Some culture which is imposed by one group on another at one historical juncture is often later internalized and the origins forgotten. Some legislation is never accepted and remains as ideology. A careful study of these processes is required when referring to culture. The second point is that serious consideration of the idea that individuals are shaped or even dominated by culture requires a careful study of a whole array of social forces, including the coercive and manipulative aspects of social organization and various social institutions. In this regard, sure methodologies for distinguishing between cultural norms and ideology have not yet been developed. It is, none the less, clear that the two are very different and that ideology accompanies power inequalities: not only is it a product of such inequalities, but in many cases it is used to create and to maintain them. For this reason, it is important to consider how societal rewards are controlled and distributed in any given society.

Assumptions provide a point of departure for any vision of society. In developing a model for the examination of Japanese society the authors argue that Japanese society is characterized by a good deal of internal variation, that alternative models of Japanese society must offer some explanation of conflict in Japanese society, that Japanese seek to maximize self-interest in a culturally defined manner and that power inequalities and ideology are important phenomena influencing both the consciousness and the behavioral choices of Japanese. The next chapter examines some of these propositions in further detail.

Chapter 13

The Stratification Framework in a Japanese Context

The multidimensional framework of social stratification developed in the preceding chapter is open to each society having its own history and culture. It is based on the assumption that an industrialized society will be stratified in a number of ways and that persons will be motivated by some notion of self-interest which will be linked to the idea of maximizing one's acquisition of societal rewards. It is possible that the way in which individuals are differentiated and the way individuals define societal rewards may vary from society to society; a close look at these two aspects of stratification is required in each social setting. In this chapter, social stratification is considered in the Japanese context. The first half focuses on the definition of societal rewards. The second half looks at ways in which the agents of stratification account for variation in several different types of behavior.

I Societal Rewards in the Japanese Context

A Income as Specific to Time and Place

The preceding chapter argued that income, power, information and status would provide useful categories in discussing societal rewards in various social contexts. Unfortunately, although a good deal has been written about income distribution, very little has been written about the distribution of other rewards. This no doubt reflects the generally held view that income can be easily measured whereas other rewards are less amenable to estimation. However, even with regard to income, much has been assumed and the task of defining income needs to be given much more attention before the stratification model can be fully tested. One of the authors has examined the definition of income in the Japanese context (Mouer: 1980a). That research is introduced here to suggest that economic utility is not so easily quantified simply by surveying monetary income, that culture may affect the definition of income, and that the meaning of economic rewards may change considerably over time.

An examination of both quantitative and qualitative evidence suggests that a considerable transformation has occurred among the Japanese in terms of the definition of economic goals over the past two or three decades. The change can be seen in the manifestos of competing intellectuals, in the issues debated at the time of national and local elections and in the demands of labor unions (Mouer: 1980a, pp. 366–483). One shift can be detected around 1970. As Table 13.1 shows, the change can be detected by comparing demands made between 1955 and 1970 with those made between 1970 and 1975.

In the first period, prime importance was attached to obtaining a steadily increasing monetary income with which to purchase basic necessities. Cultural activities and the need for psychic satisfaction were given secondary importance, and even then were commonly

Table 13.1. *Economic demands during two periods in postwar Japan*

	Period I (1955–70)		Period II (1970–80)
1	Total employment	1	Less pollution and environmental protection
2	Higher incomes and a higher standard of living	2	More leisure
3	Personal savings	3	Better housing
4	Capital investment	4	Improved safety
5	Minimal expenditure on self-defense	5	Price stability
6	Policy of exports first	6	Increase in social welfare
7	Regional development and improved communications	7	Compensation
		8	Participation

Source: Mouer (1980a), pp. 431–74.

expressed in material terms. Rapid growth after a period of relative deprivation following the war perhaps contributed to the belief that one should focus first on securing material comforts. However, over time several changes took place. Values of incomes and savings were eroded by inflation. Improvements in the levels of material consumption, especially in terms of durable goods, were in part offset by the deterioration of the living environment due to poor housing and pollution. An increasing amount of information became available in the mass media, and the leisure to think about the paradoxes of rapid growth increased. Consequently, attention came to focus on ways to guarantee civil minima which would allow more individuals to realize personal goals. It might be argued that higher concerns became possible precisely because the material standard of living improved so dramatically between 1955 and 1970.

Cole (1971a, pp. 3–4), Kōshiro (1982a, pp. 14–15) and others have put forth the idea that many workers are motivated by a scarcity mentality. This mentality is attributed to the widespread perception among the Japanese that they are still poor and need to work all out to survive economically. This is consistent with the view that the Japanese save a lot because changes in their patterns of consumption have simply not occurred as rapidly as changes in their level of income (Sumiya: 1969, vol. 1, pp. 49–87). It is also consistent with the generally accepted assertion that, given enough income, most Japanese would like to own larger homes, travel overseas and enjoy affluence in a manner similar to that described in other industrialized societies and associated with the notion of embourgoisement. This transformation can in part be seen over the past 30 years in the shift of attention among many Japanese from *obtaining* the 'three sacred treasures' (*sanshu no jingi* = fan, refrigerator and television) in the fifties, the 'three S's' (*suihanki* = rice cooker, *sentakuki* = washing machine, and *sōjiki* = vacuum cleaner) in the sixties, and the 'three C's' (car, cooler and color television) in the seventies to *enjoying* the 'three new S's' (sex, sport and the screen) in the eighties. It is estimated that in 1981 'love hotels' (generally for pre- or extra-marital sex) were used by 550 million couples or 1.1 billion persons (an average of over 13 times per adult), spending enough to average 48,000 yen per adult Japanese aged over 15 (NA: 1982). According to a survey by the Prime Minister's Office in 1980, adults spent an average of 54,000 yen on sports equipment (Kuwabara: 1982, p. 31).

Pornography also appears to be big business in Japan. However, as Tsujimura (1972) argues, it is not simply a matter of replacing the concern with making a living with the desire to enjoy life, but rather a situation in which the time devoted to leisure depends very much on income level and the ability to support leisure-time activities in addition to one's more basic needs. One key to understanding Japan's future and to forecasting the social climate will be the interesting trade-off between work and leisure and the way that trade-off is represented in the mass culture.

The gap between advertised and real rates of growth seemed to expand over the years. People came to question whether their economic well-being was really reflected in figures on total GNP or even GNP per capita. Accordingly, there was growing disillusionment with statistics. In the seventies the emphasis shifted from units of money to units of actually consumed utility. These needs included environmental criteria, social overheads and other items involving external economies. To guarantee a minimal standard of living in these terms, various new demands were made on the system, and this set of demands no doubt contributed to the increase in social tension in Japan in the late sixties and early seventies. The focus on the system also directed attention to the role of policy-makers in the Liberal Democratic Party, highly placed bureaucrats, top management in big business and union leadership. Many people seemed to have become more aware of their relationship to the leadership.[1]

Another idea linked to the shift to system demands is that of compensation or redistribution. The demand for compensation came from those who felt that they were made to bear a disproportionately large share of the external diseconomies. They have demanded some publicly recognized mechanism which would guarantee a fairer distribution through a secondary distribution.[2] When the system cannot cover the public costs or external diseconomies which occur in the course of production, forces for change emerge. In the case of Japan, there were no mechanisms for affecting a redistribution. Victims of pollution and traffic accidents have often been left to fend for themselves. Welfare and unemployment benefits have also been limited compared with standards in many similarly industrialized societies. Moreover, those who have benefited from the initial distribution have tended to resist efforts to redistribute their income according to other criteria. It is not surprising, therefore, that efforts to introduce the green card in 1982, in order to clamp down on tax evasion by those with large incomes, failed. The speed with which wealthy Japanese shifted their liquid holdings to gold and foreign bonds was amazing and deserves further study.

It is in this connection that the demand for participation arises. First, a broader base for participation in deciding upon initial distribution means that there will be fewer who can demand compensation or a further redistribution. Second, and more important, increased participation enhances the ability of the system to minimize the shifting of costs through external diseconomies. Improved feedback would enable people to know about their costs much earlier, and would thereby allow them to speak up for their interests before the first distribution is made. One key to understanding levels of consensus in Japanese society lies in the extent to which there is participation related to the initial distribution. There is room for debate on the extent to which the system of joint consultation between labor and management allows for such participation (Galenson: 1976). It is also necessary to be open to the idea that participation will take different forms in different societies (Odaka: 1975; Hanami, Kōshiro and Inagami: 1977). None the less, it is clear that Japanese management has been very wary of schemes which would give employees a vote on the board of directors or in any other way infringe upon their prerogatives as owners. For example, in the area of industrial safety, management has traditionally tended to place blame for industrial accidents on human error (i.e., the employee) rather than looking for situational factors, such as poor equipment, lack of safety measures and floor layout, for which management might be responsible (Matsuda: 1972). At the same time, management has also taken the initiative to invest in robots and other automatic machinery to decrease the number of jobs involving dirty and dangerous work (Kuwahara: 1983).

These ideas were suggested earlier by Nakayama (1975) who attempted to distinguish between economic or physical efficiency based upon private calculations in monetary terms, as defined in the narrow sense, and true or social efficiency, which involves the attainment of societal goals based upon broader concepts of utility. Indeed, as Nakayama also argues, it is precisely because of conflicting interests that progress cannot be achieved. From this perspective he argues, cooperative, participatory arrangements have meaning for many employees. There is also the problem of alienation and the need for self-expression or self-actualization in the realm of economic activity and economic needs, including the desire or need to be creative in the act of production. Yet, a major significance of participation is in closing the gap between public and private accounts.

Several themes seem common to both periods. One is the strong sense of self-interest. Individuals and organizations are very much aware of their own economic interests and are extremely sensitive to the benefits and costs arising from external economies. Many external factors cut both ways and involve several different kinds of pluses and minuses. For example, the employee working for a chemical plant knows that the future of the plant – and thereby his job and source of income – rests, at least in the short run, on the ability of the factory to dispose freely of certain harmful wastes. At the same time, he may himself be eating contaminated fish or have a relative living near the factory breathing the air his factory has polluted. The question of which consideration will prevail is not always easy to answer. Furthermore, interests are differentiated in a number of ways. Geographical location, firm size, occupation, industrial affiliation, age and sex consistently tend to determine one's relative exposure to external diseconomies and one's access to social welfare or housing.

While fitting into the overall framework of need hierarchies as developed by Maslow (1954 and 1962), an individual's current definition of self-interest is seen as being a function of two kinds of perception, as shown in Figure 13.1. One is based on a careful assessment of what can possibly be achieved. To say a Japanese manager lacks a sense of self-interest because he does not demand the swimming-pool enjoyed by his Australian counterpart ignores important differences in the situations of the two. Population densities, land costs, and the enjoyment associated with swimming vary from one society to another. The second type of perception is based on an assessment of the institutional setting and the nature of the social system itself. This also involves an evaluation in terms of possibilities, and shapes the way in which instrumental and consummatory values are assigned. Leisure has a different meaning when it is organized by the company and when the facilities are owned by private corporations than when individuals are free to do as they wish and have available public facilities at no additional cost. However, while the definition of economic rewards seems to be intricately tied to a given cultural milieu, the definition is dynamic and changes over time. While improvements in the real standard of living tend to produce a shift away from earlier goals (such as employment security) to higher-level needs (such as participation), the recessions following the oil shocks in the mid-seventies also reveal the fact that the process is not unilinear and that economic well-being in objective terms is not

Figure 13.1 *A comparison of old priorities and new demands*

Two types of perception as key variables	Concepts involved		Period I (1955–70) Old priorities	Period II (1970–80) Old priorities plus new demands
Perceptions of self-interest	Goals seen as having been achieved and now taken for granted			Higher income and welfare guarantees
	Possible goals to be achieved	instrumental	Higher monetary income	Food, clothing, house (guaranteed by life-cycle plans)
		ultimate	Basic life-cycle needs: food, clothing, house	Cultural activities and psychic satisfaction
				Private needs / Public or social needs
	The truly ultimate goal which is seen as being beyond the current realm of possibilities		Cultural activities and psychic satisfaction Private needs	
Perception of the nature of the system	Means for maximizing self-interest within the system	cross-benefit calculation	Minimization of private costs and maximization of private benefits	Close alignment of public costs and benefits with private costs and benefits
		locus of decision-making	Elites Government Business	Participatory arrangements with (1) government (2) business (3) labor and (4) the consumer
		mobility criteria	Formal educational career	Life-long education

Source: Mouer (1980a), p.478.

something which is guaranteed even in the advanced or industrialized world. At the same time, perceptions and the ability to articulate one's goals are affected by a wide range of forces: consumption patterns and the uses of leisure, the demographic composition of the population and the labor force, the industrial structure, government policy, the international flow of ideas, the international situation and the general intellectual climate in Japan. In turn all of these forces are seen by the Japanese through the lenses of their own culture.

To summarize, dissatisfaction in Japanese society in the early seventies cannot be understood without examining changes in the concept of income. Several considerations underline the heuristic value of a comprehensive definition of income, as outlined above. First is the tremendous rapidity with which Japanese social and economic organization has been transformed over the past three decades. During that period the Japanese economy expanded at a rate nearly twice that achieved by other growth economies and perhaps four or five times that achieved during the same period by the most advanced industrial nations like the United States or Great Britain. Whether one wishes to express these changes in the vocabulary of Maslow or in some other fashion, the successive annexation of new demands over time seems to be occurring. Indexes for measuring the market-basket ten years or even five years ago are no longer adequate today.

A second consideration in arguing for a comprehensive definition of income is its importance as a tool for understanding social tension. The study of alienation provides but one example of how the less frequently cited components of income affect the perceptions of large groups of people. Thus, while wage differentials in Japan narrowed quite remarkably during the sixties, the impression received by many employees was one of growing differentials. This is explained partially by referring to the different concepts of income employed at the objective and subjective levels. Simple measurements of cash income are not sufficient.

Finally, the definition of income is very much tied to our understanding of the individual's rationality and our vocabulary for discussing rationality. The debate among the substantivists and the formalists in economic anthropology has made this point abundantly clear (LeClair and Schneider, 1968). Income must be defined within a social and cultural context if more formal economic theories of optimalization are to be valid.[3]

B The Importance of Particularistic Demands within the Japanese Setting

Given the preceding discussion, it might be useful to look more carefully at the issues involved in popular disturbances in postwar Japan from January 1952 to June 1960 (Sugimoto: 1981d, pp. 77–82). During this period, 945 cases of popular disturbance erupted *outside* Tokyo and Hokkaidō. For the purposes of this analysis, disputes were classified as being particularistic, universalistic, both or neither, following the definition provided by Parsons and Shils (1951, p. 81).

Disturbances based on particularistic demands were those in which the actors demanded something for themselves on the grounds that the actors had a special right to or interest in the object demanded. These demands usually involved the receipt of some direct benefit at the cost of another party or of the community at large. In agrarian disputes, the issues related to land transfer, land use, change in territorial boundaries and other land interests (e.g., construction or expansion of American military bases in the community, water rights or irrigation problems). In the area of industrial relations, the particularistic issues commonly involved working conditions: wage increases, unfair managerial reaction to labor disputes (e.g., dismissals, suspensions and wage cuts), labor contracts, management initiatives to release redundant personnel and demands for improved working conditions.

Disturbances centered on universalistic demands were those in which broader criteria were used to justify the demands of the protest. Disturbances of this type usually involved overall ideological definitions of the situation in terms of community needs, national interest or internationalism. They included protests against the Security Treaty between Japan and the United States (1959–60), opposition to the extension of police functions (1958), and struggles against central government's increasing control over the system of education (1957–9).

As shown in Table 13.2, the particularistic type outnumbered the universalistic type during the period under enquiry, although universalistic disturbances, especially those organized by the labor unions, recorded much higher magnitudes in terms of duration and number of participants.

The fact that most particularistic disturbances concerned grievances against political authorities is conspicuous. In about two-thirds of the particularistically oriented incidents, government officials at various levels were selected as targets of protest. In less than a quarter of the incidents managers of private economic organizations were involved. Accordingly, particularistic cases were mainly political in substance. The distribution of locations of disturbance showed that confrontations took place most frequently in prefectural or municipal offices.

The strong commitment to narrowly defined self-interest can also be seen in many of the anti-pollution movements. A study of several dozen such movements (Mouer: 1980a, pp. 646–72) clearly reveals this point. Self-interest was defined by many Japanese as the avoidance of *kōgai*, a Japanese concept which is much more comprehensive than its English equivalent, pollution. Vibration, noise, dust, shadow, traffic hazards on routes commonly travelled – all these invited immediate reaction. While people were quick to become involved in local movements to fight against any diseconomy affecting their residence, many were equally quick to lose interest if the movement sought to subsume broader issues involving a wider community and thereby seemed likely to dilute the attention given to their specific demands.

Finally, the study of voting behavior by Uno (1981) is also of considerable interest. Cross-sectional data for 46 prefectures is used and the support for each of the political parties is shown to be linked to various dimensions of the quality of life as measured by a number of social indicators. Briefly stated, support for the ruling Liberal Democratic Party is strongest in those locations where social capital formation (e.g., the value added per worker in the primary sector and the percentage of value added attributed to manufacturing) is high. Its support is high where the ratio of the daytime population to the night-time population is high (e.g., the central business districts whose interests it serves). In general higher income and growth rates contributed to its support. Price inflation weakened its ability to draw votes. The Japanese Socialist Party obtained relatively more support in areas where the number of households receiving social welfare was high and relatively less where the proportion of privately owned homes was higher. Uno concludes that voting behavior is affected by the rational assessment of the extent to which the ideological goals and philosophical commitments of the parties speak to the particularistic needs of the voter in terms of his or her socio-economic situation. At the same time, the complexity of self-interest is also indicated. For example, higher unemployment and price inflation exert a negative impact on the JSP, perhaps not because of its views on those matters but because of a judgement about the actual ability of the party (as one of four opposition parties) to effect the desired

Table 13.2. *The frequency of popular disturbances with particularistic and universalistic demands in Japan: 1952–60*

Issues	Frequency	Percent
I RELATIVELY PARTICULARISTIC		
A Labor-management relations		
1 Wage increases	253	26.8
a Standard salary	152	16.1
b Bonus	115	12.2
2 Managerial actions regarding labor disputes	141	14.9
a Punishment of participants such as firing, suspension and salary cuts	96	10.2
b Lockouts	20	2.1
3 Personnel cut initiated by management	31	3.3
4 Terms of labor agreement	36	3.8
5 Specific work conditions	19	2.0
6 Denunciation of activities of management-oriented second labor union	11	1.2
B Territorial issues		
1 Merger or split of municipalities	48	5.1
2 Construction projects	14	1.5
3 American military bases	11	1.2
4 Right of water use	10	1.1
5 Boundaries of fishing areas	9	1.0
6 Boundaries of school districts	7	0.7
C Police actions		
1 Release of the arrested	74	7.8
D Unemployment problems	33	3.5

change. The interplay of judgements about instrumental goals and values concerning consummatory goals does not always produce behavior which is consistent outside the given cultural context.

C Social Control and Reward Fungibility

The stratification framework allows for societal rewards to be used as resources. This fluidity in part accounts for the permanence of patterns of structured inequality, since those who receive relatively more rewards at one point in time are able to use those rewards to influence the distribution at a later point. This influence is often exerted by controlling others. In Chapter 10 a typology according to the degree of control was developed to show that Japanese are in some ways subject to power relationships. Here the idea of control is approached from a slightly different angle to show how each of the

Table 13.2 *Continued*

Issues	Frequency	Percent
II RELATIVELY UNIVERSALISTIC		
A Peace issues		
1 Security Treaty with USA	39	4.1
2 Self-defense forces	8	0.8
3 Nuclear arms race	4	0.4
B Educational issues		
1 Enforcement of evaluation of work performance of teachers	82	8.7
2 Contents of education	38	4.0
3 Training courses for teachers	32	3.4
C Others		
1 Police duties law	26	2.8
2 Immigration law	8	0.8
III OTHERS		
1 Korean issues	38	4.0
2 Judiciary process	22	2.3
3 Taxation	17	1.8
4 Postal services	11	1.2
5 Pollution	11	1.2
6 Student affairs in schools or universities	10	1.1
7 Ballot counting procedures	7	0.7
TOTAL NUMBER OF DISTURBANCES	945	

Source: Sugimoto (1981d), pp. 79–80.

reward clusters has a political component; the acquisition of any given type of reward allows one to control others. Corresponding to the four types of reward, four types of control are briefly discussed in the Japanese context.

1 Coercive Control. The most direct mode of control involves the use of political resources. Power and authority can be used to exact certain types of behavior regardless of the will of the person being controlled. In Japan, violence has included police forces assaulting demonstrators, the inculcation of self-discipline through hard physical training under the supervision of drill-masters in Self-Defense Forces and university sports clubs, the intimidation of professors in kangaroo courts and abuse of wives and children. Institutional controls include sanctions for not paying one's income tax. Japanese without a residence card cannot enrol their children in primary school. Denied a passport or permission to use foreign exchange, some Japanese have until recent years been prevented from travelling abroad.

2 *Utilitarian Control.* Outright coercion is often unnecessary. Once a framework is established so that some types of behavior win rewards, individuals tend to make rational calculations of the likely gains and losses of each behavioral choice. This type of control is based on the carrot approach whereas coercive control leans toward the stick approach.

It may be said that utilitarian control primarily involves the distribution of economic rewards. As it does not require violence or institutional sanctions, those controlled in this way appear to be acting voluntarily. Yet the actors are subject to the manipulation of those who have economic rewards to distribute, given the risk-reward structure. This kind of control may be illustrated by the lifestyle of the *mōretsu-shain* who contributed much to Japanese economic growth in the postwar period. Many worked extremely hard for marginal promotion with the full knowledge that management selected the goals for their organizations.

3 *Cognitive Control.* Those with larger quantities of information can control others by hiding or distorting factual data. Many of the confrontations concerning pollution, including the Minamata case, were characterized by government officials and employees in private enterprises refusing to supply available information. In some cases information was deliberately destroyed and false information created, even with full knowledge that by doing so the number of pollution victims would increase. Massive hoarding on the sly by reputable enterprises and the resultant price-gouging of the consumer at the time of the oil shocks also involved the dissemination of misinformation. These activities aroused enough public anger to produce a very short-lived publicity campaign by big business to assure the public that the social responsibility of managers was being seriously studied. Exaggerated advertisements of pharmaceutical goods and incorrect content descriptions on labels on canned foods are cases where the consumer's choice has been manipulated by the dissemination of distorted information. Others have made private fortunes by obtaining government information on land development projects or by conniving to create a speculative market which could not be sustained and would leave someone else holding the baby.

There are a variety of other areas where the control of information is a key mechanism: politicians and officials leaking exclusive news to journalists; mass media rarely publishing arguments against the

Emperor system; the public being provided with very little objective data on contraceptive pills or marijuana; and the routine calls of America's nuclear submarines at Japanese ports never being fully revealed to the Japanese public. Examples of groundless rumors and demagoguery also illustrate how false information is created and used to manipulate people. At the time of the Kantō Earthquake in 1923, an ill-willed rumor had it that Koreans in Japan would take the city of Tokyo by assault. On the basis of that rumor, numerous Koreans were murdered by ordinary Japanese citizens.

4 *Symbolic Control.* One is always passing judgement consciously or unconsciously as to what is good or bad, respectable or degenerate, beautiful or ugly. Many of these judgements are influenced by the large number of symbols to which one is exposed from birth to death. To analyze the distribution of various value systems, it is useful to consider how the idea of status is manipulated.

The prevailing definition of what is beautiful influences the way people act. In Japan mannequins in department stores are often Caucasian. Cover-girls for the weekly magazines are more frequently white rather than non-Japanese Asian or black. Large breasts are presented as an attraction in many weekly magazines. English is the only foreign language taught in most secondary schools. These phenomena make us curious about how Japanese acquire a sense of aesthetics at the mass level and how decisions are made in the mass media to associate happiness, pleasure and satisfaction with the possession of certain objects, with acceptable speech patterns, mannerisms and dress and with specific types of behavior or topics of conversation.

More overt controls over the use of status symbols may be observed in the prewar *shūshin* lectures and postwar courses in morals. Subtle values are expressed in company songs, and in the inspirationals and testimonials starting the day at many companies. They are also built into the numerous placards and sign-boards seen in Japanese streets, which carry a full array of imperative statements such as 'Don't do this,' 'Let's do that,' or 'We must stop doing something else.' All are explicit forms of indoctrination, powerful forces shaping images of what constitutes proper behavior. However, this omnipresence tends to belie the notion that Japanese are voluntarily guided by a set of internalized values. Proverbs and axioms printed, not only in the margins of diaries and calendars but also in textbooks, can also be regarded as a form of symbolic control. The Government each year hands out the Emperor's awards for skill or some other worthy trait in many areas. It also decides who will be recognized as *ningen kokuhō* (national living treasures). Various companies and organizations also give rewards. In nearly all cases the recipients are chosen not only for their accomplishments but also for having acceptable behavior. By reserving kudos of this kind for very aged persons, younger people are encouraged to toe the line along the way. The important point is not that symbols exist and are used, but that the phenomenon is universal; some Japanese have much more say than others in deciding which symbols will be used with which connotations.

II Inequality and the Differentiation of Behavior

The stratification framework delineates a number of variables which account for inequality. The model is formulated on the idea that these agents of stratification reveal not only the patterns of inequality but also some of the ways in which variation occurs in the behavior and thinking of persons in a society. In the remaining portion of this chapter, several aspects of life in Japan are discussed from this angle.

A Political Attitudes

The complexity of political behavior becomes a bit clearer if we examine some of the ways in which public opinion is segmented. Table 13.3 suggests that at least seven agents of stratification help to account for some of the diversity in public opinion: geographic region, the urban-rural differential, sex, age, occupation, affiliation with a labor union and the level of educational attainment. The same seven variables can also be seen as accounting for variation in thinking on a vast variety of other issues.[4] Geographically, LDP support is significantly lower in areas with US military bases and pollution,[5] but higher in areas which have received government funds for regional development projects.[6] Looking at age groups, the very young (those under 25) and the very old are the most conservative; those in their thirties the least so.[7] Viewed occupationally, those in agriculture, corporate executives, and real-estate profiteers are among those supporting the LDP.[8]

A look at newspapers and public opinion surveys in the postwar period would suggest that these kinds of segmentation are not new or passing phenomena. For example, one survey indicated that political

Table 13.3. *Stratification variables and the perception of election issues related to the thirty-third general election for the House of Representatives (10 December 1972)*

Stratification variable	Percentage of the sample indicating that one or more issues were important	Percentage of respondents who considered one or more of the following issues important when voting										
		Security Treaty and defense	Welfare	Pollution	Rising prices	Tanaka's plan to remodel Japan	Agricultural sector of the economy	Urban problems	Other problems	Cumulative total of the percent responding to each item available as a choice	Those who did not consider any issue in voting	Unclear
Geographical area												
1. Hokkaidō	94.5	9.85	25.12	13.81	33.95	4.44	4.44	3.47	4.03	184.7	4.5	.9
2. Tōhoku	79.9	6.58	22.75	15.85	29.37	8.38	12.90	2.09	2.09	176.7	15.3	4.8
3. Kantō	90.3	8.16	27.53	18.98	28.03	4.55	4.05	7.41	1.29	202.3	8.0	1.7
4. Chūbu	84.6	5.35	29.90	15.40	32.15	3.29	9.47	2.86	1.48	155.2	13.6	1.8
5. Kinki	89.6	6.20	28.79	20.82	30.17	4.68	3.15	5.22	.98	202.3	9.0	1.4
6. Chūgoku	80.6	4.64	31.04	16.68	27.30	2.77	10.62	4.64	2.32	155.3	15.5	3.6
7. Shikoku	67.5	7.80	32.23	19.15	25.22	6.07	6.94	2.60		138.4	30.1	2.4
8. Kyūshū	78.7	7.51	31.16	15.46	29.50	3.51	7.02	4.19	1.66	162.4	15.6	5.7
City size												
The ten largest	91.2	7.11	28.22	21.81	28.31	4.26	2.06	7.44	.80	213.7	7.6	1.2
Middle-sized cities	89.8	8.32	29.36	18.54	31.43	2.94	2.83	4.46	2.12	183.9	8.2	1.9

Table 13.3. *Continued*

Stratification variable	Percentage of the sample indicating that one or more issues were important	Percentage of respondents who considered one or more of the following issues important when voting										
		Security Treaty and defense	Welfare	Pollution	Rising prices	Tanaka's plan to remodel Japan	Agricultural sector of the economy	Urban problems	Other problems	Cumulative total of the percent responding to each item available as a choice	Those who did not consider any issue in voting	Unclear
Small cities	82.3	7.01	29.26	14.89	28.68	5.45	8.34	5.33	1.04	172.6	13.8	3.5
Villages and towns	78.6	5.00	26.41	15.00	29.29	6.03	13.53	2.63	2.05	156.0	18.0	3.4
Sex												
Male	87.5	9.22	27.40	18.44	24.10	6.21	7.01	5.96	1.65	189.6	10.8	1.7
Female	83.7	4.85	29.38	16.84	35.22	2.77	5.78	3.81	1.54	162.7	13.1	3.2
Age groups												
20–24	86.8	9.30	20.57	19.98	26.16	3.78	4.11	5.86	2.41	182.7	11.6	1.9
25–29	89.0	7.55	28.04	18.41	30.11	3.55	5.43	6.27	.64	202.6	10.6	.4
30–39	89.1	7.11	26.28	17.68	32.42	4.58	4.79	5.69	1.47	190.0	9.8	1.1
40–49	87.5	7.42	26.04	18.25	30.04	5.34	6.88	4.59	1.44	187.4	11.3	1.2
50–59	84.0	5.59	30.91	17.19	29.64	3.01	7.79	3.81	1.27	173.4	11.4	4.1
60 +	74.9	5.65	34.43	14.82	24.10	5.01	9.38	3.36	2.93	139.7	16.1	7.0

Table 13.3. *Continued*

Stratification variable	Percentage of the sample indicating that one or more issues were important	Percentage of respondents who considered one or more of the following issues important when voting										
		Security Treaty and defense	Welfare	Pollution	Rising prices	Tanaka's plan to remodel Japan	Agricultural sector of the economy	Urban problems	Other problems	Cumulative total of the percent responding to each item available as a choice	Those who did not consider any issue in voting	Unclear
Occupation												
Self-employed (Ag)	81.5	4.99	21.74	8.79	24.27	5.44	33.50	.44	.82	158.2	15.9	2.6
Self-employed (nonAg)	86.2	8.41	27.64	17.02	25.00	6.85	3.09	7.98	3.49	178.0	11.4	2.4
Management	90.0	13.33	23.33	19.17	21.67	10.83	3.33	5.83	2.50	240.0	8.0	2.0
Clerical	94.1	11.36	29.34	21.03	22.45	5.17	3.45	6.32	.00	226.3	4.9	1.0
Sales and Service	86.5	7.57	28.46	18.94	20.46	6.63	3.31	4.26	21.17	100.1	8.9	3.6
Production Workers	80.6	6.07	29.57	21.38	33.52	1.84	3.45	3.67	.50	179.6	23.0	1.4
Family worker (Ag)	75.6	2.63	21.69	7.92	25.92	4.77	33.85	1.61	1.61	145.9	22.3	3.1
Family worker (nonAg)	78.8	7.19	32.05	17.25	26.82	5.24	1.47	8.10	1.69	141.2	20.5	.7
Student	94.1	15.09	19.59	23.53	13.73	9.50	1.97	13.73	1.97	300.1	3.9	
Housewife	83.0	4.25	28.79	17.72	39.16	2.39	2.33	4.14	1.22	171.6	8.5	2.5
Other	77.4	4.74	36.37	16.45	29.03	3.92	5.19	2.59	1.71	158.1	13.7	8.9

Table 13.3. *Continued*

Stratification variable	Percentage of the sample indicating that one or more issues were important	Percentage of respondents who considered one or more of the following issues important when voting									Those who did not consider any issue in voting	Unclear
		Security Treaty and defense	Welfare	Pollution	Rising prices	Tanaka's plan to remodel Japan	Agricultural sector of the economy	Urban problems	Other problems	Cumulative total of the percent responding to each item available as a choice		
Union affiliation												
Organized	92.9	10.04	28.39	21.57	25.96	4.52	3.19	5.17	.96	230.0	5.6	1.5
Non-organized	85.6	9.23	29.13	19.75	26.80	5.29	3.27	5.29	1.24	192.9	12.9	1.6
Level of education												
Middle school	80.5	5.24	27.98	16.55	31.65	3.79	9.67	3.22	1.90	158.3	15.3	4.3
High school	89.0	6.94	29.85	18.07	30.39	3.87	4.36	5.06	1.45	185.9	10.3	.9
University	94.1	11.90	36.97	10.66	21.29	8.50	3.06	9.29	1.07	251.8	4.5	1.4
Total average	85.4	6.80	27.94	17.40	29.14	4.45	6.31	4.83	1.54	179.4	12.0	2.6

Source: Kōmei Senkyo Renmei (1973), pp. 142–3.

loyalties were fairly well maintained over the years, showing that 89.1 percent of those voting for the LDP in the December 1968 general elections also voted for the same party in 1967; the corresponding percentages for the JSP, the JCP and Kōmeitō were 85.3, 80.8 and 72.8.[9] The relative persistence of these pluralized or diversified patterns of segmentation in political attitudes can perhaps be demonstrated even more convincingly by examining public opinion polls taken in the mid-fifties. For this purpose, 29 responses to 16 questions drawn randomly from public opinion surveys taken in Japan during 1955, 1956 and 1957 were analyzed by calculating the mean and standard deviation for a total of 29 values which represented the difference in the percentage responses found in twelve pairs of stratal subgroups. The results are summarized in Table 13.4.

Table 13.4. *Stratification differentials and political preference and attitudes (in terms of percentage differentials)*

Stratification variable differentials	Political support and party preference[a]		Political attitudes on political issues[b]		Respondents replying 'I don't know'[c]	
	$\bar{x}$[d]	s[e]	$\bar{X}$[d]	s[e]	$\bar{X}$[d]	s[e]
Educational differential[f] between:						
PS and JHS	11.8	4.0	10.7	6.0	21.9	6.6
JHS and SHS	5.9	3.5	6.2	4.2	10.4	3.3
SHS and College	5.1	4.5	5.1	5.0	6.7	2.1
JHS and College	7.4	4.8	10.1	8.3	16.7	3.8
Age-group differential[g] between:						
M: 20–29 and 50–59	15.9	8.6	9.7	8.8	3.4	1.8
F: 20–29 and 50–59	8.8	5.8	7.7	6.4	17.4	7.7
B: 20–29 and 50–59	10.9	8.6	8.0	5.8	3.7	6.4
Sex differential between men and women	11.7	5.4	11.8	8.4	22.8	5.8
Occupational differential[h] between:						
S and IL	5.9	4.1	9.1	5.0	11.4	3.3
Ag and S, IL, MI	8.9	5.1	6.7	5.3	11.3	5.7
S and MI	12.6	7.8	7.6	5.2	4.8	5.6
IL and MI	13.1	7.2	7.3	4.4	6.6	4.6

Notes: (a) The dates of the surveys, the questions and responses chosen are given in Appendix J, series A (Mouer 1980a).

(b) The dates of the surveys, questions and responses chosen are given in Appendix J, series B (Mouer 1980a).

(c) The dates of the surveys, the questions and responses chosen are given in Appendix J, series A and B (Mouer 1980a).

(d) $\bar{x}$ is the mean percentage differential calculated as $\dfrac{\sum_{n=i}^{N} P_1^{\,n} - P_2^{\,n}}{N}$

P_1 and P_2 represent the given percentage response by the two variable groups on a given question and N represents the total number of questions considered.

(e) s is the standard mean deviation in the percentage differentials $P_1 - P_2$, for each pairing as explained in (d).

(f) PS = primary school graduates; JHS = junior high-school graduates; SHS = senior high-school graduates; and college = college graduates.

(g) M = males; F = females; and B = both males and females.

(h) S = salaried workers; IL = industrial laborers; Ag = agricultural workers; and MI = merchants and industrialists.

Source: The questions and responses are from the public opinion polls recorded in Allan B. Cole and Naomichi Nakanishi, *Japanese Public Opinion Polls with Socio-Political Significance, 1947–1957* (published under the auspices of the Fletcher School of Law and Diplomacy, Tufts University and the Roper Public Opinion Poll Research Center, Williams College, no date). Further details are given in Mouer (1980a, pp. 614–15).

Although the number of variables is restricted, one can nevertheless see that education, age, sex and occupation contributed to the segmentation or pluralization of political behavior. Without going into more detailed multivariate analysis or designating the dimension of greatest importance, the foregoing discussion serves to substantiate the hypothesis that political polarization in Japan occurs simultaneously in a number of dimensions related to the various stratification subsystems. Thus, while both the issues and the expressive vocabulary with which they are articulated have changed over the past 20 or 30 years, major lines of cleavage reappear. At the same time, however, in order to identify correctly cleavages in society, it is important that one gives careful attention to how the issues and the nuances of vocabulary change over time. Indeed, the vocabulary which divides a nation at any one time may be that which brings it a little closer together at another time. It is our feeling that such vocabularies will be culture-specific and that they will provide an important clue for understanding how rational choices are articulated in any given society.

B The Male–Female Wage Differential

The study of inequality among males and females at work illustrates how the stratification model provides a framework for comparative study while also underlining the importance of the cultural context. Looking at just one societal reward, income, we can see that there is a large differential between the wage earnings of male and female employees, although that differential is diminishing over time (see Table 13.5). In making a comparative study of the differential two general conclusions emerged (Mouer: 1982a).

The first is that the concept of return is so culture-bound that comparisons are extremely difficult. Although Takahashi (1975) uses the Paasche formula to correct differences in the age, educational and occupational composition of the labor force in different countries to argue that the differential is still larger in Japan, the complexity of the Japanese wage system makes outright comparisons with the situation of women in other countries difficult. Consideration of wage income only may be misleading; for example, various kinds of fringe benefits (including not only tuition in flower arranging and similar niceties but travel allowances, subsidized cafeterias and various recreation facilities as well) need to be considered. At the same time, other practices such as early retirement, the difficulty of promotion, Japan's own peculiarities with regard to child care and other support institutions make the world of work for Japanese women uniquely Japanese. Some of these practices are described by Kaji (1973) and also affect the way in which the differentials are interpreted. One

Table 13.5. *The male–female wage differential in Japan: 1960–80*

Year	A Average monthly earnings	B Monthly average of bonuses	C Average monthly pay (A + B)
1960	43.5	39.9	42.8
1965	48.7	44.8	47.8
1970	51.7	48.7	50.9
1975	56.5	54.1	55.8
1980	54.6	51.7	53.8

Unit: female earnings as a percentage of male earnings.
Source: Rōdōshō Fujin Shonen Kyoku (1981), p. 85.

might also cite the large proportion (by international standards) of Japanese women who are engaged in entrepreneurial activity for which they receive profits but not wage income (Yano Tsuneo Kinenkai: 1981, pp. 38–9).

The second conclusion is that other stratification variables affect the size of the wage differential. The size of the wage differential varies according to prefecture and industry. Among those with higher levels of education it tends to be smaller. It is larger among those in their forties than those in their twenties. If four subsamples specified by age and firm size are drawn from the labor force, and if the correlation of the size differential is calculated using Pearson's r for each of the 6 subgroup pairings, as shown in Figure 13.2, cross-sectional data for 46 prefectures, 9 major industrial categories and 20 manufacturing sectors show that there is little correspondence between the four subsamples. In other words, age and firm size are important variables which seem to produce significant changes in the rank order of prefectures, industries and manufacturing sectors in terms of the size of the male–female wage differential.

Finally, the sharp division of employees by sex results in two different subcultures. Some firms which have taken the lead in hiring women for managerial positions have found that the major task of female trainees is not adopting male ways of thinking and behaving; it is rather relating to other women who continue to function in a women's world and see the female manager as someone who has

Figure 13.2 *Scheme for six-way comparisons of the male-female wage differential among four subsamples varying by age and firm size*

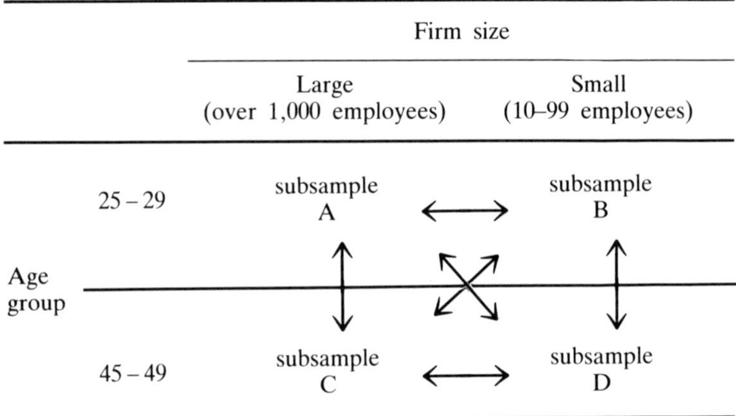

Source: Mouer (1982a), p.16.

deserted the ranks.[10] Although differences in male and female subcultures among office workers are sometimes symbolized by contrasting the tea-pouring syndrome of female employees with the after-business drinking syndrome of male employees, many of the deeper resentments and lasting images of male subcultures held by women are brought out in a recent discussion organized by Tamaru (1982).

C Language

While Japanese share the same national language (*kokugo*), many variations in usage still exist. Again, the patterns align with the common set of stratification variables. A quick glance through the short synopsis in Hayashi (1982) will easily substantiate that point.

Considerable attention has been given to differences in male and female usage. Quite apart from levels of politeness, the vocabulary used by men and women is different (Yamazawa and Takamizu: 1970). It is also clear that words, particularly adjectives, are sex-linked although Japanese grammar does not indicate gender (Kokuritsu Kokugo Kenkyūsho: 1973). While many Japanese seem to feel that differences between male and female usage have narrowed, it is also apparent that neither males nor females are in favor of further narrowing (Egawa: 1980). Moreover, the vast majority of Japanese remain capable of detecting male–female differences and seem to receive negative vibes whenever they hear women using male language (Bunka Yoron Kotoba Chōsa Gurūpu: 1980).

Another well-known source of variation in language patterns is geographical region. The distribution of family names varies from one area to another (Mitsuda 1961; Sakuma: 1972; Shibata: 1955). One investigation found that people in fishing villages have 34 words for describing waves whereas those in mountain villages have only two (Muroyama: 1978); people in northern Japan have 21 words for snow whereas those in the south have only one (Sanada: 1976). While standard Japanese is taught to all Japanese school-children and to foreigners, it is used by only 75 percent at most in everyday life, even among Tokyo residents raised in Tokyo. As one moves away from the Tokyo area, the figure drops to below 50 percent in most areas (Ōishi: 1969). Using a different data base, Kasai (1981) obtained similar findings.

Two other stratification variables also account for important differences: age and occupation. The way of saying 'thanks' seems to vary sharply, with younger people more likely to say *sumimasen* and older people saying *arigato* (Saiga: 1966). Age also explains differences among the sexes in the frequency with which persons use certain types of communication such as speaking, writing, listening and reading (Hayashi: 1974). Partially related to the tremendous rise in educational standards, especially for women, age is also an important factor in explaining the difference in male and female literacy (Nomoto: 1977) and in the ability of those migrating to cities to adopt urban patterns of speech (Kokuritsu Kokugo Kenkyūsho: 1981). Literacy also varies considerably by occupation, which is in turn linked to the level of education (Nomoto: 1977; Monbusho: 1961). People in different occupations are also perceived as using very different languages (Egawa *et al.*: 1970). Occupation is, like sex, a major determinant of which levels of formality are used in speech (Sugito: 1979). Of particular interest is the care with which employees consider their authority relationships with the person they are addressing (Sugito: 1979, pp. 35–44).

D The Crime Rate

Crime is another social phenomenon not evenly distributed across the entire population. Occupationally, the crime rate is considerably higher among unskilled process workers in manufacturing and among low-level operatives in transport and communications. It is also high among the unemployed (K. Hoshino: 1981, pp. 178–81). Juvenile delinquency also occurs more frequently among young people whose parents are in blue-collar occupations and self-employed (Matsumoto: 1975, p. 167). Obviously, it is in such households that both parents are more likely to be working and are least able financially to provide their children with the full range of consumer goods and educational opportunities available to young people in the upper middle class. Considering only the phenomenon of white-collar crime (Hoshino: 1981), it may be fruitful also to consider the unevenness with which crime is defined and justice is administered.

Education is not unrelated to the occupational hierarchy. Those with higher levels of education are much less likely to commit crimes, particularly those of a violent nature (Hoshino: 1981, pp. 179–82). Juvenile delinquency is tied to the parents' level of education (Matsumoto: 1975, p. 168). Delinquency is lowest among those whose parents have had a university education, regardless of their occupation. Among those whose parents had little education, the occupation of the parent becomes a very significant variable.

Although there has been an upsurge in female crime, especially among teenagers, in recent years, the crime rate is still seven or eight times as high among males. In addition to differences in the overall rate, attention should also be paid to qualitative differences in the type of crime (Hirose: 1981, pp. 18–25). In this regard, age should also be considered as an important variable.

Finally, urban–rural differences should be mentioned. Crime rates are particularly high in urban areas such as Tokyo, Osaka and Fukuoka. It is also interesting to notice that the rates are high in a number of peripheral areas such as Okinawa and all four prefectures in Shikoku (Keisatsuchō: 1980, pp. 224–77). With regard to juvenile delinquency the frequency of student violence against schoolteachers is most pronounced in the Kinki region (Hōmushō: 1981, pp. 292–6).

E Other Applications

The preceding sections have discussed some ways in which Japanese behavior seems to have been conditioned by agents of stratification. Whether the variation accounted for by any particular agent is more or less important in explaining some aspect of behavior in Japanese society than in another society remains to be studied, with more sophisticated techniques for analyzing variation and correlation. In concluding this section, it might be useful to consider briefly some other ways in which variation in behavior may be at least partially accounted for by stratification variables. Here we touch upon six other areas in which the stratification framework could assist in cross-cultural research.

1 The Labor Market. The so-called permanent employment system seems to be more entrenched among male white-collar employees in large corporations. Labor statistics in the seventies indicate that the separation rate is higher in medium-sized companies and lower in large corporations. Sex is also a significant variable; while the male separation rate fluctuates between 10 and 20 percent, the female rate is normally above 20 percent, reaching 30 percent in some years. Finally, it is higher for young males in their twenties and much lower for middle-aged males.

In this regard, it is also interesting to note that much of this variation can be explained in terms of the assumption that individuals seek to maximize self-interest. For male career employees whose salary increases and promotion prospects are guaranteed, it is rational to stay in the same company. For other employees who do not share the same future, however, it is often rational to leave.

The organization rate for unions also differs depending on firm size. More than 60 percent of employees in large companies with more than 500 employees are unionized, whereas only slightly above 30 percent are organized in medium-sized companies with 100–500 employees, and less than 10 percent are so organized in small companies with less than 100 employees. While certain aspects of organizational dynamics make it difficult for unionists to organize workers in the smaller firms, it is also true that workers in the large firms profit by workers in small firms not being organized; they have time and again shown a general lack of interest in the organization of such workers and have not seriously pushed for standard wages or even minimum wage legislation for an entire industry or occupational group.

2 Voting Behavior. Watanuki (1980 and 1982) reports that various types of stratification variables affect voting. These include occupational categories. The level of support for conservatives is highest among employers, merchants, farmers and fishermen, less pronounced among white-collar employees and lowest among blue-collar workers. He also notes that age, level of education, sex, industry, firm size, religion, lifestyle and other variables cited in studies on social stratification and inequality are important. However, he also argues that the importance of these variables changes over time, and that their interrelationship is such as to create a pattern of voting unique to Japan, which he refers to as Japan's cultural politics.

According to one survey of student activists in the late sixties, more than 50 percent were engaged in part-time work to support themselves, while more than 80 percent of the non-activists were reliant solely upon their parents (Tsurumi: 1968). The amount and source of economic rewards received seem to influence political behavior.

3 Family Life. The patterns of family life are also stratified. Based on fieldwork in numerous village communities in Japan, Fukutake (1949, pp. 34–48 and 69–115) generalized that there is much regional variation in community structure. He reported that vertical repressive relationships between landlords and tenants are strongest in northeastern Japan, whereas egalitarian horizontal networks among rural households were more prevalent in the southwest. Elsewhere, Befu (1971a, pp. 38–66) summarizes regional variation in marriage practices. In both cases, geographical region is the stratification variable which accounts for considerable variation in patterns of inter-household relations in agrarian communities.

4 Leisure. The use of leisure also seems to be conditioned by stratification variables. According to Atsumi (1975) who has studied interpersonal relations among male white-collar employees, potential management recruits in large companies do not engage in leisure activities as frequently as employees in medium- and small-sized companies. The elite *sararīman* in large corporations tends to see leisure outside the work setting as being related to work. Their leisure often consists of golf or eating and drinking with business contacts. Atsumi's data show that white-collar employees in small and medium companies tend to enjoy pastimes which involve gambling: horse races, bicycle races and *pachinko* (Japanese pinball machines). It can be said that small-company employees are more oriented to individualistic leisure than are workaholics in large firms, simply because they do not obtain much pay-off by devoting themselves to company work. Differences in the way leisure time is spent can also be observed between males and females, between young and old and between the urban and rural populations.

5 Popular Disturbances. From Sugimoto's data (1981d, pp. 74–6) it is clear that labor unionists, students, Koreans and farmers were the strata most represented at scenes of disturbances. These findings suggest that the stratification framework may be useful in explaining the incidence of popular protests.

It is noteworthy that the Japanese pattern just described tends to go against the findings of Kerr and Siegel (1954, pp. 191–3) for 11 industrialized democracies in the West. They maintained that miners, sailors, longshoremen and those in similarly isolated occupations are likely to strike because social isolation tends to loosen external restraining ties and increase the internal solidarity of the members in these occupations. Kornhauser (1959) contends that the persons most available for radical movements are atomized individuals alienated from the mainstream of society. According to him, those who have the fewest ties with the existing social order are most likely to engage in efforts to destroy it.

The data on Japan show that it was those in the government and the semi-public sector who became the principal driving force when labor disturbances occurred. Topping the list were members of the

Japan National Railways, schoolteachers and postal workers. These unionists represented the segment most tightly integrated into the general society. The findings of Sugimoto corroborate the findings of C. Tilly and his associates, who studied collective violence in France, Italy and Germany (Tilly *et al.*: 1975).

6 Religious Affiliation. Sociologists of religion, including Morioka (1975), have demonstrated that many of the new religions in contemporary Japan tend to draw people with specific socio-economic backgrounds. For example, Sōkagakkai, which is affiliated with Kōmeitō (the second largest parliamentary opposition party), is composed largely of owners of small firms and shops as well as younger blue-collar workers who have moved to the city from rural areas. Seichō no Ie, however, is supported mainly by persons from the middle class.

7 Suicide. Even the probability of committing suicide is not random. The research of Chikazawa (1972) indicates that the age distribution of suicides shows a peak for those in their early twenties, gradually declining but then rising to another peak for those in their sixties. Occupationally, the male suicide rate is lowest among management. In the prewar period, the suicide rate of female domestics was known to be extremely high. Again we can see patterns related to age, sex and occupation.

III Conclusions

While underlining the need for more empirical research, the preceding discussion suggests that at least some Japanese do have a sense of self-interest. It also indicates that variation in at least some kinds of Japanese behavior can be partially accounted for by various agents of stratification. With regard to the first point, not only are the Japanese individualistic or egoistic, they are also shaped by a number of factors specific to Japanese society in defining their goals. These factors include the state of the economy and the individual's perceptions of what can and cannot reasonably be expected from the system. Accordingly, the inequalities associated with each agent of stratification will probably have culturally specific meanings which will form part of the subcultures created in that dimension of stratification. At the same time, light is thrown on how aggregate behavior results from the way in which subcultures formed in one dimension cut across those in another dimension, the way in which those in strata controlling relatively more resources influence those in strata with relatively fewer resources, and the way in which changes over time in the size of the population in each stratum might produce social change. Although there may be cultural explanations for certain types of behavior, a close examination of the structural factors may well place the dynamics of culture in a better perspective.

Finally, there is a need to move away from unilinear concepts of social change based upon simplistic notions of evolution. Much of the debate concerning Japanese society has revolved around whether or not Japan measured up to other countries in terms of one criterion or another. The rapid rate of economic growth and the accelerated pace of industrialization have perhaps contributed to the idea that change is monolinear and inevitable. Until recently, the line has more often than not been pointed in the direction of American concepts and realities. Although the learn-from-Japan boom has contributed to a willingness to see change as being multidirectional, there is still the tendency to see each country moving along its own unilinear trajectory. At the same time, the very real problems of identity which seem to surface when rapid change takes place perhaps add to our willingness to accept theories which look for permanence in the uniqueness of culture and a particular history rather than in some of the universalities associated with structure.

One strength of the stratification framework is that it allows us to treat the question of national differences among societies in relation to internal differences within each of the societies being studied. This point might be illustrated by considering briefly four hypothetical individuals, two from Japan and two from Australia: Mr Tanaka (aged 55 and living in Osaka, an executive of a large pharmaceutical company), Miss Suzuki (aged 22 and living in Aomori, a factory worker for a small firm manufacturing cameras), Mr Smith (aged 50 and living in Melbourne, the managing director of a large hospital) and Miss Ryan (aged 23 and living in Cairns, a waitress at a small hotel for tourists). We then ask the question: which pair is likely to share common ideas, views and attitudes and find communication the easiest?

Conventional theories which emphasize national character and the importance of unique cultures focus attention on the similarities present between the two Japanese (Mr Tanaka and Miss Suzuki) and between the two Australians (Mr Smith and Miss Ryan) because nationality (i.e. 'Japaneseness' or 'Australianity') is seen as being the

Figure 13.3 *Third-level comparisons in cross-cultural research*

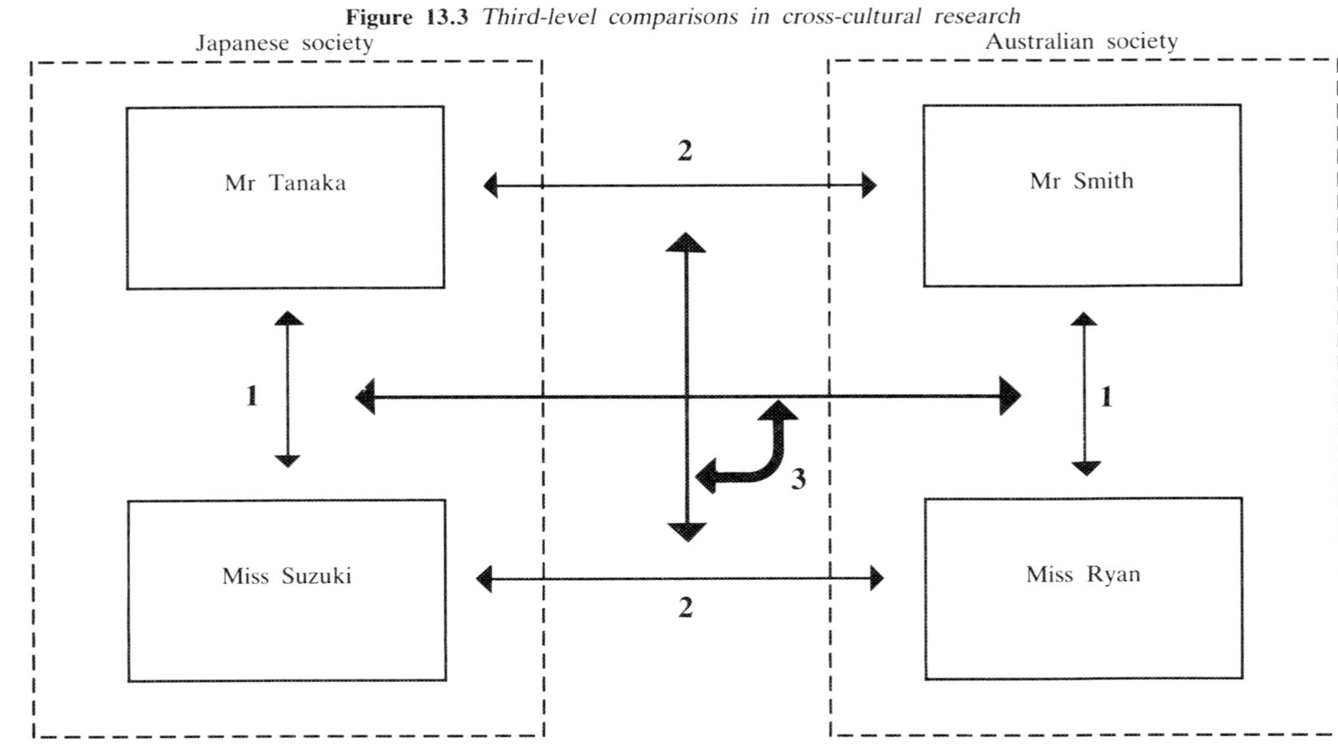

key determinant of attitudinal and behavioral patterns. Language provides a powerful means for communicating and provides a ready set of symbols with shared meanings. The stratification model recognizes nationality as one, but only one, agent of stratification and allows us to consider as a theoretical possibility the likelihood that other agents such as sex, age, firm size, occupation, location of residence and marital status may also provide grounds for communication. On this basis, the model suggests the possibility of attitudinal similarities and easy communication being present between Tanaka and Smith and between Suzuki and Ryan.

Accordingly, the stratification model raises as an explicit problem the comparison of similarities in various dimensions. As a framework for cross-cultural research, it focuses attention of internal variation and the need for third-level comparisons along the lines shown in Figure 13.3. In this manner the stratification model gives a much broader base for evaluating cultural content. It also gives us a framework for evaluating the comparability of samples from different societies before generalizing about the entire societies from which the samples are drawn. It suggests that consideration be given first (i) to variation (and similarity) in the social positions of individuals within specific societies, and then (ii) to variation (and similarity) across societies. The final step is (iii) to compare ways in which the first two types of comparison point to similarities and differences in the way that the social positions of individuals are distributed in two or more societies.

Chapter 14

Testing the Stratification Model: Some Empirical Evidence

I Introduction

The final step in constructing a new model is its testing. As a preliminary step, a variety of social phenomena were considered in the last chapter. As a further step toward ascertaining the viability of the model developed in Chapters 11 and 12 a test was devised to see how high-school students in the US and Japan perceived differences in job situations in their own country. Do they see the agents of stratification identified in the model as being relevant to understanding the way in which their own society is stratified? The test described in this chapter is not seen as the ultimate test but as an indicator of whether the same stratification model makes sense in Japanese and American societies.

Most observers accept that occupational structures similar to those found in other industrial societies do exist in Japan (Inkeles and Rossi: 1956; Ramsey and Smith: 1960; Treiman: 1977). There seems to be fairly widespread agreement that, with a few exceptions, similar occupations exist and are similarly ranked in similarly industrialized societies, including Japan. However, there is less agreement concerning the significance of these findings. Although Japanese know which occupations are, *ceteris paribus*, more prestigious, many observers maintain that the primary sense of status in Japan is not the occupational role, but the larger organization (or group) in which one occupational role is organically integrated with another. Although it has been noted that institutions commonly associated with a uniquely Japanese approach to organizing work – namely, the seniority wage system, lifetime employment and enterprise unionism – applied at best to a quarter of the Japanese labor force (Hamada: 1980, p. 39; Sumiya: 1981), those promoting the holistic view argue that the importance of such institutions lies less in their actual presence than in the fact that they are conceived culturally as an ideal by a large majority of the Japanese. While those supporting the holistic image tend to emphasize the way in which employees become totally involved with their firm (Abegglen: 1958; Ballon: 1969; Yoshino: 1968; Rohlen: 1974; Dore: 1973), others suggest that this involvement occurs not so much because of the cultural value placed on commitment and loyalty but rather for instrumental reasons related to the manipulation of organizational structures (Cole: 1971a; Bennett and Levine: 1976; Marsh and Mannari: 1976 and 1977).

In much of the literature on industrial relations in Japan, the propensity of Japanese workers to identify with and to think in terms of their company rather than their occupation has often been emphasized (Yakabe: 1977, p. 80; Nakane: 1970, pp. 2–3; Vogel: 1963, p. 264; 1967, p. 108; and 1975, pp. xx–xxi; Cole: 1971a, p. 13; Reischauer: 1978, p. 184). Recast in slightly different terms, this argument is seen as saying that classes in the Marxist sense (e.g. horizontal or occupationally based strata) are less important for understanding Japanese society than for understanding Western societies (Craig: 1975, p. 12; DeVos: 1975, p. 226; Nakane: 1970, p. 96; Reischauer: 1978, p. 160; OECD: 1977, p. 27). Most common is the simple, more limited assertion that the Japanese have especially strong ties in their firm (Rohlen: 1974, p. 16; Abegglen: 1958, p. 11; 1973, p. 62; Yoshino: 1968, p. 114; OECD: 1973b, p. 10; DeVos: 1975, p. 212; Craig: 1975, p. 31; Ballon: 1969, p. 76).

These statements are implicitly comparative. It is clear that, compared with other people, the Japanese are seen as placing a greater emphasis on the company than on occupationally defined categories. Moreover, this feature of Japanese society is seen as being related to a number of other characteristics commonly associated with the Japanese and their system of industrial relations: loyalty to the group, a relatively low emphasis on individualism, traditional or paternalistic practices in personnel management, hierarchical patterns of authority, the cultural emphasis placed on work, the value attached to the maintenance of high levels of consensus, the seniority wage system, lifetime employment, the enterprise union and greater income equality. In this regard, and not unrelated to the perspective of the sociology of knowledge, it is interesting to note the extent to which scholars characterizing Japanese society in this fashion have relied on Nakane Chie as a major source (Abegglen: 1973, pp. 22–3 and 27–8, Yoshino: 1968, pp. 204–07; Hanami: 1979, p. 138; Dore: 1973, p. 250; OECD: 1977, p. 10; Rohlen: 1974, pp. 15 and 263–4).

Despite the common acceptance of statements about the Japanese tendency to think and to organize in terms of vertically defined strata, few rigorous comparative studies have been made. Although Dore (1973), Rohlen (1974), Cole (1971a), Vogel (1963), Whitehill and Takezawa (1968) have made individual case studies in which this aspect of Japanese behavior has been noted, none has made careful international comparisons. Apart from the international comparisons of occupational status mentioned above, it is known that Japan had a rather active labor movement along occupational lines in the Meiji period (Ayusawa: 1966, pp. 59–88). Cole and Tominaga (1976) have also observed that there is enough awareness of occupational differentiation for people to pursue considerably different levels of education for different, broadly defined occupational categories. The work of Taira (1970) also demonstrated that the Japanese have been sensitive to occupational wage differentials and have consistently sought jobs with higher pay. Finally, as mentioned above in Chapter 5, Japanese wage differentials based on sex, age, occupation, industry, etc. are similar to those found in both the United States and Japan (Mouer: 1980a, pp. 235–9). Each study throws light on the question of the relative importance of one dimension or agent of stratification to another. Each adds to the growing skepticism regarding the assertions of the group model theorists about behavior in Japan.

The stratification model provides a framework for examining these propositions in a comparative perspective. While overcoming limitations inherent in case studies, the stratification model focuses attention on variation within society and, by identifying potential classes (*Klasse an sich* in Marxian terms),[1] it also highlights a number of dimensions in which loyalties or solidarities might crystallize. Unfortunately, most comparative studies of stratification (including those of Japanese society) have tended to focus on only one dimension: occupational hierarchies. For some reason the literature on stratification in the West has developed around the notion of occupationally based classes; following the Pacific War Japanese scholars with a comparative interest in stratification simply adopted that approach. Accordingly, not only cross-societal studies on occupational prestige but also those on social mobility (listed in

Glenn *et al.*: 1970, pp. 179–80) have been based on the assumption that occupational differentiation is the type of differentiation most relevant to understanding social inequality. Treiman (1977, p. 1), for example, starts out with the proposition that 'men are known by their work' and immediately assumes that the sort of work one does is defined largely by 'occupational roles'.[2] Early studies on social mobility in Japan, which were initially organized in the fifties by Odaka under the auspices of the Japanese Sociological Association and later followed up by Tominaga, Yasuda and others, were also conceived in terms of occupational categories (Odaka: 1958; Tominaga: 1968, 1970a, 1979: Yasuda: 1971).

The multidimensional model of social stratification suggests that job situations will be defined not only by occupation but also by a number of other variables including firm, industry and geographical location. These elements (and perhaps others) combine to define a given job situation. The independent importance of each element is in part demonstrated by the fact that each forms a basis for forming different types of labor unions: industrial unions; trade, craft or occupational unions; company of enterprise unions; and regional bodies of soviet-type unions. In addition to being aware of the full range of criteria which differentiate job situations, it is also important to evaluate the extent to which these criteria relate to the distribution of societal rewards.

The methodology used in this study was developed from techniques used in the early work of the National Opinion Research Center in the late forties and Lenski (1952), and then further refined for cross-cultural study of social stratification and mobility. Accordingly, the instruments developed in this research do not measure levels of class consciousness or solidarity, the extent to which Japanese and American students view the present system as ideal or the relative importance of the various factors delimiting job situations in accounting for dispersion in the distribution of societal rewards. Attention has rather been given to the construction of an index which will indicate the extent to which there is consensus among a group of individuals as to the way job situations are evaluated in terms of their access to one or more societal rewards. Job situations have been defined by one or more agents of stratification. One interest is knowing whether the use of different rewards as ranking criteria or the use of different agents to define job situations produces changes in the level of consensus.

Reputational evaluation of job situations raises a number of problems. First, the evaluations do not necessarily reflect their ranking in terms of the actual situation. Second, several types of bias are known to exist: some respondents exaggerate the status of their own job relative to others; others tend to cluster all the jobs closer together to coincide with their norms as to how things should be. Difficulties of this kind are perhaps heightened when high-school students are surveyed, because few have actually been in the labor force. Nevertheless, these students were used for several reasons, two considerations in particular were important. One was ease of administration, given tight financial and time constraints. The other was the desire to survey a population not directly involved in the labor market, in order to ensure that the views surveyed might represent broader perceptions held in society at large, images diffused into the culture and not dependent upon inside information obtained at work. Seen as a preliminary test and a pilot survey to give some indication of whether the model had any promise at all, before expending more time and energy in its application, it was felt that a rough approximation could be obtained; that there was value in seeing how far outside the place of work images of work had spread; that a carefully chosen set of high schools would allow replication in the future; and that it would provide a bench-mark which could later be checked against other populations, including even younger students, to assist in uncovering the process by which people learn through time about the way in which the social world around them is structured.

To examine the way in which jobs are perceived by American and Japanese students, a survey was designed and administered early in 1980 to 531 American high-school students and 1,023 Japanese high-school students. A rather complex format was used, along with procedures for randomizing and rotating the way in which the problems were posed. These aspects are described in the Appendix. Here only the basic findings are presented. Two basic sets of data from which some of the tables in this chapter are drawn are also given in the Appendix.

II Some Initial Findings

A The Ranking of Job Situations

Analysis of the 18 problems involving ranking yielded the results given in Table A.1 in the Appendix. As expected, there is much higher agreement in ranking job situations defined by one criterion than in ranking those defined by two. A comparison of the American and Japanese samples, however, yields some interesting results. First is the high correlation between the values registered by the two samples. It is high both for job situations defined in one dimension and for those defined in two. The rank order correlation is perfect in nearly all cases. Looking at the situations defined by one criterion, in both countries the standard deviation among the means for each of five situations is smallest for situations defined by occupation and then for those defined by firm and by geographical region. There seems to be least agreement on how to rank job situations differentiated by industry. Given the tendency of the same industry to have a unique history in each society, this finding is not particularly surprising.

Looking only at occupation-related criteria and firm-related criteria, it is interesting to note that there is slightly more agreement among the American sample on firm-linked situations and among the Japanese sample on occupation-linked situations. When job situations were defined by occupation and firm, both samples consistently referred to occupation more than to firm-related factors in ranking the situations. This tendency was slightly more pronounced among the Japanese sample. This difference in the relative significance attached to each of these two agents of stratification and the consensus with which that was done is even more evident if the ratio of the level of consensus in ranking occupations to the level of consensus in ranking firms is examined (Table 14.1).

These similarities between American and Japanese high-school students remain even when the results for three subgroups are taken from each national sample. One subsample consisted of persons coming from families with high levels of socio-economic status (SES). These households were defined as those in which the father had a tertiary education and the mother was not working. A second group came from households with low SES. These households were defined as those in which the father had a primary or secondary education and the mother was working. Finally, it has been argued that those who portray Japanese society as a fully integrated, holistic entity (emphasizing consensus and vertical relationships within firm-based groups) are really writing about a small group of white-collar elites in Japan's large-scale, bureaucratic sector. Accordingly, the third group has been labeled the Nakane ideal type. It consists of individuals from homes in which the father was an employee in a white-collar job in a large firm. In Table 14.1 the ratio of the scores for agreement on

Table 14.1. *Ratio of standard deviation means for occupational criteria to those for firm-related criteria*

Sample	For 12 problems with situations defined in one dimension				For 6 problems with situations defined in two dimensions			
	Aggregate totals	For high SES group	For low SES group	For Nakane's ideal type	Aggregate totals	For high SES group	For low SES group	For Nakane's ideal type
American high-school students (N = 531)	1.281	1.357	1.316	1.454	1.779	1.606	1.630	1.696
Japanese high-school students (N = 1,023)	1.519	1.469	1.472	1.534	2.005	2.043	1.893	1.784
Extended Japanese sample (N = 1,493)	1.573	1.580	1.477	1.504	2.151	2.104	2.055	1.967

Note: These figures for subsamples are taken from Table 5 in Sugimoto and Mouer (1982: pp. 94–9).

The figures for the aggregate totals are taken from Table A.2 in the Appendix. The uppermost figure in the far left column (1.281) was derived as follows:

$$\frac{\text{standard deviation for occupations}}{\text{standard deviation for firms}} = \frac{1.013}{0.791} = 1.281$$

To the extent that the ratio is over 1.0, the amount of agreement on occupational criteria is greater than that on firm criteria.

For the standard deviations for each situation and a fuller explanation, see the Appendix.

occupational criteria to those on firm-related criteria are given for the three subgroups. The ratio is consistently higher for situations where both occupation and firm-related factors were involved. In both societies those from households with higher SES seem consistently to refer more to occupation than to firm-related factors.

The data for Nakane's ideal type yield interesting results. For the six problems with job situations defined by occupation and firm-related factors, the difference in the level of agreement in ranking occupations and firms is smaller.

Japanese constituting the Nakane ideal type seemed to refer relatively less to occupation than did their counterparts, although they too referred more to occupation than to firm. Among the American respondents, those constituting the Nakane ideal type seemed to refer more to occupation than did persons in the other subgroups. However, the fact that those in the high SES Japanese subsample showed a pattern similar to the Nakane ideal type in America suggests that firm conclusions cannot be drawn. It seems that there are no appreciable differences between the Nakane ideal type and others in the Japanese population. Finally, it is interesting to note in the case of Japan that the addition of 470 persons from the labor force to the high-school sample yielded considerably higher ratios. This suggests that the importance of occupation in defining the job situation is somehow even more acutely perceived by those actually employed. The high-school data were also analyzed for sex and age differences. Neither variable seemed to exert influence in a consistent fashion.

B Visual Associations

Three problems involved the presentation of five pictures of individuals. Respondents were asked to match each picture with one of five job situations which were defined by occupation and firm-related factors. The results in Table 14.2 show a rather clear pattern. With one exception (the second set of standard deviations for the first problem), the results suggest that Japanese students were more likely to refer to occupation in distinguishing among the individuals pictured, whereas American students consistently referred more often to firm characteristics.

C Semantic Differentials

Although the data on semantic differentials have not been completely

Table 14.2. *Index of association involving pictures and job situations defined by occupation and firm-related factors*

Problem	Job-defining characteristics / Sample / Index of association	I Standard deviation among the percentage frequencies with which job situations were associated with a given picture		II Standard deviation among the percentage frequencies with which pictures were associated with a given job situation	
		Japanese sample of high-school students	American sample of high-school students	Japanese sample of high-school students	American sample of high-school students
1	occupation	7.0	6.3	6.6	7.3
	firm	5.7	6.5	5.7	7.1
2	occupation	9.4	3.6	11.3	3.7
	firm	5.2	5.7	4.2	5.9
3	occupation	12.8	3.7	12.5	3.7
	firm	4.7	7.3	4.8	7.2

Note: For a full explanation of how the index is calculated, refer to the Appendix, Figure A.8, and the accompanying discussion.

analyzed, the initial findings are of considerable interest. First are the fairly strong rank-order correlations between the way Americans ranked occupations and firms and the way Japanese did. Second, Japanese are again more likely than Americans to use occupation in differentiating among job situations. This is true both in terms of comparing the absolute amount of variation across occupations (as measured by the standard deviation) and in terms of comparing its importance relative to that of firm-related criteria (Table 14.3).

Third, for 18 semantic differentials which involved evaluational judgements, the Japanese sample registered higher scores for every occupation and every industry, meaning a less favorable appraisal of every job situation. One interpretation is that Japanese are less oriented to work situations or that some sense of alienation is associated with work. This is quite unexpected in the light of literature emphasizing the general commitment of the Japanese to work. Nevertheless, one should be careful not to rely too heavily on these preliminary results. There are numerous difficulties in obtaining correspondence either in the meaning of specific standard deviations or in the overall perception of what it means to be high or low on any of the scales. The results are interesting because the positioning of the positive and negative poles to the right or the left in the survey was random and because the Japanese answers were consistently toward the negative end for every pair.

D Criteria for Choosing a Job

The findings reported above are further corroborated by the data in Table 14.4 for the open-ended multiple choice question. First, the

Table 14.3. *The mean of the standard deviations across occupations and firms for each of 25 semantic differentials*

	American sample	Japanese sample
A Occupation	.3583	.4649
B Firm	.1089	.1119
C Ratio A/B	3.2900	4.1600

Note: For each of 25 semantic differentials, the mean score for each of the five occupations and each of the firms was calculated. For each set of 5 mean scores a standard deviation was calculated. This table shows the mean of those 25 standard deviations for the occupations and for the firms for each of the two national samples of high-school students. The figures for rows A and B were taken from Table A.3 in the Appendix.

Table 14.4. *Relative weightings given ten criteria for choosing a job*

	Criteria	Samples		
		(I) American high-school students N = 513	(II) Japanese high-school students N = 1,023	(III) Extended Japanese sample (including those in sample II) N = 1,493
1	The amount of income or wages paid	1.507 (–1.36)	1.691 (–1.03)	1.729 (–1.01)
2	The content of the job	1.755 (–0.85)	1.649 (–1.08)	1.702 (–1.05)
3	The chance for promotion	1.603 (–1.16)	2.083 (–0.57)	2.057 (–0.62)
4	The personalities of other people in the firm and the extent to which they are friendly	1.785 (–0.79)	2.091 (–0.56)	2.079 (–0.59)
5	The size of the firm	2.497 (0.66)	2.223 (–0.41)	2.258 (–0.38)
6	The stability of the firm, judged according to how long it has been in business	2.094 (–0.16)	2.429 (–0.16)	2.485 (–0.11)
7	Whether the firm is family owned and run or owned by stockholders and run by a board of directors	2.744 (1.16)	2.735 (0.19)	2.673 (0.12)

Table 14.4. *Continued*

		Samples		
	Criteria	(I) American high-school students N = 513	(II) Japanese high-school students N = 1,023	(III) Extended Japanese sample (including those in sample II) N = 1,493
8	The extent to which the firm's products are well known	2.328 (0.31)	2.748 (0.21)	2.727 (0.18)
9	Whether or not friends or acquaintances were working in the firm	2.586 (0.84)	3.899 (1.56)	3.952 (1.66)
10	How close the firm was to the town or city in which I grew up and/or in which my closest friends are located	2.840 (1.36)	4.145 (1.85)	4.065 (1.79)
	Mean	2.174	2.569	2.573
	Standard deviation	0.491	0.852	0.833

Notes: (1) Correlation (measured by Pearson's r with level of significance in parentheses):
Sample I and Sample II .8109 (.002)
Sample I and Sample III .8044 (.003)
Sample II and Sample III .9985 (.000)
(2) In the table Z scores are given in parentheses.

correlation between the samples for each set of 10 values is high. The Pearson's r was over 0.8 and the level of significance was well within the 1 percent mark. Second, the three items related to human relationships (items 4, 9 and 10) were given higher priority by the American sample. Finally, in selecting a job, occupationally related considerations were given clear priority by both samples. Firm-related criteria were a second consideration for students in both countries.

One interesting difference appeared in item 3, where the American sample seemed to be much more concerned with promotion. As with the semantic differentials, however, interpretation of the results is not without its difficulties. Once into the right occupational track at the time of employment, promotion may be taken for granted by the Japanese respondents. It is also possible, for example, that the English and Japanese words are not equivalent, the term having positive nuances in one language and negative ones in the other language.

III Some General Conclusions

The group model makes two claims about Japanese society. One is that it is characterized by high levels of consensus and cultural homogeneity. The other is that the Japanese more than other people attach a value to vertical relationships; at work the Japanese are typified as attaching relatively more importance to their firm than to their occupation. The chapters in Parts Two and Three presented some reasons for being skeptical about the validity of the group model. The findings presented here corroborate those doubts. The Japanese did not seem to exhibit greater consensus about how Japanese society is stratified than did Americans about their society. Furthermore, there was no indication that Japanese were more likely to think in terms of the firm as the key factor determining their job choice or as the major factor accounting for stratified inequality in their society. The research on job situations was designed primarily to test the viability of the multidimensional stratification framework as a heuristic device for understanding Japanese society. The evidence presented here suggests that the framework is viable and that students could relate to the variables introduced. To the knowledge of the researchers, there was no difference in the degree of difficulty or unnaturalness which students in the two societies felt in answering the questions.

The results suggest that stratification at work occurs in a similar fashion in Japan and the United States, or that people at least perceive that such stratification occurs in roughly similar ways. The next step is to move from the structural or phenomenological level to the ideational level. Given that both vertical and horizontal hierarchies are equally well perceived in both Japanese and American societies, is there a greater normative value associated with vertical consciousness in Japan? Can careful comparative evidence be presented to show that Japanese do indeed prefer vertical solidarities or that they feel such solidarities are more natural? If so, how are these solidarities defined? What other types of consciousness are there? How do these different kinds of class or stratal consciousness manifest themselves in Japanese society, and how do we know that one is stronger than another? At the subjective level as well, the authors believe that the multidimensional model of stratification offers a useful framework not only to ensure a representative sample, but also to provide an initial set of categories for classifying the consciousness to be studied.

Part Five

Relevance and New Directions: The Future of Japanese Studies

Chapter 15

Internationalization and Japanese Society

I Introduction

In recent years Japan's presence abroad has received increasing attention. The emergence of Japan as a world power can be traced with objective indicators such as figures on trade, foreign investment, tourism, foreign aid and levels of participation in international organizations and other forums. It can also be detected in the consciousness of Japanese and non-Japanese alike. In addition to the interest in Japan abroad, the perception of Japan as having an international presence has also developed among Japanese. Japanese studies boom and the proliferation of *nihonjinron* in Japan and abroad in part reflects the concern with Japan's economic policies and defense strategies, the increased coverage given to Japan's movements in the international arena and the renewed sense of confidence which many Japanese seem to have in discussing issues related to Japan's national interests.

The change has been not so much in the subject-matter as in the problem consciousness. Concern abroad has shifted from simply looking at Japan from afar and finding the secret of Japanese economic growth to dealing with the more practical problems involved in having direct contact with Japanese; from notions of 'Japan Incorporated' to the idea of 'Japan International'. Self-images and mass culture and their influence on the way in which Japanese perceive themselves and their society are a major component of the process now being referred to as internationalization. It is in this regard that the literature of *nihonjinron* has a particular bearing on the choices which Japanese have in directing their own lives in the years to come. It suggests that Japanese society is so unique, so different culturally, that entry into and exit from Japanese society are beyond the realm of possibility.

This, however, is not the only effect on the Japanese of the literature emphasizing Japan's uniqueness. There are several other ways in which perceptions seemed to be shaped by *nihonjinron*. One is the belief that Japanese culture is part of the biology of being Japanese. Miller (1982), for example, argues that many Japanese are prone to believe that the Japanese language and the Japanese race are the same thing.

The similarities with the climatological explanations and spiritualism of the thirties (as described above in Chapter 2) are conspicuous, and many Japanese have come to accept without question the way things are in Japan, simply because they are led to believe there is no other way. *Nihonjinron* encourages Japanese to classify reality as being either *nihonteki* (ethnically, racially or culturally Japanese) or non-Japanese. It is an all or nothing perspective which leaves little room for accommodation or international mixtures. At the same time, others are led to envisage options which in fact do not exist. For example, some Japanese talk about wanting to leave Japan; their disillusionment with Japan often derives from an overly idealized image of the West. The idealized characteristic may be Western individualism, Western democracy, Western openness or Western notions of human equality. This idealization of some Western attribute is often coupled with an equally exaggerated notion of some negative aspect of Japanese society. Here another naïve conceptualization sometimes emerges, the idea that culture is tied to a location, and that one can flee one's culture simply by leaving it behind, like an unwanted bundle abandoned in a coin locker.

The internationalization of Japanese society has in some ways occurred in circumstances not dissimilar to those described by Schell (1982) with regard to nuclear weapons: a situation characterized by the failure of people to talk openly about a phenomenon which people recognize individually as being crucial to the continuation of their society as they now know it. Although internationalization is not the only area where the perception of viable choices seems to be circumscribed by *nihonjinron*, it provides an interesting case study for learning about the interplay between ideology, values and self-perception.

This chapter differs from the others in that the kind of hard data found in some of the earlier chapters is missing. This is partly because of the shift in concern from describing realities to exploring potentialities. Conclusions are drawn in a more speculative manner from participant observation and from following the mass media in Japan over the past dozen years.

The discussion begins with a brief look at how the process of internationalization in Japanese society has been perceived. In other words, what does internationalization mean to most Japanese? Attention is then focused on the use of internationalization as an ideological concept in Japanese political culture and on the question of self-identity. The final two sections return to the broader issue of social change in Japanese society, in the light of the shift in the debate on convergence and divergence from questions regarding the emergence of appropriate or requisite cultural values and the impact of industrialization to questions concerning the cultural diffusion of ideas and the impact of internationalization. Space does not allow a comparison of how these two global forces have and will continue to affect Japanese society. The focus is more on how ideas associated with *nihonjinron* are used as ideology, a usage which facilitated Japan's industrialization. The issue here is whether this usage will also facilitate Japan's internationalization and our understanding of that process.

II Internationalism in Japan

In recent years, internationalism and the age of internationalization have come into vogue in the Japanese vocabulary. In urban commuter trains English schools are advertised as the door to the world, as the way to obtaining a global view of life, as the road to international cooperation and as the formula for being an international person. Most of the new magazines written for tomorrow's leaders project an image of keeping up internationally and bear bright English names such as *Big Tomorrow, President, Will, Brutus* or *Men's Club*. Nor is this a new phenomenon, as a quick look at the titles of older publications, at product labels or at the images created in advertising will confirm.

The term *kokusaijin* was created in the Meiji period and has come to be used sometimes in a slightly derogatory manner to refer either to an idealistic person hopelessly out of touch with reality or to one way in which the upper crust goes around putting on airs. However, the idea of being international has positive connotations for most Japanese. The term hides more than it reveals, and has served for many Japanese as a key word or convenient euphemism for referring to various aspects of foreign policy while also shifting attention away from a number of major issues which divide the Japanese.

Most discussions of internationalization in Japan center on activities rather than on ends. In leading discussions on internationalization in several major Japanese cities in 1980 and 1981, the authors found that most persons thought it was a process which they as individuals supported. However, when asked what internationalization meant to them, about ten items frequently received mention. They ranged from studying English to learning about foreign cultures, and are essentially the items (definitions) which have been cited by Befu (1981). Both sets are listed in Table 15.1. Once the list had been compiled, participants were asked to indicate whether the definitions referred to means or ends. Nearly all participants saw each item listed as representing some instrumental activity. Internationalization was seen as being a number of steps or strategies to achieve an undefined goal. Attempts to elicit a definition of the goal or to promote discussion as to why individuals attached a positive value to the set of activities they mentioned in their definition usually invited embarrassed silence and resulted either in the discussion being terminated or in a temporary lull until the leader of the session changed the subject to some other aspect of internationalization.

The experiment was repeated elsewhere with other formats, using different cross-sections of the Japanese population including some Japanese who were living overseas. Also, a number of individuals were interviewed and asked similar questions. However, the results were invariably the same: internationalization (*kokusaika*), becoming international (*kokusai shugi*) and the age of internationalism (*kokusaika jidai*) were positively evaluated and then defined as activities rather than as situations to be attained. In other words, internationalization was seen as being a desirable process of change, even though the final outcome or the end state of affairs to be attained was not clearly defined. In short, it was seen as being an activity toward some undefined end. Perhaps in most languages internationalism is an ambiguous term which generates vague notions of something good. Nevertheless, because the term is frequently used to justify various kinds of behavior in Japan as though it were a goal, its

Table 15.1 *Some definitions of the term* kokusaika *(internationalization)*

From the authors' conversations	Definitions listed in Befu's paper
To learn English	The introduction of Western ideas and practices
To speak foreign languages	Foreigners in Japan
To travel overseas	Foreign investment in Japan
To learn about foreign countries	The liberalization of trade policy
To be more friendly to foreigners visiting Japan	Japanese investment abroad
To teach more about the world in Japanese schools	Foreign language competency
To learn about the customs of other peoples	Association with foreigners
To stop behaving like economic animals	Understanding foreign cultures
To promote world peace	Allowing foreigners to teach at Japanese universities
To foster international understanding	Easing Japanese laws for naturalization
	Teaching the Japanese language to foreigners
	An improved cultural understanding of Japan
	Contributions to the world order

Note: The items in the left-hand column are responses to the question: 'What does the word "internationalization" mean to you?' Those in the right-hand column are from Befu (1981), pp. 2–12.

usage and the goals implied in its usage deserve further examination.

Given the difficulties encountered in these more formal situations with unknown persons in trying to ferret out the end-product being sought through the processes of internationalization, two other methods were tried. One was to read more carefully the mass media, without going so far as to employ content analysis. The other was to speak to acquaintances in the media and other relevant professions. The term internationalization was found to imply at least two conflicting goals. One is the smooth promotion of Japan's national interests (Yamamoto: 1981). These interests relate primarily to the achievement of Japan's economic goals overseas without rocking the boat in international waters. It has meant sending performers in the traditional arts as unofficial ambassadors, to calm the locals and to distract attention from economic difficulties or from charges that Japanese multinational companies are exploiting the local economy. This usage of internationalism tends to be associated primarily with the establishment: members of the Liberal Democratic Party, the business community and certain conservative labor leaders.

Those using internationalization can also be said to possess a discernible view about Japan's cultural uniqueness and the significance of that uniqueness. In the cultural understanding game, Japan is portrayed as a country with a culture so unique that economic conflicts of interests abroad can always be dismissed either as cultural misunderstandings or as ethnocentrism on the part of foreign negotiators. Accordingly, the responsibility for conflict resolution is shifted to the foreigner, who is advised that his salvation lies not in learning economic facts about Japanese firms or in looking at their balance sheets, but in endlessly running the gauntlet of petty customs – from bowing to knowing all the nuances of *amae* or *sō desu ne*. It is not surprising, therefore, that some contributions to the learn-from-Japan campaign focus on these aspects and provide guides. While these guides may be open to cynical comment, they are nevertheless based upon a modicum of common sense: when in Rome do as the Romans do. The full implications, however, are difficult to discern. If the guest travels to Rome and tries to accommodate himself to local customs, he is said to be cosmopolitan; on the other hand, if the host demands that visitors adhere strictly to all the house rules, he is said to be ethnocentric or at best ungracious.

The second usage assigned to the term internationalization implies a different process with a different outcome. Given the general disillusionment with nationalism following defeat in 1945, the idealism associated with notions of world peace was reinforced by the socialist movement which emerged during the occupation. The strong commitment of many Japanese to the idea of peace, their concern about nuclear weapons and their demonstrations against the Security Treaty with the United States are legend. However, when asked for a more concrete definition of their goals, those sympathetic to this type of internationalism have tended to gravitate in one of two directions: either referring vaguely to international brotherhood and goodwill among nations or outlining the way in which some form of world government might be encouraged. The common theme which links these two views together is the idea that the present situation requires a fundamental change. Moreover, it is a change which is implicitly assumed to be very intimately connected with a change in the government. It is not surprising, then, that this usage of internationalization is associated primarily with anti-establishment forces: the more leftist members of the socialist parties, certain labor leaders and persons involved in the various citizens' movements.

The ordinary citizen may not consciously distinguish clearly between these two usages of internationalization, which imply very different goals. Yet the word does seem to be used with a clear intent in mind, at least by the two groups mentioned above. The first is a committed elite with a solid grasp of *realpolitik* and the realities of Western imperialism in Asia earlier this century. Its members generally accept the nation-state system. The second group consists of those persons with a wide range of mixed and even conflicting views on the role of the state. However, they do seem to share a wariness not so much of nationalism as of the present political arrangements and the present conservative regime in Japan.

To be sure, there is also a sizable stratum of persons interested only in getting along and promoting their own self-interest. They are fairly apathetic; indeed, they are even alienated by the constant efforts of the other two to use the concept of internationalism as an ideological tool. This third group represents a segment of society which is open to a give-and-take form of interaction with foreign governments, firms and individuals, based on the notion of comparative advantage and the idea of protecting their own limited interests. For this reason, it could be crucial in determining the future direction of Japanese politics. A swing to the right in their support could bring in a reactionary government; a swing to the left could bring in a more reformist coalition government. If there is a key to how Japan will internationalize in the future, it may very well lie in our understanding of this stratum.

III The International in Japanese Political Culture

Some time ago Kunihiro (1978 and 1979) coined the words 'inter-domestic' and 'inter-mestic' to refer to the way in which essentially domestic matters in one society often have ramifications which markedly affect the essentially domestic affairs of another society. In his view, 'inter-domestication' is a global phenomenon. Perhaps the frequent political use of terms like internationalization in the Japanese context may have made it easier for a Japanese to perceive this phenomenon.

Japanese concern with international matters is characterized by frequent and extensive use of international comparisons to justify behavioral choices. One might argue that, to some extent, this is inevitable, given Japan's great dependence on foreign resources and its reliance on the goodwill of other nations in the pursuit of its economic goals. Although others have discussed propositions concerning the actual extent of Japan's dependence (Hollerman: 1967; Kojima: 1971), the focus here is not on the actual extent of Japanese dependence as measured according to some universal standard. It is on the perception that many Japanese have of their nation and their society as being dependent on external developments and on the question of whether this perception is more widely or strongly held in Japanese society than in other societies. The roots of this belief among the Japanese go back at least to the early part of the Meiji period (Nihon Rōdō Kyōkai: 1971, pp. 6–8).

There seems to be an unwritten belief that the lack of land area on a poor island with a large population influenced the Japanese national character in a manner similar to the way climate was seen as affecting national character by the climatologists of the thirties. It is often suggested as an axiom that an appreciation of these basic reasons for dependence would inevitably result in an understanding of Japanese behavior in the international arena. In Australia a fairly strong sense of dependence is felt. There is, perhaps, even a fear with regard to Asia, as reflected in past notions of the Yellow Peril and in the now lapsed White Australia policy. Nevertheless, this anxiety is not verbalized to the extent that it is in Japan. Why this concern appears to be so important for so many Japanese would certainly make an interesting study in intellectual history. Part of that account would deal with the extent to which images are created with a view not to a better understanding of the policy choices which exist in the 'inter-domestic age', but to mobilizing people to support one ideological position or another within the domestic political arena. A number of case studies clearly show how essentially domestic events in Japan have a tendency to become internationalized.

1 The Concern with Pollution. The anti-pollution movements of the early seventies provide insights on this subject.[1] Two techniques in particular seem to have been used in various combinations. One was the frequent reference to the situation outside Japan in order to lend a kind of moral authority to a political position inside Japan. The second was the direct appeal to the outside world, not so much to ask for intervention as simply to embarrass the other side.

As an example of the first type, the Muskie Law was temporarily cited to underline Japan's backwardness, and pollution was presented as a form of Japanese social dumping in countries flooded with Japanese exports. The second type can be seen in various activities designed to embarrass the Government, including the stationing of Japanese pollution victims outside the United Nations Conference on the Environment in Stockholm in June 1972 and the shepherding of tourists to pollution-hit areas in Japan. Information was supplied to anti-whaling groups outside Japan and to those in less developed countries, who could cite pollution as a form of exploitation in order to pressure Japanese multinationals for additional concessions.

The Government often diffused criticism by internationalizing the internationalizers. It offered to sponsor international gatherings; as the situation required, it cited international averages in an attempt to soften the demands of the pollution victims. With equal skill, it could also reverse its position and show how Japan was different from the rest of the world, when victims tried to use the notion of international standards to support their case. In the early stages, the victims seemed to profit from international exposure. However, that momentum was difficult to maintain, and in the latter stages the initiative was often lost to the Government and to big business. Satellite communications and the electronic media certainly facilitated, on a global scale, the use of 'inter-domestic' symbols. Access to these channels of information and the ability to advertise commercially in Japan seem to have been a great advantage for those with the necessary money and influence. Although those in the anti-pollution movements received a good deal of television coverage, they were not always able to project an international image. However, when the movements were effective, an international image was frequently present.

Beginning with *Kutabare GNP* (Down with GNP!) which occupied a full page in the Sunday edition of the *Asahi Shinbun* (Asahi Newspaper) from May to September 1970, the media launched a movement to criticize GNP. In the barrage of publications which followed, foreign opinions were important.[2] Considerable attention was given in March 1972 to the report by the Club of Rome (Meadows *et al.*).[3] An even greater stir was created in 1973 by the widely read report of the OECD on Japan's labor force policies.[4] The same can be said for the OECD report on the Japanese system of education, which again underlined the connection with high economic growth rates. The speed with which these reports were translated into Japanese and published is amazing, and can be said to reflect the deep concern of the Japanese establishment about what was being said about Japan by outsiders.[5]

Two themes appeared regularly in this campaign. One was the idea that the Japanese had become obsessed with catching up with the West and with GNP growth at any cost. The futility of doing so was underlined by reference to the fact that Japan had fallen short of the Western ideal (e.g., the Western standard of living) in many ways, despite the all-out efforts of the conservative leadership. The issue was not so much the question of whether or not to catch up, but what catching up meant. The position of the West as Japan's positive reference group was not seriously challenged; rather, the dispute concerned who was to be the true interpreter of the West. The criticism was that GNP growthmanship as promoted by the LDP had given people a false sense of catching up. It was pointed out that actually the people had been deceived. Some argued that Japan had fallen behind, particularly in terms of the quality of life. The second theme was a nebulous concern for world ecology. It arose perhaps not so much from respect for nature and the notion of Mother Earth as from a systems overview and functionalist assessment of the prospects facing Spaceship Earth and of what Japan's share of the world's finite resources might be.

2 Labor-management Relations. Another area where essentially domestic issues have been internationalized is labor-management relations. Attempts to involve the ILO in the right-to-strike issue and the strategy of arguing for shorter hours of work in the sixties by referring to shorter working hours abroad provide good examples. In the latter case, it is particularly interesting to note the view that the goal of the unions was not shorter hours of work at all, but rather a redistribution of the work between standard working hours and overtime so as to increase take-home pay.

As per capita GNP rose to the levels achieved in other countries, management too shifted its arguments. In the early sixties, it claimed that longer hours of work were appropriate in a poor country like Japan. In the late seventies, it attempted to show that Japanese did not work excessively long hours.[6] With this shift in its position, management also changed its definition of hours of work to suit its own convenience, and began to use its own international comparisons in dealing with labor. Management also used these comparisons as a device to consolidate public opinion within Japan. Various attempts were made to weaken the class consciousness of Japanese by emphasizing how the Japanese as a society were being criticized unfairly by jealous trading partners.

In looking for the motivation behind the Government's move to support shorter hours of work in the early seventies, the presence of international pressure was again important.[7] Newspapers cited an endless number of foreign opinions saying that the Japanese worked too hard.[8] Survey teams were sent overseas and various study teams made international comparisons.[9] Editorials on leisure almost invariably started with some kind of international comparison. The word 'workaholic' was imported from the United States as though it had been concocted especially for the Japanese.[10]

It has also been convenient for labor to appeal to an overseas standard in its campaign for higher wages. Within the somewhat successful framework developed for the annual wage or spring offensive, unions pushed for wages on a par with those in Europe (*Yōroppa nami chingin*) during the sixties. Once that goal had been achieved, the union movement was quick to shift its demands to having a distribution of GNP on a par with that found in Europe (*Yōroppa nami bunpairitsu*). Accordingly, during the early seventies we saw a great clamor about life-cycle needs. At the same time, the Government was quick to respond by importing quality-of-life indicators which it could manipulate with its massive array of statistics. Foreign ideas were again introduced to mobilize Japanese around domestic political issues and to control the vocabulary with which such issues could be discussed. This jostling for position can also be seen in the discussion of an incomes policy in the early seventies.

The point to be made here is that institutionalized concern with knowing about other societies is not necessarily motivated by a desire to understand other cultures. Rather, there is an instrumental concern with supporting a political (or ideological) position at home, with developing stable export markets and with obtaining reliable sources of raw materials and certain other necessary goods abroad. Further, the use of foreign ideas to promote ideological positions can be seen not only on the part of the Government, but also within the labor and socialist movements themselves. This does not mean that no Japanese see value in understanding other cultures, but suggests that the efforts of those who do need to be seen in relation to the ideological thrust of the main political actors.

IV Internationalization as a Problem of National Self-identity

In this context the recent boom in literature emphasizing Japanese uniqueness is of considerable interest in terms of understanding Japanese society and assessing the possibilities for increased Japanese participation in the international community., Because perceptions yield self-fulfilling prophecies, the way in which Japanese perceive their situation and the choices they have will in no small measure define the situation and the choices available. One might simply dismiss the literature and the images of Japanese society it projects as popular culture; however, the heavy involvement of the academic community and of the political and business establishment in promoting such images, not only at home but abroad as well, suggest that these images also contain other ideological elements. In this regard, three points deserve mention.

First are the interesting similarities with the intellectual underpinnings of prewar Japanese nationalism as found in *nihonshinkokuron, yamato damashii* or *jōiron.* The second concerns the extent to which the view of Japanese society as an integrated whole tends to serve the interests of the elites. The way in which self-fulfilling prophecies work needs little elaboration. Acceptance of such views of Japanese society encourages Japanese to accept the *status quo.* Acceptance abroad discourages well-meaning foreigners who might otherwise accept an invitation to interfere in Japan's domestic affairs. It may well be no accident that the Japanese Foreign Ministry chooses actively to promote this view of Japan abroad. Finally, it is important to note how explanations of this view have been used as a convenient negotiating tactic by Japanese in their dealings with people overseas. If the Japanese are seen by foreigners as being inscrutable and if Japanese decision-making is seen as a unique process which foreigners cannot understand, on one hand, and if the doctrine of cultural relativism is then used to defend one's own way of doing things, on the other, a tremendous barrier is placed in the way of the foreigner's understanding of, and involvement in, the activities of his or her Japanese counterparts. A mystique is created in which Japan is hidden in mist. In such misty surroundings it is easier for Japanese to parry the approaches of foreign negotiators.

The present ambiguity with regard to goals implied by the term internationalization cannot be understood apart from the self-images of Japanese themselves. These images serve the Japanese as a mirror for looking not only at themselves but also at the world around them. As we suggested above in Chapter 2, the holistic view of Japanese society as a unique entity is not new. Kawamura (1980 and 1982a) has traced its development back to the idea of *wakon kansai* in the eighteenth century. Befu (1982a) has suggested that the Meiji Restoration was accompanied by numerous developments which resulted in the West becoming the reference group for many Japanese. He has also pointed out that defeat in World War II and the subsequent occupation served to focus Japanese attention even more narrowly on the United States, arguing as follows:

> It is quite natural . . . for the group model of Japanese society, as it came to be formulated in the postwar years, to incorporate features of Japanese society which stood out in contrast to American society. Moreover, as a folk model, it was important for the group model to incorporate overt and covert contrasts with the culture which had come to play such a salient role in the everyday life of the Japanese. (Befu, 1982b, p. 190).

To some extent, this concern with identity is a natural outcome of Japan's increasing presence in the international arena. It can be seen as a defense mechanism when venturing out of one's own environs into a sometimes hostile world. It is not simply fear of the unknown in physical terms. One can study scientifically the lie of the land; it is more difficult to know the motivations of outside purposive actors whose intentions toward Japan are not always clear. Foreign actors are often perceived as working in collusion against Japan and changing the rules freely to serve their own needs. They divided China and came to Japan with unequal treaties which defined how the Japanese should receive international acceptance. In the postwar period, English has been the medium for dialogs and for commerce. Contracts are drawn up according to Anglo-Saxon law. Japan's constitution is modeled on American and Western European constitutions. The work of Japanese academics is judged largely by Americans according to whether it uses the style of analysis found in American journals.

Early on, Japanese were told that a market economy and economic competition were what was needed. Nothing could help Western democracy as much as a healthy Japanese economy based on the principles of *laissez-faire* competition. When such an economy was produced, however, Japanese were then told that the rules had changed, and that the real problem with its economy was low wages. After a decade of growth and a great improvement in wage rates, Japanese were finally told that Japan would have to open its doors to foreign goods and investment. And to help Japan achieve these goals, Americans floated the dollar in order that the yen might be revalued upwards. Wages immediately doubled in comparison with American rates and imports became much cheaper for Japan, although Japan was not to learn until later that the oil shocks were just around the corner. With higher wage rates and a more open market, the issue then became hours of work, 'rabbit hutches' and defense expenditure. No matter what the Japanese did, there always seemed to be new demands. Then came the trade friction (*bōeki masatsu*) in the spring of 1982 and the arrest of several Japanese businessmen in the United States by the FBI when the Japanese computer industry became too competitive. Popular perceptions were reinforced. The problem actually was not this or that aspect of Japanese society; it seemed rather to be simply that Japan was beating the West at its own game and that many in the West resented this. Accusations against Japan were seen as a form of sour grapes or even outright jealousy. The ultimate solution for Japan was bluntly stated by foreign citizens interviewed on the streets of their own cities in Europe and North America and widely broadcast by the media in Japan: Japan should accept its own position in the world and not be a climber. Somewhere in the unwritten rules was the statement that the international order was fine the way it was, and that non-Western societies like Japan could play fairly only by not winning. The Profesor of International Business at the Université de Paris, Yoshimori Masaru, summarized this perception as follows:

> The Japanese are damned if they do, and damned if they don't, the *Economist* of London wrote recently. The destiny of Japan as the most visible culprit does not seem to have changed much since novelist Ōgai Mori expressed this sentiment in a poem during the Russo-Japanese War: 'Win the war, and Japan will be denounced as a yellow peril. Lose it, and it will be branded a barbaric land.' It has been and

> still is difficult to be a Japanese. From the initial shock and the hasty measures to remedy the trade imbalances with the West, Japanese reaction has shifted toward increasing resentment, powerlessness and even occasional defiance against an apparently endless list of demands as well as the emotional escalation of verbal attacks by the United States and Europe. It is not a feeling but almost a conviction of most Japanese that they are being made the scapegoats for the internal economic problems of Western nations. (*JT*, 18 August 1982, p. 12).

Where this suspicion of the West came from is not clear. The view has often been advanced that views of the outside world and of foreigners were ambivalent until the end of the Tokugawa period, when the Japanese became aware of Western imperialism in Asia. At any rate, as the following quotation suggests, such suspicions had become rather widespread by the middle of the Meiji period:

> But in the Meiji years, such a pseudo-Western lifestyle was not yet so prevalent as today. It was an object of fascination and envy, but could at the same time be something to be detested. On the one hand, the repulsion was based on the traditional psychology of the Japanese people, but, on the other, even stronger was the above-mentioned suspicion of incongruity held by the conscientious intellectuals toward the so-called 'civilized' countries that were ruthlessly encroaching politically, economically, and militarily upon the Asian countries. To them it was a sheer paradox that the nations advanced in civilization should become barbaric invaders vis-à-vis retarded nations. From the viewpoint of Oriental philosophy, civilization meant a social condition characterized by a supreme moral standard without any relevance to material wealth. The following critical remark of Takamori Saigo about the Western civilization should be interpreted from this angle: namely, 'I cannot understand why the civilization of the West should be called a civilization. If theirs were a genuine civilization, the so-called civilized countries should have enlightened and helped the retarded, weak countries in Asia to become civilized. Far from it, the civilized countries of the West are invading Asian

> countries by force of arms. Why should one call them civilized countries?' (Nishio: 1982, pp. 2.3–2.4).

At the same time, there are reasons for this resentment being retained, and they lie in the constant exposure to Western ethnocentrism. In addition to the more general set of stereotypes and prejudices which are subsumed in the notion of Orientialism as described by Said (1979), Wilkinson (1981) and Minear (1980a), there are the various images of uniqueness developed specifically for Japan. Some of these were discussed in Chapters 1 and 2; they arise from the idea that Japan is a culture of contradictions euphemistically referred to as paradoxes and that Japan still does not measure up on the scales used for appraising civilizations. Among these scales, modernization, with its ideal types defined abstractly in terms of Parsonian pattern variables, is perhaps the most sophisticated. None the less, however eloquently the sentiments may have been expressed by Kipling and others, the message is still the same: East and West are worlds apart. Expressed less eloquently by MacArthur, compared with Americans 'the mental age of the Japanese is twelve.' Thus a production like the BBC's *Perspectives on Japan* is of great interest not for what it tells us about Japan but for what it tells us about Britain. Britain's own economic problems (which the Japanese like to call the British disease) could not be better underlined than by the message that Japan may be economically advanced, but is spiritually still in the dark ages. The subtle reminder is also made repeatedly in television dramas like *Roll Call, A Town like Alice* and *Shogun.* Films like *Southern Cross* and *Kagemusha* also have their impact.

Even the recent flurry of books about Japan's economic successes comes as a backhanded compliment. First and foremost, these books sell overseas for their surprise value: who would have believed that the Japanese could have achieved such growth? For a quarter of a century after the war the image of Japan remained largely unchanged: poverty, homeless and demoralized repatriates, industrial unrest and honey buckets. During the fifties and sixties the world's attention was drawn elsewhere: China, Korea, Suez, Hungary, Cuba, Vietnam, the Middle East. Then, all of a sudden, there was Japan. This time the paradox was too big to ignore. Many of the books which appeared in rapid succession from the late sixties onwards tried to explain the paradox. While Western development may have been accepted as natural or even inevitable, Japanese development was somehow out of keeping with the expectations of many Westerners.

Many of these books also became bestsellers in Japan, but not necessarily because they informed the Japanese about themselves. While many people were no doubt flattered, for some part of the joy in reading these volumes derived from knowing how little these foreign experts really knew and from baiting clever foreign research students by inviting them to comment on the extraordinary insights embedded in these books. From this point of view, folk models emphasizing Japan's uniqueness make sense as a psychological defense mechanism and as a search for dignity, two prerequisites, perhaps, for building the bridges with the past which were described in the quotation from Morley in Chapter 2 (p. 31). The national obsession with Japan's uniqueness has also been described frequently as a research problem by outsiders doing work on Japan. Indeed, the way in which this concern has been woven into the language itself is described in some detail by Miller (1982).

Why should the Japanese be any more interested than others in seriously trying to understand themselves if such understanding has little value for getting ahead in the world? Moreover, why should foreigners monopolize the vocabulary with which Japanese discuss their own experience? There is a saying, 'If you can't beat them, join them.' However, if you're constantly told that you can't join them, only a small amount of lateral thinking is necessary to refocus attention on winning at all costs, and then practicing the same kind of exclusiveness in reverse. Unfortunately, the task is not easy. The more pathological aspects produced by the psychology of catching up and winning the international sweepstake while seeking to maintain one's cultural integrity in a pure form are well described in the work of Fanon (1965, 1967a and 1967b) and, more recently, Goulet (1971) and Naipaul (1975, 1977 and 1981).

V Internationalization and Japanese Society: an Australian Perspective Once Removed

The Japanese concern with a very limited number of societies becomes clearer when we consider briefly the cultural relations between Australia and Japan. In thinking about the internationalization of Japanese society from an Australian perspective, several issues come to mind.[11] There are anxieties concerning the meaning which those leading the private and public sectors in Japan give to a frequently used term like internationalism, when they are talking about the problem of cultural differences and the need for improved international understanding. These anxieties are heightened by the confidence which many Japanese seem to have about their understanding of the Australian scene. The Japanese are often seen by many as running about in a great flurry of activity, intent on gathering data about the physical environment. They are sometimes portrayed as being intent upon manipulating, but without much interest either in explaining motivation or in understanding the local society and its culture.

The concern in *nihonjinron* with generalizing from American examples (and, to a lesser extent, from the European experience) has given many Japanese a very limited knowledge of the world. Indeed, one could argue that Australians have a better understanding of the Japanese than the Japanese do of Australians, even though Australians may have less statistical information and fewer fancy data banks. Although there have been significant changes in recent years as economic ties between Australia and Japan have deepened, and as the work of the Australia–Japan Foundation progresses, it is instructive to consider the direction and volume of cultural exchange which existed until a few years ago. Without going into an elaborate definition of culture, let it suffice to confine this discussion to the realm of ideas and the feelings generated by a given social milieu. Here we might examine briefly material expressions, artistic expressions and intellectual expressions.

The first concerns the exchange of economic goods, the artefacts produced by economic activity. Australia imports various kinds of consumer durables that are used widely throughout Japanese society: cars, household appliances, tools, machinery and electronic computers. Australians have some idea about the kinds of product Japanese workers produce and Japanese consumers purchase. There is also a sizable Japanese community in Australia, whose members are visible and easily distinguished from other Asians by dress, mannerisms and other aspects of behavior. Finally, many Australians have eaten at a local Japanese restaurant. In the other direction, however, Japan imports largely raw materials from Australia. The materials are processed and never really seen in their original form by Japanese consumers, although they may have eaten Australian beef. Moreover, the imported materials are mined in rural Australia, whereas most Australians live in large cities and do not relate to the materials or to the processes by which they are extracted. Japanese images of Australia are of kangaroos and koalas, sheep stations and the vast outback, which few Australians have seen or experienced (Atsumi: 1978). Until recently, there were no Australian restaurants in Japan, although in Tokyo today Australian cuisine is served at Matilda's in Roppongi, 'jumping meat' is advertised in Shinjuku and Australian wines have become increasingly available. The few Australians in Japan are not conspicuous as Australians and are not readily perceived as being different from Americans and other English-speakers. When speaking English, they are often asked, 'Are you from America?'

In the area of art, the Japanese Government and other organizations are constantly despatching to Australia *kabuki* troupes, arrangers of flowers, masters of the tea ceremony, *jūdō* experts and some professional *go* players. It is basically elitist or upper middle-class culture, but it comes in a steady stream. From Australia there is very little, if any, touring by performers in Japan.

Finally, in the realm of the intellectual climate there are lacunae on both sides, although Australians have access to a large number of books about Japan in English and a large number of Japanese novels in translation. The percentage of secondary-school students studying Japanese as a second language is second only to the figures for Korea. Japanese films and television programs are occasionally shown in Australia. Few Australian novels are translated into Japanese; few Japanese schools teach the Australian version of English; few Australian films or television programs are shown in Japan. Newspaper coverage is perhaps slightly more balanced (cf. Atsumi: 1978; Broinowski: 1980).

The absorption of Australian culture is not the acid test of internationalism. However, in the case of Japan its absence suggests that the concern of many Japanese with foreign ideas and international culture has been narrowly focused. We suspect that a closer examination of longitudinal data will also show that Japan's interest in Australia (in terms of coverage in the mass media, for example) is largely a function of its economic inroads into the Australian economy and its need for economic information. One wonders again whether internationalization in Japan and the call for international understanding in the case of Australia simply mean the acquisition of more information to facilitate further penetration of the Australian economy.

VI False Images and International Isolation: Some Consequences

Despite a fairly good grasp of the raw facts (e.g., reams of statistical data) concerning other societies, as long as the Japanese self-image is ideologically colored and is consciously created by Japanese leaders as a kind of self-fulfilling prophecy, the understanding which many Japanese have of other cultures may be seriously limited. As explained in the early chapters of this book, *nihonjinron* is implicitly comparative. As a kind of looking-glass not only for viewing themselves but also others, the likelihood that *nihonjinron* will transpose ideological distortions created for domestic politics onto the images which many Japanese have of the outside world is not small.

In the postwar period Japan has increasingly come into contact with the world economy and the international political situation and some Japanese are concerned with becoming international citizens, in a way which would facilitate the free movement of individuals into and out of Japan. The increasing amount of interaction with the international community means the ability to see the outside world without these ideological lenses and to assess more accurately realities outside Japan becomes an increasingly important asset. However, the promotion of *nihonjinron* as ideology and as public relations has fostered a situation in which Japan's objective internationalization has in some ways been accompanied by subjective de-internationalization.

As mentioned above, the West in general and the United States in particular are often cited as the major reference groups in much of the *nihonjinron* literature. For a small minority advocating the conflict perspective, the reference group may be the Soviet Union, China or some other society believed to have achieved a socialist state. To the extent that internationalism is a goal associated with the acquisition of a more cosmopolitan outlook, the almost exclusive concern with a very narrow range of societies undermines efforts to gain a global understanding of the world. Tsurumi (1983) observes that the Fifteen Years' War was lost not to the United States but to China and that the American occupation was a convenient interlude which allowed Japanese an opportunity to delude themselves into thinking that they had in fact lost only to the allied powers of the West and to America's military might but not to other Asians. This problem of using an idealized West as a reference group is no doubt further aggravated by the tendency to view the West as a monolith. More realistic appraisals of a particular society are replaced by generalizations which fit no one society and which even in themselves are often fallacious or of dubious validity. This means that individuals are left to act without being aware of the full range of behavioral choices.

A more serious shortcoming of *nihonjinron* is the attitude toward other cultures which it often implants. As a folk model packaged to sell to the public, there is great emphasis on the storytelling of interesting anecdotes, chosen and arranged not so much for their truth but rather for their entertainment value. While the use of anecdotes and unique phrases in the Japanese language is another facet of the sampling problem, they contribute to the idea that accuracy should be subordinated to entertainment in the production of national stereotypes. Given these attitudes, the initial concern with respecting other cultures and with the idea of cultural relativism (which has in part prompted the emphasis on unique features of Japanese society) may easily give way to the denigration of other cultures and the people who live in them. When cultural differences only are emphasized and are seen as being the overbearing reality, it is easy to find one's own meaning in the superiority of one's own culture as *the* culture and to look upon the people in the other culture as a subcategory of the human species or as culturally less developed.

Morimura (1981 and 1982) very vividly describes the way in which Japanese in Manchuria came to use Chinese captives in human experiments. The appellation *maruta* (log) was used to refer to the Chinese, a mental trick which allowed the human objects to be dehumanized and to be treated simply as biological material. One can also see this sleight of hand at work in the treatment of the *burakumin* who at one time were called non-people (*hinin*) and who even in recent history have been kept in a separate category with labels such as *yotsu* (four-legged animal) (DeVos and Wagatsuma: 1967, p. 4; Price: 1967, p. 11). To some extent similar attitudes can be seen in Japanese sex tours to Asia, the treatment of Asian entertainers in Japan and the open use of a word like *ketō* in speaking of Westerners. It is also in part built into the case of *yoko meshi* and *tate meshi*, one being natural and comfortable and the other being unnatural and uncomfortable, and into the derogatory nuance of *konketsu* (children of mixed blood).

The point here is not that the Japanese are more guilty than other people for having engaged in this kind of compartmentalization. As

Morimura (1981, pp. 231–2) and others have observed, the phenomenon is more universal; it is likely to occur whenever there is war and whenever man's inhumanity to man is being promoted. The cultural origins of the Nazi treatment of the Jewish people lie in theories of biological and cultural uniqueness. Americans returned home to the world after having fought the 'dinks' in Southeast Asia.

Inequality on an international level can certainly be understood as one type of social differentiation and as one dimension of social stratification. It is difficult to predict how theories of uniqueness will be transformed into theories of denigration. Perhaps that is why national images and stereotypes can be so frightening. We know that images are a powerful force shaping social behavior. We know nationalism can be a powerful force shaping public policy. But we do not know exactly how national images or self-identities develop or how they will affect public policy.

There is a further consideration. A good deal has been said in Japan about the need for cultural understanding. Over the past decade, however, while the amount of information about Japan has increased, so too has Japan's trade friction. One problem is that much of this information is in fact an artefact of an extensive public relations campaign. To the extent that messages consist largely of the *nihonjinron* stereotypes, however, the result may be the replacement of one kind of cultural misunderstanding with another, albeit one more suited to the interests of Japan's leadership.

For many non-Japanese there is something plastic or artificial about the images of Japanese groupism and harmony presented in the mass media and by leaders who serve as Japan's spokesmen abroad. When the lower level of strike activity in Japan in the late seventies is presented as a cultural trait of Japanese society, an incredulous picture is created in the minds of many foreigners. Given their smattering of information about student riots, assassinations, the Red Army, the anti-pollution and anti-nuclear movements, the *ampo* demonstrations, the struggle at Miike or the frustrations of the examination hell to get into a good school or university, they are confused by the clear-cut paradoxes. Rather than helping to bridge cultural differences, the *nihonjinron* type of explanation often makes the cultural gap appear to be much wider than it actually is. Sometimes the gulf is seen as being so wide that only the most fantastic assumptions about the Japanese pattern of culture can tie it all together.

The presentation of two completely opposite images and the

continual emphasis on apparent paradoxes in Japanese character contribute to the entrenchment of ambivalent attitudes toward Japan, and thereby to a certain instability. When a shift in the image of Japan occurs, it is likely to be large. One sees Japan either as a consensus-oriented society or as a fully controlled and orchestrated society. One either accepts Japanese statements about internationalizing or cynically rejects them as fancy double-talk to cover up neo-Japanese imperialism. Non-Japanese without close Japanese friends often find it difficult to deal with individual Japanese on a human basis, to say some are and some are not likeable, orchestrated, internationalizing, etc. For many Japanese, anxiety is created by being pointed one way by international public opinion on one day and then in another completely different direction only a few days later, when positive evaluative judgments made about Japan's international image suddenly change to negative criticism of some other feature of Japanese society. In the long run, Japanese efforts to establish a firm, consistent and coherent foreign policy may be frustrated by the instability of its image abroad.

Further, on a more practical level, the frustrations of Japanese attempting to learn English might be mentioned. There is, for example, an insistence in much English-language education that one must think like an English-speaker (usually a middle-class American) to speak English. One is told that one requires a cultural transfusion to be able to communicate properly in English. Unfortunately, the transfusion often consists of doses of the Western monolith found in most *nihonjinron.* The results are several. One is the myth that to talk in English one must be individualistic and aggressive, and that shy Japanese must be more outgoing in using their English. Foreigners are thus confronted with all kinds of personal questions by probing Japanese individuals on the trains of Tokyo. They are forced by overbearing Japanese into speaking English at Japanese gatherings, when the language of the occasion is obviously Japanese. Rather than communicators, the end-product of this think-Western English instruction is often a technically accomplished interpreter robot, which is aggressive and obnoxiously loud with its own brand of Japanese individualism.

The way in which some English-speaking Japanese divide the world into Japan and the West can be seen in other ways as well. Most obvious, perhaps, are T-shirts with English expressions like 'hot-lips', 'grab me' and 'kiss me', or the lyrics of many English songs. Asked if they would wear a similar shirt with Japanese lettering or sing the lyrics in Japanese, many young people reply with an embarrassed 'No!' Apart from not having a firm idea of the English meaning, there is a belief that it is all right to say whatever one wants in English because one can be one's own self in English. To some extent, this practice tends to develop unchallenged, as other Japanese around the individual in question also do not understand the English and share the same myths. The same behavior can also be found among some Japanese academics, who believe that it is fun to publish in English because they can express themselves better in such a logical language. These are often the same individuals who insist on reading everything in English (both English originals with Japanese translations and English translations of Japanese originals) because it is so much easier to understand in English.

It would be interesting to study whether language ability upon leaving Japan is a predictor of the success which Japanese foreign students and businessmen have in integrating into societies overseas. In fact, for Japanese whose study of English was linked to the cultural content approach, it may be that the reverse is the case. Their ability to communicate in English may sometimes be offset by the belief that they are so different that anything more than the most formal interaction would be impossible. In other words, the most capable communicators may be those who go abroad with little else than an open mind ready to appreciate both similarities and differences. A careful study might reveal that they turn out to be the ones who find it easiest to live in dormitories and flats with non-Japanese. It may be that somewhere along the line they had developed their own means of finding common ground on which to communicate – some simply by searching out those with similar experiences, hobbies and habits and others in a more systematic fashion by drawing a map of society similar to the one presented above in Chapters 11 through 14, in the form of a multidimensional model of stratification.

VII Internationalization and the Study of Japanese Society

Tokyo is one of the world's great cities. It has first-class museums, offers a rich variety of national cuisines and constantly draws the world's top performers. As a center for world business, Tokyo has also become a repository for information from every corner of the world. In short, it is cosmopolitan. Since rejoining the international community in the early fifties, Japan has been active in the United Nations and its various agencies, the OECD, the Club of Rome, the Trilateral Commission, the ILO, the World Bank, GATT and the International Monetary Fund. Japanese have also been enthusiastic members of Rotary International, the International Boy Scouts, the Lions Club, the Experiment in International Living and other similar bodies. The zeal with which English and other foreign languages are studied is unparalleled in the world. The number of titles translated into English by the Japanese themselves is also no small accomplishment. It would be difficult to criticize the Japanese for not being international.

At the same time, however, the alleged failure of the Japanese to internationalize is commonly discussed in the Japanese media, often with laments and sometimes with vexation. The Japanese are constantly prodding themselves to be more international. It would seem reasonable, therefore, to ask why so much self-doubt is expressed about Japan's internationalization when Japan already appears to be so internationalized. There are, no doubt, several reasons.

Internationalization is a multifarious process. Societies may be international in some regards but not in others. While few societies have been as open as Japanese society to foreign ideas, the knowledge many Japanese have of the outside world is in some ways qualitatively quite limited. As such, it is not really as formidable as it seems when we think only of the quantity of information and the number of titles imported into Japan. Although many Japanese are very sensitive to comparisons with the West, there has been a tendency to view the West as a monolith. Moreover, while such factual information has assisted Japanese businessmen intent upon knowing about functional or mechanical relationships in order to work more effectively within foreign economies, the massive amounts of quantitative data or factual information on foreign societies collected in Tokyo have not necessarily produced an understanding of the societies studied.

In Japan today there is a considerable debate on the internationalization of Japanese society. Part of the discussion is focused on identifying the consequences or ramifications of certain inevitable changes. In the past many Japanese have seen the national goal as being one of catching up or as national survival itself. Now that Japan is a front-runner and in a position where its ability to influence the survival of other countries is recognized, its leaders are increasingly being called upon to demonstrate international leadership. The international situation has changed dramatically over the last two decades and Japan can no longer depend upon the United States to lead the way; it will now begin to plot its own course. In democracies where different images and ideologies are free to compete, public opinion is an important force influencing the formation of foreign policy. For this reason, Japan's future will be shaped in part by the way in which Japanese perceive themselves and their inter-relationship with the rest of the world. However, as in any democracy, to the extent that the goals remain implicit and are not explicitly debated, they are not chosen openly by an informed public but by a small number of self-appointed decision-makers. Their judgements as to what the goals should be and the public's acceptance of their decisions will in turn be shaped by the way in which the outside world is perceived by both the leadership and the electorate.

People's lives are shaped and controlled by the stereotypes and by the national myths to which they are exposed. The decisions of political leaders and others in positions of authority are often based on such stereotypes, and particularly so at junctures where a society is facing some kind of crisis, including the search for an identity. *Nihonjinron* has provided many Japanese with a rather fixed and narrow image of the outside world. It has also been used ideologically as a means of mobilizing Japanese on domestic issues, thereby limiting the choices which Japanese have. This is not to argue that each society does not have its own national myths which are comparable to *nihonjinron.* Nor does it suggest that citizens should not be socialized to see the world as it is (i.e., as a collection of competing nation states). From this perspective, a few comments may be made about the significance of *nihonjinron* for understanding Japanese society today.

In many discussions of Japanese society, the debate on convergence and divergence is frequently mentioned. Without going into the details of that debate, it should suffice simply to state that concern with Japanese values is a core issue. From the point of view of those concerned with economic development, policies to mobilize the masses, as opposed to simply directing or leading a spontaneously motivated population, are of considerable interest. From the point of view of moving into the post-industrial era, the apparently lower crime rates, lower levels of alienation and industrial unrest, the attention given to corporate welfarism and the seemingly higher level of purposive activity also draw considerable interest. From either angle, there is concern with the trade-off between voluntarism and control. As a theory, *nihonjinron* tends to minimize the importance of or need for control and coercion. Seen as ideology, however, it tends to underline the existence of artificial devices which mobilize and channel people.

From this perspective, then, the group model places cultural blinkers on many Japanese and leads them to think they are so unique that they could not possibly survive overseas. In discussing civil rights in the Soviet Union, one commonly cited piece of evidence used to demonstrate their absence and the presence of coercive controls is the way in which the Soviet Government obstructs the emigration of those unhappy with the system. Although Japan is one of the great postwar democracies, it seems to us that the official and unofficial support given to *nihonjinron* by the government, business leaders and management, conservative politicians and the mass media serves to create psychological barriers which are invisible but none the less effective in preventing migration. It is from this perspective that the recent interest in internationalism holds a certain significance for those studying Japanese society. It is only when all Japanese feel comfortable in moving about internationally and in accepting immigrants into Japanese society that we can discuss in a meaningful way the extent to which Japanese society is characterized by uniquely high levels of social consensus.

Internationalism in this context is not the only index or even the ultimate index of how open a society is. It is only one index, but one which draws attention to restrictions on the issue of passports and foreign exchange, which in the past tended to limit the ability of Japanese to travel abroad. It makes us more sensitive to folk models which build cultural and psychological barriers, which in turn discourage people from leaving Japan. It points to the citizenship requirements that long denied Japanese citizenship to the children of Japanese women married to non-Japanese men. It registers the reluctance of the Japanese Government to accept refugees or to permit non-Japanese to be employed in tenured positions at national universities. While internationalism or even openness are not the only criteria for judging societies, such concepts are not irrelevant when seeking to explain social behavior in terms of social values. Indeed, they throw considerable light on questions concerning voluntarism and control, spontaneity and coercion, democracy and totalitarianism, nationalism and militarism, values and ideology. After all, these are the key issues in much of the debate on Japan's uniqueness, and on its role in the world today.

Chapter 16

The Future of Japanese Studies

I *Nihonjinron* as a Social Construction: a Summary

The images which people have of their own society often serve as tinted lenses through which other societies are perceived. Conversely, the images people have of other societies also serve as a looking-glass against which their own society is examined. In focusing on popular images of Japanese society, this book has identified some common themes which are held about Japanese society by Japanese and non-Japanese alike. It was argued that the most widely held view of Japanese society has tended to be characterized by stress on the ways in which Japanese society is different from all other societies. Points at which Japanese society might intersect with other societies have been denied. Several reasons for suspecting the validity of the stereotyped image of Japanese society were mentioned, and it was suggested that the popular image may have contributed to the construction of an artificial barrier which has made interaction between Japanese and non-Japanese more difficult than it need be.

While discussing the ways in which the images of Japanese society have changed over time, Chapter 2 highlighted a number of themes which have remained quite constant over time. One is the treatment of the Japanese as a homogeneous whole, the disturbing tendency to refer to the Japanese as though a concept like *Homo Japanicus* or 'the modular Japanese person' would be sufficient for discussing the individual in a society as complex and as varied as the Japanese one. A second theme is the frequent reference to the paradoxical nature of the Japanese. This has perhaps been a device to retain a holistic view of a complex society, in which different individuals do different things and occasionally come into conflict. Rather than accepting that there are several types of individuals, and perhaps a need for several theories, the Japanese have been conceived as a single monolith which incorporates all types of behavior, which inevitably become paradoxical when attributed to the same individual.

This book has not surveyed the entire library on Japanese society; rather, as a limited case study it examined only a small sample from a particular genre in the literature on Japanese society. That genre is known as *nihonjinron.* The views of Japanese society found in that sample were characterized by two common denominators. One was the tendency to argue that Japanese society is more unique than other societies. There is in this insistence a pronounced tendency to deny points at which the Japanese experience intersects with the shared experience of other peoples and to celebrate only the features of Japanese culture which are seen as being unique. The other common feature is the tendency to single out the group orientation as the dominant cultural pattern which shapes Japanese behavior at every turn. Japanese culture is seen as producing people who do not develop as ego-centered individuals. The Japanese ego is seen as being underdeveloped from the Western point of view, and the group orientation of the Japanese is often contrasted with Western individualism. The Japanese are also seen as placing an inordinate value on vertical relationships, and as subordinating themselves to the demands of a fairly structured set of patron-client or hierarchical relationships. It is argued that most Japanese have only a secondary interest in relating with persons who perform functionally equivalent roles in other hierarchies or organizations. Finally, the social preference for consensus is underlined. While the mechanism by which differing interests are aggregated is seldom discussed, it is often posited that individuals will sacrifice their self-interest to preserve harmony within the group to which they are affiliated. It is perhaps assumed that Japanese are socialized to share such similar values and that consensus can therefore be said to exist *a priori.*

There are, to be sure, other views of Japanese society. Some were introduced in Chapters 3 and 5–7. The major alternative to *nihonjinron* is a loose body of literature which emphasizes conflict in Japanese society and the role of coercion in soliciting acceptable behavior or consent in one form or another. However, much of this literature is focused on specific aspects of Japanese society, such as education, religion, the family or labor-management relations. Events contrary to expectations associated with *nihonjinron* are presented, but there is no alternative theory of Japanese society which gives an integrated explanation of the individual, interpersonal relationships and group dynamics in the way that *nihonjinron* does.

Having many of the shortcomings associated with the case study, the research presented here has been useful not so much in answering questions as in raising them. In looking at *nihonjinron*, the authors have attempted to utilize several methodologies. These included the use of government statistics, access to key informants, participant observation, surveying, the reading of secondary sources on history and immersion in the printed Japanese mass media. The initial examination of *nihonjinron* in Part Two suggested that the group model was suspect for three reasons. A variety of empirical research was introduced in Chapter 5 to indicate that there are extensive phenomena in Japanese society which the model fails to explain. In fact, the model can be interpreted as simply denying the existence of social conflict and significant intra-societal variation. Chapter 6 argued that *nihonjinron* was advanced without methodological rigor, and that its proponents presented interesting hypotheses without any mention of how the conclusions had been derived or how they might be tested. Finally, in Chapter 7, attention was given to two perspectives from the sociology of knowledge. One homed in on the mechanical problems involved in training area specialists and others who engaged in cross-cultural research, with the aim of comparing two or more societies. The second dealt with the issue of values in research on Japanese society and the interaction between ideology and knowledge. It served to clarify the model's rather consistent association with a specific ideological point of view, an emphasis which appeared again in Chapter 15.

The chapters in Parts Three and Four approached the examination of *nihonjinron* from another angle by asking whether an equally comprehensive and viable alternative model could be constructed. The first experiment was to look for examples which portrayed characteristics opposite to those found in the group model: individualism, contractual ties and control mechanisms which would fuse people together regardless of whether there were high levels of consensus or not. The argument advanced in Part Three was that such counter-examples could be found quite easily, and that they could be linked together in a coherent fashion to produce a very different image of Japanese society. The argument is not that the resulting image of Japanese society is accurate in the sense of being representative of the total of Japanese society. There is, however, an insistence that it is just as well informed as the group model, which is built on another set of isolated and arbitrarily chosen examples. The two are seen as perhaps explaining different phenomena, or different aspects of Japanese society. Neither is seen as forming a complete theory of that society.

The multidimensional model of stratification was developed in Part Four as a framework which would help to place the group model and its obverse into a more proper perspective. Reference was made to broader literature on social stratification to identify other types of variation which might be considered in supplementing the initial two-dimensional framework developed by Nakane. It was suggested that inequalities in the distribution of societal rewards had major consequences for the behavior of individual Japanese, and that stratification variables delineate groups with differential access to societal rewards, whose members share a kind of class or stratal consciousness. Without arguing whether consciousness or sense of identity with others was stronger in one dimension or another, findings from a survey among Japanese and American high-school students were introduced in Chapter 14 to indicate that the Japanese perception of how their society was objectively stratified was quite similar to that of people in at least one other major industrial society. Although the issue of class consciousness and normative judgements about various kinds of affiliation were not central foci at this stage of the research, the limited findings should serve as a corrective in one area, where the enthusiasts for *nihonjinron* have simply claimed that the consciousness, the perception and the reality of social inequality in Japan are all linked to notions of verticality, in a way which sets Japanese society completely apart from other similarly industrialized societies.

II Methodological Considerations

In the final analysis, the absence of a clear methodology and the presence of a clear ideological insistence do not in themselves invalidate the theories associated with *nihonjinron*. They do, however, provide reasons for being skeptical of such theories, and underline the need for a more careful appraisal than they have been given in the past. The real problem for the future is the development of criteria for judging between two or more competing explanations.

A more basic problem may lie in the fact that models are not meant to account for all phenomena; rather, they are judged on the basis of the closest fit for the largest number of cases. Accordingly, inaccuracy or evidence of contrary phenomena does not necessarily mean that a model is wrong. The evaluation of a model or theory involves subtle value judgements about what constitutes a close fit and about the significance of the few phenomena which are not explained. Consequently, evidence alone will not resolve the differences. The problems are more complex and return to methodological considerations at a more basic level, where the philosophy of science or, in this case, Japanese studies must be thought through very carefully. It is a problem which involves the choice of some realities for study and the exclusion of other realities from one's realm of concern. Before considering these issues, however, it might be useful to touch on some even more rudimentary considerations and explore the possibility of developing a more truly comparative methodology or multicultural perspective for the study of Japanese society.

Over many years social scientists have developed a set of criteria for evaluating a vision of the human condition. Table 16.1 introduces three lists from introductory textbooks. These are drawn largely from traditions developed in the natural sciences. Although the lists vary slightly in how they have been adapted for the social sciences, several major criteria stand out.

First, a theory must fit the known historical facts. A big problem with holistic views of Japanese society is that they generally fail to predict variation across space and time in a meaningful way. This is due largely to the fact that the holistic view of Japanese society is not laid down in a manner which allows for hypotheses to be deduced and tested. This in turn reflects the general confusion of theories with taxonomies, and of statements of fact with tautologies. Finally, there is a confusion of ideal types with actual happenings in real life, and of roles with individuals.

Provided statements are worded so that they can be tested, empirical data need to be carefully collected and organized. Different methods of recording data have different advantages and disadvantages, so the processes by which data are collected need to be explicitly stated. Methods need to be carefully chosen so that several complement each other, something which does not happen when the same method is used repeatedly, giving the same advantages and disadvantages each time. Accuracy is further improved if each experiment is repeated several times, and if variations in the values

Table 16.1. *Some fundamental concerns in evaluating theories of a society*

A The Weinsteins		B Lave and March	C Graham Sergeant
Natural science method	Human science method		
1 Factual accuracy	1 Factual accuracy	1 Truth	1 Accuracy
2 Precision	2 Precision	2 Beauty	2 Precision
3 Consistency and coherence	3 Consistency and coherence	3 Simplicity	3 Level of systematization
4 Explanation (Under what conditions do specific events appear?)	4 Adequacy (Do diverse events fall into a plausible context?)	4 Fertility	4 Relationship to recorded data
5 Prediction (Under what conditions will specific events appear?)	5 Fruitfulness (Does the image reveal new possibilities for action?)	5 Surprise	5 Objectivity
		6 Justice	6 The use of trained observers in testing
			7 The design for isolation of variables in testing

Sources: A Weinstein and Weinstein (1974), Chapter III.
B Lave and March (1975), Chapter III.
C Sergeant (1971), pp. 20–1.

obtained from repeatedly measuring the same phenomenon are meticulously studied.

The criteria are clear; however, social phenomena are not amenable to being studied in that fashion. Although there can be no scientific study of causality or other meaningful relationships without regularity, social behavior is such that regularities are difficult to observe. It is nearly impossible to observe human behavior independently in two situations which are exactly the same. The great difficulties which social science faces in this regard can be mitigated only if researchers faithfully report the conditions under which observations are made and data collected, and a conscientious effort is made to draw attention to extraneous or random variables which also affect the subjects being studied. This would allow roughly similar studies to be undertaken and the results of earlier studies to be checked.

A final concern is conceptual clarity. For communication to occur not only cross-culturally, but also across disciplines, common vocabularies must exist. This point relates to the second major conclusion that many of the concepts used for cross-cultural analysis are quite dubious. As Blumer (1956) lamented some time ago, few, if any, truly generic variables have been developed. Even the seemingly universal and clear-cut concept of sex varies from society to society, and in many cases is reduced in the process of *operationalization* to being a disparate variable. His ideas in this regard are very similar to those of Pike (1967) who developed the notion of *emic* and *etic* analyses. When international or cross-cultural comparisons are involved, concepts being studied in everyday language are often transformed in the process of translation. Seldom is there a one-to-one correspondence between the *etic* and the *emic*. This phenomenon has sometimes been referred to as the problem of operationalization. Comparative research requires a combination of both types of concept, those which are peculiar to a given society (such as *amae*, *shigoto*, *rōdōsha*, *nenkō* or *rabu hoteru*) and those which can be used rather freely in more than one cultural context (such as a person's height in centimeters and weight in kilograms or the distance in kilometers from Tokyo to Osaka). In this age of electronic data processing and extensive public surveying, many semi-*etic* concepts have also been developed (such as the age and sex composition of the population, the birth rate, the circulation of newspapers or other periodicals, the suicide rate, the number of students at tertiary institutions, the unemployment rate or even GNP itself). The difficulties may be illustrated by considering discussion of the family. The concept of the family in English does not correspond to that of the *ie* in Japanese. In some cases it may be useful to confine one's attention to the household, a rather clearly defined concept which can refer to the persons living under the same roof. The Japanese word would be *setai*. However, for investigating certain types of phenomenon, the concept of the household so defined loses its significance and no longer indicates important relationships which are perceived as the essence of living together in a given society.

The chapters in Part Three suggest that many of the variables used in comparative research need careful rethinking. This is particularly true of the Parsonian pattern variables and similar conceptual schemes used for assessing modernization, and is even more evident if we consider relatively simple concepts like income equality (Mouer: 1975b) or the level of popular disturbance (Sugimoto: 1981d). The idea that an anecdote or even a proverb can represent behavior consistent with a specific, abstract, normative concept seems dubious. Both the obverse model of Japanese society and work with the *iroho karuta* data underline these difficulties. The question of whether this is due to something inherent in the specific concepts themselves or whether our findings can be attributed to the problem of operationalization seems academic. The overwhelming reality is that the Japanese are both group-oriented and individualistic; moreover, they are group-oriented in ways Americans and Australians are not and they are individualistic in some unique ways as well. To claim that Western individualism is the true brand and Japanese individualism is something else simply returns us to the problems of defining generic variables and tautological logic, as far as the actual comparison of two cultures is involved. The use of a word like 'personhood', as suggested by Befu (1982a, p. 40) may help, but that too is likely to have only a cosmetic value. It also invites us to accept too willingly a notion like Western individualism at its face value. A closer look at the Western monolith may reveal that the concept of personhood has, even in its own cultural habitat, a certain prism-like quality; depending on the angle of refraction, some kinds of individualistic behavior may appear to be very conformist or otherwise tied to the need to belong.

The methodological problem is less one of coming up with universal concepts, although work on testing the universality of certain concepts is extremely important. The crucial requirement is that researchers be fully aware of the disparity between abstract concepts and those which are used in the everyday language of the people being studied. One of the great contributions of the *nihonjinron* literature is the elucidation of certain Japanese *emic* concepts. Its greatest shortcoming is the assumption either that these can without further thought also be used as *etic* concepts (as in saying that Japan is *tate* and the West is *yoko*) or that the concepts are so unique that no cross-cultural comparisons can be made, aside from the statement that qualitative differences exist. The message is important: there is a certain *arbitrariness* in the way in which concepts have been used by many comparative researchers. Modernization, industrialization, urbanization, rationalization, centralization: to what extent is there a Western or American *emic* bias in the way these concepts have been defined?

The loose fit between *etic* and *emic* concepts becomes even looser if ambiguity characterizes the abstract concepts we start with. In other words, the variables used in cross-cultural research need to be carefully designed so that comparisons can in fact be made. Approaches which rely on linguistic reductionism often argue that the uniqueness of a language results in the uniqueness of social concepts in a given society. The end result is the obfuscation of the major analytical variables, and often the conclusions that such variables do not exist. At the same time, we need to be sensitive to the difficulty (indeed, perhaps even the impossibility) of generating Blumer's generic variables. Nevertheless, the analysis of variance is central to social science. Without meaningfully defined cross-cultural variance there can be no comparative study within the framework of scientific analysis.

While being aware of the need for more methodological rigor, the kind of guidelines set out in Table 16.1 remain ambiguous. They also fail to address two major issues. One is that intellectual history as a scientific endeavor depends upon the observation of behavior assumed to reflect certain thought processes. Truly creative genius in social science, therefore, may lie less in the verification of facts than in the ability to identify convincingly the links which exist between the phenomenological and ideational levels of existence. The inadequacies of the *nihonjinron* literature and the debates they have stimulated seem to suggest not only that social science must be firmly based upon scientific methods, but also that much more than scientific method is required if the study of society is to be a fruitful or liberating endeavor, as defined by the Weinsteins (1974). To the extent that social science is concerned with potentially verifiable statements about human behavior, as opposed to philosophical or normative statements, it must begin with scientific method, and still go beyond a narrow concern with such methodologies alone. As Nisbet (1976) reminds those in sociology, both the sense of problem consciousness which makes sociology relevant and the spark of perception which yields the most profitable insights often come not from the rigorous application of scientific method but from the intuition characteristic of the artist. Nevertheless, while being keenly aware of the need for intuition and the vital role it fulfills, there is also a need for the more mundane work which is required before provocative speculation can be treated as theory.

A more basic doubt about the guidelines shown in Table 16.1 is that they do not come to grips with the special difficulties involved in cross-cultural research. At the same time, those actually involved in the comparative study of Japanese society have not sought to initiate their own discussion of these issues. As social science itself is fundamentally comparative, it is often simply assumed that cross-cultural comparisons involve little more than adding an extra dimension. It is often assumed that such comparisons add a degree of difficulty, but that they do not make the research qualitatively different enough to require a qualitatively different methodology.

While this study has not thrown light on methodological issues of this kind, it has underlined the difficulties involved in making cross-cultural comparisons. Reality is complex; so too are the ways of classifying it. Area studies have evolved from attempts to understand other societies on their own ground, but have never addressed a number of key issues involved in knowing or in comparing cross-culturally. Part of the problem lies in the failure to articulate clearly the goal of cross-cultural studies; part lies in the failure to confront the qualitatively different methodological problems raised when another culture is brought into one's field of vision. The answers are beyond the authors; however, with the hope that these issues will receive more attention in the future, the remaining pages are used to float a few naïve ideas about the problems involved in studying or describing Japanese society in a comparative perspective.

III Toward a Methodology for the Study of Japanese Society

Area studies developed rapidly in the United States following the Second World War. Without discussing the complex array of factors which accounted for the emergence of area studies, the rationale behind such an approach is obvious: social behavior cannot be understood apart from its cultural, historical and institutional context. However, a specific methodology did not evolve; at best, area studies became a loosely formulated approach in which language study and immersion in the foreign culture were seen as major prerequisites for understanding. This usually meant that a preparatory period of reading about the society and its history, with some exposure to the language, was followed by an extended stay in the society being studied. At the same time, advocates of the area studies approach have not considered this training as a methodological problem. They have not argued that understanding of a foreign society will vary directly with the researcher's language ability or the length of time spent submerged in that society. In fact, many would warn that understanding is actually reduced by 'over-identity' with the foreign culture being studied and the loss of objectivity which accompanies going native.

The failure of area specialists to articulate the need for a distinct methodology has made it difficult to legitimize area studies as an independent means of inquiry. One consequence of this failure is reinforcement of the view that serious social scientists do not major in area studies. This in turn has tended to result in the study of foreign societies being seen simply as a challenging enterprise in which the methods of a traditional discipline applied to one's own society are simply extended for use abroad in a rather mechanical fashion. The major intellectual problems in studying a foreign society then become entry into the society, the translation of material into the researcher's language and the inclusion of an additional variable or set of variables so that the nation can be properly categorized. Those coming to an area from a discipline tend to place little emphasis on mastering the language or knowing the historical context fully.

A major task for those wishing to develop Japanese studies as a legitimate academic enterprise is the formulation of a methodology which can be shown to produce a view of Japanese society which is markedly different from that of those tied solely to a discipline and from the one associated with those having simply a cultural overview and a grasp of the language. While the study of *nihonjinron* clearly highlights the methodological weaknesses of those without a firm grounding in the social sciences, at least two considerations suggest that the solution will require more than the mere addition of rigorous social science methodology to the areas studies approach. There are doubts about the efficacy of social science itself as a method which can enlighten us about social phenomena. In addition to the well-known problems – the difficulty of replicating observations, the natural reaction of people to being studied and the inevitability of the observer being part of the social situation – are more fundamental doubts regarding the extent to which methodological purity produces accurate facts without understanding, narrow empirical studies with a high level of technical sophistication but with little relevance to obtaining an overview of the social system and the essence which distinguishes one society and/or culture from another. To what extent does the mechanization of research resemble the efforts of the scientist to produce wine by chemically duplicating the process of fermentation in stainless steel vats?

The more basic question for area specialists, however, concerns the qualitative differences which characterize cross-cultural research. One major difference is created by the need to bridge two languages. The problem is not simply one of mastering two languages, but of building *etic* concepts or meta-categories for making comparisons. This problem is further complicated by the problem of international stratification, which tends to be accompanied by a hierarchical order of cultures.

Few *etic* concepts are truly cross-cultural; most are *emic* concepts which have predominated because of the dominant position of scholars, who have systematized a whole set of related concepts in a superior, but nonethless culturally bound, fashion and who have been able to persuade others of that superiority. The product of the *etic–emic* distinction and various kinds of inequalities among nation states and their constituent social sciences is a form of cultural or intellectual imperialism. As suggested above in Chapter 4, *nihonjinron* can in part be understood as a reaction against the tendency of American scholars of modernization to overwhelm the international intellectual community with concepts which appear to be *etic* but are still quite *emic*ally American. At the same time, as Sibatani (1982) observes, two related points require emphasis. First, the same process of competition among sub-*emic* concepts can be seen within American intellectual life, suggesting that American *emic* concepts may not be even as American as they are made out to be. Second, while serving as a corrective to American cultural imperialism, *nihonjinron* can also be seen as a reflection of Japanese nationalism and as an attempt to project certain Japanese *emic* concepts into comparative discussions of Japanese society as major concepts for discussing Japanese phenomena. As early as the twenties, Takata Yasuma had begun to develop a rather sophisticated systems theory not too dissimilar from the one developed later by Talcott Parsons. One can speculate on how modernization theory would have developed had Japan won the war. May be the rationalism of Japanese bureaucracy and the strong individualism of Japanese leaders would have been stressed. The victor's justice extends beyond the writing of history at war trials; it confers on the victors the right to attach the labels 'theory' to their stereotypes and '*etic*' to their *emic* concepts.

In a world characterized both by growing interdependence and a strengthening of the role of the nation state, interest in promoting area studies stems not only from a vague concern with cosmopolitan values and a belief in the merits of a liberal education. Intellectual activity too is being internationalized and there is room for anxiety about how ideas are and will be diffused. Stereotypes can be powerful; public opinion does shape public policy, although policy-makers also form popular images. As illustrated by the Japanese textbook issue in the summer of 1982, education is no longer only a domestic issue. For persons to be informed citizens in the late twentieth century, to make intelligent choices and to take a responsible political role in their own society, it is imperative that they know something about other societies. However, since the domestic policies of one society have come increasingly to impinge upon the choices of people in other societies, capriciousness and isolation in learning about other societies is likely to yield policies based on misunderstanding and to foster unnecessary tensions between societies. The tendency of many Japanese to dismiss the trade friction with the United States early in 1982 simply as Western misunderstanding resulting from cultural differences and American ethnocentrism is a case in point. Basic conflicts of interest are perceived only as instances of cultural misunderstanding; serious interest in cultural understanding is circumscribed by theories which *a priori* assume Japan's cultural uniqueness and do not invite a careful questioning of the interests of other people which may emerge from shared values (e.g., low unemployment).

In this context, those in area studies can have a special impact on the images which are formed about their own area of interest. Their work can affect the images of persons living in the area and of persons living outside the area. They have an opportunity to contribute to the internationalization of education in the societies with which they have contact. One choice is to develop more multicultural perspectives. In promoting such perspectives, however, it will be necessary to think carefully not only about the goals of area studies, but also about the relationship of social structures to the production of international or multicultural knowledge.

From this perspective, a sociology of Japanology would serve well the study of Japanese society. One of the motifs associated by Berger (1963) with the sociological enterprise is that of debunking. However, as Lee (1978) has suggested, social scientists are reluctant to give their own activities, including their notions of professionalism and their behavior as professionals, the same dispassionate scrutiny given to the society they study. Occasionally a book like Said's causes the professionals to think, but too often the pause is but a momentary diversion from on-going research interests. While it is clear that the conception, construction and testing of even a single model is a huge enterprise which cannot be carried out by one individual and which will require the cross-cultural cooperation of many engaged in Japanese studies, it also seems apparent that cooperative ventures will require the type of organization which institutionalizes itself in terms of accepted paradigms and ideologies. A healthy sense of introspection and an ability to take a cynical, though humorous, look at our shortcomings as researchers will become increasingly important as Japanese studies are organized by professional bureaucracies. Given the generosity of the government and many private enterprises in Japan, the learn-from-Japan boom has produced a multimillion-dollar industry. This will undoubtedly result in larger amounts of information about Japan becoming widely available. Whether the end-product of more information is a deeper understanding of Japan will depend upon the ability of those with funds to develop mechanisms which will guarantee that a variety of models can compete. It is also this concern which projects us beyond the question of 'Knowledge from what?' and focuses our attention on even more fundamental issues: 'Knowledge by whom?', 'Knowledge for whom?' and 'Why knowledge at all?'

IV Toward the Internationalization of Japanese Studies

How does one interject a more multicultural perspective into the comparative study of Japan? In trying to answer this question, one finds that a good deal has been written on how to study other societies and on how to carry out fieldwork, but that there are few works on how to make cross-cultural comparisons. Perhaps because the core of social science itself is seen as being the comparison, the problem of cross-cultural comparisons is assumed to be one of simply another comparison.

One would like to think that comparative studies in general are moving in the direction of more multicultural perspectives without any special discussion or policy. Table 16. 2 gives a very superficial overview of how several methodologies for comparative studies might be categorized. Five types of methodology are delineated, and arranged from the least sophisticated (type I) to the most sophisticated (type V). One interesting question is whether comparative studies in general and Japanese studies in particular are progressing from type I to type V. Even fairly early on in Japanese studies one can find writers such as Hearn (1904) and Lloyd (1911) at the beginning of the century and Embree (1972) and Allen (1938) in the thirties using the methods associated with type III. Their work was done well before Benedict's (1946) which is associated with type II. On the individual level, many comparative researchers would see intellectual growth in their own scholarship, growth which occurred less as the result of shifting from one stage to another and more from accumulating skills which allowed them to combine and fine tune the methods associated with types I, II and III.

Another related set of questions asks whether type V methodology produces superior findings. The sequence from type I to type V is characterized by increasing sophistication in the use of a second and/or third language and increasing involvement on an equal basis of researchers from more than just one culture. These attributes may be seen as contributing not only to the internationalization of methodology in the narrowest sense (e.g., the gathering of data), but also to the cultural diversification of the problem consciousness and presentation consciousness which are an integral part of research methodology in the broader sense.

Relevant to this questioning is the possibility that *etic* concepts may be generated from the *emic* vocabulary of the Japanese. The first task in developing a kind of Esperanto of comparative concepts is testing for universality, not only among different societies but also within a given society or macro-cultural context. Too many grandiose theories have developed on the assumption that the concepts were universal even in a single society. The framework developed in Chapter 12 allows us to see a society in the larger setting

Table 16.2 *Typology of methodologies for comparative research*

Type	Approach	Location for studying foreign society	Number of investigators involved	Number of countries which investi-gator(s) actually experience	Person representative of methodology	Primary methodology and type of data	Languages used	Audience for which research is published
I	Bibliographic research (comparisons are implicit)	Only in investigator's own country (library)	1	1 (investi-gator's own country)	Max Weber Emile Durkheim	(1) reading travelogs and literature from the other societies (often in translation) (2) reading the research of others	(1) reading ability in investigator's own native language (2) reading ability in language of the foreign society studied desirable but seldom possessed	persons in the investigator's own society
II	The study of immigrants (comparisons may be explicit but are usually implicit)	Only in investigator's own country	1	1 (investi-gator's own country)	Ruth Benedict	(1) interviewing, surveying, and participant observation (often with interpretation) (2) reading secondary sources in one's own language (often in translation)	(1) investigator's own native language (2) speaking and listening in language of the foreign society being studied desirable, but seldom possessed	persons in the investigator's own society

III	Fieldwork (comparisons may be explicit and some usually are, but many implicit comparisons are also made)	in investigator's own society and in the other societies being studied	1 (although the investigator may sometimes hire research assistants)	*2 or more* (1) investigator's own country plus the other societies being studied	Alexis de Tocqueville John Embree most Ph.D. candidates	(1) analyzing various kinds of documentary evidence (including government statistics) (2) interviewing, surveying and participant observation (3) relying on key informants	(1) investigator's own native language (especially to obtain data sources (2) and (3)) (2) importance of speaking, listening and reading in language recognized (3) there is still a considerable reliance on translation and interpretation in many cases	persons in the investigator's own society
IV	Joint research (most comparisons are explicit)	(1) each investigator does research primarily in his or her country of responsibility	*2 or more* (1) one in each country studied	*1 or more* (1) if possible, principal investigator visits all countries being compared	(1) many of those involved in empirical studies of moderniza- tion	(1) various kinds of data with an emphasis on obtaining comparable data	(1) each investigator uses fully own native language for his or her own country's research	(1) primarily persons in the society of the primary investigator

Table 16.2 *Continued*

Type	Approach	Location for studying foreign society	Number of investigators involved	Number of countries which investigator(s) actually experience	Person representative of methodology	Primary methodology and type of data	Languages used	Audience for which research is published
		(2) comparisons result from the exchange of each country's data (3) in some cases researchers may be sent out to the field from the country of the primary investigator	(2) one person is usually recognized as the principal investigator (3) research is usually designed by the principal investigator		(2) students and primary investigator (especially when students come from the countries being studied)	(2) comparisons often made by simply juxtaposing country reports, some parts of which are comparable and others of which are qualitatively different (3) one gathering (conference) of participants seen as desirable but not necessary	(2) communications are carried out in language of the principal investigator (3) funds are often available in project's budget to pay for translation of papers by secondary investigators into language of principal investigator (4) considerable correspondence of languages is assumed	(2) secondary investigators usually free to prepare translation for persons in their own society, but to appear after publication in primary language and funds are seldom allocated in project budget

V	Collaborative research (explicitly comparative)	each investigator does research primarily in his or her own country; exchange visits seen as desirable	*2 or more* (1) one in each society studied (2) no principal investigator (3) research designed by all investigators	each investigator is encouraged to spend considerable time in as many of the countries studied as possible	?	(1) eclectic methods encouraged with an emphasis on obtaining comparable data (2) integrated comparisons sought (3) emphasis on building multicultural *etic* concepts (4) gathering of participants seen as necessary for planning and for final analysis (5) emphasis on problem consciousness which makes research in some (though perhaps different) ways relevant to each society studied	(1) each investigator fluent in at least two languages relevant to societies being studied (2) ideal is for each investigator to be able to correspond in his or her own language or at least to have a choice of two or three other languages	(1) publication of initial findings in each language is seen as important methodology for obtaining feedback (2) ideal is for final report to be published simultaneously in each society studied

of international stratification, where citizenship is also an important variable accounting for social inequality. The multidimensional model of stratification makes us sensitive to the fact that certain concepts express a universally shared meaning only within one society, while other concepts have a certain universality across several societies but only among members of one stratum (such as managers or women) within any given society.

Whether the internationalization of Japanese studies is viewed as necessary or even desirable will, of course, depend upon one's goals. In Japanese studies, goals have seldom been made clear, although one virtue of works by authors like Benedict (1946) and Vogel (1979a) is that the initial goals are fairly well explained, even if the assumptions behind them are not fully explored by either the authors or the readers. In most works on Japanese society by non-Japanese, however, it is not clear whether the goal is an understanding of Japanese society for its own sake or whether Japan is seen as an interesting case study for throwing light on theories relevant to understanding the author's own society. Many non-Japanese doing research on Japan spend the major portion of their time teaching about Japanese society. Often the goal in this teaching is not that of making their students experts on Japan, but rather simply one of exposing them to aspects of another society which may serve as a mirror for understanding and evaluating their own society better.

There are also those who dismiss the notion of value-free research and become involved in research to assist policy-makers of specific political persuasions. However, their research is often presented without an open discussion of the political goals the research is intended to serve. It is the authors' belief that the researcher's feedback and the reader's understanding would be greatly enhanced by clearer statements of the goals guiding each piece of research. Research requires that various kinds of choices be made; knowledge of which choices were made is crucial to understanding and evaluating the methodologies employed.

V The Study of Japan as a Personal Concern: Research as a Set of Choices

The term Japanese society is often used as though it referred to a commonly perceived phenomenon. This perhaps reflects the tendency to view this society as a monolith. However, various constraints prevent us from studying all of Japanese society; in most cases our knowledge of it is limited to selected information on selected aspects. At the same time, however, the search for relevance often gives way to the belief that limited insight into one aspect of society will yield a glimpse of some more generalized social reality. There seems to be a reluctance to admit that research is largely of personal rather than of social relevance.

In recent years the authors have received several survey forms from prominent bodies interested in promoting Japanese studies. In seeking the view of Japanophiles, the goals have invariably been stated as being the improved dissemination of information about Japan so that more people will obtain a correct understanding of Japan. The explanation immediately drew to mind Mitchell's discussion (1976, p. 161) of thought control and his very brief reference to the establishment of the Cabinet Information Division in 1937. Behind that move was the desire to provide newspapermen with correct data which would quite naturally guide their thoughts into the proper channels. Quite apart from the actual content of that understanding, there is the assumption that there is a correct view, a simplistic belief that Japanese society is a single reality, a physical monolith against which various descriptions can be tested to determine the extent of correspondence.

In debating the nature of social reality in Japan, it is easy to assume that the study of society is an exercise in social photography, and that each participant has tried to take a picture of the same thing. Accordingly, when the results differ, the discussion often focuses on the mechanics of photography: different lenses, different settings, different film. In many cases, however, the subjects being photographed are themselves rather different. Much of our academic training is focused on the mechanical difficulties; less attention is given to the actual choice of a subject.

Brief consideration of the study of Mount Fuji may illustrate some of these problems. Although most Japanese have a general image of a snow-capped, conical pyramid, close questioning will reveal that there are significant variations. Is it possible to rank the images of Mount Fuji in terms of criteria such as accuracy? The lines which delineate the gentle slopes, the erosion and the snow change as the angle of viewing is rotated from Fuji City to Numazu, Shūzenji, Gotenba, Kōfu and Minobu. Even from the same location Mount Fuji will take on different appearances as the seasons change. Indeed, even on a given day, the position of the sun may be an important variable.

Kawamura Tokitarō, who later took the name Katsukawa Shunrō, spent a good portion of his life studying Mount Fuji. Through woodblock prints, he sought to capture the essence of Mount Fuji. *Fugaku Sanjūrokkei* (Thirty-six Views of Mount Fuji) and *Fugaku Hyakkei* (One Hundred Views of Fuji) represent his years of work. At the age of 75 he made the following observation (Kikuchi: 1970, pp. 105–06):

> From the age of six I began drawing the shapes of things. By the time I reached the age of about half-a-hundred, I began to produce quite inept pictures, and even at the age of seventy I produced nothing of any worth. When I became seventy-three I began to be able to understand the basic form of animals and plants. By the time I become eighty, I will have made some progress; at ninety I will be able to know the secrets of the art, at one hundred my work will be praiseworthy, and many years later I will be able to produce true living likenesses. I only hope I will live long enough to accomplish all this.

The 'Mad Old Man of Art', who later became known as Hokusai, appreciated the difficulty of capturing the essence of Mount Fuji. He was thoroughly familiar with the different angles, seasons and times of day. He had experimented with a wide range of technologies – different paints, woods, chisels, paper. However, there was one other important variable in his prints of Fuji: human existence. All 46 views in the first collection (which is known as *Thirty-six Views*) show people in the foreground. Moreover, the people are working people in social organizations. In other words, for Hokusai Mount Fuji was more than a physical lump of lava covered with snow, flora and fauna; Fuji had a social existence which lay in the significance it held for Japanese intent on making a day-to-day living. Mount Fuji had not only an objective existence, but also a subjective relevance for all who saw it.

The problem is that the relevance Mount Fuji held for people varied from person to person. It is possible, then, that Mount Fuji has a thousand different meanings when viewed by a thousand people. In that case, what is the reality known as Mount Fuji? Does it consist only of the elements common to all views? Or should it be conceived as being the composite mosaic or collage which is produced simply by accumulating all the views? In either case, what happens to that reality should some of the thousand die, or should others come to see Mount Fuji for the first time? What happens if some who viewed Mount Fuji forget something observed and remembered yesterday, change their evaluation of some aspect of the mountain, or begin to fantasize about how the peak used to look? The reality of Mount Fuji is different again for those concerned with whether it will erupt in the near future.

Mountains are easy. When the object of study is a society composed of purposive human beings, there are complex interactions between the objective and subjective dimensions. The object itself attaches a subjective significance to its own objective existence. How can such a changeable substance be studied scientifically? Or does the source of understanding still lie in an undefined ability to put together insights from a succession of impressionistic peeps at a merry-go-round of life?

In recent years the value of the social sciences has been increasingly questioned. Quite apart from lingering doubts about the status and credibility of the social sciences as science, there are also doubts about the relevance of the social sciences for those living in society (Jones: 1982; Berger and Kellner: 1982). Why is there so much disagreement with regard to the paradigm in even a single discipline like sociology? Why can't social scientists solve even a few of the social problems plaguing modern society? It is within this larger questioning of social science that a harder look at the goals of Japanese studies is required. Although Japanese studies are a booming business today, does the boom reflect an increase in the desire to understand Japanese society, or is it only a surface phenomenon limited to a change in the ideological vocabulary through which perceptions of national interest and of economic necessity are expressed in a changing world? What will tomorrow's graduates in Japanese studies be told when the market for their knowledge and understanding of Japan collapses? To the extent that Japanese studies are organized to implant in students unrealistic expectations about what can be learned from Japan, it might be wise to think through more carefully the goals set for research on Japan. Although collective agreement may not be achieved, individual goals can be made explicit and time saved by focusing more sharply on the substantive issues. While defining goals, it would be well to reconsider carefully the complexity of the realities known as Japanese society.

If social reality in general is seen as a collage of several different realities, the study of Japanese society can be understood better as involving explicit choices among several different kinds of reality. Four kinds of choice come immediately to mind. One decision is whether to study existing phenomena or potential phenomena. Social reality includes the various latent potentials which societies and individuals have for the future. Reality at this level is more than the simple extrapolation of annual growth rates in GNP. It involves the study of human and social potential for kindness, endurance, aggression, mobilization, cooperation. Answers may sometimes be found in anthropological studies of small minority groups and sometimes even in the adventures of a lone explorer or navigator. Explorations into a glorious past and even romantic visions of the noble savage very often focus on this kind of reality. A good deal of *nihonjinron* takes on a new significance when understood not as moralizing ideology but as a statement of potential. If the study of potential is the goal, then attention is not on statements of what Japanese society is, but arguments about what it could be. Just as some people may ask 'Why?' others may ask 'Why not?'

A second choice is between information and understanding. Information can result in a good explanation of many things. Functional explanations, for example, often rely heavily on information. To industrialize (e.g., to have six factories which can produce, say, a total of 521,984 vehicles annually), one can calculate the various types and quantities of manpower and resources needed. If a certain number of workers are to live in a given area, the demand for housing and the amount of environmental disruption can be predicted. Mechanisms can be conceived for moving people from one location to another. This kind of knowledge is different from that which has understanding as its goal. What do people feel when they move or are moved from one place to another? How do people classify cars, as powered bicycles for enjoying one's leisure better or as mechanical horses for facilitating heavier workloads? Why, when production seems to be expanding so smoothly, is there a sudden strike or a sense of alienation? Although we can obtain relatively abundant data on income distribution, such data are not always useful in explaining changes in the perceptions of inequality or even in explaining how it feels to be rich or poor in a given society.

The paradoxical image of the Japanese may in part result from a failure to distinguish between these two types of knowledge. Such a failure reflects and fosters a belief that information about easily observed and objective realities corresponds to an understanding of less tangible and subjective realities. Accordingly, student riots amid unprecedented prosperity and political scandals amid national consensus are treated as paradoxical. It is not always clear whether *nihonjinron* is about consent (people not openly protesting about a situation in which they feel compelled to behave in some manner) or about consensus (people thinking it is good to behave in such a way). Many of the debates about Japanese society would be better focused if this choice were more clearly explained.

A third choice is between the macro and the micro. It is often not clear whether the value of a case study (of which an anecdote may be a sub-category) lies in its relevance for understanding a larger set of events (in which the case study is a sample) or in its relevance for ascertaining historical fact. The evaluative criteria are very different: the latter involves a search for an absolute truth and whether a particular event occurred; the former involves an investigation of the probabilities with which a number of similar events have occurred. There are times when we want to know exactly what a Tōjō or a Yamashita did; there are also times when we may want to know about the behavior common to a large number of Japanese generals with certain backgrounds. The questions involved in solving a crime and bringing its perpetrator to justice are often quite different from those involved in removing crime from society. The answers to one set of questions may sometimes offer fruitful avenues for speculation in seeking answers to questions in the other set. But to assume simply that the answers are the same is to give rein either to conspiracy theories or to guilt by association. It is easy to forget introductory lectures in economics and anthropology about the fallacy of composition or misplaced concreteness.

There are also choices involving the treatment of persons studied. To what extent are they to be treated as friends, and to what extent are they to be used as informants? Who do we study and for whom do we publish? Quite apart from the moral or ethical issues, there are more fundamental questions concerning the role of empathy as part of a methodology for understanding. Working in the Japanese context, the extensive involvement of social scientists in the mass media highlights not only the use of academic research for ideological ends and commercial profit, but also the possibilities of carrying on an active dialogue with the people studied as an integral part of one's research methodology.

VI Toward a Moratorium on *Nihonjinron*

The study of one's own society presents enormous challenges. The study of another society is an even more formidable undertaking. The comparison of two different societies is fraught with still more difficulties. At the same time, the study of one's own society tends to lose meaning without reference to other societies, as indicated by the fact that many of the categories we use to describe a single society have meaning only when they are defined in terms of a scale which is implicitly comparative.

Understanding requires careful strategies and time; we live increasingly in a world that requires quick answers. As the pollution problem revealed some time ago, new kinds of pollution are produced and then replaced before they can be properly researched and scientifically understood. People also come and go.

When individuals die, their death is often left as a personal tragedy without any links to larger social causes ever being established. However, not all the pollution was new. Disputes concerning the pollution of the Ashio and Fuji Rivers occurred at the end of the last century. The pollution at Minimata was noted in the fifties. However, there is again a time lag and then a sudden demand for explanations and remedies. The same phenomena can be seen with regard to the organization of tertiary education and the student movement of the late sixties. Such contingencies invite easy answers, euphemisms and historical generalizations. But even more, they invite apologies from those who chose simply to look the other way while there was still time.

When an entire nation is involved, the sense of urgency is even more pronounced, but so too is the willingness to accept easy answers. This is particularly true when people in one society have outdated and stereotyped images of the people in others. This is, in part, what occurred when Japan suddenly appeared on the doorstep of the United States and Europe with a formidable economy, while most people in the respective societies still had prewar or immediate postwar images of Japan. The Japanese automobile industry took 20 years to build and had an accumulative impact; public concern abroad with Japan's automobile industry and the high unemployment rates in their own countries has occurred only in the last 5–10 years or so. The same can be said for the sudden increase of direct Japanese foreign investment, which was produced by an economic machine assembled over several decades. No wonder that the steady progress from 1950 to 1970 appeared as a miracle when it was conceived as having occurred overnight. And no wonder that people are willing to accept quite incredible explanations to close the gap without challenging their basic ethnocentric assumptions.

Accelerated changes within Japanese society and the rapidity with which Japan's international relations have been transformed over the past two decades are undoubtedly sources of a new awareness. There is a large array of phenomena which we suddenly wish to understand. *Nihonjinron* represents one attempt to provide such an understanding. Although its shortcomings have increasingly become evident with the benefit of time and hindsight, *nihonjinron* has inspired people not only with its support for narrow nationalistic ideologies and its parochial contribution to the national identity of many Japanese, but also with its call for a more cosmopolitan outlook and its concern for cultural relativism as a viable ideal. At the same time, there is a danger that inspiration will turn into fundamentalist religious belief, that an understanding based on narrowly defined *emic* concepts tied to the unique cultural symbols of one nation will give way to manipulation, and that ideas about national differences will degenerate into simplistic stereotypes of national character. Quite apart from their association with the conditions for war, developments like this tend to obfuscate international understanding and the development of social science as a humanistic enterprise.

The dangers associated with knowledge can be mitigated by renewed efforts in our research to distinguish more clearly between personal goals and social requisites. The failure to make such a distinction leaves us more susceptible to theories which reify society and culture. Although the unique features of Japanese society can be dredged up *ad infinitum*, we wonder whether it might not be more profitable to leave such activities in abeyance until some of the more fundamental questions of purpose and method have been sorted out and until there has been an opportunity to scrutinize the hypotheses thus far presented by the *nihonjinron* theorists. If we are in a position to choose among several knowledges but have the resources and time to produce only one, why create a knowledge which will serve only as a barrier to the cultural integration of the Japanese into the world community? Why choose a knowledge which aims to lead people by presenting a particular way of doing things as being culturally predestined rather than a vision which might stimulate people to think of their potential in terms of various new options? Why produce a knowledge which tends to deny people choices that would otherwise be theirs? In the minds of the authors these are questions with which all who seek to understand Japan and its place in the world today must grapple.

Appendix

Methodology for the Survey of Job Situations

I Operationalization

1 The Ranking of Job Situations. As an instrument to measure the extent to which respondents were willing and able to differentiate among various job situations, the survey was constructed to specify the two major parameters involved when structured social inequality occurs: criteria according to which respondents were to rank job situations and the characteristics which delimit each job situation. The criteria for ranking job situations consisted mainly of access to one or more types of societal rewards. In some cases specific criteria were not given and a more general evaluation of total status was used. Job situations were fully or partially delineated in several ways by reference to an occupational category, an industrial category, the size of the firm, the name of the firm, geographical location or some combination of these. Job situations were defined in terms of male situations in the two countries, to minimize the effect of sex roles and their association with different types of career pattern.

Eighteen hypothetical contexts were created. For each respondents were asked to rank in order five job situations according to their share of income (6 items), status (3), power (1), information (1) or some mixture of these (7). The job situations used in 12 contexts were defined by only one agent of stratification: occupation (in 4 problems), firm (in 3), industry (in 3) or geographical location (in 2). In six contexts they were defined by some combination of firm-related factors and occupation. The two approaches are illustrated by the examples in Figures A.1 and A.2 respectively. The items in

Figure A.1. *Hypothetical contexts with sets of five job situations defined in one dimension*

PROBLEM 8

Five business firms are listed below. Which firms pay their employees the best incomes? Giving each firm a different number from '1' for the firm offering its employees the best incomes to '5' for the firm offering its employees the lowest incomes, please rank these five firms in terms of your general impression as to the income they pay their employees.

______ Fujitsū

______ Casio

______ Sharp

______ Tōshiba

______ IBM

PROBLEM 18

Assuming that each of the five occupations listed below pays exactly the same income, and further assuming that you have a family and were given a chance for your child to enter one of these occupations, which one would you choose for him or her? Giving each occupation a different number from '1' for your first choice to '5' for your last choice, please rank these five occupations in terms of the extent to which you would be happy having your son or daughter enter them.

______ university professor

______ corporation executive

______ a movie actor

______ a race-car driver

______ a small shop owner

Problem 8 (Figure A.1) are from the Japanese version; comparable American companies were substituted for the American version. The job situations are differentiated only by the names of the employing companies and the respondents were asked to rank the situations in terms of income. In Problem 18, however, the job situations are defined in terms of occupations and the respondent was asked to rank them in terms of his own criteria (without income being a consideration). The same occupations were used in both the American and Japanese versions. In Problem 3 (Figure A.2) the job situations are defined by a firm and an occupation, and respondents are asked to rank each job in terms of an incumbent's likely access to general information about Japanese society. In Problem 5, the job situations are again defined by firm-related variables (i.e., industrial activity and size) and occupation; they are to be ranked in terms of the business knowledge or money-making acumen associated with the type of person likely to be in such a job. Again, proper nouns were transposed into equivalents; firm size, industry and occupation were translated directly.

In order to overcome the problems of a bias being built into the order in which the job situations appear, several precautions were taken. First, the order in which the job situations were listed was randomized. Second, five different versions were printed, each with a different randomized ordering, so structured that no one situation appeared in the same position in more than one version. Third, in order to avoid the problem of interpreting answers to problems where the job situations were defined by two agents of stratification, a scheme for randomized rotated pairings was devised. The scheme is shown in Figure A.3.

If each job situation in a set of five ($S_1 \ldots S_5$) is respectively defined by a unique combination of occupational category ($O_1 \ldots , O_5$) and firm characteristics ($F_1 \ldots F_5$) and then ranked, it is difficult to know whether the ranking of S was determined by O or by F. Accordingly, even though the combinations were randomly listed, it might be the overall way in which the combinations emerged (i.e., the unique set of pairings) which determined the way in which the situations were ranked. For this reason five different sets of five pairings were formed to yield 25 unique combinations, constructed from five occupationally related criteria and five firm-related criteria, so that no two definitions of a job situation ($S_n = O_i + F_j$) would be the same. In other words, five versions of the survey were produced to yield five unique sets with 25 unique pairings so that the value [i,j] was never

Figure A.2. *Hypothetical contexts with sets of five job situations defined in two dimensions*

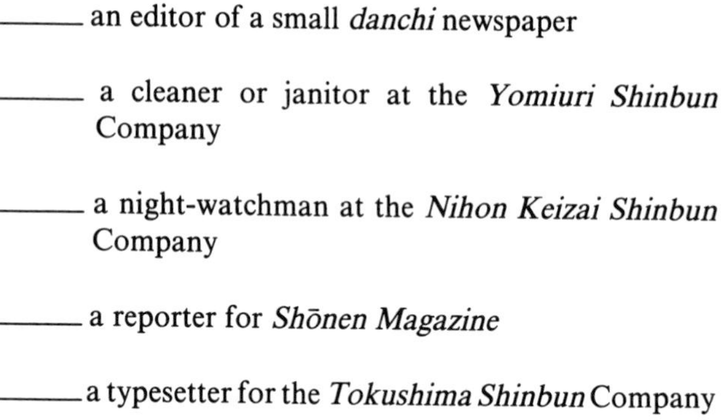

PROBLEM 3

Suppose that you are a spy from a foreign country, and that you have been instructed to obtain as much information as possible about how Japanese society works. Imagine that you have met a person who will introduce you to the five individuals listed below. With whom would you try to become close friends for your espionage purposes? Please rank the following five from '1' for the most helpful to '5' for the least helpful to indicate who you feel would best assist you in achieving your goal.

_____ an editor of a small *danchi* newspaper

_____ a cleaner or janitor at the *Yomiuri Shinbun* Company

_____ a night-watchman at the *Nihon Keizai Shinbun* Company

_____ a reporter for *Shōnen Magazine*

_____ a typesetter for the *Tokushima Shinbun* Company

duplicated and each element appeared at least once in each set. In tabulating the results, the values for each of the five occupations ($O_1 \ldots O_5$) and for each of the firm-related criteria ($F_1 \ldots F_5$) could then be factored out. Figure A.3 shows one possible set of five job situations which have been defined by occupation and firm-related factors.

2 Other Measures. A number of other formats were also used to verify the findings on how job situations were ranked. Three

PROBLEM 5

Suppose that you have just received an inheritance of 50 million yen with the stipulation that you set up a small supermarket or grocery store with one of the following persons as a partner. Assuming that you have decided to accept the 50 million yen and set up the small business with one of the following persons, please rank the persons listed below from '1' for the person most useful from the viewpoint of making your business a success to '5' for the person least likely to contribute to the store's financial success.

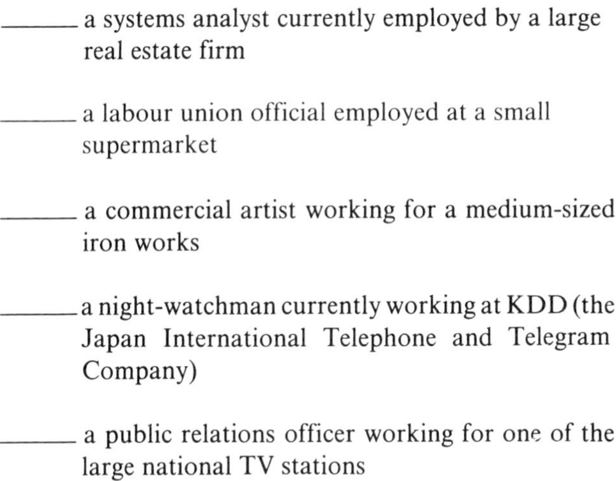

______ a systems analyst currently employed by a large real estate firm

______ a labour union official employed at a small supermarket

______ a commercial artist working for a medium-sized iron works

______ a night-watchman currently working at KDD (the Japan International Telephone and Telegram Company)

______ a public relations officer working for one of the large national TV stations

problems were posed in which the respondents were given five pictures of individuals taken from Japanese and American weekly magazines, newspapers, cartoons and comic-books for adults. The five were drawn randomly from a pool of about 100 pictures and the same set was used for both the American and Japanese surveys, with the rotation techniques described above. As shown in Figure A.4, after each set of pictures, five job situations were given. Respondents were asked to match each picture with a job situation. In all three

Figure A.3. *The definitions of one set of five job situations rotated to yield five sets*

The blue survey form	The green survey form	The yellow survey form	The white survey form	The pink survey form
$O_3 + F_3$	$O_3 + F_4$	$O_4 + F_1$	$O_3 + F_1$	$O_3 + F_2$
$O_4 + F_4$	$O_5 + F_1$	$O_1 + F_3$	$O_2 + F_5$	$O_1 + F_5$
$O_5 + F_5$	$O_4 + F_5$	$O_5 + F_2$	$O_1 + F_4$	$O_4 + F_3$
$O_1 + F_1$	$O_2 + F_3$	$O_2 + F_4$	$O_4 + F_2$	$O_2 + F_1$
$O_2 + F_2$	$O_1 + F_2$	$O_3 + F_5$	$O_5 + F_3$	$O_5 + F_4$

Note: The occupations and firms might be defined as follows

O_1 = sales manager
O_2 = personnel manager
O_3 = financial analyst
O_4 = maintenance engineer
O_5 = president and owner

F_1 = a large multinational corporation
F_2 = a traveling circus
F_3 = a small department store
F_4 = a medium-sized manufacturing firm
F_5 = a large public corporation (a statutory authority)

problems, the job situations were defined by occupation and firm-related factors. The system of rotation and randomization explained above was used again.

Another test consisted of the battery of semantic differentials shown in Figure A.5. Respondents were asked to rate each of five job situations in terms of 25 pairs of semantic differentials. The five job situations were defined by occupation and firm-related variables. The two components were rotated and the situations were randomized as explained above.

Finally, respondents were given a list of ten possible criteria for ranking job situations. They were asked to score each item from '1' for very important to '5' for unimportant, in terms of choosing a job. The format for this question is given in Figure A.6. The criteria were randomly ordered but the ordering of the list remained the same for all five versions of the survey.

Figure A.4. *An example of a problem using picture identification*

PROBLEM 15

Below five photographs are shown. The photographs were blurred on purpose to see if you could still identify the individuals in the photographs well enough to guess which picture fits which of the persons described below.

Use the numbers (from 1 to 5) under the photographs to indicate which picture goes best with which individual.

______ sales manager for a large multinational corporation

______ personnel manager for a traveling circus

______ financial analyst for a small department store

______ maintenance engineer for a medium-sized manufacturing firm

______ president and owner of a large public corporation (a statutory authority)

Figure A.5. *Semantic differentials and job situation*

PROBLEM 26

A PERSONNEL MANAGER AT A SHOE MANUFACTURING FIRM
(An example)

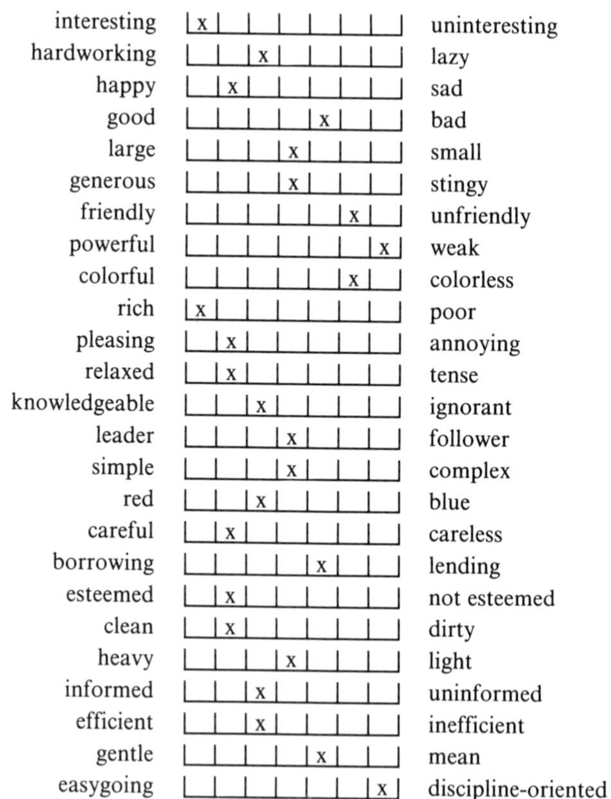

interesting	x							uninteresting
hardworking			x					lazy
happy		x						sad
good					x			bad
large				x				small
generous				x				stingy
friendly						x		unfriendly
powerful							x	weak
colorful						x		colorless
rich	x							poor
pleasing		x						annoying
relaxed		x						tense
knowledgeable			x					ignorant
leader				x				follower
simple				x				complex
red			x					blue
careful		x						careless
borrowing					x			lending
esteemed		x						not esteemed
clean		x						dirty
heavy				x				light
informed			x					uninformed
efficient			x					inefficient
gentle					x			mean
easygoing							x	discipline-oriented

Figure A.6. *Open-ended multiple response question*

PROBLEM 22

Below a number of criteria often used in deciding whether to accept a job offer are listed. Using a scale of '1' for 'very important', '2' for 'somewhat important', '3' for 'slightly important', '4' for 'not very important', and '5' for 'not important at all', please indicate which criteria are important to you personally in choosing a job. Unlike the other problems, you may use any number as frequently as you wish. For example, if all of the considerations listed below are all very important, place a '1' in front of all of them; if none are of any importance at all place a '5' in front of all of them.

______ whether the firm is family owned and run or whether it is owned by stockholders and run by a board of directors

______ the chance for promotion

______ the personalities of other people in the firm and the extent to which they are friendly

______ the extent to which the firm's products are well known

______ the size of the firm

______ the amount of income or wages paid by the firm

______ the stability of the firm, judged according to how long it has been in business

______ the content of the job

______ how close the firm is to the town or city where you grew up, went to school and now have your closest friends

______ whether or not other friends or acquaintances are working in the firm

______ other (please specify)

II The Tabulations

1 The Ranking of Job Situations. An index was developed which would indicate the levels of consensus or agreement concerning the ordering of a given set of five job situations. As the five job situations in each problem were to be ranked from 1 to 5, the index needed to indicate how often a particular job situation received the same ranking. The first step was to calculate the average ranking for each job situation. Since the rankings ranged between 1 and 5, the resulting averages were between 1.0 and 5.0. For each set of five situations the standard deviation among the mean rankings was calculated. For situations defined by two criteria (firm and occupation), the average rank order was calculated for each job situation classified by occupation and then again for each job situation classified according to the firm-related variable.

To explain the procedure further, several hypothetical results are given in Figure A.7. Three samples are presented: sample A with two cases, sample B with two cases and sample C with five cases. For all three samples the responses of the first case are assumed to be the same and are given in the extreme left column. In the first sample, the second respondent ranked the job situations ($S_1 \ldots S_5$) in exactly the same manner as the first respondent. The averages thus become 1.0, 2.0, 3.0, 4. 0 and 5.0. The standard deviation among these means is 1.4142 (the square root of 2.0). Sample A indicates the maximum amount of dispersion which could occur among the means were everyone to rank the five job situations in exactly the same way. The two respondents in sample B rank the same set of situations in exactly the opposite way. The average ranking for each is 3.0. Since there would be no dispersion among the means, the standard deviation among the mean rankings (3,3,3,3 and 3) equals zero (0.0). In other words, for a sample of two individuals our measure varies between the 1.4142 for a perfect positive correlation and 0.0 for a perfect negative correlation. The perfect correlation can be equated with full consensus. In this case, however, the notion of negative correlation is more difficult to grasp. This is because the survey is designed to show clustering, not correlation. Accordingly, when many cases are involved, as in the third sample, considerable dispersion comes to represent agreement rather than correlation; and the lack of dispersion (e.g., a small standard deviation near zero) comes to represent not a negative correlation but perfect randomness in the

Figure A.7. *Some hypothetical rankings of job situations: three samples with indices of consensus*

		Possible rank orders of other respondents and the sample average for each job situation								
		Sample I		Sample II		Sample III				
Job situation	Rank order of first respondent for all samples	Rank order of second respondent	Average for the sample	Rank order of second respondent	Average for the sample	Rank order of second respondent	Rank order of third respondent	Rank order of fourth respondent	Rank order of fifth respondent	Average for the sample
A	1	1	1	5	3	2	3	4	5	3
B	2	2	2	4	3	3	4	5	1	3
C	3	3	3	3	3	4	5	1	2	3
D	4	4	4	2	3	5	1	2	3	3
E	5	5	5	1	3	1	2	3	4	3
Index of consensus (standard deviation)			1.4142 ($\sqrt{2}$)		0					0

answers of the respondents. Accordingly, the higher the standard deviation, the greater the consensus among members of the sample as to how a particular set of five job situations ought to be ranked.

2 Other Measures. For the three problems with pictures, a measure of concentration was needed to indicate the extent to which people felt that a given job description went with a given picture. To obtain such a measure the absolute frequencies with which a given job was associated with each of the pictures were recorded. The absolute frequencies were converted to row and column percentages. The standard deviation among the five percentage frequencies for each picture and for each job situation was calculated, and the mean of each set of five standard deviations was taken as the concentration index. The two examples in Figure A.8 show the extremes of high concentration (e.g., high agreement) and no concentration (e.g., no agreement or complete randomness).

Finally, the response for each of the 25 semantic differentials was given a score between 1.0 and 7.0; the scores for each occupation and each firm were factored out and the means were calculated. The mean scores for each of the five occupations and for each of the five firms were calculated. The procedure for doing this can be understood by carefully examining Figure A.9. The standard deviation for the five means for the occupations (see box D under 'Tabulations' in Figure A.9) was calculated and then compared with that for the firms. In the example given here, the larger standard deviations (2.00 and 2.33) for occupations suggest that this was the major consideration in evaluating the job situations.

Finally, with the open-ended multiple response question, the mean score was calculated for each choice. The possible range was between 1.0 for 'very important' and 5.0 for 'not important at all'.

III Sampling Procedures

The survey was administered to 531 American high-school students, 1,023 Japanese high-school students and 470 young Japanese company employees at a seminar house. A two-stage quota cluster sample was used. The first stage involved the choice of the high schools and the second involved the choice of particular classes. Although the choice of institutions was determined largely by the contacts of the researchers, an attempt was made to obtain a fairly

Figure A.8. *Examples of how to calculate the concentration index using percentage frequencies*

A Perfect concentration

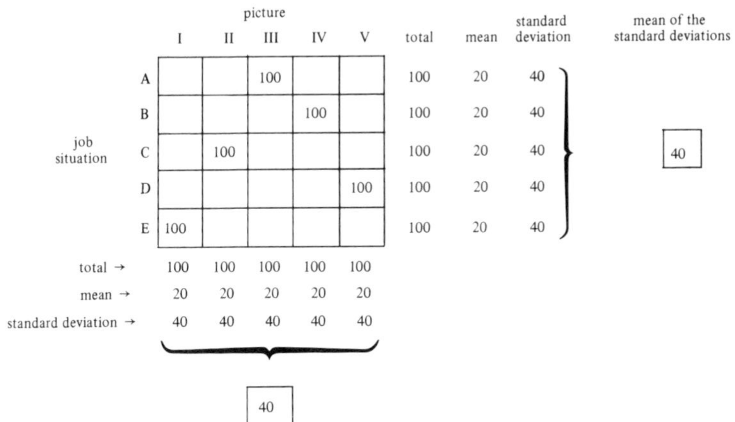

job situation	I	II	III	IV	V	total	mean	standard deviation
A			100			100	20	40
B				100		100	20	40
C		100				100	20	40
D					100	100	20	40
E	100					100	20	40
total →	100	100	100	100	100			
mean →	20	20	20	20	20			
standard deviation →	40	40	40	40	40			

mean of the standard deviations: 40 (rows); 40 (columns)

B Perfect randomness (the absence of concentration)

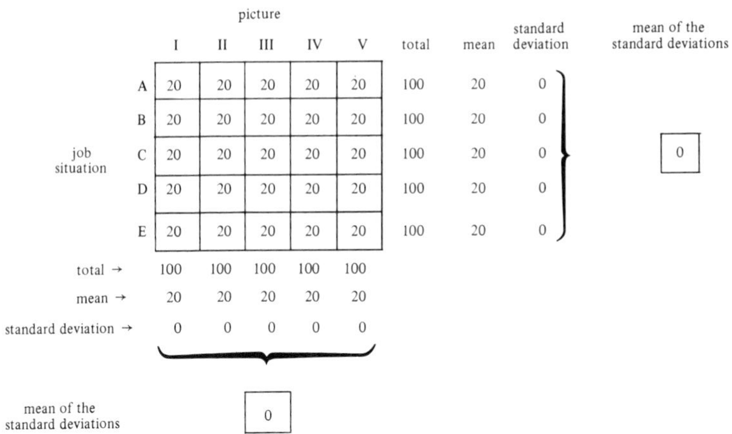

job situation	I	II	III	IV	V	total	mean	standard deviation
A	20	20	20	20	20	100	20	0
B	20	20	20	20	20	100	20	0
C	20	20	20	20	20	100	20	0
D	20	20	20	20	20	100	20	0
E	20	20	20	20	20	100	20	0
total →	100	100	100	100	100			
mean →	20	20	20	20	20			
standard deviation →	0	0	0	0	0			

mean of the standard deviations: 0 (rows); 0 (columns)

Figure A.9. *Example of tabulations for semantic differentials for a sample of two*

Responses

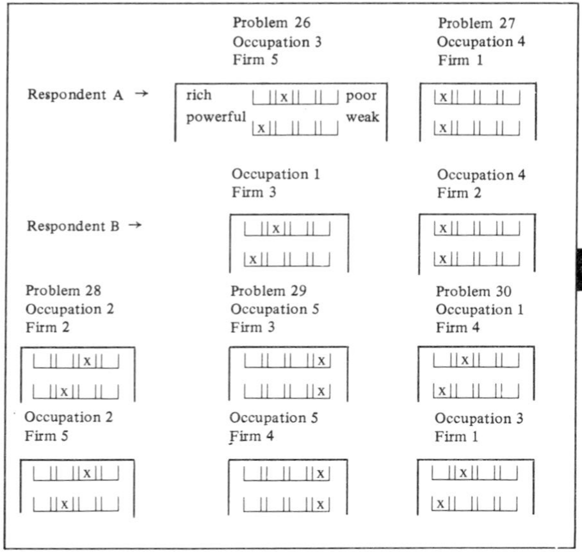

Respondent A →

Problem 26
Occupation 3
Firm 5

rich — poor
powerful — weak

Problem 27
Occupation 4
Firm 1

Respondent B →

Occupation 1
Firm 3

Occupation 4
Firm 2

Problem 28
Occupation 2
Firm 2

Problem 29
Occupation 5
Firm 3

Problem 30
Occupation 1
Firm 4

Occupation 2
Firm 5

Occupation 5
Firm 4

Occupation 3
Firm 1

Tabulations

A Scoring

|x||x||x||x|
1 2 3 4 5 6 7

B Respondent A's scores

Semantic differential	Scores									
	Occupation					Firm				
	1	2	3	4	5	1	2	3	4	5
1. rich/poor	3	5	3	1	7	1	5	7	3	3
2. powerful/weak	1	3	1	1	7	1	3	7	1	1

C Respondent B's scores

Semantic differential	Scores									
	Occupation					Firm				
	1	2	3	4	5	1	2	3	4	5
1. rich/poor	3	5	3	1	7	3	1	3	7	5
2. powerful/weak	1	3	1	1	7	1	1	1	7	3

D Sample scores

Semantic differential	Scores										Standard deviation	
	Occupation					Firm						
	1	2	3	4	5	1	2	3	4	5	Occu-pations	Firms
1. rich/poor	3.0	5.0	3.0	1.0	7.0	2.0	3.0	5.0	5.0	4.0	2.00	1.17
2. powerful/weak	1.0	3.0	1.0	1.0	7.0	1.0	2.0	4.0	4.0	2.0	2.33	1.20
AVERAGE											2.17	1.19

broad cross-section. Of the eight high schools chosen in Japan, seven were in the Tokyo area and one was in a rural capital. The seven in Tokyo included an elite university preparatory school for boys, an elite university preparatory school for girls, a mixed coeducational university preparatory public school, a manual arts school for boys, a school for girls not going on to tertiary institutions, an average private school for girls and a public school in a lower socio-economic neighbourhood. In the United States, all schools were coeducational and public; one was from a rural country town, one was in an upper middle-class suburb near a major city, one was from a lower socio-economic neighbourhood and the fourth was from a provincial center with a population over a hundred thousand. Given the problems of representation with cluster and quota sampling, biographical data were obtained on sex, age and various aspects of the household, including the houehold's income levels and the education of the parents. The percentage distribution of the two samples for some of these variables is given in Table A.1.

IV Some First-order Statistics

The basic first-order statistics generated from the raw data are given in Tables A.2 and A.3. Further breakdowns for the three sub-populations mentioned in the text are presented elsewhere (SM: 1982a).

Table A.1. *Percentage distribution of the respondents according to sample and selected biographical characteristics*

Variable and Categories	Sample		
	I American high school students N = 531	II Japanese high school students N = 1023	III Extended Japanese population N = 1493
A Sex			
Males	35.8	46.2	50.3
Females	41.6	48.0	41.3
No answer	22.6	5.8	8.4
B Age			
-15	6.6	0.0	0.0
16	3.0	10.7	7.4
17	44.4	55.7	38.2
18	26.9	29.2	20.3
19 +	10.5	0.3	21.9
No answer	8.6	4.1	12.2
C Birthplace			
Same municipality	29.9	48.2	41.1
Same prefecture/state	31.3	23.0	18.8
Other prefecture/state	24.3	23.5	34.0
No answer	14.5	5.3	4.1
D Father's education			
Primary	3.0	3.7	7.0
Secondary	42.9	46.7	49.6
Tertiary	33.7	38.9	30.6
No answer	20.4	10.7	12.8
E Size of father's firm			
More than 1,000 employees	20.0	27.2	25.3
100–1,000	23.9	15.2	15.0
20–100	12.8	13.6	13.3
Less than 20	12.1	23.3	22.4
No answer	31.2	20.7	24.0
F Mother's education			
Primary	1.5	2.9	8.1
Secondary	48.4	69.1	65.6
Tertiary	28.6	16.7	12.9
No answer	21.5	11.3	13.4
G Employment status of mother			
Working	50.3	45.2	43.4
Not working	11.9	47.3	46.9
No answer	37.8	7.5	9.7

Table A.2. *Index of rank order consensus for job situations*

A Situation defined in one dimension

Problem characteristics			Samples					
			(I) American high-school students N = 513		(II) Japanese high-school students N = 1023		(III) Extended Japanese sample (including those in sample II) N = 1493	
Stratification variable defining job situation	Problem number	Societal rewards used as criteria for ranking job situations	(a) Standard deviation among rankings for sets of five job situations	(b) Mean of standard deviations for given stratification variable	(a) Standard deviation among rankings for sets of five job situations	(b) Mean of standard deviations for given stratification variable	(a) Standard deviation among rankings for sets of five job situations	(b) Mean of standard deviations for stratification variable
1 Company	8	Income	0.882		0.540		0.527	
	12	Mixed	0.901	0.791	0.970	0.747	0.928	0.714
	19	Mixed	0.590		0.731		0.688	
2 Occupation	4	Income	0.772		1.170		1.150	
	14	Income	1.278		1.396		1.391	
	11	Mixed	1.223	1.013	1.211	1.135	1.210	1.123
	18	Mixed	0.788		0.764		0.740	
3 Industry	1	Income	0.454		0.714		0.706	
	23	Income	0.460	0.412	0.489	0.507	0.517	0.513
	24	Mixed	0.322		0.317		0.316	
4 Geographical region	2	Income	0.626		0.419		1.138	
	13	Mixed	0.777	0.702	0.453	0.801	0.483	0.811

Table A.2. *Continued*

B Situation defined in two or more dimensions

Problem characteristics			Samples					
Stratification variable defining job situation	Problem number	Societal rewards used as criteria for ranking job situations	(I) American high-school students N = 513		(II) Japanese high-school students N = 1023		(III) Extended Japanese sample (including those in sample II) N = 1493	
			(a) Standard deviation among rankings for sets of five job situations	(b) Mean of standard deviations for given stratification variable	(a) Standard deviation among rankings for sets of five job situations	(b) Mean of standard deviations for given stratification variable	(a) Standard deviation among rankings for sets of five job situations	(b) Mean of standard deviations for stratification variable
1 Company-related criteria	3	Information	0.321		0.790		0.770	
	6	Status	0.219		0.086		0.096	
	9	Status	0.471		0.500		0.465	
	17	Status	0.288	0.376	0.224	0.388	0.181	0.365
	5	Income/status	0.432		0.484		0.449	
	20	Power	0.475		0.243		0.229	
2 Occupations	3	Information	0.443		0.614		0.648	
	6	Status	0.775		1.150		1.139	
	9	Status	0.794		0.713		0.737	
	17	Status	0.549	0.669	0.463	0.778	0.435	0.785
	5	Income/status	0.578		0.563		0.590	
	20	Power	0.876		1.164		1.158	

C Ratio of standard deviation means for occupational criteria to those for firm-related criteria

	(I)	(II)	(III)
1 Seven problems in A with situations defined in one dimension	1.283	1.519	1.573
2 Six problems in B with situations defined in two dimensions	1.779	2.005	2.151

Note: Additional data on three sub-populations are presented elsewhere, in SM (1982a, pp. 94–9)

Table A.3. *Mean rankings of occupations and firms on 25 semantic differentials*

Semantic differential		Occupation							Firm						
	Sample	A	B	C	D	E	Mean	Standard deviation	A	B	C	D	E	Mean	Standard deviation
Interesting/	JP	4.72	2.91	4.90	4.24	4.67	4.29	0.7223	4.30	4.26	4.30	4.27	4.30	4.29	0.0179
Uninteresting	US	3.64	3.17	3.60	3.71	4.56	3.74	0.4534	4.06	3.55	4.03	3.54	3.49	3.73	0.2179
Hardworking/	JP	3.35	3.35	3.42	3.23	2.87	3.24	0.1968	3.35	3.15	3.45	3.00	3.27	3.24	0.1567
lazy	US	2.86	2.50	2.67	2.68	3.04	2.75	0.1844	3.05	2.64	2.74	2.71	2.61	2.75	0.1452
Happy/	JP	3.75	3.14	4.33	3.58	4.83	3.73	0.6231	3.97	3.78	4.11	3.87	3.88	3.92	0.1162
sad	US	3.12	3.06	3.54	3.32	3.84	3.38	0.2866	3.57	3.27	3.46	3.24	3.33	3.37	0.1237
Good/	JP	3.77	3.17	4.20	3.60	4.30	3.81	0.4118	3.80	3.77	3.93	3.77	3.77	3.81	0.0621
bad	US	2.88	2.75	3.28	3.09	3.33	3.07	0.2238	3.20	2.97	3.08	3.00	3.06	3.06	0.0791
Large/	JP	4.26	4.24	4.25	3.80	5.34	4.38	0.5116	4.43	4.17	4.51	4.61	4.18	4.38	0.1769
small	US	3.69	3.82	3.19	3.37	3.99	3.61	0.2929	3.68	3.44	3.49	4.02	3.46	3.62	0.2184
Generous/	JP	4.41	3.76	4.44	3.77	4.50	4.18	0.3369	4.22	4.09	4.19	4.21	4.17	4.18	0.0465
stingy	US	3.53	3.39	3.83	3.56	3.66	3.59	0.1462	3.61	3.57	3.69	3.57	3.53	3.59	0.0442
Friendly	JP	3.89	3.76	3.92	3.59	3.22	3.68	0.2560	3.67	3.66	3.75	3.56	3.72	3.67	0.0650
unfriendly	US	2.37	2.79	3.37	3.09	3.02	2.93	0.3348	3.04	2.92	3.05	2.76	2.85	2.92	0.1111
Powerful/	JP	4.27	4.61	4.01	3.67	4.99	4.31	0.4590	4.51	4.11	4.41	4.47	4.06	4.31	0.1887
weak	US	3.27	3.73	2.37	2.93	4.30	3.32	0.6612	3.46	3.24	3.27	3.47	3.16	3.32	0.1238
Colorful/	JP	4.76	2.80	4.98	4.41	5.50	4.49	0.9160	4.61	4.37	4.60	4.41	4.46	4.49	0.0982
colorless	US	3.26	2.92	3.58	3.64	3.97	3.48	0.3537	3.61	3.53	3.59	3.25	3.42	3.48	0.1327
Rich/	JP	3.84	3.43	4.59	3.77	5.47	4.22	0.7308	4.26	4.05	4.32	4.35	4.11	4.22	0.1179
poor	US	3.57	3.58	3.46	3.81	4.58	3.80	0.4063	3.84	3.70	3.90	3.79	3.75	3.80	0.0694
Pleasing/	JP	3.94	3.46	4.16	3.74	3.77	3.81	0.2317	3.77	3.86	3.84	3.81	3.80	3.82	0.3162
annoying	US	3.07	2.99	3.72	3.54	3.54	3.37	0.2880	3.46	3.35	3.47	3.15	3.40	3.37	0.1164

Table A.3. *Continued*

Semantic differential		Occupation							Firm						
	Sample	A	B	C	D	E	Mean	Standard deviation	A	B	C	D	E	Mean	Standard deviation
Relaxed/	JP	4.55	4.22	4.46	4.00	4.14	4.28	0.2071	4.34	4.26	4.22	4.27	4.31	4.26	0.0460
tense	US	3.37	3.38	4.26	3.81	3.42	3.65	0.3470	3.68	3.63	3.82	3.49	3.61	3.65	0.1071
Knowledgeable/	JP	3.77	3.57	4.08	3.76	4.99	4.03	0.5052	4.01	3.92	4.10	4.13	3.96	4.02	0.0802
ignorant	US	2.71	2.73	2.67	2.98	3.91	3.00	0.4678	3.16	2.93	3.05	2.93	2.91	3.00	0.0958
Leader/	JP	3.81	4.38	4.27	3.36	5.61	4.29	0.7545	4.35	4.11	4.47	4.35	4.14	4.28	0.1374
follower	US	2.87	3.55	2.06	2.65	4.69	3.16	0.8997	3.21	3.05	3.20	3.11	3.22	3.16	0.0668
Simple/	JP	4.24	4.83	3.88	3.97	3.15	4.01	0.5211	4.05	4.04	4.00	3.90	4.08	4.01	0.0626
complex	US	3.82	4.02	4.29	3.65	3.05	3.77	0.4167	3.70	3.75	3.75	3.82	3.84	3.77	0.0511
Red/	JP	4.31	3.86	4.04	3.93	4.62	4.15	0.2797	4.41	3.93	4.25	4.01	4.16	4.15	0.1663
blue	US	4.04	3.99	3.87	3.88	4.06	3.97	0.0794	3.94	3.89	4.03	3.95	4.02	3.97	0.0524
Careful/	JP	2.89	3.07	3.65	3.35	4.22	3.44	0.4690	3.37	3.36	3.57	3.54	3.33	3.43	0.0873
careless	US	2.70	2.41	2.77	2.78	3.30	2.79	0.3641	2.82	2.83	2.87	2.76	2.67	2.79	0.0698
Borrowing/	JP	4.53	3.74	3.73	4.51	3.08	3.92	0.5467	4.01	4.02	3.83	3.72	4.00	3.92	0.1256
lending	US	4.12	3.97	3.95	3.85	3.54	3.89	0.1933	3.90	3.94	3.85	3.86	3.87	3.88	0.0326
Esteemed/	JP	3.94	3.99	4.43	3.64	5.34	4.27	0.5924	4.27	4.18	4.47	4.28	4.14	4.27	0.1141
not esteemed	US	3.38	3.31	3.18	3.36	4.13	3.47	0.3363	3.58	3.41	3.55	3.41	3.42	3.47	0.0750
Clean/	JP	3.66	3.06	4.26	3.78	4.50	3.85	0.5011	3.87	3.96	3.92	3.69	3.83	3.85	0.0954
dirty	US	2.28	2.66	3.09	3.22	3.37	2.92	0.3996	3.04	2.91	3.24	2.54	2.85	2.92	0.2307
Heavy/	JP	3.88	4.61	4.04	3.65	5.09	4.25	0.5246	4.34	4.14	4.34	4.50	3.95	4.25	0.1902
light	US	3.79	4.10	3.33	3.57	3.94	3.75	0.2716	3.82	3.84	3.64	3.96	3.49	3.70	0.1740
Informed/	JP	4.00	3.98	4.42	3.86	5.40	4.33	0.5059	4.35	4.19	4.53	4.38	4.21	4.33	0.1240
uninformed	US	2.55	2.79	2.45	2.95	3.88	2.92	0.5093	3.03	2.85	3.01	2.89	2.83	2.92	0.0826

Table A.3. *Continued*

Semantic differential	Sample	Occupation A	B	C	D	E	Mean	Standard deviation	Firm A	B	C	D	E	Mean	Standard deviation
Efficient/ inefficient	JP	3.42	3.64	3.92	3.36	4.01	3.67	0.2598	3.65	3.61	3.78	3.71	3.60	3.67	0.0672
	US	2.34	2.35	2.51	2.50	3.04	2.55	0.2217	2.62	2.50	2.62	2.44	2.54	2.54	0.0697
Gentle/ mean	JP	3.94	3.59	3.98	3.58	3.27	3.67	0.2621	3.69	3.70	3.71	3.56	3.71	3.67	0.0576
	US	3.14	3.12	4.13	3.73	3.28	3.48	0.3925	3.54	3.48	3.64	3.26	3.48	3.48	0.1237
Easygoing/ discipline-oriented	JP	4.73	4.47	4.27	4.23	3.83	4.31	0.2968	4.35	4.23	4.16	4.24	4.37	4.27	0.0787
	US	3.62	3.33	4.41	3.98	3.26	3.72	0.4283	3.69	3.81	3.82	3.52	3.76	3.72	0.1101
Mean of the standard deviations	JP							0.4649							0.1119
	US							0.3583							0.1089

Abbreviations: JP = Japan
US = United States

Occupations: A = personnel manager
B = designer
C = labour union leader
D = foreman
E = cleaner

Firms: A = a fountain pen manufacturer
B = a shoe manufacturer
C = a seat cover manufacturer
D = a dress manufacturer
E = a furniture manufacturer

Notes

Chapter 1, pp. 1–18

[1] This debate has evolved over the years. In addition to its earlier concern with the way in which technological change seemed to produce occupational structures similar to those found in other industrialized societies (Inkeles and Rossi: 1956; Ramsey and Smith: 1960), a whole range of issues, including structured international inequalities, have now begun to receive careful consideration (Meyer *et al.*: 1975). No longer is there simply a narrow interest in strategies for development or in the consequences of industrialization; attention has shifted to larger issues defining the human condition and to neo-evolutionary theories of civilization. The debate now raises key questions confronting social philosophers over the ages; issues brought to the fore by modern war and the concern with fascism, democracy and the role of ideology; issues explored by the utopians, who spoke of the unity of mankind and international socialism. In more recent times, the debate has involved those who are interested in how the communications revolution and the diffusion of ideas are affecting the world. Finally, for social critics like V. S. Naipaul (1980), the true essence of the debate lies in its warnings about the potential of nationalism to isolate the Third World into self-defeating, fundamentalist parochialism. To the extent that interest in Japan abroad has focused on Japan's economic expansion and the prospects for Japan's remilitarization (including the hegemony that implies) or on its imperialist expansion earlier in the twentieth century, the kind of issues raised more recently by the debate on convergence and divergence have a particular relevance.

[2] Papers from the symposium, along with an introductory chapter and three overviews, appear in a special issue of *Social Analysis* (SM, eds: 1982) which can be obtained from the Department of Anthropology, University of Adelaide, GPO Box 498, Adelaide, South Australia 5001.

Chapter 2, pp. 21–63

[1] In this regard it is ironic that Abegglen himself has often, rightly or wrongly, been associated with the stereotyped notion that all Japanese employees exactly fit the concept of life-time employment. While one might be sympathetic in view of the fact that he has perhaps been over-used as a point of departure for many subsequent writers, one should not overlook his close association with the notion of 'Japan, Incorporated' which has enjoyed considerable vogue in America.

[2] See also Bellah (1957, p. 183). For a critique of Bellah's views, see Mouer and Fodella (1970).

[3] For example, see a cross-section of the coverage given Japan in *Newsweek*: Oh, The Pride of Nissan!' (3 May 1971), p. 46; 'Japan: the Computerized Bulldozer', (17 July 1972), pp. 15–19; or 'The Japanese Yen for Work' (26 March 1973), p. 40. Also refer to Jay (1972) and Frankland (1972).

[4] See, for example, 'Japanese Society Probed in Keen Study by Expert', *AEN* (13 April 1971), p. 6; or P. N. Mason (1971), 'Key Unlocks Japanese Society', *JT* (28 April 1971), p. 9. For similar reviews in academic journals see Lee (1971), Caldarola (1972) and Smith (1971). For a more reserved discussion, see Levine (1976). For two rather critical reviews, see Cole (1971b) and Befu (1971b).

[5] The appeal of this superficial treatment of Japanese society can be seen in the fact that three years after the publication of *The Emerging Japanese Superstate,* Kahn was still able to reiterate comfortably his predictions for Japan. This is perhaps due to the fact that the book is addressed to an American need to respond to Japan's sudden presence in the international economy. Also see Jameson (1973) or the following press release from Associated Press: 'Futurologist Kahn Predicts Japan Will Become First Post-industrial Society', *JT* (21 July 1973), p. 12. Although the early views of Kahn have been

somewhat modified over time, the major assumptions about Japanese society remain largely unchanged (Kahn and Pepper: 1979).

[6] 'A Special Strength: A Survey of Japan', *Economist* (31 March 1973), pp. 7–67. The section entitled 'The Most Unmarxist Society' is merely a recapitulation of Nakane Chie's thinking, referring to her book *Japanese Society* as 'perhaps the most important book written about Japan in the past few years'.

[7] Also in early 1972, the Union Bank of Switzerland, in its study entitled 'Japan – Dynamic Force in the Industrial World', states that 'Japan seems well on its way to becoming the superpower of the future'. Quoted from an Associated Press release in *AEN* (18 January 1972), p. 1. At an even later date, Henry C. Wallich writes that in 'the early 1980's, if not before, the average citizen of Japan will have a higher income than the average American. At present, the per capita GNP of Japan is a little more than $3000 against $4400 in the U.S. If Japan can maintain its present growth rate of 8 to 10 percent, it is a question of only a few years.' Quoted from 'Japan and the U.S.' *Newsweek* (16 April 1973), p. 47. Finally, there is the claim of Maurice Stans, US Commerce Secretary, that the 'Japanese economy could very well surpass that of the United States over the next 20 years'. Quoted from a UPI release reported in *JT* (9 December 1969), p. 8. For example, despite the revaluation of the yen in late 1971, Kanamori (1972), deputy director of the Economic Research Institute of the Economic Planning Agency, was in the following year still predicting that by 1985 average per capita GNP would be $13,574 for the Japanese as compared with only $10,750 for the Americans and $4,165 for the British.

[8] One might also consult the volume put out by the Boston Consulting Group and edited by Abegglen (1970), particularly the 'Executive Summary', pp. 1–25, and Chapter 4, 'Japan, Incorporated: Government and Business Relationship', pp. 71–82.

[9] For example, in addition to the items given above in note 3, consider Peter Ward's 'Dark Side of the Rising Sun' *Australian* (1–2 March 1980), p. 9. At the same time, it should also be noted that there has been a great improvement in the coverage given to Japan in Australia, for example. In 1982 a full 28-page supplement 'Special

Report: Japan' was published without the use of a single trite headline in the *Australian* (28 May), pp. 21–48.

[10] From an interview reported in *Nihonjin o Kangaeru-Fujūbun na Ko no Kakuritsu* (Some Thoughts on the Japanese: a Case of the Underdeveloped Ego), *NKSC* (22 January 1972), p. 22. Based on his viewing of the movie *Love Story*, the film made from Erich Segal's popular novel, Kunihiro also concludes that Americans can never say they are sorry because to say so would be an admission of guilt or fault which would put the cold, calculating individual in American society on the defensive and hinder his ability to maximize his own self-interest.

[11] For those with more than a superficial knowledge of Japan, the real questions do not concern these successes. Rather, as Najita (1980), Shibata (1979) and others have noted in criticizing Vogel, there have been very conspicuous failures. One issue, then, is how to obtain an overall balance sheet, and the indices of net national welfare developed in Japan in the mid-seventies (Tōkyo-to: 1972; Keizai Shingikai: 1973; Kanamori: 1976; Uno: 1977) reflect the need for considering both sides of the ledger. A more complex question, however, concerns the extent to which the positive and negative aspects can be separated or isolated in terms of specific social structures. Those arguing for learning from Japan have tended to assume that one can borrow only the good without the bad. Another view would be that the social structures involved (or perhaps even necessary) in producing Japanese successes are inherently so structured that they will also simultaneously produce the diseconomies which are also associated with the Japanese experience (Yoneyama and SM: 1980). This is a point also made by Bix (1980) and others.

Chapter 3, pp. 64–83

[1] Three bibliographies of work on conflict in English were appended to an earlier publication of the authors (SM eds: 1982, pp. 14–17).

[2] For a rather detailed explanation of the *Rōnōha-Kōzaha* debate, see Koyama (1953) and Ōuchi Hyōei (1970, particularly Chapters II and III). Many of the arguments were set forth by one group in a

journal entitled *Rōnō*, which was begun in December 1927 and included the contributions of Yamakawa Hitoshi, Inomata Tsuneo, Arahata Kanson, Suzuki Mosaburō, Kushida Tamizō, Ōuchi Hyōei, Sakisaka Itsurō, Arisawa Hiromi, Uno Kōzō, Aono Suekichi and Tsuchiya Takao. The basic foundation upon which the Kōza group argued can be found in an eight-volume history of Japanese capitalism edited by Noro (1932–33). Members of this group included Noro Eitarō, Hirano Yoshitarō, Yamada Moritarō, Yamada Katsujirō, Hani Gorō, Kobayashi Yoshimasu, Watanabe Masanosuke and Hattori Shirō. For a short discussion in English of the debate between these two groups, see Beckmann (1962b).

[3] Inaba (1972) suggests that Tominaga has been the most influential scholar to present the argument that class conflict disappears as the particularistic values of capitalist society are replaced by the more universalistic and participatory values of complex organizations in mass society.

[4] The first of Kazehaya's two volumes was initially published in 1937 and is a classic, with its detailed historical treatment of the development of Japan's social policy in the prewar period. Republished in 1951 with additional chapters covering the years during the war and a second volume on the occupational reforms in the immediate postwar years, Kazehaya shows how social policy is constantly watered down by the government's ability to act independently of the business community. Kishimoto relies heavily on Kazehaya's work, but usually makes his points from a more orthodox Marxist approach – more theoretical and less historical.

[5] The outline of poverty research in the early postwar years has followed closely the outline of Ichibangase (1958, pp. 94–118), who lists about 350 items dealing with poverty in Japan which were published between 1945 and 1955. Anyone interested in this issue should certainly begin by consulting this bibliography.

[6] On this point, consult the discussion on social stratification in Chapter 11.

[7] Given the ready availability of this literature in English, only a brief summary of some major themes in the Japanese literature is provided in this section.

Chapter 4, pp. 84–95

[1] For example, Wakata Kyōji's paper, *Nihonteki Seiji Rīdāshippu* (Japanese-style Political Leadership) was roundly criticized at the annual conference of the Japanese Political Science Association (Nihon Seijigaku Kenkyūkai) held at Kansai Gakuin University, 27–8 March 1982. It was clear that the platitudes about groupism and consensus had lost their magic for the political scientists gathered at that particular conference.

[2] In examining the individual criteria for that subjective judgement, the question then becomes: 'Enough antagonism, cohesiveness and awareness for what?' The obvious answer is for social tension to occur. But again, 'How much social tension?' If the answer is 'to produce significant social change or revolution,' definitions are again asked in an endless round *ad infinitum.* 'Significance' is much like Thoreau's 'beauty'; it is very much in the eye of the beholder.

Chapter 5, pp. 99–128

[1] This approach was further developed by Lenski (1966) as a means of understanding not only the distribution of social rewards, but also social class (cf. Chapter 12). The approach was later utilized in a modified form by Cutright (1967) to make international comparisons of inequality to test Lenski's theory on inequality and stages of development. Although there are several reasons for disagreeing with Cutright's choice of variables to obtain his distributions, such debate is reserved for another occasion.

[2] It should be noted that the number of groups associated with any one approach to analysis varies. The comparability of the GCRs for any one set of categories is improved to the extent that the categories are numerous, the number of categories is the same and that the population is distributed evenly among the categories.

[3] For example, see the excellent surveys of occupational earnings taken by the National Personnel Authority for use in setting wage rates for public servants: Jinjiin Kyūyokyoku (Bureau of Salaries, National Personnel Authority), ed., *Minkan Kyūyo no Jittai* (Actual State of Salaries in Private Industry) (Tokyo: Ōkurashō Insatsukyoku, published annually).

[4] For some background on this point, see Umemura (1967 and 1971). In English the idea of a uniquely Japanese system of seniority wages was made popular by Abegglen (1958).

[5] The GCR was calculated for the US for both March 1974 and March 1975 data. The two GCRs were exactly the same up to four significant places to the right of the decimal. The 1975 data is from the Bureau of the Census, Statistical Abstract 1975 (Washington, DC: Government Printing Office, 1976), p. 398. The data for 1974 are from the same Bureau, 'Household Money Income in 1974,' p. 100.

[6] On the relative weighting of years of service and age, see Nakamura (1975).

[7] The data for the US are taken from the Bureau of the Census, *Statistical Abstracts 1975,* p. 398; and the Bureau's 'Household Money Income in 1974,' p. 10.

Chapter 6, pp. 129–55

[1] On the distinction between *emic* terms or concepts embedded in the categories of a given language and the *etic* typologies developed to bridge the differences among languages when cross-cultural analysis is conducted, see Pike (1967).

[2] Although the recent supplement to *The Oxford English Dictionary* by Burchfield (1976, Vol. II, p. 287) cites a slightly earlier usage in 1827, for many years it was commonly accepted that the earliest usage of 'individualism' was H. Reeve's 1835 translation of de Tocqueville's *Democracy in America* as recorded in Murray *et al.* (1970, Vol. V, p. 224). Although, slightly later, the usage associated with *Democracy in America* has certainly been more widely known than that found in the earlier example. It is also interesting to note than individualism was then defined as a phenomenon whereby persons sever themselves from the masses of society and draw apart with their friends and family. In translating de Tocqueville's volume, individualism was used not to refer to autonomous individuals but to indicate a special kind of groupism and the joining of associations which de Tocqueville felt was peculiar to America.

[3] Although the quotes used above are from the English version (1973), her references (1972a) were to the original edition (1967a).

[4] Some caution is required when interpreting the figures in Table 6.1. A citation is simply a record that someone referred to a specific volume. It does not mean that the volume received favorable comment. Nevertheless, the number of citations may be used as *one* means of gauging the importance attached to a volume by others since they could simply have ignored the volume.

In this regard, the name of Ronald Dore should be mentioned. Among non-Japanese scholars the depth and range of his scholarship on Japanese society are legend. As the figures in Table N.1 show, his work is frequently cited. He was not included for analysis, owing to the fact that his work had focused on specific aspects of Japanese society; he has not written an overview of Japanese society, although his *British Factory – Japanese Factory* makes reference to the group model. Even when Dore's views on Japanese society are pulled together, they form a vision considerably more sensitive to intra-societal variation and the subtle complexities of Japanese society than the vision generally associated with the advocates of *nihonjinron* who are being examined here.

[5] Some variation in the two sets of findings for each volume resulted from inconsistencies in the way the two referees classified data. However, the overall correlation between findings for the English and Japanese versions was striking. One idea was simply to average them together, but in the end a subjective choice was made between the two referees, based on the detail and overall sense of consistency which seemed to characterize their recording of the data.

Chapter 7, pp. 156–88

[1] For some information about the Japanese labor market for university academics, see Cummings (1980) or Shinbori (1965).

[2] Of course, such decisions are also influenced by ideas in each society as to which other societies constitute that society's positive reference group.

[3] During the sixties an average of nearly a hundred Japanese union leaders were sent to the United States each year. Since these figures are only for those who were programed through the American Department of Labor, usually on full or partial grants from the State Department, they do not include all persons visiting the United States

Table N.1. *The number of citations of works by Dore*

Book	Year											
	1970	1971	1972	1973	1974	1975	1976	1977	1978	1979	1980	1981
City Life In Japan (58/67/71)	5	3	2	6	6	6	6	6	5	3	1	5
Land Reform in Japan (59/66)	3	3	2	4	2	3	3	4		3	3	1
Education in Tokugawa Japan (65/67)	7	3	8	3	3	1	2	4	4	2	3	3
Aspects of Social Change (67/73)	7	2	1	1	1	1	4	1	4	1		
British Factory/Japanese Factory (73/74)				1	18	14	15	15	25	15	14	21
Diploma Disease (76/77/78)								4	16	12	17	22
Shinohata (78)									1	3	3	4
TOTAL number of citations	27	18	18	22	34	35	46	46	66	50	58	69

from Japanese labor unions. The figures given here were calculated from carbon copies of data sheets supplied by the Bureau of International Labor Affairs, US Department of Labor, Washington, DC, in the fall of 1974.

[4] See Sugimoto (1978a, p. 276) and the last chapter of Stockwin (1975) on Japanese political culture.

Chapter 8, pp. 191–210

[1] *Gairai Jiten* (Dictionary of Borrowed Words) lists 27,000 items adopted from other languages. Some are very technical expressions, but others like apāto, depāto, naitā and *terebi* are very much a part of everyday life in Japan and involve no resistance at all. It would be a stretch of the imagination and of common logic to suggest that the true values of most Japanese emphasized riding in a palanquin or living in a thatched house (*gassho zukuri*) as opposed to a ferroconcrete de luxe apartment simply because words for those items existed in Japanese several hundred years ago. Many of these words are also used in advertising precisely because they capture an old value and give it a new twist. Certainly sleight of hand is involved, and the cost of using foreign symbols to replace those in the vernacular often obfuscates one's identity and one's ability to communicate with others, as we mention below in Chapter 15. Finally, those who cite the borrowing of *puraibashī* and use it to contrast Japan with the West seldom mention that the word has also been borrowed directly from English for use in many other European languages. An extension of the logic applied to *purabashī*, however, would suggest that many non-English-speaking Europeans are not individualistic.

Chapter 9, pp. 211–33

[1] The idea of the contract being *tatemae* (in principle only but not of any real consequence) is often given by the real estate agent to help the uniformed foreigner to deal with his surprise. An American student once tested the idea by suggesting that the notion of *tatemae* could be elevated to an even higher level, as in his college community back home, by simply agreeing that the contract had been signed in principle and that the actual signing in ink was perfunctory. The argument made little headway and the agent rang later to say the flat had been rented to another person.

Chapter 11, pp. 275–91

[1] In Chapter 12 consideration is given to the definition of class. Unfortunately, there seems to be little argument on how this term is used in much of the literature on social stratification. In the next chapter, class is defined to indicate a concept close to Marx's notion of *Klasse für sich*. However, in this chapter the term is used in a rather loose fashion to express the ideas of other authors.

[2] For the most part, studies on social status in postwar Japan have accepted this assumption. The work done by the Research Committee of the Japanese Sociological Assoc. in 1955 (Okada and Nishihara: 1965) and the later studies done by that group in 1965 (Tominaga: 1969 and 1970b) and in 1975 (Tominaga: 1979) were developed on the assumption that occupation is the major determinant and the best index of social status or social standing in contemporary industrialized societies.

[3] For a brief description of the *sararīman* who make up the new middle class, see Vogel (1963, pp. 4–11).

[4] Quoted from an interview with Gerald Curtis, 'Trying to Destroy "Japan, Inc." Myth', *AEN* (7 February 1973), p. 3. This point is also made by Stockwin (1982).

[5] This point was once made in a lecture by Ronald Dore at the International House of Japan in Tokyo on 16 September 1970 (Dore: 1970) and is also raised in his contribution to the well-known report of the OECD (1973). With regard to the financial status of the parents of newly entering university students, see *Funsōgo no Tōdaiseizō* (A Portrait of the Student Body at the University of Tokyo following the 1968–9 Struggles) *NKSC* (10 December 1970), p. 22; *Yūmeikō Shingakusō no Shūhen* (The Strata Moving up to the Famous Schools), *NKSC* (9 April 1973), p. 6; and *Kyōikuhi Saitenken* (Another Look at the Costs of Education), *NKSY* (26 February 1974), p. 7.

[6] This is not the first attempt to provide such a meta-typology. As Marsh (1982) notes approvingly, Blau (1977) had earlier classified these variables (which he labelled parameters) as being 'nominal' and 'graduated'.

[7] Aruga and Nakane used this pair of terms in slightly different contexts. Aruga, for example, used *tate* to refer to the links which created a sense of identity with the rural agricultural community. Nakane is more concerned with the firm. Nevertheless, common to both views is a concern with the need for a more sophisticated picture of stratification in more than one dimension. The distinction is further confused by the tendency to use *tate* colloquially to refer to Japanese things and *yoko* to refer to Western things, as in *tatemeshi* (Japanese food) and *yokomeshi* (Western food). This seems to have derived from the observation that Japanese is traditionally written down the page (*tate*) whereas Western languages are written across the page (*yoko*). However, in the use of these terms as analytical concepts there is a sleight of hand whereby in the Japanese Nakane's vertical solidarities come to be subconsciously associated with being Japanese, and her horizontal solidarities, with being Western.

[8] For a good introduction to this discussion see Evans (1971, pp. 40-4).

[9] See, for example, Wellemeyer (1974, p. 228). Also see the series of studies done by Heidrick and Struggles, a firm of management consultants based in Chicago. The following are available as 10–12-page pamphlets: *Profile of a President* (1972), *Profile of the European Chief Executive and his American Counterpart* (1969), *Profile of a Chief Marketing Executive* (1971), *Profile of a Chief Financial Officer* (1970), *Profile of a Chief Research and Development Executive* (1973). This literature would tend to suggest that the extent of mobility in the United States has been exaggerated. Although labor turnover is higher in the United States, the data cited here would suggest that there are two groups of executives there – those who have been with their firms for 25 years or longer and those who have been with the firm less than five years. This pattern would be similar to that found in Japan, with those of short duration having come from Government (through the practice of *amakudari*) or from related firms (*keiretsu kigyō*).

[10] The term 'lifetime employment' is commonly used to describe incorrectly employment patterns in Japanese firms. Even the substitute 'career employment' does not describe well a situation in which the average length of employment even for males in firms with over 1000 employees from 1971 to 1975 was between 6.8 years (using

statistics for the rate of exit) and 10.7 years (using the figures for the rate of entry). The corresponding figures for firms with 300–999 employees are 5.4 and 7.7; 100–299 employees, 4.7 and 5.7; 30–99 employees, 4.6 and 5.3 years; and 5–29 employees, 5.0 and 5.9 years. The figures on rates of entry and exit were taken from Rōdōshō (1976, p. 25).

Chapter 12, pp. 292–327

[1] Like the word 'status', 'hierarchy' has come to have two meanings, one being a general reference to inequality and ranking in terms of access to social rewards and the other being a reference to a specific set of authority relationships and rankings in terms of access to one type of societal reward, power. For a discussion of the dual usage assigned to 'status', see notes 7 and 9 below.

[2] The term 'societal reward' is preferred to the term 'social reward' because, in addition to the nuance that the creation of such utility involves a social arrangement, it also contains the nuance that the creation of rewards is the result of belonging to a system. There is not space here to discuss fully all the implications which follow from conceiving society as a system. The most important, perhaps, is the assumption that there is some measure of consensus among members of either the social system itself, or at least among members of one of its subgroups existing in a stratified society. To assume that each individual had completely different goals would result in an anarchic picture of society and make measures of reward distribution problematic, if not impossible.

[3] Ordinarily, the utilities produced by a hermit for his own consumption would not be counted as a societal reward, to the extent that he is outside the social system. However, to the extent that he is part of a larger society which is, in an institutionalized fashion, denied his services, or which allows him to deny the use of certain of his resources to others, his uses of time and resources result in societal rewards for himself. As population densities increase and the realm of the natural economy diminishes, such recluses are subsumed within the social system.

[4] Unfortunately, Weber used the term 'class' in his references to the economic dimensions. Thus, many writers today use the term 'class'

to refer only to economic strata or an individual's status (ranking) in terms of his economic functions.

[5] It is not crucial at this stage whether the typology contains three or four categories. The categories serve only as convenient labels. The four-category typology seems to have a number of heuristic advantages. To the extent that current distributions affect future access, the clear delineation of information as a separate type of reward resolves some of the central issues in the debate on the culture of poverty. For a brief introduction to that debate, refer to the five items appearing in Ritzer (1972, pp. 469–499). In many ways the culture of poverty can be better understood as being the poverty of the information necessary to make informed choice. The delineation of information as a separate reward may also contribute to the making of a conceptual distinction between culture and ideology, an issue discussed at the end of this chapter.

[6] Perhaps this reflects the fact that much economic behavior in the ordinary sense involves interaction within the framework of political organization and also the fact that power tends to involve a zero-sum type of calculation. On this concept of power, see Parsons (1965) or Thurlow (1980).

[7] Here it must be noted that Warner's use of status tends to subsume segmental status judgements as total status judgements. Thus, it may easily be argued that Warner's model does not fit into this category. The authors tend to go along with that view, but feel that the common tendency to associate Warner with the delineation of social status is well enough entrenched to warrant its inclusion as a status-based reward model. At the same time, the differentiation between total and segmental judgements leads to still other problems which go beyond the scope of this book, but are relevant to the delineation of the various societal rewards themselves.

[8] One notable exception is Lenski (1966). Some of his ideas are discussed below in the section on social class.

[9] To distinguish among the variables used for classifying roles and individuals, three different concepts have been introduced: traits, roles and features. The term 'roles' is perhaps self-explanatory, and is used in a narrow sense to indicate functionally relevant roles and

achievement-oriented criteria. Occupation is one example. The term 'trait' is used to indicate other acquired characteristics which generally differentiate people but which are not generally associated with the delineation of functional roles. One's ethnic background or place of education are examples. Finally, the term 'features' refers to inherited physical attributes such as race or beauty. In this regard, it should be noted that social role is defined in the broadest sense to indicate the behavior associated with a social position. See Woodland (1968).

[10] For want of a better term, these characteristics are referred to as agents of stratification. Other authors have variously referred to them as demographic variables, stratification variables and parameters.

[11] One should also note that theoretical models in the social sciences are not meant to explain every case, but to yield generalizations or guidelines which will explain some percentage of all cases. The higher the percentage, the more reliable, or the more regularly applicable the model or theory.

[12] Accordingly, the size of the percentage of the population in each of the boxes shown in Figure 11.2 will be different for each of the societies just mentioned.

[13] Although altruism and acts of kindness towards others can also be interpreted as satisfying some individual psychological needs, serious thought needs to be given to the possibility of people being motivated by considerations other than self-interest. There is a danger that the notion of self-interest and societal rewards may become so broadly defined as to include everything. The assumption is then no longer a hypothesis subject to testing; it is simply true by definition or tautological reasoning.

Chapter 13, pp. 328–59

[1] Consequently, cleavage between decision-makers and non-decision-makers (between the capitalists and the workers or between the elite and the masses, to use Marxist terminology), or between the leadership and the participants in the system widened during this period. This dimension can best be seen in anti-pollution, consumer and student movements. Income was not the only issue in these

conflicts, but it was one which was closely tied to demands on the system.

[2] On the concept of primary and secondary distribution, see Kurabayashi (1973).

[3] The substantists have argued that the economics of scarcity and monetized markets (e.g., money-making) are of little use in understanding much of the economic activity in many primitive economies and, by inference, significant aspects of modern economies. Among several coming to the defense of the formal economists, LeClair (1962) argues that 'whatever may have been the view of classical (19th century) economists, contemporary economists have long since adopted a broader view of the nature of human wants.' In support of his argument he cites Stigler's *The Theory of Price* (1946):

> The concept of an 'economic man' does not imply (as almost all of its critics state) that the individual seeks to maximize money or wealth, that the human soul is a complex cash register. It does not affect the formal theory . . . in the least whether the individual maximizes wealth, religious piety, the annihilation of crooners or his waistline.

He also quotes from Machlup who in the same year (1946) wrote as follows:

> In short, economists no longer believe, if they ever did, that human wants are confined, in market societies, to material wants, not do they assume this to be true of any society. Nor is an assumption of the materialistic nature of human wants a necessary element in contemporary economic theory.

[4] See, for example, Nihon Chiiki Kaihatsu Sentā (1970), the monthly publication of the Prime Minister's Office, *Yoron Chōsa* (Public Opinion Surveys), or any others of a variety of publications in this area.

[5] *ASC* (30 June 1971), p. 12.

[6] *YSC* (12 December 1972), p. 5.

[7] *AEN* (26 December 1969), p. 1; and *ASC* (8 December 1972), p. 21.

[8] *AEN* (4 November 1972), p. 1; *YSC* (12 December 1972), p. 5; and *ASC* (5 December 1972), p. 2.

[9] Murata Kiyoshi, 'Voting Behavior' *JT* (25 December 1969), p. 12.

[10] This view was revealed in an interview with one of the authors by a male manager who was in charge of the women managers' trainee programme at a large department store in Japan.

Chapter 14, pp. 360–73

[1] In referring to *Klasse an sich* in Marxian terms, the emphasis is on the abstract concept (groups of people in society which share some objective similarity determining in part their access to societal rewards) and not to the particular groups identified by Marx as being the most likely to become *Klasse für sich* (such as those delineated by their relationship to the means of production).

[2] Although Treiman is not perfectly clear on this point, and does seem to recognize that 'occupational prestige is not the only basis of rank,' he does not define the other bases or relate them to the ranking of work situations, thereby leaving the impression that work is categorized mainly, if not solely, in terms of occupation.

Chapter 15, pp. 377–404

[1] The comments here are drawn from the literature mentioned in Chapter 5 with regard to conflict in Japan.

[2] For the Asahi volume see Asahi Shinbun Henshūbu (1971). For the literature which followed see Yano and Yamazaki (1972), Itō (1972), Yomiuri Shinbunsha (1971). In the preface to their volume, Yano and Yamazaki write that dissatisfaction with the standard of living will become increasingly pronounced among the people as better statistics become available, which will allow for better international comparisons.

[3] For example, see 'The 'Crisis of Mankind'', *AEN* (25 March 1972), p. 4; or *Kono Chikyū: 50 Nen Saki no Shigen Kokatsu* (This World: Resources Dried up in another 50 Years), *ASC* (4 May 1972), p. 4. These are just two examples of the kind of articles which flooded the Japanese press in 1972.

[4] The report recommended that the Japanese Government rethink its priorities, particularly with reference to the trade-off between continuing high economic growth rates and improved welfare for the labor force. The report strongly suggested that Japan's rapid economic growth was in no small measure assisted by three institutions: lifetime employment (*shūshin koyō*), the seniority wage system (*nenkō joretsu chingin*), and the enterprise-based labor union (*kigyōbetu kumiai*). In the view of the OECD investigations, the dual structure which created have and have-nots within the labor force, as well as certain restrictions on the individual's freedom of movement, seem to have been particularly important on the negative side.

[5] This phenomenon can be verified by considering the difference in publication dates: two months for the first one (March and May) minus one month for the second (December and November) and ten months (December and September) for the third. The importance attached to them can also be substantiated by looking at the translators and publishers which are listed in the bibliography.

[6] See, for example *NKSC* (12 January 1981), p. 3.

[7] See, for example, an even earlier editorial in the *JT*:

> There are some excellent reasons why the nation's political and industrial leaders should urge adoption of the five-day week – a position they have but lately moved toward. Sensitive to foreign criticism that Japan is disrupting world economic balances, and particularly to charges of dumping, they recognize that measures must be taken to counter the image of cheap labor in this country. This pressing problem has given a sense of urgency that has not been seen before to the purpose of the five-day week (3 April 1971, p. 14).

[8] See *ILO no Yūkyū Kyōiku* The ILO on Paid Educational Leave), *SRN* (13 March 1972), p. 2, and *SRN* (2 April 1973), p. 2; or *Ōshū*

Gokakoku no Tabi kara (A Visit to Five European Countries), *SRN* (13 November 1972), p. 3. Similar articles can be found in the leading national papers.

[9] On a survey taken by the Foreign Ministry, see '5-Day Workweek', *JT* (10 February 1973), p. 14. In the fall of 1972 the Japan Institute of Labor sent its team abroad. See *Shū Itsukasei no ato ni Kurumono* (After the Five-day Workweek), *NRKZ* (vol. 15, no. 4: April 1973), pp. 2–16. Other examples are readily available.

[10] See 'Japanese Workaholics', *AEN* (28 July 1973), p. 4; and 'Japanese are "Workaholics"', *AEN* (5 May 1972), p. 4.

[11] In mentioning Australian perspectives, the authors do not pretend to speak for Australians. As a Japanese and an American who have spent roughly the last third of their adult lives working in the Australian context, they believe that they have gained a perspective somewhat different from that obtained earlier in Japan and the United States. Although still very much in the process of learning about the Australian academic tradition, none the less they feel that they have been intellectually stimulated and enriched by the years spent living there and wish to label the resultant perspective 'Australian'. If there is an Australian perspective on Japanese society, it may be delineated by the greater awareness of authority relationships and institutional histories in the study of society. For a fuller exposition of these themes, see the volumes edited by SM (1982) and MS (1982c) which contain papers given at a symposium on 'Alternative Models for Understanding Japanese Society' held in conjunction with the first national conference of the Japanese Studies Association of Australia in May 1980.

References

Abegglen, James C.
1958 *The Japanese Factory: Aspects of its Social Organization.* Glencoe, Ill.: Free Press.
1970a 'The Economic Growth of Japan.' *Scientific American* (vol. 222, no. 3: March), pp. 31–7.
1970b 'An Anatomy of Japan's Miracle Economy.' *The Washington Post* (15 March), p. 83.
1970c *Business Strategies for Japan.* Tokyo: Sophia University.
1973 *Management and Worker: the Japanese Solution.* Tokyo: Kodansha International.
1974 *Nihon no Keiei kara Nani o Manabuka* (What can be Learned from Japanese Management), translated by Urabe Tomi and Mori Yoshiaki. Tokyo: Daiyamondosha.

Adachi, James S.
1973 'Japanese Like to Live, Work in Groups: Japanese People are Different.' *JT* (1 December), p. 11.

Aida, Yūji
1970 *Nihonjin no Ishiki Kōzō* (The Structure of the Japanese Consciousness). Tokyo: Kōdansha.
1977 *Nihon Jinzairon: Shidōsha no Jōken* (A Theory of Japanese Human Potential: Prerequisites for Leaders). Tokyo: Kōdansha.

Aizawa, Hisashi
1976 *Nihonjinron no Tame ni* (A Contribution to *Nihonjinron*). Tokyo: Ushio Shuppansha.

Akiyama, Kenji
1982 'Kikai no Fubyōdō' (The Inequality of Opportunity). In *Nihon no Shinchūkansō* (Japan's New Middle Strata), edited by Ariyoshi Hiroyuki and Hamaguchi Haruhiko. Tokyo: Waseda Daigaku Shuppanbu, pp. 162–90.

Akiyama, Kenjirō, Mori, Hideo, and Yamashita, Takeshi, eds.
1960 *Gendai Nihon no Teihen: Saikasō no Hitobito* (At the Bottom of Contemporary Japanese Society: The People of the Lowest Strata).

4 vols. Tokyo: San-ichi Shobō.
Alker, Hayward R., and Russett, Bruce M.
1968 'Indices for Comparing Inequality.' In *The Use of Quantitative Data in Cross-National Research,* edited by Richard L. Merritt and Stein Rokkan. New Haven, Conn.: Yale University Press, pp. 349–72.
Allardt, Erick
1968 'Theories about Social Stratification.' In *Social Stratification,* edited by J. A. Jackson. Cambridge: Cambridge University Press, pp. 14–24.
Allen, G. C.
1938 *Japan: the Hungry Guest.* London: Allen and Unwin.
Allison, Paul D.
1978 'Measures of Inequality.' *American Sociological Review* (vol. 43, no. 6: December), pp. 865–80.
Amano, Katsufumi
1982 'Rainichi Kisha' (Foreign Correspondents Visiting Japan). *MSC* (2 October), p. 5.
Ames, Walter J.
1981 *Police and Community in Japan.* Berkeley, Cal.: University of California Press.
Anonymous
1971 'Generation Gap, Money Lack Plagues Japanology in U.S..' *AEN* (28 December), p. 6.
1982 'Rabuhoteru Hyakka' (A Guide to Love Hotels). *Da Kāpo* (vol. 2, no. 8: 20 April), pp. 98–9.
1982b 'Learning from Japan.' *Asiaweek* (5 November), pp. 29–37.
Aoi, Kazuo; and Naoi, Yū
1974 'Sociology.' *An Introductory Bibliography for Japanese Studies* (vol. 1, part 1), pp. 49–67.
Aoki, Kōji
1967 *Meiji Nōmin Sōjō no Nenjiteki Kenkyū* (Chronological Study of Agrarian Disturbances in Meiji Japan). Tokyo: Shinseisha.
1968 *Nippon Rōdō Undōshi Nenpyō, Dai Ikkan, Meiji Taishō Hen* (Chronological Tables of Japanese Labor Movements, vol. I, the Meiji and Taishō Periods). Tokyo: Shinseisha.
1971 *Hyakushō Ikki Sōgō Nenpyō* (Comprehensive Chronological Tables of Peasant Rebellions in Tokugawa Japan). Tokyo: San-ichi Shobō.
1977 *Taishō Nōmin Sōōjō Shiryō Nenpyō* (Historical Documents and Chronological Tables of Peasant Revolts in Taishō Japan). 3 vols. Tokyo: Gannandō.
Aonuma, Yoshimatsu
1962 *Shin Chūkan Kaikyū no Shakaiteki Seikaku* (The Social Characteristics of the New Middle Class). Sanshokki Monograph no. 171.

Tokyo: Keiō University.

1965 *Nihon no Keieisō: Sono Shusshin to Seikaku* (The Managerial Class in Japan: its Background and Character). Tokyo: Nihon Keizai Shinbunsha.

Apter, David

1965 *The Politics of Modernization.* Chicago, Ill.: University of Chicago Press.

Araki, Hiroyuki

1973 *Nihonjin no Kōdō Yōshiki* (Japanese Patterns of Behavior). Tokyo: Kōdansha.

Arisawa, Hiromi

1955 'Chingin Kōzō to Keizai Kōzō: Teichingin no Igi to Haikei' (Wage Differentials and the Structure of the Economy: Some Background Factors Related to the Minimum Wage). In *Chingin Kihon Chōsa* (A Study of Wages), edited by Nakayama Ichirō. Tokyo: Tōyō Keizaisha.

Ariyoshi, Sawako

1972 *Kōkotsu no Hito* (The Ecstatic Ones). Tokyo: Shinchōsha.

1975 *Fukugō Osen* (Compound Pollution). 2 vols. Tokyo: Shinchōsha.

Armstrong, Rodney

1980 'The American Press and Japan.' *Keio Communication Review* (vol. 1), pp. 73–86.

Aruga, Kizaemon

1943 *Nihon Kazoku Seido to Kosaku Seido* (The Japanese Family System and Tenant System). Tokyo: Iwanami Shoten.

Asahi Jānaru, ed.

1982 'Me de Miru Amerika de no "Nihon no Hyōban"' (Looking at the American Evaluation of Japan). *AJ* (18 June), pp. 26–30.

Asahi Shinbunsha

1971 *Kutabare GNP* (Down with GNP!). Tokyo: Asahi Shinbunsha.

1972 *28 Years in the Guam Jungle: Sergeant Yokoi Home From World War II.* Tokyo: Japan Publications.

1975 *Shin Binbō Monogatari* (The Story of the New Poverty). Tokyo: Asahi Shinbunsha.

Asahi Shinbunsha, ed.

1974a *Shisō o Aruku* (Back through Japan's Intellectual History). 2 vols. Tokyo: Asahi Shinbunsha.

1974 *Wagashisaku Wagafūdo* (Our Lives, Our Thoughts: 19 Autobiographical Sketches). Tokyo: Asahi Shinbunsha.

Asō, Makoto

1967 *Erīto to Kyōiku* (Elite and Education). Tokyo: Fukumura Shoten.

Association of Japanese Geographers, ed.

1980 *Geography of Japan.* Tokyo: Teikoku Shoin.

Atsumi, Reiko

1975 *Personal Relationships of Japanese White-collar Company*

Employees. Ph.D. dissertation, University of Pittsburgh.

1978 'Images of Australia and Australians as Reflected in the Japanese Mass Media.' Paper presented at the Second National Conference of the Asian Studies Association of Australia, University of New South Wales, Sydney, 14–18 May.

1979 '*Tsukiai*—Obligatory Personal Relationships of Japanese White-Collar Company Employees.' *Human Organization* (vol. 38, no. 1: Spring), pp. 63–70.

1982 'Patterns of Personal Relationships: a Key to Understanding Japanese Thought and Behaviour.' In *Japanese Society: Reappraisals and New Directions,* edited by Yoshio Sugimoto and Ross Mouer as a special issue of *Social Analysis* (nos. 5/6: December 1980), pp. 63–78.

Austin, Lewis

1967 'The Izumi Syndrome: Aspects of Political Socialization and Political Culture in Japan.' Cambridge: duplicated paper for the Center for International Studies, Massachusetts Institute of Technology.

Awanohara, Susumu

1982 'In pursuit of an Ideal.' *FEER* (12 February), pp. 45–6.

Ayusawa, Iwao R.

1966 *A History of Labor in Modern Japan.* Honolulu, Hawaii: East-West Center Press.

Azumi, Koya

1969 *Higher Education and Business Recruitment in Japan.* New York: Teachers College Press, Columbia University.

Azumi, Koya, and Hull, Frank

1982 'Technology, Organization and Alienation in Japanese Factories: a Contradiction of the Blauner Thesis.' Paper presented to the International Colloquium on the Comparative Study of Japanese Society, Noosa Heads, Queensland, Australia: 29 January–6 February.

Azumi, Koya, Hull, Frank, and Hage, Gerald

1981 'Organization Designs in an Age of High Technology: A Comparison between Japan and the U.S.' Paper presented to the Seminar on the Challenge of Japan's Internationalization: Organization and Culture, Kwansei Gakuin University Seminar House, Santa, Hyōgo-ken, 30 June–5 July.

Baba Kōnōsuke

1981 *Fukushi Shakai no Nihonteki Keitai* (Japanese Forms of the Welfare Society). Tokyo: Tōyō Keizai Shinpōsha.

Ballon, Robert J.

1968 'Japan's Life-Time Remuneration System.' *Bulletin of the Industrial Relations Section, Socio-Economic Institute,* no. 16. Tokyo: Sophia University.

1969 'Participative Employment.' In *The Japanese Employee,* edited by Robert J. Ballon. Tokyo: Sophia University, pp. 63–76.

Ballon, Robert J., ed.

1969 *The Japanese Employee.* Tokyo: Sophia University in collaboration with the Charles E. Tuttle Company.

1979 *Nihongata Bijinesu no Kenkyū* (Some Research on Japanese-Style Business). Tokyo: Purejidentosha.

Baltzell, E. Digby

1964 *The Protestant Establishment: Aristocracy and Caste in America.* New York: Vintage Books.

Barnett, Arnold, Abraham, Michael, and Schimmel, Victor

1979 'Airline Safety: Some Empirical Findings.' *Management Science* (vol. 25, no. 11: November), pp. 1045–56.

Barnlund, Dean C.

1975 *Public and Private Self in Japan and the United States: Communicative Style of Two Cultures.* Tokyo: The Simul Press.

Bayley, David H.

1976 *Forces of Order: Police Behavior in Japan and the United States.* Berkeley, Cal.: University of California Press.

Beardsley, Richard K., Hall, John W., and Ward, Robert E.

1959 *Village Japan.* Chicago, Ill.: University of Chicago Press.

Beckmann, George M.

1962a *The Modernization of China and Japan.* New York: Harper and Row.

1962b 'Japanese Adaptations of Marx-Leninism: Modernization and History.' *Asian Cultural Studies* (no. 3: October), pp. 103–14.

1969 *The Japanese Communist Party: 1922–1945.* Stanford, Cal.: Stanford University Press.

Befu, Harumi

1971a *Japan: an Anthropological Introduction.* San Francisco: Chandler.

1971b 'Japanese Society by Chie Nakane.' *American Journal of Sociology* (vol. 77, no. 1: July), pp. 174–6.

1974 'Power in Exchange: the Strategy of Control and Patterns of Compliance in Japan.' *Asian Profile* (vol. 2, nos. 5/6: October/December), pp. 601–22.

1977 'Power in the Great White Tower.' In *The Anthropology of Power,* edited by R. D. Fogelson and R. M. Adams. New York: Academic Press, pp. 77–87.

1980 'The Group Model of Japanese Society and an Alternative.' *Rice University Studies* (vol. 66, no. 1: Winter), pp. 169–87.

1981 'The Internationalization of Japan and *Nihon Bunkaron.*' Paper presented to the Seminar on the Challenge of Japan's Internationalization: Organization and Culture, Kwansei Gakuin University, Santa, Hyōgo-ken, 30 June–5 July.

1982a 'A Critique of the Group Model of Japanese Society.' In *Japanese*

Society: Reappraisals and New Directions, edited by Yoshio Sugimoto and Ross Mouer as a special issue of *Social Analysis* (nos. 5/6: December 1980), pp. 29–43.

1982b 'Alternative Steps: the Next Step.' In *Japanese Society: Reappraisals and New Directions,* edited by Yoshio Sugimoto and Ross Mouer as a special issue of *Social Analysis* (nos. 5/6: December 1980), pp. 188–93.

1982c 'A Theory of Social Exchange as Applied to Japan.' Paper presented to the International Colloquium on the Study of Japanese Society, Noosa Heads, Queensland, Australia, 29 January–6 February.

1982d 'Emic-Etic Issues in the Context of Japanese Studies.' Paper presented to the International Colloquium on the Study of Japanese Society, Noosa Heads, Queensland, 29 January–6 February.

Befu, Harumi, Kawamura, Nozomu, Sugimoto, Yoshio, and Mouer, Ross

1980 'Machigai darake no Nihonjinron' (New Models for Understanding Japanese Society). *AJ* (vol. 22, no. 36: 12 September), pp. 26–33.

Bellah, Robert N.

1957 *Tokugawa Religion.* New York: Free Press.

Bendasan, Isaiah

1970 *Nihonjin to Yudayajin* (The Japanese and the Jews). Tokyo: Yamamoto Shoten.

1972 *The Japanese and the Jews,* translated by Richard L. Gage. Tokyo: Weatherhill.

Benedict, Ruth

1946 *The Chrysanthemum and the Sword.* Boston, Mass.: Houghton Mifflin.

Bennett, John W., and Levine, Solomon B.

1976 'Industrialization and Social Deprivation: Welfare, Environment and Post-Industrial Society in Japan.' In *Japanese Industrialization and Its Social Consequences,* edited by Hugh Patrick (with Larry Meissner). Berkeley, Cal.: University of California Press, pp. 439–492.

Berger, Michael

1982 'A Trade Imbalance Made in America?' *San Francisco Chronicle* (10 March), p. C-1.

Berger, Peter

1963 *Invitation to Sociology: a Humanistic Perspective.* Ringwood: Penguin Books.

Berger, Peter L, and Kellner, Hansfried

1982 *Sociology Reinterpreted: an Essay on Method and Vocation.* Harmondsworth: Penguin Books.

Béteille, André

1969 'Introduction'. In *Social Inequality: Selected Readings,* edited by André Béteille. Baltimore, Md.: Penguin Books, pp. 9–14.

Béteille, André, ed.

1969 *Social Inequality: Selected Readings.* Baltimore, Md.: Penguin Books.

Birnbaum, Norm

1953 'Conflicting Interpretations of the Rise of Capitalism: Marx and Weber.' *British Journal of Sociology* (vol. 4, no. 2: June), pp. 125–41.

Bix, Herbert

1978 'Kawakami Hajime and the Organic Law of Japanese Fascism.' *Japan Interpreter* (vol. 12, no. 1: Winter), pp. 118–33.

1980 'Japan at the End of the Seventies: the Treatment of the Political in Recent Japanology.' *Bulletin of Concerned Asian Scholars* (vol. 12, no. 1: January–March), pp. 53–60.

Black, Cyril Edwin, *et al.*, eds.

1975 *The Modernization of Japan and Russia.* New York: Free Press.

Blau, Peter M.

1977 *Inequality and Heterogeneity: a Primitive Theory of Social Structure.* New York: Free Press.

Blaug, Mark

1976 *An Introduction to the Economics of Education.* London: Allen Lane.

Blumer, Herbert

1956 'Sociological Analysis and the "Variable".' *American Sociological Review* (vol. 21, no. 6: December), pp. 683–90.

Bottomore, T. B.

1976 *Sociology as Social Criticism.* New York: Morrow.

Broadbridge, Seymour

1966 *Industrial Dualism as a Problem of Economic Growth and Structural Change.* Chicago, Ill.: Aldine.

Brochier, Hubert

1965 *Le Miracle Economique Japonais* (The Economic Miracle of Japan). Paris: Calmann-Lévy.

Broinowski, Richard

1980 'Problems of Communicating Japan to Australia: The Media.' Paper delivered to the Third National Conference of the Asian Studies Association of Australia, Griffith University, Brisbane, 24–29 August.

Brooks, Harvey

1972 'What's Happening to the U.S. Lead in Technology?' *Harvard Business Review* (vol. 50, no. 4: May–June), pp. 110–18.

Brzezinski, Zbigniew

1972 *The Fragile Blossom.* New York: Harper and Row.

Bunka Yoron Kotoba Chōsa Gurūpu

1980 'Gendaijin no Hanashi Kotoba' (Spoken Japanese in Contemporary Japan). *NHK Bunken Geppō* (vol. 32, no. 2: February), pp. 1–15.

Buraku Kaihō Dōmei Ōsaka-fu Rengōkai, ed.

1974 *Gendai no Buraku Kaihō Undō* (The Burakumin Liberation Movement in contemporary Japan). Osaka: Buraku Kaihō Kenkyūsho.

Buraku Kaihō Kenkyūsho, ed.

1981 *Gendai Yūwa Kyōiku Hihan* (A Critique of Contemporary Education for Integrating the Burakumin). Osaka: Kaihō Shuppansha.

Burchfield, R. W.

1976 *A Supplement to the Oxford English Dictionary.* Oxford: Clarendon Press.

Caldarola, Carlo

1972 '*Japanese Society* by Chie Nakane.' *Pacific Affairs* (vol. 44: no. 4: Winter, 1971–1972), pp. 618–21.

Chalmers, Norma

1981 'Japanese Perspectives on Australian Industrial Relations.' *Research Paper* no. 16. Brisbane: Centre for the Study of Australian-Asian Relations, Griffith University.

Chalmers, Norma, and Mitchie, Steven J.

1982 'Business and Media Perceptions of Japan: A Queensland Case Study.' *Research Paper* no. 17. Brisbane: Centre for the Study of Australian-Asian Relations, Griffith University.

Chikazawa, Kei-ichi

1972 *Jisatsu no Kenkyū* (A Study of Suicide). Tokyo: Kurieitosha.

Choo, H. C.

1975 'Some Sources of Relative Equity in Korean Income Distribution: a Historical Perspective.' In *Income Distribution, Employment and Economic Development in Southeast and East Asia,* vol. I, edited by the Japan Economic Research Center and the Council for Asian Manpower Studies. Tokyo: Japan Economic Research Center, pp. 48–72.

Clark, Burton R.

1968 'The Study of Educational Systems.' In *Encyclopedia of the Social Sciences,* edited by David L. Sills. New York: Macmillan and Free Press, vol. 4, pp. 509–11.

Clark, Gregory

1977 *Nihonjin: Yunīkusa no Gensen* (The Japanese: Origins of a Nation's Uniqueness), translated by Ikegami Chizuko. Tokyo: Saimaru Shuppankai.

1981 'The People are the Enterprise.' *PHP* (vol. 12, no. 12: December), pp. 31–58.

Clark, Rodney C.

1979 *The Japanese Company.* New Haven, Conn.: Yale University Press.

Clifford, William

1976 *Crime Control in Japan.* Lexington, Mass.: D. C. Heath.

Cole, Allan B.
1956 *Japanese Society and Politics: the Impact of Social Stratification and Mobility on Politics. Boston University Series in Political Science,* no. 1. Boston, Mass.: Boston University.
Cole, Allan B., Totten, George O., and Uyehara, Cecil H.
1966 *Socialist Parties in Postwar Japan.* New Haven, Conn.: Yale University Press.
Cole, Robert E.
1971a *Japanese Blue Collar.* Berkeley, Cal.: University of California Press.
1971b '*Japanese Society* by Chie Nakane.' *Journal of Asian Studies* (vol. 30, no. 3: May), pp. 678–9.
1972a 'Amerika no Nihon Rōshi Kankeikan to Genjitsu' (The American View of Labor-Management Relations in Japan and the Reality). *NRKZ* (vol. 14, no. 8: August), pp. 27–33.
1972b 'Permanent Employment in Japan: Facts and Fantasies.' *Industrial and Labor Relations Review* (vol. 26, no. 1: October), pp. 615–30.
1979 *Work, Mobility and Participation: a Comparative Study of American and Japanese Industry.* Berkeley, Cal.: University of California Press.
Cole, Robert E., and Tominaga, Ken-ichi
1976 'Japan's Changing Occupational Structure and Its Significance.' In *Japanese Industrialization and Its Social Consequences,* edited by Hugh Patrick (with Larry Meissner). Berkeley, Cal.: University of California Press, pp. 53–95.
Colfax, J. David, and Roach, Jack L., eds.
1971 *Radical Sociology.* New York: Basic Books.
Collins, Randall
1975 *Conflict Sociology: toward an Explanatory Science.* New York: Academic Press.
Connerton, Paul
1977 *Critical Sociology.* Ringwood: Penguin Books.
Cook, Alice
1966 *Japanese Trade Unionism.* Ithaca, N.Y.: Cornell University Press.
Cooper, Gary M.
1976 *Would You Care to Comment on That Sir?* Tokyo: Nihon Keizai Shinbunsha.
Cotgrove, Stephen
1967 *The Science of Society.* London: Allen and Unwin.
Craig, Albert M.
1975 'Functional and Dysfunctional Aspects of Government Bureaucracy.' In *Modern Japanese Organization and Decision-Making,* edited by Ezra Vogel. Berkeley, Cal.: University of California Press, pp. 3–32.
Craig, Albert M., and Shively, Donald H., eds.
1970 *Personality in Japanese History.* Berkeley, Cal.: University of

California Press.

Crawcour, Sydney

1977 'The Japanese Employment System: Past, Present and Future.' Research Paper (March). Canberra: Australia-Japan Economic Research Project.

1982 'Alternative Models of Japanese Society: an Overview.' In *Japanese Society: Reappraisals and New Directions,* edited by Yoshio Sugimoto and Ross Mouer as a special issue of *Social Analysis* (nos. 5/6: December 1980), pp. 184–7.

Cummings, William K.

1972 *Nihon no Daigaku Kyōju* (The Changing Academic Marketplace and University Reform in Japan), translated by Iwauchi Ryōichi and Tomoda Yasumasa. Tokyo: Shiseidō.

1980 *Education and Inequality in Japan.* Princeton, N.J.: Princeton University Press.

Cutright, Phillips

1967 'Income Distribution: A Cross-National Analysis.' *American Sociological Review* (vol. 32, no. 4: August), pp. 562–78.

Dahrendorf, Ralf

1969a 'Social Structure, Group Interests and Conflict Groups.' Reprinted from *Class and Class Conflict in Industrial Society* in *Structured Social Inequality: A Reader in Comparative Social Stratification,* edited by Celia Heller. New York: Macmillan, pp. 488–96.

1969b 'On the Origin of Inequality among Men.' In *Social Inequality: Selected Readings,* edited by André Béteille. Baltimore, Md.: Penguin Books, pp. 30–40.

Dai-hyaku Seimei (Dai-hyaku Life Insurance)

1981 'Shufu no Risō no Rōōfujinzō' (Housewives' Ideal Images of Old Women). In *Nippon Nandemo 10-ketsu* (Japan's Top Ten in Every Field), edited by Shūkan Daiyamondo. Tokyo: Daiyamondosha, p. 32.

Davis, Kingsley, and Moore, Wilbert E.

1945 'Some Principles of Stratification.' *American Sociological Review* (vol. 10, no. 2: April), pp. 242–9.

Davis, Paul A.

1978 'Long-Term Contracts with Japan.' *Research Paper,* no. 50. Canberra: Australia-Japan Economic Relations Research Project.

Davis, Winston

1982 'Japan as "Paradigm": Imitation vs. Insight.' *Christianity and Crisis* (20 September), pp. 254–60.

Dawe, Alan

1970 'The Two Sociologies.' *British Journal of Sociology* (vol. 21, no. 2: June), pp. 207–18.

Deacon, Richard

1982 *A History of the Japanese Secret Service.* London: Frederick Muller.

De Vera, Jose M.

1982 'Communication between Japan and Europe: The Next Decade.' In *Papers Presented at the Fifth Kyushu International Cultural Conference.* Fukuoka: Fukuoka UNESCO Association, pp. D3.1-D3.6.

DeVos, George A.

1972 'Apprenticeship and Paternalism: Psychological Continuities Underlying Japanese Social and Economic Organization.' Paper presented at the Colloquium, Center for Japanese and Korean Studies, University of California, Berkeley, Cal., 12 December.

1973 *Socialization for Achievement: Essays on the Cultural Psychology of the Japanese.* Berkeley, Cal.: University of California Press.

1975 'Apprenticeship and Paternalism.' In *Modern Japanese Organizations and Decision-Making,* edited by Ezra Vogel. Berkeley, Cal.: University of California Press, pp. 210–27.

DeVos, George A., and Wagatsuma, Hiroshi

1967 *Japan's Invisible Race: Caste in Culture and Personality.* Berkeley, Cal.: University of California Press.

Doi, Takeo

1962 'Understanding Japanese Personality Structure.' In *Japanese Culture: Its Development and Characteristics,* edited by Robert J. Smith and Richard K. Beardsley., Chicago, Ill.: Aldine, pp. 132–9.

1967 'Giri-Ninjo: An Interpretation.' In *Aspects of Social Change in Modern Japan,* edited by Ronald P. Dore. Princeton, N.J.: Princeton University Press, pp. 327–34.

1971 *Amae no Kōzō* (Patterns of Dependence). Tokyo: Kōbundō.

1973 *The Anatomy of Dependence,* translated by John Bester. Tokyo: Kodansha International.

Dōmeki, Kyōsaburō

1982 'Nihon no Bunka Chizu: Japan' (A Cultural Map of Nihon: 'Japan'). *ASY* (23–27 August), p. 5.

Dore, Ronald P.

1958 *City Life in Japan.* Berkeley, Cal.: University of California Press.

1965 *Education in Tokugawa Japan.* London: Routledge and Kegan Paul.

1967 'Introduction.' In *Aspects of Social Change in Modern Japan,* edited by Ronald P. Dore. Princeton, N.J.: Princeton University Press, pp. 3–24.

1970 'The Future of Japan's Meritocracy.' *Bulletin* (of the International House of Japan) no. 26: October, pp. 30–50.

1971 'Commitment–To What, by Whom and Why?' In *Social and Cultural Background of Labor-Management Relations in Asian Countries.* Proceedings of the 1971 Asian Regional Conference on

Industrial Relations held in Tokyo during March. Tokyo: Japan Institute of Labor, pp. 106–26.

1973 *British Factory–Japanese Factory: the Origins of Diversity in Industrial Relations.* Berkeley, Cal.: University of California Press.

Douglas, Roger

1979 'Data on Demonstrations in Australia.' Unpublished data, Department of Legal Studies, La Trobe University.

Dower, John W.

1975a 'E. H. Norman and the Uses of History. ' In *Origins of the Modern Japanese State: Selected Writings of E. H. Norman,* edited by John Dower, New York: Pantheon Books, pp. 3–101.

1975b 'Occupied Japan as History and Occupation History as Politics.' *Journal of Asian Studies* (vol. 34, no. 2: February), pp. 485–504.

Downard, J. Douglas

1978 'Survey of Former Japan Foundation Fellowship Recipients.' Mimeographed paper.

Dowsey, Stuart, ed.

1970 *Zengakuren: Japan's Revolutionary Students.* Berkeley, Cal.: University of California Press.

Duke, C. Benjamin

1966 'The Karachi Plan — Master Design for Compulsory Education.' *International Review of Education* (vol. 12, no. 1), pp. 73–9.

Earhart, H. Byron

1974 *Religion in the Japanese Experience: Sources and Interpretations.* Belmont, Cal.: Dickenson.

Egawa, Kiyoshi

1980 'Gendai-jin no Hanashi Kotoba' (Colloquial Language of Contemporary Japanese). *Kotoba Shirīzu 12: Hanashi Kotoba* (Colloquial Japanese). Tokyo: Bunkachō.

Egawa, Kiyoshi, Takada, Makoto, and Nemoto, Kesao

1970 'Madoguchi no Kotoba to Ishiki' (Some Subjective Dimensions of the Vocabulary Used at Work). *Gengo Seikatsu* (no. 223: April), pp. 28–39.

Eguchi, Eiichi, *et al.*

1979 *Sanya: Shitsugyō no Gendaiteki Imi* (Sanya: Being Unemployed in Contemporary Times). Kyoto: Miraisha.

Embree, John F.

1972 *Suye Mura: a Japanese Village.* Chicago, Ill.: University of Chicago Press.

1978 *Nihon no Mura-Suemura* (Suye Mura: A Japanese Village). Tokyo: Nihon Keizai Hyōronsha.

Eunson, Roby

1965 *100 Years: the Amazing Development of Japan Since 1860.* Tokyo: Kodansha International.

Evans, Robert, Jr.
1971 *The Labor Economics of Japan and the United States.* New York: Praeger.

Fanon, Franz
1965 *The Wretched of the Earth*, translated by Constance Farrington, New York: Grove Press.
1967a *Black Skin, White Masks*, translated by Charles L. Markmann. New York: Grove Press.
1967b *A Dying Colonialism*, translated by Haakon Chevalier. New York: Grove Press.

Farmer, John S., and Henley, W. E.
1965 *Slang and its Analogues: Past and Present.* New York: Kraus Reprint Corporation. Originally published by Routledge and Kegan Paul (London), 1890–1904.

Frankland, Mark
1972 'Strange Forces Drive Japan: What Lies Beneath the Country's Superficial Similarities with the West.' An article originally published in the *Observer* (London) and subsequently reprinted in *AEN* (11 October), p. 5.

Frazer, Patrick, and Vittas, Dimitri
1982 *The Retail Banking Revolution.* London: Michael Lafferty.

Fudesaka, Hideyo
1983 *Yūzai: Tanaka Kakuei* (Tanaka Kakuei: Guilty!). Tokyo: Tōkei Shuppan.

Fujii, Toshiko, and Takahashi, Hisako
1972 *Fujin Rōdō no Chishiki* (Basic Information about Women at Work). Tokyo: Nihon Keizai Shinbunsha.

Fujita, Wakao
1955 *Dainikumiai* (The Second Union). Tokyo: Nihon Hyōron Shinsha.
1972 *Nihon no Rōdō Kumiai* (Japanese Labor Unions). Tokyo: Nihon Rōdō Kyōkai.

Fujiwara, Hajime, Hayakawa, Sei, and Matsuzawa, Hirobumi
1982 *Nihonjinron no Otoshiana* (The Shortcomings of *Nihonjinron*). Tokyo: Yamate Shobō.

Fukada, Yūsuke
1975 *Shin Seiyō Jijō* (An Updated Report on the West). Tokyo: Hokuyōsha.
1976 *Seiyō Kōsai Shimatsu* (The State of the Dialogue with the West). Tokyo: Bungei Shunjū.

Fukutake, Tadashi
1949 *Nihon Nōson no Shakaiteki Seikaku* (The Social Characteristics of Japanese Agricultural Communities). Tokyo: Tokyo Daigaku Shuppankai.

1974 *Japanese Society Today.* Tokyo: University of Tokyo Press.

Funabashi, Naomichi

1971a 'Kijun Seikeihi Settei no Konnichiteki Ishiki' (The Relevance of Setting up Criteria for Measuring the Standard of Living Expenses). In *Kijun Seikatsuhi no Kenkyū* (Research on Standard Living Expenses), edited by Funabashi Naomichi. Tokyo: Nihon Rōdō Kyōkai, pp. 3–11.

1971b *Tenkanki no Chingin Mondai* (The Japanese Wage System at a Turning-point). Tokyo: Nihon Hyōronsha.

Galbraith, John Kenneth

1956 *American Capitalism: the Concept of Countervailing Power.* Boston, Mass.: Houghton Mifflin.

Galenson, Walter, and Odaka, Kōnosuke

1976 'The Japanese Labor Market.' In *Asia's New Giant,* edited by Hugh Patrick and Henry Rosowski. Washington, DC: Brookings Institute, pp. 587–671.

Gendai Shakaigaku Kaigi, ed.

1980 *Nihon Shakairon* (Theories of Japanese Society). A special issue of *Gendai Shakaigaku* (Contemporary Sociology) (vol. 7, no. 1: June).

Genji, Keita

1972 *The Guardian God of Golf and other Humorous Stories,* translated by Hugh Cortazzi. Tokyo: Japan Times.

George, Aurelia

1982 'The Comparative Study of Interest Groups in Japan: The Need for an Institutional Framework.' Paper presented to the International Colloquium on the Comparative Study of Japanese Society, Noosa Heads, Queensland, Australia, 29 January–6 February.

Gerzon, Mark

1982 *A Choice of Heroes: The Changing Faces of America's Manhood.* Boston, Mass.: Houghton Mifflin

Gibney, Frank

1982 *Miracle by Design.* New York: Times Books.

Glazer, Nathan

1974 'From Ruth Benedict to Herman Kahn: The Postwar Japanese Image in the American Mind.' *Bulletin* (of the International House of Japan) no. 32, pp. 22–5.

1975 'From Ruth Benedict to Herman Kahn: The Postwar Japanese Image in the American Mind.' In *Mutual Images: Essays in American-Japanese Relations,* edited by Akira Iriye. Cambridge, Mass.: Harvard University Press, pp. 138–68.

Glenn, Norval D., Alston, Jan P., and Weiner, David

1970 *Social Stratification: a Research Bibliography.* Berkeley, Cal.: Glendessary Press.

Gordon, Milton

1958 *Social Class in American Sociology.* Durham, N.C.: Duke University Press.

Goulet, Denis

1971 *The Cruel Choice: a New Concept in the Theory of Development.* Philadelphia, Penn.: Atheneum.

Greenstein, Fred I.

1982 *The Hidden-Hand Presidency: Eisenhower as Leader.* New York: Basic Books.

Guillain, Robert

1970 *The Japanese Challenge: Race to the Year Two Thousand,* translated from French by Patrick O'Brian. Philadelphia, Penn.: Lippincott.

Gunji, Kazuo

1982 *NHK Zankoku Monogatari* (The Cruel Story at NHK). Tokyo: Ēru Shuppansha.

Hadley, Eleanor M.

1970 Antitrust in Japan. Princeton, N.J.: Princeton University Press.

Haga, Yaichi

1938 *Kokuminsei 10-ron* (Ten Discourses on Japanese National Character). Tokyo: Fuzanbō.

Hall, Edward T.

1959 *The Silent Language.* Garden City, N.Y.: Doubleday.

Hall, John W.

1965a 'Changing Concepts of the Modernization of Japan.' In *Changing Japanese Attitudes toward Modernization,* edited by Marius B. Jansen. Princeton, N. J.: Princeton University Press, pp. 7–41.

1965b 'Education and Modern National Development.' In *Twelve Doors to Japan,* edited by John Whitney Hall and Richard K. Beardsley. New York: McGraw-Hill, pp. 384–426.

1966 *Government and Local Power in Japan 500 to 1700: a Study Based on Bizen Province.* Princeton, N.J.: Princeton University Press.

1971 'Thirty Years of Japanese Studies in America.' *Transactions of the Sixteenth International Conference of Orientalists in Japan.* Tokyo: Tōhō Gakkai, pp. 22–35.

Hall, John W., and Beardsley, Richard K.

1965 *Twelve Doors to Japan.* New York: McGraw Hill.

Halliday, Jon

1975 *A Political History of Japanese Capitalism.* New York: Pantheon Books.

Halliday, Jon, and McCormack, Gavan

1973 *Japanese Imperialism Today.* London: Penguin Books.

Halloran, Richard

1970 *Japan: Images and Realities.* Tokyo: Charles E. Tuttle.

Hamada, Tomoko

1980 'Winds of Change: Economic Realism and Japanese Labor

Management.' *Asian Survey* (vol. 20, no. 4: April), pp. 397–408.
Hamaguchi, Eshun
1982 *Kanjin Shugi no Shakai: Nihon* (Japan: The Society of Interactive Persons). Tokyo: Tōyō Keizai Shinpōsha.
Hamaguchi, Eshun, ed.
1982 *Nihon no Aida gara* (The 'Interpersonalness' of the Japanese). A special issue of *Gendai no Esupuri* (no. 178: May).
Hanami, Tadashi
1971 'The Characteristics of Labor Disputes and Their Settlements in Japan: In Order to Examine the Functions and Cultural Norms in Japan.' In *Social and Cultural Background of Labor-Management Relations in Asian Countries.* Proceedings of the 1971 Asian Regional Conference on Industrial Relations held in Tokyo during March. Tokyo: Japan Institute of Labor, pp. 206–20.
1973 *Rōdō Sōgi: Rōshi Kankei ni Miru Nihonteki Fūdo* (Industrial Disputes: the Japanese Element in Industrial Relations). Tokyo: Nihon Keizai Shinbunsha.
1979 *Labour Law and Industrial Relations in Japan.* Deventer: Kluwer.
1981 *Labor Relations in Japan Today.* Tokyo: Kodansha International.
Hanami, Tadashi, Kōshiro, Kazutoshi, and Inagami, Takeshi
1977 'Worker Participation in Management Today.' *Japan Labor Bulletin* (vol. 16, no. 8: August), pp. 5–8; (vol. 16, no. 9: September), pp. 5–8.
Hane, Mikiso
1982 *Peasants, Rebels, and Outcasts: the Undesirable of Modern Japan.* New York: Pantheon Books.
Harada, Shūichi
1968 *Labor Conditions in Japan.* New York: AMS Press.
Hasegawa, Nyozekan
1966 *The Japanese Character: a Cultural Profile,* translated by John Bester. Tokyo: Kodansha International.
Hasegawa, Takuya
1979 *Saikin no Waisetsu Shuppan: 1963–1979* (Recent Pornographic Publications: 1963–1979). Tokyo: San-ichi Shobō.
Hatano, Seiichi
1963 *Time and Eternity,* translated by Suzuki Ichirō. Tokyo: Japanese Government Printing Bureau.
Havens, Thomas R. H.
1982 *Artist and Patron in Postwar Japan: Dance, Music Theatre and the Visual Arts.* Princeton, N.J.: Princeton University Press.
Hayashi, Michiyoshi, and Sano, Yoshiko
1974 *Kinrin Sōon: Chiisana Oto no Bōryoku to no Tatakai* (Neighborhood Noise Pollution: Struggle against Noise Problems). Tokyo: Nippō.
Hayashi, Ōki, *et al.* eds.

1982 *Zusetsu Nihongo* (A Guide to the Study of the Japanese Language). Tokyo: Kadokawa Shoten.

Hayashi, Shirō

1974 *Gengo Hyōgen no Kōzō* (The Structure of Expression in Language). Tokyo: Meiji Shoin.

Hazama, Hiroshi

1964 *Nihon Rōmu Kanri Kenkyū* (Studies on Japanese Personnel Practices). Tokyo: Daiyamondosha.

1971 *Nihonteki Keiei Shūdan Shugi no Kōzai* (The Japanese Approach to Management: Strengths and Weaknesses). Tokyo: Nihon Keizai Shinbunsha.

Hazama, Shinjirō

1960 'Shin Chūkan Kaikyū no Mondai' (The Problem of the New Middle Class). *Nihon Hōgaku* (vol. 26, no. 5: December), pp. 27–49.

Hearn, Lafcadio

1913 *Japan: An Interpretation* (New Impression 1913, Reprinted 1956). New York: Macmillan.

Hedberg, Hakan

1970 *Nihon no Chōsen: 1980-nendai no Keizai Chōtaikoku* (The Japanese Challenge: Superstate of the 1980s), translated from Swedish by Sekiguchi Yasushi. Tokyo: Mainichi Shinbunsha.

Heller, Celia

1969 'General Introduction.' In *Structured Social Inequality: a Reader in Comparative Social Stratification,* edited by Celia Heller. New York: Macmillan, pp. 1–6.

Hidaka, Rokurō

1960 *1960-nen 5-gatsu 19-nichi* (May 19, 1960). Tokyo: Iwanami Shoten.

1980 *Sengo Shisō o Kangaeru* (Reflections on Postwar Japanese Thought). Tokyo: Iwanami Shoten.

1982a 'Nihonjinron ni Tsuite' (On *Nihonjinron*). Foreword in *Nihonjinron ni Kansuru 12-shō* (Twelve Chapters on *Nihonjinron*), edited by Ross E. Mouer and Yoshio Sugimoto. Tokyo: Gakuyō Shobō, pp. 3–5.

1982b 'Nihon no Masukomi no Zeze-Hihi Shugi' (Middle-of-the-roadism of Japanese Mass Media). Paper presented to the International Colloquium on the Comparative Study of Japanese Society, Noosa Heads, Queensland, Australia, 29 January–6 February.

Higgins, Ronald

1980 *The Seventh Enemy: the Human Factor in the Global Crisis.* Sydney: Pan Books.

Higuchi, Kiyoyuki

1972 *Nihon no Chie no Kōzō* (The Structure of Japanese Intelligence). Tokyo: Kōdansha.

Hijikata, Kazuo

1982 '"Nihon Bunkaron" no Bunkashi' (Cultural History of 'Theories of Japanese Culture'). *Yuibutsuron Kenkyū* (no. 6: April), pp. 25–35.

Hirai, Tomio
1981 *Nihonteki Chisei to Shinri* (The Psychology and Intelligence of the Japanese). Tokyo: Mikasa Shobō.

Hirose, Katsuyo
1981 *Josei to Hanzai* (Females and Crime) Tokyo: Kongō Shuppan.

Hitotsubashi Keizai Kenkyūsho (Hitotsubashi Economic Research Institute), ed.
1961 *Nihonkeizai Tōkei: Tōkei ni yoru Sengo no Bunseki no Tame ni* (Japan's Economic Statistics: with an Emphasis on Those Necessary for Analyzing the Postwar Years). Tokyo: Iwanami Shoten.

Hodges, Harold
1964 *Social Stratification.* Cambridge, Mass.: Schenkman.

Hodgson, James D.
1977 *The Wondrous Working World of Japan.* Washington, D.C.: American Enterprise Institute.

Hollerman, Leon
1967 *Japan's Dependence on the World Economy: the Approach Toward Economic Liberalization.* Princeton, N.J.: Princeton University Press.

Hōmushō Hōmu Sōgō Kenkyūsho (Ministry of Justice, General Research Institute), ed.
1981 *Hanzai Hakusho* (White Paper on Crimes). Tokyo: Ōkurashō Insatsukyoku.

Honda, Katsuichi
1968 *Senjō no Mura* (From a War-torn Village). Tokyo: Asahi Shinbunsha.
1970 *Amerika Gasshūkoku* (The United States of America). Tokyo: Asahi Shinbunsha.

Honda, Katsuichi, ed.
1979 *Kodomotachi no Fukushū* (Revenge of the Children). 2 vols. Tokyo: Asahi Shinbunsha.

Horie, Masanori
1962 *Nihon no Rōdōsha Kaikyū* (The Working Class in Japan). Tokyo: Iwanami Shoten.

Horie, Masanori, ed.
1969 *Nihon no Hinkon Chitai* (Japan's Poverty Areas). 2 vols. Tokyo: Shin Nihon Shuppansha.

Horowitz, David, ed.
1971 *Radical Sociology: an Introduction.* San Francisco, Cal.: Canfield Press.

Horvats, Andrew
1978 'The Myth of the "Unique" Japanese.' *PHP* (vol. 9, no. 5: May), pp. 73–81.

Hoshino, Akira
1981 'The Future of Japanese Identity.' Paper prepared for the Seminar

on the Challenge of Japan's Internationalization: Organization and Culture, Kwansei Gakuin University Seminar House, Santa, Hyōgo-ken, 30 June–5 July.

Hoshino, Kanehiro

1981 *Hanzai Shakaigaku Genron* (The Basic Principles of a Sociological Theory of Deviant Behavior). Tokyo: Tachibana Shobō.

Hosoi, Wakizō

1947 *Jokō Aishi* (The Tragic History of the Factory Girls). Tokyo: Kaizōsha.

Huddle, Norie, Reich, Michael, and Stiskin, Nahum

1975 *Island of Dreams: Environmental Crisis in Japan.* Tokyo: Autumn Press.

Huffman, James L.

1980 *Politics of the Meiji Press.* Honolulu, Hawaii: University of Hawaii Press.

Ichibangase, Yasuko

1958 'Tei Shotoku Kaisō ni kansuru Kenkyū no Keifu' (An Outline of Previous Research on the Low Income Strata). In *Nihon no Hinkon: Bōdārain Kaisō no Kenkyū* (Poverty in Japan: a Study of the Borderline Stratum), edited by Nihon Shakai Fukushi Gakkai (The Association for Social Welfare in Japan). Tokyo: Yūhikaku.

Ide, Sakuo, and Takeuchi, Atsuhiko

1980 'Jiba Sangyō: Localized Industry.' In *Geography of Japan,* edited by the Association of Japanese Geographers. Tokyo: Teikoku Shoin, pp. 299–319.

Ienaga, Saburō

1977 *Ichi Rekishi Gakusha no Ayumi* (A Personal History of a Historian). Tokyo: Sanseidō.

Iida, Tsuneo

1979 *Nihonteki Chikarazuyosa no Saihakken: Nihon Keizairon no Jōshiki o Naosu* (Toward a Rediscovery of Japan's Real Strengths: a Reappraisal of Commonly Accepted Explanations of the Japanese Economy). Tokyo: Nihon Keizai Shinbunsha.

1981 *Watakushi no Keizaigaku Hihan* (A Personal Critique of Economics). Tokyo: Tōyō Keizai Shinpōsha.

Ikeda, Makoto

1970 *Nihon Kikaikō Kumiai Shiron* (The History of the Founding of the Japan Machinists' Union). Tokyo: Nihon Hyōronsha.

Ikeda, Makoto, and Ōmae, Sakurō

1966 *Nihon Rōdō Undō Shiron: Taishō 10-nen no Kawasaki Mitsubishi Kōbe Ryō Zōsenjo Sōgi no Kenkyū* (Studies on the History of the Japanese Labor Movement: the 1921 Strikes at the Kōbe Shipbuilding Plants of both Kawasaki and Mitsubishi). Tokyo: Nihon Hyōronsha.

Ikumi, Takuichi, Imai, Noriyoshi, and Nagasu, Kazuji, eds.
1966 *Gendai Nihon Shihonshugi Kōza* (Lectures on Capitalism in Postwar Japan). 3 vols. Tokyo: Nihon Hyōronsha.

Imahori, Seiji
1974 *Gensuibaku Kinshi Undō* (The Movement Against Atomic and Hydrogen Bombs). Tokyo: San-ichi Shobō.

Inaba, Michio
1972 'Gendai Shakai no Toraekata' (Approaches to the Study of Modern Society). In *Kaikyū Shakairon* (Social Stratification), edited by Tsujimura Akira. *Shakaigaku Kōza* (Lectures in Sociology), vol. 13. Tokyo: Tokyo Daigaku Shuppankai, pp. 11–30.

Inagaki, Masami
1972 *Heieki o Kyohi shita Nihonjin* (The Japanese who Refused to be Conscripted). Tokyo: Iwanami Shoten.

Inagaki, Yoshihiko, Ishino, Hiroshi, and Saijō, Katsuya
1981 'Chūgakusei no Gengo Kankaku (The Sense of Language Developed among Middle-school Students). *NHK Bunken Geppō* (vol. 31, no. 5: May), pp. 25–36.

Inkeles, Alex, and Rossi, Peter
1956 'National Comparisons of Occupational Prestige.' *American Journal of Sociology* (vol. 61, no. 4: January), pp. 329–39.

Inoguchi, Rikihei, Nakajima, Tadashi, and Pineau, Roger
1958 *The Divine Wind.* New York: Ballantine Books.

Inoguchi, Takashi
1980 'Economic Conditions and Mass Support in Japan: 1960–1976.' In *Models of Political Economy,* edited by P. Whiteley. London: Sage, pp. 121–51.
1981 'Explaining and Predicting Japanese Elections, 1960–1980.' *Journal of Japanese Studies* (vol. 7, no. 2: Summer), pp. 285–318.

Inoue, Kiyoshi
1963–6 *Nihon no Rekishi* (Japanese History). 3 vols. Tokyo: Iwanami Shoten.
1969 *Taishōki no Seiji Shakai* (Politics and Society in Taishō Japan). Tokyo: Iwanami Shoten.

Inoue, Kiyoshi, and Watanabe, Tōru, eds.
1959–61 *Kome Sōdō no Kenkyū* (Study of Rice Riots). 5 vols. Tokyo: Yūhikaku.

International House of Japan
1974 *Japanese Social Science Works: a Bibliography of Translations, English, French and German.* Tokyo: International House of Japan.

Iremonger, John, Merritt, John, and Osborne, Graeme, eds.
1973 *Strikes: Studies in Twentieth Century Australian Social History.* Sydney: Angus and Robertson.

Irokawa, Daikichi
1979 *Santama Jiyū Minken Shiryōshū* (Collection of Historical Documents of Civil Rights Movements in the Santama Region). Tokyo: Yamato Shobō.
Irokawa, Daikichi, Ei, Hideo, and Arai, Katsuhiro
1970 *Minshū Kenpō no Sōzō* (The Creation of the People's Constitution). Tokyo: Hyōronsha.
Ishida, Hideo
1976 *Nihon no Rōshi Kankei to Chingin Kettei* (Wage Determination and Labor-Management Relations in Japan). Tokyo: Tōyō Keizai Shinpōsha.
Ishida, Takeshi
1970 *Nihon no Seiji Bunka–Dōchō to Kyōsō* (Japanese Political Culture: Conformity and Competition). Tokyo: Tokyo Daigaku Shuppankai.
1971 *Japanese Society.* New York: Random House.
Ishihara, Shū
1913 *Jokō to Kekkaku* (Girl Factory Hands and Tuberculosis). Tokyo: Kokka Igakukai.
Ishikawa, Hiroshi, and Ujikawa, Makoto
1961 *Nihon no Howaitokarā* (Japan's White-collar Group). Tokyo: Nihon Seisansei Honbu.
Isomura, Eiichi, ed.
1962 *Nihon no Suramu* (Japan's Slums). Tokyo: Seishin Shobō.
Itasaka, Gen
1971 *Nihonjin no Ronri Kōzō* (The Logical Structure of the Japanese). Tokyo: Kōdansha.
Itō, Mitsuharu
1972 *Seikatsu no Naka no Keizaigaku* (The Economics of Everyday Living). Tokyo: Asahi Shinbunsha.
Iwao, Sumiko, Hagiwara, Shigeru, and Mouer, Ross
1980 'Ōsutoraria no Daigakusei no Tainichi Imji' (The Image of Japan held by Australian University Students). In *Nihon Shakai Shinri Gakkai Dai 21 Taikai* (Proceedings of the Japanese Association of Social Psychologists). Nishinomiya: Kwansei Gakuin Daigaku, pp. 35–38.
Iwata, Ryūshi
1977 *Nihonteki Keiei no Hensei Genri* (Basic Principles in the Structure of Japanese-style Management). Tokyo: Bunshindō.
1978 *Gendai Nihon no Keiei Fūdo* (Managerial Style in Modern Japan). Tokyo: Nihon Keizai Shinbunsha.
1980 *Nihonteki Sensu no Keieigaku: Jikkan kara no Shuppatsu* (For a Japanese Theory of Management: Subjective Experience as a Starting-point). Tokyo: Tōyō Keizai Shinpōsha.
1981 *Gakurekishugi no Hatten Kōzō* (The Development of a Philosophy Emphasizing School-based Careers). Tokyo: Nihon Hyōronsha.

1982 'Nihonteki Keiei o Kangaeru' (Some Thoughts on Japanese-style Management). *NKSY* (10 June), p. 3.

Iwauchi, Ryūichi

1980 *Gakurekishugi wa Hōkai Shitaka* (Has the Emphasis on School-based Careers Waned?). Tokyo: Nihon Keizai Shinbunsha.

Jameson, Sam

1973 'A Look at Japan's Financial Future with Herman Kahn.' *JTW* (15 September), p. 10.

Jansen, Marius B.

1965 'Changing Japanese Attitudes toward Modernization.' In *Changing Japanese Attitudes toward Modernization,* edited by Marius B. Jansen. Princeton, N.J.: Princeton University Press, pp. 44–89.

Japan Culture Institute (Nihon Bunka Kenkyūsho)

1971 *Great Historical Figures of Japan.* Tokyo: Nihon Bunka Kenkyūsho.

Jay, Peter

1972 'Face of Asia behind Western Mask.' An article originally published in *The Times* (London) and reprinted in *AEN* (29 June), p. 5; (30 June), p. 5.

Johnson, Chalmers

1972 *Conspiracy at Matsukawa.* Berkeley, Cal.: University of California Press.

1975 'Japan: Who Governs? An Essay on Official Bureaucracy.' *Journal of Japanese Studies* (vol. 2, no. 1: Autumn), pp. 1–28.

1978 *Japan's Public Policy Companies.* Washington, DC: American Enterprise Institute.

1982 *MITI and the Japanese Miracle: the Growth of Industrial Policy, 1925–1975.* Stanford, Cal.: Stanford University Press.

Johnson, Sharon

1982 'Japan Comes to the Campus.' *This World* (a supplement to the *San Francisco Chronicle,* 16 May), p 24.

Jones, George E., with English, Carey W.

1982 'Social Sciences: Why Doubts are Spreading Now.' *U.S. News and World Report* (31 May), pp. 70–1.

Kagayama, Takashi

1970 *Teishotokusō to Hihogosō* (The Low-income Strata and Welfare Recipients). Kyoto: Minerva Shobō.

Kahl, Joseph A., and Davis, James A.

1955 'A Comparison of Indexes of Socio-Economic Status.' *American Sociological Review* (vol. 20, no. 3: June), pp. 317–25.

Kahn, Herman

1970 *The Emerging Japanese Superstate: Challenge and Response.* Englewood Cliffs, N.J.: Prentice Hall.

Kahn, Herman, and Pepper, Thomas

1978 *Soredemo Nihon wa Seichō Suru: Hikanbyō Dasshutsu no Susume*

(Even so Japan will Grow: the Escape from Pessimism), translated by Ueno Akira *et al.* Tokyo: Saimaru Shuppankai.

1979 *The Japanese Challenge: the Success and Failure of Economic Success.* New York: Thomas Y. Crowell.

Kaji, Etsuko

1973 'The Invisible Proletariat: Working Women in Japan.' *AMPO* (no. 18: Autumn), pp. 45–58.

Kajinishi, Mitsuhaya, Ōshima, Kiyoshi, Katō, Toshihiko, and Ōuchi, Tsutomu, eds.

1953 *Nihon ni okeru Shihonshugi no Hatten* (Development of Capitalism in Japan). 13 vols. Tokyo: Tokyo Daigaku Shuppankai.

Kakegawa, Tomiko, ed.

1976 *Shisō Tōsei* (Thought Control). *Gendaishi Shiryō* (Materials and Documents on Modern History), vol. 42. Tokyo: Misuzu Shobō.

Kamata, Satoshi

1973 *Jidōsha Zetsubō Kōjō–Aru Kisetsukō no Nikki* (Deadened at the Auto Plant: the Diary of a Seasonal Employee). Tokyo: Gendaishi Shuppansha.

1974 *Rōdō Genba no Hanran–Hachi Kigyō ni Miru Gōrika to Rōdō no Kaitai* (Rebellion on the Job: Rationalization and Labor Disorganization at Eight Firms). Tokyo: Daiyamondosha.

1977 *Shokuba ni Tatakai no Toride o* (Focus on the Embattled Fortress at Work). Tokyo: Satsukisha.

1980 *Rōdō Genba: Zōsenjo de nani ga Okotta ka.* (At the Place of Work: What Goes on at the Shipbuilding Yards). Tokyo: Iwanami Shoten.

1982 '"Kyōiku Kōjō" no Kodomotachi' (Children in 'Education Factories'). *Sekai* (no. 440: July), pp. 224–39.

Kamishima, Jirō

1975 *Nihonjin no Hassō* (The Thought Processes of the Japanese). Tokyo: Kōdansha.

Kanamori, Hisao

1972 'Affluence Awaits Japan if She Avoids Pitfalls.' *AEN* (1 April), p. 6.

1976 *Keizai Seichō to Fukushi: GNP and NNW* (Economic Growth and Social Welfare: GNP and NNW). Tokyo: Nihon Keizai Shinbunsha.

Kanda, James

1978 'Methods of Land Transfer in Mediaeval Japan.' *Monumenta Nipponica* (vol. 33, no. 4: Winter), pp. 379–405.

Kaneko, Yoshio

1980 'The Future of the Fixed-Age Retirement System.' In *The Labor Market in Japan,* edited by Nishikawa Shunsaku and translated by Ross Mouer. Tokyo: University of Tokyo Press, pp. 104–23.

Kano, Masanao

1974 'Kinu no Michi to Seishun' (Youth and the Silkroad). In *Shisō o Aruku* (Back through Japan's Intellectual History), edited by Asahi Shinbunsha. Tokyo: Asahi Shinbunsha, vol. 2, pp. 95–117.

Kaplan, Eugene J.

1972 *Japan: The Government–Business Relationship.* Washington, DC: US Government Printing Office.

Karsh, Bernard, and Cole, Robert

1968 'Industrialization and the Convergence Hypothesis: Some Aspects of Contemporary Japan.' *Journal of Social Issues* (vol. 24, no. 4: October), pp. 45–63.

Kasai, Hisako

1981 'Hyōjungo-kei no Zenkoku Bunpu' (Regional Distribution of Patterns of Standard Japanese). *Gengo Seikatsu* (no. 354: July) pp. 52–5.

Kataoka, Yōko

1982 'Yurusenu Mondaiji Tsūhō Seido' (The Unacceptable Practice of Reporting Problem Children). *MSC* (13 October), p. 4.

Katō, Hidetoshi

1957 *Chūkan Bunka* (Middle-brow Culture). Tokyo: Heibonsha.

Katō, Hiroyuki

1882 *Jinken Shinsetsu* (New Theory on People's Rights). Reprinted in vol. 5 of *Meiji Bunka Zenshū* (Collection of Cultural Writings in Meiji Japan, 1967.) Tokyo: Nihon Hyōronsha.

Katō, Shūichi

1956 *Zasshu Bunka* (Hybrid Culture). Tokyo: Kōdansha.

1976 *Nihonjin to wa Nanika* (What are the Japanese?). Tokyo: Kōdansha.

Katō, Shūichi, and Miyazaki, Isamu

1982 '"Hogosha" ga "Higaisha" ni Tenjita Amerika no Senryōsha Ishiki' (When the Protected become the Victims: the Occupation Consciousness of Americans). *AJ* (26 March), pp. 10–17.

Kawai, Takeo

1973 'Gendai Nihon no Kaikyū Kōzō no Henka to Howaito Karā Sō: 1955-nen–1970-nen' (Changes in the Class Structure of Postwar Japan and the White-collar Stratum: 1955–1970). *Hōgaku Kenkyū* (vol. 46, no. 9: September), pp. 31–85

Kawakami, Hajime

1949 *Binbō Monogatari* (The Story of the Poor). Third edition. Tokyo: Iwanami Shoten.

1964 *Gendai Nihon Shisō Taikei* (Series on Modern Japanese Thought). Vol. 19. Tokyo: Chikuma Shobō.

Kawamura, Nozomu

1975 *Nihon Shakaigakushi Kenkyū* (Studies in the History of Japanese Sociology). 2 vols. Tokyo: Ningen no Kagakusha.

1980 'Sociology and Society in Early Modern Japan.' Monograph no. 6 in *La Trobe Sociology Papers*, Department of Sociology, La Trobe University, Bundoora, Victoria, Australia.

1982a 'The Historical Background of Arguments Emphasizing the

Uniqueness of Japanese Society.' In *Japanese Society: Reappraisals and New Directions*, edited by Yoshio Sugimoto and Ross Mouer as a special issue of *Social Analysis* (nos. 5/6: December 1980), pp. 44–62.

1982b *Nihonbunkaron no Shūhen* (Some Arguments on Theories of Japanese Culture). Tokyo: Ningen no Kagakusha.

1982c 'The Transition of the Household System in Modernizing Japan.' Mimeographed paper.

Kawasaki, Jirō

1969 *Japan Unmasked.* Tokyo: Charles E. Tuttle.

1973 *Alien Rice.* Tokyo: Charles E. Tuttle.

1975 *Japon sans Voiles* (Japan Unmasked). Paris-Limoges: Lavauzelle.

Kawashima, Takeyoshi

1950 *Nihon Shakai no Kazoku-teki Kōōsei* (Family System of Japanese Society). Tokyo: Nihon Hyōronsha.

Kazehaya, Yasoji

1973 *Nihon Shakai Seisakushi* (The History of Social Policy in Japan). 2 vols. Tokyo: Aoki Shoten.

Keisatsuchō (Police Agency), ed.

1982 *Keisatsu Hakusho* (Police White Paper). Tokyo: Ōkurashō Insatsukyoku.

Keizai Shingikai (Economic Advisory Council)

1973 *NNW Kaihatsu Iinkai Hōkoku: Atarashii Fukushi Shihyō NNW* (Report of the Sub-Committee to Develop the Concept of NNW as a New Measure of Welfare). Tokyo: Ōkurashō Insatsukyoku.

Keller, Suzanne

1963 *Beyond the Ruling Class: Strategic Elites in Modern Society.* New York: Random House.

Kerr, Clark, Dunlop, John T., Harbison, Frederick H., and Myers, Charles A.

1960 *Industrialism and Industrial Man.* Cambridge, Mass.: Harvard University Press.

1963 *Indasutoriarizumu* (Industrialism), translation supervised by Nakayama Ichirō. Tokyo: Tōyō Keizai Shinpōsha.

Kerr, Clark, and Siegel, Abraham

1954 'Interindustry Propensity to Strike: An International Comparison.' In *Industrial Conflict*, edited by Arthur Kornhauser *et al.* New York: McGraw-Hill, pp. 186–212.

Kikuchi, Sadao

1970 *Hokusai.* Osaka: Hoikusha.

Kinmonth, Earl H.

1981 *The Self-Made Man in Meiji Japanese Thought.* Berkeley, Cal.: University of California Press.

Kishimoto, Eitarō

1955 *Kyūbōka Hōsoku to Shakai Seisaku: Shakai Seisaku kara Shakai*

Hoken e (The Law of Impoverishment and Social Policy: from Social Policy to Social Insurance). Tokyo: Yūhikaku.

1967 *Rōdō Keizai to Shakai Seisaku* (Social Policy and the Labor Economy). Kyoto: Mineruva Shobō.

1969 'Sengo ni okeru Nenkō Chingen no Saihen to Kigyō-betsu Kumiai' (The Reorganization of the Wage System in the Postwar Period and the Enterprise Union). In *Rōdō Keizairon Nyūmon* (An Introduction to Labor Economics), edited by Kishimoto Eitarō. Tokyo: Yūhikaku, pp. 261–301.

Kishimoto, Eitarō, ed.

1969 *Rōdō Keizairon Nyūmon* (An Introduction to Labor Economics). Tokyo: Yūhikaku.

Kitahara, Taisaku

1975 *Buraku Kaihō no Rosen* (Strategies for Liberation of the Burakumin). Kyoto: Buraku Mondai Kenkyūsho Shuppanbu.

Kitamura, Kazuyuki

1972 'The Student Movement.' In *Higher Education and Student Problems*, edited by Kokusai Bunka Shinkōkai. Tokyo: Kokusai Bunka Shinkōkai, pp. 207–29.

Kluckhohn, Florence R., and Strodtbeck, Fred L.

1961 *Variations in Value Orientations*. Evanston, Ill.: Peterson.

Kobayashi, Takiji

1968 *Kōjō Saibō* (The Factory Cell). Tokyo: Shin Nippon Shuppansha.

1969 *Kani Kōsen/Fuzai Jinushi* (The Crab-canning Ship and the Absentee Landlord). Tokyo: Aoki Shoten.

1973 *The Factory Ship and the Absentee Landlord*, translated by Frank Motofuji. Tokyo: University of Tokyo Press.

Kobayashi, Tetsuya

1981 *Kaigai Shijo Kyōiku, Kikoku Shijo Kyōiku* (Education for Japanese Children Overseas and Education for Japanese Children Returning to Japan). Tokyo: Yūhikaku.

Kodomotachi ni Sekai ni! Hibaku no Kioku o Okurukai (The Hiroshima-Nagasaki Publishing Committee).

1978 *Hiroshima-Nagasaki: Genbaku no Kiroku* (A Record of the Atomic Bombings at Hiroshima and Nagasaki). Tokyo: Kodomotachi ni Sekai ni! Hibaku no Kiroku o Okurukai.

Koe naki Koe no Kai

1962 *Mata Demo de Aō* (Let us Meet in Demonstrations Again). Tokyo: Tokyo Shoten.

Kogawa, Tetsuo

1981 'Japan as Manipulated Society.' *Telos* (no. 49: Fall), pp. 138–40.

1982 *Media no Rōgoku* (Media Control). Tokyo: Shōbunsha.

Koike, Kazuo

1976 *Shokuba no Rōdō Kumiai to Sanka: Rōshikankei no Nichibei Hikaku* (Labor Unions and Participation at the Shop Level: a

Comparison of Labor-Management Relations in Japan and the US). Tokyo: Tōyō Keizai Shinpōsha.

1981 *Nippon no Jukuren* (Development of Job Skills in Japan). Tokyo: Yūhikaku.

1982 'QC Sākuru Katsudō no Shojōken–Chōki o Kangaeta Kojin no Kōdō' (Some Factors Affecting Behaviour in Quality Control Circles: a Long-term Perspective on Individual Behavior). Paper presented to the International Colloquium on the Comparative Study of Japanese Society, Noosa Heads, Queensland, Australia: 29 January–6 February.

Koike, Kazuo, and Watanabe, Ikuo

1979a 'Wagakuni no Kyōiku Seido to Kigyō' (The Japanese System of Education and the Business Enterprise). In *Nijūichi Seiki no Rōdō to Shakai: Rōdō Seikatsu no Ningenka o Mezashite* (Work and Society in the Twenty-First Century: For the Humanization of Life at Work), edited by Masamura Kimio *et al.* Tokyo: Gendai Sōgō Kenkyū Shūdan, pp. 193–262.

1979b *Gakureki Shakai no Kyozō* (The School-based Career Society: Fact and Fantasy). Tokyo: Tōyō Keizai Shinpōsha.

Kojima, Kenji

1973 'Atarashii Hinkon to Rōdō Kumiai Undō' (The New Poverty and the Labor Movement). In *Kōza Gendai Nihon Shihonshugi* (Lectures on Capitalism in Postwar Japan), edited by Okakura Koshirō *et al.*, Tokyo: Aoki Shoten, vol. 2, pp. 197–224.

Kojima, Kiyoshi

1971 *Japan and a Pacific Trade Area*. Berkeley, Cal.: University of California Press.

Kokumin Seikatsu Sentā, ed.

1981 *Shōhisha Undō no Genjō to Kadai* (Present and Future Problems of Consumer Movements). Tokyo: Keisō Shobō.

Kokuritsu Kokugo Kenkyūsho

1973 *Shakai Kōzō to Gengo no Kankei ni tsuite no Kisoteki Kenkyū* (Basic Studies of the Relationship between Social Structure and Language). Tokyo: Shūei Shuppan, vol. 3.

1981 *Dai Toshi no Gengo Seikatsu–Bunseki-hen* (Linguistic Life in Large Cities: the Analysis). Tokyo: Sanseidō.

Kokushō, Iwao

1928 *Hyakushō Ikki no Kenkyū* (A Study of Peasant Uprisings). Tokyo: Iwanami Shoten.

Kōmei Senkyo Renmei (Association for Promoting Fair Elections)

1973 *Shūgiin Giin Sōsenkyo no Jittai. Yoron Chōsa Kekka Shiryō: Dai 33-kai Shōwa 47-nen 12-gatsu 10-ka Shikkō* (Realities of the Thirty-third General Election for the House of Representatives on 10 December 1972: Data on the Public Opinion Survey). Tokyo: Kōmeio Senkyo Renmei.

Komuro, Naoki
1982 *Nihon 'Shūgō' Shugi no Maryoku* (The Magical Power of Japanese 'Groupism'). Tokyo: Daiyamodosha.

Kornhauser, William
1959 *The Politics of Mass Society.* New York: Free Press.

Kōsai, Yutaka, and Ogino, Tarō
1980 *Nihon Keizai Tenbō* (Some Views on the Japanese Economy). Tokyo: Nihon Hyōronsha.

Koschmann, J. Victor, ed.
1978 *Authority and the Individual in Japan: Citizen Protest in Historical Perspective.* Tokyo: University of Tokyo Press.

Kōshiro, Kazutoshi
1980 'The Economic Impact of Disputes in the Public Sector.' In *The Labor Market in Japan: Selected Readings*, edited by Nishikawa Shunsaku. Tokyo: University of Tokyo Press, pp. 236–54.
1982a 'Ryōkō na Koyō Kikai no Kishōsei to Nihonteki Rōshi Kankei' (The Scarcity of Good Jobs and Japanese Industrial Relations). *NRKZ* (vol. 24, no. 1: January), pp. 4–13.
1982b 'Industrial Relations in the Japanese Automobile Industry.' *Discussion Paper* no. 82–5. Yokohama: Center for International Trade Studies, Faculty of Economics, Yokohama National University.

Koyama, Hirotake
1953 *Nihon Shihonshugi Ronsōshi* (A History of the Debate on Japanese Capitalism). 2 vols. Tokyo: Aoki Shoten.
1982 *Kōza Konnichi no Nihon Shihonshugi* (Lecture Series on Capitalism in Contemporary Japan). 10 vols. Tokyo: Ōtsuki Shoten.

Kōza Konnichi no Nihon Shihonshugi Henshū Iinkai (The Committee to Edit the Lecture Series on Contemporary Japanese Capitalism), ed.
1982 *Kōza Konnichi no Shihonshugi* (Lecture Series on Capitalism in Contemporary Japan). Tokyo: Ōtsuki Shoten.

Kozeki, Sanpei
1960 *Sakushu to Hinkon no Shakai Mondai* (Exploitation and Poverty as Social Problems). Vol. 1 of *Gendai Nihon no Shakai Mondai* (Social Problems in Modern Japan). Kyoto: Chūbunsha.

Krauss, Ellis, S.
1974 *Japanese Radicals Revisited: Student Protest in Postwar Japan.* Berkeley, Cal.: University of California Press.

Krookow, Christian, Graf, von
1970 'Die Japanische Herausforderung.' Published in *Gewerkschaftliche Monatsheft*, the leading organ of the DGB (the West German Labor Federation). Our knowledge of this article comes from a review by Ōtsuka Ken-ichi, 'C.G. von Kurokkuou Chō-Nihon no Chōsen' (The Japanese Challenge by C. G. von Krookow), *NRKZ* (no. 146: May 1971), pp. 70–8.

Kublin, Hyman

1964 *Asian Revolutionary: the Life of Sen Katayama*. Princeton, N.J.: Princeton University Press.

Kuhn, Thomas

1970 *The Structure of Scientific Revolutions*. Chicago, Ill.: University of Chicago.

Kunihiro, Masao

1978 *Intāmesuchikku Eiji* (The 'Inter-domestic' Age). Tokyo: Sōseiki.

1979 'The Interdomestic Age.' *PHP* (vol. 10, no. 6: June), pp. 6–16 and 77–8.

1980 *Nihonjin wa Kokusaijin ni Nareruka* (Can the Japanese be Internationalists?). Tokyo: Seikyō Shinbunsha.

Kunugi, Teruo

1982 'Shingapōru no Sōdai na Jikken' (The Great Singapore Experiment). *Shūkan Asahi* (28 May), pp. 35–8.

Kurabayashi, Yoshimasa

1973 'Wagakuni ni okeru Shotoku to Tomi no Kaisō-betsu Bunseki' (An Analysis of Income and Wealth Classes in Japan), *Shūkan Tōyō Keizai*, special issue on income distribution (no. 3764: 4 October), pp. 69–73.

Kuwabara, Takeo

1982 'Gendai Shakai ni okeru Supōtsu: Naze, Ima Totemo Ninki ga Arunoka' (Sports in Contemporary Japanese Society: Why Are They so Popular?). *Ekonomisuto* (vol. 60, no. 28: 11 May), pp. 30–8.

Kuwahara, Yasuo

1983 'Technological Change and Industrial Relations in Japan.' Forthcoming in *Bulletin of Comparative Labor Relations*.

Kuznets, Simon

1963 'Quantitative Aspects of the Economic Growth of Nations, *Economic Development and Cultural Change* (vol. 11, no. 2, part 2: January), pp. 1–80.

Kyōkasho Kentei Soshō o Shiensuru Zenkoku Renrakukai, ed.

1967–81 *Ienaga Kyōōkasho Saiban* (Professor Ienaga's Lawsuit against the Government Authorization System for School Textbooks). Tokyo: Bun-ichi Sōgō Shuppan.

Landecker, Werner

1960 'Class Boundaries.' *American Sociological Review* (vol. 25, no. 6: December), pp. 868–77.

1963 'Class Crystallization and Class Consciousness.' *American Sociological Review* (vol. 28, no. 2: April), pp. 219–29.

Large, Stephen, S.

1972 *The Yūaikai 1912–1919: Rise of Labor in Japan*. Tokyo. Sophia University Press.

Lave, Charles A., and March, James G.

1975 *An Introduction to Models in the Social Sciences.* New York: Harper and Row.

LeClair, Edward E.

1962 'Economic Theory and Economic Anthropology.' *American Anthropologist* (vol. 64, no. 6: December), pp. 1179–203.

LeClair, Edward E., and Schneider, Harold K., eds.

1968 *Economic Anthropology: Readings in Theory and Analysis.* New York: Holt, Rinehart and Winston.

Lebra, Takie Sugiyama

1976 *Japanese Patterns of Behavior.* Honolulu, Hawaii: University of Hawaii Press.

Lee, Alfred McLung

1966 *Multivariant Man.* New York: Braziller.

1978 *Sociology for Whom?* New York: Oxford University Press.

Lee, O. Young

1978 'Nihonjin no Shiranai Nihon' (The Japan the Japanese do not Know). *Ajia Kōron* (vol. 7, no. 4: April), pp. 72–9.

1982 '*Chijimi-Shikō' no Nihonjin* (The Japanese Are Oriented to 'Making Things Smaller'). Tokyo: Gakuseisha.

Lee, Tosh

1971 'Chie Nakane, *Japanese Society.' Annals* (vol. 395: May), pp. 212–13.

Lenski, Gerhard

1952 'American Social Classes: Statistical Strata or Social Groups.' *American Journal of Sociology* (vol. 58, no. 2: September), pp. 139–44.

1954 'Status Crystallization: a Non-vertical Dimension of Social Status.' *American Sociological Review* (vol. 19, no. 4, August), pp. 405–13.

1956 'Social Participation and Status Crystallization.' *American Sociological Review* (vol. 21, no. 4: August), pp. 458–64.

1966 *Power and Privilege: a Theory of Social Stratification.* New York: McGraw-Hill.

Levine, Solomon B.

1958a 'Japan's Labor Problems and Labor Movement: 1950–1955.' A supplement to Ōkōchi Kazuo's *Labor in Modern Japan.* Economic Series no. 18. Tokyo: The Science Council of Japan, Division of Economics, Commerce and Business, pp. 86–117.

1958b *Industrial Relations in Postwar Japan.* Urbana, Ill.: University of Illinois Press.

1967 'Postwar Trade Unionism, Collective Bargaining, and the Japanese Social Structure.' In *Aspects of Social Change in Modern Japan*, edited by Ronald P. Dore. Princeton, N.J.: Princeton University Press, pp. 245–89.

1976 '*Japanese Society* by Chie Nakane and *Japanese Blue Collar* by Robert Cole.' *Comparative Studies in Society and History* (vol. 18),

pp. 119–25.
Levine, Solomon, B., and Kawada, Hisashi
1980 *Human Resources in Japanese Industrial Development.* Princeton, N.J.: Princeton University Press.
Levine, Solomon B., and Taira, Koji
1978 'Conflict and Cooperation in Japanese Industry: Is There Conflict?' Unpublished mimeographed paper.
Levy, Marion J.
1969 *Modernization and the Structure of Societies: a Setting for International Relations.* Princeton, N.J.: Princeton University Press.
Lifton, Robert Jay, Katō, Shūichi, and Reich, Michael, R.
1979 *Six Lives Six Deaths: Portraits From Modern Japan.* New Haven, Conn.: Yale University Press.
Lim, Chong-Yah
1982 *Learning from the Japanese Experience.* Singapore: Maruzen Asia.
Lipset, Martin
1963 *The First New Nation.* New York: Basic Books.
Liu, Tong Lin, Yang, Xu Guang, and Wang, Qi Heng
1982 *Ribende Xingzheng Guanli* (Japanese Industrial Management). Beijing: Renmin Chubanshe.
Liu, Zhon Quan, and Jiang, Xiao Ruo
1982 'Nihon Kindaika ni okeru Shakai Shokōzō no Sōgo Kankei' (The Interrelationship of Social Structures in Japan's Modernization). Paper presented to the International Colloquium on the Comparative Study of Japanese Society, Noosa Heads, Queensland, Australia: 29 January–6 February.
Lloyd, Arthur
1911 *Every-day Japan.* London: Cassell and Company.
Lockheimer, Roy
1969 'On the Eve of Japan's Next Rendezvous with Destiny: Basic Tensions May Produce Turmoil.' *Field Staff Reports: East Asian Reports* (American Universities Field Staff) (vol. 16, no. 3: February), pp. 1–14.
Lockwood, William W.
1965 'Prospectus and Summary.' In *The State and Economic Enterprise in Japan,* edited by William W. Lockwood. Princeton, N.J.: Princeton University Press, pp. 3–14.
Low, Albert
1982 *Zen and Creative Management.* New York: Playboy Paperbacks.
Lummis, C. Douglas
1982 *A New Look at the Chrysanthemum and the Sword.* Tokyo: Shōhakusha.
Lynd, Robert S., and Lynd, Helen Merrell.
1929 *Middletown.* New York: Harcourt, Brace.

McCormack, Gavan
1982 '1930s Japan: Fascist?' In *Japanese Society: Reappraisals and New Directions*, edited by Yoshio Sugimoto and Ross Mouer as a special edition of *Social Analysis* (nos. 5/6: December 1980), pp. 125–43.
McDonnell, John
1980 'Understanding Japan.' In *Australia and Asia: the Capricornia Papers*. Research Paper no. 10. Brisbane: Centre for the Study of Australian-Asian Relations, Griffith University.
McGown, Valerie
1982 'Paternalism: a Definition.' In *Japanese Society: Reappraisals and New Directions*, edited by Yoshio Sugimoto and Ross Mouer as a special edition of *Social Analysis* (nos. 5/6: December 1980), pp. 102–24.
Magofuku, Hiromu
1981 'America Loves to Teach, Hates to Learn: Enthusiasm and Welcome for Foreign Students not Matched by Effort to Study Other Countries.' *JT* (26 April), p. 4.
Magota, Ryōhei
1972 'Chingin Taikei no Hendō' (Changes in Wage Structure). In *Chingin: Sono Kako, Genzai, Mirai* (The Past, Present and Future of the Japanese Wage System), edited by Kaneko Yoshio. Tokyo: Nihon Rōdō Kyōkai, pp. 153–208.
Mainichi Shinbunsha, ed.
1977 *Shinkokusaijin no Shutsugen* (The Appearance of the New Internationalist). Tokyo: Mainichi Shinbusha.
Manabe, Kazufumi
1981 'Gaikoku Kyōikusho ni Miru Nihon' (Japan as Seen in Foreign Textbooks). *Kangaku Jānaru* (no. 39: 25 September), p. 8.
Mannari, Hiroshi
1974 *The Japanese Business Leaders*. Tokyo: University of Tokyo Press.
Mannari, Hiroshi, and Abegglen, James
1971 'Gendai Nihon no Keieisha-zō–1960–1970' (A Portrait of Management in Modern Japan: 1960–1970). *NRKZ* (vol. 13, no. 6: August), pp. 2–14.
Mannari, Hiroshi and Befu, Harumi, eds.
1983 *The Challenge of Japan's Internationalization: Organization and Culture*. Tokyo: Kodansha International.
Mannheim, Karl
1954 *Ideology and Utopia*. London: Routledge and Kegan Paul.
March, Robert
1979 'The Australia-Japan Sugar Negotiations.' *Research Paper* no. 56. Canberra: Australia-Japan Economic Relations Research Project.
1982 'Melodrama in Japanese Negotiations: Doing Business in Japan Requires a Different Kind of Gamesmanship.' *WINDS* (inflight magazine of Japan Air Lines, April), pp. 23–9.

Marsh, Robert M.
1982 'A Macrosociological Theory of Japanese Social Structure.' Paper prepared for the International Colloquium on the Comparative Study of Japan, Noosa Heads, Queensland, Australia: 30 January–6 February.

Marsh, Robert M., and Mannari, Hiroshi
1976 *Modernization and the Japanese Factory.* Princeton, N.J.: Princeton University Press.
1977 'Organizational Commitment and Turnover: a Prediction Study.' *Administrative Science Quarterly* (vol. 22, no. 1: March), pp. 57–76.

Marshall, Byron
1967 *Capitalism and Nationalism in Prewar Japan: the Ideology of the Business Elite: 1868–1941.* Stanford, Cal.: Stanford University Press.

Marshall, Robert C.
1981 'Kōkan Kankei Moderu ni yoru Nihon Shakai no Kaimei' (An Understanding of Japanese Society within the Framework of the Social Exchange Model). A special issue of *Shūkan Tōyō Keizai* (no. 57: 10 July), pp. 114–23.

Maruyama, Magoroh
1980 'Mindscapes and Science Theories.' *Current Anthropology* (vol. 21, no. 5: October), pp. 589–600.

Maruyama, Masao
1956 *Gendai Seiji no Shisō to Kōdō* (Thought and Behavior in Modern Japanese Politics). Tokyo: Miraisha.
1963 *Thought and Behavior in Modern Japanese Politics.* London: Oxford University Press.
1965 'Patterns of Individuation and the Case of Japan: a Conceptual Scheme.' In *Changing Japanese Attitudes toward Modernization*, edited by Marius B. Jansen. Princeton, N.J.: Princeton University Press, pp. 489–531.
1974 *Studies in the Intellectual History of Tokugawa Japan*, translated by Mikiso Hane. Tokyo: University of Tokyo Press.

Masamura, Kimio
1968 *Gendai Nihon Keizai-ron* (Theories about the Contemporary Japanese Economy). Tokyo: Hyōronsha.
1972 *Keizai Taisei no Sentaku* (Options in Choosing Economic Systems). Tokyo: Tōyō Keizai Shinpōsha.

Maslow, Abraham
1954 *Motivation and Personality.* New York: Harper and Row.
1962 *Toward a Psychology of Being.* New York: Van Nostrand.

Masuzoe, Yōichi
1982 *Nihonjin to Furansujin: 'Kokoro wa Hidari Saifu wa Migi no Ronri'* Japanese and the French: The Logic of Liberal Humanism and Conservative Financing). Tokyo: Kōbunsha.

Matsubara, Haruo
1973 'Seikatsu Taikei to Seikatsu Kankyō: Seikatsu to Komyuniti' (A Systems Approach to Lifestyles and Social Environment: Livelihood and the Community). In *Seikatsu Kōzō no Riron* (The Theory of Lifestyles and Living Patterns), edited by Aoi Kazuo, Matsubara Haruo and Fukuda Yoshiya. Tokyo: Yūhikaku, pp. 95–138.
1974 *Nihon Shōnen no Ishiki Kōzō: 'Fuan' to 'Fuman' no Mekanizumu* (The Conscience of Young Japanese: the Mechanism of Anxiety and Dissatisfaction). Tokyo: Kōbundō.
Matsuda, Yasuhiko
1972 'The Prevention of Industrial Accidents in Japan.' *Japan Labor Bulletin* (vol. 11, no. 1: January), pp. 5–8; (vol. 11, no. 2: February), pp. 4–8.
Matsumoto, Shin-ichi
1981 '"Japanesuku" Būmu Shikake no Butaiura "Kenkyū"' (Research on Behind-the-scenes Efforts to Create a Japanesque Boom). *Uwasa no Shinsō* (December), pp. 62–8.
Matsumoto, Yoshio
1975 'Shakai Kōzō to Hanzai' (Social Structure and Crimes). In *Hanzai Shakaigaku* (Criminology), edited by Nihon Hanzai Shakai Gakkai. Tokyo: Yūhikaku, pp. 163–72.
Matsushita, Keiichi
1959 *Gendai Seiji no Jōken* (Conditions of Contemporary Politics). Tokyo: Chūō Kōronsha.
Matsuyama, Yukio
1982 'Japan in the World: Understanding of Other Peoples Needed.' *AEN* (22 September), p. 7.
Meadows, Donella H., Meadows, Dennis L., and Behiens, William W., III
1972a *The Limits of Growth: a Report for the Club of Rome's Project on the Predicament of Mankind.* New York: Universe Books.
1972b *Seichō no Genkai* (Limits of Growth), translated by Ōkita Saburō. Tokyo: Daiyamondosha.
Merton, Robert
1957 *Social Theory and Social Structure.* Glencoe, Ill.: Free Press.
1973 *The Sociology of Science: Theoretical and Empirical Investigations.* Chicago, Ill.: University of Chicago Press.
Meyer, John W., Boli-Bennett, John, and Chase-Dunn, Christopher.
1975 'Convergence and Divergence in Development.' *Annual Review of Sociology* (no. 1), pp. 223–46.
Miller, Roy Andrew
1982 *Japan's Modern Myth: the Language and Beyond.* Tokyo: Weatherhill.
Mills, C. Wright
1956a *The Sociological Imagination.* New York: Oxford University Press.
1956b *The Power Elite.* New York: Oxford University Press.

Milward, Peter
1980 *Nihonjin no Nihon Shirazu* (The Japan Most Japanese Never Know), translated by Bekku Sadanori. Tokyo: Seishun Shuppansha.
1978 *Igirisujin to Nihonjin* (The English and the Japanese), translated by Bekku Sadanori. Tokyo: Kōdansha.
1980 *Oddities in Modern Japan: Observations of an Outsider.* Tokyo: Hokuseidō Press.
Minakata, Kumagusu
1971–5 *Minakata Kumagusu Zenshū* (Complete Collection of Works of Minakata Kumagusu). 10 vols and 2 additional issues. Tokyo: Heibonsha.
Minami, Hiroshi
1953 *Nihonjin no Shinri* (The Psychology of the Japanese People). Tokyo: Iwanami Shoten.
1971 *The Psychology of the Japanese People*, translated by Albert R. Ikuma. Tokyo: University of Tokyo Press.
1980 *Nihonjinron no Keifu* (The Development of 'Nihonjinron'). Tokyo: Kōdansha.
Minami, Renpei
1981 *Kensetsugyōkai Aku no Kōzu* (The Construction Industry: Corrupt Structure). Tokyo: Ēru Shuppansha.
Minear, Richard H.
1972 *Victor's Justice: the Tokyo War Crimes Trial.* Tokyo: Charles E. Tuttle.
1980a 'Orientalism and the Study of Japan.' *Journal of Asian Studies* (vol. 30, no. 3: May), pp. 507–17.
1980b 'The Wartime Studies of Japanese National Character.' *Japan Interpreter* (vol. 15, no. 1: Summer), pp. 36–59.
Mitchell, G. Duncan
1968 'Model.' In *A New Dictionary of Sociology*, edited by G. Duncan Mitchell. London: Routledge and Kegan Paul, p. 127.
Mitchell, Richard Hanks
1967 *The Korean Minority in Japan.* Berkeley, Cal.: University of California Press.
1976 *Thought Control in Prewar Japan.* Ithaca, N.Y.: Cornell University Press.
Mitsuda, Shin-ichirō
1961 'Ōi Myōji Ōi Namae' (Common Given Names and Common Family Names). *Gengo Seikatsu* (no. 118, July), pp. 42–6.
Miyagi, Hirosuke
1970 *Atarashii Kaikyū-Chishiki Rōdōsha to Sono Shūhen* (The New Class: the Expert, the Technician and Other Professional Workers). Tokyo: Daiyamondosha.
Miyaji, Sōshichi
1963 *Hadaka ni Sareta Nihon Keizai: Kokusai Shakai wa Amakunai*

(The Japanese Economy Exposed: the Tough International Community). Tokyo: Tōyō Keizai Shinpōōsha.

Miyamoto, Ken

1975 'A Woman for the Blue Stockings.' *Japan Interpreter* (vol. 10, no. 2: Autumn), pp. 190–204.

Miyamoto, Musashi

1982 *The Book of Five Rings*, translated from Japanese to English by Nihon Services Corporation. New York: Bantam Books.

Miyanohara, Seiichi, Maruki, Masaomi, Igasaki, Akio, and Fujioka, Sadahiko, eds.

1979 *Shiryōō: Nihon Gendai Kyōikushi* (Documents: Contemporary History of Japanese Education). Revised edition. 3 vols. Tokyo: Sanseidō.

Miyashita, Tadako

1980 *Zen-mō Haha no Kiroku* (A Blind Mother's Record). Tokyo: Banseisha.

Miyazaki, Yoshikazu

1980 'Excessive Competition and the Formation of *Keiretsu*.' In *Industry and Business in Japan*, edited by Kazuo Saitō. London: Croom Helm, pp. 53–73.

Monbushō (Japan Ministry of Education).

1961 *Kokumin no Yomi-kaki Nōryoku* (Measures of National Literacy). Tokyo: Ōkurashō Insatsukyoku.

Moore, Barrington

1966 *Social Origins of Dictatorship and Democracy*. Boston: Beacon Press.

Mori, Jōji

1972 *Nihonjin–Kara Nashi Tamago no Jigazō* (The Japanese: A Self-image of an Egg without a Shell). Tokyo: Kōdansha.

Mori, Kōjirō

1951 *Shakai Seisaku Joron* (An Introduction to Social Policy). Tokyo: Nihon Hyōronsha.

1953 *Seikatsu Suijun* (The Standard of Living). Vol. 5 of *Keizagaku Shin Taikei* (The New Series on Economics). Tokyo: Kawade Shobō.

Morikawa, Hidemasa

1973 *Nihongata Keiei no Genryū* (The Origins of Japanese-style Management). Tokyo: Tōyō Keizai Shinpōsha.

1980 *Nihongata Keiei no Tenkai* (The Development of Japanese-style Management). Tokyo: Tōyō Keizai Shinpōōsha.

Morimura, Sei-ichi

1981 *Akuma no Hōshoku* (Feast of the Devils). Tokyo: Kōbunsha.

1982 *Zoku Akuma no Hōshoku* (A Continuation of the Feast of the Devils). Tokyo: Kōbunsha.

Morioka, Kiyomi

1975 *Religion in Changing Japanese Society.* Tokyo: University of Tokyo Press.

Morishima, Michio

1982 *Why has Japan Succeeded? Western Technology and the Japanese Ethos.* Cambridge University Press.

Morley, James William

1971 'Introduction: Choice and Consequence.' In *Dilemmas of Growth in Prewar Japan*, edited by James William Morley. Princeton, N.J.: Princeton University Press, pp. 3–30.

Morris, Ivan

1975 *The Nobility of Failure: Tragic Heroes in the History of Japan.* New York: New American Library.

Mosca, Gaetano

1939 *Ruling Class.* New York: McGraw-Hill.

Mouer, Ross

1973a 'Pollution in Japan.' *Japan Foundation Newsletter* (vol. 1, no. 2: October), pp. 9–10.

1973b 'Kakei Chōsa ni okeru Shotoku Bunpu to Setaiinsū no Kanren' (An Examination of the Relationship Between Household Size and the Distribution of Income Using the FIES Data). *Mita Gakkai Zasshi* (vol. 66, no. 10: October), pp. 16–34.

1973c 'Income Distribution in Japan: An Examination of the Family Income and Expenditure Data, 1963–1971 (I).' *Keio Economic Studies* (vol. 10, no. 1: Spring), pp. 87–109.

1974a 'Income Distribution in Japan: An Examination of the Family Income and Expenditure Data, 1963–1971 (II).' *Keio Economic Studies* (vol. 11, no. 1: Spring), pp. 9–28.

1974b 'Income Distribution in Japan: An Examination of the Family Income and Expenditure Data, 1963–1971 (III).' *Keio Economic Studies* (vol. 11, no. 2: Fall), pp. 21–34.

1975a 'Nihon ni okeru Ka-i Taikeibetsu no Shotoku Bunpu no Jōkyō-Kakei Chōsa Kenkyū o Tsūjite' (A Subsystems Approach to Income Distribution in Japan Using the FIES Data), *Kikan Riron Keizaigaku* (vol. 26, no. 1: April), pp. 30–43.

1975b 'Fubyōdō ni Taisuru Shakai no Nintai Gendo' (The Social Limits of Inequality). *Keizai Kenkyū* (vol. 26, no. 2: April), pp. 108–17.

1976 'Kokusai Rōdō Undō to Komyunikēshon no Yakuwari' (The International Labor Movement and the Role of Communications). *NRKZ* (vol. 18, no. 8: August), pp. 2–8.

1978 'Conservative and Radical Approaches in the Literature on Japanese Society.' Paper presented to the Second National Conference of the Asian Studies Association of Australia, University of New South Wales, Sydney, 14–18 May.

1980a 'Income and Distribution in Japan with an Emphasis on the

Households of Employees in Urban Japan: an Inquiry into the Methodology of Commonly Accepted Approaches to Understanding Japanese Society.' Ph.D. thesis, Fletcher School of Law and Diplomacy, Medford, Massachusetts, USA.

1980b 'Can We Generalize about Women's Lower Wages? An Examination of Some Japanese Data.' Paper presented to the Women and Labour Conference, Melbourne, 17–19 October.

1981a 'Japanese Society: Stereotypes and Realities'. *Dentsu Japan: Marketing/Advertising* (No. 18: January), pp. 26–30.

1981b 'Nihon Shakai no Hikaku Kenkyū–Ima no Jōkyō to Kongo no Kadai ni Tsuite' (The Comparative Study of Japanese Society: the Present Situation and Future Prospects). *Gakujutsu Kokusai Kōryū Sankō Shiryō-shūū* (International Academic Exchange Monograph Series), no. 65, February. Tokyo: Meiji University.

1981c 'Ichikawa Fusae and Women in Japan.' *Women in Asia Newsletter* (vol. 1, no. 2: November), pp. 4–6,

1982a 'Nihon ni okeru Danjokan no Chingin Kakusa' (Male-Female Wage Differentials in Japan). *NRKZ* (vol. 24., no. 2: February), pp. 12–22.

1982b 'Japanese Society: Industrialization, Internationalization and Social Change.' In *Modern Society in Japan*. Orientation Seminars on Japan, no. 8. Tokyo: Japan Foundation.

1982c 'The Significance of Studying Japanese Society.' *World Review* (vol. 21, no. 2: June), pp. 60–85.

Mouer, Ross, and Fodella, Gianni

1970 'Economic Thought in Tokugawa Japan.' *KBS Bulletin* (no. 102: June-July), pp. 1–23; (no. 104: October-November), pp. 1–16; (no. 105: December-January 1971), pp. 1–15.

Mouer, Ross, and Sugimoto, Yoshio

1979a 'Kutabare Japanorojī–"Nihonjin Dōshitsuron" no Hōhōōronteki Mondaiten' (The Limits of Theories Emphasizing the Homogeneous Nature of the Japanese: Some Comments on the Need for Analyzing the Dimensions of Inequality and Variance). *Gendai no Me* (vol. 20, no. 6: June), pp. 134–45.

1979b 'Doi Takeo Setsu e no Hōhōronteki Gimon' (A Methodological Critique of the Research of Doi Takeo). *Gendai no Me* (vol. 20, no. 9: September), pp. 200–13.

1980 'Nihon Shakairon no Saikōchiku o Mezashite' (Toward a New Theory of Japanese Society). *Kikan Kuraishisu* (no. 6: Winter), pp. 200–08.

1982a 'Reappraising Images of Japanese Society.' In *Japanese Society: Reappraisals and New Directions*, edited by Yoshio Sugimoto and Ross Mouer as a special issue of *Social Analysis* (nos. 5/6: December 1980), pp. 5–19.

1982b *Nihonjin wa 'Nihonteki' ka* (A Reconsideration of the Arguments about Japanese Society). Tokyo: Tōyō Keizai Shinpōsa.

Mouer, Ross, and Sugimoto, Yoshio, eds.

1982c *Nihonjinron ni Kansuru 12-shō* (Twelve Chapters on the Japanese). Tokyo: Gakuyō Shobō.

Murakami, Hyōe, and Harper, Thomas, J., eds.

1978 *Great Historical Figures of Japan.* Tokyo: Japan Culture Institute.

Murakami, Hyōe, *et al.*

1982 *Japanese Culture in America: an Investigation into Methods of its Dissemination.* Tokyo: Japan Culture Institute.

Murakami, Masako

1967 'Zaisei ni yoru Shotoku Bunpai' (Income Distribution and the Effects of Fiscal Policy). In *Keizai Seichō to Zaisei Kin-yū Seisaku* (Economic Growth and Fiscal-Monetary Policy), edited by Fujino Shōzaburō and Udagawa Akihito. Tokyo: Keisō Shobō, pp. 242–6.

Murakami, Yasuaki, Kumon, Shunpei, and Satō, Seizaburō

1979 *Bunmei to Shite no Ie Shakai (Ie* Society as Civilization). Tokyo: Chūō Kōronsha.

Muroyama, Toshiaki

1978 'Gyogyō Shakai no "Nami" no Goi' (The Vocabulary for "Wave" in Fishing Communities). *Kokugo Bungaku-kō* (no. 78: April), pp. 33–42.

Murray, James A. H., *et al.*, eds.

1970 *The Oxford English Dictionary: Being a Corrected Re-issue with an Introduction, Supplement and Bibliography of A New English Dictionary on Historical Principles.* Oxford: Clarendon Press. The third printing of the 1933 original.

Nagasawa, Kikuya

1982 *Sanseidō Kanwa Jiten* (The Sanseidō Japanese Dictionary for Chinese Characters). Third edition. Tokyo: Sanseidō.

Nagasu, Kazujii, and Masamura, Kimio

1966 'Dai Niji Sekai Taisengo no Nihon Shihon Shugi–Sono Keizai Seichō to Kōzō Henka no Shotokuchō' (Japanese Capitalism Since World War II; Some Special Characteristics of Economic Growth and Structural Change). In *Gendai Nihon Shihon Shugi Kōza*, vol. 1, edited by Ikumi Takuichi *et al.* Tokyo: Nihon Hyōronsha, pp. 1–41.

Nagata, Akira, and Nagata, Tomoko

1980 *Kaigai Chūzai Kazoku Repōto* (Japanese Families Living Overseas: a Report). Tokyo: Nihon Keiei Shuppankai.

Naipaul, Vidiadhar Surajprasad

1975 *Guerrillas.* New York: Knopf.

1977 *India: a Wounded Civilization.* New York: Random House.

1980 'People are Proud of Being Stupid.' *Newsweek* (18 August), p. 38.

1981 *Among the Believers: an Islamic Journey.* New York: Knopf.

Najita, Tetsuo
1980 'Must We Copy Japan?' *New York Review of Books* (vol. 27, no. 2: 21 February), pp. 33–5.
Najita, Tetsuo, and Koschmann, J. Victor, eds.
1982 *Conflict in Japanese History: the Neglected Tradition.* Princeton, N. J.: Princeton University Press.
Naka, Mamoru
1979 *Habatsu Kankaku to Bosu no Jōken* (The Instinct of Factionalism and the Conditions of the Bosses). Tokyo: Hyōgensha.
Nakajima, Makoto
1968 *Zengakuren.* Tokyo: San-ichi Shobō.
Nakamura, Akira
1982 *Kōjō ni Ikiru Hitobito* (The People Who Live in the Factory). Tokyo: Gakuyō Shobō.
Nakamura, Atsushi
1975 'Kigyōnai Chingin Kōzō no Bunseki.' *Tōyō Keizai*, special issue (no. 31: 29 January), pp. 45–52. This later appeared as 'Intra-Firm Wage Differentials' in *The Labor Market in Japan: Selected Readings*, edited by Nishikawa Shunsaku. Tokyo: University of Tokyo Press, 1980, pp. 202–15.
Nakamura, Hajime
1960 *The Ways of Thinking of Eastern Peoples.* Tokyo: Japanese Government Printing Bureau.
1964 *Ways of Thinking of Eastern Peoples: India, China, Tibet, Japan.* Revised English translation edited by Philip P. Wiener. Honolulu, Hawaii: East-West Center Press.
Nakamura, Kikuo
1973 *Nihonjin o Ugokasu Mono* (Motivation in the Japanese). Tokyo: Nihon Kyōbunsha.
1974 'The "Japanese" in "Japanese Politics", translated by Ross Mouer. *Keio Journal of Politics* (vol. 1, no. 1: Spring), pp. 1–17.
1976 'The Style of Leadership in Japan.' *PHP* (vol. 7, no. 12: December), pp. 53–60.
Nakamura, Tomoko
1976 *'Fūryū Mutan' Jiken Igo: Henshūsha no Jibunshi* (After the 'Fūryū Mutan' Incident: a Personal History of an Editor). Tokyo: Tabata Shoten.
Nakane, Chie
1964 'Nihonteki Shakai Kōzō no Hakken' (The Discovery of a Truly Japanese Social Structure). *Chūō Kōron* (vol. 79, no. 5: May), pp. 48–85.
1965 'Towards a Theory of Japanese Social Structure: a Unilateral Society.' *Economic Weekly* (Bombay) (vol. 17: February), pp. 197–216.
1967a *Tate Shakai no Ningen Kankei: Tan-itsu Shakai no Riron*

(Interpersonal Relationships in a Vertically Structured Society: a Theory for Understanding a Homogeneous Society). Tokyo: Kōdansha.

1967b *Kinship and Economic Organization in Rural Japan.* New York: The Humanities Press.

1970 *Japanese Society.* London: Weidenfeld and Nicolson.

1971 *On the Characteristics of the Japanese and Japanese Society.* Tokyo: Nihon Kokusai Kyōiku Kyōkai.

1972a *Tekiō no Jōken: Nihonteki Renzoku no Shikō* (Conditions of Adaptation: the Japanese Sense of Continuity). Tokyo: Kōdansha.

1972b *Human Relations in Japan.* Tokyo: Ministry of Foreign Affairs.

1973 *Japanese Society.* Revised edition. Harmondsworth: Penguin Books.

1974 *La Société Japonaise*, translated from the 1970 original into French by Laurence Ratier, with a preface by Michel Crozier. Paris: Armand Colin.

1975 'Fieldwork in India–A Japanese Experience.' In *Encounter and Experience: Personal Accounts of Fieldwork*, edited by André Béteille and T. N. Madan. Honolulu: The University Press of Hawaii, pp. 13–26.

1978 *Tateshakai no Rikigaku* (The Dynamics of Vertical Society). Tokyo: Kōdansha.

1982a *Riben Shehui* (Japanese Society), translated into Chinese by Xu Zhen and Zhu Jun Ling. Tianjin: Tianjin Renmin Chubanshe.

1982b *Sangkon Yipun* (Japanese Society), translated into Thai by Vichien Athichartkarn and Theeravat Kuhaprema and edited by Surichai Wun-gaeo as Monograph no. 15 of the Institute of Asian Studies, Chulalongkorn University. Krungthep (Bangkok): Saru-Muan-Chon.

Nakano, Tadayoshi

1982 *Yogosareta Mitsukoshi no Eikō* (The Stained Honor of Mitsukoshi). Tokyo: Ēru Shuppansha.

Nakayama, Ichirō

1960 *Nihon no Kōgyōka to Rōshi Kankei* (Japanese Industrialization and Industrial Relations). Tokyo: Nihon Rōdō Kyōkai.

1974 *Rōshi Kankei no Keizai Shakaigaku* (The Socio-economics of Labor-Management Relations). Tokyo: Nihon Rōdō Kyōkai.

1975 *Industrialization and Labor-Management Relations in Japan*, translated by Ross Mouer. Tokyo: Japan Institute of Labor.

Nakayama, Ichirō, Ōkōchi, Kazuo, and Ballon, Robert J.

1965 'Nihon no Rōshi Kankei' (Labor-Management Relations in Japan). In *Nihon no Rōshi Kankei* (Labor-Management Relations in Japan), edited by Nihon Rōdō Kyōkai. Tokyo: Nihon Rōdō Kyōkai, pp. 7–36.

Nakayama, Masakazu
1972 *Nihongo ni Yoru Keiei–Hon-yaku Keiei kara no Dappi* (Management with the Japanese Language: a Step Away from Foreign Management Practices). Tokyo: Nihon Nōritsu Kyōkai.

Namiki, Nobuyoshi, ed.
1981 *Nihon Shakai no Tokushitsu* (The Special Characteristics of Japanese Society). Tokyo: Nihon Keizai Kenkyū Sentā.

Naruse, Tatsuo
1982 'Sengo Nihon Shihonshugi to Kokumin Seikatsu Yōshiki' (Capitalism in Postwar Japan and the Lifestyle of the People). In *Kōza Konnichi no Nihon Shihonshugi* (Lecture Series on Capitalism in Contemporary Japan), vol. 9, edited by Kōza Konnichi no Nihon Henshū Iinkai. Tokyo: Ōtsuki Shoten, pp. 10–38.

Needham, Rodney
1979 *Symbolic Classification.* Glencoe, Ill.: Scott, Foreman.

Neustupný, J. V.
1979 'The Study of Japan in Australia: Applicability in the New Paradigm.' Paper presented to the Seminar on Employment Prospects for Australian Graduates in Japanese, Sydney, 30–31 August.

1982a 'On Paradigms in the Study of Japan.' In *Japanese Society: Reappraisals and New Directions*, edited by Yoshio Sugimoto and Ross Mouer as a special issue of *Social Analysis* (nos. 5/6: December 1980), pp. 20–8.

1982b 'Kaisō Gengo to iu Kabe' (Stratification of Language as a Barrier to Communication). *Gengo* (vol. 11, no. 10: October), pp. 49–57.

NHK Hōsō Yoron Chōsasho, ed.
1975 *Zusetsu Sengo Yoronshi* (A Visual Survey of Public Opinion in Postwar Japan). Tokyo: Nihon Hōsō Shuppan Kyōkai.

1981 Kokumin Seikatsu Jikan Chōsa (A National Survey of Daily Time Consumption). Tokyo: Nihon Hōsō Shuppan Kyōkai.

Nihon Chiiki Kaihatsu Sentā (The National Regional Development Center), ed.
1970 *Nihonjin no Kachikan* (Values and Attitudes of the Japanese). Tokyo: Shiseidō.

Nihon Gakujutsu Kaigi
1963 *Nihonjin no Seikaku Kenkyūhon* (A Book of Research on the Japanese Character). Tokyo: Nihon Gakujutsu Kaigi.

Nihon Hōsō Shuppan Kyōkai, ed.
1980 *Nihon no Shōhisha Undō* (Consumer Movements in Japan). Tokyo: Nihon Hōsō Shuppan Kyōkai.

Nihon Rōdō Kyōkai (Japan Institute of Labor), ed.
1971 *70-nendai no Chingin Dōkō: Chingin Yōkyū no Mokuhyō o Saguru* (The Direction of Wages in the Seventies: The Decision on Wage Demands). Tokyo: Nihon Rōdō Kyōkai.

Nihon Rōdō Sōhyōgikai, ed.
1974 *Sōhyō 20-nenshi* (A Twenty-year History of Sōhyō). 2 vols. Tokyo: Rōdō Junpōsha.
Nihon Senbotsu Gakusei Shuki Henshū Iinkai, ed.
1949 *Kike Wadatsumi no Koe* (Listen to the Voice of the Sea). Tokyo: Tokyo Daigaku Kyōdō Kumiai Shuppanbu.
Nihon Shakai Gakkai (The Japan Sociological Association), Chōsa Iinkai (Research Team)
1958 *Nihon Shakai no Kaisōteki Kōzō* (Social Stratification in Japan). Tokyo: Yūhikaku.
Niijima, Atsuyoshi
1978 *Yamagishizumu Kōfuku Gakuen: Yūtopia o Mezasu Komyūn* (Yamagishi-ism Happiness School: Commune for Utopia). Tokyo: Hongō Shuppansha.
Nippon Steel Corporation, Personnel Development Office
1982 *Nihon: Sono Sugata to Kokoro* (Nippon: The Land and Its People). Tokyo: Gakuseisha.
Nisbet, Robert
1976 *Sociology as an Art Form*. New York: Oxford University Press.
Nishi, Toshio
1982 *Unconditional Democracy: Educational Policies in Occupied Japan: 1945–1952*. Stanford, Cal.: Hoover Press.
Nishibe, Susumu
1975 *Soshio-Ekonomikkusu* (Socio-Economics). Tokyo: Chūō Kōronsha.
Nishida, Kitarō
1960 *A Study of Good*, translated by V. H. Vigliemo. Tokyo: Japanese Government Printing Bureau.
1973 *Art and Morality*, translated by David A. Dilworth and Valdo H. Vigliemo. Honolulu, Hawaii: University of Hawaii Press.
Nishikawa, Shunsaku
1974 'Joshi Rōdōryokuritsu no Hendō Yūin' (An Explanation of in the Labor-Force Participation Rate of Women). *NRKZ* (vol. 16, no. 5: May), pp. 12–21.
Nishimura, Hiromichi
1970 *Nihon no Chingin Mondai* (The Wage Problem in Japan). Kyoto: Mineruva Shobō.
Nishio, Yōtarō
1982 'Nihon Kindaishi ni okeru Taigaikan' (The International Outlook of the Japanese in the Meiji Era). In *Papers Presented at the Fifth Kyushu International Cultural Conference*. Fukuoka: Fukuoka UNESCO Association, pp. A2.1–A2.7.
Nishiyama, Sen
1972 *Gokai to Rikai: Nihonjin to Amerikajin* (Misunderstanding and Understanding: a Comparison of Japanese and Americans). Tokyo: Saimaru Shuppankai.

1979 *Tsūyakujutsu to Watashi* (Personal Encounters and the Art of Interpretation). Tokyo: Purejidentosha.

Nitta, Jirō

1971 *Hakkōdasan Shi no Hōkō* (Death March at Mt. Hakkōda). Tokyo: Shinchōsha.

Noguchi, Tasuku, Katayama, Goichi, and Arakawa Kunihisa, eds.

1973 *Gendai Nihon no Kabushiki Gaisha* (The Joint-stock Corporation in Contemporary Japan). Tokyo: Nan-undō Shinzansha.

Nomoto, Kikuo

1977 'Nihonjin no Yomikaki Nōryoku' (Literary Levels of the Japanese). In *Kokugo Kokuji Mondai.* (Problems with the Language and Japanese Characters). Iwanami Kōza Nihongo (The Iwanami Series on the Japanese Language), vol. 3. Tokyo: Iwanami Shoten.

Nomura Sōgō Kenkyūsho (Nomura Research Institute)

1978 *Nihonjinron: Kokusai Kyōchō Jidai ni Sonaete* (Theories of the Japanese: the Groundwork for an Era of International Cooperation). A special issue of *Refarensu* (no. 2).

Norbeck, Edward

1965 *Changing Japan.* New York: Holt, Rinehart and Winston.

Norman, E. H.

1975 *Origins of the Modern Japanese State: Selected Writings of E. H. Norman*, edited by John Dower. New York: Pantheon Books.

Noro, Eitarō, ed.

1932–3 *Nihon Shihon Shugi Hattatsushi Kōza* (A History of the Development of Japanese Capitalism). Tokyo: Iwanami Shoten.

Nozawa, Masanori

1965 'Sengo Nihon no Rōdōsha Kaikyū no Kōsei' (The Composition of the Working Class in the Postwar Period). *Keizai Hyōron* (vol. 21, no. 8: August), pp. 120–47.

Obi, Keiichirō

1968 'Rōdō Kyōkyū Riron: Sono Kadai oyobi Kasetsu no Gan'i.' *Mita Gakkai Zasshi* (vol. 61, no. 1: January), pp. 1–25. An English translation of this essay has appeared as 'The Theory of Labor Supply: Some New Perspectives and Some Implications' in *The Labor Market in Japan: Selected Readings*, edited by Nishikawa Shunsaku. Tokyo: University of Tokyo Press, 1980, pp. 41–66.

Oda, Makoto

1974 *Beheiren towa Nanika* (What is the Citizens' Association for Peace in Vietnam?). Tokyo: Chikuma Shobō.

1982 'Kaku o Koeru Rinri to Ronri no Sōsei e' (Toward the Formulation of Ethics and Logic Which Go Beyond Nuclear Weapons). *AJ* (vol. 24, no. 13: 26 March), pp. 124–8; (vol. 24, no. 14: 2 April), pp. 10–14.

Oda, Makoto, ed.

1969 *Jiritsusuru Shimin* (Independent Citizens). Tokyo: Asahi Shinbunsha.

Odaka, Kunio
1958 *Shokugyō to Kaisō* (Occupation and Social Strata). Tokyo: Mainichi Shinbunsha.
1965 *Nihon no Keiei* (Management in Japan). Tokyo: Chūō Kōronsha.
1975 *Toward Industrial Democracy: Management and Workers in Modern Japan.* Cambridge, Mass.: Harvard University Press.

Odaka, Kunio, and Nishihara, Shigeki
1975 'Social Mobility in Japan: a Report on the 1955 Survey of Social Stratification and Social Mobility in Japan.' *East Asian Cultural Studies* (vol. 4: March), pp. 83–126.

Ōe, Shinobu
1978 *Kaigenrei* (Martial Law). Tokyo: Iwanami Shoten.

Ogata, Sadako
1980 *Kokuren kara no Shiten: 'Kokusai Shakai to Nihon' o Kangaeru* (A View From the United Nations: Some Thoughts on International Society and Japan). Tokyo: Asahi Ibuningu Nyūsusha.

Ogawa, Noboru
1969 'Chinrōdō no Riron' (Wage Labor). In *Rōdō Keizairon Nyūmon* (An Introduction to Labor Economics), edited by Kishimoto Eitarō. Tokyo: Yūhikaku, pp. 21–44.

Ōhashi, Kaoru
1962 *Toshi no Kasō Shakai: Shakai Byōrigakuteki Kenkyū* (Lower-class Society in Urban Japan: a Pathological Approach). Tokyo: Seishin Shobōō.

Ōhashi, Ryūken
1971 *Nihon no Kaikyū Kōsei* (The Class Composition of Japan). Tokyo: Iwanami Shoten.

Ohmae, Ken-ichi
1982 *The Mind of the Strategist: the Art of Japanese Business.* New York: McGraw-Hill.

Oikawa, Hiroshi
1967 *Dōzoku Soshiki to Sonraku Seikatsu* (Dōzoku Organization and Village Life). Tokyo: Miraisha.

Ōishi, Hatsutarō
1969 'Tokyo-jin no Hyōjungo Shiyō–Sono Ishiki Chōsa' (Usage of Standard Japanese among Tokyoites: Survey of their Consciousness). In *Saeki Umetomo Hakushi Koki Kinen Kokugogaku Ronshū* (A Collection of Essays on the Japanese Language on the Seventieth Birthday of Professor Saeki Umetomo), edited by Saeki Umetomo Hakushi Koki Kinen Kokugogaku Ronshū Kankōkai. Tokyo: Hyōgensha, pp. 697–725.

Ojimi, Yoshihisa
1975 'A Government Ministry: The Case of the Ministry of International Trade and Industry.' In *Modern Japanese Organization and Decision-making*, edited by Ezra Vogel. Berkeley, Cal.: University of California Press, pp. 101–12.

Oka, Hideaki
1967 *How to Wrap Five Eggs.* Tokyo: Weatherhill.
1975 *How to Wrap Five More Eggs.* Tokyo: Weatherhill.

Okakura, Koshirō, Hayashi, Naomichi, Taguchi, Fukuji, and Shimada, Yutaka, eds.
1973 *Kōza Gendai Nihon Shihon Shugi* (Lectures on Capitalism in Postwar Japan). 4 vols. Tokyo: Aoki Shoten.

Okamoto, Hideaki
1971 'Shanai Hendō to Rōōdōsha Ishiki–Kumiai Undō ni okeru Sedai no Mondai' (Social Change and Attitudes among Labor: the Generation Gap as a Factor in the Union Movement). *NRKZ* (vol. 13, no. 1: January), pp. 14–29.
1972 'Industrialization: Environment and Anti-pollution Movements: a Case.' *Japan Labor Bulletin* (vol. 11, no. 11: November), pp. 4–12.
1973 'The Social Responsibility of the Enterprise: some Proposals by Keizai Dōyūkai.' *Japan Labor Bulletin* (vol. 12, no. 11: November), pp. 4–10; (vol. 12, no. 12: December), pp. 6–12.

Ōkōchi, Kazuo
1940 *Shakai Seisaku no Kihon Mondai* (The Major Tasks of Social Policy). Tokyo: Nihon Hyōron Shinsha. (A revised edition came out in 1954.)
1949 *Shakai Seisaku Sōron* (The General Theory of Social Policy). Tokyo: Yūhikaku.
1952a *Shakai Seisaku no Keizai Riron* (The Economic Principles of Social Policy). Tokyo: Nihon Hyōron Shinsha.
1952b *Reimeiki no Nihon Rōdō Undō* (The Dawning of the Labor Movement in Japan). Tokyo: Iwanami Shoten.
1958 *Labor in Modern Japan.* Economic Series no. 18. Tokyo: The Science Council of Japan, Division of Economics, Commerce and Business Administration.
1964 *Binbō Monogatari* (The Story of Poverty). Tokyo: Bungei Shunjū Shinsha.
1970 *Kurai Tanima no Rōdō Undō* (The Labor Movement in Darkness). Tokyo: Iwanami Shoten.

Ōkōchi, Kazuo, and Matsuo, Hiroshi
1965–73 *Nihon Rōdō Kumiai Monogatari* (A History of Japanese Labor Unions), 5 vols. Tokyo: Chikuma Shobō.

Okonogi, Keigo
1978 'Nihonjin no Ajase Conpurekkusu.' (The Ajase Complex of the Japanese) *Chūō Kōron* (vol. 93, no. 6: June), pp. 90–123. An English translation appeared as 'The Ajase Complex of the Japanese: the Depth Psychology of the Moratorium People,' *Japan Echo* (vol. 5, no. 4: Winter 1978), pp. 88–105; (vol. 6, no. 1: Spring 1979), pp. 104–18.

1979 *Moratoriamu Ningen no Jidai* (The Age of the Moratorium People). Tokyo: Chūō Kōronsha.

Okudaira, Yasuhiro, ed.

1973 *Chian Ijihō* (Public Peace Preservation Law). *Gendaishi Shiryō* (Resource Materials on Modern History), vol. 45. Tokyo: Misuzu Shobō.

O'Neill, John

1972 *Sociology as a Skin Trade: Essays toward Reflexive Sociology.* New York: Harper and Row.

Ono, Akira

1973 *Sengo Nihon no Chingin Kettei: Rōdō Shijō no Kōzō Henka to Sono Eikyō* (Wage Determination in Postwar Japan: the Effect of Structural Change in the Labor Market). Tokyo: Tōyō Keizai Shinpōsha.

Ono, Tsuneo

1979 'Takokuseki Kigyō no 'Tekiō Kōdō' Patān no Kenkyū' (Research on How Multinational Enterprises Adapt to Local Conditions). *NRKZ* (vol. 19, no. 1: January), pp. 28–40.

Ono, Tsuneo, Nishikawa, Tadashi, and Fujii, Tokuzō

1976 *Kanrishoku no Chingin–Sono Kangaekata to Kimekata* (The Philosophy and Criteria Determining the Wages of Company Executives). Tokyo: Nihon Keieisha Dantai Renmei.

Onoda, Hiroo

1974 *No Surrender: My Thirty-year War*, translated by Charles S. Terry. Tokyo: Kodansha International.

Ōoka, Shōhei

1957 *Fires on the Plains*, translated by Ivan Morris. Tokyo: Charles E. Tuttle.

Organization for Economic Cooperation and Development

1971 *Reviews of National Policies for Education: Japan.* Paris: OECD.

1972 *Nippon no Kyōiku Seisaku* (Education Policy in Japan), translated by Fukashiro Junrō. Tokyo: Asahi Shinbunsha.

1973a *OECD Tainichi Rōdō Hōkokusho* (The OECD Report on Labor in Japan), translated by the Rōdōshō (Ministry of Labor). Tokyo: Nihon Rōdō Kyōkai.

1973b *Manpower Policies in Japan.* Paris: OECD.

1973c *Education and Policy Planning in Japan.* Paris: OECD.

1977 *The Development of Industrial Relations in Japan: Some Implications of the Japanese Experience.* Paris: OECD.

Origuchi, Shinobu

1972–4 *Origuchi Shinobu Zenshū* (Complete Works of Origuchi Shinobu). 31 vols. Tokyo: Chūō Kōronsha.

Osada, Kōichi

1981 'Seikatsu Ishiki' (Middle-class Consciousness). In *Nihon no Shinchūkansō* (Japan's New Middle Strata), edited by Ariyoshi

Hiroyuki and Hamaguchi Haruhiko. Tokyo: Waseda Daigaku Shuppanbu, pp. 105–61.

Ōshita, Eiji

1983 *Dokyumento Mitsukoshi* (A Documentary on Mitsukoshi). Tokyo: San-ichi Shobō.

Ossowski, Stanislav

1956 'Old Nations and New Problems: Interrelations of Social Structure in Modern Society.' *Transactions of the Third World Congress of Sociology* (vol. 3) pp. 18–25.

1963 *Class Structure in the Social Consciousness*, translated by Sheila Patterson. New York: Free Press.

Ōtsuka, Hisao

1948 *Kindaika no Ningen-teki Kiso* (The Human Foundation of Modernization). Tokyo: Iwanami Shoten.

Ōtsuka, Hisao, Kawashima, Takeyoshi, and Doi, Takeo

1976 *'Amae' to Shakai Kagaku (Amae* and the Social Sciences). Tokyo: Kōbundō.

Ōuchi, Hyōei

1970 *Keizaigaku 50-nen* (Fifty Years of Economics). Vol. 1. Tokyo: Tokyo Daigaku Shuppankai.

Ōuchi, Tsutomu

1970 *Gendai Nihon no Rōdō Keizai* (The Labor Economy in Present-day Japan). Tokyo: Nihon Hyōronsha.

1971 *Gendai Nihon Keizairon* (Theories of the Economy in Present-day Japan). Tokyo: Tokyo Daigaku Shuppankai.

Ouchi, William G.

1981a *Theory Z: How American Business Can Meet the Japanese Challenge.* New York: Avon Books.

1981b *Seorī Z: Nihon ni Manabi, Nihon o Koeru* (Theory Z: Learning from the Japanese and Meeting Their Challenge), translated by Tokuyama Jirō *et al.* Tokyo: CBS Sonī Shuppan.

Ōyama, Atsushiko, ed.

1979 *Nihon Daizasshi* (Major Magazines in Modern Japan). 5 vols. Tokyo: Ryūdō Shuppan.

Ozaki, Robert S.

1978 *The Japanese: a Cultural Portrait.* Tokyo: Charles E. Tuttle.

Ozaki, Shigeo

1980 *Amerikajin to Nihonjin* (Americans and Japanese). Tokyo: Kōdansha.

Packard, George

1966 *Protest in Tokyo.* Princeton, N.J.: Princeton University Press.

Paeng, Won-Soon

1982 'Nihon to Ajia Shokokukan no Komyunikēshon Gyappu' (Communication Gap between Japan and Other Asian Countries). In

Papers Presented at the Fifth Kyushu International Cultural Conference. Fukuoka: Fukuoka UNESCO Association, pp. D2.1–D2.8.

Pareto, Vilfredo

1935 *Mind and Society: a Treatise on General Sociology*, translated by A. Livingston and A. Bongiorno. 4 vols. New York: Dover.

1968 *The Rise and Fall of Elites*. Ottawa: Bedminster.

Parsons, Talcott

1951 *The Social System*. New York: Free Press.

1954a 'A Revised Analytical Approach to the Theory of Social Stratification.' In *Essays in Sociological Theory*, edited by Talcott Parsons. Revised edition. New York: Free Press, pp. 418–27.

1954b 'Social Classes and Social Conflict in the Light of Recent Sociological Theory.' In *Essays in Sociological Theory*, edited by Talcott Parsons. Revised edition. New York: Free Press, pp. 323–35.

1964a 'A Revised Approach to the Theory of Social Stratification.' In *Essays in Sociological Theory: a Collection of Parsons' Essays*. New York: Free Press, pp. 418–27.

1964b 'Social Classes and Social Conflict in the Light of Recent Sociological Theory.' In *Essays in Sociological Theory: a Collection of Parsons' Essays*. New York: Free Press, pp. 328–9.

1965 'On the Concept of Political Power.' In *Class, Status and Power: Social Stratification in Perspective*, edited by Rienhard Bendix and Seymour Martin Lipset, second edition. New York: Free Press, pp. 240–65.

1970 'Equality and Inequality in Modern Society, or Social Stratification Revisited.' In *Social Stratification: Research and Theory for the 1970s*, edited by Edward O. Laumann. Indianapolis, Ind.: Bobbs-Merrill, pp. 13–72.

Parsons, Talcott and Shils, Edward, eds.

1951 *Toward a General Theory of Action*. Cambridge, Mass.: Harvard University Press.

Pascale, Richard Tanner, and Athos, Anthony G.

1981 *The Art of Japanese Management*. New York: Simon and Schuster.

1981b *Japanīzu Manējimento: Nihonteki Keiei ni Manabu* (Japanese Management: Learning from Japanese Management), translated by Fukada Yūsuke. Tokyo: Kōōdansha.

Passin, Herbert

1980 *Japanese and the Japanese*. Tokyo: Kinseidō.

Pearce, Joan

1982 'The Other Side of Narita.' *WINDS* (vol. 4, no. 6: November), pp. 4–14.

Peters, Thomas, and Waterman, Robert

1982 *In Search of Excellence: Lessons from America's Best-run Companies*. New York: Harper and Row.

Phelps, Tracy, and Azumi, Koya
1976 'Determinants of Administrative Control: A Test of a Theory with Japanese Factories.' *American Sociological Review* (vol. 41, no. 1: February), pp. 80–94.
Phillips, Derek
1971 *Knowledge from What?: Theories and Methods in Social Research.* Chicago, Ill.: Rand McNally.
Pike, Kenneth L.
1967 *Language in Relation to a Unified Theory of the Structure of Human Behavior.* Revised edition. The Hague: Mouton.
Plimpton, Jack
1982 'West Meets East in Japan.' *Limousine City Guide* (vol. 3, no. 3: July), pp. 3–6.
Price, John
1967 'A History of the Outcast: Untouchability in Japan.' In *Japan's Invisible Race: Caste in Culture and Personality*, edited by George DeVos and Hiroshi Wagatsuma. Berkeley, Cal.: University of California Press, pp. 6–30.
Price, William
1971 *The Japanese Miracle and the Yen.* New York: John Day.
Pucik, Vladimir
1980 'Japanese Management not so Inscrutable after All.' *JT* (24 February), p. 12.
1981 'Nihonteki Keieiron ni Kagakuteki Genmitsusa o' (Applying Scientific Methodological Rigor to the Testing of Japanese Theories About Japanese Management Practices). *NKSC*(21 January), p. 11.
Pucik, Vladimir, and Hatvany, Nina
1982 'Management Practices in Japan: An Integrated System Focusing on Human Resources.' In *Japanese Society: Reappraisals and New Directions*, edited by Yoshio Sugimoto and Ross Mouer as a special issue of *Social Analysis* (nos. 5/6: December 1980), pp. 63–78.
Pulvers, Roger
1979 'Japan: a Key to Understanding the Western Mind.' *Japan Foundation Newsletter* (vol. 7, no. 5: December/January), pp. 8–12.

QC Sākuru Honbu, ed.
1971 *QC Sākuru Katsudō Unei no Kihon* (An Introduction to the Administration of QC Circle Activities). Tokyo: Nihon Kagaku Gijutsu Renmei.

Ramsey, Charles E., and Smith, Robert, J.
1960 'Japanese and American Perceptions of Occupations.' *American Sociological Review* (vol. 65, no. 2: March), pp. 475–82.
Reischauer, Edwin

1947 *Japan: Past and Present.* London: Duckworth.
1970 *Japan: the Story of a Nation.* New York: Knopf.
1971 'Generation Gap, Money Lack Plague Japanology in U.S.' *AEN*(28 December), p. 6.
1978 *The Japanese.* Cambridge, Mass.: Belknap Press, Harvard University Press.
1979 *Za Japanīzu* (The Japanese), translated by Kunihiro Masao. Tokyo: Bungei Shunjū.
1980 *Ribenren* (The Japanese), translated into Chinese by Meng Sheng De and Liu Wen Tao. Shanghai: Shanghai Yiwen Chubanshe.

Richardson, Bradley M., and Ueda, Taizō
1981 *Business and Society in Japan: Fundamentals for Businessmen.* New York: Praeger.

Rikō, Mitsuo, Mori, Seiichi, and Sone, Yasunori
1980 *Manjō-ichi to Tasūketsu* (Unanimous Consensus and Majority Rule). Tokyo: Nihon Keizai Shinbunsha.

Ritzer, George, ed.
1972 *Issues, Debates and Controversies: an Introduction to Sociology.* Boston, Mass.: Allyn and Bacon.

Rōdōshō (Japanese Ministry of Labor)
1975 *Rōdō Hakusho: Shōwa 50-nenban* (The 1975 White Paper on Labor). Tokyo: Ōkurashō Insatsukyoku.

Rōdōshō, Daijin Kanbō Tōkei Jōhōbu (Bureau of Statistical Information, Secretariat of the Minister, Japanese Ministry of Labor)
1976 *Koyō Dōkō Chōsa Hōkoku* (Report on the Survey of the Employment Situation). Tokyo: Ōkurashō Insatsukyoku.
1982 *Rōdō Tōkei Yōran* (A Handbook of Labor Statistics). Tokyo: Ōkurashō Insatsukyoku.
Annual *Chingin Kōzō Kihon Tōkei Chōsa Hōkoku* (The Report on the Basic Survey of the Wage Structure). Tokyo: Rōdō Daijin Kanbō Tōkei Chōsabu.

Rōdōshō, Fujin Shōnenkyoku (Bureau for Women and Minors, Japanese Ministry of Labor)
1981 *Fujin Rōdō no Jittai* (White Paper on Working Women). Tokyo: Ōkurashō Insatsukyoku.

Rōdō Undōshi Kenkyūkai (Association for Research on the Labor Movement)
1972 *Senryōka no Rōdō Sōgi* (Labor Disputes during the Years of the Occupation). Tokyo: Rōdō Junpōsha.
1973 *Senryōka Rōdō Undō no Bunseki* (An Analysis of the Labor Movement during the Occupation). Tokyo: Rōdō Junpōsha.

Rohlen, Thomas P.
1974 *For Harmony and Strength: Japanese White-collar Organization in Anthropological Perspective.* Berkeley, Cal.: University of California Press.

1975 'The Company Work Group'. In *Modern Japanese Organization and Decision-making*, edited by Ezra Vogel. Berkeley, Cal.: University of California Press, pp. 185–209.

Runciman, W. G.

1967 *Relative Deprivation and Social Justice*. London: Routledge and Kegan Paul.

Sahashi, Shigeru

1980 *Nihonjinron no Kenshō* (An Examination of *Nihonjinron*). Tokyo: Seibundō Shikōsha.

Said, Edward W.

1979 *Orientalism*. New York: Vintage Books.

Saiga, Hideo

1966 'Sunao ni "*Arigatō*" to Iō' (A Proposal for Using *Arigatō*). *IDE* (no. 54: March), pp. 44–5.

Sakaguchi, Ango

1968 *Nihon Bunka Shikan* (A Personal View of Japanese Culture), edited by Satō Tadao. Tokyo: Hyōronsha.

Sakuma, Hide

1972 *Nihonjin no Sei* (Japanese Surnames). Tokyo: Rikugei Shobō.

Salamon, Sonya

1975 'The Varied Groups of Japanese and German Housewives.' *Japan Interpreter* (vol. 10, no. 2: Autumn), pp. 151–70.

Salvador, Gloria S., and Eduarte, Rolly F.

1982 'The Productivity Improvement Circles: Concepts, Features, Objectives, Benefits.' A pamphlet prepared for the Productivity and Development Center, a government organization in the Philippines.

Sameda, Toyoyuki

1966 *Nikushoku no Shisō* (The Thought Patterns of the Meat-Eaters). Tokyo: Chūō Kōronsha.

Sanada, Fumi

1976 *Etchū Gokasan Hōgen Goi: Tenshō Chishō ni Kansuru Kotoba* (The Local Dialect in Etchū Gokasan: Words about the Climate and Nature). Privately published.

Sano, Yōko

1967 'An Analysis of Industrial Wage Differentials.' *Keio Business Review* (no. 6), pp. 29–43.

1970 *Chingin Kettei no Keiryō Bunseki* (A Quantitative Analysis of Wage Determination). Tokyo: Tōyō Keizai Shinpōsha.

1972 'Keizai Seichō to Shotoku Kakusa' (Economic Growth and Income Differentials). *Chingin Jitsumu* (vol. 9, no. 212: 1 April), pp. 48–52.

Satō, Tadao

1982 *Currents in Japanese Cinema*, translated by Gregory Barrett. Tokyo: Kodansha International.

Scalapino, Robert A.

1967 *The Japanese Communist Movement, 1920–1966.* Berkeley, Cal.: University of California Press.

Schell, Jonathan

1982 *The Fate of the Earth.* New York: Knopf.

Schonberger, Richard

1982 *Japanese Manufacturing Techniques: Nine Hidden Lessons in Simplicity.* New York: Free Press.

Schwantes, Robert S.

1974 'Japan's Cultural Policies.' In *Japan's Foreign Policy, 1868–1941: a Research Guide,* edited by James W. Morley. New York: Columbia University Press, pp. 153–83.

Schweisberg, Dave

1982 'The "Japanning" of America.' *JT* (20 October 1982), p. 16.

Sekiguchi, Takeo

1983 *Tanaka Kakuei Shiron* (Tanaka Kakuei: a Personal Theory). Tokyo: Shinnihon Shuppansha.

Senda, Minoru

1980 'Territorial Possession in Ancient Japan: The Real and the Perceived.' In *Geography of Japan,* edited by the Association of Japanese Geographers. Tokyo: Teikoku Shoin, pp. 101–20.

Sengoku, Tamotsu

1974 *Nihonjin no Ningenkan* (The Japanese View of People). Tokyo: Nihon Keizai Shinbunsha.

1982 *Nihon no Sararīman: Kokusai Hikaku de Miru* (The Salaried Employee in Japan: Some International Comparisons). Tokyo: Nihon Hōsō Shuppankai.

Sergeant, Graham

1971 *A Textbook of Sociology.* London: Macmillan.

Shaw, Ellen Torgerson

1982 'Hi! Care for a Drink? A Meatball? My Script? Me?' *TV Guide* (vol. 30, no. 21: 22 May), pp. 43–6.

Shibata, Mitsuzō

1983 *Hō no Tatemae to Honne* (Avowed Principles and Actual Practices in Japanese Law). Tokyo: Yūhikaku.

Shibata, Takeshi

1955 'Nihonjin no Jinmei' (Japanese Surnames). In *Kōza Nihongo Dai 2-kan: Nihongo no Kōzō* (Lectures on Japanese (II): The Structure of Japanese), edited by Nakamura Michio. Tokyo: Ōtsuki Shoten, pp. 125–45.

Shibata, Toshiharu

1979 *'Japan As Number One: Lessons for America.'* Book review in *Japan Quarterly* (vol. 26, no. 4: October-December), pp. 550–2.

Shibushiwan Kōgai Hantai Renraku Kyōgikai (The Joint Consultative Committee of Organizations Opposing the Pollution of Shibushi Bay).

1982 *Aru Kaihatsu Hantai Undō* (An Account of One Movement against

Regional Development). Tokyo: Gakuyō Shobō.
Shiga, Shigetaka
1937 *Nihon Fūkeiron* (A Theory of Japanese Landscape). Tokyo: Iwanami Shoten.
Shillany, Ben Ami
1982 *Politics and Culture in Wartime Japan.* Oxford: Oxford University Press.
Shiloh, Ruth
1976 *Yudayashiki Ikujihō* (Jewish Child-rearing), translated by Edagawa Kōichi. Tokyo: Goma Shobō.
Shimada, Haruo
1974 'The Structure of Earnings and Investment in Human Capital: A Comparison between the United States and Japan.' Ph.D. dissertation, University of Wisconsin.
1980 'The Japanese Employment System.' *Japanese Industrial Relations Series* no. 6. Tokyo: Japan Institute of Labor.
Shimahara, Nobuo
1971 *Burakumin: a Japanese Minority and Education.* The Hague: Martinus Nijhoff.
Shimizu, Ikutarō
1948 *Shakaigaku Kōgi* (Lectures on Sociology). Tokyo: Iwanami Shoten.
Shimodaira, Hiromi
1973 'Hinkon Seikatsu Kenkyū no Hōhō ni Kansuru Nōto' (Some Remarks on the Methodology of the Poverty and Livelihood Research Projects). *NRKZ* (vol. 15, no. 5: May), pp. 35–47.
Shinbori, Michiya
1965 *Nihon no Daigaku no Kyōju Shijō: Gakubatsu no Kenkyū* (The Labor Market at Japan's Universities: A Study of Academic Factions). Tokyo: Tōyōkan Shuppansha.
Shinoda, Yūjirō
1977 *Nihonjin to Doitsujin: Nekoze Bunka to Mune o Haru Bunka* (Japanese and Germans: the Culture of Bowing and the Culture of Putting out one's Chest). Tokyo: Kōbunsha.
1979 *Shimaguni to Nihonjin: Meishi Shakai to Tatami no Seishin* (The Island Country and the Japanese: The Name Card Society and the Spirit of the Tatami Mat). Tokyo: Kōbunsha.
1980 *Nihonjin yo Sokoku Bunka o Ushinauna* (Japanese! Don't give up your Cultural Heritage). Tokyo: Nihon Kōgyō Shibunsha.
Shinohara, Miyohei
1972 *Structural Changes in Japan's Economic Development.* Tokyo: Kinokuniya.
Shinotsuka, Eiko
1980 'Josei no Rōdō Shijō to Chingin Kakusa' (The Labor Market for Women and the Male-female Wage Differential). *ESP* (no. 99: July), pp. 16–21.

Shiota, Shōbei
1969 'Senryōka no Rōdō Undō' (The Labor Movement under the Occupation). In *Nihon Rōdō Undō no Rekishi to Kadai* (Issues in the History of the Japanese Labor Movement), edited by Rōdō Undōshi Kenkyūkai (Association for Research on the Labor Movement). Tokyo: Rōdō Junpōsha, pp. 74–109.

Shiotsuki, Yaeko
1972 *Kimono no Hon* (A Book on Kimonos). Tokyo: Kōbunsha.

Shiroyama, Saburō
1976 *Mainichi ga Nichiyōbi* (Every Day is Sunday). Tokyo: Shinchōsha.
1981 *Ikinokori no Jōken* (Conditions of Survival). Tokyo: Kōdansha.

Shisō no Kagaku Kenkyūkai, ed.
1959–62 *Tenkō* (Forced Conversion). 3 vols. Tokyo: Heibonsha.

Shively, Donald H.
1971 'Editor's Preface.' In *Tradition and Modernization in Japanese Culture*, edited by Donald H. Shively. Princeton, N.J.: Princeton University Press, pp. xiii–xvii.

Sibatani, Atuhiro
1981 *Imanishi Shinkaron Hihan Shiron* (An Exploratory Critique of the Evolution Theory of Professor Imanishi). Tokyo: Asahi Shuppansha.
1982 'A Personal Overview of the Noosa Heads Colloquium.' *Dialogue* (vol. 2, no. 1: March), pp. 10–11.

Sinh, Vinh
1982 'Japan in the World of the 1980s: A Historical Perspective.' In *Papers Presented at the Fifth Kyushu International Cultural Conference*. Fukuoka: Fukuoka UNESCO Association, pp. A3.1–A3.11.

Skeat, Walter W.
1910 *An Etymological Dictionary of the English Language*. Oxford: Clarendon Press. (Reprint 1961).

Smith, Eugene W., and Smith, Aileen
1975 *Minamata: Words and Photographs*. New York: Holt, Rinehart and Winston.

Smith, Lilian
1961 *Killers of the Dream*. New York: Norton.

Smith, Robert J.
1961 'Japanese Rural Community: Norms, Sanctions and Ostracism.' *American Anthropologist* (vol. 63, no. 3: June), pp. 522–33.
1971 '*Japanese Society* by Chie Nakane.' *American Anthropologist* (vol. 73, no. 6: December), pp. 1318–19.

Sōka Gakkai, Youth Division
1982 *Peace is Our Duty: Atrocities caused by War*. Tokyo: Japan Times.

Sone, Yasunori
1981 'Nihon – "Manjō Itchi Shakai" setsu no Kyokō' (The Fiction of Unanimous Consensus in Japanese Society). *Shūkan Tōyō Keizai*

(Kindai Keizaigaku Shirīzu, no. 57: 10 July), pp. 64–73.
1982a 'Seiji no Keizaigaku to Minshushugi no Kosuto' (The Economics of Political Behavior and the Costs of Democracy). In *Seiji no Keizaigaku* (The Economics of Political Behavior), edited by Shiratori Rei. Tokyo: Daiyamondosha, pp. 229–65.
1982b 'Nihon no Rieki Shūdan to Seijiteki Kettei Katei' (Interest Groups and Decision Making in Japan). Paper presented to the International Colloquium on the Comparative Study of Japanese Society, Noosa Heads, Queensland, Australia, 29 January–6 February.

Song, Du-Yul
1982 'Is the Japanese Model an Alternative?' *Telos* (no. 52: Summer), pp. 56–62.

Sōrifu Tōkeikyoku (Bureau of Statistics, Office of the Japanese Prime Minister)
1972 *Kigyō Tōōkei Chōsa: 1972* (Survey of Places of Employment: 1972). Tokyo: Ōkurashō Insatsukyoku.
1981a *Nihon no Tōkei* (Statistics of Japan). Tokyo: Ōkurashō Insatsukyok
1981b *Kakei Chōsa Nenpō 1980* (Annual Report on the Family Income and Expenditure Survey: 1980). Tokyo: Ōkurashō Insatsukyoku.
1982 *Kokusai Tōkei Yōran* (A Handbook of World Statistics). Tokyo: Ōkurashō Insatsukyoku.

Sorokin, Pitirim
1959 *Social Change and Mobility*. New York: Macmillan.

Sparks, D. E.
1972 'Nihon ni Okeru Shakai Hendō to Rōrei Mondai' (Social Change and Old Age in Japan). *NRKZ* (vol. 14, no. 12: December), pp. 47–61.

Spengler, Joseph J.
1953 'Changes in Income Distribution and Social Stratification: a Note.' *American Journal of Sociology* (vol. 41, no. 2: November), pp. 247–59.

Steiner, Kurt, *et al.*, eds.
1980 *Political Opposition and Local Politics in Japan*. Princeton, N.J.: Princeton University Press.

Steven, Rob
1979 'The Japanese Bourgeoisie.' *Bulletin of Concerned Asian Scholars* (vol. 11, no. 2: April–June), pp. 2–24.
1980 'The Japanese Working Class.' *Bulletin of Concerned Asian Scholars* (vol. 12, no. 3: July–September), pp. 38–58.

Stirling, Peter
1981 'Learning to Live with Japan, Inc.' *Australian Business* (30 July), pp. 40–55.

Stockwin, J. A. A.
1975 *Japan: Divided Politics in a Growth Economy*. New York: Norton.
1982 'Understanding Japanese Politics.' In *Japanese Society: Reappraisals*

and New Directions, edited by Yoshio Sugimoto and Ross Mouer as a special issue of *Social Analysis* (nos. 5/6: December 1980), pp. 144–53.

Stucki, Lorenz

1978a *Japans Herzen denken anders* (The Different Way the Japanese Think). Bern and München: Scherz Verlag.

1978b *Kokoro no Shakai: Nihon* (Japan: a Society which Stresses the Heart), translated by Ōkushi Kiyoko. Tokyo: Saimaru Shuppankai.

Sturmthal, Adolf, and Scoville, G., eds.

1973 *The International Labor Movement in Transition: Essays on Africa, Asia, Europe and South America.* Urbana, Ill.: University of Illinois Press.

Sugimoto, Yoshio

1975a 'Surplus Value, Unemployment and Industrial Turbulence: A Statistial Application of the Marxian Model to Post-war Japan'. *Journal of Conflict Resolution* (vol. 19, no. 1: March), pp. 25–47.

1975b 'Structural Sources of Popular Revolts and the Tōbaku Movement at the Time of the Meiji Restoration.' *Journal of Asian Studies* (vol. 34, no. 4: August), pp. 875–89.

1976 'Land Reform and Agrarian Disturbance: the Case of the American Occupation of Japan.' *Australian Journal of Politics and History* (vol. 22, no. 1: April), pp. 51–61.

1977a 'Labor Reform and Industrial Turbulence: the Case of the American Occupation of Japan.' *Pacific Sociological Review* (vol. 20, no. 1: October), pp. 492–514.

1977b 'Comparative Analysis of Industrial Conflict in Australia and Japan.' In *Sharpening the Focus*, edited by R. D. Walton. Brisbane: Griffith University, pp. 198–219.

1978a 'Quantitative Characteristics of Popular Disturbances in Post-Occupation Japan (1952–1960).' *Journal of Asian Studies* (vol. 37, no. 2: February), pp. 273–91.

1978b 'Measurement of Popular Disturbance.' *Social Sciences Research* (vol. 7, no. 3: September), pp. 284–97.

1978c 'Myths Reiterated.' *Hemisphere* (vol. 22, no. 4: April), pp. 14–15.

1979 '"Languagism" in Japanese Studies.' *Japanese Language Teaching Newsletter* (no. 3: Winter), pp. 10–11.

1980a '"Nihon Tokushu Shūdan-setsu" no Kōzui no Nakade' (Amid the Prevalence of the 'Uniquely Japanese Groupism' Theory). *AJ* (vol. 22, no. 46: November), pp. 10–14.

1980b Book Review of William Clifford, *Crime Control in Japan. Asian Studies Association of Australia Review* (vol. 4, no. 1: July), pp. 76–7.

1980c 'Value Differentiation in Japanese Proverbs: the Case of *Iroha Karuta*.' Paper presented to the Third National Conference of the Asian Studies Association of Australia, Griffith University,

Brisbane, 24–29 August.
1981a 'Nihonbyō toshiteno Hataraki Chūdoku' (Workaholism as the Japanese Disease). *AJ* (vol. 23, no. 13: March), pp. 30–4.
1981b 'Gendai Nihon ni okeru Fashizumu no Ne: "Nihonjinron" to "Kokusaikaron" no Shiya kara' (Sources of Japanese Fascism Today: from the Perspectives of Japanology and Internationalization Theories). *Shisō no Kaguku* (vol. 7, no. 2: May), pp. 58–64.
1981c 'Kokunai Mondai toshiteno Kokusaika Jidai' (The Internationalization Theory as Applied to Domestic Issues). *MSY* (6 March), p. 7.
1981d *Popular Disturbance in Postwar Japan.* Hong Kong: Asian Research Service.
1982a 'Bunka Gyappu o Kangaeru: Keizai Kokusai-shugi to Bunka Kokusui-shugi no Kyōsei' (The Cultural Gap in Trade Friction between Japan and the West: Symbiosis of Economic Internationalism and Cultural Nationalism). *Ekonomisuto* (vol. 60, no. 24: June), pp. 130–5.
1982b 'Nihon Raisan-ron no Shōwa no Naka de' (The Chorus of Theories Praising Japan's Achievements). *MSY* (25 January), p. 4. Translated into English and published in the *International House of Japan Bulletin* (vol. 2, no. 3: Summer), pp. 3–4 and *The Asia Record* (May).
1982c 'Japanese Society and Industrial Relations.' In *Industrial Relations in Japan*, by Yoshio Sugimoto, Haruo Shimada, and Solomon B. Levine. Melbourne: Japanese Studies Centre, pp. 1–20.

Sugimoto, Yoshio, and Mouer, Ross
1979a 'Nakane Chie Setsu e no Hōhōronteki Gimon' (Some Methodological Problems in the Theory of Nakane Chie). *Gendai no Me* (vol. 20, no. 7: July), pp. 124–35.
1979b 'A Discussion Paper on the Limits of Japanology as a Paradigm for Understanding Japanese Society.' Paper delivered to a seminar organized by the Australia-Japan Economic Relations Research Project, Australian National University, Canberra, on 12 November.
1979c 'Japanology: a Methodological Dead End for Theories Assuming Uniformity Among the Japanese.' *Griffith Translation Series* no. 2. Brisbane: School of Modern Asian Studies, Griffith University.
1980a 'Some Questions Concerning Commonly Accepted Stereotypes of Japanese Society.' *Research Paper* no. 64. Canberra: Australia-Japan Economic Relations Research Project.
1980b 'The Future of Japanese Studies: Philosophy, Journalism, Science or Art?' *Center News* (vol. 4, no. 8: March), pp. 1–6.
1981 *Japanese Society: Stereotypes and Realities.* Melbourne: Japanese Studies Centre.
1982a 'Multiple Dimensions in the Delineation of Job Situations in Japan and the United States.' In *Japanese Society: Reappraisals and New Directions*, edited by Yoshio Sugimoto and Ross Mouer as a special

issue of *Social Analysis* (nos. 5/6: December 1980), pp. 79–101.

1982b 'Competing Models for Understanding Japanese Society: Some Reflections on New Directions.' In *Japanese Society: Reappraisals and New Directions*, edited by Yoshio Sugimoto and Ross Mouer as a special issue of *Social Analysis* (nos. 5/6: December 1980), pp. 194–204.

1982c 'Toward the Comparative Study of Japan.' *Australia-Japan Foundation Newsletter* (vol. 2, no. 1: April), pp. 14–16. Also in the *Center News* of the Japanese Studies Center of the Japan Foundation (vol. 7, no. 2: June), pp. 2–4.

Sugimoto, Yoshio, and Mouer, Ross, eds.

1982 *Japanese Society: Reappraisals and New Directions*. A special issue of *Social Analysis* (nos. 5/6: December 1980). Adelaide: University of Adelaide.

Sugito, Seiju

1979 'Shokuba Keigo no Ichijittai–Hitachi Seisakusho de no Chōsa kara' (The Use of Polite Language at Work: a Report on the Survey at Hitachi Manufacturing). *Gengo Seikatsu* (no. 328: April), pp. 30–44.

Sumii, Sue

1961 *Hashi no Nai Kawa* (River without a Bridge). Tokyo: Shinchōsha.

Sumita, Yutaka

1965 *Shakai Seisaku Kōgi* (An Introduction to Social Policy). Tokyo: Miraisha.

Sumitomo Corporation

1982 *Aspects of Japanese Culture, Tradition and Behavior*. Tokyo: Sumitomo Corporation.

Sumiya, Mikio

1954 'Chinrōdō no Riron ni Tsuite' (On the Theory of Wage Labor). *Keizaigaku Ronshū* (vol. 23, no. 1: October), pp. 22–69.

1965 *Rōdō Keizairon* (The Theory of Labor Economics). Tokyo: Nihon Hyōronsha.

1969 *Nihonjin no Keizai Kōdō* (The Economic Behavior of the Japanese). 2 vols. Tokyo: Tōyō Keizai Shinpōsha.

1974 'Rōdō Mondai Kenkyū no Kihonteki Shikaku: Chinrōdō no Riron o Megutte' (Toward a New Foundation for the Study of Labor Problems: Some Thoughts about the Debate on the Theory of Wage Labor). *Shisō* (no. 600: June), pp. 741–60.

1981 'Nihonteki Rōshi Kankeiron no Saikōchiku' (Restructuring the Theory of Industrial Relations in Japan). *NRKZ* (vol. 23, no. 1: January), pp. 1–3.

Suzuki, Eitarō

1971 *Suzuki Eitarō Chosakushū* (Collection of the Writings of Suzuki Eitarō). 6 vols. Tokyo: Miraisha.

Suzuki, Masashi, and Inoue, Kiyoshi

1956 *Nihon Kindaishi* (The History of Modern Japan). Tokyo: Gōdō Shuppansha.

Suzuki, Yukio

1974 'Keizai Ronri kara no Gyōsei Shidō no Kōzai' (Merits and Demerits of Administrative Guidance Based on Economic Logic). *Jichi Kenshū* (no. 167: July), pp. 24–30.

Tada, Tetsunosuke

1975a 'Sukiyaki.' *Encyclopedia Japonica.* Revised edition. Tokyo: Shōgakukan, vol. 10, pp. 262–3.

1975b 'Nabe Ryōri' (Boiled Pot Dishes). *Encyclopedia Japonica.* Revised edition. Tokyo: Shōgakukan, vol. 13, pp. 664–5.

Taira, Koji

1970 *Economic Development and the Labor Market in Japan.* New York: Columbia University Press.

Taishō Kaijō Kasai

1981 'Chūnen Sararīman no Sukina Kotowaza' (Proverbs which Middle-Aged Salaried Employees are Fond of). In *Shūkan Daiyamondo Bessatsu: Nippon Nandemo 10-Ketsu.* Tokyo: Daiyamondosha, p. 33.

Takagi, Nobuyuki

1982 '"Nihon ni Manabe" Uchidasu Mareshia' (Malaysia on the Road to Learning from Japan). *Ekonomisuto* (14 June), pp. 119–23.

Takahashi, Chōtarō

1959 *Dynamic Changes of Income and its Distribution in Japan.* Written with the collaboration of Iochi Ryōtarō and Emi Kōichi. Tokyo: Kinokuniya.

Takahashi, Kō

1970 *Nihonteki Rōshi Kankei no Kenkyū* (Studies of Japanese-style Industrial Relations). Revised edition. Tokyo: Miraisha.

Takahashi, Nobuko

1975 'Women's Wages in Japan and the Question of Equal Pay.' *International Labour Review* (vol. 111, no. 1: January), pp. 51–68.

Takahashi, Tetsu, *et al.*

1983 'Shunin Kenkyūin ni Miru Zunō Shūdan no Puro Ishiki: Saifujō Shita Nihon no Shinku Tanku' (The Re-emergence of Japan's Think Tanks: What the Pros Think–A Report on a Survey of Senior Research Officers). *AJ* (21 January), pp. 22–6.

Takano, Shirō

1970 *Gendai no Hinkon to Shakai Hoshō* (Poverty in Present-day Society and Social Guarantees). Tokyo: Chōbunsha.

Takasuga, Yoshihiro, and Teranishi, Jirō

1974 'Economics.' *An Introductory Bibliography for Japanese Studies* (vol. 1, part 1), pp. 29–48.

Takata, Yasuma

1934 *Hinja Hisshō* (The Inevitable Victory of the Poor). Tokyo: Chikuma Shobō.

Takatori, Masao

1975 *Nihonteki Shikō no Genkei* (The Origins of Japanese Thought). Tokyo: Kōdansha.

Takayama, Noriyuki

1980 Fubyōdō no Keizai Bunseki (The Economic Analysis of Inequality). Tokyo: Tōyō Keizai Shinpōsha.

Takayanagi, Shun-ichi

1976 'In Search of Yanagita Kunio.' *Monumenta Nipponica* (vol. 31, no. 2: Spring), pp. 165–78.

Takemae, Eiji

1970 *Amerika Tainichi Rōdō Seisaku no Kenkyū* (Studies of America's Labor Policy for Japan). Tokyo: Nihon Hyōronsha.

Takemura, Ken-ichi, ed.

1977 *Nihon no Jōshiki wa Sekai no Hijōshiki* (Japanese Common Sense is Absurd in the World Scene). Tokyo: Daiyamondosha.

Takemura, Ken-ichi, and Clark, Gregory

1979 *Yunīkuna Nihonjin* (The Unique Japanese). Tokyo: Kōdansha.

Takenaka, Yasukazu

1977 *Nihonteki Keiei no Genryū* (The Origins of Peculiarly Japanese Patterns of Management). Kyoto: Mineruva Shobō.

Takeuchi, Hiroshi, and Asō, Makoto, eds.

1982 *Nihon no Gakureki Shakai wa Kawaru* (The School-based Career Society will Change). Tokyo: Yūhikaku.

Takeuchi, Naoichi

1972 *Shōhisha Undō Sengen* (A Proclamation for Consumer Movements). Tokyo: Gendai Hyōronsha.

Takeuchi, Yō

1980 *Kyōsō no Shakaigaku: Gakureki to Shōshin* (The Sociology of Competition: School Career and Promotion). Tokyo: Sekai Shisōsha.

Takeuchi, Yoshimi

1952 *Nihon Ideorogī* (Japanese Ideology). Tokyo: Chikuma Shobō.

Takezawa, Shin-ichi, and Whitehill, Arthur M.

1981 *Work Ways: Japan and America.* Tokyo: Japan Institute of Labor.

Tamaru, Misuzu

1982 'Konna Jōshi o Motsu Fukō' (The Unpleasantness of Having this Person over Me). *Bungei Shunjū* (vol. 60, no. 7: July), pp. 220–8.

Tanaka, Hiroshi, ed.

1963 *Hachijōkoku Jidai no Nippon Keizai* (The Japanese Economy under Article Eight). Tokyo: Daiyamondosha.

Tanaka, Yasuo

1981 *Nantonaku Kurisutaru* (Nevertheless Glistening). Tokyo: Kawade Shobō Shinsha.

Teihen no Kai (The Group at the Bottom), ed.
1961 *Doya-Sanya o Chūshin ni* (Shanty Town: a Look at Sanya). Tokyo: San-ichi Shobō.
Thurlow, Lester C.
1980 *The Zero-Sum Society*. New York: Basic Books.
Thurston, Donald R.
1973 *Teachers and Politics in Japan*. Princeton, N.J.: Princeton University Press.
Tilly, Charles, Tilly, Louise, and Tilly, Richard
1975 *The Rebellious Century, 1830–1930*. Cambridge, Mass.: Harvard University Press.
Titmuss, Richard
1962 *Income Distribution and Social Change*. London: Allen and Unwin.
Toba, Kin-ichirō
1978 *Futatsu no Kao no Nihonjin: Tōnan Ajia no naka de* (The Two Faces of the Japanese: A Report from Southeast Asia). Tokyo: Chuō Kōronsha.
Tōbata, Seiichi, ed.
1966 *The Modernization of Japan*. Tokyo: Institute of Asian Economic Affairs.
Tokyo Metropolitan Government
1972 *Minor Industries and Workers in Tokyo*. Tokyo Metropolitan Government Municipal Library Series, no. 8. Tokyo: Tokyo Metropolitan Government.
Tōkyo-to Kikaku Chōseikyoku (Tokyo Metropolitan Government, Policy Planning Bureau)
1972 *Kijunten Hōshiki ni yoru Fukushi Shihyō Sakusei no Kokoromi* (A Proposal for a Measure of Social Welfare Using a Formula Based on Basic Standards). Tokyo: Tokyo Metropolitan Government.
Tominaga, Ken-ichi
1965 *Shakai Hendō no Riron* (The Theory of Social Change). Tokyo: Iwanami Shoten.
1968 'Social Mobility in Tokyo.' In *Comparative Perspectives on Stratification: Mexico, Great Britain, Japan*, edited by Joseph A. Kahl. Boston, Mass.: Little, Brown, pp. 180–94.
1969 'Trend Analysis of Social Stratification and Social Mobility in Contemporary Japan.' *The Developing Economies* (vol. 7, no. 4: December), pp. 471–98.
1970a 'Shakai Idō no Sūsei Bunseki–1955–1965' (An Analysis of Social Mobility in Japan: 1955–1965). *Shakaigaku Hyōron* (vol. 21, no. 1: July), pp. 2–24.
1970b 'Studies of Social Stratification and Social Mobility in Japan: 1955–1967.' *Rice University Studies* (vol. 56, no. 4: Fall), pp. 133–49.
1973 'Social Mobility in Japan – Prewar and Postwar.' *Japan Interpreter* (vol. 8, no. 3: Autumn), pp. 374–86.

Tominaga, Ken-ichi, ed.

1979 *Nihon no Kaisō Kōzō* (The Structure of Social Stratification in Japan). Tokyo: Tokyo Daigaku Shuppankai.

Tosaka, Jun

1937 *Nihon Ideorogīron* (On Japanese Ideology). Expanded edition. Tokyo: Hakuyōsha.

Totten, George

1966 *The Social Democratic Movement in Prewar Japan*. New Haven, Conn.: Yale University Press.

Totten, George, and Wagatsuma, Hiroshi

1967 'Emancipation: Growth and Transformation of a Political Movement.' In *Japan's Invisible Race*, edited by George DeVos and Hiroshi Wagatsuma. Berkeley, Cal.: University of California Press, pp. 33–67.

Toyota, Toshio

1970 'Education in the Modernization of Japan and Asia.'*Review of International Affairs* (vol. 21, no. 493: 20 October), pp. 19–21.

Treiman, Donald J.

1977 *Occupational Prestige in Comparative Perspective*. New York: Academic Press.

Tsuda, Masumi

1968 *Nenkōteki Rōshi Kankeiron* (The Theory of Japanese-style Industrial Relations). Kyoto: Mineruva Shobō.

1976 *Nihonteki Keiei no Yōgo* (The Vindication of Japanese-style Management). Tokyo: Tōyō Keizai Shinpōsha.

1977 *Nihonteki Keiei no Ronri* (The Logic of Japanese-style Management). Tokyo: Chūō Keizaisha.

Tsujimura, Kōtarō

1972 'Rōdō Jikan Tanshuku wa Seisan o Bōgai Shieru ka.' *Keizai Hyōron* (vol. 2, no. 12: November), pp. 56–67. This was later published as 'The Effect of Reductions in Working Hours on Productivity,' in *The Labor Market in Japan: Selected Readings*, edited by Nishikawa Shunsaku. Tokyo: University of Tokyo Press, 1980, pp. 67–83.

Tsukushi, Tetsuya

1982 *Sekai no Nihonjinkan* (Views of the Japanese from around the World). Tokyo: Jiyū Kokuminsha.

Tsunoda, Tadanobu

1978 *Nihonjin no Nō: Nō no Hataraki to Tōzai no Bunka* (The Brain Structure of the Japanese: Functions of the Brain and Eastern and Western Culture). Tokyo: Taishūkan.

Tsurumi, Kazuko

1968 'The Japanese Student Movement (1): its Milieu.' *Japan Quarterly* (vol. 15, no. 4: October/December), pp. 430–55.

1970 *Social Change and the Individual: Japan before and after Defeat in*

World War II. Princeton, N.J.: Princeton University Press.

1972 *Kōkishin to Nihonjin* (Curiosity and the Japanese). Tokyo: Kōdansha.

Tsurumi, Shunsuke

1980 'A Glimpse of Wartime Japan.' *Center for East Asian Studies Occasional Papers*, no. 7. Montreal: McGill University.

1982 *Senjiki Nihon no Seishinshi* (Intellectual History of Wartime Japan). Tokyo: Iwanami Shoten.

1983 *Japanese Conceptions of Asia.* Melbourne: Japanese Studies Centre.

Tsurumi, Shunsuke, Ono, Nobuyuki, and Eakes, Yan

1972 *Sensō no Kikai o Tomero*! (Stop the War Machine!). Tokyo: San-ichi Shobō.

Tumin, Melvin

1953 'Some Principles of Stratification: A Critical Analysis.' *American Sociological Review* (vol. 18, no. 4: August), pp. 387–94.

1967 *Social Stratification: the Forms and Functions of Inequality.* Englewood Cliffs, N.J.: Prentice-Hall.

Uchiyama, Hideo

1982 'The Actualities of State and Democracy in Japan.' In *Papers Presented at the Fifth Kyushu International Cultural Conference.* Fukuoka: Fukuoka UNESCO Association, pp. B3.1–B3.10.

Ueki, Emori

1879 *Minken Jiyūron* (On People's Rights and Liberty). Reprinted in *Meiji Bunka Zenshū* (Collection of Cultural Writings in Meiji Japan), vol. 2, 1967. Tokyo: Nihon Hyōronsha, pp. 181–96.

Uemura, Naomi

1980 *Uemura Naomi Bōken* (Adventures of Uemura Naomi). Tokyo: Mainichi Shinbunsha.

Ui, Jun

1968 *Kōgai no Seijigaku* (The Politics of Pollution). Tokyo: Sanseidō.

1971–4 *Kōgai Genron* (An Introduction to Environmental Studies). 3 vols. Tokyo: Aki Shobō.

Ui, Jun, Miyamoto, Ken-ichi, and Miyamoto, Akira

1971 *Kōgai: Genten kara no Kokuhatsu* (Pollution: a Protest from the Grass Roots). Tokyo: Kōdansha.

Umemura, Mataji

1967 'Nenkō Chingin ni Tsuite.' *Keizai Kenkyū* (vol. 18, no. 2: April), pp. 160–3. This was later published as 'The Seniority-Merit Wage System in Japan,' in *The Labor Market in Japan: Selected Readings*, edited by Nishikawa Shunsaku. Tokyo: University of Tokyo Press, 1980, pp. 177–87.

1971 'Nenkō-Shotoku Purofiru no Kokusai Hikaku' (Some International Comparisons of Income Profiles and Seniority Wages). *Keizai*

Kenkyū (vol. 22, no. 3: July), pp. 271–5.

Umesao, Tadaō

1957 'Bunmei no Seitai Shikan Josetsu' (An Introduction to the Ecological Theory of the History of Civilizations). *Chūō Kōron* (vol. 72, no. 2: February), pp. 32–49.

1967 *Bunmei no Seitai Shikan* (An Ecological View of the History of Civilizations). Tokyo: Chūō Kōronsha.

Umetani, Shun-ichirō

1980 'Present Japanese Employment and Wage Structure.' *Japan Labor Bulletin* (vol. 19, no. 11: November), pp. 4–10.

United States, Department of Labor, and Japan, Ministry of Labor and Ministry of International Trade and Industry

1966 *Wages in Japan and the United States: Report on the Joint United States-Japan Wage Study.* Washington, DC: US Government Printing Office.

Uno, Kimio

1977 'An Econometric Model of Social Indicators and its Application to Social Policies: a Japanese Experience.' *Nihon Keizai Kenkyū* (no. 6: August), pp. 17–38.

1981 'Quality of Life and Voting Behavior in Japan: 1960–1979.' *Nihon Keizai Kenkyū* (no. 10: March), pp. 28–38.

Uno, Yoshiyasu, ed.

1982 *Kokusai Masatsu no Mekanizumu: Ibunka Kussetsu Riron o Megutte* (The Mechanism Explaining International Friction: an Examination of the Theory of Cultural Refractions). Tokyo: Saiensusha.

Uyehara, Cecil H.

1959 *Leftwing Social Movements in Japan: an Annotated Bibliography.* Tokyo: Charles E. Tuttle.

Valliant, Robert B.

1974 'The Selling of Japan: Japanese Manipulation of Western Opinion, 1900–1905.' *Monumenta Nipponica* (vol. 29, no. 4: Winter), pp. 415–38.

Van Zandt, Howard F.

1970 'Japanese Culture and the Business Boom.' *Foreign Affairs* (vol. 48, no. 2: January), pp. 344–57.

1972 'Learning to Do Business with "Japan, Inc.".' *Harvard Business Review* (vol. 50, no. 4: July-August), pp. 83–92.

Vogel, Ezra

1963 *Japan's New Middle Class.* Berkeley, Cal.: University of California Press.

1967 'Kinship Structure, Migration to the City, and Modernization.' In *Aspects of Social Change in Modern Japan*, edited by Ronald P. Dore. Princeton, N.J.: Princeton University Press, pp. 91–111.

1970 *Japan's New Middle Class*. Revised edition. Berkeley: University of California Press.
1975 'Introduction: Toward More Accurate Concepts.' In *Modern Japanese Organizations and Decision-making*, edited by Ezra Vogel. Berkeley, Cal.: University of California Press, pp. xiii–xxv.
1979a *Japan as Number One*. Cambridge, Mass.: Harvard University Press.
1979b *Japan Azu Nanbāwan* (Japan as No. 1), translated by Hironaka Wakako and Kimoto Akiko. Tokyo: TBS Buritanika.
1980a *Japan as Number One: Lessons for America*. Tokyo: Charles E. Tuttle.
1980b *Riben Minglie Diui* (Japan as Number One), translated into Chinese by Guying, Zhangke and Danliu. Beijing: Shijie Zhishi Chubanshe.

Wade, Nicholas
1982 'Beaten at Our Own Game: What to Learn from Japan's Victory in the 64K RAM Race.' *New York Times* (9 March), p. A22.
Wagatsuma, Hiroshi
1967 'Postwar Political Militance.' In *Japan's Invisible Race*, edited by George DeVos and Hiroshi Wagatsuma. Berkeley, Cal.: University of California Press, pp. 68–87.
Wakamori, Tarō
1973 *Tennōsei no Rekishi Shinri* (Historical Psychology of the Emperor System). Tokyo: Kōbundō.
Wakata, Kyōji
1981 *Gendai Nihon no Seiji to Fūdo* (Japanese-style Politics). Kyoto: Mineruva Shobō.
Ward, Robert E.
1968 'Introduction.' In *Political Development in Modern Japan*, edited by Robert E. Ward. Princeton, N.J.: Princeton University Press, pp. 3–9.
Ward, Robert E, and Rustow, Dankwart A., eds.
1964 *Political Modernization in Japan and Turkey*. Princeton, N.J.: Princeton University Press.
Watanabe, Shōichi
1976 *Chiteki Seikatsu no Hōhō* (Methods for Intellectual Activity). Tokyo: Kōdansha.
1980 *Nihon Soshite Nihonjin: Sekai ni Hiruinaki 'Donbyakushō Hassō' no Chie* (Japan and the Japanese: The Wisdom in the Unique Thought Processs of the 'Uncivilized Peasants' in Japan). Tokyo: Shōdensha.
Watanabe, Shōichi, ed.
1975 *Nihon no Eichi* (Japanese Intelligence). Tokyo: Nihon Kyōbunsha.
Watanuki, Jōji
1967 'Daitoshi Jūmin no Seijiishiki' (The Political Consciousness of

Residents in Large Cities). *NRKZ* (vol. 9, no. 1: January), pp. 11–23.
1980 'Social Structure and Voting Behavior in Japan.' *Research Paper* no. A-41. Tokyo: Institute of International Relations for Advanced Studies on Peace and Development in Asia, Sophia University.
1982 'Social Structure and Voting in Japan: a Multidimensional Approach to the Study of Ideology and Voting Behaviour.' In *Japanese Society: Reappraisals and New Directions*, edited by Yoshio Sugimoto and Ross Mouer as a special issue of *Social Analysis* (nos. 5/6: December 1980), pp. 170–83.

Watsuji, Tetsurō
1935 *Fūdo* (Climatology). Tokyo: Iwanami Shoten.
1962 *A Climate: a Philosophical Study*, translated by Geoffrey Bownas. Tokyo: Japanese Government Printing Bureau.
1971 Second edition. Tokyo: Hokuseido Press.

Weber, Max
1958 'Class, Status and Power.' In *From Max Weber: Essays in Sociology*, translated by H. H. Gerth and C. Wright Mills. New York: Oxford University Press, pp. 180–5.

Weinstein, Deena, and Weinstein, Michael A.
1974 *Living Sociology: a Critical Introduction.* New York: David Mackay.

Wellemeyer, Marilyn
1974 'The Class the Dollars Fell On,' *Fortune* (vol. 89, no. 5: May), pp. 225–9.

Wessolowski, W.
1969 'The Notions of Strata and Class in Socialist Society,' translated from Polish by André Béteille. In *Social Inequality: Selected Readings*, edited by André Béteille. Baltimore, Md.: Penguin Books, pp. 125–33.

Whitehill, Arthur M., Jr., and Takezawa, Shin-ichi
1968 *The Other Worker: a Comparative Study of Industrial Relations in the United States and Japan.* Honolulu, Hawaii: East-West Center Press.

Whiting, Robert
1977 *The Chrysanthemum and the Bat.* Tokyo: Permanent Press.

Whymant, Robert
1982a 'Children May Never Learn Truth of Japanese Brutality in China.' *TDY* (22 August), p. 7.
1982b 'Strangers in a Strange Land.' *TDY* (3 October), p. 5.

Wigmore, John Henry
1967–70 *Law and Justice in Tokugawa Japan.* 10 parts. Tokyo: Kokusai Bunka Shinkōkai.
1969–75 *Law and Justice in Tokugawa Japan.* 12 vols. Tokyo: University of Tokyo Press.

Wilcox, Claire
1966 *Economies of the World Today: Their Organization, Development and Performance.* New York: Harcourt, Brace and Jovanovich.
Wild, Ronald
1974 'Social Stratification or Statistical Exercises?' In *Social Change in Australia: Readings in Sociology*, edited by Don Edgar. Melbourne: Cheshire, pp. 227–35.
Wilkinson, Endymion
1981 *Misunderstanding: Europe vs. Japan.* Tokyo: Chūō Kōronsha.
Will, George
1982 'Country's Conflicting Desires.' *Daily Bangor News* (22 December), p. 10.
Wilson, James Q.
1978 *Varieties of Police Behavior: the Management of Law and Order in Eight Communities.* Cambridge, Mass.: Harvard University Press.
Wilson, Robert, and Hosokawa, Bill
1980 *East to America.* New York: Morrow.
Woodland, D. J. A.
1968 'Role.' In *A Dictionary of Sociology*, edited by G. Duncan Mitchell. London: Routledge and Kegan Paul, pp. 148–52.
Wootton, Barbara
1962 *Social Foundations of Wage Policy.* London: Allen and Unwin.
Woronoff, Jon
1979 *Japan: the Coming Economic Crisis.* Tokyo: Lotus Press.
1980 *Japan: the Coming Social Crisis.* Tokyo: Lotus Press.
1981a *Japan's Wasted Workers.* Tokyo: Lotus Press.
1981b *Maboroshi no Han-ei Nippon* (The Illusion of Prosperity: Japan), translated by Nomura Jirō. Tokyo: Kōdansha.
Wrong, Dennis H.
1969 'Social Inequality without Stratification.' In *Structured Social Inequality: a Reader in Comparative Social Stratification*, edited by Celia Heller. New York: Macmillan, pp. 513–20.

Yabu, Keizō
1982 'Sensō no Kizuato' (The Scars of War). *ASY* (26 July), p. 5.
Yakabe, Katsumi, ed.
1977 *Labor Relations in Japan: Fundamental Characteristics.* Tokyo: Ministry of Foreign Affairs.
Yakura, Hisayasu, Sada, Tomoko, Matsuno, Osamu, and Ide, Magoroku
1982 'Kyōiku Genba no Fukenkō' (Unhealthy Education in Progress). *Sekai* (no. 440: July), pp. 240–57.
Yamada, Ichirō
1976 *Nihonteki Keiei no Hihan* (A Critique of Japanese Management). Tokyo: Daisan Shuppan.

Yamagishi, Toshio, and Brinton, Mary C.
1980 'Sociology in Japan and *Shakai-Ishikiron.*' *American Sociologist* (vol. 15, no. 4: November), pp. 192–207.
Yamagishikai, ed.
1973 *Z-Kakumei Shūdan Yamagishikai* (The Z Revolution Group Yamagishikai). Tokyo: Rukku Bukkusu.
Yamaguchi, Masayuki
1972 *Gendai Shakai to Chishiki Rōdō* (Modern Society and Knowledge-intensive Work). Tokyo: Shin Nihon Shuppansha.
Yamamoto, Mitsuru
1981 'Nihon ga Kokusai Shakai de Ikiru Jōken' (Some Conditions for Japan to Survive as a Member of the International Community). *Ekonomisuto* (no. 2389: 13–20 January), pp. 10–16.
Yamamoto, Shichihei
1979a *Kinben no Tetsugaku: Nihonjin o Ugokasu Genri* (The Philosophy of Hard Work: Principles Which Motivate the Japanese). Kyoto: PHP Kenkyūsho.
1979b *Nihonjin-teki Hassō to Seiji Bunka* (Japanese Thought Patterns and Political Culture). Tokyo: Nihon Shoseki.
1979c *Nihon Shihonshugi no Seishin* (The Spirit of Japanese Capitalism). Tokyo: Kōbunsha.
Yamamoto, Shichihei, and Komuro, Naoki
1981 *Nihonkyō no Shakaigaku* (A Sociology of Belief in Japan). Tokyo: Kōdansha.
Yamamoto, Shigemi
1972 *Aa Nomugi Tōge* (At Last, the Nomugi Pass). Tokyo: Asahi Shinbunsha.
Yamamoto, Yūjirō
1980 *Shin Kokufuron* (A New Theory of the Wealth of Nations). Tokyo: Ōesu Shuppansha.
Yamanaka, Tokutarō, ed.
1971 *Small Business in Japan's Economic Progress.* Tokyo: Asahi Evening News.
Yamanouchi, Kazuo
1977 *Gyōsei Shidō* (Administrative Guidance). Tokyo: Kōbunsha.
Yamashiro, Aki, ed.
1979 *Nihonteki Keiei no Kōchiku* (The Structure of Japanese-style Managment). Tokyo: Bijinesu Kyōiku Shuppan.
Yamazaki, Harunari
1966 'Sengo Nihon ni okeru Kaikyū Kōsei no Hendō' (Changes in the Class Composition of Postwar Japan). In *Gendai Nihon Shihon Shugi Kōza*, edited by Ikumi *et al.* Tokyo: Hyōronsha, vol. 2, pp. 255–81.
Yamazaki, Toyoko
1965 *Shiroi Kyotō* (The White Tower). Tokyo: Shinchōsha.

1969 *Zoku Shiroi Kyotō* (The Second Volume of the White Tower). Tokyo: Shinchōsha.

Yamazawa, Kayoko, and Takamizu, Takae

1969 'Josei Kotoba Higashi to Nishi' (East-West Differences in Female Japanese Language). *Kyōritsu Joshi Daigaku Tanki Daigaku Bunka Kiyō* (no. 13: December). pp. 140–56.

Yanaga, Chitose

1968 *Big Business in Japanese Politics.* New Haven, Conn.: Yale University Press.

Yanaga, Teizō, Nagahara, Keiji, Fujishima, Toshio, and Kajinishi, Mitsuhaya, eds.

1965 *Nihon Keizaishi Taikei* (An Outline of Japanese Economic History). 6 vols. Tokyo: Tokyo Daigaku Shuppankai.

Yanagida, Kunio

1962–64 *Teihon Yanagida Kunio-shū* (The Standard Collection of Writings of Yanagida Kunio). 31 vols. Tokyo: Chikuma Shobō.

Yano, Ichirō, ed.

1981 *Sūji de Miru Nihon no 100-nen* (Figures on Japan's Last Hundred Years). Tokyo: Kokuseisha.

Yano, Seiya, and Yamazaki, Mitsuru

1972 *Shōhisha Binbō no Tsuiseki: Nihonjin no Yokkyū Fuman wa Dokokara Kuruka* (Looking at the Impoverished Japanese Consumer: Sources of Need Frustration in Japan). Tokyo: Tōyō Keizai Shinpōsha

Yano Tsuneo Kinenkai

1981 *Nihon no Hyakunen* (A Century of Japanese Statistics). Tokyo: Kokuseisha.

Yasuba, Yasukichi

1975 'Anatomy of the Debate on Japanese Capitalism.' *Journal of Japanese Studies* (vol. 2, no. 1: Autumn), pp. 63–82.

Yasuda, Saburō

1971 *Shakai Idō no Kenkyū* (Research on Social Mobility). Tokyo: Tokyo Daigaku Shuppankai.

1973 'Gendai Nihon no Kaikyū Ishiki' (Class Consciousness in Modern Japan). In *Gendai Nihon no Kaikyū Ishiki* (Class Consciousness in Modern Japan), edited by Yasuda Saburō. Tokyo: Yūhikaku, pp. 201–10.

1980 'Nihon Shakairon Bunken Mokurokusho' (A Bibliography of Works on Japanese Society). *Gendai Shakaigaku* (vol. 7, no. 1), pp. 74–87.

Yokoyama, Gennosuke

1949 *Nihon no Kasō Shakai* (The Lower Classes in Japan). Tokyo: Chūō Rōdō Gakuen.

Yomiuri Shinbunsha, ed.

1971 *Denaose Keizai Ōkoku: Nihon no Kokumin Mokuhyō o Kangaeru*

(Rethink the Meaning of Being an Economic Power: Goals of the Japanese People). Tokyo: Daiyamondosha.

Yoneyama, Shōko, Sugimoto, Yoshio, and Mouer, Ross

1980 'Some Further Research on Stereotypical Images of Japanese Society: Report on a Content Analysis of *Japan as Number One* and *The Japanese.*' Paper presented to the Third National Conference of the Asian Studies Association of Australia, Griffith University, Brisbane, 24–29 August.

Yoneyama, Toshinao

1976 *Nihonjin no Nakama Ishiki* (The Japanese Sense of Comradeship). Tokyo: Kōdansha.

Yoshikawa, Eiji

1981 *Musashi*, translated from Japanese by Charles S. Terry. New York: Harper and Row.

Yoshimoto, Takaaki

1959 *Geijutsuteki Teikō to Zasetsu* (Artistic Resistance and Philosophical Breakdown). Tokyo: Miraisha.

Yoshimura, Masaharu

1961 *Jiyūka to Nihon Keizai* (Liberalization and the Japanese Economy). Tokyo: Iwanami Shoten.

Yoshino, Michael

1968 *Japan's Managerial System: Tradition and Innovation.* Cambridge, Mass.: MIT Press.

Yoshisato, Naoaki

1982 'Shakai Hoshō no Taikeika Kyūmu' (The Necessity of Systematizing Japanese Social Welfare). *ASC* (8 July), p. 4.

Yūki, Masaharu

1970 *Gunki Hatameku Moto ni* (Beneath the Army's Unfurled Banner). Tokyo: Chūō Kōronsha.

Zhang, Kening

1982 'A Brief Introduction to the Recent Chinese Press Coverage of Japan.' Paper presented to the International Colloquium on the Comparative Study of Japanese Society, Noosa Heads, Queensland, Australia, 29 January–6 February.

Index

Abegglen, James C., 24, 35-6, 50, 55, 56
  business elites, 279
  seniority wages, 287, 460
academic life, 158-63
Akahata, 81
Akiyama, Kenjirō, 78
Akiyama, Minoru, 236-239
alienation, 5, 79
  in firms, 101, 103-6, 365
Allen, G.C., 419
aloofness, *see* social distance
'Alternative Models for Understanding Japanese Society' — Symposium, Australia (1980), 14
amae psychology, 14, 33, 130, 138
Amano, Katsufumi, 178
America, *see* United States of America
Ampo demonstrations, 67, 91, 108
Ampo News, 175. *See also* US–Japan Security Treaty
anthropology, 23-6
anti-nuclear movement, 71, 378
anti-pollution movements, 67, 69, 82, 337
Aoi, Kazuo, 161
Aoki, Kōji, 108
Aonuma, Yoshimatsu, 277, 279
area studies, vi, 24, 27, 414-417
Arisawa, Hiromi, 100
Ariyoshi, Sawako, 159
Aruga, Kizaemon, 43, 44, 283, 465
Asahi Shinbun, 195, 385
Aso, Makoto, 101, 279
Athos, Anthony G., 38
Atsumi, Reiko, 101, 355
Austin, Lewis, 33
Australia
  group model of Jap. society, 90-1
  industrial conflict compared with Japan, 111-14, 173-4
  relations with Japan, 7, 165, 393-395
  television, 197, 226
  White policy, 384
  Australia–Japan Foundation, viii, 394
  Australian Business, 91
autobiographies, 198-199
Azumi, Koya, 103, 280

BBC: *Perspectives on Japan*, 392
Ballon, Robert J., 88, 163, 287
Baltzell, E. Digby, 310-311
Basic Survey of the Wage Structure (BSWS), 119-23
Bayley, David H., 38, 241
Beardsley, Richard K.: *Twelve Doors to Japan*, 9
Befu, Harumi
  exchange theory, 14
  internationalism, 380-81, 389
  Japan: an Anthropological Introduction, 9
  on marriage practices, 355
nihonjinron as 'folk model', 162

'paternalistic neglect', 230
personhood, 412
on self-interest, 101, 325
behavior, inequality and the differentiation of, 342-356
Beiheiren (anti-Vietnam War group), 67, 242
Bellah, Robert N., 27
Bendasan, Isaiah, 33
Benedict, Ruth: *The Chrysanthemum and the Sword*, 8, 45, 62
comparative methodology, 419, 420, 424
on Jap. concern with being watched, 239-41
Berger, Peter, 418
biographies, 198-199
Birnbaum, Norm, 324
Blau, Peter M., 464
Blumer, Herbert, 411
Brinton, Mary C., 161
Broadbridge, Seymour, 120
business corporation, *see* firm

Camus, Albert, 326
censorship, 244
Chalmers, Norma, 100
character, national, 49-52, 231-233, 284
stereotypes, 1-18
Chichibu Rebellion, (1884), 67
Chikazawa, Kei-ichi, 356
children, 196, 259, 261
China, 2, 37, 158
Choo, H.C., 118
Chuō Kyōiku Shingikai, 258
citizens' movements, 29, 69-71
civil rights debate, 69
Clark, Gregory, 88, 163
class, social, 92-3, 314-22
in Jap. society, 277-78
Clifford, William, 38-9
climate, 42, 384
Cole, Robert E., 167, 178, 179
on class, 277, 362
on loyalty to firm, 288, 330
on unions, 254
Communists, 47, 67. *See also* Japan Communist Party
company, *see* firm
competitiveness, 32, 101, 228, 235
Conference on Modern Japan, 27-32
conflict theories, 10, 64-83, 88-95, 406 *See also* disturbances, popular
consensus model, 14, 21-62, 84-8, 406
doubts about, 10-12, 95
conservation movement, 71
consumer movements, 67
contractual relationships, 211-234, 407
control, social, 5, 234-271, 407
as reward fungibility, 338-42
Cooper, Gary M., 195
corruption, 245
Cotgrove, Stephen, 22
Craig, Albert M., 195
Crawcour, Sydney, 170, 177
crime, 263-4, 352-3
cultural relativism, 56-63, 431
Cummings, William K., 163
Curtis, Gerald, 278
Cutright, Phillips, 459

Dahrendorf, Ralf, 298, 300, 305
Dai-hyaku Seimei, 195
Davis, Kingsley, 305
Davis, Winston, 38, 173, 182
De Vos, George A., 33
democratization theory, 44-7
deviancy, *see* crime
Dilemmas of Growth, *see Conference on Modern Japan*
disturbances, popular, 66-71, 106-11, 336-338, 355-6. *See also* citizens' movements
Doi, Takeo, 10, 86, 88
content analysis, 143-51
psychology of *amae*, 33, 130, 138
Dore, Ronald P., 461-3
City Life in Japan, 24
industrialization, 4, 36, 287
Douglas, Roger, 106
Downard, J. Douglas, 165
dumping, social (*bōeki masatsu*), 3, 172-3, 385

eating arrangements, 229-30
Economist, The, 11, 35, 221
economy, Japanese, 1-3, 390, 392-3
demands in, 329-30
exploitation in, 74-80
education, 3, 5, 218
Government control of, 111, 177, 240
private, 207-8
role in social stratification, 280
social control in, 256-63
Egawa, Taku, 198
elites, 15, 49-52, 65, 278
business, 279, 285, 355, *See also*

sararī man
Embree, John F., 23, 419
emic concepts, 133, 411-13, 416, 419
employment
contract, 222
investigation pre-, 252
lifetime, 48, 109
ethnocentrism accusation, 171, 173, 382, 417
ethnography, 42-3, 159
etic concepts, 133, 411-13, 416, 419

family, 223, 412
kinship unit, 321, 354-5
register (*koseki*), 241
Family Income and Expenditure Survey (FIES), 116-18
Fanon, Franz, 2, 393
Farmer, John S., 228
firm,
commitment to, 15, 230, 330
controls within, 252-256
role of, 281-288
foreign exchange restrictions, 241, 407
Frazer, Patrick, 221
Fujita, Wakao, 81, 254
Fukada, Yūsuke, 176
Fukutake, Tadashi, 354
Japanese Society Today, 9
Fukuzawa, Yukichi, 233
Seiyō Jijō (*The Western Situation*), 40
Funabashi, Naomichi, 79

GNP criticism movement, 385-7
Galbraith, John Kenneth, 320
Garai Jiten (*Dictionary of Borrowed Words*), 463
Gekkan Yoron Chōsa (*Monthly Review of Survey Data*), 159
Genji, Keita: 'The Translator', 171
Glazer, Nathan, v, 25, 26, 34
Gordon, Milton, 299
Goulet, Denis, 2, 393
Government, Japanese, 177-81
control, 240-242
resistance to, 208
Greenstein, Fred I., 220
group models, 54-63, 406
doubts about, 10-12
rethinking, 114-15
Gunji, Kazuo, 254
gyōsei shidō (administrative guidance), 243-5

Hakone Conference, 1960: Modernization of Japan, 47, 64, 165
Hall, John W., 23-4, 31-2, 257
Government and Local Power in Japan 500-1700, 23
Twelve Doors to Japan, 9
Hamaguchi, Eshun, 51
Hanami, Tadashi, 256
Harper, Thomas J., 195
Hasegawa, Takuya, 40, 268
Hatano, Seiichi, 177
Hatvany, Nina, 254
Hayashi, Megumi, 280
Hayashi, Ōki, 351
Hazama, Hiroshi, 287
Hearn, Lafcadio, 419
Heller, Celia, 305
Henley, W.E., 228
heroes, 195-200
Hidaka, Rokurō, iv, 162, 250
Higgins, Ronald, 18
Higuchi, Kiyoyuki, 51
Hokusai, 426
holistic approach, *see* group models
Honda, Katsuichi, 159
Horie, Masanori, 278
Nihon no Rōdōsha Kaikyū, 91
Horvats, Andrew, 180
Hosoi, Wakizō, 74
Hull, Frank, 103
Human Relations in Japan (Jap. Foreign Ministry), 177

Ichibangase, Yasuko, 458
Ichikawa, Fusae, 195
Ienaga, Saburō, 260
Iida, Tsuneo, 102
Inaba, Michio, 458
Inagaki, Yoshihiko, 155
income, 328-36
distribution, 115-28 *See also* wages
India, 125
Government sponsored business meeting with Japan, 225
individualism, 191-210, 407
Indochina, 174
industrial relations, 36, 48, 250, 336 *See also* labor-management relations
industrialization, 2-6, 48
inequality, social, 5, 71-81, 82
and differentiation of behavior, 342-7, 408
on international level, 398
Inoguchi, Rikihei, 101, 102

Inoue, Kiyoshi, 65, 108
internationalization (*kokusaika*)
  and Jap. society, 6-7, 52-4, 377-404
  of Jap. studies, 418-24
interpreters, 161
Irokawa, Daikichi, 68, 223
Ishida, Hideo, 100
Ishida, Takeshi, 29, 32
  Japanese Society, 9
Ishihara, Shū, 74
Ishikawa, Hiroshi, 159, 277
Itch, Noe, 247
Iwanami, 163
Iwata, Ryūshi, 102, 287
Iwauchi, Ryūichi, 102
'Izumi Syndrome', 33

Japan Communist Party, 66, 242, 347
Japan Foundation, iii, vii, 166, 181
Japan Interpreter, 175
Japan Quarterly, 175
Japan Socialist Party, 47, 66, 337, 347
Japan Teachers Union
  struggle with Ministry of Education, 67-8, 257, 262-3
Japanese Ministry of Labor (*Rōdopshō*), 120-7
Japanese Sociological Association, 279, 363
Japanese Studies Association of Australia, vii
Japanology, 142-55
  sociology of, 156-84
Jewish culture, 34
jishukusei (self-regulation), 244
job situations, survey of perceptions of,
  US-Jap. comparison, 360-64: case study, 433-50; conclusions, 372-3
jobs, *see* employment
Johnson, Sharon, 9, 37

Kagayama, Takashi, 278
Kahn, Herman, 3, 34-5, 455
  The Emerging Japanese Superstate, 35
Kaji, Etsuko, 349
Kamata, Satoshi, 159, 262, 288
  Jidōsha Zetsubō Kōjō, 176
kamikaze pilots, 249
Kanamori, Hisao, 456
Kaneko, Yoshio, 253
Karachi plan, 2
Kasai, Hisako, 351
Katō, Hidetoshi: *Chūkan Bunka*, 47
Katō, Hiroyuki, 69
Katō, Shūichi, 46, 197
Katsukawa, Shunrō (Hokusai), 426
Kawada, Hisashi, 37
Kawai, Takeo, 278
Kawakami, Hajime, 74
Kawamura, Nozomu, 41, 163, 389
Kawamura, Tokitarō, *see* Katsukawa, Shunrō
Kawashima, Takeyoshi, 32, 44
Kazehaya, Yasoji, 72, 458
Keller, Suzanne, 310-11
Kennan, George, 182
Kerr, Clark, 48, 355
Kinmonth, Earl H., 195
Kishimoto, Eitarō, 72, 76
Kobayashi, Takiji, 74
Kodansha, 163
Koe naki Koeno Kai (Group representing the Voiceless Voices), 70
Koike, Kazuo, 100, 101, 103-4
Kojima, Kenji, 289
Kojima, Yoshio, 245
Kokugaku movement, 39, 88
Kōmeitō, 347, 356
Korea, 109, 118, 165
Kornhauser, William, 355
Kōsai, Yutaka, 102
Kōshiro, Kazutoshi, 103, 184, 330, 332
Kotoku, Kosui, 247
kotowaza (proverbs or wise sayings), 134-6, 151-5
Kotowaza-Meigen Jiten (Dictionary of Proverbs and Famous Sayings), 151
Krishner, Bernard, 90
Kuhn, Thomas, 157
kumi shakai (organized society), 264-7
Kunihiro, Masao, 6, 383, 457
Kunihiro, Tetsuya, 50, 131
Kuroda, Toshio, 280

labor, 353-4
  legislation, 81, 250
  -management relations, 287, 386-7
  movement, 66, 67, 80-1
Landecker, Werner, 289
language, English
  literature on Japan, 86, 91
  problems of learning, 399-400
  use in Japan, 160, 389
language, Japanese

abstraction in, 232
importance of written word, 216-219
need for proficiency in, 17, 165-7
and personhood, 208-9
reductions in, 134-6
variations in usage, 351-2
Lave, Charles A., 410
LeClair, Edward E., 335, 469
leaders, 195-200
Learn-from-Japan boom, 3-4, 36-9, 173, 418
Lebra, Takie Sugiyama, 34, 135
Lee, Alfred McLung, 210, 418
Lee, O. Young, 132
leisure, 200-205, 207, 355
Lenski, Gerhard, 85, 459
social stratification, 298, 300, 320-1, 363
Levine, Solomon B., 37, 100
Liberal Democrat Party (LDP), 331, 337, 342, 347
Litton, Robert Jay, 197
Lloyd, Arthur, 419
Lockheed scandal, 243, 245
Lockheimer, Roy, 29, 179
Lockwood, William W., 28
Lummis, C. Douglas, 62
Lynd, Helen Merrel, 298, 300
Lynd, Robert S., 298, 300

McCormack, Gavin, 134
McGowan, Valerie, 134
Machlup, F., 469
Magofuku, Hiromu, 56, 232
Manchuria
biological experiments on Chinese, 41, 249, 397
Mannari, Hiroshu, 103, 279
Mannheim, Karl, 269
March, James G., 410
marriage contract, 225-6
Marsh, Robert M., 103, 464
Marshall, Byron, 27
Marshall, Robert C., 101, 325
Maruyama, Masao, 29, 30, 44, 47
Marxism, 31-2, 64-6, 317
in Japanese intellectual life, 12, 91, 159
Masamura, Kimio, 65, 66
Maslow, Abraham, 333
Matsubara, Haruo, 73
Matsumoto, Seichō, 197
Matsuyama, Yukio, 182
media, mass, 88-90, 160, 197, 199, 381
Merton, Robert, 141, 157
Mexico, 125
Miki, Kiyoshi, 250
Miller, Roy Andrews, 167, 177, 179, 378, 393
Mills, C. Wright, iv, 269, 279
Milward, Peter, 163
Minakata, Kumagusu, 43
Minami, Hiroshi, 33
Minear, Richard H., 8, 392
Mishima, 199
Mitchell, Richard Hanks, 425
Miyagi, Hirosuke, 277
Miyamoto, Musashi, 173
The Book of Five Rings, 38
Miyanohara, Seichi, 257
mobility, social, 279-281
modernization theory, 27-32, 47-9, 60, 416-17
Moore, Wilbert E., 305
Mori, Jōji, 50
Mori, Kōjirō, 71, 75
Mori, Ōgai, 233
Moriji, Shigeo, 280
Morimura, Sei-ichi, 249, 397, 398
Morioka, Hiroshi, 235-9
Morioka, Kiyomi, 356
Morley, James Wiliam, 29, 31, 32
Morris, Ivan, 195
Mosca, Gaetano, 279
Motoori, Norinaga, 39
Mouer, Ross, vii, 22, 48, 91, 116, 130, 329, 348, 349, 366, 412, 447, 450, 455, 457, 463
Murakami, Hyōe, 181, 195
mure shakai (associated society), 264-267

NHK (Hōsō Yoron Chōsasho), 182, 218, 244
Naipaul, Vidiadhar Surajprasad, 18, 59
internationalism, 393, 454
naishinsho (confidential appraisals of students), 258
Nakamura, Hajime, 45, 177
Nakamura, Kikuo, 33, 196
Nakane, Chie, 86, 88, 362
content analysis, 143-51
family, 222
Japanese Society, 34, 59, 137, 139, 177, 456
tautologies in, 136-7
uniqueness, 6, 60
verticality, 11, 32, 134, 465: and

role of the firm, 281-8
Nakayama, Ichirō, 48, 256
on prestige, 295, 332
Nakayama, Masakazu, 287
Namiki, Nobuyoshi, 51
Naoi, Yū, 161
National Opinion Research Center, 363
Natsume, Sōseki, 233
Needham, Rodney, 271
Neustupny, J.V., 17, 167
Newsweek, 34, 90, 174, 456
nihonjinron (or *nihonron*; *nihonshakairon*), vi, 22
as a controlling myth, 169-84, 377-9, 388, 431
doubts about methodological validity, 97-184
false images, 396-400, 402
stages in development of, 56-63, 88, 158-63, 428
summary, 405-8
See also consensus model; group models; uniqueness; verticality
Nisbet, Robert, 414
Nishibe, Mitsuru, 102
Nishida, Kitaro, 177
Nishikawa, Shunsaku, 100, 281
Nishio, Yotarō, 391-2
Nitobe, Inazō, 161
Nitta, Jirō, 249
Nomura Research Institute, 87
Norman, E.H., 277
nuclear weapons
movement against, 71, 378
victims of, 69

OECD, 287, 386
Obi, Keiichirō, 100
occupational classifications, 323
Odaka, Kunio, 288, 363
Ōe, Shinobu, 247
Ogai, Mori, 390
Ogawa, Noboru, 78
Ogino, Tarō, 102
Ōhashi, Ryūken, 278
Nihon no Kaikyū Kōsei, 91
Oka, Hideyaki; *How to Wrap Five Eggs*, 193
Okada, Shigeru, 220
Okamoto, Hideaki, 288
Ōkōchi, Kazuo, 72, 75, 76-7
Okonogi, Keigo, 138
Omi Spinning Mills, 253
Ono, Akira, 100
Ono, Tsuneo, 101
Onoda, Hiroo, 198
Ōoka, Shōhei: *Nobi* (Fires on the Plain), 248
orientalism, 8, 59, 177, 392
Origuchi, Shinobu, 42
Ōsugi, Sakae, 247
Ōtsuka, Hisao, 45
Ouchi, William G., 38
overseas residence, 243, 403
Ozaki, Robert S., 140

Pareto, Vilfredo, 279
Parsons, Talcott, 27, 60, 321, 336
Pascale, Richard Tanner, 38
passports, 243, 403
peace movement, 31, 70, 382
See also anti-nuclear movement
People's Daily (Chinese), 2
personhood, *see* self-identity
Perspectives on Japan (BBC), 392
Peters, Thomas, 184
Phelps, Tracy, 103
Philippines, the, 37, 254
Pike, Kenneth L., 411
police, 109, 240, 264
box (*kōban*), 241-2
Police Duties Act (1958, 1959), 111
political attitudes, 342-9
the international in, 383-8
pollution, 384-6
bureaucratic indifference to, 4, 245, 246, 251
noise, etc, 71, 337, 430
See also anti-pollution movement
pornography, 244, 330
poverty, 74-80
privacy (*puraibashi*), 4, 205-8
property, private, 205-8
psychology, Japanese, 33
Public Security Police Act (1900), 240
Pucik, Vladimir, 100, 101, 254

quality control circles (QC), 179, 182, 254

racism, 41
ranking, social, 292-304
regulations, public, 245-7
Reischauer, Edwin, 88, 141
content analysis, 143-51
group model, 10, 30, 86
religion, 115, 199-200, 356
research
cross-cultural, 414, 416-24

foreign on Japan, 163-8
goals, 424-9
sources of funds, 162-3, 244
residential registry (*jumin tōruku*), 241
rewards, societal, 292-304, 408
and cultures, 323-4
in Jap. society, 328-42
rice riots (1918), 67, 70, 108
Rikō, Mitsuo, 101
Rōdōshō, *see* Japanese Ministry of Labor
roles, social, 115, 304-6
Rōnō, 458
Rōnōha-Kōzaha debate, 65, 457
Runciman, W.G., 294
rural sociology, 43

Said, Edward W., 8, 177
Orientalism, 59, 392
Saimaru, 163
Sameda, Toyoyuki, 51
Sano, Yōko, 100, 119
sararī man, 325, 355
Schell, Jonathan, 378
Schweisberg, Dave, 182
Science Council of Japan, 87
Scoville, G., 132
security consciousness, 242-3
Security Treaty, *see* US-Japan Security Treaty
seishin (Individual surviving on his own), 198, 211
self-identity, 33, 208-9, 388-93
self-interest, 14, 82, 333
motivation, 8, 324-6
Sengoku, Tamotsu, 131
Sergeant, Graham, 410
sex tours, 7, 53
Shiloh, Ruth, 131
Shils, Edward, 336
Shimada, Haruo, 100, 288
Shimodaira, Hiromi, 278
Shinbun Kyōjaum 178
Shiroyama, Saburō: *Mainichi ga Nichiyōbi*, 230
shishōsetsu (private novel), 199
Shisō no Kagaku Kenkyūkai, 158
Shively, Donald H., 195
shnihonbunkaron, *see nihonjinron*
Shūkan Bunshun, 176
Sibatani, Atuhiro, 416
Siegel, Abraham, 355
Singapore, 37, 254
Slaughter, Murray, 197
Smith, Aileen, 251
Smith, Eugene W., 251
Smith, Lilian: *Killers of the Dream*, 268
Social Analysis, vii, 455
social distance, 227-33
in research, 159-61
social policy Center, University of Tokyo, 278
Social Sciences Citation Index, 143
Sōka Gakkai, 249
Sone, Yasunori, 101
Sōrifu Tōkeikyoku, 203
Sorokin, Pitirim, 283
Spengler, Joseph J., 119
Stans, Maurice, 456
Stigler: *The Theory of Price*, 469
Stirling, Peter, 174
Stockwin, J.A.A., 278, 463, 464
stratification, social, 275-92
agents of, 306-8
multidimensional framework, 292-327, 424
strikes, 67
Japan compared with Australia, 173-4
students, 261-2
demonstrations, 10, 29, 67, 69, 82, 109
Sturmthal, Adolf, 132
Subversive Activities Prevention Act (1952), 111
Sugimoto, Yoshio, vii, 22, 91, 106-15, 130, 151, 152, 261, 267, 338-9, 355, 366, 412, 447, 450, 455, 457
suicide, 356
See also kamikaze pilots
Sumitomo Corporation, 176
Sumiya, Mikio, 73, 100, 324
Suzuki, Ichirō, 233
Suziki, Masashi, 65
Suziki, Yukio, 243-4
Suziki, Zenko, 219

Tachi, Minoru, 280
Taigyaku Jikken, 247
Taira, Koji, 100, 118, 362
Taishō Kaijō Kasai, 230
Takahashi, Chōtarō, 118
Takahashi, Nobuko, 349
Takamori, Saigo, 391
Takano, Shirō, 79
Takashima, 238-9
Takasuga, Yoshihiro, 161
Takata, Yasuma, 417

Takayama, Noriyuki, 116
Takeuchi, Hiroshi, 101
Takeuchi, Yō,
Takeuchi, Yoshimi, 158
Takezawa, Shin-ichi, 287
Tamaru, Misuzu, 351
Tanaka, Ichirō, 237
Tanaka, Kakeui, 6
Tanaka, Yasuo, 102
tautologies, 136-9
tenko (forced conversion), 158, 244, 250
Teranishi, Jirō, 161
textbook issue, 53, 177, 260
Tilly, Charles, 106, 107, 356
Tilly, Richard, 106, 107
Time, 36
Todaisha (Lighthouse Society), 250
Tokuyama, Jirō, 34, 174
Tokyo, 400-401
  University of, 163
Tominaga, Ken-ichi, 48, 458
  education for occupation, 362
  Japanese and firm, 287
  social mobility, 279, 280-281, 363
Tarabāyu, 225
translation syndrome, 160-1
Treiman, Donald J., 363, 470
Tsuda, Masumi, 287
Tsujimura, Kōtarō, 330
Tsukushi, Tetsuya, 87
Tsunoda, Tadanobu, 51
Tsurumi, Shunsuke, 158, 396
Tumin, Melvin, 296, 305

US Department of Labor
  study of wage structures, 120-7
US–Japan Security Treaty, 47, 109, 336
  revision (1960), 111
Ueki, Emori, 69
Uemura, Naoki, 194
Ui, Jun, 82
Ujihara, Shop¯jiro, 281
Ujikawa, Makoto, 277
Umemura, Mataji, 100, 288
Umesao, Tadao, 46
Umetani, Shun-ichirō, 100
Union Bank of Switzerland: 'Japan — Dynamic Force in the Industrial World', 456
unionism, 336
  enterprise, 48, 109
uniqueness of Japanese, 1, 6, 11, 60, 406
  history of, 39-41
United Kingdom, 124
United Nations Conference on the Environment, Stockholm (1972), 385
United States of America, 187-8
  job situation perceptions compared with Japanese, 360-64, 372-3

  QC circles, 254
  relationship with Japan, 181-4, 389-90
  study of Japan, 9, 12, 22-39, 164
  technology and alienation comparison, 103-6
universities, 101
  foreign staff in, 260, 403
Uno, Kimio, 337
Uno, Kōzō, 66
Utah Foundation, vii

Van Zandt, Howard F., 36
vertical society, 11, 14, 32, 54, 134, 406, 465
  and role of firm, 283
Vietnam War, 12, 141
  movement anti-, 67. *See also* Beiheiren
violence, physical, 247-52
Vittas, Dimitri, 221
Vogel, Ezra, 88, 140, 424
  on class, 277
  content analysis, 143-51
  on education, 137, 231
  on group model, 3, 10, 86
  Japan as Number One, 11, 37, 59
  Japan's New Middle Class, 11
volition, culture and ideology, 326-7
voting behavior, 101, 337, 354

wages
  male–female differential, 349-51
  offensives, 29, 66, 111, 387
  seniorty, 48, 100, 123, 287
Wallich, Henry C., 456
Ward, Peter, 456
Washington Post, 35
Watanabe, Ikuo, 101
Watanabe, Shōichi: *Cheteki Seikatsu no Hōhō* (Approaches to an Intellectual Life), 139
Watanabe, Torū, 108
Watanuki, Jōji, 101, 354
Waterman, Robert, 184
Watsuji, Tetsurō, 33, 42, 177

Weber, Max, 59, 293
Weinstein, Deena, 410, 413
Weinstein, Michael A., 410, 413
welfare, 331
  corporatism, 36, 287
Wesselowski, W., 299, 300
West, the
  idealization of, 40, 45-7, 378, 386
  as a monolith, 16, 132-3, 397
  suspicion of, 390-3
Whitehill, Arthur M., 287
Whiting, Robert, 39
Whymant, Robert, 179
Wigmore, John Henry, 223
Wild, Ronald, 289
Wilkinson, Endymion, 392
Wilson, James Q., 271
Winds, 175
women, 5, 31
  Jap. marrying foreigners, 171, 403
  rights in marriage, 225-6
  wages, 123, 349-51
  at work, 100, 224

Yakabe, Katsumi, 177, 287
Yakura, Hisayasu, 261
Yamagishi, Toshio, 161
Yamagishikai movement, 70
Yamaguchi, Masayuki, 277
Yamamoto, Shichihei, 169
Yamamoto, Shigemi: *Ah Nomugi Tōge*, 253
Yamamoto, Yūjirō, 169
Yamazaki, Mitsuru, 470
Yamazaki, Toyoko, 159
  Shiroi Kyotō, 219
Yanaga, Chitose, 279
Yanagida, Kunio, 42
Yano, Seiya, 470
Yasuda, Saburō, 87, 281, 363
Yokoi, Shōchi, 198
Yokota, Testuji, 251
Yokoyama, Gennosuke, 74
Yoneyama, Toshinao, 101, 115
Yoshimori, Masaru, 391
Yoshimoto, Takaaki, 158
Yoshisato, Naoki, 251
Yūki, Masaharu: *Gunki Hatameku Moto ni*, 249

8 FEB 2 2 1988